Kitchen Traditions

The Lions Clubs Cookbook

**A special collection of favorite recipes
from Lions Clubs members
across the nations.**

Compiled by
**Cookbooks Unlimited
Loveland, Colorado**

Published and Printed By
Cookbook Publishers, Inc.
P.O. Box 15920
Lenexa, Kansas 66285-5920

ISBN 0-9638796-1-8

First Printing   July 1994   10,000 books

A recipe that is not shared with others
will soon be forgotten,
but when it is shared
it will be enjoyed by future generations.

DEDICATION

We dedicate this book to all Lions Clubs members . . . those very special people who are committed to building a brighter future for their community and their fellow man.

Our very sincere thanks go to all those members who so generously contributed their favorite recipes for this outstanding cookbook. Without their help, this book would have never been possible.

Some of the recipes included here are treasured family keepsakes, and some are new. However, they all reflect the love of good cooking. We hope you will enjoy the many outstanding and treasured recipes on the following pages.

Sincere thanks from,

Francis & Linda Sedlacek
Cookbooks Unlimited

Lionism Through the Years . . .

The International Association of Lions Clubs began as the dream of Chicago businessman Melvin Jones. He believed that local business clubs should expand their horizons from purely professional concerns to the betterment of their communities and the world at large.

Jones' own group, the Business Circle of Chicago, agreed. After contacting similar groups around the country, an organizational meeting was held on June 7, 1917 at the LaSalle Hotel in Chicago. The new group took the name of one of the groups invited, the "Association of Lions Clubs," and a national convention was held in Dallas in October of that year. In all, nine states were represented at Dallas—Arkansas, California, Colorado, Illinois, Louisiana, Missouri, Oklahoma, Tennessee, and Texas. A constitution, by-laws, objects, and code of ethics were approved.

Just three years after its formation, the organization became international when the first club in Canada was established in 1920. Major international expansion continued as clubs were established, particularly throughout Europe, Asia, and Africa during the 1950s and 1960s.

The year 1918 saw an important "first" in Lionism. Volume 1, Number 1, of *THE LION Magazine* was published in November, with Melvin Jones as editor. It contained 28 pages and, of course, had a small circulation. Today there are 20 editions of *THE LION*, in 15 languages.

Lions International entered the 1920s with a spirit of confidence and boundless energy. By the end of the decade, Lions Clubs were organized in every state of the union at the time, and in Mexico, China, and almost every province in Canada, making the Association truly international. Membership stood at nearly 80,000 and club strength at over 2,200. The International

Headquarters had moved from Melvin Jones' crowded office, where he and his wife did most of the paperwork, to new, spacious quarters in downtown Chicago. A full-time staff of 33 was employed to manage and coordinate details and records of the growing Association.

Perhaps the single event having the greatest impact on the Association's service commitment occurred in 1925 when Helen Keller addressed the Lions at their international convention in Cedar Point, Ohio. It was there that she challenged Lions to become "knights of the blind in the crusade against darkness."

In the 1950s, the motto "We Serve" was officially adopted as tens of thousands of civic-minded men joined Lions Clubs throughout the world.

In 1990 Lions launched their most aggressive sight preservation effort to date: SightFirst. The U.S. $130 million dollar program strives to rid the world of preventable and reversible blindness by closing the gap between existing health care services and those that remain desperately needed.

Broadening its role in international understanding, the association helped the United Nations form the Non-Governmental Organizations sections in 1945, and continues to hold consultative status today. Each year, during The Lions With The United Nations ceremonies, an award is presented to the grand prize winner of the Lions International Peace Poster Contest.

Since those first years, the association has grown to include nearly 1.4 million men and women in more than 40,000 clubs located in nearly 180 countries and geographical areas. Lions Clubs International celebrated 75 years of service in 1992.

Lions Clubs International

Service History — Worldwide, Lions Clubs are recognized for their service to the blind and visually impaired. This service began through a challenge issued by Helen Keller to become "knights of the blind in the crusade against darkness" during the Lions' 1925 International Convention.

Primary Program "SightFirst" — Established in 1990, SightFirst works to prevent and reverse blindness worldwide by closing the gap between existing health care services and those that remain desperately needed.

More than $13 million (U.S. dollars) has already been granted for at least 40 projects including: cataract surgery outreach programs in nine Latin American countries; 5 national eyeglass recycling centers in the U.S.; cataract surgery eyecamps in Pakistan, Kenya and India; and new eye hospitals and training facilities in Barbados, India, Malawi, Mali, and Sri Lanka.

Financial support for SightFirst projects is provided by Campaign SightFirst, which depends on the fundraising activities of local clubs, donations by individual Lions, and the contributions of governments, foundations, and corporations.

In 1993-94 Lions everywhere are participating in an effort to raise a minimum of $130 million (U.S. dollars) for the establishment of SightFirst projects during "The Year of Campaign SightFirst."

Other Sight-Related Activities — In addition to the SightFirst program, Lions Clubs continue to support other sight-related activities:

❦ In the U.S., Canada, and United Kingdom, Lions cosponsor with 460 LensCrafters stores *Give the Gift of Sight,* a special holiday used eyeglass collection and recycling program.

❦ Lions provide 600,000 free professional glaucoma screenings and make 25,000 corneal transplants possible each year.

❦ Lions establish and support a majority of the world's eye banks, hundreds of clinics, hospitals, and eye research centers worldwide.

❦ Lions provide thousands each year with free quality eye care, eyeglasses, Braille-writers, large print texts, white canes, and guide dogs.

International Youth Programs — Lions make a strong service commitment to youth through several international programs:

❦ Lions-Quest Program: Through the Lions-Quest "Skills For Adolescence" curriculum, pre-teenagers in 24,000 schools in 28 countries have developed skills to help make healthy decisions and resist pressures to use drugs and alcohol. In the U.S. and Canada, 7,500 schools have implemented the "Skills For Growing" program for kindergarten through fifth grades.

❦ Lions International Peace Poster Contest: Each year 200,000 students, ages 11 to 13, from nearly 40 countries participate. The winner of the fifth annual contest, "Environment for Peace," was an 11-year-old girl from Indonesia.

❦ Leo Program: Lions Clubs in 118 countries sponsor more than 4,500 Leo clubs worldwide. The more than 113,000 members, ages 12 to 28, perform various community service activities and support a special worldwide Literacy and Culture project.

❦ International Youth Exchange: In 1991-92 more than 3,700 students, ages 16 to 22, stayed with Lion host families in 62 countries.

Lions Clubs International Foundation — Lions Clubs International Foundation (LCIF) is the charitable branch of Lions Clubs International. LCIF disburses donated funds in the form of grants for humanitarian services, disaster relief, and vocational assistance. LCIF also initiated the Campaign SightFirst fundraising effort that supports the association's SightFirst program.

Lions Clubs—United in Purpose

As individuals, Lions are people of tireless drive, uncommon spirit, and ambitious goals. United in efforts through more than 40,000 individual clubs around the world, Lions Clubs International is a strong organization with a proud history of accomplishment.

But the Lions' efforts and our future ability to serve the growing population of those in need in local communities, across our country and around the world, depend on the involvement of a new generation of Lions. A generation of individuals committed as we are to eradicating reversible blindness, preserving the environment, and building self-esteem in young people. A generation that knows that we can accomplish great things if we work together.

As Lions, our goal is to make a difference—and we have—over and over again with programs that succeed.

Service to people who are blind and who are visually impaired has always been one of our most significant programs. Today, the Lions *SightFirst* program is dedicated to eradicating preventable and reversible blindness worldwide. Lions operate the vast majority of eye banks throughout the world and have donated hundreds of millions of dollars toward research, training, and rehabilitation for people who are blind.

Lions make a difference.

New Dimensions

For all of us, personal time is a valuable commodity. How you choose to spend your time is an important consideration. *Volunteering as a Lion can make a difference for you too.*

We believe that time invested with a Lions Club yields an invaluable return: an added dimension to your personal and professional life. While providing the framework for you to serve your community, a Lions Club also offers opportunities for individual growth.

Leadership Ability — Whether you lead a meeting, spearhead a fundraising effort, or organize a project, Lions Clubs provide opportunities to learn the skills that get the job done. Increased self-confidence and self-esteem flow naturally from making things happen when you work with your Lions Club.

Business Skills — You can improve your public speaking and presentation skills while you communicate with others on important social issues. First-hand experience in budgeting projects, planning activities, and motivating others in your Lions Club can also enhance your professional abilities.

Networking — Interact with other professionals who have come together through Lions Clubs to work toward common goals and to have a meaningful impact on your community.

> Join a Lions Club and make a
> difference in your life and the lives
> of countless others.

More than ever, people with vision problems, our senior community, our youth, and the disadvantaged around the world need your help.

Our commitment to serve holds strong. You can help.

By participating in a local Lions Club, you can help meet pressing needs in your own community and have a meaningful impact on the health and well-being of people around the world.

For more information, contact your local Lions Club (look for address or phone number in the back of this cookbook.)

Or contact Lions International Headquarters at:

300 - 22nd Street
Oak Brook, IL 60521-8842
Phone: (708) 571-5466

TABLE OF CONTENTS

SNACKS, APPETIZERS, BEVERAGES 1

BREAKFAST AND BRUNCH 47

SOUPS AND SANDWICHES 67

SALADS 109

VEGETABLES 153

ENTREES 201

CASSEROLES AND MAIN DISHES 303

BREADS 377

CAKES AND FROSTINGS 431

PIES AND PASTRIES 505

COOKIES, BARS, CANDIES 537

DESSERTS 603

MISCELLANEOUS 647

FAVORITE RECIPES
FROM MY COOKBOOK

Recipe Name	Page Number

FOOD QUANTITIES FOR 25, 50, AND 100 SERVINGS

FOOD	25 SERVINGS	50 SERVINGS	100 SERVINGS
Rolls	4 doz.	8 doz.	16 doz.
Bread	50 slices or 3 1-lb. loaves	100 slices or 6 1-lb. loaves	200 slices or 12 1-lb. loaves
Butter	½ lb.	¾ to 1 lb.	1½ lb.
Mayonnaise	1 c.	2 to 3 c.	4 to 6 c.
Mixed filling for sandwiches (meat, eggs, fish)	1½ qt.	2½ to 3 qt.	5 to 6 qt.
Mixed filling (sweet-fruit)	1 qt.	1¾ to 2 qt.	2½ to 4 qt.
Jams & preserves	1½ lb.	3 lb.	6 lb.
Crackers	1½ lb.	3 lb.	6 lb.
Cheese (2 oz. per serving)	3 lb.	6 lb.	12 lb.
Soup	1½ gal.	3 gal.	6 gal.
Salad dressings	1 pt.	2½ pt.	½ gal.
Meat, Poultry, or Fish:			
Wieners (beef)	6½ lb.	13 lb.	25 lb.
Hamburger	9 lb.	18 lb.	35 lb.
Turkey or chicken	13 lb.	25 to 35 lb.	50 to 75 lb.
Fish, large whole (round)	13 lb.	25 lb.	50 lb.
Fish, fillets or steaks	7½ lb.	15 lb.	30 lb.
Salads, Casseroles, Vegetables:			
Potato salad	4¼ qt.	2¼ gal.	4½ gal.
Scalloped potatoes	4½ qt. or 1 12x20" pan	8½ qt.	17 qt.
Mashed potatoes	9 lb.	18-20 lb.	25-35 lb.
Spaghetti	1¼ gal.	2½ gal.	5 gal.
Baked beans	¾ gal.	1¼ gal.	2½ gal.
Jello salad	¾ gal.	1¼ gal.	2½ gal.
Canned vegetables	1 #10 can	2½ #10 cans	4 #10 cans
Fresh Vegetables:			
Lettuce (for salads)	4 heads	8 heads	15 heads
Carrots (3 oz. or ½ c.)	6¼ lb.	12½ lb.	25 lb.
Tomatoes	3-5 lb.	7-10 lb.	14-20 lb.
Desserts:			
Watermelon	37½ lb.	75 lb.	150 lb.
Fruit cup (½ c. per serving)	3 qt.	6 qt.	12 qt.
Cake	1 10x12" sheet cake 1½ 10" layer cakes	1 12x20" sheet cake 3 10" layer cakes	2 12x20" sheet cakes 6 10" layer cakes
Whipping cream	¾ pt.	1½ to 2 pt.	3 pt.
Ice Cream:			
Brick	3¼ qt.	6½ qt.	12½ qt.
Bulk	2¼ qt.	4½ qt. or 1¼ gal.	9 qt. or 2½ gal.
Beverages:			
Coffee	½ lb. and 1½ gal. water	1 lb. and 3 gal. water	2 lb. and 6 gal. water
Tea	1/12 lb. and 1½ gal. water	⅙ lb. and 3 gal. water	⅓ lb. and 6 gal. water
Lemonade	10 to 15 lemons, 1½ gal. water	20 to 30 lemons, 3 gal. water	40 to 60 lemons, 6 gal. water

SNACKS, APPETIZERS, BEVERAGES
SNACKS AND APPETIZERS

TORTILLA ROLL-UPS

8 oz. pkg. cream cheese
8 oz. sour cream
3 green onions, diced
1 small can green chili peppers,
  chopped

4 oz. finely ground Cheddar
  cheese
Garlic powder to taste
8 to 10 flour tortillas

Combine all ingredients, except tortillas. Spread on tortillas and roll into log. Slice to desired size. Serve with picante sauce for dipping.

Judy Roby, Plattsmouth Lions Club
Plattsmouth, Nebraska, USA

HIDDEN VALLEY RANCH PINWHEELS

2 (8 oz.) pkg. cream cheese,
  softened
1 (1 oz.) pkg. Hidden Valley Ranch
  original dressing mix
2 green onions, minced

4 (12 inch) flour tortillas
1 (4 oz.) jar diced pimento
1 (4 oz.) can diced green chiles
1 (2.2 oz.) can sliced black olives

Mix first 3 ingredients. Spread on tortillas. Drain vegetables and blot dry on paper towel. Sprinkle equal amounts of remaining ingredients on top of cream cheese. Roll tortillas tightly. Chill for at least 2 hours, then cut the rolls into 1 inch pieces. Discard ends. Serve with spirals facing up. Makes 3 dozen.

Footnote: Three or 4 tablespoons of picante sauce can be used in place of the Ranch dressing.

Kathy Steffan, Independence Eastview Lions Club
Independence, Missouri, USA

MEXICAN MESS

8 oz. cream cheese
Small chip dip (I use French
  onion)
1 pkg. dry taco seasoning, divided
Diced tomatoes
½ green pepper

Small onion
Celery
Black olives, fresh mushrooms
  (optional)
1 pkg. shredded cheese

Mix together cream cheese and dip. Place in plate with lip. Sprinkle with ½ package dry taco mix. Layer ingredients, one at a time. Sprinkle with shredded cheese, then other ½ package of taco mix. Refrigerate. Serve with favorite tortilla chips.

Pam Sedlar, Onekama Lions Club
Onekama, Michigan, USA

GUACAMOLE

1 avocado (soft to the touch)
½ small onion, chopped
1 Tbsp. lemon juice

½ clove garlic, minced
Salt and pepper (to taste)

Cut avocado in half; remove seed and scoop out pulp with a spoon into a small bowl. Add remaining ingredients and mash with a fork. Cover and refrigerate until ready to serve. Tastes best if the flavors are allowed to blend. Serve with corn chips. Makes about 1 cup.

This recipe is adapted from the one Kenyi, a Peruvian Lions-Youth Exchange Student, made for us.

Rosemary Kish, Downriver Pride Lions Club
Lincoln Park, Michigan, USA

MEXICAN LAYER DIP

1 can refried beans
4 or 5 green onions, chopped
½ head lettuce, finely chopped
2 small tomatoes, chopped
1 (8 oz.) pkg. shredded Cheddar
    cheese

1 (8 oz.) ctn. guacamole dip
1 small jar picante sauce
1 (8 oz.) ctn. sour cream
1 small jar chopped black olives

Spread refried beans in bottom of 1 or 2 inch deep Pyrex dish. Sprinkle chopped onions over beans; spread lettuce over onions. Sprinkle chopped tomato over lettuce. Spread guacamole dip over tomatoes. Sprinkle grated cheese over dip. Shake picante sauce over cheese. Drop, then spread sour cream over picante sauce. Sprinkle chopped black olives over sour cream. Serve with favorite chips.

Let me do it now - for I shall not pass this way again.

Frances B. Blount, Saginaw Lions Club
Saginaw, Texas, USA

FIVE LAYERED DIP

Bean dip
Avocados
Lemon juice
Salt
Pepper

Sour cream
Taco seasoning
Sliced green and black olives
Shredded Cheddar cheese

1. Bottom layer: Spread dip.
2. Next layer, avocados mashed with seasoning (lemon, salt, pepper).
3. Top with sour cream mixed with taco seasoning
4. Sprinkle with sliced green and black olives.
5. Top with shredded Cheddar cheese.

Pauline Sammons
Waldo, Arkansas, USA

SUPER CHALUPA DIP

1 lb. ground beef
1 large onion, chopped
1 tsp. salt
¼ tsp. pepper
1 Tbsp. chili powder
1 to 2 (1 lb.) cans refried beans
Hot sauce (desired amount for
    spicing up)

1 to 2 (4 oz.) cans diced green
    chilies
3 c. shredded Cheddar cheese
1 (7 oz.) can green chili salsa
¼ c. chopped green onion
1 can chopped black olives
Guacamole dip
1 c. sour cream

Brown meat and onion in large skillet; drain. Add salt, pepper, chili powder, refried beans, hot sauce, and half of the green chilies. Mix well. Pour meat mixture into large baking dish. Top with layers of remaining green chilies, cheese, and salsa.

CHILI CON QUESO DIP

2 (16 oz.) cans Mexican style
    tomatoes
2 lb. Velveeta cheese

1 (16 oz.) bottle salsa (medium)
8 oz. pkg. hot pepper cheese

Pour tomatoes into pan at medium heat. Break large tomatoes into small pieces. Cut cheese into 1 inch cubes. Add everything to pot. Heat slowly till melted. Serve with nacho chips or seasoned crackers. Leftover must be refrigerated. Can be warmed in microwave.

Walter E. Loomis, North Jackson Lions Club
Jackson, Michigan, USA

CHILI CON QUESO DE NEW MEXICO

2 lb. Velveeta cheese
1 small onion, finely chopped

1 (4 oz.) can chopped green chilies
1 (4 oz.) can green chili salsa

Combine all ingredients in a 1½ quart saucepan and heat on low till cheese is melted, stirring to blend.

Serve warm with tortilla chips. Reheat as needed to maintain proper consistency.

This recipe was used by the wife of former Governor Mechem of New Mexico and leftovers are rare.

Clark Leedy (Joanne)
Reno, Nevada, USA

❧

As long as you have a window, life is exciting.

ARMADILLO EGGS (STUFFED JALAPENOS)

11 oz. can jalapenos
1 lb. Monterey Jack cheese,
 grated
1 c. Bisquick

1 lb. sausage
1 pkg. Shake 'n Bake for pork
3 eggs, beaten

Slice peppers in halves lengthwise and remove seeds. Stuff pepper halves with half of grated cheese. Make a dough with remaining cheese, Bisquick, sausage, and eggs. Make a small patty from dough and roll around stuffed peppers, then roll in Shake 'n Bake to coat. Place on cookie sheet. Bake 20 to 25 minutes at 350°.

Lion Jane McCune, Huffman Lions Club
Huffman, Texas, USA

NACHOS DELUXE

1 pkg. nacho chips
1 lb. ground beef
1 pkg. taco seasoning
1 c. refried beans
2 c. shredded Co-Jack cheese

1 c. salsa
1 c. chopped tomatoes
¼ c. chopped green onion
¼ c. sliced black olives
1 c. sour cream

Brown ground beef and drain off fat. Mix taco seasoning and meat together according to package instructions. Add refried beans to mixture and simmer for 10 minutes.

In a large baking dish, cover bottom with layer of chips. Spoon ½ meat mixture over chips, then ⅓ salsa over meat and chips, then sprinkle ½ cup cheese. Repeat layers and cover with last layer of chips. Sprinkle remaining salsa and cheese over top. Bake for 10 to 15 minutes at 325°. Remove from oven and sprinkle tomatoes, green onions, and black olives over top. Scoop sour cream onto center of nacho dish for dipping.

BURRITO BITES

1 (8 oz.) pkg. cream cheese
4 green onions, finely chopped
1 small can green chili peppers,
 chopped (unseeded) and
 drained

¼ tsp. garlic powder
1 large pkg. flour tortillas

Combine the ingredients in a food processor and mix until smooth. Spread thinly on a large package of Aztec flour tortillas. Roll up and cut into small bites. Serve on toothpicks to dip in Mexican salsa.

Mrs. Lion Robert (Margaret) Logan, Canton Lions Club
Canton, Georgia, USA

CRISP WON TON

1 lb. ground pork or pork sausage	2 tsp. soy sauce
½ lb. raw shrimp, diced	1 Tbsp. salt
¼ c. water chestnuts, chopped	2 (12 oz.) pkg. won ton wrappers
½ c. green onions, chopped	

In bowl, combine ingredients, except wrappers. Place ½ to 1 teaspoon of mix in center of wrapper. Fold into rectangles or triangles. Moisten edges with water and seal by pressing together. Fry in hot oil until brown. Drain on paper towels.

Violet M. Heslep, Huffman Lioness Club
Huffman, Texas, USA

STUFFED CELERY

1 pkg. cream cheese	Dash of salt and pepper
1 small pkg. regular Port cheese	Dash of Worcestershire sauce

Cut washed celery into 3 inch pieces and stuff with above mixture.

Uncle Don Drew, Westbrook Lions Club
Westbrook, Maine, USA

GREEN PEPPER APPETIZER

4 large bell peppers	½ tsp. basil leaves
⅓ c. vinegar	1 crumbled bay leaf
¼ c. minced onion	1 (6 oz.) pkg. smoked Cheddar
½ tsp. salt	cheese, grated
¼ tsp. black pepper	⅓ c. melted butter
½ c. olive oil	60 saltine or Ritz crackers
1 clove garlic, minced	

Place peppers in a 400°F. oven until the skin puffs (10 to 25 minutes). Remove stems, seeds, and peel, then slice into small strips. Combine vinegar, oil, salt, pepper, oil, garlic, basil, and bay leaf in a small bowl. Add pepper slices and marinate overnight in the refrigerator. Combine cheese and melted butter in a bowl. Mix well and chill. To serve, let guests spread cheese on cracker, then top with pepper. Makes 60 appetizers.

Sarah Wehling, Bothell Lions Club
Bothell, Washington, USA

Do all you can and trust God to do what you cannot.

TEXAS CAVIAR

1 can black-eyed peas with jalapenos, drained
1 can field peas with snaps, drained
3 fresh chopped tomatoes
½ red onion, chopped
½ bell pepper, chopped
1 bottle Wish-Bone lite Italian dressing
2 avocados, finely chopped

Mix all ingredients, except avocados. Chill 3 hours or overnight. Before serving, stir in finely chopped avocados. Serve with tortilla chips.

Lion Jane McCune, Huffman Lions Club
Huffman, Texas, USA

CALIFORNIA CAVIAR

1½ c. chopped ripe olives
1 Tbsp. chopped anchovies
2 tsp. lemon juice
1 tsp. olive oil
⅓ c. sour cream
1 Tbsp. chopped green onion
1 Tbsp. chopped mild red pepper (can use pimiento)
Lettuce leaves

Mix olives, anchovies, olive oil, and lemon juice. Cover tight in plastic container and refrigerate at least 3 hours or overnight. When ready to serve, turn out onto a lettuce lined dish. Top with sour cream, then sprinkle with green onions and red peppers. Serve with cracker or chips.

Mary Jane Childers, Ponderosa Lions Club
Clovis, California, USA

SAUSAGE BALLS

1 lb. sausage
3½ c. Bisquick
1 (10 oz.) pkg. shredded cheese (about 1½ c. - we prefer mild Cheddar cheese)

Mix together above ingredients with hands and form into small balls. Place on ungreased cookie sheet. Bake 15 or 20 minutes in 350° oven. Makes about 100 balls.

Billy W. Higginbotham, McMinnville Lions Club
McMinnville, Tennessee, USA

A small town is a place where the only automatic teller is the town gossip.

COWBOY JERKY

5 lb. lean beef strips
4 oz. salt
½ oz. garlic powder
½ oz. black pepper

Pinch of cure salt
2 Tbsp. liquid smoke
2 qt. water

Cut beef strips about ¼ inch thick. Make brine, combining all ingredients.

Soak meat in brine approximately 6 hours or longer. Remove meat from brine and hang up or lay out flat to dry.

Can be done at room temperature or put in oven at no more than 150°.

Leonard Knudsen, Otis Lions Club
Otis, Colorado, USA

HOMEMADE BEEF JERKY

1½ to 2 lb. beef flank
1 clove garlic, crushed
⅓ c. soy sauce

⅛ tsp. salt
⅛ tsp. pepper

1. Slice meat lengthwise with the grain into ¼ inch pieces.
2. Combine remaining ingredients and mix with meat strips. Let stand 15 to 20 minutes.
3. Drain and arrange in a single layer on a rack set in shallow baking pan.
4. Bake in 150° oven or at lowest oven temperature for at least 12 hours.
5. Store in airtight container.

Better than store bought.

Lion Fred Taniguchi, Caruthers Lions Club
Caruther, California, USA

COCKTAIL MEATBALLS

1½ lb. ground beef
1 small onion, minced
Dash of garlic salt
½ tsp. salt
Dash of pepper

1 tsp. Worcestershire sauce
1 tsp. soy sauce
1 tsp. mustard pickle relish
1 jar pickled onions
Toothpicks

Mix all ingredients, except onions. Form into balls. Fry in lightly greased pan until done. Serve with 1 onion per 1 meatball per toothpick. Makes 26 or more.

Option: Toss with toasted sesame seeds.

May be made ahead and frozen. Good to use in a lighted chafing dish.

Sarah Wehling, Bothell Lions Club
Bothell, Washington, USA

COCKTAIL MEAT BALLS

Meat Balls:

1 lb. lean ground beef
⅓ c. dry bread crumbs
¼ c. ground onion
⅓ c. skim milk

1 egg white, beaten
¼ tsp. salt
¼ tsp. allspice
⅛ tsp. pepper

In a medium bowl, mix beef, bread crumbs, onion, milk, egg white, salt, allspice, and pepper. Shape into tiny balls and place on jelly roll pan or baking sheet with sides. Bake until brown at 400° for 12 to 15 minutes. Can be frozen till ready to use.

Yogurt Sauce:

3 tsp. low sodium beef flavored
   bouillon granules
1½ c. water

1 Tbsp. cornstarch
½ c. plain lowfat yogurt

Shortly before serving, dissolve bouillon granules in water. Mix cornstarch with 1 tablespoon yogurt and stir into remaining yogurt. Add yogurt to bouillon. Add meat balls and heat gently.

The yogurt mixture may look curdled at first, but it will become creamy as it simmers.

One meat ball equals 20 calories, 0.8 g fat, 5 mg cholesterol, and 24 mg sodium.

MICROWAVE MEATBALL APPETIZERS

1 lb. ground beef
1 egg, beaten
½ c. fine bread crumbs
3 Tbsp. milk or water
1 tsp. salt

¼ tsp. paprika
⅛ tsp. pepper
1 bottle of your favorite bar-b-que,
   sweet and sour or spaghetti
   sauce

Mix all ingredients (except sauce) together and shape into 12 balls. Arrange in a circle along the outer edge of a glass pie plate. Microwave on HIGH 7 to 8 minutes, rearranging halfway through cooking time.

Top with your favorite bar-b-que, sweet and sour or spaghetti sauce. Skewer with colored toothpicks. Makes 12 appetizer meatballs.

Pessimist: a person who takes life with a grain of sulk.

BOURBON HOT DOGS
(Hors d'oeuvres)

Combine and bring to a boil:

¾ c. bourbon (rum may be used)   ½ c. brown sugar
½ c. catsup   1 tsp. grated onion

Add 1 pound wieners, cut into ½ to ¾ inch pieces. Freeze in sauce. Reheat to serve.

John J. Hess, Clarence Center Lions Club
Clarence Center, New York, USA

BARBECUE COCKTAIL WIENERS

16 oz. barbecue sauce (original   Dry onion (as desired)
    flavor)   2 Tbsp. brown sugar
10 oz. grape jelly

Simmer 10 minutes. Add cocktail wieners and simmer 10 minutes longer.

Marge Klabunde, Brownton Lions Club
Brownton, Minnesota, USA

VEGETABLE PIZZA

2 (8 oz.) tubes crescent rolls   1½ tsp. dill weed
2 (8 oz.) cream cheese   2 Tbsp. minced onion
1 c. mayonnaise

Vegetables: Can use green pepper, carrots, celery, radishes, tomatoes, cauliflower, broccoli, ripe olives (chopped), or shredded cheese.

Place unrolled rolls flat on a 17x11 inch cookie sheet. Pinch edges together. Bake 10 minutes or until lightly browned. Cool.

Mix cream cheese, mayonnaise, dill weed, and onion well. Spread on pastry. Put whatever veggies you like on top.

Cover with plastic wrap and chill well. Cut in small squares to serve as appetizer or use as snack dish. I use carrots (grated), radishes, cauliflower, and broccoli. Top with chopped ripe olives and shredded cheese. Makes a delicious and colorful dish.

Dorothy Wimmer, Rock Falls Lions Club
Sterling, Illinois, USA

❦

It takes a great deal of wisdom to recognize it in someone else.

VEGETABLE PIZZA

2 pkg. Pillsbury crescent rolls
2 (8 oz.) pkg. cream cheese
¾ c. mayonnaise
1 pkg. Hidden Valley Ranch
   dressing
Diced mushrooms

Broccoli
Cauliflower
Chopped black olives
Fresh tomatoes
Shredded Mozzarella cheese
Shredded Cheddar cheese

Crust: Pat crescent rolls onto ungreased cookie sheet. Bake as directed. Cool.

Mix cream cheese, dressing, and mayonnaise; spread on cooled crust. Spread diced and chopped vegetables thinly on cream cheese mixture. Garnish with shredded cheese. Cut into bite-size squares. *Delicious!*

ITALIAN PIE

1 lb. ground beef
½ c. chopped onion
½ tsp. salt (optional)
½ tsp. pepper
1 (8 oz.) can tomato sauce

1 (10 oz.) can onion soup
4 oz. Cheddar cheese, grated
1 can crescent rolls
½ c. sour cream (can substitute
   with Ricotta cheese)

Brown beef and onions together. Drain liquid. Add salt, pepper, tomato sauce, and onion soup. Pour all ingredients into greased baking dish (approximately 9x13 inches). Top with sour cream and grated cheese. Unroll crescent rolls. Place on top to make a crust. Bake at 375° for 25 to 30 minutes. Serve with salad.

Martha Johnson, Dolley Madison Lions Club
Greensboro, North Carolina, Guilford County, USA

The poorest of all men is not the man without a cent.
It is the man without a dream.

FRUIT PIZZA

½ c. butter
¼ c. powdered sugar
1 (8 oz.) pkg. cream cheese
⅓ c. sugar
1 tsp. vanilla
Fruit of your choice (strawberries
    melon, pineapple, kiwi,
    blueberries, mandarin
    oranges, apples, etc.)

2 Tbsp. corn starch
¼ c. sugar
1 tsp. lemon juice
1 c. fruit juice and water

Crumb crust: Mix together ½ cup butter, 1 cup flour, and ¼ cup powdered sugar. Press into small pizza pan or 13x9 inch pan to form crust. Bake for 15 minutes at 350°.

Combine one 8 ounce package cream cheese, ⅓ cup sugar, and 1 teaspoon vanilla. Spread on cooled crust. Layer fruit of your choice in artistic pattern over cream cheese layer.

Sauce: Combine 2 tablespoons cornstarch, ¼ cup sugar, 1 teaspoon lemon juice, and fruit juice and water to equal 1 cup. Cook until clear. Cool and pour over fruit. Refrigerate.

PINEAPPLE CHUNKS

1 (16 oz.) can pineapple chunks
1 lb. bacon

Toothpicks

Wrap chunks with ½ slice bacon. Hold with toothpick. Broil in oven till bacon is cooked. Use La Choy sweet and sour sauce and plum sauce for dipping.

Walter E. Loomis, North Jackson Lions Club
Jackson, Michigan, USA

SPICED PEARS

29 oz. can pear halves, drained
1½ c. honey
½ c. vinegar
3 (3 inch) cinnamon sticks
3 whole cloves

½ to 1 tsp. red or green food
    coloring
1 qt. jar (an empty mayonnaise or
    salad dressing jar is
    perfect)

Place pear halves in 1 quart jar. Heat remaining ingredients until syrup boils. Remove from heat. Add food coloring. Pour on pears; cool. Cover and refrigerate at least 8 hours. Pears will be fully colored in 12 hours. Store no longer than 8 days. Makes 1 quart. Easy to prepare. You can also substitute apricot halves, peach halves, or pineapple chunks in this recipe and *no* food coloring is necessary.

Rosemary Kish, Downriver Pride Lions Club
Lincoln Park, Michigan, USA

MICROWAVE CURRIED FRUIT

1 (20 oz.) can apricots, drained
1 (20 oz.) can pineapple chunks,
   drained
1 (20 oz.) can pear halves, drained
1 (20 oz.) can peach halves,
   drained

1 c. golden raisins
⅓ c. butter
½ tsp. curry powder
¾ c. firmly packed brown sugar
10 maraschino cherries, halved
½ c. toasted almonds

Arrange fruit in a 12x8x2 inch baking dish. Melt butter in a 1 cup measure. Stir in curry powder and brown sugar. Microwave on HIGH for 1 minute. Spoon over fruit. Microwave for 10 minutes on HIGH, basting and turning dish several times. Add cherries and nuts just before serving. Serve warm, reheating if necessary.

Phyllis Hillis, McMinnville Lions Club
McMinnville, Tennessee, USA

CHESTNUT WRAP AROUND
(Microwaveable to heat)

1 (8 oz.) can whole water
   chestnuts, drained
1 (1 lb.) pkg. bacon, sliced and cut
   in halves (not lengthwise)

¼ c. sesame seeds
Toothpicks

    Sauce:

1 c. catsup
½ c. sugar

1 c. vinegar
½ tsp. celery salt

Wrap ½ strip bacon around each chestnut and secure with toothpick. Put in a baking dish. Add sauce and bake at 350°F. until bacon is cooked (20 or more minutes). Serve warm. Sprinkle with sesame seeds.

This is a pleasant appetizer on cold, rainy nights. I have never seen it served anywhere else.

Sarah Wehling, Bothell Lions Club
Bothell, Washington, USA

WRAPPED WATER CHESTNUTS

1 can water chestnuts (whole)
1 lb. bacon, cut into thirds
½ c. mayo

½ c. bar-b-q sauce
½ c. brown sugar

Wrap bacon around chestnuts and hold with toothpicks. Put in oven on cookie sheet. Bake in oven at 350° for 30 minutes (until bacon is browned, but not hard); drain grease. Mix together mayo, sauce, and sugar. Pour over chestnuts and heat through.

Pam Sedlar, Onekama Lions Club
Onekama, Michigan, USA

WATER CHESTNUTS

2 (6 oz.) cans whole water
   chestnuts
1 lb. bacon
Toothpicks

Wrap chestnuts in ½ slice bacon. Hold with toothpick. Broil in oven till bacon is cooked. Use La Choy sweet and sour sauce and plum sauce for dipping.

Walter E. Loomis, North Jackson Lions Club
Jackson, Michigan, USA

DEVILED EGGS

12 eggs, hard-boiled and chilled
2 to 3 Tbsp. mayonnaise
Mustard to taste
Nutmeg

Cut eggs in halves lengthwise. Take yolks out of egg whites and mix in bowl with mayonnaise and mustard. Refill egg whites with yolk mixture. New and improved "Hooter Girl" idea: Sprinkle nutmeg on top. Chill and serve.

"Another Hooter Girl original!!" This was mother's recipe (Ms. Jen Long).

Mgr. Bill Acquario, Clarence Center Lions Club
Clarence Center, New York, USA

ROASTED GARLIC

6 heads garlic
Salt and pepper
1 qt. boiling water

Parboil the heads of garlic for 2 or 3 minutes. Remove from water. Sprinkle with salt and pepper. Wrap in foil. Bake in a 400° oven for 30 minutes.

After cooking, squeeze the cloves from out of the papery skin and eat plain or spread on crusty French bread.

Very interesting taste and consistency. Very mild-tasting. A good "conversation piece."

Lion Claire Cloon, Aurora Eastgate Lions Club
Aurora, Colorado, USA

STUFFED EGGS

12 hard cooked eggs
1 c. (8 oz. can) cooked crabmeat,
   flaked
1 c. finely chopped celery
2 Tbsp. finely chopped green
   pepper
1 Tbsp. French salad dressing mix
⅓ c. dairy sour cream

Slice eggs in halves (lengthwise). Remove yolks and mash well. Combine yolks with crabmeat, celery, green pepper, salad dressing, and sour cream. Blend well. Fill egg whites. Chill until serving time.

Kathryn Reiker, Silver Run-Union Mills Lions Club
Westminster, Maryland, USA

STUFFED MUSHROOMS

3 lb. fresh mushrooms
1 lb. hot pork sausage
3 (8 oz.) cans tomato sauce

⅓ c. vermouth
1 tsp. oregano

In saucepan, simmer tomato sauce, vermouth, and oregano. Remove stems from mushrooms (freeze for later use). Stuff caps with sausage. Bake on cookie sheet at 350° for ½ hour. Baked mushrooms are then added to sauce. Best if allowed to marinate for a few hours. Serve hot. Can be frozen.

TUNA FISH MOLD

2 env. Knox unflavored gelatine
1 can cream of asparagus soup
8 oz. cream cheese, softened
1 Tbsp. lemon juice
1 c. mayonnaise

1 small onion, chopped
1 green pepper, chopped
2 cans (6⅛ oz.) tuna, drained and
    flaked
½ c. cold water

Dissolve gelatine in ½ cup cold water. Heat soup and add to gelatine mixture. In large bowl, mix cream cheese, lemon juice, mayonnaise, onion, pepper, and tuna. Add soup-gelatine mixture. Mix well. Turn into a mold and refrigerate until firm. Unmold onto a serving plate. Serve with crackers. This makes a lot and fills the large Tupperware ring mold. I prepare this the day before serving and refrigerate it overnight.

Violet M. Heslep, Huffman Lions Club
Huffman, Texas, USA

TUNA PATE

1 (8 oz.) softened cream cheese
2 Tbsp. chili sauce
2 Tbsp. parsley flakes
1 tsp. minced onion

½ tsp. hot pepper sauce
2 cans tuna, well drained
Dash of garlic

Blend all ingredients. Chill 3 hours. Shape as suited and serve with crackers or cocktail breads.

Dona Bayless, Craigsville Lions Club
Craigsville, West Virginia, USA

The best thing about the future is that it comes only a day at a time.

SALMON MOLD

Served as appetizer or salad luncheons.

8 to 16 oz. canned or fresh salmon
8 oz. cream cheese
1 Tbsp. lemon juice
1 pkg. unflavored gelatin
2 Tbsp. minced onion

2 tsp. liquid smoke
1 tsp. salt
Dash of pepper (use white pepper
  if wanted)

Dissolve gelatin per package. Mix all rest of ingredients. Mold. I use a fish shaped mold. I surround this with fresh parsley, lemon slices and half a stuffed green olive for the eye of the fish. Serve with crackers.

Sarah Wehling, Bothell Lions Club
Bothell, Washington, USA

SHRIMP MOUSSE

1 small can shrimp, drained
1 can cream of mushroom soup
1 (8 oz.) pkg. cream cheese
1 env. Knox gelatine
¼ c. water

1 c. mayonnaise (not Miracle
  Whip)
⅓ c. celery, chopped
⅓ c. onion, chopped

Melt soup and cream cheese together over low heat. Remove from heat. Dissolve gelatine in water. Add gelatine and mayonnaise to soup mixture. Stir well, then fold in remaining ingredients. Put in 4 cup mold and chill to set. Serve with party pumpernickel.

SHRIMP DIP

1 (8 oz.) cream cheese, softened
⅓ c. mayo or salad dressing
1 Tbsp. lemon juice
Cocktail sauce

1 (4½ oz.) can well drained shrimp
¾ c. chopped celery
¼ c. chopped green onion
1 tsp. dill weed (optional)

Mix till well blended the cheese, mayo, and lemon juice. Stir in remaining ingredients. You can either leave in bowl or put on serving dish and form into shape. Top with cocktail sauce and refrigerate 1 to 2 hours. Serve with fresh vegetables or crackers.

Judy Stork, Arlington Lions Club
Arlington, Nebraska, USA

❧

If you want free service, you have to first pay for a warranty.

SHRIMP DIP

12 oz. cream cheese
1 small diced onion
2 Tbsp. mayonnaise
2 Tbsp. lemon juice
2 Tbsp. Worcestershire sauce

Dash of garlic salt
1 bottle chili sauce
1 can shrimp (or crabmeat)
Parsley
Ritz crackers

Cream together cream cheese, onion, mayonnaise, lemon juice, Worcestershire sauce, and garlic salt. Spread over a large tray or 2 small trays. Spread chili sauce over bottom layer. Top with shrimp (may mash to go farther) or shredded crabmeat. Sprinkle with parsley. Serve with Ritz crackers.

Note: This dip freezes well and may be made up well ahead of time.

SHRIMP DIP

1 (6 oz.) canned shrimp
1 (10 oz.) can shrimp soup

1 (3 oz.) pkg. cream cheese

Mix all ingredients and allow to set before using.

Walter E. Loomis, North Jackson Lions Club
Jackson, Michigan, USA

SPINACH BREAD

1 round whole sourdough French
    bread
2 bags sourdough bagettes
2 boxes frozen chopped spinach
1 large and 1 small container sour
    cream

1 bunch green onions
1 box Knorr leek soup mix
5 Tbsp. mayonnaise
4 stalks celery

1. Defrost spinach; drain well.
2. Slice top off of round French bread. Cut out center of bread, leaving ½ inch all around.
3. Mix together leek soup mix, sour cream, and mayonnaise.
4. Chop green onions and celery. Add to sour cream mixture. Add drained, chopped spinach. Mix thoroughly.
5. Put spinach mixture into round French bread.
6. Slice bagettes and place around French bread or serve in a basket next to dip.

❧

The greatest trouble with an idle rumor is that it doesn't remain so.

SPINACH DIP

2 c. fresh spinach, chopped, or 1 (10 oz.) pkg. frozen chopped spinach
1 bunch green onions
1 (8 oz.) can water chestnuts, sliced
1 pkg. Knorr vegetable soup mix
2 tsp. reduced-calorie mayonnaise
1¼ c. plain nonfat yogurt
½ c. shredded carrots
1 round loaf rye or sourdough bread

If using frozen spinach, thaw and squeeze out water. Combine all ingredients and chill in fridge for at least 3 hours before serving. Hollow out loaf of bread. When ready to serve, put dip in hollowed out loaf and use bread cubes made from loaf for dipping. Yield: 3½ cups.

Diabetes exchange: 4 tablespoons equals 1 vegetable, ½ fat exchange.

Rebecca Mergaert, North Jackson Lions Club
Sault Ste. Marie, Ontario, Canada

ONION DIP

1 (16 oz.) sour cream
1 pkg. onion soup mix

Just mix in bowl and serve.

Mix ahead of time for best flavor, then stir before using.

Walter E. Loomis, North Jackson Lions Club
Jackson, Michigan, USA

WATER CHESTNUT DIP

3 oz. cream cheese
1½ c. sour cream
½ c. coarsely chopped water chestnuts
¼ c. sliced pimento stuffed olives
1 (0.6 oz.) env. Italian salad dressing

Blend cream cheese and sour cream until smooth. Add remaining ingredients. Great with chips or crackers.

Mrs. Lion George (Dianne) Murphy, Canton Lions Club
Canton, Georgia, USA

DILL DIP

⅔ c. sour cream
⅔ c. mayonnaise
1 Tbsp. finely chopped parsley
1 Tbsp. instant minced onion
1 Tbsp. dried dill weed
¼ tsp. dry mustard

Combine all ingredients; mix well. Chill. Serve as a dip for assorted fresh vegetables. Yield: 1½ cups.

Mrs. Lion Robert (Margaret) Logan, Canton Lions Club
Canton, Georgia, USA

CURRY DIP
(The easy way)

1 c. mayonnaise
1½ tsp. curry powder
⅔ tsp. dry mustard

⅔ Tbsp. lemon juice
⅛ tsp. salt

Blend and chill. Makes 1 cup. Serve with raw vegetables.

Makes a nice presentation in a basket (the vegetables in the basket). I use celery and carrot strips, mushrooms, radishes, cauliflower, and broccoli pieces.

I have served this for years and people always say they have never tasted anything like it.

Sarah Wehling, Bothell Lions Club
Bothell, Washington, USA

REUBEN DIP

2 c. mayonnaise
1 small chopped onion
5 pkg. Buddig corned beef, cut in
   small strips

1 lb. Swiss cheese, grated

Put above mixture in casserole and top with sauerkraut. Bake at 350° for 35 minutes. Good served with pumpernickel bagel chips.

Mrs. Tom (Nancy) Sweet, Elburn Lions Club
Elburn, Illinois, USA

BUENO SAUSAGE DIP

1 lb. pork sausage, cooked and
   crumbled
1½ pkg. (12 oz.) cream cheese,
   softened

1 small can chili peppers,
   chopped

Cook sausage thoroughly, crumbling as you cook over low heat. Add softened cream cheese and stir constantly. Add chopped green chilies and serve warm with nacho chips.

I've had party guests look for the Visionware this dip was made in just to have a last lick.

Lion Jane Huber, Greensboro-Dolley Madison Lions Club
Greensboro, North Carolina, USA

❧

If something goes without saying, it's best to let it.

SAUSAGE DIP

1 lb. hot sausage
1 to 1½ lb. hamburger

1 chopped onion

Brown and drain the above ingredients; put in crock pot.

Add the following:

1 can crushed tomatoes
1 (2 lb.) box Velveeta cheese,
   chopped into hunks

1 can cream of mushroom soup

Let simmer until cheese melts and serve right from crock pot with chips.

Pattie Cundiff, Hodgenville Lions Club
Hodgenville, Kentucky, USA

SAUSAGE DIP

1 lb. ground beef
1 lb. pork sausage
2 lb. Velveeta cheese, softened
1 onion, minced

1 (7½ oz.) can Old El Paso
   jalapeno relish
1 can cream of mushroom soup
1 tsp. garlic powder

Cook ground beef and sausage together until lightly browned. Drain off excess fat. Add the melted cheese, onion, soup, and relish. Add garlic powder last. Serve hot with chips.

Janie Fox, Saginaw Lions Club
Saginaw, Texas, USA

HOT SAUSAGE DIP

1 lb. ground beef
1 lb. hot pork sausage
2 lb. Velveeta cheese
1 can Old El Paso jalapeno relish

1 can cream of mushroom soup
1 small onion, minced, or 2 Tbsp.
   dried minced onion flakes
1 tsp. garlic powder

Brown ground beef and sausage together in a 5 quart saucepan; drain off excess fat. Add cubed cheese to browned and drained meats to start melting. Add onion, soup, and relish. Add garlic last. Stir and simmer for 5 minutes. (Strips of dry roasted pepper and green bell pepper may be added to use as decoration on top.) Serve dip warm with chips of your choice.

Frances B. Blount, Saginaw Lions Club
Saginaw, Texas, USA

Giving is an exercise that makes a healthy heart.

LINDA'S DIP

8 avocados
1 bunch green onions
1 small can black olives
1 small can green olives
1 c. mayonnaise
2 large cans refried beans

32 oz. sour cream
1½ tsp. lemon juice
6 tomatoes
2 packs taco seasoning mix
1½ lb. Cheddar cheese
3 bags tortilla chips

Spread layer of beans in a flat casserole dish. Smash avocados in bowl; add lemon juice and mayonnaise. Spread this layer on top of beans. Mix sour cream, taco seasoning, and chopped green onions. Spread this over avocados. Slice olives, grate cheese, and dice tomatoes. Sprinkle grated cheese over entire layer. Add olives and tomatoes. Will serve at least 25. Cut in half for smaller gathering. *Serve cold.*

BACON CHEESE DIP

4 slices bacon
2 Tbsp. flour
1 c. milk
1 garlic clove
8 oz. Monterey Jack cheese, shredded (2 c.)

4 oz. Cheddar cheese, shredded (1 c.)
1 tsp. dry or prepared mustard
½ tsp. Worcestershire sauce
Dash of hot pepper sauce

Fry bacon; crumble and set aside. In bacon drippings, stir flour. Add milk and garlic; stir until smooth. Cook on HIGH in microwave for 3 to 4 minutes until thickened, stirring once. Discard garlic. Stir cheeses into mixture. Cook on MEDIUM for 4 to 6 minutes until smooth, stirring once. Stir in mustard, Worcestershire sauce, pepper sauce, and bacon bits. Mixture will thicken as it stands.

To reheat and thin slightly, cook on MEDIUM for 1 to 2 minutes. Stir once.

COTTAGE CHEESE PINEAPPLE DIP

1 (16 oz.) can crushed pineapple
24 oz. cottage cheese
4 Tbsp. Cool Whip

1 medium box orange pineapple jello

Drain pineapple until almost dry. Add pineapple to cottage cheese. Add Cool Whip and jello. Stir and serve cold. The dip will last up to 10 days in refrigerator. Serve with crackers. Serves from 5 to 10.

What's the use of having an enemy if you can have a friend?

PEPPERONI PIZZA DIP

1 (8 oz.) cream cheese, softened
½ c. dairy sour cream
1 tsp. crushed oregano
⅛ tsp. garlic powder
⅛ tsp. crushed red pepper
  (optional)

½ c. pizza sauce
½ c. chopped pepperoni
¼ c. sliced green onion
¼ c. chopped green pepper
½ c. shredded Mozzarella cheese

In small mixer bowl, beat together cream cheese, sour cream, oregano, garlic powder, and red pepper. Spread evenly in a 9 to 10 inch quiche dish or pie plate. Spread pizza sauce over the top. Sprinkle with pepperoni, onion, and green pepper. Bake at 350° for 10 minutes. Top with cheese. Bake for 5 minutes more or until cheese is melted and mixture is heated through. Serve with pepper strips, broccoli flowerets, carrot strips, or crackers. Makes 1½ cups (138 calories).

PIZZA DIP

1 (8 oz.) cream cheese
1 jar Pizza Quick sauce
1 pkg. pepperoni (slices)
1 small can sliced black olives,
  drained

1 bunch green onions, chopped
1 large pkg. Mozzarella cheese

Spread softened cream cheese in the bottom of a 9x13 inch pan. Pour pizza sauce over cream cheese. Layer sliced pepperoni over sauce. Layer chopped green onions over pepperoni. Sprinkle Mozzarella cheese on top and bake at 350° for approximately 30 minutes or until cheese is melted and bubbly.

Patti Cundiff, Hodgenville Lions Club
Hodgenville, Kentucky, USA

VEGETABLE DIP

2 c. plain yogurt
1 c. fat free/cholesterol free real
  mayonnaise (not substitute)
1 Tbsp. parsley flakes (dried or
  fresh)
1 tsp. dried minced onion or fresh
  chives, chopped

1 tsp. dill weed
1 tsp. Beau Monde
½ tsp. garlic powder
½ tsp. lite salt
4 drops of Tabasco sauce

Place coffee filter in a strainer over pan. Spoon yogurt onto coffee filter. Cover and refrigerate overnight. Pour yogurt cheese from coffee filter to bowl. Discard liquid in pan. Add remaining ingredients to yogurt cheese and mix well. Store, covered, in refrigerator. Keeps 2 weeks.

Serve with fresh vegetables such as carrot sticks, celery, peppers, cucumber, broccoli, cauliflower, tomatoes, etc., or with bread sticks. Makes 2 cups of dip.

VEGGIE DIP

8 oz. cream cheese
1 tsp. prepared mustard
½ tsp. celery salt (or to taste)

1 small tomato
1 small green pepper
6 slices bacon

Beat cream cheese and mustard till smooth. Add celery salt. Dice tomato and green pepper; add to cream cheese. Cook bacon crisp and crumble; mix into cream cheese mixture.

Carol Tagliapeitra, Eden Lions Club
Eden, Wisconsin, USA

BEAN DIP

1 c. mayonnaise
1 c. sour cream
1 can black olives
1 pkg. taco mix

10 green onions
3 cans Frito-Lay bean dip
Nacho chips

Mix bean dip and taco mix. Spread in 9x13 inch pan. Spread chopped green onions on top. Mix mayonnaise and sour cream. Spread on top of onions. Top off with sliced black olives. Serve with nacho chips or flavored crackers.

Walter E. Loomis, North Jackson Lions Club
Jackson, Michigan, USA

TACO DIP

1 to 1½ lb. ground meat
1 onion, chopped
1 pkg. taco mix
1 can green chilies, chopped
1 to 2 cans refried beans

10 to 12 oz. shredded Cheddar
   cheese
1 small bottle taco sauce
Tortilla chips

Brown meat and onions; drain grease. Add taco mix and chilies. In large casserole (glass is best), layer refried beans, meat mixture, cheese, and taco sauce. Bake at 350° for 20 minutes. Remove from oven and let set 10 minutes. Place tortilla chips around casserole for decoration as well as in a dish beside the dip.

This recipe works very well with ground turkey and ground venison.
Patti M. Montague, Richfield Township Lions Club
Davison, Michigan, USA

❦

In the good old days, people quit spending when they ran out of money.

TUNA VEGETABLE SPREAD

½ c. grated carrots
½ c. finely chopped celery
¼ c. finely chopped green onion
1 (6½ oz.) can tuna in water,
    drained

2 Tbsp. reduced-calorie
    mayonnaise
¼ c. plain nonfat yogurt
1 tsp. Worcestershire sauce
¼ tsp. pepper

Combine carrots, celery, onions, and tuna in small bowl. Add remaining ingredients and mix well. Serve with raw vegetables and crackers. Yield: About 2 cups.

Good snack for diabetics. Four tablespoons equals 1 lean meat exchange. Yummy.

Rebecca Mergaert, North Jackson Lions Club
Sault Ste. Marie, Ontario, Canada

CRABBIES

1 stick (4 oz.) margarine or butter
1 (5 oz.) jar Old English cheese
    spread
1½ tsp. mayonnaise
½ tsp. garlic salt

½ tsp. seasoned salt
1 lb. backfin crabmeat, picked
    over to remove cartilage
6 English muffins, split

Let margarine and cheese spread soften to room temperature. Mix together all ingredients. Stir in crabmeat last. Spread on split muffins. Cut into sixths and broil until bubbly and slightly crisp. May be made ahead and put into freezer until ready to use.

The greatest calamity is not to have failed, but to have failed to try!
Lois Peregoy (Mrs. Jerry), Silver Run-Union Mills Lions Club
Westminster, Maryland, USA

"HANKY-PANKIES"

1 lb. ground beef
1 lb. roll sausage (Jimmy Dean)
1 lb. Kraft Velveeta cheese

1 medium size onion, chopped
    small
1 loaf party rye

Brown ground beef, roll sausage, and onion. Pour off all excess fat. Chop up cheese and add to meat mixture. Continue to cook until cheese is melted and mixed well with meat. Remove from heat and allow to partially cool. Mixture can then be spread on rye bread (good amount). Breads can then be placed on cookie sheet and browned under broiler for immediate use, or placed in freezer until frozen and then placed into plastic bags. They then become excellent snacks for any occasion. I use either hot sausage or Mexican Velveeta (depends on how spicy you like them). "Easy to fix, enjoyed by everyone."

Lion Jerry Wilson, Onekama Lions Club
Kaleva, Michigan, USA

POLISH MISTAKES

1 lb. hamburger
1 lb. lean sausage
1 lb. Velveeta cheese
1½ Tbsp. oregano

2 Tbsp. Worcestershire sauce
1 tsp. garlic powder
2 small loaves or 1 large loaf party
  rye bread

Brown separately the hamburger and sausage; drain fat. Mix the meats and seasonings. Cut cheese in small pieces and add to mixture. Cook on low heat and stir until melted. Spread on bread. Warm in oven at 350° for about 10 minutes. May be stacked and frozen in layers.

Marilyn Merrill, Whitestown Lions Club
Whitestown, Indiana, USA

SMITHFIELD HAM SAUSAGE
AND BACKFIN CRAB SPREAD

1 (12 oz.) roll Smithfield ham
  sausage (2 Tbsp. water)
1 lb. backfin crabmeat
1 Tbsp. Old Bay seafood
  seasoning

½ c. mayonnaise
1 tsp. black pepper (optional)

Place broken up ham sausage into frying pan. Cook until browned, stirring to separate while it browns. Drain off fat. Add *2 tablespoons water.* Clamp lid on and steam until water evaporates. Set aside to cool. Pick over crabmeat to remove shell and transfer to mixing bowl. Process ham sausage till minced fine. Transfer to mixing bowl. Add black pepper and toss to blend. Fold in mayonnaise and chill. Serve on dish in a mound surrounded by crackers, using parsley or lemon slice to garnish.

This is a less salty version of Charles Henry Gray's recipe passed on to me by my sister who works at Smithfield Packing Co., Smithfield, Virginia.
Lion Vivian Quinlan, Mathews Lions Club
Mathews, Virginia, USA

Having it all doesn't necessarily mean having it all at once.

HEARTY PARTY RYES

6 oz. cream cheese
3 Tbsp. sour cream
4 to 5 drops of hot sauce
2 Tbsp. grated Parmesan cheese
1 c. grated Swiss cheese
10 slices bacon, fried crisp and
    crumbled

6 to 7 green onions, cut up thin
    (use greens)
⅔ c. chopped up black olives
1 loaf party rye

Let cream cheese soften at room temperature for about 1 hour, then blend in sour cream and hot sauce. Add Parmesan cheese, Swiss cheese, and bacon; stir up well. Add onions and black olives; mix by hand together.

Spread thickly on party rye. Put on cookie sheet to bake. Bake in oven at 350° for 10 to 12 minutes.

Can be made ahead, baked, and then well cooled, then freeze and reheat after thawing for about 5 minutes to heat through.

Everyone loves this snack. Never had a recipe that was so sought after!! This is an original!

Mrs. Dick (Pam) Jahns, Elburn Lions Club
Elburn, Illinois, USA

LIVERWURST SPREAD

½ lb. Braunschweiger, softened
12 oz. cream cheese, softened
1 Tbsp. Worcestershire

½ small onion, diced
1 tsp. melted butter

Mix together well. Chill. Serve with crackers.

Sherry Swinehart, Whittemore Lioness Club
Whittemore, Michigan, USA

HOLIDAY PIE

1 (8 oz.) pkg. cream cheese
2 Tbsp. milk
1 (2½ oz.) jar dried chipped beef
¼ c. walnuts

3 Tbsp. minced onion
2 Tbsp. minced bell pepper
8 oz. sour cream
½ tsp. black or white pepper

Blend softened cream cheese with milk. Add cut up beef. Add remaining ingredients. Put in Pyrex dish. Add walnuts to top. Bake at 350° for 15 minutes. Let set for 10 minutes. Serve with crackers or corn chips.

Mrs. Lion George (Dianne) Murphy, Canton Lions Club
Canton, Georgia, USA

ROAST BEEF ROLL-UPS
(Appetizer)

5 oz. jar dried beef (one brand is
   by Armour)
8 oz. cream cheese, softened

1 tsp. dill weed
1 tsp. horseradish (mild or hot)

Mix cheese, dill, and horseradish. Spread thinly on slices of beef. Roll up and stick with toothpick, then slice into bite-size pieces. Cover and chill until serving. May be made ahead. Makes a dinner plate full.

This recipe is quite old; never a leftover.

Sarah Wehling, Bothell Lions Club
Bothell, Washington, USA

HEAVENLY DIP (HOT)
(Chipped beef-pecan)

2 (8 oz.) cream cheese
2 c. (1 pt.) sour cream
4 Tbsp. milk
4 Tbsp. dried onion flakes (or
   fresh)
½ c. chopped green pepper
½ c. chopped red pepper
6 oz. dried sliced beef

1 Tbsp. basil
1 Tbsp. oregano
1 Tbsp. salt
1 Tbsp. pepper
1 c. chopped pecans
½ stick margarine (or butter)
Taco or chips (plain) or crackers
   (to dip)

Blend the first 3 ingredients until smooth (hand or blender). Mix next 7 dried items into the soft mixture. Break beef in small pieces. Melt margarine and lightly saute pecans. Put ⅔ pecans in dip. Place mixture in rectangular glass dish (9x13 inches). Sprinkle ⅓ cup on top. Bake at 325° for 20 minutes. Be prepared to make this as a favorite for any occasion!

Dotty Parker, Huffman Lions Club
Huffman, Texas, USA (Harris)

CHIPPED BEEF CHEESE SPREAD

1 tsp. dried minced onion flakes
1 (8 oz.) pkg. cream cheese,
   softened
2 Tbsp. mayonnaise

1 to 3 Tbsp. milk
1 (3 oz.) pkg. dried chipped beef,
   chopped up
¼ c. chopped green olives

Mix softened cream cheese with dried minced onion flakes. Add mayonnaise to the cream cheese and minced onion flakes; mix well. Add 1 to 3 tablespoons milk to the cream cheese mixture to give it a smooth texture, but not to make soupy. Add the dried chopped chipped beef and chopped green olives to the cream cheese mixture. Refrigerate for 3 to 4 hours. Serve with variety of crackers.

CHIPPED BEEF BALL

1 jar dried beef
1 bunch green onions, chopped
1 tsp. Accent

8 oz. cream cheese
1 tsp. Worcestershire sauce
¼ tsp. garlic salt

Chop beef in the blender. Mix ½ beef with onions and tops and other ingredients. Roll ball in rest of beef. Serve with crackers.

Whatever you dislike in another person, be sure to correct in yourself.
Betty Arnold, Rock Hill Lions Club
Rock Hill, South Carolina, USA

BAKED CREAM CHEESE APPETIZER

1 (4 oz.) can refrigerated crescent
   dinner rolls
1½ tsp. minced fresh dill weed or
   ½ tsp. dried whole dill weed

1 (8 oz.) pkg. cream cheese
1 egg yolk, beaten
Fresh dill weed sprig (garnish)

Unroll dough on a lightly floured surface; press seams together to form a 12x4 inch rectangle. Sprinkle and gently press minced dill weed onto top of cream cheese. Place cream cheese, dill weed side down, in center of dough; bring up sides of dough snugly around cheese, pinching to seal.

Place, seam side down, on a lightly greased baking sheet. Brush with egg yolk. Bake at 350° for 20 to 22 minutes. Garnish if desired. Serve warm with crackers. Yields 16 appetizer servings.

A warm knife makes cheese easier to slice.
Mrs. Charlotte M. Garner, Pascagoula Evening Lions Club
Pascagoula, Mississippi, USA

HOT OLIVE CHEESE PUFFS

1 c. soft shredded sharp cheese
½ c. flour
½ tsp. Worcestershire sauce
3 Tbsp. soft butter

1 tsp. paprika
Dash of salt
24 to 36 medium size stuffed
   green olives

Cream cheese and butter together. Blend all ingredients, except olives. Mold a slightly rounded teaspoon of cheese and butter dough around each olive, covering completely. Bake on ungreased cookie sheet at 400°F. for 12 minutes. Let stand to cool 5 minutes before serving.

Marie E. Ohlinger, Blandon (Lioness) Lions Club
Blandon, Pennsylvania, USA

❦

Some people are like blisters. They don't show up until the work is done.

CHEESE BALL

1 (8 oz.) cream cheese
1 (8 oz.) Cheddar cheese
1 (4 oz.) Blue cheese
1 tsp. chives
1 tsp. parsley flakes
1 tsp. hydrated onions

1 Tbsp. chopped pimentos
1 (3 oz.) pkg. chopped chipped
    beef
Nuts (any kind - use later; set
    aside)

Mix well all ingredients. Form into ball shape. Coat ball with nuts. Chill. (Very good.)

Thelma Bankert (Mrs. Melvin), Silver Run-Union Mills Lions Club
Littlestown, Pennsylvania, USA

ALL OCCASION CHEESE BALL

1 (8 oz.) pkg. cream cheese
2 tsp. lemon dill seasoner
2 Tbsp. crushed pineapple,
    drained

2 Tbsp. finely chopped bell
    pepper, onions, and olives
3 Tbsp. walnuts, chopped

Mix together and form into ball. Roll in coconut or more crushed walnuts. (Pecans can also be used.) Decorate for the occasion - Easter, Christmas, etc.

Jack and Ruth Graham, Lyman Lions Club
Lyman, Wyoming, USA

CHEESE ROLL

2 (8 oz.) pkg. cream cheese
½ pkg. Blue cheese (4 oz.)
1 tsp. garlic salt

2 tsp. chopped green peppers
2 tsp. pimentos
Toasted almonds

Roll in ball and then roll in toasted almonds. Put in foil and refrigerate to chill.

Bertha Smith, President, Parkway Lions Club
Panama City, Florida, USA

SPECIAL CHEESE BALL

2 (8 oz.) cream cheese
1 (8 oz.) can crushed pineapple
2 c. chopped pecans or English
    walnuts

2 Tbsp. minced onion
1 tsp. salt

Soften cream cheese. Stir in pineapple, onions, salt, and ½ of nuts. Form ball. Roll in rest of nuts. Put in frididaire. Keeps for several weeks.

Jeanne Wait, Whitestown Lions Club
Whitestown, Indiana, USA

CHEESE BALL

2 pkg. cream cheese
1 small chopped onion
½ tsp. paprika

2 sticks oleo
½ tsp. salt

Let cream cheese and oleo soften at room temperature for a couple of hours. Mix all ingredients thoroughly. Form into a ball. Roll in chopped walnuts. Top with cherry. Bon Appetit.

Kitchen hint: Cut down on cholesterol by substituting equal parts of applesauce for oil needed in recipe. Works great. Tastes great.
Robin DeShano, Lioness Whittemore Lions Club
Whittemore, Michigan, USA

CHEESE BALL

2 (8 oz.) bars cream cheese,
  softened
1 small jar dried beef (use half)
1 c. crushed pecans

1 (4 oz.) shredded Cheddar
  cheese
1 pkg. Hidden Valley Ranch
  dressing

Mix all ingredients well. Place 1 cup crushed pecans on wax paper; roll cheese ball in pecans until coated. Makes 2 or 1 big cheese ball.
Laura East, Mt. Airy Foothills Lions Club
Mt. Airy, North Carolina, USA

JIM'S CHEESE BALL

2 (8 oz.) cream cheese
1½ sticks butter
1 container Kraft Cracker Barrel
  Cheddar cheese spread

1 small onion, minced
2 c. chopped walnuts or pecans

Mix ingredients together. Form in ball and roll in the nuts.
Lion Jim Fisher, Rootstown Lions Club
Rootstown Township, Rootstown, Ohio, USA

CHEESE LOG

2 large pkg. cream cheese
10 oz. Cheddar cheese, grated
1 tsp. garlic powder
1 Tbsp. Worcestershire sauce

2 Tbsp. liquid smoke
Chopped pecans
Paprika (optional)

Soften the cream cheese. Mix the ingredients. You may add finely chopped pecans to the roll and dust with paprika or you may omit putting the pecans in the mix and roll the mix in the pecans instead. Refrigerate a few hours before serving. Make the rolls the size to fit on a Ritz cracker or make a cheese ball.
Janie Fox, Saginaw Lions Club
Saginaw, Texas, USA

CHEESE BALL OR SPREAD

1 (8 oz.) pkg. Philadelphia cream cheese
1 (5 oz.) jar Kraft Roka Blue cheese spread
1 (5 oz.) jar Kraft bacon cheese spread
1 Tbsp. Worcestershire sauce
1 Tbsp. dry minced onion
1 Tbsp. chopped stuffed olives
2½ oz. pkg. chopped pecans

Mix and chill overnight. Form into ball and roll in chopped pecans. For spread, add ½ cup butter or oleo and omit nuts.

You may substitute any flavor cheese spread you desire.

Mrs. Carl (Jane) Lechlitner, Baugo Lions Club
Elkhart, Indiana, USA

SUNGREN'S CHEESE BALL

2 (8 oz.) cream cheese (room temperature)
1 cube butter
1 small can chopped ripe olives, drained
1 small jar Cheez Whiz

Mix and chill. Shape into a ball, then roll in any chopped nuts.

Nut options: Pecans, peanuts, or walnuts.

This is a friend's recipe, who loves simple, easy preparation.

Sarah Wehling, Bothell Lions Club
Bothell, Washington, USA

HAM AND CHEESE BALL

8 oz. pkg. cream cheese
¼ c. mayonnaise
2 (8 oz.) tins Burns flaked ham
2 Tbsp. chopped parsley
1 tsp. minced onion
¼ tsp. dry mustard
¼ tsp. Tabasco
½ c. chopped walnuts

Beat cheese and mayonnaise until smooth. Stir in next 5 ingredients. Cover and chill several hours. Form into 2 medium size balls. Roll in nuts to coat. Freezes well.

Can be made into a log for Christmas. Place on lettuce.

This recipe we have every Christmas for our staff party.

Isabelle Templeton, Jasper Mountain Lions Club
Jasper, Alberta, Canada

If at first you don't succeed, try out for second.

PINEAPPLE CHEESE BALL

2 (8 oz.) cream cheese
1 (8½ oz.) crushed pineapple,
  drained
2 c. finely chopped pecans

¼ c. chopped green peppers
2 tsp. chopped onions
¼ tsp. salt

Put salt and cheese in bowl and mix. Add remaining ingredients, except for 1 cup pecans. Mix well. Make/shape into ball - ball will be soft. Refrigerate for approximately 1 hour or until slightly firm. Roll in remaining pecans to coat ball. Keep refrigerated until ready to use.

Dona Bayless, Craigsville Lions Club
Craigsville, West Virginia, USA

PINEAPPLE CHEESE BALL

2 (8 oz.) pkg. cream cheese,
  softened
2 Tbsp. finely chopped onion
1 Tbsp. seasoning salt

2 c. chopped pecans
¼ c. finely chopped green pepper
1 (8½ oz.) can crushed pineapple,
  drained

In a medium bowl, beat cream cheese with a fork. Gradually stir in crushed pineapple, 1 cup pecans, green pepper, onion, and seasoning salt. Shape into a ball and roll in the remaining nuts. Wrap in plastic wrap and refrigerate until well chilled (overnight). Place cheese ball on serving tray and garnish with pineapple slices, cherries, or parsley. Surround with crackers.

This is a big hit for mid-winter hospitality rooms.
Lion Jane Huber, Greensboro Dolley Madison Lions Club
Greensboro, North Carolina, USA

PINEAPPLE CHEESE BALL

1 small can crushed pineapple,
  drained
2 pkg. (8 oz.) cream cheese,
  softened
1 c. pecans, chopped

3 Tbsp. finely chopped onion
1 tsp. salt
1 tsp. chopped chives
1 c. pecans (to roll ball in)

Beat cream cheese by hand until smooth, then stir in pineapple, pecans, chives, onions, and salt. Shape into ball and roll in the other cup of pecans. Wrap in plastic wrap. Chill for at least 3 hours.

Janice P. Baynard, Dolley Madison Lions Club
Greensboro, North Carolina, USA

❦

Don't judge people by their relatives.

CHEESE DUMPLINGS

Dough:

2 c. flour   **3 large eggs**

Make a large well in center of flour and drop in eggs. Work flour into eggs. You should have a fairly stiff dough. You may have a little flour left in bowl, but this is okay. Set aside to rest while you make filling.

Filling:

1 (24 oz.) ctn. cottage cheese,   **2 eggs**
  drained

Mix cottage cheese with eggs.

Topping:

1 lb. thick sliced bacon, diced   **6 large onions, sliced**

Fry bacon till crisp. Lift out bacon bits with a slotted spoon. Pour off and reserve about ½ of the grease. Fry onions in bacon grease until soft and clear. Do not brown. Use reserved bacon grease only if onions seem too dry. Add bacon bits to onions before serving.

Bring a large pot of salted water to a boil. Divide dough into 2 or 3 portions for easy handling. Roll each portion ⅛ inch thick. Cut into 2 inch squares. Put a spoonful of filling on square and fold over into 3 corner package. Dampen edges of dough and seal with fingers or fork.

Drop 12 at a time into boiling water and cook until done, a few minutes after they float to the top. Cook until dough is "al dente." Remove and keep warm. Top with onion-bacon topping and serve.

CHEESE PUFFS

May be frozen. Do not thaw before baking.

4 oz. cream cheese, softened   **⅛ tsp. cayenne pepper**
¾ tsp. grated onion   **4 Tbsp. grated Parmesan cheese**
¼ c. mayonnaise   **Party rye**
1 Tbsp. chopped chives

In mixing bowl, combine cream cheese, onion, mayonnaise, chives, pepper, and Parmesan cheese. Mix well. Spread on party rye. Bake at 350° for 15 minutes.

John J. Hess, Clarence Center Lions Club
Clarence Center, New York, USA

❦

A man's ability is usually rated by what he finishes, not by what he starts.

MINIATURE BACON-CHEESE QUICHE

1 egg, beaten
½ c. milk (can use skim milk)
1 tsp. pepper
½ c. shredded Cheddar cheese
½ c. shredded Muenster cheese

2 slices bacon, cooked and
  crumbled
1 Tbsp. minced onion
1 Tbsp. minced green pepper

Pastry Shells:

1 (3 oz.) pkg. cream cheese
6 Tbsp. margarine, softened

1½ c. all-purpose flour

Combine ingredients and stir well; pour into prepared pastry shells. Bake at 350° for 20 minutes. Yield: 2½ dozen.

Pastry Shells: Combine cream cheese and margarine, blending until smooth. Add flour and mix well. Shape dough into 30 (1 inch) balls. Place in lightly greased miniature muffin pans. Shape each into shell. Prick bottom and sides with fork. Bake at 400° for 5 minutes. Let cool.

Mrs. Lion George (Dianne) Murphy, Canton Lions Club
Canton, Georgia, USA

KAHLUA CARAMEL CORN

2 qt. popped corn
½ c. Kahlua
1 c. sugar

2 Tbsp. cider vinegar
3 Tbsp. butter
¾ c. cashews

After popping corn, keep it warm in low oven. Heat Kahlua, sugar, and vinegar to boiling, stirring until sugar dissolves. Add butter and boil just to hard crack stage (300°). Pour over warm corn; add nuts and cool. Can be stored in airtight container for several weeks. Do not refrigerate.

Nancy Fausett, Lyman Lions Club
Lyman, Wyoming, USA

MICROWAVE KARMEL CORN

4 qt. popped corn
1 large paper grocery bag
½ c. butter
1 c. brown sugar

¼ c. light corn syrup
½ tsp. salt
1 tsp. vanilla
¾ tsp. baking soda

Place popped corn in paper bag. Mix butter, brown sugar, corn syrup, and salt in bowl. Microwave mixture on HIGH for 4 minutes. Stir twice while cooking in microwave oven. Add vanilla and baking soda. Stir mixture until foamy. Pour over popcorn in bag. Shake bag well. Place bag inside microwave oven. Cook on HIGH for 1½ minutes. Shake. Cook on HIGH for 1 minute. Shake. Cook on HIGH for 30 seconds. Shake. Spread on cookie sheet to cool.

Margery J. Bradbury, Moweaqua Lions Club
Moweaqua, Illinois, USA

CARAMEL CORN

1½ c. white sugar
½ c. white corn syrup
½ lb. butter (butter works best)

16 c. popped corn
1 c. dry roasted peanuts (optional)

Pop corn and set aside in large stainless steel bowl. Add peanuts. (Do not use plastic.) Place sugar, corn syrup, and butter in heavy saucepan; bring to boil. Cook to 300° or hard crack. Mixture will turn light brown. Pour syrup mixture over popcorn and peanuts. Toss well. Pour mixture out on wax paper. *Cool.*

I am Luanne Shafer, wife and mother of 3 sons. We live on the family farm. We raise wheat, cattle, sheep, ducks, and chickens. I am a Master Food Preserver and FCE member. I am the County Vice President. I use this recipe as a gift and make about 20 recipes each Christmas. I can't remember where I got it, but have had it for years. Great make ahead gift for bake sales also. Simple but good. Enjoy.

Luanne Shafer, Otis Lions Club
Otis County, USA

POPCORN BALLS

1 c. molasses
1 Tbsp. vinegar
1 tsp. soda

½ tsp. salt
4 qt. popcorn
½ c. peanuts

Boil molasses, vinegar, soda, and salt until it tests brittle in cold water. Pour the molasses mixture over the popcorn and mix. Grease hands and form into balls.

Ursula J. Harrington, Westbook Lions Club
Westbrook, Maine, USA

POPCORN CAKE

1 gal. popped popcorn
1 lb. salted peanuts
1 lb. M&M's

1 lb. marshmallows
½ c. vegetable oil
½ c. butter

Melt marshmallows, butter, and vegetable oil in saucepan over low heat. Put popcorn, M&M's, and peanuts in a large bowl; mix together. When marshmallows are melted well, pour it over popcorn mixture and mix well. Pour in greased Bundt or tube cake pan and let cool. You may cool in refrigerator for a few minutes.

I fixed this for a goodie day at work and everyone really liked it. I also fixed it for the Christmas holidays and it looked festive with the M&M's.

Faye Blount, Levelland Lioness Club
Levelland, Texas, USA

Lose an hour in the morning and you will be all day hunting it.

POPCORN

Candied Popcorn:

6 qt. plain popped popcorn	**2 Tbsp. water**
¾ c. light corn syrup	**4 c. (1 lb.) powdered sugar**
¼ c. butter or margarine	**1 c. tiny marshmallows**

In 3 quart saucepan, combine all ingredients, except the popcorn. Cook and stir over low heat until mixture comes to a boil. Pour over popcorn and toss to coat. Cool and store in airtight container. Yield: 6 quarts.

Caramel Corn:

12 qt. plain popped popcorn	**2 lb. packed brown sugar**
1 lb. peanuts (optional)	**½ c. dark corn syrup**
2 c. butter or margarine	**½ c. molasses**

Put popcorn in 2 bowls. In a 5 quart saucepan, combine all ingredients, except the popcorn. Bring to a boil over medium heat; boil and stir for 5 minutes. Pour half of syrup over each bowl of popcorn and stir to coat. Turn coated popcorn into a large roasting pan. Bake at 250° for 1 hour. Remove from oven and break apart while warm. Cool. Yield: 12 quarts.

"Life is what you make it."
Lion Kathleen Schatz Dague, Aurora Eastgage Lions Club
Aurora, Colorado, USA

CANDIED WALNUTS

¼ c. butter, melted (½ stick)	**¼ tsp. salt**
1 egg *white*	**½ lb. shelled walnuts**
½ c. granulated sugar	

Preheat oven to 300°. Place melted butter in 13x9 inch pan. In small bowl with mixer at high speed, beat egg white, gradually adding sugar and salt. Beat until stiff peaks form. Fold in nuts. Spread mixture in buttered pan. Bake for 30 to 40 minutes, turning nuts and shaking pan frequently until nuts are slightly browned and crisp. Cool nuts in pan on wire rack for a few minutes. Turn out on heavy brown paper to cool completely.

The future is purchased by the present.

GARBAGE MIX

5 to 6 c. Corn Chex
5 to 6 c. Rice Chex
5 to 6 c. Crispix
5 to 6 c. Cheerios
5 to 6 c. pretzels (thin stick)
1 (1 lb.) can Spanish peanuts
1 lb. pecans

2½ sticks margarine
⅔ c. oil
5 tsp. garlic salt
Few shakes of Tabasco sauce
4 tsp. salt
5 tsp. Worcestershire sauce

Mix cereal, nuts, and pretzels in a large baking pan. Bring margarine, oil, garlic salt, Tabasco, Worcestershire, and salt to a full boil. Stir and spoon over cereal mixture. Stir mixture thoroughly. Bake at 300° for 1 hour, stirring every 15 minutes. Cool. This freezes well. The recipe serves a crowd or makes enough for many parties.

PEOPLE CHOW

1 (12 oz.) pkg. chocolate chips
1 c. peanut butter
1 stick margarine

1 box Crispix cereal
3 c. powdered sugar

Melt chocolate chips, peanut butter, and margarine. Pour over cereal. Put ½ the powdered sugar and ½ the mixture in Ziploc plastic bag. Shake until coated evenly. Pour out on waxed paper. Repeat process (powdered sugar and mixture) in bag. Store mixture in covered container. This recipe is delicious and very easy to make. Even "little Lions" can make this.

Lion Theresa Hill, Hector Lions Club
Hector, Minnesota, USA

LOWER CALORIE GRANOLA

3 c. rolled oats
1½ c. wheat germ
¼ c. dry milk
¼ c. chopped nuts or seeds
½ c. raisins

⅓ c. safflower oil
⅓ c. honey
¼ tsp. cinnamon
1 tsp. vanilla extract

Mix oats, wheat germ, dry milk, and chopped nuts in large bowl. Heat and stir oil and honey in small saucepan until blended (about 2 minutes). Remove from heat and stir in cinnamon and vanilla. Drizzle mixture over oat mixture and stir well. Spread on 2 cookie sheets and bake at 300° for 10 minutes. Remove and stir well. Store in container and enjoy.

Bertha Smith, President, Pakway Lions Club
Panama City, Floria, USA

BEVERAGES

CRANBERRY-GRAPE SPRITZER
(Punch)

1 (12 oz.) can Welch's frozen
   cranberry juice cocktail
   concentrate, thawed
3 cans (4½ c.) club soda, chilled

2 (25.4 oz.) bottles Welch's
   sparkling red or white grape
   juice
Chilled orange slices

In punch bowl, gently stir together cranberry juice cocktail concentrate and club soda; add sparkling grape juice. Garnish with orange slices. Serve immediately in ice-filled glasses. Makes about 15 (¾ cup) servings.

Marie E. Ohlinger, Blandon Lioness Club
Blandon, Pennsylvania, USA

LIME PUNCH

1 large box lime Jell-O
2 c. boiling water
1½ c. sugar
1 small can frozen concentrated
   orange juice

1 large can unsweetened
   pineapple juice
6 c. cold water

Mix boiling water and box of lime Jell-O. Mix well. Add sugar, then add rest of the ingredients. This mixture makes 5 quarts. Freeze this mixture, then 2½ hours before serving time, remove from freezer. Add 2 quarts ginger ale, Sprite, or Atreat-Treatum. Mixture should be slushy. Very refreshing drink.

Verna M. Habecker, Baroness Stiegle Lioness Club
Lititz, Pennsylvania, USA

PARTY FRUIT PUNCH

6 very ripe bananas
1 c. sugar
12 oz. frozen condensed orange
   juice (mix with water it
   called for)

1 large (48 oz.) can pineapple juice
10 oz. pkg. frozen or fresh
   strawberries
5 qt. ginger ale

Put bananas in blender. Add 1 cup sugar. Add frozen orange mix, pineapple juice, and 5 quarts ginger ale in a gallon jar. Add strawberries that have been cut in halves.

This is great for a wedding.

Shirley Caterbury, Eastmont Lions Club
East Wenatchee, Washington, USA

PUNCH FOR 100 PEOPLE

2 (12 oz.) frozen orange juice
2 (12 oz.) frozen lemonade
2 (46 oz.) pineapple juice
7 qt. water

6 c. sugar
4 small pkg. strawberry Kool-Aid
4 qt. ginger ale

Make a syrup of water and sugar. Add orange juice, lemonade, pineapple juice, and strawberry Kool-Aid. Put in large container and chill well. When ready to use, add punch mixture and ginger ale in equal proportions (such as 2 quarts ginger ale to ½ of punch mixture). Everyone loves this punch. It has gone to many a shower, reception, and party. Can be made ahead and stored for days.

Lioness Dora T. Poythress, Lawrenceville Lioness Club
Lawrenceville, Virginia, USA

PERFECT PARTY PUNCH

1 chilled (64 oz.) ctn. Dole country
    raspberry
1 chilled (64 oz.) bottle Cran-Apple
    juice
1 (2 liter) bottle lemon lime soda

3 fresh lemons
3 fresh limes
1 (750 ml) bottle white wine
    (optional)

Cut 1 lemon and 1 lime into thin slices. Remove seeds. Arrange alternating slices of fruit in the bottom of a 3½ cup ring mold. Pour in enough juice to barely cover fruit. Freeze until set. Add enough juice to fill mold. Freeze overnight. Squeeze juice from remaining lemons and limes into large punch bowl. Add rest of ingredients and stir to mix. Unmold frozen ring and float in punch. Makes 35 (6 ounce) servings.

Kathy Gallant, Westbook Lions Club
Westbrook, Maine, USA

It's hard to say which is worse -
having a child who doesn't practice his music lessons, or one who does.

LUSCIOUS PUNCH

2 c. sugar   1 c. instant tea

> Mix with water to taste.

> Add:

1 sliced lemon   1 sliced orange
1 sliced lime

> Allow to set overnight. Take out fruit.

> Add:

1 large can frozen grape juice   2 (12 oz.) cans frozen orange juice
3 cans frozen pineapple juice

> Refrigerate.

> When ready to serve, add:

3 qt. chilled ginger ale   1 sliced lime
1 sliced lemon   1 sliced orange

> Serves lots!

Peg Turner, Rootstown Lions Club
Rootstown, Ohio, USA

BLUE JAY PUNCH

6 (12 oz.) cans frozen lemonade   6 (48 oz.) cans pineapple juice
12 (12 oz.) cans frozen orange   12 oz. ginger ale
   concentrate   Alcohol (add if desired)
1½ c. maraschino cherry juice

Thaw frozen juices slightly and mix with other juices. Add ginger ale just before serving. This large quantity (approximately 100 glasses) may be divided into 2 punch bowls, with alcohol being added to one bowl.

Howard Fleming, PDG A-2, Otter Valley Lions Club
Otterville, Ontario, Canada

A song in the heart will put a smile on the face.

BANANA SLUSH PUNCH

2 c. sugar
6 c. water
1 (6 oz.) can frozen pure orange
   juice
½ c. fresh lemon juice

2 (12 oz.) cans frozen pure
   pineapple juice
6 large bananas (not overripe),
   mashed
6 bottles ginger ale

Combine all ingredients (except ginger ale) into an 8 quart container. Stir well to blend. Freeze in large or small containers. Before serving, scoop slush into a goblet or ice tea glass. Pour ample amount of ginger ale over slush and stir until mixture forms a smooth consistency. Garnish with a fruit slice or assorted bowl or punch bowl. Yields 6 quarts.

Very good punch for wedding receptions and a very good drink for hot days.
Lion Ethel D. Parr, Mt. Holly Springs Lions Club
Gardners, Pennsylvania, USA

FIRST NIGHT FREEZES

12 oz. can frozen lemonade
   concentrate, thawed
12 oz. can frozen limeade
   concentrate, thawed
1 c. powdered sugar

4 egg whites
6 c. crushed ice
1 qt. club soda
Lime slices
Coarse salt

In a 4 quart, no metal container, combine lemonade, limeade, powdered sugar, egg whites, and crushed ice. Mix well. Cover and freeze, stirring occasionally. Remove from freezer for 30 minutes before serving. Spoon 2 cups slush mixture into blender; add 1 cup club soda. Blend until frothy. To serve, rub rim of glass with lime slice. Dip rim of glass in coarse salt; fill glass. Garnish with lime slice. Makes 24 servings.

Bob Swett, Westbrook Lions Club
Westbrook, Maine, USA

SLUSH

2½ c. orange juice
5 bananas, mashed
4 c. sugar

½ c. lemon juice
4 c. pineapple juice
6 c. water

Combine sugar and water. Heat until sugar is dissolved. Remove from heat; cool. Combine with remaining ingredients. Freeze. To serve: Fill glass half full of slush and pour on 7-Up or Sprite.

Valerie Borecky, Lyman Lions Club
Lyman, Wyoming, USA

EGGNOG

15 eggs, separated
2 c. sugar
10 oz. rum
6 oz. brandy

2 c. blended whisky
1½ qt. whipping cream
1 qt. half & half
2 tsp. vanilla

Beat egg yolks and add the sugar. When blended, add the alcohol and set aside. Beat the whipping cream till thick and mix with the half & half. Fold this into the alcohol mixture and add the vanilla. Beat the egg whites until they peak and fold both ingredients together. Chill for 24 hours in covered container. Stir before serving. Makes 175 ounces or about 35 servings.

William M. Davidson, IV, Statesboro Lions Club
Statesboro, Georgia, USA

WOODY'S REVENGE

32 oz. orange-pineapple juice
14 oz. rum
3 oz. apricot brandy
3 oz. vodka
4 oz. grain alcohol

4 oz. cherry juice
3 oz. lemon juice
6 oz. apricot nectar
2 tsp. powdered sugar

Mix all ingredients together in a large jar. Place ice in glasses and fill with mixture. Garnish with orange slices and cherries. Be careful of the second drink.

William M. Davidson, IV, Statesboro Lions Club
Statesboro, Georgia, USA

RUM GOODIES

1 qt. rum
1 qt. pineapple juice
1 qt. orange juice
1 qt. lemon juice (aid)
1 qt. Hawaiian juice (punch)
1 qt. white wine

2 small cans apricot nectar
1 small can peach nectar
1 bottle coconut flavoring
Orange slices, pineapple slices
Cherries

Mix all liquid ingredients in a large container. Place crushed ice in the glasses and garnish with the fruit. Pour punch into the glasses and serve.

This recipe was made for parties, etc., when my wife and I were stationed at the Navy Base, Guantanamo Bay, Cuba. Coconut Rum Liqueur was used instead of the flavoring.

William M. Davidson, IV, Statesboro Lions Club
Statesboro, Georgia, USA

❦

Love is always an appropriate gift.

IRISH CREAM

1 can sweetened condensed milk
½ pt. heavy cream or 1 pt. half &
    half
¼ c. milk

1 Tbsp. chocolate syrup
1 tsp. instant coffee
8 shots (1 oz. shots) whiskey

Dissolve instant coffee in just a little boiling water and cool. Mix everything together and enjoy!

Better than Bailey's.

Rev. Fred Gilbert, Dannemora Lions Club
Dannemora, New York, USA

FLY ME TO CANCUN MARGARITA

1 can frozen limeade
1 can tequila

½ can Triple Sec
Ice

Fill blender with ice. Pour in all liquids. Blend. Serve in chilled glasses with salted rims.

Faith Spivey, Manteno Lions Club
Manteno, Illinois, USA

KAHLUA

4 c. water
4 c. sugar
1 Tbsp. Hershey's syrup
½ tsp. glycerin

¾ c. instant coffee
1 fifth vodka
1 vanilla bean, chopped fine

Boil water and sugar for 15 minutes. Take off heat. Add coffee slowly, then syrup and vanilla bean. Cool. Add vodka and glycerin. Let stand for 2 to 3 weeks.

Louie Lampron, Westbrook Lions Club
Westbrook, Maine, USA

GRANDMA'S FERMENTED GRAPE WINE

Pick, wash, and mash grapes, adding enough water to bring juice over the grapes. Let stand 24 hours. Press out pulps. Put in bags and strain the juice. Add as much water as there is juice.

To every gallon of mixture, add 3 pounds sugar. Stir until dissolved, then don't stir anymore. Let stand 7 days, skimming every morning, then drain off and strain. Put in jugs. Keep lightly capped 3 to 4 days, then cap tight. Leave until March undisturbed (if you can). Strain and put back into jugs. Ready to use. We use 4 gallon crock jars and glass jugs.

Lion Jack Hamilton, Graysville/Proctor Lions Club
Proctor, West Virginia, USA

STRAWBERRY DAIQUIRI

2 (10 oz.) pkg. frozen strawberries,
    thawed and blended
1 (12 oz.) can frozen orange juice,
    thawed
2 c. sugar

9 c. water
2 pkg. unsweetened Kool-Aid
1 pt. gin, rum or vodka
7-Up (added later into glass)

Mix all ingredients in a 5 quart ice cream pail. Stir well! Freeze 24 hours before serving. Fill glass ½ to ⅔ full with daiquiri mixture. Add 7-Up to fill glass.

RaNaye Baumgarten, Brownton Lions Club
Brownton, Minnesota, USA

MARGARITAS

6 oz. frozen limeade concentrate
6 oz. tequila

3 oz. Triple Sec
2 egg whites

Put all ingredients in blender; fill to top with ice and blend until smooth.

Optional: Stir in salt rimmed glasses and garnish with lime wedges.

RaNaye Baumgarten, Brownton Lions Club
Brownton, Minnesota, USA

NEW YEAR'S NECTAR

3 cinnamon sticks
1 tsp. whole cloves
6 whole allspice
46 oz. can apple juice

12 oz. can apricot nectar
6 oz. can frozen lemonade
    concentrate, thawed

Tie all spices in cheesecloth bag. In large saucepan, combine apple juice, apricot nectar, and lemonade concentrate; add spice bag. Bring to a boil; reduce heat and simmer for 10 minutes. Remove spice bag. Serve hot in mugs or cups. Makes 16 (4 ounce) servings.

Bob Swett, Westbrook Lions Club
Westbrook, Maine, USA

❦

Some people make the world special just by being in it.

HOT WASSAIL

4 spice (orange) tea bags
1 gal. cider
2 qt. orange juice
1½ c. sugar

1 qt. cranberry juice
4 cinnamon sticks
½ c. candy hearts
12 whole cloves

Pour 1 quart boiling water over 4 spice (orange) tea bags. Steep for 4 minutes. In large pot, combine tea with cider, orange juice, cranberry juice, and sugar. Bring to a boil, then reduce heat to simmer. Add cinnamon sticks, candy hearts, and cloves. Simmer for 30 minutes. Remove cloves before serving. Makes 2 gallons.

Option: Put 12 cloves in a whole orange and add to pot.

Mary Levecque, Westbrook Lions Club
Westbrook, Maine, USA

FRESH HOMEMADE LEMONADE

1 Tbsp. grated lemon rind
1 c. lemon juice (4 or 5 lemons)
1 c. sugar
4½ c. water

1 lemon, sliced
Ice cubes
Mint leaves or sliced lemon for
  garnish

Lemon Syrup: Prepare and mix first 3 items. Stir to dissolve sugar. Keep in a covered container in fridge until ready to use. For a pitcher of lemonade, use all the lemon syrup and 4½ cups water with lemon slices. For a glass full, use 3 tablespoons syrup in glass and ice. Fill with water. Use a piece of mint leaf or slice of lemon for garnish.

Club soda can be substituted for water for a sparkling and refreshing drink.

Walter E. Loomis, North Jackson Lions Club
Jackson, Michigan, USA

CAPPUCCINO MIX

1 c. instant coffee creamer
1 c. instant chocolate drink mix
⅔ c. instant coffee crystals

½ c. sugar
½ tsp. ground cinnamon
¼ tsp. ground nutmeg

Combine all ingredients. Mix well. Store in an airtight container. To prepare one serving, add 3 tablespoons mix to 6 ounces hot water. Stir well. Yields 3 cups dry mix.

Rena Lesser, Mitchell Lioness Club
Mitchell, South Dakota, USA

❦

Nobody has ever measured how much the heart can hold.

SPICED TEA MIX

1 c. instant tea
2 c. Tang orange drink mix
1½ c. white sugar

¾ c. Wyler's lemonade mix
1 tsp. cinnamon
1 tsp. cloves

Mix all ingredients together and store in a tight container. Use 2 teaspoons (more or less to suit taste) to 1 cup of boiling water.

Kenneth Strohbehn, Gladbrook Lions Club
Gladbrook, Iowa, USA

❦

An expert is one who will know tomorrow
why the things he predicted yesterday didn't happen today.

❦ ❦ ❦

The shortest recorded period of time lies between
the minute you put some money away for a rainy day
and the unexpected arrival of rain.

❦ ❦ ❦

Thanks to the Interstate Highway System,
it is now possible to travel across the country from coast to coast
without seeing anything.

❦ ❦ ❦

It takes as much courage to have tried and failed
as it does to have tried and succeeded.

Notes

It's easy to identify people who can't count to ten.
They're in front of you in the supermarket express lane.

Breakfast
and
Brunch

MICROWAVE HINTS

1. Place an open box of hardened brown sugar in the microwave oven with 1 cup hot water. Microwave at high for 1½ to 2 minutes for ½ pound or 2 to 3 minutes for 1 pound.
2. Soften hard ice cream by microwaving at 30% power. One pint will take 15 to 30 seconds; one quart, 30 to 45 seconds; and one-half gallon, 45 seconds to one minute.
3. One stick of butter or margarine will soften in 1 minute when microwaved at 20% power.
4. Soften one 8-ounce package of cream cheese by microwaving at 30% power for 2 to 2½ minutes. One 3-ounce package of cream cheese will soften in 1½ to 2 minutes.
5. Thaw frozen orange juice right in the container. Remove the top metal lid. Place the opened container in the microwave and heat on high power 30 seconds for 6 ounces and 45 seconds for 12 ounces.
6. Thaw whipped topping...a 4½ ounce carton will thaw in 1 minute on the defrost setting. Whipped topping should be slightly firm in the center but it will blend well when stirred. Do not overthaw!
7. Soften jello that has set up too hard - perhaps you were to chill it until slightly thickened and forgot it. Heat on a low power setting for a very short time.
8. Dissolve gelatin in the microwave. Measure liquid in a measuring cup, add jello and heat. There will be less stirring to dissolve the gelatin.
9. Heat hot packs in a microwave oven. A wet fingertip towel will take about 25 seconds. It depends on the temperature of the water used to wet the towel.
10. To scald milk, cook 1 cup milk for 2-2½ minutes, stirring once each minute.
11. To make dry bread crumbs, cut 6 slices bread into ½-inch cubes. Microwave in 3-quart casserole 6-7 minutes, or until dry, stirring after 3 minutes. Crush in blender.
12. Refresh stale potato chips, crackers, or other snacks of such type by putting a plateful in the microwave oven for about 30-45 seconds. Let stand for 1 minute to crisp. Cereals can also be crisped.
13. Melt almond bark for candy or dipping pretzels. One pound will take about 2 minutes, stirring twice. If it hardens while dipping candy, microwave for a few seconds longer.
14. Nuts will be easier to shell if you place 2 cups of nuts in a 1-quart casserole with 1 cup of water. Cook for 4 to 5 minutes and the nut meats will slip out whole after cracking the shell.
15. When thawing hamburger meat, the outside will many times begin cooking before the meat is completely thawed. Defrost for 3 minutes, then remove the outside portions that have defrosted. Continue defrosting the hamburger, taking off the defrosted outside portions at short intervals.
16. To drain the fat from hamburger while it is cooking in the microwave oven (one pound cooks in 5 minutes on high), cook it in a plastic colander placed inside a casserole dish.
17. Cubed meat and chopped vegetables will cook more evenly if cut uniformly.
18. When baking large cakes, brownies, or moist bars, place a juice glass in the center of the baking dish to prevent a soggy middle and ensure uniform baking throughout.
19. Since cakes and quick breads rise higher in a microwave oven, fill pans just half full of batter.
20. For stamp collectors: Place a few drops of water on stamp to be removed from envelope. Heat in the microwave for 20 seconds and the stamp will come right off.
21. Using a round dish instead of a square one eliminates overcooked corners in baking cakes.
22. When preparing chicken in a dish, place meaty pieces around the edges and the bony pieces in the center of the dish.
23. Shaping meatloaf into a ring eliminates undercooked center. A glass set in the center of a dish can serve as the mold.
24. Treat fresh meat cuts for 15 to 20 seconds on high in the microwave oven. This cuts down on meat-spoiling types of bacteria.
25. A crusty coating of chopped walnuts surrounding many microwave-cooked cakes and quick breads enhances the looks and eating quality. Sprinkle a layer of medium finely chopped walnuts evenly onto the bottom and sides of a ring pan or Bundt cake pan. Pour in batter and microwave as recipe directs.
26. Do not salt foods on the surface as it causes dehydration (meats and vegetables) and toughens the food. Salt the meat after you remove it from the oven unless the recipe calls for using salt in the mixture.
27. Heat leftover custard and use it as frosting for a cake.
28. Melt marshmallow creme in the microwave oven. Half of a 7-ounce jar will melt in 35-40 seconds on high. Stir to blend.
29. Toast coconut in the microwave. Watch closely because it browns quickly once it begins to brown. Spread ½ cup coconut in a pie plate and cook for 3-4 minutes, stirring every 30 seconds after 2 minutes.
30. Place a cake dish up on another dish or on a roasting rack if you have difficulty getting the bottom of the cake done. This also works for potatoes and other foods that don't quite get done on the bottom.

BREAKFAST AND BRUNCH

ABBLESCIBERS
(Danish)

3 eggs
2 c. buttermilk
2 c. flour

¾ tsp. salt
1 Tbsp. sugar
1½ tsp. baking powder

Separate 3 eggs. Beat egg whites till stiff. Beat egg yolks and add 2 cups buttermilk. Stir. Sift 2 cups flour, ¾ teaspoon salt, 1 tablespoon sugar, and 1½ teaspoons baking powder, then add to buttermilk mixture. Stir and fold in egg whites. Bake on top of stove in Abblesciber pan, that has been greased and heated. Turn batter slowly with toothpick as it browns, forming a ball. You can roll the pancake like balls in sugar or dip into syrup or jelly. Fruit can also be added to batter in pan.

Bonnie Wilson, Onekama Lions Club
Onekama, Michigan, USA

NANCY'S HOT FRUIT

1 large can peaches
1 large can chunk pineapple

1 large can pears, sliced
1 medium jar maraschino cherries

Topping:

1 jar applesauce
1 stick melted margarine
⅔ c. sugar

2 Tbsp. cornstarch
¾ c. chopped pecans

Mix and drain first 4 ingredients. Mix topping ingredients, except nuts, and pour over fruit mixture. Put pecans on top.

Betty Patterson, Kosciusko Lions Club
Kosciusko, Mississippi, USA

QUICHE LORRAINE

4 slices cooked bacon
1 (9 inch) pie shell
1 c. shredded Swiss cheese
3 beaten eggs

¼ tsp. salt
Dash of nutmeg
2 tsp. plain flour or cornstarch

Cook pie shell in a 450° oven for 5 minutes. Reduce oven to 325°. Take pie crust out and crumble bacon into shell. Add Swiss cheese. In bowl, beat eggs; mix in milk, salt, nutmeg, and flour. Pour over bacon and cheese. Bake in 325° oven until set and brown.

Glenn E. Bunch, Jr., PDG 31-H, Snow Hill Lions Club
Snow Hill, North Carolina, USA

SOUTHWESTERN QUICHE

1 (4 oz.) can chopped chilies
½ lb. grated Cheddar cheese
4 eggs

1 c. Bisquick or biscuit mix
¼ tsp. salt
1 c. light cream or canned milk

Put chilies in bottom of 9 inch square dish. Sprinkle cheese on top. Whip 4 eggs with fork. Add biscuit mix and salt. Beat until smooth. Slowly add cream. Pour over cheese. Bake at 350° for 30 to 45 minutes. Double and use cake pan. Good luck.

Lion Maybelle Lorenc, Amarillo Centennial Lions Club
Amarillo, Texas, USA

CHEESY SAUSAGE QUICHE

1 lb. regular sausage
½ c. onion, chopped
⅓ c. green pepper, chopped
1½ c. cheese, grated (Colby or
   Cheddar)
1 Tbsp. flour
1 Pet-Ritz deep dish pie crust shell

2 eggs, beaten
1 c. Pet evaporated milk
1 Tbsp. parsley flakes
¾ tsp. seasoned salt
¼ tsp. garlic salt
¼ tsp. pepper

Preheat oven to 375°. In medium skillet, fry sausage until cooked. Remove sausage and drain on paper towel. Reserve 2 tablespoons fat. Saute onion and green pepper in reserved fat 2 to 3 minutes. Combine cheese and flour. Stir in sausage, green pepper, and onion. Spread in pie crust shell. Mix remaining ingredients and pour into shell. Bake on cookie sheet 35 to 40 minutes or until browned and filling is set. Serves 6.

The bottom layer can be frozen, thawed when ready to use, and the top added when ready to cook.

Sherry Parker, Decatur Lions Club
Decatur, Texas, USA

EASY TURKEY QUICHE

2½ to 3 c. leftover stuffing or 1 (6
   oz.) pkg. stuffing mix
1 c. chopped cooked turkey
1 c. shredded Swiss cheese

4 beaten eggs
1 (5½ oz.) can evaporated milk
⅛ tsp. pepper

Press leftover stuffing or mix into 9 inch pie plate or quiche dish to form crust. Bake at 400° for 10 minutes. Combine meat and cheese. In another bowl, beat eggs, milk, and pepper; sprinkle meat and cheese on baked crust. Pour egg-milk mixture on top layer. Bake for 30 to 35 minutes in a 350° oven, until center is set. Let stand for 10 minutes. Garnish with tomato wedges. Serves 6.

Anna Gilman, Westbrook Lions Club
Westbrook, Maine, USA

SPINACH QUICHE

2 frozen 8 inch pie crusts
1 pkg. frozen chopped spinach,
   thawed and drained
   (uncooked)
1½ c. cream
1½ c. milk
6 eggs

1 minced onion or dried flakes
½ c. flour
1½ tsp. salt
½ tsp. pepper
½ tsp. nutmeg
8 oz. shredded Swiss cheese

Combine all other ingredients in bowl. Pour over cheese and spinach. Sprinkle cheese and spinach over pastry in pie plate.

Mary Mason, Hedgesville Lions Club
Hedgesville, West Virginia, USA

GREEN CHILI QUICHE

1 pie shell
½ lb. hamburger
¼ c. onion, chopped
1 (14 oz.) can drained green chilies
2 c. grated Cheddar cheese

3 eggs, beaten
¼ tsp. salt
1 c. half & half
¼ tsp. garlic salt

Cook hamburger with onion. Drain. Sprinkle into pie shell. Cover meat with grated cheese and chilies. Mix eggs, salts, and half & half. Pour over meat and cheese mixture. Bake at 375° for 35 minutes.

Terry Jones, Kosciusko Lions Club
Kosciusko, Mississippi, USA

WALT'S VEGETABLE QUICHE

4 large mushrooms
1 medium potato
1 medium onion
5 eggs
3 c. beet green (tops)
3 Tbsp. flour
2 Tbsp. oleo or butter
½ lb. American or Cheddar grated
   cheese

¼ tsp. garlic powder
¼ tsp. spike seasoning
12 oz. cottage cheese
1 c. milk
2 Tbsp. oil
Salt and pepper to taste

Wash clean beet tops. Chop into 1 inch pieces. Boil till tender. Drain. Chop onion and mushrooms. Saute in 2 tablespoons oil. Add grated potato and garlic powder; cook until onion is done (transparent). Add cooked green mix. Put into greased 9x13 inch pan. Blend flour, milk, oleo, and spike seasoning. Pour into pan. Spread cottage cheese over that. Sprinkle ½ of grated cheese next. Beat eggs thoroughly and add to top. Sprinkle rest of grated cheese on top. Bake at 350° to 375° for 45 minutes. (You can use leftover boiled potatoes - just mash with fork.)

Walter E. Loomis, North Jackson Lions Club
Jackson, Michigan, USA

SAUSAGE AND EGG CASSEROLE

8 slices fresh bread, cubed
1 to 1½ lb. ground pork sausage,
   browned and drained
2 c. grated Cheddar cheese
1 (4 oz.) can mushroom stems and
   pieces, drained

4 eggs, beaten
¾ tsp. dry mustard
3 c. milk
1 can cream of mushroom soup

Place cubed bread in greased 9x13 inch baking pan. Layer meat over bread. Sprinkle the cheese and mushrooms over top. Combine beaten eggs, dry mustard, and 2½ cups milk; pour over ingredients in pan. Cover and refrigerate at least 3 hours or overnight. When ready to bake, combine the soup and remaining ½ cup milk; pour over all. Bake in preheated oven at 300° for 1½ hours. Serves 12.

Note: Turkey or ham also work well.

Lion J.J. Hauger, Siren 27-E-1 Lions Club
Siren, Wisconsin (Burnett), USA

CHEESY EGG BAKE

2 cans cream of chicken soup
1 c. milk
4 tsp. instant minced onion
1 tsp. prepared mustard
8 oz. (2 c.) shredded Swiss cheese

12 eggs
12 (½ inch) thick slices French
   bread, buttered and halved
Snipped parsley

In a saucepan, combine soup, milk, onion, and mustard. Cook and stir until smooth and heated through. Remove from heat; stir in cheese until melted. Pour 1 cup of sauce into each of two 10 x 6 x 1¾ inch (or thereabouts) baking dishes. Break 6 eggs into sauce in each casserole. Carefully spoon remaining sauce around eggs. Stand French bread slices around edges of casseroles with crusts up. Bake in 350° oven for 20 minutes or until eggs have set. Garnish with snipped parsley. I prefer sharp Cheddar cheese in place of the Swiss. Goes great with bacon, juice, coffee, and potatoes for a Sunday Brunch. Serves 12.

Ellen Ostrand, Lady Lions of Rohnert Park
Rohnert Park, California, USA

COUNTRY BRUNCH CASSEROLE

10 slices bread, cut in cubes
2 thick slices ham, cubed
2 to 3 Tbsp. chopped onion
6 eggs

3 c. milk
2 c. grated Cheddar cheese
Salt and pepper to taste

Butter 9x13 inch pan. Spread bread cubes in pan. Sprinkle ham and grated Cheddar cheese on top of bread cubes. Sprinkle with onion. In large bowl, beat eggs, milk, salt, and pepper. Pour over mixture in pan. Cover with foil and refrigerate overnight. Bake at 350° for 40 to 45 minutes.

Mrs. Jerry (Nancy) Lagerstrom, Plattsmouth Lions Club
Plattsmouth, Nebraska, USA

EGG STRATA

6 slices white bread (trim off
    crusts)
3 c. chopped ham
6 oz. shredded Cheddar cheese

8 eggs
2½ c. milk
¼ c. melted margarine

Butter 6 slices of bread. Place in 9x13 inch pan, buttered side down. Add ham and cheese. Beat eggs; add milk. Pour over bread, ham, and cheese. Melt ¼ cup margarine and drizzle over top. Bake in 350° oven for 1 hour.

Recipe can be made the night before, covered, and then baked in the a.m. Serves 8. It's delicious!

Lioness Cate Piti, Mitchell Lioness Club
Mitchell, South Dakota, USA

FAVORITE BREAKFAST CASSEROLE

1 lb. *hot* pork sausage
10 slices bread, cubed
1 c. shredded sharp Cheddar
    cheese
1 c. shredded mild Cheddar
    cheese
1 c. shredded Monterey Jack
    cheese

4 eggs
2½ c. milk
1 (10 oz.) can cream of chicken
    soup with mushrooms
½ c. milk

Brown sausage in skillet, stirring until crumbly; drain. Layer bread, sausage, and cheese in greased 9x13 inch baking pan. Combine eggs and 2½ cups milk in bowl; mix well. Pour over layered mixture. Refrigerate, covered, overnight. Preheat oven to 375°. Combine soup and ½ cup milk in bowl. Pour over casserole. Bake, covered, for 30 minutes. Uncover; bake for 40 to 50 minutes longer. Yield: 10 to 12 servings.

Lion Karen Stowers, Amarillo North Lions Club
Amarillo, Texas, USA

Marriage should be a duet - when one sings, the other claps.

ONE DISH BREAKFAST

9 beaten eggs
Dash of black pepper
¼ tsp. oregano
3 slices bread, cubed
1 c. sharp Cheddar cheese, shredded
1 c. Monterey Jack cheese, shredded

2 Tbsp. finely chopped green pepper
3 c. milk
½ tsp. salt
1 lb. sausage, browned and well drained
1 c. Swiss cheese, shredded

Mix eggs, green pepper, pepper, salt, oregano, and milk. Set aside. Toss bread cubes, sausage, and part of the cheese together. Place in a 9x13 inch baking dish. Pour liquid mixture on the top of the bread. Sprinkle remaining cheese on the top. Cover and place in refrigerator overnight. In the morning, uncover and bake at 350° for 45 minutes. Serves 8 to 10. Wonderful to make even when there is only two people at home since it keeps well and can be reheated in the microwave.

Dolores (Lori) Avram, Georgetown Evening Lions Club
Georgetown, Texas, USA

WINE AND CHEESE OMELET CASSEROLE

1 large loaf French bread, torn up
6 Tbsp. oleo, melted
¾ c. Swiss cheese, shredded
½ lb. Monterey Jack cheese, shredded
12 slices hard salami or ham, chopped
16 eggs
3¼ c. milk

½ c. dry white wine
4 large green onions, chopped
1 Tbsp. Grey Poupon mustard
¼ tsp. ground pepper
⅛ tsp. red pepper
2 c. sour cream (large ctn. and small ctn.)
Parmesan cheese

Butter two 9x13 inch baking dishes. Spread bread on bottom. Drizzle with oleo. Layer Swiss, Monterey Jack, and salami or ham. Beat together eggs, milk, wine, green onions, mustard, pepper, and red pepper until foamy. Pour over the cheese. Cover dish with foil and refrigerate overnight. Remove from refrigerator 30 minutes before baking. Bake casserole at 325° for 45 minutes, covered. Spread sour cream and Parmesan cheese. Bake, uncovered, 10 minutes. Great for brunch! Makes 24 servings.

Store cheese in a tightly covered container with sugar cubes to prevent mold.

Mrs. Charlotte M. Garner, Pascagoula Evening Lions Club
Pascagoula, Mississippi, USA

❧

Life is like a bridge - cross over it but don't establish yourself upon it.

OVEN OMELET

¼ c. butter
1½ doz. eggs
1 c. sour cream

1 c. milk
2 tsp. salt
1 c. milk

Mix 1½ dozen eggs, 1 cup room temperature sour cream, 1 cup milk, and 2 teaspoons salt until well blended. Heat oven to 325°. Melt ½ cup butter in a 9x13 inch pan in oven. Remove and tilt to coat the bottom of the dish. Pour eggs into pan and bake 30 to 35 minutes until set but moist. Eggs will rise and then fall even when out of oven. Cut in squares. Serves 12.

Pat Tulloch, Bedford Heights Lions Club
Bedford Heights, Ohio, USA

BRUNCH EGG CASSEROLE

4 c. croutons
2 c. shredded Cheddar cheese
Any meat (cooked bacon,
    sausage, or ham)
8 eggs

4 c. milk
¾ tsp. salt
¾ tsp. prepared mustard
Pepper to taste

Grease a 9x13 inch pan. Combine 4 cups croutons, 2 cups shredded Cheddar cheese, any meat (cooked bacon, sausage or ham crumbled or cubed), and mushrooms. Sprinkle on bottom of greased pan.

In bowl, mix 8 eggs, 4 cups milk, ¾ teaspoon salt, ¾ teaspoon prepared mustard, and pepper to taste. Beat and pour over crouton mixture. (At this point, you may refrigerate overnight.) Bake at 350° for 1 hour.

Mrs. Mike (Shirley) Stoffa, Elburn Lions Club
Elburn, Illinois, USA

CHILI EGG PUFF

10 eggs
½ c. flour
½ tsp. salt
1 Tbsp. baking powder
1 lb. Jack cheese, grated

1 pt. small curd cottage cheese
½ c. butter, melted
2 (4 oz.) cans chopped green
    chilies

Beat eggs until light. Fold everything into the beaten eggs. Bake in a 9x13 inch buttered pan in a 350° oven for 35 to 40 minutes.

Joyce Butcher, Reno Plumb Lane Lions Club
Reno, Nevada, USA

❧

The best thing a man can put on his crop or his kids is his own shadow.

TORTILLA EGG CASSEROLE

8 to 10 (7 inch) flour tortillas
1½ lb. hot pork sausage or
    chorizo, browned and
    drained
4 c. shredded Cheddar cheese
12 eggs, slightly beaten
4 c. milk

½ tsp. salt
½ tsp. chili powder
½ tsp. cumin
Salsa or taco sauce, heated
Sour cream
Sliced green onion

Heat oven to 325°. Arrange tortillas to cover bottom and sides of greased 13x9 inch and 9 inch square baking dish. (If necessary, cut tortillas in halves.) Sprinkle with browned sausage and cheese. In large mixer bowl, place eggs. Beat at low speed until slightly beaten. Add milk, salt, chili powder, and cumin. Continue beating until well mixed. Pour over sausage and cheese. Bake for 45 to 55 minutes or until knife inserted in center comes out clean. Serve with heated salsa and a dollop of sour cream; sprinkle with green onion. Yield: 12 to 14 servings.

Note: The 9 inch square pan will be done before the 13x9 inch pan. Check for doneness in 9 inch pan at minimum time. Do not overcook.

Elsie Mae Jensen, Brownton Lions Club
Brownton, Minnesota, USA

CHEESY SPINACH BRUNCH

6 eggs
24 oz. small curd cottage cheese
1 (10 oz.) pkg. frozen chopped
    spinach, well drained
3 Tbsp. flour

¼ c. butter, softened
1 c. Swiss or Colby cheese, grated
1 Tbsp. instant minced onion
½ tsp. salt

In large bowl, beat eggs. Add remaining ingredients and stir to combine. Pour into a 1½ or 2 quart lightly greased casserole. Bake at 350° for 50 to 55 minutes or until knife inserted near center comes out clean. Garnish with tomato wedges. Makes 6 to 8 servings.

To keep cottage cheese longer (after opened), turn upside down in refrigerator.

Elsie Mae Jensen, Brownton Lions Club
Brownton, Minnesota, USA

If you must doubt, doubt your doubts - never your beliefs.

HAM AND CHEESE OVEN BAKED OMELETTE

12 slices white bread
3 c. diced ham
8 oz. pkg. Cheddar cheese
Salt, pepper (dash)

6 eggs
2½ c. milk
½ c. melted butter
1 tsp. dry mustard (optional)

Remove crust from bread. Butter 1 side. Place, buttered side down, in 9x13 inch pan. Cover bread with ham. Place cheese over ham. Dice remaining bread and spread over cheese. Beat eggs, milk, salt, and pepper. Pour over bread mixture. Press down with hands until moisture is absorbed. Dribble butter over all of it. Cover pan and refrigerate overnight. Bake 1 hour covered and 15 minutes uncovered at 350°.

May use other meats in place of ham.

RaNaye Baumgarten, Brownton Lions Club
Brownton, Minnesota, USA

EASY BREAKFAST

1½ lb. hamburger, browned
1 doz. eggs, beaten
1 can mushrooms

½ lb. Velveeta cheese, sliced
½ c. green pepper
Onion

Put hamburger in bottom of greased 9x13 inch pan. Add beaten eggs, green peppers, onions, and mushrooms. Top with sliced cheese. Bake at 350° for 20 to 25 minutes.

RaNaye Baumgarten, Brownton Lions Club
Brownton, Minnesota, USA

SAUSAGE AND EGG CASSEROLE

6 eggs
2 c. milk
6 slices white bread
1 tsp. salt

1 tsp. dry mustard
1 lb. mild sausage
1 c. grated cheese

Crumble and lightly brown sausage. Drain off grease and cool. In mixing bowl, beat eggs. Add milk, salt, and mustard; beat until mixed. Add cubed bread and stir. Add cheese and sausage; put into baking dish, 8x12 inches. Put in refrigerator overnight. Bake 45 minutes at 350°F. Let set a few minutes after removing from oven. Cut into squares.

Barb Barton, Baugo Lions Club
Elkhart, Indiana, USA

❦

The surest way to get somewhere is to know where you are going.

EGG AND SAUSAGE SOUFFLE

6 eggs, beaten slightly
2 c. milk
1 tsp. dry mustard
1 c. Bisquick baking mix

½ tsp. dried oregano leaves
1 lb. bulk sausage, browned and
    drained
1 c. shredded Cheddar cheese

Mix all ingredients and cover. Put in refrigerator overnight. Heat oven to 350°. Pour into a greased 2 quart casserole and bake until knife inserted in center comes out clean, about 1 hour. Serves 6.

Convenience! You can make it a day ahead. Can be used for brunch or a light supper.

Lioness Louise Little, Bailey Mountain Lioness Club
Conifer, Colorado, USA

GRITS SOUFFLE

3 c. water
¾ c. grits (quick)
2 eggs, beaten
½ lb. sharp English cheese,
    grated

Salt to taste
¾ stick margarine

Cook grits in boiling water and salt. Add grated cheese and margarine. When slightly cool, add beaten eggs and mix. Bake in a greased casserole at 350°F. for 45 minutes. Double to serve 8 to 10, using only 1 stick margarine.

W. Harold Arnett, Reno Plumb Lane Lions Club
Reno, Nevada, USA

SAUSAGE-ONION SQUARES

1 lb. mild pork sausage
1 large onion, chopped
2 c. Bisquick
¾ c. milk
2 eggs

2 tsp. caraway seed
1½ c. sour cream
¼ tsp. salt
¼ tsp. paprika

Cook sausage and onion until sausage is browned and onion is tender; drain. Combine Bisquick, milk, and 1 egg; mix well. Spread mixture in greased 13x9x2 inch baking dish. Sprinkle with caraway seed, then top with sausage mixture. Combine sour cream, salt, and 1 egg; blend well and pour over sausage mixture, then sprinkle with paprika. Bake at 350° for 25 to 30 minutes. Cut into squares. This is great with scrambled eggs.

As you walk on the sands of time, take care what your footprints reveal: So the imprint you leave may be that of a soul, and not that of a heel!

Peggy Alewine, Rock Hill Lions Club
Rock Hill, South Carolina, USA

SAUSAGE BREAKFAST CASSEROLE

6 slices bread
Butter or margarine
1 lb. bulk sausage
1½ c. (6 oz.) shredded Longhorn
  cheese

6 eggs, beaten
2 c. half & half
1 tsp. salt

Remove crusts from bread; spread slices with butter. Place in a greased 13x9x2 inch baking dish and set aside.

Cook sausage until browned, stirring to crumble. Drain well. Spoon over bread slices and sprinkle with cheese. Combine eggs, half & half, and salt; mix well. Pour over cheese. Cover casserole and chill overnight. Remove from refrigerator 15 minutes before baking. Bake casserole, uncovered, at 350° for 45 minutes or until set. Makes 8 servings.

I use pork sausage with this recipe. This is a favorite breakfast of my family and easy to prepare.

Doris Stuller (Mrs. Ed), Silver Run-Union Mills Lions Club
Westminster, Maryland, USA

BREAKFAST CASSEROLE

Fry 1 pound hot sausage and 1 pound bacon.

10 slices bread, cubed
2 c. grated sharp cheese (8 oz.)
1 tsp. salt
1 tsp. dry mustard

8 eggs
1 qt. milk
Worcestershire sauce (to taste)

Butter 11x14 inch dish. Layer with ½ the bread cubes,1 cup cheese, all of the meat, and the remaining cheese. Beat the eggs and milk together; pour over layered ingredients. Can be covered and put in the refrigerator overnight at this point. Bake, uncovered, at 325° for 45 to 60 minutes. Serves 10 to 12.

Makes a great brunch dish to serve with fruit and muffins for weekend guests.

Mrs. Lion Robert (Margaret) Logan, Canton Lions Club
Canton, Georgia, USA

❦

Happiness can be thought, taught, and caught - but not bought

BRUNCHY EGG CASSEROLE

Egg Dish:

½ c. Velveeta cheese (1 c.),
    shredded
4 to 6 slices bacon
¼ c. chopped onion
1 doz. eggs, slightly beaten

½ tsp. salt
1 (4 oz.) can mushroom slices
3 slices bread, cubed, and 2 Tbsp.
    oleo

Dice and fry bacon. Drain grease. Saute onion with bacon. Scramble eggs to soft stage. Fold in bacon, onion, mushrooms, and eggs into White Sauce. Pour into 12 x 7 x 2½ inch baking dish. Cover with buttered bread cubes. Sprinkle with paprika. Cover and refrigerate overnight. Bake, uncovered, at 350° for 30 minutes.

White Sauce:

2 Tbsp. butter or oleo
2 Tbsp. flour

2 c. milk

Combine and heat until it starts to thicken. Add cheese.

This is our breakfast dish we serve at our church for Easter breakfast. Everybody loves it.

BREAKFAST CASSEROLE

10 to 12 eggs
12 oz. Cheddar cheese, grated
2 (4 oz.) cans chopped green
    chilies

Salt and pepper

Spread grated cheese in 9x13 inch pan that has been buttered. Spread green chilies evenly over cheese. Beat eggs and add salt and pepper to taste. Pour eggs over cheese and chili peppers and bake at 350° for 25 to 30 minutes or until set. Cut into squares and serve.

Arvella James, White Deer Lions Club
White Deer, Texas, USA

Joy is not in things; it is in us.

EGG CASSEROLE

3 Tbsp. butter
2 medium onions, chopped
1 lb. fresh mushrooms
2 green peppers
12 slices white bread, crusts
    trimmed off
2 c. Cheddar cheese, shredded

1 lb. boiled ham, chopped
8 eggs
2 c. milk
1 Tbsp. Worcestershire sauce
1 tsp. salt
¼ tsp. pepper

Brown onions, green peppers, and mushrooms in butter. Place 6 slices bread in bottom of 9x13 inch greased pan as a lining. Place half of the ham and a third of the cheese on the bread. Place half of the browned vegetable mixture on the cheese. Repeat layers, starting with the bread; end with a cheese layer on top.

Mix together the eggs, milk, Worcestershire sauce, salt, and pepper. Pour over the layers, making sure that all bread and the corners are covered with the egg mixture. Cover and refrigerate overnight. Remove cover and check corners to make sure bread is covered with egg mixture. If not, add more milk mixed with an egg. Bake, uncovered, at 350° for 50 to 60 minutes or until egg is set. Let stand for 10 minutes before cutting to serve.

EGG-SAUSAGE CASSEROLE

6 eggs
2 tsp. Worcestershire sauce
Dash of Tabasco
6 to 8 slices bread
Instant onions
3 c. milk

½ tsp. salt
1 lb. sausage (Jimmy Dean)
2 c. grated Cheddar or Colby
    cheese
1 (4 oz.) can chopped green chilies
    (optional)

Trim crusts from bread and place in a buttered 9x13 inch pan. Sprinkle onion flakes and cheese over bread. Brown sausage and green chilies; drain and sprinkle over bread. Mix remaining ingredients well and pour on top. Cover and let stand overnight in refrigerator. Bake at 350° for 30 to 40 minutes.

Great for Christmas morning brunch and we have used for our church's Easter breakfast. Can be spicy or toned down according to your taste.

Keep your happiness in circulation!

ARMADILLO EGGS

1 lb. pork sausage
1 c. shredded cheese (Monterey
   Jack, Colby, or Longhorn)
1½ c. Bisquick
2 jars Trappy jalapeno peppers,
   seeded

Monterey Jack cheese, cut to fit
   inside peppers
Flour
2 eggs, beaten
Shake 'n Bake (any flavor) or
   cracker crumbs

Preheat oven to 350°. Combine first 3 ingredients to a sausage ball texture. Drain jalapeno peppers and fill each pepper with Jack cheese. Wrap each pepper with the sausage mixture. Roll in flour; dip in egg. Roll in Shake 'n Bake or cracker crumbs. Put on cookie sheet and bake for 30 to 40 minutes.

For the people who love a *hot* appetizer, these are a delicious treat. Enjoy.
Lion Karen Stowers, Amarillo North Lions Club
Amarillo, Texas, USA

EGGS O'BRIEN
(Microwave)

4 slices bacon, cut in halves
3 c. frozen hash browns with
   onions and peppers (12 oz.)
1 Tbsp. butter

½ tsp. salt
⅛ tsp. pepper
4 eggs
Paprika

Place bacon in 9 inch microwaveable pie plate. Cover with a paper towel. Microwave on HIGH for 3 minutes or till crisp. Set bacon aside. Drain off all but 1 tablespoon drippings.

Into drippings in pie plate, stir potatoes, butter, salt, and pepper. Microwave on HIGH for 7 minutes or till potatoes are almost tender, stirring twice. Crumble bacon and stir into potatoes. With the back of a spoon, make 4 shallow depressions in potato mixture. Place an egg in each hollow. Cover tightly with plastic wrap, turning one edge back. Microwave at 50% for 6 to 8 minutes or till eggs are almost done. Remove from oven. Sprinkle with paprika if desired.

Arrange whatever pieces come your way.

BAKED CHEESE AND EGGS

2 Tbsp. butter
6 green onions (with some top),
   sliced
1 c. cheese (Cheddar or
   Monterey), shredded

6 eggs
6 Tbsp. half & half
Salt and pepper
Paprika

Brush six 6 ounce custard cups with butter. Divide green onions and half the cheese evenly among the custard cups. Carefully break eggs onto the cheese. Pour 1 tablespoon half & half over each egg. Sprinkle egg with salt, pepper, remaining cheese, and the paprika. Cook, uncovered, at 325° oven until desired doneness for 20 to 22 minutes for soft set yolks. Great for brunch. Serves 6.

For a spicier version, substitute picante sauce for half & half.

BREAKFAST PIZZA

1 lb. bulk pork sausage
1 pkg. refrigerated crescent rolls
1 c. frozen loose pack hash
   browns, thawed
1 c. shredded sharp Cheddar
   cheese

5 eggs
¼ c. milk
½ tsp. salt
2 Tbsp. grated Parmesan cheese
⅛ tsp. pepper

In a skillet, cook sausage; drain. Place rolls on ungreased 12 inch pizza pan with points toward center. Press over bottom and up sides of points form crust. Seal perforation. Spoon sausage over crust. Sprinkle with hash browns. Top with Cheddar cheese.

In bowl, beat eggs, milk, salt, and pepper; pour over crust. Sprinkle with Parmesan cheese. Bake at 375° for 25 to 30 minutes. Serves 6.

Mrs. Tom (Nancy) Sweet, Elburn Lions Club
Elburn, Illinois, USA

BREAKFAST PIZZA

1 lb. pork sausage
1 c. cooked rice
1 (8 count) pkg. refrigerated
   crescent rolls
4 eggs, slightly beaten

¼ c. milk
½ tsp. salt
⅛ tsp. pepper
½ c. shredded Cheddar cheese
½ c. shredded Mozzarella cheese

Brown and drain sausage; mix with rice. Separate crescent rolls and place, side by side, in pizza pan. Press together to form a crust. Combine eggs, milk, and seasonings. Set aside. Spoon rice and sausage mixture over crust. Top with cheeses and pour egg mixture over all. Bake in a 350° oven for 30 minutes. Serves 6 to 8.

BREAKFAST PIZZA

1 (8 count) crescent rolls
1 lb. sausage
1 c. Cheddar cheese
1 c. Mozzarella cheese
6 eggs

½ c. milk
Salt
Pepper
Oregano

Press rolls in pizza pan, fluting up edges. Bake at 375° for 5 minutes on lower rack. Brown sausage and drain grease. Sprinkle sausage and cheeses over crust. Mix eggs, milk, salt, and pepper. Pour over sausage and cheese. Sprinkle with oregano. Bake at 350° for 30 to 35 minutes on lower rack.

Phyllis Hillis, McMinnville Lions Club
McMinnville, Tennessee, USA

FARMER'S BREAKFAST

2 Tbsp. margarine
4 medium potatoes, cooked and
  chopped
1 to 2 c. cooked meat, cut into
  small pieces

6 eggs, beaten
1 c. cheese, grated (Colby,
  American or other)
¼ c. chopped onion (optional)

Saute onion in large skillet. Fry potatoes and meat until heated through. Add beaten eggs to meat and potatoes. Add cheese. Cook slowly until eggs are set. Stir occasionally. Serve hot. Serves 6.

LEFSE

3½ c. boiled and mashed potatoes
¼ c. melted butter
½ tsp. salt

1 c. flour
¼ c. half & half
½ tsp. sugar

Combine potatoes, butter, and salt; set aside to cool. Add flour, half & half, and sugar when you are ready to roll. Roll as thin as possible. Bake on pancake or lefse grill. Turn once. When baked, stack rounds and cover with cloth so they won't dry out.

❦

When helping one another, both are strong.

HAM AND POTATO BREAKFAST

1 pkg. Betty Crocker hash browns
1½ c. shredded Cheddar cheese
1 c. finely chopped ham
½ c. sliced green onions
1½ c. water
1 c. milk

1 tsp. salt
1 tsp. dry mustard
Dash of ground red pepper
5 eggs, beaten
Paprika

Heat oven to 350°. Mix all ingredients, except paprika, in large bowl. Pour into ungreased rectangular baking dish, 12x17x2 inches. Sprinkle with paprika. Bake, uncovered, until knife inserted in center comes out clean. Bake for 40 to 45 minutes.

PANCAKES

2 c. flour
1 c. oat bran
6 tsp. baking powder
3 Tbsp. white sugar
1 tsp. salt

3 eggs
3 Tbsp. Mazola oil
3 c. milk (whole milk)
1 orange with peel

Blend dry ingredients together. Blend egg, oil, milk, and orange in a blender. Mix in dry ingredients.

Chesley Bull, Eastpont Lions Club
Eastpont, Newfoundland, Canada

POTATO PANCAKE

2 large potatoes, grated
½ yellow onion, chopped fine
2 slices boiled ham, diced
2 stalks green onion, sliced fine
⅛ c. small dried shrimp, soaked
    for 1 hour

¼ c. cornstarch
¼ c. milk
1 tsp. salt
¼ tsp. Accent
Dash of pepper
2 eggs

Combine all ingredients thoroughly. Drop by tablespoonfuls into a hot oiled skillet. Fry until golden brown and set on one side, then turn and fry on other side until golden and until potatoes are cooked. Serve hot.

Great for breakfast.

Lion Greg Marsh, Caruthers Lions Club
Caruthers, California, USA

❧

Formula for youth: Keep your enthusiasm and forget your birthdays.

CRISP ZUCCHINI PANCAKES

3 medium zucchini, trimmed and
shredded (about 1 lb.)
¾ tsp. salt
1 medium onion, finely chopped
(about ½ c.)

1 Tbsp. unsalted butter
2 eggs, slightly beaten
¼ c. unsifted all-purpose flour
⅛ tsp. pepper
Vegetable oil for frying

Place zucchini in colander. Sprinkle with ½ teaspoon salt. Set aside for 30 minutes. Squeeze as much liquid as possible from zucchini with your hands. Reserve. Saute onion in hot butter over medium high heat until softened, about 3 minutes. Transfer reserved zucchini and onion to large bowl. Stir in eggs, flour, remaining ¼ teaspoon salt, and pepper. Pour oil into clean skillet to a depth of ⅛ inch and heat. Drop slightly rounded teaspoonfuls of the batter into oil. Flatten to 3 inch diameter with back of spoon. Cook, turning once until golden brown. Remove with slotted spoon. Drain on paper towels.

WALT'S FAVORITE HOT CAKES

1 c. quick oats
1½ c. buttermilk (or soured)*
¼ c. brown sugar
2 eggs
¼ c. butter or margarine, melted
(soft)

1 c. flour (white, all-purpose)
1 tsp. salt
1 tsp. baking soda

Put oat and milk in bowl. Let stand 10 minutes. Stir in brown sugar and rest of ingredients. Beat eggs. Mix well. Don't beat. Spoon batter onto griddle and cook just like regular hot cakes.

* Add 2 tablespoons vinegar to fresh milk to sour, but buttermilk makes best cakes.

Walter Loomis, North Jackson Lions Club
Jackson, Michigan, USA

CINNAMON FRENCH TOAST

½ c. "Egg Beaters"
½ c. skim milk
½ tsp. vanilla

12 diagonally cut slices French
bread (½ inch thick)

Spray nonstick skillet. Heat to 350°. In shallow dish, combine "Egg Beaters," milk, cinnamon, and vanilla. Beat well. Dip bread in mixture, coating both sides. Cook in skillet about 2 to 3 minutes on each side until golden brown. Serve with powdered sugar or lite syrup.

Kathy Gallant, Westbrook Lions Club
Westbrook, Maine, USA

STUFFED FRENCH TOAST

1 loaf bread, cubed*
1 (4 oz.) cream cheese, grated
   (optional)

8 eggs
⅓ c. honey
1⅓ c. milk

Mix eggs, honey, and milk; set aside. In a 9x13 inch greased pan, evenly layer half of bread cubes, then grated cheese and top with rest of bread. Pour egg mixture over bread. Cover and leave in refrigerator overnight. In morning, remove cover and bake at 350° for 35 to 40 minutes. Serve with butter and syrup. A little sprinkle of icing sugar and cinnamon is a nice touch. Serves 6 to 8. Recipe cut in half works well.

This recipe is great when the family is together Christmas morning. The work's done the night before.

  * Works best if bread is not fresh.

Lori Ann Symington, Edmonton Golden Gate Lions Club
Edmonton, Alberta, Canada

FRENCH TOAST SUPREME

½ c. butter
2 Tbsp. white corn syrup
1 c. brown sugar
French bread or Texas toast

5 eggs
1 c. Carnation milk
1 tsp. vanilla
¼ tsp. salt

Boil together butter, corn syrup, and brown sugar for 1 minute. Grease a 9x13 inch pan and put the caramel mixture in bottom. Slice French bread about 1 inch thick or use Texas toast. Put slices close together on top of the caramel sauce. Beat together eggs, milk, vanilla, and salt. Pour over the top of the bread. Cover and refrigerate overnight. Bake at 350° for 45 minutes. When ready to serve, turn the pieces over and the caramel will be on top. *A good brunch recipe.*

WAFFLE RECIPE

2 c. sifted all-purpose flour
2 Tbsp. sugar
1 tsp. salt
3 tsp. baking powder

2 eggs, separated
1¾ c. sweet milk
4 Tbsp. melted butter or other
   shortening

Sift dry ingredients together into mixing bowl. Add egg yolks and milk slowly, beating until batter is smooth. Add melted shortening and fold in stiffly beaten egg whites. Bake in waffle iron.

Grace Stuffle (Mrs. John), Silver Run-Union Mills Lions Club
Westminster, Maryland, USA

BLIZZARD FRUIT

2 to 3 bananas
1 (No. 10) can chunk pineapple

½ c. shredded coconut
½ c. Cool Whip

Cut bananas into ½ inch chunks. Mix all ingredients. Serve or chill and serve. Serves 4.

Served at breakfast at the Farmstead Bed and Breakfast, Route 236, Eliot, Maine, Owner John Lippincott.

John Lippincott, Eliot Lions Club
Eliot, Maine, USA

PIPERADE

3 onions
2 red bell peppers
1 green bell pepper
16 oz. can plum tomatoes

4 cloves garlic
¼ c. olive oil
1½ tsp. salt
½ tsp. pepper

Slice onions. Cut peppers into strips. Drain and chop tomatoes. Mince garlic. Heat oil in a frying pan over medium heat. Add onions and peppers; cook until soft (about 15 minutes). Add remaining ingredients; cover and simmer until vegetables are very soft, about 20 minutes. Uncover and continue cooking until liquid evaporates, 5 to 10 minutes. Serve with omelettes.

Lion Carol Neely, Graysville/Proctor Lions Club
Proctor, West Virginia, USA

QUICK BREAKFAST ROLLS

2 pkg. refrigerator biscuits
⅔ c. brown sugar
½ c. nuts
Handful of butterscotch chips

1 tsp. cinnamon
⅓ c. butter
2 Tbsp. water

Cut biscuits into fourths and place in an 8x8 inch pan. Mix remainder of ingredients in saucepan and heat till all is melted and blended. Stir frequently. Pour over biscuit pieces. Bake at 350° for 10 to 15 minutes.

There is no one luckier than he who thinks he is.

Soups
and
Sandwiches

A HANDY SPICE AND HERB GUIDE

ALLSPICE-a pea-sized fruit that grows in Mexico, Jamaica, Central and South America. Its delicate flavor resembles a blend of cloves, cinnamon, and nutmeg. USES: (Whole) Pickles, meats, boiled fish, gravies; (Ground) Puddings, relishes, fruit preserves, baking.

BASIL-the dried leaves and stems of an herb grown in the United States and North Mediterranean area. Has an aromatic, leafy flavor. USES: For flavoring tomato dishes and tomato paste, turtle soup; also use in cooked peas, squash, snap beans; sprinkle chopped over lamb chops and poultry.

BAY LEAVES-the dried leaves of an evergreen grown in the eastern Mediterranean countries. Has a sweet, herbaceous floral spice note. USES: For pickling, stews, for spicing sauces and soup. Also use with a variety of meats and fish.

CARAWAY-the seed of a plant grown in the Netherlands. Flavor that combines the tastes of anise and dill. USES: For the cordial Kummel, baking breads; often added to sauerkraut, noodles, cheese spreads. Also adds zest to French fried potatoes, liver, canned asparagus.

CURRY POWDER-a ground blend of ginger, turmeric, fenugreek seed, as many as 16 to 20 spices. USES: For all Indian curry recipes such as lamb, chicken, and rice, eggs, vegetables, and curry puffs.

DILL-the small, dark seed of the dill plant grown in India, having a clean, aromatic taste. USES: Dill is a predominant seasoning in pickling recipes; also adds pleasing flavor to sauerkraut, potato salad, cooked macaroni, and green apple pie.

MACE-the dried covering around the nutmeg seed. Its flavor is similar to nutmeg, but with a fragrant, delicate difference. USES: (Whole) For pickling, fish, fish sauce, stewed fruit. (Ground) Delicious in baked goods, pastries, and doughnuts, adds unusual flavor to chocolate desserts.

MARJORAM-an herb of the mint family, grown in France and Chile. Has a minty-sweet flavor. USES: In beverages, jellies, and to flavor soups, stews, fish, sauces. Also excellent to sprinkle on lamb while roasting.

MSG (MONOSODIUM GLUTAMATE)-a vegetable protein derivative for raising the effectiveness of natural food flavors. USES: Small amounts, adjusted to individual taste, can be added to steaks, roasts, chops, seafoods, stews, soups, chowder, chop suey, and cooked vegetables.

OREGANO-a plant of the mint family and a species of marjoram of which the dried leaves are used to make an herb seasoning. USES: An excellent flavoring for any tomato dish, especially pizza, chili con carne, and Italian specialties.

PAPRIKA-a mild, sweet red pepper growing in Spain, Central Europe, and the United States. Slightly aromatic and prized for brilliant red color. USES: A colorful garnish for pale foods, and for seasoning Chicken Paprika, Hungarian Goulash, salad dressings.

POPPY-the seed of a flower grown in Holland. Has a rich fragrance and crunchy, nut-like flavor. USES: Excellent as a topping for breads, rolls, and cookies. Also delicious in buttered noodles.

ROSEMARY-an herb (like a curved pine needle) grown in France, Spain, and Portugal, and having a sweet fresh taste. USES: In lamb dishes, in soups, stews, and to sprinkle on beef before roasting.

SAGE-the leaf of a shrub grown in Greece, Yugoslavia, and Albania. Flavor is camphoraceous and minty. USES: For meat and poultry stuffing, sausages, meat loaf, hamburgers, stews, and salads.

THYME-the leaves and stems of a shrub grown in France and Spain. Has a strong, distinctive flavor. USES: For poultry seasoning, croquettes, fricassees, and fish dishes. Also tasty on fresh sliced tomatoes.

TURMERIC-a root of the ginger family, grown in India, Haiti, Jamaica, and Peru, having a mild, ginger-pepper flavor. USES: As a flavoring and coloring in prepared mustard and in combination with mustard as a flavoring for meats, dressings, salads.

SOUPS AND SANDWICHES
SOUPS

GONE ALL DAY STEW

1 (10¾ oz.) can tomato soup
(undiluted)
1 c. water or red wine
¼ c. all-purpose flour
2 lb. beef cubes, fat trimmed (1 or
2 inches in size)
3 medium carrots, cut in 1 inch
diagonal slices
6 white or yellow boiling onions,
quartered
4 medium potatoes, cut into 1½
inch chunks

½ c. celery, cut into 1½ inch
chunks
12 whole large fresh mushrooms
2 beef bouillon cubes
1 Tbsp. Italian herb seasoning mix
(or 1 tsp. each of leaf
oregano, thyme, and
rosemary)
1 bay leaf
Pepper to taste

Mix soup, water, and flour until smooth. Combine with remaining ingredients in a covered roasting pan. Bake at 275° for 4 to 5 hours. When ready to serve, adjust seasoning if desired. Serve over noodles or with a crunchy bread like French or Italian to soak up the gravy.

This is great for the working woman and has everything in that you need for a meal.

Doris Stuller (Mrs. Ed), Silver Run-Union Mills Lions Club
Westminster, Maryland, USA

GONE ALL DAY STEW

1 (10¼ oz.) can tomato soup
(undiluted)
1 c. water or red wine
¼ c. flour
2 lb. stew meat
3 carrots, cut in 1½ inch chunks

12 whole large fresh mushrooms
2 beef bouillon cubes
1 Tbsp. Italian herb seasoning or
1 tsp. each oregano, thyme,
rosemary, and 1 bay leaf
3 grinds fresh pepper

Mix together soup, water, and flour until smooth. Combine with remaining ingredients. Bake in roaster at 275° for 4 to 5 hours. Makes 8 servings.

Diabetic exchange - 1 serving: 3 protein, 1 bread, 2 vegetables, ½ fat, 10 grams fat, 311 calories, 660 mg sodium, 103 mg cholesterol, 26 g carbohydrates, and 29 g protein.

Marge Sabin, Rootstown Lions Club
Rootstown Township, Rootstown, Ohio, USA

OVEN STEW

1½ lb. cubed beef, dredged in flour
   and browned in 1 Tbsp. oil
1 qt. whole tomatoes
2 c. celery, sliced diagonally
2 c. carrots, sliced diagonally
1 bell pepper, cubed
2 c. onions, cubed (can use small
   frozen onions)

½ c. bread crumbs
2 Tbsp. tapioca
1 c. red or white wine
2 tsp. Perk
8 peppercorns
1 bay leaf
Sprig of parsley and rosemary

Combine all of the above ingredients and place in a 250° oven for 4 hours. Add 4 potatoes, cubed, and 1 cup frozen peas. Continue baking at 350° for 1 hour.

Put vegetable oil on the wire of your hummingbird feeder - no ants.
Joann Geist, Fallbrook Lioness Club
Fallbrook, California, USA

WICKY WACKY STEW

1 lb. ground round
¼ c. minced onion
1 green pepper, diced
1 can cream of mushroom soup

1 can vegetable soup
2 cans water
1½ c. macaroni

Brown meat, onion, and pepper. Add remaining ingredients. Cover and simmer 45 minutes.

Evelyn Steele, Lyman Lions Club
Lyman, Wyoming, USA

MOM'S BEEF STEW

3 lb. shoulder stew beef or favorite
   beef
2 cans vegetarian vegetable soup
   (undiluted)

3 or 4 carrots, cut up
3 to 4 potatoes, quartered
Water to cover meat

Brown meat in Dutch oven. Add the above ingredients. Cook on top of stove in Dutch oven for 1 or 2 hours. When the meat is tender, thicken gravy. May add more water if needed. Serve with cabbage salad or other green salad. Rye bread is served.

A favorite meal in this family - a dinner complete in one pot.
Mrs. George E. Ducar, East Syracuse Lions Club
East Syracuse, New York, USA

One thing you can give and still keep is your word.

HEARTY MEATBALL AND VEGETABLE STEW

The steamed cabbage wedges arranged around the edge of the serving platter complement the stew. (Very pretty.)

1 lb. bulk pork sausage	2 stalks celery, sliced
2 Tbsp. oil	1 large (1 c.) onion, sliced
¼ c. flour	1 (12 oz.) can whole kernel corn
⅛ tsp. pepper	(undrained)
1 c. water	2 c. water
1 (10¾ oz.) can condensed	1 medium head cabbage, cut into
chicken broth	8 wedges
3 carrots, sliced	

Shape pork sausage into 25 balls. In large skillet, brown meatballs in oil, carefully turning. Remove meatballs from skillet. Reserve 2 tablespoons meat drippings in skillet; stir in flour and pepper. Gradually add 1 cup water and chicken broth. Cook until mixture boils and thickens, stirring constantly. Add carrots, celery, onion, and meatballs. Simmer, uncovered, for 20 to 30 minutes or until vegetables are tender and stew is thickened, stirring occasionally. Add corn and heat thoroughly.

In large saucepan, heat 2 cups water to boiling; add cabbage. Cover and cook for 8 minutes or until crisp tender. Drain. Arrange cabbage wedges in a ring, cut side down, around edge of serving platter. Spoon stew into center of cabbage ring. Serves 6 to 8.

BRUNSWICK STEW

1 chicken	1 pkg. lima beans
1 lb. ground pork	2 cans stewed tomatoes, minced
1 lb. ground beef	2 c. instant potatoes
1 pkg. corn	1 can tomato sauce

Cover chicken with water and boil. (Salt and pepper to taste.) Remove from stock. Pick the chicken and chop the meat. Brown the pork and beef; add all 3 meats back to the chicken stock. Add remaining ingredients and simmer until thick. Serve with BBQ or goes well by itself.

William M. Davidson, IV, Statesboro Lions Club
Statesboro, Georgia, USA

The miracle is this - the more we share, the more we have.

ELEPHANT STEW

Elephant (medium to large size)
Salt and pepper to taste

Rabbits (optional)
Brown gravy

Cut elephant into bite-size pieces (takes about 2 months). Add enough brown gravy to cover. Cook over an open fire about 4 weeks at 465°. Serves 2,000 to 4,000 people. If more guests are expected, 2 rabbits may be added; however, most people don't like hare in their stew.

Lloyd E. Wright, Georgetown Lions Club
Georgetown, Ohio, USA

PHEASANT STEW WITH BAKING POWDER DUMPLINGS

2 boned pheasants
1 c. chopped onion
6 to 8 carrots, sliced

1 c. chopped celery
1 can green beans
Flour with salt and pepper to taste

Brown bite-size pieces of floured pheasant. In cooker, add carrots, onion, celery, and beans. Add enough water to form a thin gravy. Season to taste. Simmer a good 4 hours. When ready, add dumplings. Can add cornstarch mixture to thicken gravy if necessary.

Baking Powder Dumplings:

2 c. flour
1 tsp. salt
2 tsp. baking powder
2 Tbsp. parsley

½ c. chopped green onions
1 egg, beaten
Milk

Beat 1 egg in measuring cup and fill with milk to make 1 cup. Beat into flour mixture. Drop by spoons into boiling stew. Cover tightly and return to boil. Reduce heat (don't lift cover). Simmer for 12 to 15 minutes.

Be wary of the person who urges an action
in which he himself incurs no risk.

WINTER WHITE CHILI

1 large onion, chopped (about 1 c.)
1 clove garlic, finely chopped
¼ c. (½ stick) margarine or butter
4 c. cooked chicken, cut into ½ inch cubes (about 5 or 6 breasts)
3 c. water
2 Tbsp. chopped fresh cilantro (or 1 Tbsp. if dried)
1 Tbsp. chopped fresh or 1 tsp. dried basil leaves
3 tsp. chicken bouillon granules
2 tsp. ground red chilies
¼ tsp. ground cloves
2 (16 oz.) cans Great Northern beans (undrained)
1 medium tomato, chopped (about ¾ c.)
Tortilla chips

Cook onion and garlic in margarine in 4 quart Dutch oven, stirring frequently, until onion is tender. Stir in remaining ingredients, except tomato and chips. Heat to boiling; reduce heat. Cover and simmer 1 hour, stirring occasionally. Serve with tomato and chips. Makes 6 servings.

Note: I used 1 teaspoon chili powder instead of red chilies and omitted cloves. I put in a can of Mexican style stewed tomatoes instead of fresh tomato.

If you like hot, try this.

Phyllis Hillis, McMinnville Lions Club
McMinnville, Tennessee, USA

WEDNESDAY'S CHILI

1½ lb. ground round
2 Tbsp. oil
½ tsp. salt
1 (10 oz.) Campbell's onion soup
1 Tbsp. chili powder
2 tsp. cumin powder
½ tsp. pepper
1 (21 oz.) can kidney beans
1 (6 oz.) can tomato paste
1 (8 oz.) can tomato sauce

Brown ground round in 2 tablespoons oil in 10 inch skillet till well browned. Crumble beef. Dust in ½ teaspoon salt. Pack beef firmly into skillet. Cover and heat 20 minutes on low.

Meanwhile, put onion soup through blender 1 minute. Add to the beef. Mash beef with fork till it looks like rice. Simmer 5 minutes, covered, on low. Add chili powder, cumin powder, and pepper.

Transfer to 2½ quart saucepan. Add kidney beans (undrained), tomato paste, and tomato sauce. Heat thoroughly (about 20 minutes) just to let flavors blend. This is so quick and delicious. Serve with corn bread.

Nicki Florentine, Silver Run-Union Mills Lions Club
Westminster, Maryland, USA

❧

Deal with the faults of others as gently as with your own.

TEXAS JAILHOUSE CHILI

1 c. sliced onions
1 diced green pepper (sweet)
1 diced chili pepper (hot)
3 peeled, minced garlic cloves
3 Tbsp. cooking oil
2 lb. round steak (large cubes)
3 c. boiling water

1 (16 oz.) can whole tomatoes
5 Tbsp. chili powder
½ c. cold water
1 tsp. salt
2 Tbsp. sugar
1 large can kidney beans

Cook onion, green pepper, and chili powder in oil in large skillet until tender. Add meat. Cook, uncovered, over medium heat until browned. Add boiling water, tomatoes, chili powder (mixed to a smooth paste with the cold water), salt, sugar, and garlic. Cover and cook slowly, simmering 1½ hours until meat is tender. Add a little hot water from time to time if mixture thickens too rapidly before meat is done. Finally, add kidney beans and heat, then taste and add more salt or chili powder if desired. Makes about 6 servings.

As a kid spending winters in Texas, I developed an early taste for "Tex-Mex." This chili is so named because it was the main fare for countless prisoners in Texas jails and prisons at the time.

Jack Laflin, Hartford Host Lions Club
Hartford, Connecticut, USA

BEST EVER CROCK POT CHILI!

2 lb. ground beef
2 medium onions, chopped
1 tsp. salt
¼ tsp. pepper
4 Tbsp. chili powder
½ tsp. cayenne (red) pepper

2 cans tomato soup
1 can tomatoes, chopped into
    pieces (and juice)
2 cans dark red kidney beans
2 cans chili hot beans
1 c. (or more) tomato juice

Brown ground beef and onions. Drain well. Mix all ingredients together in crock and simmer on HIGH temperature for 5 hours or so.

This recipe is for a 5 quart crock pot. You can cut it in half for smaller pot. This is a favorite among the members of St. John's for our annual soup and chili dinner! It's so easy and tastes so good!

Learn to enjoy little things - there are so many of them.

HOBO CHILE

2 lb. ground chuck
3 (27 oz. size) cans red kidney
   beans
4 to 5 Tbsp. chile powder
⅛ tsp. oregano
1 bay leaf
2 to 3 onions

4 to 6 chiles (red)
1 sq. Baker's unsweetened
   chocolate
½ c. tomato juice
4 or 5 garlic cloves
2 Tbsp. olive oil
¼ Tbsp. salt

Brown onions and garlic in large Dutch oven pan in olive oil. Add and brown meat. Add kidney beans. Add all other ingredients, beginning with chili powder. Bring to boil. Add whole square Baker's chocolate. Turn to simmer for 2 to 3 hours. Make sure it is unsweetened chocolate. It takes the sting out but keeps the flavor in.

James C. Doud, Reno Plumb Lane Lions Club
Reno, Nevada, USA

There are many perfectly normal people in the world,
but none of them ever appear on TV talk shows.

❦ ❦ ❦

When properly nourished and internalized,
your thoughts will become a reality in your world.
Thoughts are extremely powerful.

❦ ❦ ❦

Accomplishing the impossible means only
that the boss will add it to your regular duties.

REGULATORS CHILI

8 long, dried red chiles
4 dried smoked habanero chiles (optional)
1 (12 oz.) bottle Dos Equis beer
1 Tbsp. fresh ground cumin
1 Tbsp. black pepper
2 Tbsp. dried oregano, crumbled
1 Tbsp. fresh-ground coriander seeds
9 large cloves garlic, minced and mashed
3 Tbsp. mole paste
1 tsp. cayenne pepper
2 bay leaves
1 lb. lean bacon, cut in 1 inch pieces
5 large onions, peeled and coarsely chopped
¾ c. olive oil
3 lb. lean boneless beef chuck, cut in ½ inch cubes
3 lb. lean boneless pork roast, cut in large cubes
½ c. mild red chili powder
1 Tbsp. hot red chili powder
6 c. beef stock or water
⅓ c. masa harina flour
⅓ c. lard, bacon drippings, or olive oil

Remove stems and seeds from dried chiles. Simmer in beer 15 minutes in a covered pan. Fry bacon crisp and set aside. Remove all but ⅓ cup bacon drippings and saute onions until limp and golden. Remove onions. Set skillet aside.

Remove reconstituted chiles from beer to a blender, then add enough beer to blend a thick, smooth paste on medium speed. Place paste and remaining beer in saucepan, warming until just hot. Remove from heat. Add cumin, black pepper, oregano, garlic, mole paste, coriander, cayenne pepper, and bay leaf. Stir and cover; set aside.

In large, high-sided skillet, heat olive oil to brown small amounts of meat on high. (It will take about 5 batches.) Add bacon drippings if needed. In a medium-hot heavy skillet, stir together dry chili powders, lowering heat and stirring constantly to brown and enrich the chile flavor. Stir into steeping beer mixture. Remove bay leaves. Combine the beer mixture, browned meat, bacon, onions, and beef stock or water into a large chili pot. Simmer slowly about 2 hours. To thicken, whisk masa harina and heated oil or lard with 2 cups liquid from chile, then pour all back into pot, stirring until thick. Taste and salt and pepper, if needed, then simmer 20 minutes more. Serves 12.

Hint: Zap the sauteed onions with a sprinkle of Chili Pepper Vodka and the browned meat with a bit of "sippin" whiskey or a spritz of liquid smoke.

President Paula Tannacito, El Cajon Highway Lions Club
On behalf of the Club's Western Group, The Regulators
El Cajon, California, USA

❦

Putting your best foot forward at least keeps it out of your mouth.

CHILI WITH YELLOW BEANS
(Low calorie)

1 lb. lean ground beef
16 oz. tomatoes
1 can tomato soup
1 tsp. salt

1 tsp. chili powder
¼ c. chopped onion
1 can wax beans, drained
¼ tsp. pepper

Brown beef and onion in large skillet. Drain fat. Stir in rest of ingredients and heat to a boil. Reduce heat; cover and simmer for 25 to 30 minutes. Makes 6 (1 cup) servings (190 calories each).

VEGETABLE CHILI

6 Tbsp. olive oil, divided
2 medium or 1 large zucchini (do not peel), cut into ½ inch cubes
2 small onions, sliced
4 cloves garlic, finely chopped
2 large red or green bell peppers, cored and diced
1 (32 oz.) can tomatoes (undrained)
1 lb. fresh tomatoes, cut in 1 inch cubes

2 Tbsp. chili powder
2 tsp. ground cumin
2 tsp. dried basil
2 tsp. ground pepper
½ tsp. salt
¼ c. dried parsley
¼ c. dried dill weed
3 c. canned dark red kidney beans, drained, or hot chili beans
2 Tbsp. lemon juice

Heat 4 tablespoons oil in large skillet over medium heat. Add zucchini. Saute till just tender. Remove zucchini to large heavy pot. Add remaining 2 tablespoons oil to skillet over low heat. Add onions, garlic, and peppers; saute until just wilted, about 10 minutes. Transfer mixture, including oil, to large pot.

Place pot over low heat. Add undrained canned tomatoes, fresh tomatoes, chili powder, cumin, basil, pepper, salt, parsley, and dill. Cook, uncovered, stirring often for 30 minutes. Stir in canned beans and lemon juice; cook for 15 minutes. Stir well. Yield: 8 or more servings.

❧

The world steps aside for the man who knows where he is going.

MEATLESS CHILI

2 Tbsp. corn oil
1½ c. chopped onion
3 cloves garlic, minced
2 Tbsp. chili powder
½ tsp. ground cumin
1 c. diced carrots
1 green pepper, chopped
2 (14½ oz. to 16 oz.) cans
   tomatoes in juice
   (undrained)

1 (16 oz.) can chickpeas, drained
1 (15 oz.) can kidney beans,
   drained
1 (10 oz.) pkg. frozen corn, thawed
1 to 2 pickled jalapeno peppers,
   chopped

In 5 quart saucepan, heat corn oil over medium heat. Add onions, garlic, chili powder, and cumin; saute 5 minutes or until tender. Add carrots and green pepper; saute 2 minutes. Add tomatoes with juice, crushing tomatoes with spoon.

Stir in chickpeas, kidney beans, corn, and jalapeno peppers. Bring to boil. Reduce heat; cover and simmer 30 to 35 minutes. If desired, serve with rice. Makes eight 1½ cup servings. Guests enjoyed this recipe when served at our table. We served it over rice as suggested.

Alice (Mrs. Seth) Swift, Bloomington Lions Club
Bloomington, Illinois, USA

CHEEZY VEGETABLE CHILI

2 garlic cloves, minced
1 large green or red pepper,
   chopped
½ lb. fresh mushrooms, sliced
½ c. chopped onion
2 Tbsp. oil
1 can crushed tomatoes
1 can tomato sauce
1 tsp. ground cumin and 2 Tbsp.
   chili powder

1 can kidney beans, drained
1 can Bush's hot chili beans with
   sauce
1½ c. diced zucchini
1 pkg. frozen corn (or 1 can
   drained)
1½ c. shredded Cheddar cheese

Cook and stir garlic, pepper, mushrooms, and onion in oil till tender. Add tomatoes, tomato sauce, chili powder, and cumin. Heat to boil. Reduce to low heat; add beans, zucchini, and corn. Simmer 15 minutes. Add 1 cup cheese. Stir until melted. Use rest of cheese on top of chili when serving.

This recipe came from my daughter, Lisa Hickok. A little hint: Use a big pot. Makes a lot. Good for a crowd (or big family) on a Michigan winter day.
Pam Sedlar, Onekama Lions Club
Onekama, Michigan, USA

❦

There aren't enough crutches in the world for all the lame excuses.

CHILI CHICKEN

2 c. cut-up cooked chicken
1 (15 oz.) can tomato sauce
2 (15 oz.) cans spicy chili beans
  (undrained)
1 (8 oz.) can whole kernel corn
  (undrained)

Bisquick dumplings (below)
½ c. shredded Cheddar cheese (2
  oz.)

Mix chicken and tomato sauce in 4 quart Dutch oven. Heat to boiling and reduce heat. Cover and simmer 5 minutes, stirring occasionally. Stir in beans and corn. Heat to boiling and reduce heat to low. Prepare dumplings. Drop by 12 spoonfuls onto hot chili. Cook, uncovered, 10 minutes. Cover and cook 10 minutes longer. Sprinkle with cheese. Cover and cook 3 minutes till cheese is melted.

Dumplings: Mix 1½ cups Bisquick baking mix, ½ cup corn meal, and ⅔ cup milk till soft dough forms. Makes 6 servings.

Note: Stir in desired amount of chili powder with beans.

Lois Gnuse, Arlington Lions Club
Arlington, Nebraska, USA

BUTTER BEAN SOUP

1 lb. canned butter beans
Water
1 medium size onion, chopped
1 to 2 celery ribs, sliced
1 c. diced smoked turkey

1 (16 oz.) can tomatoes
1 tsp. dried thyme
1 tsp. salt (optional)
½ tsp. ground black pepper

Combine butter beans with 2 quarts water, onion, celery, and turkey. Cover. Over low heat, gently simmer until beans are soft and skins start to burst, about 2½ hours. During last hour of cooking time, add tomatoes with liquid, thyme, salt (if desired), and pepper. Makes 6 main-course servings or 8 to 10 first-course servings.

Carolyn Mason, Hedgesville Lions Club
Hedgesville, West Virginia, USA

❦

A well-beaten path may not be the right way.

GRANMA JO'S CALICO BEAN SOUP AND MIX

Beans: Purchase 12 or more 1 pound packages of various beans and lentils. Mix and package 2 cups per Ziploc Baggie and place the following bean recipe with it.

1 lb. beans	1 qt. whole tomatoes
1 qt. chicken broth	Sprigs of parsley, rosemary
1 c. onions, chopped	1 Tbsp. Perk
1 c. celery, chopped	2 Tbsp. sugar
1 c. carrots, chopped	10 peppercorns
1 c. bell pepper, chopped	3 dry red peppers
1 c. potatoes, chopped	1 ham hock
3 cloves garlic, chopped	

Rinse beans and ham hock. Place in crock pot or large pan. Add all other ingredients plus an additional quart of water. Bring to a boil and turn down to low. Simmer for 4 hours. Add 1 cup red wine or ½ cup vinegar; simmer until beans are tender. Serve with Mexican Corn Bread.

I add 1 tablespoon onion, bell pepper, pimento, 1 cup cream corn, and ½ cup crumbled bacon to your favorite corn bread mix or recipe. I make my beef or chicken broth, no salt, and defatted and freeze 2 cups in Baggies. I cook all my rice, noodles, and vegetables in broth.

Joann Geist, Fallbrook Lioness Club
Fallbrook, California, USA

BEAN, SAUSAGE, AND BRANDY SOUP

1 c. carrots, slivered	½ c. brandy (your favorite kind)
1 c. celery, chopped	4 sausages, garlic or ¾ lb. hot
½ c. onion, chopped	dogs
1 Tbsp. butter	1 (30 oz.) can chili beans
1 (10½ oz.) can consomme or bouillon	1 (1 lb.) can stewed tomatoes

Saute carrots, celery, and onion slowly in the butter for 5 minutes. Add the consomme and ¼ cup brandy. Heat to simmer, cover, and cook for 5 minutes. Cut the sausage or hot dogs into generous bite-size pieces and add to the soup. Cook for an additional 5 minutes. Coarsely mash 1 cup of the beans and add to the soup, along with the balance of the beans, tomatoes, and the remaining brandy. Simmer for 5 minutes longer. I don't know where this recipe came from, but it has been a main meal for me for years. Serve it with sourdough bread. Makes 2 quarts.

Bill Ostrand, Rohnert Park Lions Club
Rohnert Park, California, USA

You aren't stuck where you are unless you decide to be.

GARBANZO BEAN SOUP

3 cans garbanzo beans
1 chorizos sausage, cut up
4 potatoes, cubed

1 ham bone
2 qt. water
1 tsp. salt

Mix ingredients. Cook slowly for 3 hours.

Stanley Clarke Wyllie, Mad River Lions Club
Riverside, Ohio, USA

MAGIC BEAN SOUP

1 (16 oz.) pkg. dried beans and
    lentils
5 c. water
1 (28 oz.) can stewed tomatoes
1 (9 oz.) pkg. frozen green beans
1 large onion, chopped

3 carrots, peeled and sliced
½ c. chopped green pepper
1 Tbsp. Worcestershire sauce
¼ tsp. oregano
2 cloves garlic, minced

Wash and soak beans overnight. Pour off water from beans. Add 5 cups of fresh water and all of the other ingredients. Bring to a boil. Reduce heat and simmer 1 hour or until beans are tender.

Crock pot method: Soak beans in water overnight. Pour off water and add 5 cups of fresh water to the soaked beans. Add rest of ingredients. Cook on LOW for 10 to 12 hours or until beans are tender.

PORTUGUESE BEAN SOUP

½ lb. smoked ham
1 Portuguese sausage
1 c. navy beans, soaked overnight
    in water
1 large carrot, cut in pieces

2 medium potatoes, cut in pieces
1 large onion, sliced
Salt to taste
6 c. water
1 can tomato sauce

1. Boil the 6 cups of water and tomato sauce with beans for 1 hour or until beans are tender.
2. Add other ingredients and cook until tender.
3. Season with salt and pepper. You may add spaghetti or macaroni to the above for bulk.

Best bean soup from the old country.

Lion Tony Silverira, Caruthers Lions Club
Caruthers, California, USA

Prosperity is located within you.

GOULDSBORO STEAK SOUP

¼ lb. margarine
1 c. flour
½ tsp. pepper
1 tsp. Accent
1½ tsp. Kitchen Bouquet
1 qt. to 1 c. water
½ c. celery, chopped

1 Tbsp. beef base
½ c. carrots, chopped
½ c. onions, chopped
1 c. mixed vegetables
½ lb. or 8 oz. tomatoes, chopped
1 c. ground chuck

Brown meat and drain. Parboil onions, carrots, and celery. Melt margarine in 2 quart pan and add flour. Mix. Add water and stir while heating until thickened; continue stirring. Add Accent, pepper, beef base, and tomatoes. Cook 1 minute. Add Kitchen Bouquet, rest of vegetables, and meat. Cook on medium heat for 30 minutes, stirring occasionally.

Note: Soup may be frozen for later use.

W. Leeman, Gouldsboro Lions Club
Gouldsboro, Pennsylvania, USA

HAMBURGER BARLEY SOUP

1 lb. hamburger
5 c. water
32 oz. canned tomatoes, broken
   up
1 medium onion, diced
1 c. chopped carrots
1 c. chopped celery

½ c. pearl barley
¼ c. catsup
1 beef bouillon cube
1 tsp. seasoned salt
1 tsp. dry crushed basil
1 bay leaf
Salt and pepper to taste

In 3 quart pan, brown meat. Drain off fat. Add water and undrained tomatoes. Put in everything else in order, except the salt and pepper. Bring to boiling. Reduce heat and simmer, covered, for 2 hours. When done, season with salt and pepper to taste. Remove bay leaf. Makes 6 servings.

The secret of dealing successfully with a child is not to be his parent.

CHRISTMAS EVE SOUP

½ lb. ground beef
1 small potato, diced
1 small onion, diced
2 ripe tomatoes, chopped
2 green chilies, chopped
1 tsp. oregano
1½ tsp. chili powder

½ tsp. salt
½ tsp. garlic powder
½ tsp. cumin
1¾ qt. hot water
4 beef bouillon cubes
⅓ c. flour
⅓ c. cold water

Saute ground beef, potato, onion, tomato, green chilies, and spices until beef is cooked through. Dissolve bouillon cubes in hot water. Add to beef. Simmer until potato is done. Mix flour and cold water; add slowly to soup. Boil 10 minutes. Garnish with tortilla chips and Cheddar cheese before serving. Serves 4 to 6. Chicken and chicken bouillon may be substituted for the beef and beef bouillon.

CHICKEN, MEAT, VEGE, NOODLE SOUP

1 (17 oz.) can sweet peas
1 (10 oz.) can onion soup
1 (14 oz.) beef broth
1 (14 oz.) can chicken broth
1 (1 lb. 2 oz.) can chunky soup
1 lb. fresh mushrooms
4 large carrots
4 large celery stalks

1 medium size onion
1 lb. beef stew
2 c. water
1 can whole kernel corn
4 large potatoes
Salt and pepper
8 oz. pkg. egg dumplings

Into a large kettle, empty sweet peas, onion soup, beef broth, chicken broth, chunky soup, whole kernel corn, and 2 cups water. Cut beef stew into ½ inch cubes; brown in skillet. Drain and set aside. Chop mushrooms, carrots, celery, onion, and potatoes into ¼ inch cubes. Put all chopped vegetables and stew in kettle. Heat to boiling, then turn down heat and simmer for 2 hours with cover on kettle. Add 1 more cup of water. Dumplings should be cooked according to package directions. Add egg dumplings and salt and pepper to taste. Serve. Serves 6 to 8.

LEMON CHICKEN SOUP

6 c. chicken broth
1 c. diced cooked chicken
½ c. diced carrots
½ c. chopped yellow onion

1½ Tbsp. lemon juice
½ tsp. lemon-pepper seasoning
4 oz. spaghetti noodles or fresh
   egg noodles

Bring broth to a boil. Add chicken, carrots, chopped onion, lemon juice, and lemon pepper seasoning. Allow to simmer until the vegetables are tender, about 20 minutes. Snap spaghetti noodles into 1 to 2 inch pieces. Add noodles to the soup and simmer until noodles are tender, about 10 minutes. Serves 4.

SOUP SUPREME

1½ qt. water
1½ c. chopped celery
1½ c. chopped carrots
1 (20 oz.) pkg. frozen broccoli
1½ c. chopped onion

1 c. diced potato
6 chicken bouillon cubes
2 cans cream of chicken soup
1 lb. Velveeta, cubed

In a large kettle, heat water and dissolve bouillon cubes. Add potatoes, onion, celery, and carrots. Cook 15 minutes or until done. Add frozen broccoli and cook another 10 minutes. Add soup and cheese. Stir over low heat until cheese is melted. Serves 10 to 12.

Ellen Olson, Lion, Plattsmouth Lions Club
Plattsmouth, Nebraska, USA

CREAMY CHICKEN-VEGETABLE CHOWDER

2 c. chopped cooked chicken
1 (10¾ oz.) can cream of potato
   soup (undiluted)
1 (10¾ oz.) can cream of chicken
   soup (undiluted)
1 (11 oz.) can Mexican style corn
   (undrained)
1 (4 oz.) jar sliced mushrooms
   (undrained)

1 (4 oz.) can chopped green chiles
   (undrained)
1½ c. milk
1 (11 oz.) can chicken broth
⅓ c. sliced green onions
1½ c. (6 oz.) shredded Cheddar
   cheese
Sliced green onions (garnish)

Combine first 9 ingredients in a Dutch oven, stirring well. Cook over medium heat 5 to 8 minutes or until thoroughly heated. Remove from heat; add cheese, stirring until cheese melts. Garnish, if desired, and serve immediately. Yields 9 cups.

Before grating cheese, add a little oil on the grater and it will be easier to wash.

Mrs. Charlotte M. Garner, Pascagoula Evening Lions Club
Pascagoula, Mississippi, USA

❧

The speed of the leader determines the rate of the pack.

CHICKEN TORTELLINI SOUP

6 c. water
3 (10¾ oz.) cans condensed
  chicken broth
1 (10¾ oz.) can condensed cream
  of chicken soup
2 c. cubed, cooked chicken
1 c. chopped onions
1 c. sliced carrots

½ c. dry vermouth or water
2 garlic cloves, minced
½ tsp. basil leaves
½ tsp. oregano leaves
9 oz. pkg. frozen cut broccoli,
  thawed
7 oz. pkg. cheese tortellini
Grated Parmesan cheese

In large saucepan or Dutch oven, combine water, chicken broth, soup, chicken, onions, carrots, vermouth or water, garlic, basil, and oregano. bring to a boil. Add tortellini. Simmer, uncovered, 30 minutes. Add broccoli. Simmer an additional 5 to 10 minutes or until broccoli is tender. Serve with cheese. Makes 10 servings.

CHICKEN CORN SOUP

1 (6 lb.) oven stuffer chicken
Celery and onion (if desired)
1 gal. corn

½ doz. chopped eggs
2 qt. cubed potatoes
3 Tbsp. parsley

Cook chicken with celery and onion until done. Pick meat off the bones. Discard skin and bones. Cut meat into small pieces. Add corn, potatoes, and parsley into broth; cook until potatoes are soft. Add hard-boiled eggs and cut up chicken. Salt and pepper to taste.

Rubbing alcohol will remove ball-point pen marks.
Lion Ethel D. Parr, Mt. Holly Springs Lions Club
Gardners, Pennsylvania, USA

CHICKEN SUCCOTASH SOUP

½ lb. bacon, cut up
2 to 3 lb. boneless skinless
  chicken thighs, cut up
3 lb. potatoes, cut up
2 lb. bag mixed vegetables

2 Tbsp. or 2 cubes chicken
  bouillon
Garlic and seasoned salt to taste
8 to 9 qt. water

Put bacon and chicken in 12 quart soup pot. Brown meat and drain. Add rest of ingredients. Cover and cook on medium heat for about 1 hour. Stir occasionally. Turn heat to low and cook an additional hour. Serves about 12 people. This freezes well.

Alternate method. Cook bacon and chicken. Put all in large crock pot. Cook all day on LOW.

VOMACK - CZECH VEGETABLE AND CREAM SOUP

4 medium size potatoes
1 c. water
Dash of salt
½ c. fresh dill
2 c. frozen cut green beans
1 Tbsp. butter
Dash of salt and pepper

¼ c. water
1½ Tbsp. flour
1 to 1½ c. cream
3 Tbsp. vinegar
4 poached eggs
Paprika

Peel and cut the potatoes in 1 inch cubes. Boil the potatoes in 1 cup water, dash of salt, and ½ of the ferny ends of fresh dill. Cover and boil until potatoes are tender.

Meanwhile, cook the green beans until tender in ¼ cup water, the butter, salt, and pepper. Blend the flour with 1 cup cream. Combine the cooked vegetables. Slowly add the flour and cream. Cook on low heat for a minute.

Gradually add vinegar. If soup is too thick, add more cream. Put the soup in 4 open soup bowls and gently lift a poached egg to the top of each bowl of soup and sprinkle with paprika. The dill gives this delicious soup it's characteristic flavor. It is a complete meal. Serves 4.

OLD-FASHIONED VEGETABLE SOUP

2 c. beef or chicken broth
2 c. (16 oz.) can tomatoes
½ c. water
⅓ c. chopped onion
⅓ c. chopped celery
1 c. cubed potatoes

1 c. sliced carrots
1 c. (8 oz. can) peas or corn
1 c. shredded cabbage
¼ tsp. pepper
⅛ tsp. basil
½ tsp. salt

Bring broth to boil in large pot. Add vegetables and seasonings; bring to second boil. Cover and simmer 30 minutes or longer. Yield: 6 servings.

Gladys Filla, Yakima West Valley Lions Club
Cowiche, Washington, USA

The best exercise is meeting people halfway.

CREAMY VEGETABLE SOUP

½ c. grated onion
2 Tbsp. oil
1 c. chopped celery
2 (only) grated carrots
½ medium head cauliflower
2 Tbsp. minced parsley
6 c. chicken broth

¼ c. butter
¾ c. flour
2 c. milk
1 c. half & half
Salt to taste
1 c. cream

Bouquet garni - Tie in cheesecloth bag:

2 bay leaves
1 tsp. tarragon

½ tsp. peppercorn

Saute onion in oil. Add celery and carrots. Cook over low heat for 2 minutes. Stir in cauliflower and parsley. Simmer for 12 minutes. Add chicken broth and bouquet garni. Bring to a boil; reduce to low heat and simmer 5 minutes.

Meanwhile, melt butter in heavy pan; add flour to make a roux. Gradually add milk. Stir with a whisk so mixture is smooth. Remove and add half & half. Stir white sauce into simmering soup. Simmer until cauliflower is tender, about 10 minutes.

Remove bouquet garni; mix some hot soup into cream, then add to the rest of the soup. Serve. Garnish with sprig of parsley.

This recipe may be doubled or tripled and some frozen. Only 1 bouquet garni need be added.

WINTER VEGETABLE SOUP

2 tsp. olive oil
1 c. slivered onions
½ c. sliced carrots
½ c. diced pared parsnips
1 clove garlic, minced
2 large vegetarian vegetable
    bouillon cubes
2 tsp. dried marjoram

3 oz. penne or mostaccioli or ziti
1 c. green beans
2 c. sliced mushrooms
2 c. finely chopped Swiss Chard,
    shredded
1 Tbsp. plus 1 tsp. grated
    Parmesan cheese

I. In large saucepan, heat oil; add onion, carrot, parsnip, and garlic. Cook over medium high heat, stirring frequently, until onions are transparent, about 5 minutes.

II. Crumble in bouillon cubes and marjoram. Add 5 cups water and bring to boil. Add pasta and green beans. Return to boil. Reduce heat to simmer, partially covered, for 15 minutes. Add mushrooms and Swiss Chard. Simmer for 5 minutes longer. Makes 4 servings. Sprinkle with Parmesan cheese.

Mildred Butts, Mt. Clemens Lioness Club
Mt. Clemens, Michigan, USA

POTATO SOUP

6 medium potatoes (about 2 lb.)
5 c. cold water
1 carrot, washed, scraped, and
   pared
1 leek, washed thoroughly (white
   part only)
1 stalk celery, cut into pieces
1 medium onion, sliced

2 tsp. salt
¼ tsp. white pepper
¼ tsp. thyme
¼ tsp. marjoram
1 bay leaf
1 beef bouillon cube
2 Tbsp. butter
3 Tbsp. all-purpose flour

In a heavy saucepan (3 quarts) with a tight cover, place the potatoes, cut into ¼ inch slices, with the water and salt. Cover and bring to a boil. Reduce heat. Add carrot, leek, celery, onion, pepper, thyme, marjoram, and bay leaf. Cover and cook for 1 hour, or until veggies are tender.

With a slotted spoon, remove the carrot, leek, onion, celery and bay leaf. Discard. Remove 1 cup of the potato broth. With a potato masher, mash the remaining potato mixture until it becomes a fine mush. Dissolve bouillon in the reserved broth. Heat butter over low heat. Mix in flour and stir until bubbly. Add the bouillon mixture gradually to the butter mixture, stirring constantly. Pour the mixture into the soup and mix well. Return to boiling, then simmer gently for 5 to 10 minutes. Makes about 2½ pints of soup.

OLD-FASHIONED POTATO SOUP

8 potatoes, cubed
Salt and pepper to taste
½ c. flour
¼ c. milk

1 qt. milk
1 Tbsp. butter
1 egg, well beaten

Boil potatoes until soft. Drain. Add milk and beat thoroughly. Season to taste. Work butter into flour; add egg and milk. Drop by teaspoonfuls into hot milk. Cover saucepan and cook about 10 minutes. Serve at once. Serves 4.

Kathy Dobson, Mt. Airy Foothills Lions Club
Mt. Airy, North Carolina, USA

Never let failure go to your head.

TACO SOUP

2 lb. ground beef or turkey
1 onion, chopped
1 can kidney beans
1 can jalapena pinto beans
1 can plain pinto beans
1 can hominy

2 cans stewed tomatoes
1 can Ro-Tel tomatoes
1 pkg. taco seasoning
1 pkg. Hidden Valley Original
    Ranch dressing (dry)
1 can water (if needed)

Saute ground meat and chopped onion; drain fat. Add remaining ingredients. Simmer, covered, at least 30 minutes. Good over tortilla chips, rice or plain.

Quick, easy, and delicious - and healthy!

Billie Medley, Huffman Lioness Club
Huffman, Texas, USA

TACO SOUP

Brown 2 pounds ground chuck with 1 diced onion.

Dump in:

2 cans Ranch Style beans
1 can tomatoes

1 can Ro-Tel tomatoes
1 can whole kernel corn

Add:

1 env. Lawry's taco seasoning
1 env. Hidden Valley Ranch
    dressing

Simmer 45 minutes. Serve with crackers or corn bread and salad. Freezes well.

Janie Fox, Saginaw Lions Club
Saginaw, Texas, USA

We'd worry a lot less about what people think of us
if we realized they almost never give us a thought.

SLOW COOKER TACO SOUP

6 c. water
½ c. uncooked white or brown rice
   (not instant)
1 lb. lean hamburger
1 pkg. taco seasoning mix
2 medium grated carrots
1 c. chopped celery
½ small green pepper, chopped

1 small onion, chopped
1 (16 oz.) can undrained red
   kidney beans
1 (16 oz.) can undrained whole
   kernel corn
1 undiluted can tomato soup
½ tsp. cumin seed
2 Tbsp. salsa

Put 6 cups of lukewarm water and the uncooked rice in the slow cooker; cover, turning to HIGH setting.

Meanwhile, brown hamburger. While it is cooking, chop celery, green pepper, and onion. Add them and the grated carrots to the slow cooker and stir.

When meat is brown, drain and add the undrained red kidney beans, corn, and tomato soup to the ingredients in the slow cooker. Stir. After meat has simmered with the taco seasoning, add the cumin seed and salsa to the soup in the slow cooker. Stir and cover. Turn on LOW and cook all day.

Enjoy with corn bread or chips and salsa on the side. Makes 8 servings.

Variations:

1. Vegetarians can omit the hamburger.
2. Use leftover rice and simmer on top of stove for 10 to 15 minutes.

VENUS DE MILO MINESTRONE SOUP

1 lb. hamburg
1 onion, chopped
2 stalks celery, chopped
2 qt. water
1 medium can stewed tomatoes
1 small can tomato sauce (Hunt's)
2 cans Veg-All with liquid (16 oz.)
   or 2 cans peas and carrots

Pinch of red pepper flakes
Salt
Pepper
Garlic salt
1 c. orzo (pasta)
Grated cheese

Boil crumbled hamburg, onion, celery, and water together. Add salt, pepper, garlic salt, red pepper flakes, orzo, and stewed tomatoes (with juice), tomato sauce, and Veg-All. Simmer until orzo is done. Top with grated cheese.

Great on a cold or gloomy day.

Nancy Gouveia, Berkley Lions Club
Berkley, Massachusetts, USA

Our lives are what our thoughts create.

WILD RICE SOUP

1 c. wild rice
3 to 4 c. water (or chicken broth)
1 tsp. salt (omit salt if using broth)
2 c. cooked wild rice
1 large onion, finely diced
1 large carrot, finely diced
1 rib celery, finely diced

1 c. finely diced meat (chicken or turkey)
½ c. butter or margarine
4 Tbsp. flour
8 c. chicken broth
Salt and white pepper to taste
1 c. light cream or half & half

Wash wild rice by rinsing well in cold water and draining. Place washed wild rice in heavy saucepan with water. Bring to boil; reduce heat and simmer, covered, for 40 to 50 minutes or until rice is tender and most of the grains have split slightly. Drain any excess liquid and fluff with a fork.

Prepare the wild rice. In a 4 or 5 quart soup kettle, saute onion, carrot, celery, and meat in margarine or butter for about 3 minutes or until the vegetables have softened slightly. Sift in the flour, a little bit at a time, stirring and cooking until the flour is blended in well, but do not let it brown.

Slowly add the chicken broth, stirring until all the flour-butter mixture is blended well. Add the wild rice. Adjust seasonings as desired. Heat thoroughly. Add the cream or half & half and reheat gently, but do not boil.

CREAMY WILD RICE SOUP

½ c. chopped onion
4 Tbsp. butter
5 Tbsp. flour
3 c. chicken broth
2 c. milk or half & half

½ c. slivered almonds
2 c. cooked wild rice (½ c. raw rice)
½ c. grated carrots
Salt and pepper to taste

In medium saucepan, saute onion till soft. Add flour and bring to boil, stirring until smooth. Add chicken broth and bring to a boil. Reduce heat and simmer 10 to 15 minutes. Heat milk or half & half (do not boil). Add to soup mixture and stir. Add almonds and cooked wild rice and salt and pepper to taste. Simmer for 20 minutes. Serve very warm.

Dorothy L. Anderson, Mitchell Lioness Club
Mitchell, South Dakota, USA

Experience gives the test first and the lesson afterward.

SPLIT PEA WITH HAM SOUP

2 c. dried split peas
1½ qt. water
1 ham bone (about 1½ lb.)
1 onion, sliced
1 c. sliced celery
1 c. grated carrots

1½ tsp. salt
1 tsp. crushed basil
¼ c. oleo
¼ c. flour
2 c. milk

In a large saucepan, combine peas, water, bone, onion, celery, carrots, salt, and basil. Bring to boiling; reduce heat and simmer for 1½ to 2 hours. Stir flour into melted oleo in a separate saucepan. Cook until bubbly. Gradually add milk, stirring constantly. Bring to boiling. Cook for 1 minute. Stir white sauce into soup. Serves 8.

TZVIVELLE RIVEZ SOUP - ONION RIVEL SOUP

4 medium onions, diced
5 to 6 c. beef broth

Salt and pepper to taste
4 Tbsp. oleo or butter

Rivels:

1 egg, beaten

Flour

Melt oleo and saute onions until brown (don't burn). Add broth or water and bouillon. Bring to boil, then simmer.

To make rivels: Add flour to egg and mix with fork until crumbly. Bring broth back to a boil. Drop rivels in while stirring to prevent sticking together. Simmer, covered, for 10 to 15 minutes so rivels cook and soup thickens.

A delicious soup for Lent as chicken broth can be used also.
Walter E. Loomis, North Jackson Lions Club
Jackson, Michigan, USA

ONION SOUP

¼ c. butter
4 c. thinly sliced onion
4 cans (101, 2 oz.) beef broth
4 to 6 slices French bread (1 inch
   thick)

¼ c. grated Gruyere cheese
2 Tbsp. grated Parmesan cheese

In a large skillet, saute onions in butter until golden, not browned, for 8 minutes. In medium saucepan, combine beef broth and saute onion; bring to boiling. Reduce heat and simmer, covered, for 30 minutes. In broiler, toast French bread. Sprinkle each slice with grated cheeses, dividing evenly. Broil just until cheese is bubbly, about 1 minute. To serve, pour soup into individual soup bowls. Float toast on top, cheese side up.

Dave Bernier, Westbrook Lions Club
Westbrook, Maine, USA

COCKA-LEEKIE SOUP

1 cube butter
5 stalks leeks, diced
2 yellow onions, diced
½ stalk celery, diced

2 qt. chicken bouillon
2½ lb. potatoes
1 pt. half & half
Salt and pepper to taste

In large pan, melt butter over low heat. Add diced vegetables and cook until soft. Season to taste. Add chicken stock and cook 1½ hours over medium heat. Add diced potatoes and cook 45 minutes. Beat with mixer. Add half & half and return to heat. Serve with sour cream and sprinkle with parsley. I've cooked this recipe in the pressure cooker, after adding chicken stock and potatoes together, pressure for 20 minutes.

Darrell F. Fowler, Plumb Lane Lions Club
Reno, Nevada, USA

MUSHROOM SOUP
(Slovak style)

3 Tbsp. butter
2 small onions, chopped
⅛ c. flour
½ lb. fresh chopped mushrooms

4 beef bouilllon cubes
10 c. hot water
Salt to taste

Optional:

1 (10 oz.) pkg. sq. noodles

Sauerkraut juice to taste

Melt butter. Add onion and brown slightly. Add flour and brown. When flour is brown, add water, slowing stirring slowly to dissolve flour mixture. Add all of the water. Add fresh, cleaned chopped mushrooms and simmer for 20 minutes. Add bouillon cubes and salt. Taste. Simmer till mushrooms are tender, about 10 minutes more. Cook noodles and serve with sauerkraut juice on the side. Add to each persons taste.

CABBAGE PATCH SOUP

1 lb. ground beef
3 slices bacon, diced
½ c. diced celery
1 (16 oz.) can tomatoes
¼ c. margarine
1½ c. water

1 onion, thinly sliced
1 can red kidney beans
Salt and pepper to taste
1 tsp. chili powder
2 c. shredded cabbage

Brown beef and bacon; drain. Drain and rinse kidney beans. Combine all ingredients and simmer for 1½ hours. Amounts of bacon, water, and cabbage can be varied as desired. Serves 4 to 6.

RED CABBAGE SOUP

1 lb. diced onions
1 lb. diced green bell peppers
2 (No. 303) cans okra
2 (No. 303) cans whole tomatoes
1 qt. crushed tomatoes
4 celery spears, chopped fine
6 large carrots, sliced ¼ inch
2 lb. mixed soup vegetables
1 small head red cabbage, cut in half

1 large meaty soup bone
2 lb. beef chuck, cut into 1 inch squares
Black pepper*
Garlic salt*
Celery seeds*
Parsley*
Chives*
¼ c. sugar

Fill pot ⅓ full of water. Bring to a boil. Add soup bone and boil no longer than 10 minutes. Remove soup bone and give it to your best dog. Too much boiling of soup bone will make soup too greasy. Add onions, peppers, carrots, and meat. Boil until carrots are tender. Reduce heat to simmer; add okra, celery, tomatoes, and soup vegetables. When soup has reached a steady simmer, add spices and sugar. Now place red cabbage on top of soup. Simmer until cabbage is grey, or about 30 minutes. Remove cabbage and give to your boiled cabbage lover. Simmer soup for 30 more minutes. Serve with crackers. You will need a large soup pot. The red cabbage will leak all the red color into the soup.

* Add the above spices to your taste.

Parroll Winton Boyer, Stewartstown Lions Club
Stewartstown, Pennsylvania, USA

ZUCCHINI SOUP

1 lb. Italian sweet or hot sausage, casings removed
2 c. celery, sliced
2 lb. zucchini, sliced ½ inch
1 c. chopped onions
2 (28 oz.) cans tomatoes
2 tsp. salt

1 tsp. Italian herbs
1 tsp. oregano
1 tsp. sugar
1 tsp. basil
¼ tsp. garlic powder
2 green pepprs, cut in ½ inch

Brown sausage in large Dutch oven. Drain off fat. Add celery. Cook 10 minutes, stirring occasionally. Add remaining ingredients, except green peppers. Simmer, covered, for 20 minutes. Add green peppers and cook, covered, for 10 minutes. Makes 3½ quarts.

❧

If it's worth doing, it's worth doing well.

CREAM OF TOMATO SOUP

2 Tbsp. margarine
½ tsp. salt
⅛ tsp. pepper
4 Tbsp. flour
2 c. lowfat milk
2 c. fresh or canned tomatoes

½ c. water
2 tsp. sugar
2 whole cloves
¼ tsp. salt
1 Tbsp. chopped onion
⅛ tsp. soda

Make a white sauce of first 5 ingredients. Melt, in a 1½ to 2 quart saucepan, margarine. Add flour, salt, and pepper. Mix well and add milk slowly. Bring to a boil, stirring constantly. Keep hot while preparing tomatoes. Blanch and peel tomatoes if fresh. Measure into saucepan. Add water, sugar, cloves, salt, and chopped onion. Boil 20 minutes. Strain (if desired). Add ⅛ teaspoon soda. Stir well. Pour into white sauce. Stir. Serve immediately. Serves 2 to 4.

CHINESE EGG DROP SOUP - DUN FAR TONG

1 egg, beaten
2 drops of vegetable oil
1 qt. chicken stock (may use 4
    bouillon cubes in water)
¾ tsp. salt (omit if using bouillon
    cubes)

¼ tsp. sugar
Thinly sliced green onion
1 Tbsp. cornstarch, mixed in a
    little water

Bring stock to boiling; thicken with cornstarch. Turn heat off. Add egg slowly, stirring constantly. Add seasoning and onion. Serves 4.

This is a favorite in oriental restaurants, but rarely served in a Chinese home. When I was a child, my German mother made it for Sunday dinner, but you won't find it in German cookbooks. It is also called "Egg Flower Soup."

ICED GAZPACHO - COLD SOUP

1 c. Campbell's tomato juice
½ c. chicken broth
1 c. diced zucchini
1 small cucumber, peeled,
    seeded, and diced
½ c. green pepper
⅓ c. diced celery

¼ c. diced onion
2 Tbsp. lime juice
1 Tbsp. red wine vinegar
2 tsp. seeded and firmly chopped
    jalapeno pepper
1 medium clove garlic, minced

Combine and refrigerate (covered) 4 hours.

Pam Sedlar, Onekama Lions Club
Onekama, Michigan, USA

MOUNT SEYMOUR LENTIL SOUP

1½ c. brown lentils
Small ham bone
1 bay leaf
Salt and pepper to taste
1 can stewed tomatoes
1 small onion, cut

1 tsp. butter
1 tsp. wine vinegar (to taste)
About 3 inches garlic salami, cut
   into tiny pieces
6 c. water

1. Wash lentils thoroughly and place in a pot.
2. Add ham bone and bay leaf.
3. Add water (enough that the lentils are covered).
4. Bring to boil, cover, and simmer till lentils are soft.
5. Put stewed tomatoes and most of the lentils plus broth in a blender.
6. Discard bone and bay leaf.
7. When mixture is in liquid form, pour back in pot.
8. In a frying pan, slightly brown cut up onion. Put in pot. Add salami and stir.
9. Add water if too thick. Season with salt and pepper. Add vinegar. Stir and reheat.

John Pavlik, Mount Seymour Lions Club
North Vancouver, British Columbia, Canada

PASTA FAGIOLI SOUP

1 lb. hamburger
1 lb. can undrained Northern
   beans
2 cans (14 oz.) sliced stewed
   tomatoes
2 cans (14 oz.) clear beef broth
1 lb. jar Prego spaghetti sauce (no
   substitute)
½ rib celery, thinly sliced

1 medium onion, chopped
2 c. small spiral pasta (uncooked)
1 c. carrots, cut in slivers the size
   of a match
Kidney beans (optional)
Salt and pepper to taste
Red pepper to taste (if you like a
   spicy hot taste)

Cook hamburger, onion, celery, and carrots in Dutch oven pot until the red goes out of the meat. Add the rest of the ingredients. Bring to a boil; turn heat to low and cook until the pasta is tender, about 30 minutes or less. Can add water to make a thinner soup. Makes a lot. Can be frozen.

Janie Fox, Saginaw Lions Club
Saginaw, Texas, USA

Each day is a little life. Live it to its fullest.

ELEPHANT SOUP

1 large elephant (African is best)
600 gal. hot water
4 pecks onions, finely chopped
2 bu. potatoes, peeled and sliced
4 shovels salt
2 shovels white pepper

24 bottles Worcestershire sauce
15 bottles rum (or more if cooking
　time is longer)
Coke to taste
8 qt. peanut oil (optional)*

Mix 1½ ounces of rum with Coke; drink. Wash and dry elephant (don't use shampoo as this will spoil flavor). Chop into bite-size chunks. In back of 1 ton truck and trailer, pour hot water. Immediately seal all cracks to prevent leaks. Have another rum and Coke and add elephant, potatoes, and other ingredients. Allow to simmer.

Meanwhile, finish first bottle of rum. Stir mixture, using canoe paddle or 10 H.P. out-board motor. When guests arrive, start them off with remaining rum.

This recipe has been tried and tested, especially the rum. Will serve 200 people. If more soup is needed, increase the rum.

* The peanut oil won't really add to soup, but it's the way the elephant would have wanted it!

Steve Kovach, Keystone Lions Club
Brandon, Manitoba, Canada

FISH STEW

½ lb. bacon
1½ to 2 lb. haddock
5 potatoes, peeled
1 large onion
2 stalks celery

1 lb. shrimp
1 large can tomato juice
Pepper to taste
Parsley to taste

Fry bacon in large Dutch oven or heavy soup pot until crisp. Remove and drain most of grease from pot. Layer thinly sliced peeled potatoes, chopped onion and celery, and haddock that has been cut into bite-size pieces. Repeat layers and crumble bacon on top. Pour tomato juice on top. Cook over low heat until vegetables are tender. Add cleaned shrimp and cook 15 minutes longer. Serve.

When you dislike yourself, you insult those who love you.

SHRIMP BISQUE

1 c. water
1 c. chopped celery
1 c. diced potato
¼ c. chopped onion
½ tsp. salt

1 (4½ oz.) can shrimp, drained and
   chopped, or 1 c. chopped
   fresh shrimp
2 Tbsp. butter
Snipped parsley

In large saucepan, combine water, celery, potatoes, onion, salt, and pepper. Bring to a boil. Reduce heat and simmer, covered, for 15 minutes or until potatoes are tender, stirring occasionally.

Combine milk and flour till smooth; stir into potato mixture along with shrimp and butter. Cook and stir till thickened and bubbly. Garnish with parsley. Makes 4 servings.

Tom O'Dell, Hodgenville Lions Club
Hodgenville, Kentucky, USA

SEAFOOD BISQUE

3 c. half & half
⅓ stick butter
Salt and pepper to taste
1 oz. sherry
¼ to ½ tsp. grated lemon peel

1 or 2 Tbsp. corn starch to thicken
Oysters, grated cooked shrimp,
   minced clams, or crabmeat
   (only one)

Heat half & half in a saucepan along with the butter. Add corn starch, salt, and pepper to taste. As the bisque thickens, add the lemon peel and seafood of choice. (Amount of seafood is decided by the preparer of this recipe.) Wait 1 to 2 minutes and remove from heat. Add the sherry and serve. Have extra sherry available for anyone who wishes to add a little more. May add extra corn starch for thicker bisque.

William M. Davidson, IV, Statesboro Lions Club
Statesboro, Georgia, USA

A sweater is a garment worn by a child when his mother feels chilly.

FISH CHOWDER

6 slices bacon
½ c. chopped onion
1½ c. boiling water
½ tsp. salt
½ c. flour
½ c. diced celery

1 lb. haddock, cut into 1 inch
   pieces
2 c. cubed potatoes (2 or 3
   medium)
½ c. oleo
4 c. milk

Cook bacon until crisp. Drain and crumble. Saute celery and onion in bacon drippings until tender. Add fish, potatoes, water, and seasonings; simmer for 10 to 12 minutes until potatoes are tender. Melt oleo in a Dutch oven; stir in flour. Cook until smooth, stirring constantly. Remove from heat. Gradually stir in milk. Bring to a boil over medium heat, stirring constantly. Boil and stir for 1 minute. Stir in fish mixture and add bacon.

Jackie Broaddus, Westbrook Lions Club
Westbrook, Maine, USA

NEW ENGLAND CLAM CHOWDER

4 medium potatoes, diced
1 medium onion, diced
2 Tbsp. butter
¼ c. diced salt pork or butter
2 c. water

2 c. milk (park cream or canned
   milk for richer chowder)
1 c. clams*
Salt and pepper to taste

In heavy kettle, brown salt pork and remove. If using butter, just heat. Add onions and cook until transparent. Add raw potatoes and onion with water; cook until tender. If canned clams are used, use juice as part of water. Add clams and simmer. Add milk which has been heated in separate pan. Add salt, pepper, and butter and it is ready to eat. Place salt pork scraps on for garnish.

* Minced or chopped canned clams may be used.

Uncle Don Drew, Westbrook Lions Club
Westbrook, Maine, USA

Democracy without morality is impossible.

CLAM CHOWDER SOUP

8 slices bacon, chopped
3 potatoes, peeled and diced
¼ c. finely chopped onion
5 Tbsp. flour
1 tsp. salt (optional)

¼ tsp. dried thyme leaves
  (optional)
⅛ tsp. pepper
1 (6½ oz.) can minced clams
3 c. milk

Place bacon in a large casserole. Microwave on HIGH for 4 minutes or until crisp. Remove bacon, reserving drippings. Drain bacon on paper towel and set aside. Stir in potatoes and onion into bacon drippings. Cover and microwave on HIGH for 7 minutes or until potatoes are tender, stirring every 3 minutes. Stir in flour, salt, thyme, and pepper. Drain clams, reserving juice. Blend clam juice and milk into potato mixture. Microwave on HIGH for 7 minutes, or until mixture thickens, stirring every 2 minutes. Crumble bacon into mixture. Stir in clams.

CHEESE SOUP

1½ c. broccoli (fresh or frozen)
1½ c. cauliflower
1 medium onion, diced
1½ c. zucchini, sliced (optional)
4 c. water

4 chicken bouillon cubes
1 lb. Velveeta cheese, cubed (light
  Velveeta may be used)
2 cans cream of chicken soup
1 can water

Boil on low the first 6 ingredients for ½ hour. Continue low boil and add Velveeta cheese, 2 cans cream of chicken soup, and 1 can of water. Stir occasionally, making sure all ingredients are blended well (about 10 minutes). For thinner soup, add more water. Salt and pepper to taste or diet. Makes 5 to 7 servings.

CHEESE SOUP

1½ c. carrots
1½ c. potatoes
1½ c. celery
1½ qt. water
1 frozen pkg. broccoli and
  cauliflower mixture

2 cans cream of chicken soup
5 chicken bouillon cubes
1 lb. Velveeta cheese

Cook carrots, potatoes, and celery in water until done, about 15 minutes. Add broccoli and cauliflower mixture; cook 6 minutes more. Add the cream of chicken soup, the bouillon cubes, and the Velveeta cheese. Stir gently until blended well. I use a 6 quart container. This is a good, rich soup, and keeps well in the refrigerator.

Mrs. James P. Liebl, Offerle Dist. SW Kansas Lions Club
Offerle, Kansas, USA

CHEDDAR CHOWDER

2 c. water
2 c. diced potatoes
½ c. diced carrots
½ c. diced celery

¼ c. chopped onion
1 tsp. salt
¼ tsp. pepper

Boil 12 minutes.

White Sauce:

¼ c. oleo
¼ c. flour
2 c. milk

2 c. shredded Cheddar cheese
1 c. cubed ham

Make White Sauce. Melt oleo. Add flour and stir until smooth. Add milk and cook until thick. Add cheese. Stir until melted. Add to vegetables (not drained). Add ham. Do not boil.

This will serve 4 people. I usually triple this recipe for company. Increase flour to 1 cup. This not only tastes wonderful - it makes the kitchen smell wonderful as well.

Gertrude Hayden, Moweaqua Lions Club
Moweaqua, Illinois, USA

VEGETABLE CHOWDER

3 c. water
3 chicken-flavored bouillon cubes
4 medium potatoes, peeled and
    diced
1 medium onion, sliced
1 c. thinly sliced carrots
½ c. diced green pepper
⅓ c. butter or margarine

⅓ c. all-purpose flour
3½ c. milk
4 c. (1 lb.) shredded sharp
    Cheddar cheese
1 (2 oz.) jar diced pimento, drained
¼ tsp. hot sauce (optional)
Salt and pepper to taste

Combine water and bouillon cubes in a Dutch oven; bring to a boil. Add vegetables; cover and simmer 12 minutes, or until vegetables are tender. Melt butter in a heavy saucepan over low heat; add flour, stirring until smooth. Cook 1 minute, stirring constantly. Gradually add milk; cook over medium heat, stirring constantly, until thickened and bubbly. Add cheese, stirring until melted. Stir cheese sauce, pimento, and hot sauce into vegetable mixture. Cook over low heat until thoroughly heated (do not boil). Makes 10 (1 cup) servings.

Mrs. Lion Jack (Carolyn) Weaver, Canton Lions Club
Canton, Georgia, USA

You become what you think about.

MEAT BALL CHOWDER

2 lb. ground beef
2 tsp. seasoned salt
⅛ tsp. pepper
2 eggs, slightly beaten
¼ c. parsley
¼ c. fine cracker crumbs
2 Tbsp. milk
3 Tbsp. flour
1 Tbsp. salad oil
4 to 6 onions, cut in eighths

6 c. tomato juice
6 beef bouillon cubes
6 carrots, sliced (3 c.)
3 to 4 potatoes, diced (2 to 3 c.)
¼ c. long grain rice
1 Tbsp. sugar
2 tsp. salt
2 bay leaves
½ to 1 tsp. marjoram (optional)
1 (12 oz.) can Mexicorn

Combine meat, seasoned salt, pepper, eggs, parsley, cracker crumbs, and milk. Mix thoroughly. Form into balls about the size of a walnut. Makes about 40.

Dip in flour. Heat oil in 8 to 10 quart kettle. Lightly brown meat balls on all sides (or drop unbrowned in boiling vegetables). Add remaining ingredients (except add corn last 10 minutes of cooking). Bring to slow boil for 30 minutes or until vegetables are tender. (If dinner must wait, turn off heat at this point.) Makes 6 to 7 quarts.

MEXICAN CHICKEN CORN CHOWDER

¼ c. chopped onion
1 clove garlic, finely chopped
3 Tbsp. margarine or butter
1½ lb. skinned boneless chicken
  breasts, cut into bite-size
  pieces
1 c. water
2 tsp. chicken-flavor instant
  bouillon or 2 chicken-flavor
  bouillon cubes

1 tsp. ground cumin
2 c. (1 pt.) half & half
1 (16 oz.) can cream style corn
1 (4 oz.) can chopped green chilies
  (undrained)
1 c. (4 oz.) shredded Monterey
  Jack cheese
Hot pepper sauce to taste
Chopped tomatoes, sliced green
  onions, and cilantro

In large saucepan, cook onion and garlic in margarine until tender; add chicken, water, bouillon, and cumin. Bring to a boil. Reduce heat; cover and simmer 15 minutes. Add half & half, corn, chilies, cheese, and hot pepper sauce. Cook and stir until cheese melts and mixture is hot. Garnish with tomatoes, green onions, and cilantro. Refrigerate leftovers. Makes about 2 quarts. Rich and delicious!

David W. Lacy, Quitman Lions Club
Quitman, Mississippi, USA

Your thoughts are all seeds that you plant.

GAZPACHO
(Served chilled)

⅓ c. wine vinegar
1 Tbsp. Worcestershire sauce
1 tsp. curry powder
2½ c. tomato juice
2 cans stewed tomatoes
Chopped celery

1 cucumber, cubed
½ green pepper, chopped
1 medium onion, chopped
1 Tbsp. parsley
Salt and pepper to taste
Garlic salt to taste

Mix all ingredients together and chill before serving. This is wonderful to serve on a hot day.

Shirley Ward, Levelland Lions Club
Levelland, Texas, USA

ROADKILL ELEPHANT SOUP

1 elephant
3 bay leaves

1 lb. salt (approx.)
1 rabbit (optional)

Carefully retrieve elephant from road, watching for other traffic - elephants or cars. Skin and cut up elephant, allowing sufficient time to carve bite-size pieces. Save trunk as you might need it to store leftovers. Cook in iron pots over open fires, using water to cover. Add bay leaves and salt to taste. Add rabbit *only* if crowd at feast is too large for pure elephant dish - because some people will object to hare in their soup!

Lion Howard Stringham, North Jackson Lions Club
Jackson, Michigan, USA

❤

Before repeating anything "a little bird" told you,
be sure it wasn't a cuckoo.

SANDWICHES

EGG SANDWICH FILLING

10 eggs
1½ tsp. dry mustard
¾ tsp. salt
¼ tsp. pepper
¾ tsp. curry powder

2 Tbsp. onion
2 tsp. lemon juice
Chives and parsley to taste
Mayonnaise

Hard boil eggs. Shell eggs. Chop eggs as small as possible, then add all dry ingredients and mix together. Add lemon juice, then mayonnaise until right consistency to spread.

Decorating hint: In a small photo album, put samples of colours in each room.

Dianne Crayston, Jasper Mountain Lions Club
Jasper, Alberta, Canada

CHIPPED HAM SANDWICHES

½ c. brown sugar
1 c. water
4 Tbsp. ketchup
1 Tbsp. mustard, dissolved in
    water

1 Tbsp. vinegar
Salt and pepper ("dash")
1 lb. chipped ham
Kaiser rolls or any type sandwich
    rolls

In a large saucepan, combine all ingredients, except ham. Stir mixture while bringing to a boil. Add chipped ham and lower heat. Serve in kaiser or any type of sandwich rolls.

Mrs. Jeff Crosby, Exeter Township Lions Club
Exeter, Pennsylvania, USA

Seek to find the best in the worst, to discover the great in the small,
to see beauty in the plain and to detect the elegant in the simple.

CREAMED CHIPPED BEEF
(On toast)

1 or 2 pkg. chipped beef
1 can cream of mushroom soup
(undiluted)
1 can cream of chicken soup
(undiluted)
¼ to ½ c. Parmesan cheese

2 or 3 hard-boiled eggs, cut up
Chopped or grated onion (1 Tbsp.
or to taste)
Frozen peas (½ to 1 c. or green
pepper - optional)*
Hunk of Velveeta cheese

Heat soup a little (till smooth). Add rest of ingredients. Serve on toast.

I'm sure everybody has heard of this recipe (under a different name years ago!!!). This is just a little fancier.

* If using frozen peas, thaw a little. (Can also use canned peas.)

Pam Sedlar, Onekama Lions Club
Onekama, Michigan, Manistee, USA

RUNZAS
(Makes 55 to 75 Runzas)

Dough:

1¼ oz. dry yeast
2 qt. warm water
14 oz. sugar
1 oz. (1½ Tbsp.) salt

2 lb. 6 oz. flour
8 eggs
5 oz. melted shortening
5 lb. 8 oz. flour

Sprinkle yeast over water. Let stand for 5 minutes. Add sugar, salt, and 2 pounds and 6 ounces flour. Beat on medium speed until smooth. Add eggs and shortening. Continue beating. Add remaining 5 pounds and 8 ounces flour to make a soft dough. Knead for 5 minutes. Cover and let rise until double. Punch down. Divide dough into 4 or 5 balls. Roll out each ball and cut into 4x6 inch rectangle (about 3 ounces of dough). Or, weigh out 3 ounce portions and roll each one out individually. For a smaller Runza, weigh 2½ ounces of dough.

Place ⅔ to 1 cup of filling on dough. Fold lengthwise and pinch edges of dough securely to seal. Place on baking sheet with sealed edges down. Bake 25 to 30 minutes at 400°F.

Filling:

15 lb. ground beef
15 lb. cabbage
3 large chopped onions
¼ c. Worcestershire sauce
(optional)

2 oz. salt
1 tsp. pepper

Brown and drain beef. Steam cabbage and onion until slightly underdone. Add seasonings and vegetables to ground beef. Mix lightly.

PIMENTO CHEESE SANDWICHES

½ lb. mild Cheddar cheese
1 small can pimentos

2 hard-boiled eggs
1 Tbsp. grated onion

Dressing:

½ c. heavy cream
1 Tbsp. sugar
1 Tbsp. flour

2 Tbsp. vinegar
1 egg, beaten

Grate first 4 ingredients; set aside. In a double boiler, mix all dressing ingredients. Cook until mixture thickens, then pour over other ingredients. Stir until thoroughly mixed. Can be served while still warm.

Take 4 slices of bread (sandwich) and spread 3 sides, then put together. Take sharp knife and slice off all 4 sides. Slice into 3 parts (called Ribbon Sandwiches).

Roger Gage, Decatur Lions Club
Decatur, Texas, USA

SUPER BOWL SUPER SANDWICH

2 loaves frozen bread dough,
    thawed
8 oz. deli sliced ham
8 oz. deli sliced turkey
8 oz. deli sliced pastrami
8 oz. deli sliced salami
1 c. grated Cheddar cheese
1 c. grated Swiss cheese
1 c. grated Monterey Jack cheese

2 Tbsp. Dijon mustard
1 (8 oz.) can mushroom stems and
    pieces, drained
1 tsp. dried parsley
½ tsp. Italian seasoning
½ tsp. garlic powder
½ tsp. onion powder
1½ Tbsp. poppy seeds
1½ Tbsp. sesame seeds

Defrost unopened bread in refrigerator overnight. Lightly grease 10½ x 15 inch jelly roll pan. On a lightly floured surface, roll 1 loaf of bread into a 15 x 5 inch wide rectangle. Spread 1 tablespoon of mustard on dough to within ½ inch of all edges. Layer the meat and cheese in the following order: Ham, Cheddar, turkey, Swiss, pastrami, Monterey Jack, and salami. On the Swiss layer, add the combined mushrooms, parsley, Italian seasoning, garlic powder, and onion powder. Spread the remaining mustard on the salami layer. Brush edges of dough with water. Roll second loaf into 15 x 5 inch rectangle. Place over top of meat, gently stretching down to pinch dough edges together. Brush loaf with water and sprinkle with poppy and sesame seeds. "Stir" this up before the game starts. At the end of the first quarter, put in a preheated 375° oven. Bake 25 to 30 minutes. Serve warm at half-time. Makes 20 slices.

❦

Refuse to let an old person move into your body.

PIZZA SANDWICH

1 lb. lean ground beef
½ c. grated Parmesan cheese
¼ c. finely chopped onion
1 (6 oz.) can tomato paste
1 tsp. salt
½ tsp. oregano
⅛ tsp. pepper

1 loaf French bread, cut in half
   lengthwise
5 slices Cheddar cheese, sliced
   diagonally
¼ c. chopped black olives
   (optional)

Combine all ingredients thoroughly, except bread, Cheddar cheese, and olives. Spread beef mixture on each half of bread; place on cookie sheet. Broil 5 inches from heat for 10 to 12 minutes. Remove from oven. Top with cheese and olives. Broil for 1 minute longer or until cheese melts.

Eight hard rolls may be substituted for French bread.

HOT CRAB SANDWICH

4 slices French bread or buns,
   toasted
1 lb. crab or imitation crab
¼ c. celery, diced fine
1 Tbsp. onion, diced fine
3 Tbsp. reduced fat mayo
Perk seasoning and pepper to
   taste

1 Tbsp. pimento
4 slices lowfat cheese
Sprigs of parsley
4 stuffed olives
1 Tbsp. Dijon mustard

Combine crab, celery, onion, pimento, mayonnaise, and seasoning. Toast the bread. Spread Dijon mustard on each piece. Place crab mixture on buns, then cheese slice. Broil until heated through and cheese is melted. Place an olive in center and a sprig of parsley.

Perk is a no salt seasoning that has many spices in it.

Joann Geist, Fallbrook Lioness Club
Fallbrook, California, USA

Don't wait to have a good day. Make one.

CRABMEAT SPECIAL ON ENGLISH MUFFINS

2 English muffins
Butter
6 oz. (180 g) crabmeat (canned or fresh)
3 Tbsp. mayonnaise

Fresh lemon juice
Salt
Freshly ground pepper
1 large tomato, sliced thin
4 slices Swiss cheese

Split and toast the muffins and butter them while they are warm. Drain the crabmeat; toss with mayonnaise and a few drops of lemon juice and salt and pepper to taste. Spread evenly over the muffin halves; cover with tomato slices and top with cheese. Slip under the broiler until the cheese melts and is bubbly.

Ms. Nancy Dutterer, Silver Run-Union Mills Lions Club
Thurmont, Maryland, USA

VEGETABLE SANDWICH

⅓ c. minced celery
⅔ c. grated carrots
¼ c. grated onion
¼ c. green pepper, minced
¼ c. cucumber, minced

8 oz. creamed cheese
Dash of salt
2 Tbsp. lemon juice
Mayonnaise

Blend cream cheese at room temperature with enough mayonnaise to make it spread easily. Add vegetables. Let stand overnight. Makes 10 or more sandwiches.

One minute of keeping your mouth shut is worth an hour's explanation.
Mary Murphy, Rock Hill Lions Club
Rock Hill, South Carolina, USA

BURGER BUNS

1 c. catsup
½ c. water
2 Tbsp. sugar
2 Tbsp. cider vinegar
2 tsp. prepared mustard
2 Tbsp. butter

1 c. chopped onion
2 lb. hamburger
Salt to taste
Pepper to taste
1 can chicken gumbo soup

Make a sauce of catsup, water, sugar, vinegar, and mustard. Mix well and put into small jar. May be stored in refrigerator. Melt butter in pan. Add onion. Cook until done. Add hamburger, salt, and pepper. Fry until meat is browned and done. Add chicken gumbo soup (undiluted). Add the sauce or as much as desired (I use about ½ of the sauce for 2 pounds of hamburger). Simmer for at least 15 minutes. Fill between buns. *Enjoy!*

SLOPPY JOES

1½ lb. ground beef
1 large onion, chopped
1 green pepper, chopped
2 Tbsp. sugar

1 Tbsp. cider vinegar
¾ c. catsup
2 Tbsp. mustard
1 tsp. salt

Brown the beef, onion, and pepper. Combine next 5 ingredients. Add to beef mixture. Cover and simmer ½ hour to 45 minutes.

Debra Payne, Bloomington Lions Club
Bloomington, Illinois, USA

SLOPPY JOES

2 lb. hamburger
1 can jellied cranberry sauce
1 onion, chopped
1 (12 oz.) bottle Heinz chile sauce

2 Tbsp. brown sugar
1 Tbsp. lemon juice
8 hamburger buns

Brown hamburger and onion. Drain well. Add remaining ingredients and simmer 30 minutes on top of stove. Serves 8.

Jim Tulloch, Bedford Heights Lions Club
Bedford Heights, Ohio, USA

CHICKEN BAR-B-Q SANDWICHES

3 lb. chicken
1 c. chili sauce
1 c. water
1 onion, chopped
2 Tbsp. brown sugar

3 Tbsp. vinegar
2 Tbsp. Worcestershire sauce
1 tsp. dry mustard
1 tsp. salt

Cook chicken. Cut into small pieces. Mix all other ingredients together for sauce and simmer for 30 minutes. Add chicken and simmer several more minutes. Serve on hamburger buns.

Marian Matthias (Mrs. Glenn), Silver Run-Union Mills Lions Club
Westminster, Maryland, USA

Love brings people close no matter how great the distance.

Notes

*A person all wrapped up in himself
generally makes a pretty small package.*

Salads

IRON FROM SOME COMMON FOOD SOURCES

Food	Amount	Iron (mg.)
Egg	1	1.1
Meat, lean	3 oz.	(approx.) 3.0
Mature beans and peas (legumes), nuts		
Almonds, Brazil nuts, cashew nuts, walnuts	¼ cup	(approx.) 1.5
Beans, common varieties, cooked, drained	1 cup	4.9
Lentils, cooked	1 cup	3.2
Peas, dry, cooked	1 cup	4.2
Vegetables		
Lima beans, immature, cooked	1 cup	4.3
Carrots, cauliflower, sweet corn	1 cup	(approx.) 1.0
Greens, cooked	1 cup	(approx.) 2.5
Peas, green, cooked	1 cup	2.9
Sweet potato	1 med. lg.	1.0
Tomato, cooked	1 cup	1.2
Fruits		
Apricots and peaches, dried, cooked	1 cup	5.1
Berries, fresh	1 cup	(approx.) 1.5
Dates, dry, cut	½ cup	2.6
Grape juice	1 cup	0.8
Prunes, dried, softened	4 medium	1.1
Prune juice, canned	1 cup	10.5
Raisins, dried	½ cup	2.8
Watermelon	Wedge 4x8 inch	2.1
Grain Products		
Bread, enriched	1 slice	(approx.) 0.6
Flour and meal, whole or enriched, dry	¼ cup	(approx.) 1.0
Spaghetti and macaroni, enriched, dry	⅓ cup	(approx.) 1.0
Wheat germ	¼ cup	1.8
Syrup, dark	1 Tbsp.	(approx.) 1.0
Sugar, brown	1 Tbsp.	.5

SALADS

BEAN SALAD

1 can shoe peg corn, drained
1 can French style green beans,
    drained
1 can small peas, drained
1 c. chopped celery
1 c. chopped onion

1 c. sugar
1 tsp. salt
¾ c. vinegar
¼ c. water
¼ c. vegetable oil

Mix all ingredients together. Best if let stand overnight before serving.

Elma Frederick, Cuba Lions Club
Cuba, Illinois, USA

THREE BEAN SALAD

1 can yellow wax beans
½ c. green peppers, chopped
1 purple onion, cut into rings
1 can green beans
1 can red beans

¾ c. sugar
⅔ c. vinegar
⅓ c. salad oil
1 tsp. salt
1 tsp. pepper

Combine all the beans, green peppers, and onion rings. Mix together the remaining ingredients. Toss with bean mixture. Chill overnight.

Debbie Abbott, Lyman Lions Club
Lyman, Wyoming, USA

SWEET AND SOUR BEAN SALAD

1 can green beans
1 can wax beans
1 can baby lima beans
1 can kidney beans
1 c. celery, cut in thin 1 inch strips
1 green pepper, cut in thin 1 inch
    strips

1 small jar pimento strips
2 medium onions, sliced and
    separated into rings
Salt and pepper
1½ c. sugar
1 c. vinegar
½ c. oil

Drain canned beans (I wash the kidney beans) and place in a large bowl. Add celery, pepper, pimento, and onion, Mix well. Combine oil, vinegar, and sugar in pan; bring to a boil. Set aside to cool. When cool, pour over bean mix. Refrigerate overnight.

If you are in a hurry, you can pour the vinegar mixture over the beans while still hot. In fact, I like the recipe better this way. You can fiddle with the amounts of sugar, oil, and vinegar to find the most pleasing proportion. The salad tastes entirely different the second day when the beans have had a chance to marinate.

Ellen Ostrand, Lady Lions of Rohnert Park Lions Club
Rohnert Park, California, USA

BROCCOLI SALAD

2 lb. broccoli (tips only)
6 slices bacon, crisp and
   crumbled
¼ c. chopped green onions
½ c. sunflower seeds

½ c. raisins
1½ Tbsp. wine vinegar
¼ c. sugar
¾ c. mayonnaise

Cut tips of broccoli into bite-size chunks. Fry (or microwave) bacon until crisp. Blot to remove grease. Crumble. Add to broccoli along with onion, seeds, and raisins in large bowl. Combine wine vinegar, sugar, and mayonnaise. Pour over broccoli mixture.

Make at least 45 minutes before serving, preferably several hours. Keeps for several days in the refrigerator. Sweet red onion can be substituted for green.

Lou Jenkins, Ponderosa Lions Club
Auberry, California, USA

BROCCOLI-CAULIFLOWER SALAD

1 large head broccoli
1 large head cauliflower
1 medium sweet onion
½ box white raisins (7½ oz.)

1 (8 oz.) can water chestnuts,
   sliced
1 (15½ oz.) can pineapple tidbits

Dressing:

1 c. mayonnaise
⅓ c. sugar

1 Tbsp. white vinegar
3 Tbsp. pineapple juice

Wash and cut broccoli into small pieces. Wash and cut cauliflower into individual flowerets. Dice onion very fine. Drain pineapple and water chestnuts. Mix dressing until sugar is dissolved. Pour dressing over vegetables and mix thoroughly. Cover and refrigerate overnight for best flavor. Serves 8. Can be left in refrigerator for several days. Good with any meat entree.

Clara W. Stephens, Verona Lions Club
Verona, Mississippi, USA

Real friends believe in your dreams as much as you do.

BROCCOLI-CAULIFLOWER SALAD SUPREME

3 bunches fresh broccoli, broken
    into heads
1 small head cauliflower, broken
    in florets
1 lb. fresh sliced mushrooms
1 large sweet onion, sliced into
    rings

3 tomatoes, cut wedges for color
4 tsp. bacon bits
1 small jar Catalina lite dressing
Salt and pepper to taste

Combine broccoli, cauliflower, mushrooms, and onion. Pour dressing over and let stand 1 hour. Add tomato wedges and half of bacon bits. Toss and turn into serving bowl. Sprinkle rest of bacon bits over and serve.

This is a great hit with our Lions Club.
Lion Chester Kudla and Lion Jack Buchard, Onekama Lions Club
Onekama, Michigan, USA

HAM BROCCOLI SALAD

Leftover cooked ham, cubed
4 small tomatoes, chopped
4 pieces (cooked) broccoli,
    chopped and cooked

2 to 4 oz. pine nuts, toasted
Mayonnaise
Salt and pepper (optional)

Toss all ingredients. Chill and serve.
Sarah Wehling, Bothell Lions Club
Bothell, Washington, USA

CABBAGE SALAD

1 medium head cabbage,
    shredded
1 small onion, chopped
½ can pimento, chopped
½ bell pepper, chopped
1 c. sugar

½ c. salad oil
½ c. water
1 c. vinegar
½ tsp. salt
½ tsp. black pepper

Combine cabbage, onion, pimento, and pepper. Over this, pour a mixture of the sugar, oil, water, vinegar, salt, and pepper. Let stand at least 2 hours before serving. Keep in refrigerator. The secret of this salad is in the shredding. Shred about ⅛ inch thick. Good as long as it lasts.

Janie Fox, Saginaw Lions Club
Saginaw, Texas, USA

❧

Conflict cannot survive without your participation.

CARROT SALAD

1 env. unflavored gelatin
¾ c. orange juice

1 c. grated carrots
1 (8 oz.) can crushed pineapple

Place gelatin in ¼ cup orange juice to soften. Pour remaining ½ cup orange juice in pan. Bring to boil. Add heated juice to gelatin mixture. Stir till gelatin is dissolved. Add carrots, pineapple, and pineapple juice. Stir well. Pour into mold. Refrigerate until firm. Serves 6.

One serving equals 51 calories or 1 fruit exchange.

Lion Rae Hamilton, Graysville/Proctor Lions Club
Proctor, West Virginia, USA

CARROT MEDLEY SALAD
(From my friend, Mable Garrison)

2 lb. carrots (whole), peeled and
boiled 15 minutes

3 small onions, sliced thin
1 green or red pepper, sliced thin

Sauce:

1 can Campbell's tomato soup
½ c. vinegar
½ c. salad oil
¼ c. sugar

1 tsp. Worcestershire sauce
¼ tsp. prepared mustard
1 tsp. salt
1 tsp. pepper

Refresh hot carrots by draining them, then cover with cold water to cool. Drain thoroughly. Slice into ¼ inch rounds. Toss with onions and peppers. Prepare sauce by bringing all ingredients (except soup) to a boil. Add soup and while stirring over medium high heat, allow to boil "up" to blend. Pour over vegetables. Toss and chill. Holds well for several days in refrigerator. This salad gets rave reviews wherever it is served.

Lion Vivian Quinlan, Mathews Lions Club
Mathews, Virginia, USA

CAULIFLOWER SALAD

1 head lettuce, shredded
1 head cauliflower, cut in small
pieces
⅓ c. shredded Cheddar cheese
1 small onion, diced

1 lb. bacon, fried and cut in small
pieces
⅓ c. sugar
4 Tbsp. mayonnaise (I use Miracle
light)

Put the above ingredients in layers as they are listed. Let set 2 hours in refrigerator, then toss before serving.

Lion Reva Hendrix, Conway Lions Club
Conway, Missouri, USA

DEWEY LIONS COLE SLAW

To serve 25:

4 lb. green cabbage
1 medium white onion
1 small green bell pepper
1 c. white sugar
½ c. salad oil

1 c. white vinegar
1 tsp. celery seeds
1 tsp. mustard seeds
½ tsp. noniodized salt

To serve 600:

100 lb. green cabbage
10 lb. white onions
5 lb. green bell peppers
25 lb. white sugar
6 qt. salad oil

2½ gal. white vinegar
10 oz. celery seeds
10 oz. mustard seeds
4 oz. noniodized salt

Method is the same for 25 serving and 600 serving amounts.

Shred or grate the cabbage, onions, and peppers. In a cooking container, mix the sugar, salad oil, vinegar, celery seeds, mustard seeds, and salt; heat to a boil. Stir well. Allow the liquid mixture to cool and while still warm, pour over the shredded vegetable mixture. Mix the vegetable/liquid mixture well. Allow to cool and refrigerate. Allow to "set" for 24 hours. Use covered glass or plastic containers. Keeps well up to 10 days.

Slaw chef is Noel James, retired school principal. Dewey Lions like to cook; primary fundraisers are food-related - school concessions, cooking for "events", concession trailer.

Charlie Ellis, Treasurer, Dewey Lions Club
Dewey, Oklahoma, USA

OVERNIGHT COLESLAW

12 c. shredded cabbage (1
    medium head)
1 green pepper, chopped

1 medium red onion, chopped
2 carrots, shredded
1 c. sugar

Dressing:

2 tsp. sugar
1 tsp. dry mustard
1 tsp. celery seed

1 tsp. salt
1 c. vinegar
¾ c. vegetable oil

In a large bowl, combine first 4 ingredients. Sprinkle with sugar. Set aside. In a saucepan, combine dressing ingredients; bring to a boil. Remove from the heat and pour over vegetables, stirring to cover evenly. Cover and refrigerate overnight. Stir well before serving. Yield: 12 to 16 servings. Very tasty coleslaw.

Shirley Hagyard, Russell Lions Club
Russell, Manitoba, Canada

MARINATED COLE SLAW

1 large head cabbage (about 2 lb.)
1 large onion
1 green pepper
1 c. sugar
1 c. vinegar

½ c. liquid shortening
1 tsp. salt
1 tsp. celery seed
1 tsp. dry mustard

Chop cabbage, onion, and green pepper. Place in large bowl to cover. Pour sugar over this. Do not stir. Boil vinegar, shortening, salt, celery seed, and dry mustard. Pour this over cabbage mixture. Do not stir. Let sit for 4 hours at room temperature. Chill. Keeps very well for a week or more.

Glenn E. Bunch, Jr., Snow Hill Lions Club
Snow Hill, North Carolina, USA

REFRIGERATOR SLAW

1 large head cabbage, chopped
1 c. green pepper, chopped
1 c. onion, chopped
⅔ c. sugar
⅔ c. cider vinegar

2 tsp. celery seed
2 tsp. dry mustard
1 tsp. salt
2 Tbsp. sugar
⅔ c. olive oil

In large bowl, add cabbage, onion, and green pepper, then sprinkle on ⅔ cup sugar. Set aside. In saucepan, heat ⅔ cup cider vinegar, celery seed, mustard seed, salt, and sugar to a boil and cool. Pour the above mixture over cabbage mixture and toss. Pour ⅔ cup olive oil over all and toss lightly. Refrigerate overnight and then enjoy. Keeps 7 to 10 days in refrigerator. Good with anything.

Pat Lamb, Moweaqua Lions Club
Moweaqua, Illinois, USA

FREEZER SLAW

1 medium head cabbage,
    shredded
1 tsp. salt
Grated carrots
1 green pepper, chopped

1 c. vinegar
2 c. sugar
1 tsp. celery seed
¼ c. water
1 tsp. mustard seed

Boil 1 minute the vinegar, sugar, celery seed, ¼ cup water, and mustard seed. Let cool until lukewarm. Pour over slaw. Put into freezer containers.

Margaret Ann Dunlap and Patricia Samuel, Chesterfield Bay Lions Club
Mt. Clemens, Michigan, USA

❦

What you think and talk about turns into action.

FREEZER COLE SLAW

1 large head cabbage
2 carrots

1 pepper

Grate and sprinkle with 1 tablespoon salt. Mix and let stand 1 hour. Squeeze and drain.

Bring to boil:

2 c. white sugar
¾ c. water
¾ c. vinegar

1 tsp. celery seed
1 tsp. mustard seed

After liquid is cool, pour over vegetables. Put in box. Freeze.
Lion Bob Riggenbach, Graysville/Proctor Lions Club
Proctor, West Virginia, USA

COOL CORN SALAD

¼ c. dairy sour cream
¼ c. mayonnaise
1 Tbsp. prepared mustard
2 tsp. white vinegar
1 tsp. sugar
¼ tsp. salt
⅛ tsp. pepper

1 (17 oz.) can golden whole kernel
  corn, drained
1 (2 oz.) jar sliced pimientos,
  drained and diced
2 carrots, peeled and grated
½ c. diced onion

Make dressing by combining sour cream, mayonnaise, mustard, vinegar, sugar, salt, and pepper in a medium bowl. Add remaining ingredients; toss to blend. Cover and refrigerate 1 hour. Serves 4 to 6 people.

1. To vary, I use a smaller can of yellow corn and add a can of whole white corn, drained.
2. You can also add a small can of sliced black olives.

This recipe is different and I always get great reviews.
Joyce "Jaci" Kopetski, Riverdale Lions Club
Riverdale, Georgia, USA

CORN BREAD SALAD

2 pkg. corn bread mix
8 to 10 slices crisp cooked bacon
1 large onion (little green onions
  are good)

2 large tomatoes, cut up (or cherry
  tomatoes)
1 bell pepper
1 c. mayonnaise

Cook corn bread and crumble in a bowl. Crumble crisp cooked bacon in the corn bread and add rest of ingredients. Mix well. Will keep in refrigerator for 7 to 10 days. Yellow corn meal corn bread mix is really colorful.
Faye Blount, Levelland Lioness Club
Levelland, Texas, USA

CUCUMBER SALAD

5 medium cucumbers
3 medium tomatoes
1 medium onion

⅓ to ½ c. salad oil
Salt and pepper to taste

Peel and slice cucumbers. Dice tomatoes and onion. Mix all ingredients. Marinate 2 to 3 hours in refrigerator.

Alice E. Wood, Eden Lions Club
Eden, Wisconsin, USA

LETTUCE LAYERS

Lettuce
½ c. chopped celery
½ c. chopped green peppers
1 c. chopped green onions
1 (10 oz.) pkg. frozen green peas

1 to 1½ c. mayonnaise
2 Tbsp. sugar
4 to 6 oz. shredded cheese
Bacon bits

Shred lettuce to fill large bowl half full. Add next 3 ingredients. Cook peas; drain and cool. Add peas and spread mayonnaise on top. Sprinkle sugar on mayonnaise. Add shredded cheese and spread bacon bits on top. Cover with plastic wrap. Refrigerate at least 8 hours.

Good with anything or just by itself.

Margarett Westberg, Apache Lions Club
Apache, Oklahoma, USA

CHEESE STUFFED LETTUCE

1 medium head lettuce
1 (3 oz.) pkg. cream cheese
¾ c. cottage cheese
½ c. grated raw carrots
⅛ tsp. black pepper

3 Tbsp. chopped bell pepper
¼ c. pecans
¼ tsp. salt
⅛ tsp. celery salt
⅛ tsp. minced onion

Cut out core of lettuce and make cavity for the stuffing. You may have to cut the hole larger to get all the stuffing in the cavity. Combine all the ingredients and fill the cavity well. Wrap tightly with Saran Wrap. Chill overnight. Take out and unwrap; cut in 4 or 8 wedges, depending on how large the head of lettuce is. Serve the cut wedges with French dressing drizzled over top. Very good and different.

Mrs. Charlotte M. Garner, Pascagoula Evening Lions Club
Pascagoula, Mississippi, USA

Look at every obstacle as an opportunity.

LENTIL SALAD

1 lb. lentils
¾ c. oil (canola oil is preferred)
¼ c. wine vinegar
1 clove garlic, mashed
1 large chopped onion
1 green pepper, chopped

2 tomatoes, chopped
½ tsp. seasoned salt
½ tsp. black pepper
½ tsp. Worcestershire sauce
¼ tsp. Tabasco sauce

Sort and rinse lentils in large saucepan. Cover with water. Bring to boil, reduce heat, and simmer lentils, covered, for 20 minutes. Drain lentils and pour into large bowl. Pour in oil and vinegar. Mix with lentils and allow to cool. Add all remaining ingredients and mix gently. Store in refrigerator. Makes 6 to 8 servings.

SWEET ONION SALAD

6 medium sweet onions
1 c. water
2 tsp. salt
¾ c. sugar

1 c. vinegar
2 tsp. celery seed
1 c. (approx.) mayonnaise
Salt and pepper to taste

Thinly slice the sweet onions. Mix the water, salt, sugar, and vinegar. Pour over sliced onions and marinate 3 to 4 hours. Drain. Mix together mayonnaise, celery seed, and salt and pepper to desired taste.

Marinated onions will keep in original solution for about 2 weeks in fridge.
Walter E. Loomis, North Jackson Lions Club
Jackson, Michigan, USA

PEA SALAD

1 (10 oz.) pkg. frozen peas, cooked
   and cooled
½ c. green onions, sliced
1 c. grated Cheddar cheese

2 sweet pickles, chopped
2 Tbsp. pickle juice
½ c. chopped pecans
Mayonnaise

Combine all ingredients and stir in mayonnaise to desired consistency. Easy and fun.

Joyce "Jaci" Kopetski, Riverdale Lions Club
Riverdale, Georgia, USA

❦

Every job you do is a portrait of you.

POTATO SALAD

5 lb. potatoes
1 bunch celery, chopped fine

1 large onion
1½ doz. eggs (save 3 for top)

Mix together:

1 qt. Miracle Whip (light)
¾ or whole bottle *Henri's* sweet or
   sweet and sour
¼ c. sweet pickle juice

¼ c. sugar
1 large spoon mustard
Accent (1 tsp. or shake 5 or 6
   times)

Lillian Kataja, Onekama Lions Club
Onekama, Michigan, USA

POTATO SALAD

4 c. cubed and boiled potatoes
½ c. chopped onion
½ c. chopped celery
½ c. chopped green pepper
½ c. grated carrots
1 chopped cucumber

1 dill pickle, chopped
2 tsp. prepared mustard
½ tsp. salt
1 tsp. garlic powder
½ c. mayonnaise
Paprika

Combine vegetables, mustard, and seasonings. Toss lightly with mayonnaise. Sprinkle with paprika. Makes 12 servings.

GERMAN POTATO SALAD

4 c. hot diced potatoes
½ c. chopped celery
1 medium size onion, chopped
1 Tbsp. chopped parsley
1½ tsp. salt
1 Tbsp. flour

2 Tbsp. fat
⅓ c. sugar
⅓ c. vinegar
¼ tsp. pepper
⅔ c. water
8 strips bacon, chopped

Fry bacon. Fry chopped onion in hot fat until light brown. Add flour and blend, then add sugar, salt, vinegar, water, celery, and parsley. Bring to a boil, stirring constantly. Pour dressing over the diced potatoes. Sprinkle with pepper and serve hot. Serves 8.

Self-trust is the first secret of success.

Gloria A. Hershberger, Aurora Eastgate Lions Club
Denver, Colorado, USA

❦

Examine what you believe to be impossible, and then change your beliefs.

GREEK POTATO SALAD

12 cooked potatoes, pared
24 oz. cottage cheese
2 c. sour cream
2 c. mayonnaise
2 medium red onions, chopped

3 or 4 stalks celery, chopped
1 Tbsp. Greek seasoning
½ to 1 Tbsp. blended salad
   seasoning
Sliced black olives for garnish

In a large bowl, combine potatoes, cottage cheese, sour cream, mayonnaise, onions, and celery. Season with Greek seasoning and salad seasoning. Cover and refrigerate for 2 or 3 days for the flavors to blend. Garnish with black olives. Serves 12.

The longer this blends, the better it gets!!!
Dan Steffan, Independence Eastview Lions Club
Independence, Missouri, USA

DILL POTATO SALAD

5 lb. small red potatoes, cooked
   and quartered (don't peel)
2 c. green onions, chopped
2 c. celery, chopped
1 red pepper, slivered

Fresh dill to taste
1 bottle red wine vinegar
⅓ c. Paul Newman's Italian
   dressing

Mix all ingredients together, except the red pepper, the night before. Add the red pepper just before serving.

Good to make for a picnic - don't have to worry about spoiling in hot weather.
Mrs. Bill (Jan) Callaghan, Elburn Lions Club
Elburn, Illinois, USA

CURRIED RICE SALAD

1 jar marinated artichoke hearts
½ green pepper
1 box chicken flavored Rice-A-
   Roni

12 olives
5 green onions (tips and all)

1. Prepare Rice-A-Roni as directed, using 2½ cups water.
2. Drain artichokes. *Save liquid.*
3. To the artichoke liquid, add ½ cup mayonnaise, ¼ cup sour cream, scant 1 teaspoon curry powder, and ½ teaspoon salt.
4. Chop or slice fine artichokes, green pepper, onions, and olives.
5. Mix all together and place in dish or mold. Chill several hours before serving. Keeps well in fridge. In place of sour cream, you might want to use all mayonnaise.

Donna S. Reitz, Sykesville Lions Club
Sykesville, Pennsylvania, USA

SPINACH SALAD

Fresh, washed, paper towel dried, torn spinach
Fresh rings of red onion
1 to 2 small cans mandarin oranges, drained

1 small can frozen orange juice concentrate

Salad Dressing:

1 can orange juice concentrate
1 c. oil
4 Tbsp. vinegar

2 Tbsp. sugar
2 tsp. dry mustard
A dash of Tabasco

This is one recipe I used as a beginner because it was so easy and uniformly turns out the same. That was 30 years ago and it is still popular at church functions.
Sarah Wehling, Bothell Lions Club
Bothell, Washington, USA

SPINACH-STRAWBERRY SALAD

1 lb. fresh spinach

1 qt. fresh strawberries

Dressing:

¾ c. sugar
⅓ c. vinegar
¼ c. poppy seed (optional)
1 tsp. salt

1½ Tbsp. grated onion
1 tsp. dry mustard
1 c. salad oil

Wash, drain, and clip spinach ends. Wash, hull, and halve or quarter strawberries. Combine in blender (or shake in jar) dressing ingredients (except oil). Slowly add oil. Toss lightly.

Hint: I make dressing ahead of time and refrigerate. Add to spinach and berries just before serving. (Will wilt, but still tastes good!)
Pam Sedlar, Onekama Lions Club
Onekama, Michigan, USA

TOMATO SALAD

6 to 8 medium tomatoes
1 c. diced onion
1 c. diced green pepper
Salt and pepper to taste
½ c. vinegar

1½ c. sugar
¼ c. oil
¼ tsp. basil leaves or Italian seasoning

Cut tomatoes into chunks. Add onion and green pepper; salt and pepper. Mix remaining ingredients and add to vegetables. Chill 2 to 3 hours.
Helen O'Brien, Eden Lions Club
Eden, Wisconsin, USA

COUNTRY STUFFED TOMATOES

2 c. frozen petite peas or fresh
    peas
1 c. shredded sharp Cheddar
    cheese

1 stalk celery, finely chopped
2 Tbsp. minced green onion
4 large, ripe tomatoes
Lowfat Ranch dressing

Defrost the peas. If using fresh peas, cook briefly until barely tender. Drain and cool. Combine peas with cheese, celery, and onion. Bring tomatoes to room temperature if chilled. Combine ½ to ¾ cup dressing with peas. Hollow out tomatoes, reserving pulp for soups or sauces. Fill tomatoes with pea salad. Chill 30 minutes. Serve on bed of lettuce. Serves 4.

Lion Karen Stowers, Amarillo North Lions Club
Amarillo, Texas, USA

GEORGIA VEGETABLE SALAD

1 can white corn
1 can English peas
1½ c. chopped celery
1 small pkg. slivered almonds,
    toasted
⅓ c. sugar
¼ c. dark vinegar

½ c. salad oil
1 can La Choy fancy Chinese
    vegetables
1 can cut green beans
1 medium sweet onion
1 tsp. salt
1 tsp. pepper

Drain canned vegetables. Mix with celery, onion, and almonds. Mix corn, green beans, English peas, sugar, vinegar, salad oil, salt, and pepper. Pour over vegetables. Marinate for several hours.

Bonita K. Blakey, Moweaqua Lions Club
Moweaqua, Illinois, USA

SALATA HORIATIKI - VILLAGE SALAD

4 medium size tomatoes
2 slender, young green
    cucumbers
1 sweet green pepper

2 medium size onions, sliced
150 g Feta cheese
6 olives

For the dressing·

½ c. olive oil
¼ c. vinegar

½ tsp. dry mustard
Salt

Cut tomatoes into wedges. Peel cucumber thinly and halve lengthwise. Cut in 1 cm (½ inch) slices. Wash, core, and seed pepper; remove white membrane. Halve and cut into thick strips. Separate onion slices into rings. Place prepared ingredients in a bowl. Dice the Feta cheese and put on top with the olives. Serves 6.

Dressing: Shake and mix well. Pour on dressing just before serving.

George Nicolaides, PDG, Nicosia Lions Club
Nicosia, Cyprus

TACO SALAD

1 lb. hamburger
Catalina dressing
1 green pepper, chopped
2 medium tomatoes, wedged
  small

1 onion, chopped
8 oz. shredded Cheddar cheese
1 bag Nacho cheese Doritos
Lettuce (optional)

Brown hamburger and drain. Mix ¼ cup Catalina dressing; let set for 2 hours in refrigerator. Mix hamburger, green pepper, tomatoes, onion, cheese, and bag of crushed Doritos (or as many chips as desired). Add ¾ to 1 cup dressing (until moist). Serve immediately.

Prepare other ingredients and place in refrigerator until ready to use. When hamburger has chilled for 2 hours, then just put together.

Michelle (Shelly) Robinson, Randall/Cushing Lioness Club
Cushing, Minnesota, USA

CHICKEN SALAD

17 oz. pkg. macaroni rings,
  cooked
3 c. cooked and cubed chicken or
  turkey
1 c. grated carrots
1 c. diced celery
1 medium diced onion

½ c. sliced radishes
½ c. diced green pepper
½ c. sliced green olives
½ c. parsley
1 tsp. salt
Dash of pepper

Dressing:

1½ c. salad dressing
¼ c. lemon juice
½ c. sugar

1 tsp. salt
Dash of pepper

Mix well. Pour over meat the macaroni rings and vegetables. Can be made a day in advance. Will keep several days.

Elaine Dahlke, Brownton Lions Club
Brownton, Minnesota, USA

ITALIAN SALAD

1 box large shells
1 lb. Genoa salami
½ lb. Provolone
½ lb. Swiss cheese

1 can large olives
1 green pepper
Large tomatoes
1 bottle Italian dressing

Cook shells; drain and cool. Cut cheese and meat into small pieces, then add to shells. Add oil and mix.

Dave Birnier, Westbrook Lions Club
Westbrook, Maine, USA

CHINESE CHICKEN SALAD

Dressing:

6 Tbsp. white vinegar
½ c. salad oil
2 tsp. salt
1 tsp. pepper

4 Tbsp. sugar
½ tsp. monosodium glutamate
(MSG - optional)
Few drops of sesame oil (optional)

Additional ingredients:

Salad vegetables (head lettuce,
leaf lettuce, etc.)
Fried won ton pi

Cooked chicken (or ham, cold
cuts, etc.)

Combine all ingredients, except the oil (dressing). Shake well, then add oil.

Wash salad vegetables. Drain. Cut chicken (can use KFC without skin) into 1 x ½ inch strips and sprinkle over vegetables. Also sprinkle won ton pi (skin of a won ton fried and broken into small ¼ inch pieces) on vegetables. Toss salad with dressing. Sesame seed may be sprinkled over top.

Eugene Pei, S.W. Denver Lions Club
Denver, Colorado, USA

CHINESE CHICKEN SALAD

4 chicken breasts or 6 thighs
5 stalks green onions, cut into
slivers
1 head lettuce, shredded
Chinese salt (5 spice salt)
Colman's dry mustard, mixed into
a paste

Coriander (Chinese parsley)
Rice sticks, deep-fried
Sesame oil
Oil for frying

Deep-fry chicken and shred. Season with salt, mustard, and sesame oil. Combine lettuce, parsley, and green onion. Toss with seasoned chicken and rice sticks when ready to serve. Leftover fried chicken or BBQ chicken may be used. You may also use fried won ton skin strips instead of rice sticks. Makes a great meal by itself.

Lion Ed Flores, Caruthers Lions Club
Caruthers, California, USA

Never be satisfied with good if better is possible.

GRILLED TARRAGON CHICKEN SPINACH SALAD

4 chicken breasts (boneless,
    skinless)
2 (12 oz.) pkg. spinach, cleaned
1 red pepper, julienned

1 yellow pepper, julienned
1 pt. mushrooms, sliced
1 red onion, diced

Marinade:

½ c. tarragon
1 c. red wine vinegar

1 c. white wine
4 oz. olive oil

Dressing:

4 eggs
1 c. sugar

1 c. red wine vinegar
1 pt. corn oil

    1. Marinade: Reduce tarragon in vinegar. Add wine and oil. Marinate chicken breasts 2 hours.
    2. Make dressing: Combine all ingredients. Heat in double boiler till thickened. Keep warm.
    3. Grill chicken breasts and slice julienne.
    4. Toss chicken, vegetables, and enough dressing to coat. Serve.

Makes a great summer outdoors dinner.

Vans Harbor Inn, Onekama Lions Club
Onekama, Michigan, USA

SUPER CHICKEN SALAD

3 lb. chicken breasts
1 (8 oz.) pkg. cream cheese,
    softened
2 Tbsp. mayonnaise
¾ c. pecans, chopped

1 Tbsp. onion, grated
2 Tbsp. sweet pickle juice
1 c. celery, finely chopped
¼ tsp. curry powder
Salt and pepper to taste

    Cook chicken and debone. Coarsely chop. Combine cream cheese and mayonnaise until smooth. Add pecans, onion, pickle juice, celery, curry powder, salt, and pepper. Stir until well blended. Combine chicken and cream cheese mixture. Mix until well blended. Serve on lettuce leaves.

Mrs. Lion Robert (Margaret) Logan, Canton Lions Club
Canton, Georgia, USA

A diamond is a piece of coal that finished what it started.

HOT CHICKEN SALAD

2 Tbsp. chopped onion
2 c. diced chicken
1 c. mayonnaise
1 c. chopped celery

½ tsp. salt
1 c. grated cheese
Potato chips

Mix first 5 ingredients together lightly. Add crushed potato chips and grated cheese on top. Cook at 350° for 10 minutes. Serve with sweet salad.

People are lonely because they build walls instead of bridges.
Carole Choate, Rock Hill Lions Club
Rock Hill, South Carolina, USA

CHICKEN SALAD SUPREME

2½ c. cooked chicken, diced
1 c. celery, chopped
1 c. white seedless grapes, sliced
½ c. lightly toasted almonds, chopped

2 Tbsp. minced parsley (or parsley flakes)
1 tsp. salt
1 c. mayonnaise

Thoroughly mix all ingredients. Chill. Serve on lettuce leaf.

If you're too busy to laugh
You are too busy, period.

Bettie Patterson, Kosciusko Lions Club
Kosciusko, Mississippi, USA

EXOTIC CHICKEN SALAD

4 c. cubed chicken
1 c. slivered almonds
1 c. sliced water chestnuts, drained
1 c. diced celery

1 c. pineapple chunks, drained
1½ c. mayonnaise
1 tsp. curry
1 Tbsp. soy sauce
1 Tbsp. lemon juice

Mix last 4 ingredients together and chill. Prepare and mix salad ingredients. Fold in dressing mixture. Garnish with coconut or more almonds.

Joyce Butcher, Reno Plumb Lane Lions Club
Reno, Nevada, USA

Tomorrow exists so that you don't have to do it all today.

FANTASTIC LUNCHEON SALAD

1 egg, separated
1 can condensed cream of
  chicken soup
1½ Tbsp. gelatin, soaked in ½ c.
  water
½ c. chopped peanuts

3 c. diced cooked chicken
¾ c. diced celery
2 Tbsp. minced onion
⅓ c. sweet mixed pickles, diced
⅓ c. mayonnaise

Beat egg white until stiff. Heat soup and egg yolk together. Add soaked gelatin and stir to dissolve (approximately 3 minutes). Chill slightly, then add remaining ingredients with the beaten egg white last. Pour into a 1 quart mold which has been lightly oiled. May use loaf dish and decorate by placing olives in bottom of pan. Spoon chicken mixture carefully over this. Place in refrigerator overnight. Serves 8 to 10 people. With loaf dish, slice lemon real thin and place in bottom of pan, then spoon chicken over this. Really gives a good flavor.

Melba J. Gray, Eastlake Lions Club
Birmingham, Alabama, USA

WEST INDIES CRAB SALAD

1 lb. crabmeat
1 medium onion, chopped fine

Salt and pepper

Marinade:

½ c. Wesson oil
3 oz. cider vinegar

4 oz. ice water

Put layers of onion and crab in bowl. Pour over oil first, vinegar second, and water last. Marinate in refrigerator 2 to 12 hours. Serve in bowl over lettuce. Salt and pepper as needed.

Lion Lynne Harvey, Biloxi Lions Club
Biloxi, Mississippi, USA

JELLIED SHRIMP SALAD

1 pkg. cherry jello
2 c. tomato juice
1 tin shrimp
½ c. finely chopped celery

½ Tbsp. vinegar
½ tsp. grated onion
¼ c. grated carrots

Heat tomato juice and dissolve jello in it. Chill until partially set. Add remaining ingredients. Pour into jelly mould.

Terry Pister, Prince Albert Down Town Lioness Club
Prince Albert, Saskatchewan, Canada

All the abundance you want is already here - you just have to notice it.

SEAFOOD SALAD

8 oz. garden variety rotini spiral
    pasta
5 green onions, sliced
2 stalks celery, diced
½ medium green pepper, chopped
¼ c. (or more) black olives, sliced
1 (6 oz.) can shrimp
4 to 6 frozen crab sticks, thawed
    and sliced
½ c. grated Colby or Cheddar
    cheese
1 c. mayonnaise
½ c. Miracle Whip
Salt and pepper to taste

Cook pasta as directed on package. Rinse and cool. Combine mayonnaise and Miracle Whip. Toss with the rest of the ingredients. Chill. Serve on a bed of lettuce with crackers or bread of choice.

Lion Dean made this up.

Children are like wet cement - whatever is dropped on them leaves an impression.

Lion Dean E. Meisinger, Plattsmouth Lions Club
Plattsmouth, Nebraska, USA

SHRIMP MOUSSE

1 can mushroom soup
1 env. Knox gelatine
1 Tbsp. water
1 c. mayonnaise
1 c. shrimp
½ c. chopped green onions
½ c. chopped celery

In a small saucepan, heat the soup, water, and gelatine until warm. Stir. Add other ingredients. Mix well. Pour into mold or pan. Chill for 8 hours. Serve with crackers. This is excellent. Crabmeat can be used also. This recipe serves about 8. I usually double it.

Floyd N. Johnston, Plumb Lane Lions Club
Reno, Nevada, USA

SALMON SALAD

1 piece jicama, peeled and diced
1 can salmon, drained and flaked
½ tsp. dill weed
½ c. sunflower seeds, husked
Mayonnaise to taste

Line a platter with red rimmed lettuce. Mix all together. Mound on platter. Cover with plastic wrap. Chill.

Optional serving tips: Capers, boiled eggs, lemon slices.

I created this recipe one sunny afternoon for lunch to use up some fresh salmon I received from my son-in-law, a Ballard (Seattle) fisherman. Around here, there are so many Norwegians, they call Ballard "Snoose Junction."

Sarah Wehling, Bothell Lions Club
Bothell, Washington, USA

TUNA MACARONI SALAD

1 (7 oz.) pkg. macaroni, cooked
   and drained
1 c. (6½ oz. can) tuna, drained
2 c. (16 oz.) can peas, drained
1 c. (4 oz.) diced cheese
5 hard-boiled eggs, diced

½ c. diced celery
½ c. diced green pepper
½ c. minced onion
¼ c. diced pimento (optional)
¾ to 1 c. salad dressing or
   mayonnaise

Combine all ingredients, except dressing. Add enough dressing to moisten. Chill 2 hours.

Gladys Filla, Yakima West Valley Lions Club
Cowiche, Washington, USA

MACARONI SALAD

Dressing:

1 can Eagle Brand milk
2 c. Miracle Whip

1 c. sugar
¾ c. vinegar

Additional ingredients:

2 (7 oz.) boxes macaroni, salted,
   cooked, and drained
1 medium cucumber, diced
1 medium green pepper, diced
1 medium onion, chopped
2 or 3 carrots, grated

1½ c. celery, diced
Chopped cauliflower (enough to
   taste)
1 small pkg. radishes, cut in
   halves and sliced

Mix Eagle Brand milk, Miracle Whip, sugar, and vinegar with mixer until creamy. In large bowl, add the other ingredients. Add dressing and mix well. This salad is delicious. Nice to make for company as it makes a large amount. Keeps well in refrigerator for several days.

Donna Amsler, Cuba Lions Club
Cuba, Illinois, USA

"COMPANY'S COMIN" MACARONI SALAD

3½ c. cooked macaroni (1⅓ c. raw)
1 c. frozen petite peas
½ c. sliced black olives
3 Tbsp. finely chopped scallions

½ c. shredded carrots
½ c. finely sliced radishes
1 pkg. dry Italian dressing
1 c. mayonnaise

Cook and drain any style macaroni. Mix dry dressing mix with mayonnaise. Add other ingredients. Mix together gently. Combine with macaroni. Chill at least 2 hours or overnight. I like to use "tricolored pasta" or even tortellini as a change.

Bunny Creo, Merritt Island Lions Club
Merritt Island, Florida, USA

SPAGHETTI SALAD

7 oz. uncooked vermicelli
¾ c. mayonnaise or salad
  dressing
1 Tbsp. soy sauce
1 tsp. salt
1 tsp. prepared mustard
¼ tsp. garlic powder
Dash of white pepper
16 oz. bean sprouts (canned or
  fresh)

3 oz. mushrooms (canned)
1 medium stalk celery, sliced
  (about ¼ c.)
⅓ c. green pepper, chopped
1 small onion, chopped
1 c. frozen green peas, thawed
Spinach or lettuce leaves

Break vermicelli into 2 inch pieces; cook as directed on package. Do not overcook. Rinse under cold water; drain.

Mix mayonnaise, soy sauce, salt, mustard, garlic powder, and white pepper in large bowl. Stir in *all* other ingredients and mix well. Refrigerate 3 hours. Serve on spinach or lettuce leaves.

Sally McGlone, Noon Lions Club
Emporia, Kansas, USA

SPAGHETTI SALAD

1 lb. spaghetti
1 large bottle Zesty Italian
  dressing
1 (or ½) jar salad seasoning

Onions, cucumber, green pepper,
  tomatoes, bacon bits, etc.
  (optional)

Cook spaghetti according to directions. Mix together spaghetti, optional ingredients, salad seasoning, and dressing. Toss and refrigerate. Use large bowl, as in Tupperware "fix and mix."

Great for summertime picnics, etc. (Can make ahead of time.)
Pam Sedlar, Onekama Lions Club
Onekama, Michigan, USA

❦

If a man has common sense, he has all the sense there is.

SPAGHETTI SALAD

1 lb. spaghetti
1 cucumber
1 red onion
1 green pepper
3 tomatoes
1 (8 oz.) bottle sweet spicy French
    dressing

1 (8 oz.) bottle Zesty Italian
    dressing
1 bottle dry Salad Supreme
    seasoning

Break spaghetti in 1 inch pieces. Cook in salt water. Drain and rinse in cold water. Cut vegetables in small pieces. Add dressing and seasoning. Make night before and chill.

Lioness Arlis Odland, Mitchell Lioness Club
Mitchell, South Dakota, USA

PASTA-APPLE SALAD

4 eggs, beaten
1 c. powdered sugar
¼ c. lemon juice
1 (20 oz.) can crushed pineapple
½ tsp. celery seed
1½ c. cooked pasta (small shell or
    small regular macaroni)

1 (4 oz.) ctn. frozen whipped
    topping plus 1 c.
3 large apples, chopped (not
    peeled)
½ c. miniature marshmallows
½ c. chopped pecans or walnuts

Combine eggs, powdered sugar, and lemon juice in heavy-bottomed pan. Cook over medium heat until thickened, stirring frequently. Cool. Add drained pineapple, cooked pasta, marshmallows, and celery seed. Refrigerate overnight. The next day, add whipped topping, chopped apples, and nuts. Refrigerate. Serves 12.

Don and Anna Mae Mehmen, Parkersburg Lions Club
Parkersburg, Iowa, USA

ROSAMARINA SALAD

¾ c. sugar
2 Tbsp. flour
2 eggs
½ tsp. salt
½ lb. Rosamarina noodles,
    cooked and drained

2 cans chunk pineapple
1 can mandarin oranges
1 jar maraschino cherries, drained
1 (16 oz.) container Cool Whip

Cook sugar, flour, eggs, and salt with juice from pineapple and oranges until thick. Cool. Pour cooked sauce over cooked noodles, which have been drained. Cool overnight. Add fruit and Cool Whip. Serve in trifle bowl. Serves 16.

Lion Amy Serpentini, Royalton Hills Lions Club
North Royalton, Ohio, USA

NOODLES WITH COTTAGE CHEESE

1 pkg. noodles (wide)
1 box uncreamed cottage cheese
Butter

Sugar
Cinnamon

Boil a package of noodles. Drain and rinse off with cold water, then pour melted butter over all. In alternate layers, place noodles. Sprinkle cottage cheese, sprinkle cinnamon, and lastly sprinkle sugar over all. Repeat if desired. *Delicious.*

Mrs. Laurie Kovach, Brandon Crocus Lions Club
Brandon, Manitoba, Canada

CURRIED FRUIT

1 large can pears
1 large can peaches or apricots
1 large can chunk pineapple
1 small jar maraschino cherries

¾ c. light brown sugar
1 tsp. curry powder
1 stick oleo

Drain fruit thoroughly. (This is very important.) Mix all together in baking dish. Melt butter. Add sugar and curry. Pour over top of fruit and bake 1 hour at 325°, uncovered. Serves 8 to 10. Good with any meat dish.

Terry Jones, Kosciusko Lions Club
Kosciusko, Mississippi, USA

FRUIT SALAD

1 (29 oz.) can sliced peaches,
  drained
1 (20 oz.) can pineapple chunks
  (undrained)
1 (11 oz.) can mandarin oranges,
  drained
1 (6 oz.) jar maraschino cherries,
  drained, blotted on paper
  towel, and cut in halves

2 sliced bananas
2 kiwi, peeled and sliced
1 (3 oz.) instant lemon pudding
  mix

Mix together all ingredients and refrigerate overnight. Keeps well for 2 to 3 days. Serves 10 to 12.

Mrs. Lion Robert (Margaret) Logan, Canton Lions Club
Canton, Georgia, USA

Positive thoughts keep you in harmony with the world around you.

FRUIT SALAD

1 medium size can peach halves
1 medium size can pears
1 medium size can chunk
   pineapple
1 small can mandarin oranges or
   2 fresh oranges

Small portion green seedless
   grapes
2 bananas
1 small can frozen orange juice
   (undiluted)

Drain all fruits well. Mix. Add grapes. Pour orange juice over fruit. Let set a few hours or overnight. Before serving, add the bananas. (Can be added ahead of time. The orange juice keeps them from turning dark.)

Pearl M. Bridgman, Moweaqua Lions Club
Moweaqua, Illinois, USA

5-MINUTE FRUIT SALAD

1 (20 oz.) can fruit cocktail,
   drained
1 (16 oz.) can pineapple chunks,
   drained
1 large can mandarin oranges,
   drained

1 c. drained juice
2 Tbsp. lemon juice
1 (3¾ oz.) pkg. lemon instant
   pudding mix (dry)
2 bananas, sliced

Drain fruits, measuring out the 1 cup juice. Set the juice aside. Combine fruit cocktail, pineapple, and oranges with the lemon juice. Chill well. Mix the dry pudding with the cup of juice. Just before serving, add the pudding mixture and bananas to the chilled fruit. Stir well and serve.

Life itself can't give you joy unless you really will it. Life just gives you time and space - it's up to you to fill it.

Dorothy Krueger, Emporia Sundowners Lions Club
Emporia, Kansas, USA

COOKED FRUIT SALAD

1 large can peaches
2 cans mandarin oranges
1 can pineapple tidbits
3 Tbsp. orange juice

1 (4 oz.) pkg. tapioca pudding mix
1 (4 oz.) pkg. instant vanilla
   pudding mix

Drain juices from fruit. Bring juices to a boil. Cut peaches into bite-size pieces while juices are cooking. Add both pudding mixes to boiled juice and pour over all the fruit. Chill and serve.

Vickie Nash, East Prospect Lions Club
East Prospect, Pennsylvania, USA

SLEET SALAD

1 (16 oz.) box R-F acini de pepe
1 c. sugar
2 Tbsp. flour
½ tsp. salt
1¾ c. pineapple juice
2 eggs, beaten
1 Tbsp. lemon juice
1 (12 oz.) ctn. lite Cool Whip
1 (16 oz.) ctn. vanilla yogurt
3 (11 oz.) cans mandarin oranges, drained

2 (20 oz.) cans pineapple tidbits, drained
1 (20 oz.) can crushed pineapple, drained
1 c. miniature marshmallows (white or colored)
1 c. flaked coconut (optional)
Sliced bananas (optional)
Maraschino cherries for topping (red and green are pretty for Christmas)

Bring 3 quarts of water to boil with 1 to 2 teaspoons salt and 1 tablespoon cooking oil. Add acini de pepe. Cook at rolling boil approximately 8 minutes. Drain acini de pepe; rinse with cold water and drain thoroughly. Cool to room temperature.

For pudding mixture: Combine sugar, flour, and salt. Gradually stir in pineapple juice (which has been drained from the cans of pineapple) and beaten eggs. Cook over moderate heat, stirring until thickened. Add 1 tablespoon lemon juice and cool to room temperature. Combine this egg mixture with acini de pepe. Mix lightly but thoroughly. Refrigerate 8 hours or overnight in airtight container. Add the remaining ingredients of Cool Whip, yogurt, and drained canned fruit. Refrigerate until ready to serve. This recipe is easy to make and keeps good in the refrigerator for 1 to 2 weeks.

FROZEN FRUIT SALAD

3 (No. 3) cans fruit cocktail
1 small can crushed pineapple
1 (8 oz.) pkg. cream cheese
2 tsp. lemon juice

½ c. mayonnaise
½ c. sugar
2 ripe bananas, mashed
Pinch of salt

Open cans and drain fruit in colander. Cream mayonnaise, cream cheese, and sugar together. Fold into fruit. Season with lemon juice and pinch of salt. Pour into baking cups which have been placed in muffin tins. Freeze. Serve as needed.

The most valuable gift you can give another is a good example.
Rosa Brafford, Rock Hill Lions Club
Rock Hill, South Carolina, USA

How much you love living shows in your life.

FROZEN CRANBERRY FRUIT SALAD

2 (3 oz.) pkg. cream cheese
2 Tbsp. sugar
2 Tbsp. mayonnaise
1 (1 lb.) can whole berry cranberry
  sauce

½ c. chopped pecans
1 (15¼ oz.) can drained, crushed
  pineapple
½ c. Cool Whip

Cream together cheese and sugar; stir in mayonnaise. Fold in cranberry sauce, pineapple, nuts, and Cool Whip. Pour into paper-lined muffin tins and freeze until firm. When they are firmly frozen, transfer them to a plastic bag and keep in freezer until ready to use. When serving, remove cups, tear off paper, and invert on lettuce bed on plate. Goes well with any chicken dish.

Mrs. Lion Robert (Margaret) Logan, Canton Lions Club
Canton, Georgia, USA

EASY FRUIT SALAD

3 (16 oz.) sugar free fruit cocktail
1 (20 oz.) can crushed pineapple
1 (6 oz.) can frozen orange juice

1 jar maraschino cherries
4 firm bananas, chopped

Mix all together. Chill for several hours.

This is very good for family reunions or parties. Bananas do not turn brown.
Gloria Bonager, East Prospect Lions Club
East Prospect, Pennsylvania, York County, USA

APRICOT SALAD

1 (6 oz.) apricot jello
1 (8 oz.) cream cheese
½ c. sugar
1 (No. 2) can crushed pineapple
  (11 oz. or so)

1 small non-dairy whipped
  topping
1 c. cold water

Cook sugar and pineapple till rapid boil. Remove from heat. Whip in cream cheese, then jello dry and then water. When slightly thickened in refrigerator, then mix in defrosted whipped topping. Mold and chill for at least 8 hours. You may add ½ cup chopped nuts for a different salad.

Glenn Bunch, Jr., PDG 31-H, Snow Hill Lions Club
Snow Hill, North Carolina, USA

We can only give away to others what we have inside ourselves.

PURPLE LADY SALAD

1 large or 2 regular boxes black
    raspberry Jell-O
1½ c. hot water
1 (No. 303) can blueberries and
    juice

1 (No. 303) can crushed pineapple
2 env. powdered Dream Whip

Dissolve Jell-O and water. Add fruit and mix. Prepare Dream Whip as directions on box. Stir into Jell-O mixture and set.

Glen Cox, Emporia Noon Lions Club
Emporia, Kansas, Lyon County, USA

MARY SALAD

1 pkg. Dream Whip, fixed
    according to directions

1 small jar Kraft pimento spread
1 c. marshmallows

In separate bowl, drain:

1 medium can pineapple chunks

1 can mandarin oranges

Fix Dream Whip. Mix in Kraft pimento spread. Add fruit, then marshmallows. Chill.

Glenn E. Bunch, Snow Hill Lions Club
Snow Hill, North Carolina, USA

AMBROSIA SALAD

3 c. miniature marshmallows
1 large can pitted dark sweet
    cherries
2 small cans mandarin orange
    sections

1 large can chunk pineapple
1 large container sour cream
¼ c. broken walnuts

Drain all the canned ingredients. Mix everything together. Chill and serve. Can be made the night before.

Can use maraschino cherries also. At Christmas time, use green and red cherries.

Marilyn Brailsford, President, Lincoln Blackstone Valley Lions Club
Lincoln, Rhode Island, USA

How beautiful a day can be when kindness touches it.

MYSTERY SALAD

1 (No. 2) can cherry pie filling
1 (No. 2) can drained crushed
   pineapple
1 (11 oz.) can mandarin oranges,
   drained
¼ c. coarsely chopped walnuts

1 c. miniature marshmallows
1 (14 oz.) can sweetened
   condensed milk
1 (8 oz.) container whipped
   topping

Mix all ingredients. Sprinkle with nuts. Cover and refrigerate.

Bev Hofer, Mitchell Lioness Club
Mitchell, South Dakota, USA

24-HOUR SALAD

2 beaten eggs
4 Tbsp. sugar
2 c. fruit cocktail, drained
2 c. canned mandarin oranges
2 c. canned crushed pineapple,
   drained

2 c. marshmallows
2 bananas, thinly sliced
4 Tbsp. vinegar
2 Tbsp. butter or margarine
1 c. whipped cream

Put eggs in double boiler. Add vinegar and sugar. Stir while cooking until thick and smooth. Remove from heat. Add butter and let cool, then fold in whipped cream and fruit mixture. Pour into bowl and let sit in fridge 24 hours (12 hours minimum). This salad *must* be on the menu for all special occasions in our family.

Dianne Crayston, Jasper Mountain Lions Club
Jasper, Alberta, Canada

DARK CHERRY SALAD

8 oz. softened cream cheese
16 oz. can dark sweet pitted
   cherries
1 large can pineapple tidbits

2 c. miniature marshmallows
9 oz. ctn. Cool Whip
¼ c. juice*

Drain pineapple and cherries. Reserve ¼ cup juice. Blend juice into cream cheese. Stir in fruit. Fold in whipped cream and marshmallows. Chill.

* From pineapple and cherries.

Barbara Allison, Moweaqua Lions Club
Moweaqua, Illinois, USA

Be willing to let anything happen.

PINK LEMONADE SALAD

Small can frozen lemonade (add
   pink coloring)
1 box regular Cool Whip
1 small can crushed pineapple,
   drained

1 can Eagle Brand milk
48 Ritz crackers, crushed
1 stick oleo

Melt 1 stick oleo. Add to crushed Ritz crackers. Press in long baking dish. Bake 7 minutes at 350°. Keep some crumbs for top. Mix together remaining ingredients and pour over crumbs. Let set in refrigerator overnight.

Henrietta Helle, Cuba Lions Club
Cuba, Illinois, USA

CONGEALED BUTTERMILK SALAD

1 (20 oz.) can crushed pineapple
   (no sugar added)
1 (6 oz.) pkg. orange jello (no
   sugar)

2 c. lowfat buttermilk
1 (8 oz.) ctn. lite Cool Whip
½ c. pecans, chopped

Heat pineapple, including juice, to boil. Sprinkle jello in the pineapple and stir until dissolved. Let cool and add buttermilk. Chill in refrigerator until mixture is partially set. Fold in Cool Whip. Add nuts. Pour in 8x12 inch Pyrex dish and place in refrigerator until serving time.

Howard Cook, Shively Lions Club
Louisville, Kentucky, USA

SUNSHINE SALAD

1 c. raisins
1 (20 oz.) can crushed pineapple
   (packed in its own juice,
   undrained)

1 lb. carrots

Combine raisins and crushed pineapple. Grate or shred carrots. Stir together carrots and the raisins and pineapple mixture. Cover and chill before serving.

Lion Jim Cunningham, Graysville/Proctor Lions Club
Glen Easton, West Virginia, USA

❧

You can't give a hug without getting one in return.

LOW CALORIE DUMP SALAD

1 large pkg. cherry or strawberry
  Jell-O
1 (20 oz.) can crushed pineapple
  in own juice

1 (12 oz.) ctn. light Cool Whip
1 (12 oz.) ctn. lowfat cottage
  cheese

Dump Jell-O powder and other ingredients into a bowl and mix well. Chill and serve on lettuce leaf.

Use anytime, but especially good on a hot summer day.

Zeta L. Adams, Craigsville Lions Club
Craigsville, West Virginia, USA

GORGONZOLA AND APPLE SALAD

1 red apple, cored and cubed
1 green apple, cored and cubed

Green leaf lettuce

Dressing:

½ c. crumbled Gorgonzola cheese
¼ c. olive oil
2 Tbsp. fresh lemon juice
1 scallion, finely chopped

½ Tbsp. Dijon style mustard
Salt and pepper to taste
1 Tbsp. chopped parsley

Prepare apples and place them in a salad bowl with enough torn lettuce for 4 servings.

For the dressing, mix the cheese, oil, lemon juice, scallions, mustard, salt, and pepper. Pour over salad and mix. Sprinkle on the parsley.

Mrs. Tom (Nancy) Sweet, Elburn Lions Club
Elburn, Illinois, USA

PINK SALAD

1 lb. can crushed pineapple
1 large or 2 small boxes
  strawberry jello

½ c. sugar
1 lb. cottage cheese (small curd)
8 oz. container Cool Whip

Heat pineapple slowly (juice and all). Add jello and ½ cup sugar. Dissolve jello and sugar completely. Set aside to cool. Mix cottage cheese and Cool Whip well. Add to gelatin mixture and let set. Makes a 9x9 inch pan.

Carol Morgan, Moweaqua Lions Club
Moweaqua, Illinois, USA

Forgiveness is an act of self-love.

138

PINK SALAD

1 large can crushed pineapple
1 can cherry pie filling
2 c. pecan pieces
1 can Eagle Brand milk

1 pkg. coconut
2 c. miniature marshmallows
1 large container Cool Whip

Mix milk and Cool Whip with mixer about 2 minutes. Fold in rest of ingredients in large bowl. Keep refrigerated.

Linda Hartley, President, Lyman Lions Club
Lyman, Wyoming, USA

BANANA SALAD

Bananas
2 c. peanuts
2 Tbsp. flour
⅔ c. sugar

⅔ c. cream
2 Tbsp. vinegar
2 eggs

Dressing: Combine flour, sugar, cream, and eggs. Cook over medium heat until thickened and cool. Add vinegar. When ready to serve, layer in serving bowl the sliced bananas, dressing, and chopped peanuts. Repeat until bowl is full.

Barb Allison, Moweaqua Lions Club
Moweaqua, Illinois, USA

JAMES SALAD

2 (3 oz.) pkg. raspberry jello
1 pkg. frozen raspberries
1 can whole cranberry sauce

1 small can crushed pineapple
(*not* drained)

Dissolve jello in 1 cup hot water. Add raspberries, cranberry sauce, and pineapple. Pour into 11x7 inch Pyrex. Makes 8 servings.

Dorothy V. Wipreed, Bothell Lions Club
Bothell, Washington, USA

RASPBERRY DESSERT SALAD

2 (3 oz.) pkg. raspberry gelatin
15 oz. raspberries and juice
1 (15 oz.) can crushed pineapple
    with juice
1 (8 oz.) pkg. cream cheese,
    softened

1 c. sour cream
½ c. sugar
½ tsp. vanilla extract

Dissolve gelatin in 2 cups boiling water in bowl; cool. Stir in fruit. Pour into 9x13 inch dish. Chill until firm. Combine remaining ingredients in bowl; beat until smooth. Spread over gelatin. Chill until serving time. Cut into squares.

Rose Ann Maue, Onekama Lions Club
Onekama, Michigan, USA

RASPBERRY MOLD

1 large box raspberry Jell-O
1 can whole cranberry sauce
3 c. boiling water
20 oz. can crushed pineapple with
   juice

8 oz. container Cool Whip
A handful crushed walnuts
   (optional)

Mix Jell-O and boiling water until Jell-O is completely dissolved. Refrigerate 1½ hours, then mix Jell-O and Cool Whip with mixer. Fold in cranberry sauce, pineapple, and nuts. Pour into mold and refrigerate. (You will need a bowl that will hold 12 cups.) This dish is nice as a side dish with ham or turkey.

Ann M. Kennedy, Gouldsboro Lions Club
Gouldsboro, Pennsylvania, USA

7-UP SALAD

9½ oz. 7-Up
15 large marshmallows
1 (8 oz.) pkg. Philadelphia Brand
   cream cheese
1 (3 oz.) pkg. lime or strawberry
   Jell-O

1 (2 lb.) can crushed pineapple,
   drained
1 c. nuts, chopped
1 (4 oz.) container Cool Whip

Heat 7-Up and marshmallows. Stir until marshmallows are melted. Mix cream cheese and Jell-O with mixer. Stir in drained pineapple, nuts, and 7-Up mixture. Refrigerate until set, but not firm. Add one 4 ounce container Cool Whip.

Strawberries may be substituted for pineapple.

HEAVENLY SALAD

Dissolve 3 ounces lime gelatin in 1 cup boiling water.

Add:

1 c. drained crushed pineapple
2 Tbsp. grated onion

3 Tbsp. grated carrots
½ green pepper, minced

Mix separately 1 jar pimiento cheese spread, 1 cup salad dressing, and 1 small can shrimp, drained. Add to the first mixture and pour into mold.

Dorothy V. Wipreed, Bothell Lions Club
Bothell, Washington, USA

Your behavior results from the thoughts that precede it.

GOLDEN GLOW SALAD

Dissolve:

1 pkg. lemon Jell-O in 1 c. boiling
  water
1 c. pineapple juice

½ tsp. salt
1 Tbsp. vinegar

Let stand until it starts to make Jell-O. Add 1 cup pineapple, diced and drained. Use 1 small can crushed pineapple, drained. Add water to pineapple juice to make the 1 cup. Add 1 cup grated raw carrots and ½ cup nuts.

Ursula J. Harrington, Westbrook Lions Club
Westbrook, Maine, USA

CHERRY COLA SALAD

¾ c. water
¾ c. sugar
1 can cherry pie filling
1 (6 oz.) box cherry gelatin
1 can crushed pineapple and juice

1 Tbsp. lemon juice
1 can cold cola soft drink (about 1
  c.)
½ c. chopped nuts

Combine water and sugar; bring to a boil. Add pie filling and return to a boil. Pour boiling mixture over gelatin, stirring to dissolve. Add pineapple and juice, lemon juice, cola, and nuts. Pour in 9x13 inch pan and chill. Serves 8 to 10.

CONGEALED STRAWBERRY SALAD

½ c. cold water
1 pkg. unflavored gelatin
2 (6 oz.) pkg. strawberry jello
2 c. hot water
2 (10 oz.) boxes frozen sweetened
  strawberries

2 ripe bananas, mashed
1 small can crushed pineapple,
  drained
½ c. chopped pecans
1 c. sour cream

Empty package of plain gelatin over ½ cup cold water and set aside. Make jello with 2 cups hot water; cool. Add plain gelatin that has dissolved and all other ingredients, except sour cream. Mix well and pour ½ of the mixture in a square pan (approximately 9x12 inches). Let set until firm in refrigerator. Spread with the sour cream, then add the remaining jello mixture and place in refrigerator several hours. To serve, cut into squares and serve on lettuce leaf.

Thomas Bland, Kosciusko Lions Club
Kosciusko, Mississippi, USA

No one can know enough to be a pessimist.

CHRISTMAS SALAD

2 pkg. strawberry Jell-O
2 c. boiling water
2 (10 oz.) pkg. frozen strawberries
2 ripe mashed bananas

1 small can crushed pineapple,
  well drained
1 small ctn. sour cream

Pour half of mixture in dish and chill till firm. Spread sour cream on top and add other half of Jell-O mixture.

Janice P. Baynard, Dolley Madison Lions Club
Greensboro, North Carolina, USA

BLUEBERRY SALAD

2 (3 oz.) pkg. black raspberry or
  grape jello
2 c. boiling water

1 c. blueberry pie filling
1 (15 oz.) can pineapple
  (undrained)

Topping:

1 (8 oz.) pkg. cream cheese
½ c. sugar

½ c. sour cream
Nuts

Mix all ingredients together in rapidly boiling water. Place in large glass dish. Chill until jelled.

Topping: Mix cream cheese, sugar, and sour cream. Pour over jello mixture. Sprinkle with nuts.

Martha Johnson, Dolley Madison Lions Club
Greensboro, North Carolina, Guilford County, USA

CHERRY PORT JELLO

Jello:

1 (1 lb.) can dark sweet cherries
2 Tbsp. sugar
1 pkg. unflavored Knox gelatine

3 Tbsp. lemon juice
⅓ c. Port wine

Topping:

1 c. sour cream
3 Tbsp. powdered sugar

½ tsp. vanilla
Slivered almonds

Drain cherries; save syrup and add water to make 1⅓ cups liquid. Add sugar to liquid and heat. Soften gelatin in lemon juice and dissolve into liquid, then add Port. Chill till slightly thickened, then add cherries and chill till firm. Stir topping (sour cream, powdered sugar, and vanilla) together. Place on top of jello. Garnish with slivered almonds.

Owen E. Moore, Merritt Island Lions Club
Merritt Island, Florida, USA

CHERRY NUT CONGEALED SALAD

1 (3 oz.) pkg. cherry jello
1 c. hot water
1 small can crushed pineapple,
   chilled

1 can cherry pie filling, chilled
1 c. chopped pecans

Topping:

1 (8 oz.) pkg. cream cheese
⅓ c. granulated sugar

1 c. sour cream
1 tsp. vanilla flavoring

Dissolve jello in hot water. Add pie filling, pineapple, and nuts. Place in refrigerator until salad starts to set up, then stir several times. Pour into a chilled Pyrex dish. Let mixture congeal until firm, then spread with topping.

Make topping by heating together the softened cream cheese and sugar. Fold in sour cream and vanilla. Spread over the top of the salad. Keep chilled until served.

Of all the dust thrown in men's eyes, gold dust is the most blinding.
Mrs. Boyd Bradley (Frances), Rock Hill Lions Club
Rock Hill, South Carolina, USA

CHERRY CONGEALED SALAD

1 (6 oz.) pkg. cherry jello
1 can cherry pie filling
1 large can crushed pineapple

1 c. nuts
1 c. chopped apples
2 c. hot water

Pour hot water over jello and stir until dissolved. Add other ingredients and mix well. Pour into 9x12 inch Pyrex dish and chill for several hours. Serves 10 to 12.

Mrs. Lion Robert (Margaret) Logan, Canton Lions Club
Canton, Georgia, USA

EASY MANDARIN PINEAPPLE SALAD

1 (3 oz.) pkg. vanilla pudding
   (cook and serve)
1 (3 oz.) pkg. instant vanilla
   pudding
1 (3 oz.) pkg. orange Jell-O

3 c. hot water
1 can mandarin oranges
1 small can pineapple tidbits
2 c. miniature marshmallows
1 small container Cool Whip

Combine puddings and Jell-O with hot water. Cook over medium heat until thick and clear. Cool completely. When cool, add Cool Whip, mandarin oranges, pineapple, and marshmallows. Chill 30 minutes. Serves 8.

TROPICAL ORANGE SALAD

1 (6 oz.) pkg. orange Jell-O
2 c. boiling water
1 small can frozen orange juice
2 small cans mandarin oranges,
   drained
1 large can crushed pineapple
   (not drained)

1 pkg. vanilla instant pudding
1 c. milk
1 (8 oz.) container Cool Whip
Nuts (optional)

Dissolve gelatin in boiling water. Add orange juice concentrate, oranges, and pineapple. Put in a 9x13 inch glass dish. Chill until set. Beat pudding and milk. Fold in whipped topping and spread on Jell-O layer. Top with nuts. Refrigerate until ready to serve. Serves 12.

Marge Wilson, Plattsmouth Lions Club
Plattsmouth, Nebraska, USA

STRAWBERRY PRETZEL SALAD

1½ c. crushed pretzels
½ c. chopped pecans
3 Tbsp. sugar
¾ c. margarine
8 oz. cream cheese
1½ c. boiling water
1 c. sugar

8 oz. Cool Whip
2 (10 oz.) pkg. frozen strawberries
   (with juice)
1 large can crushed pineapple
   with juice
1 large pkg. Jell-O (strawberry)

Mix well the pretzels, pecans, margarine, and 3 tablespoons sugar; bake in a 9x13 inch pan at 350° for 10 minutes and cool completely. (This is the bottom layer of salad.) Cream cheese and blend in 1 cup sugar. Add Cool Whip, mixing well. Spread over cooled pretzel mix.

Dissolve jello in the boiling water. Add frozen strawberries and pineapple. Chill until slightly thickened and pour over Cool Whip layer. Chill overnight before serving. This can be used for either a salad or a dessert and goes a long way.

Beverly Foster, East Lake Lions Club
Birmingham, Alabama, USA

❦

You are sowing the flowers of tomorrow in the seeds of today.

STRAWBERRY PRETZEL SALAD

2 c. crushed pretzels
3 Tbsp. sugar
¾ c. melted oleo
8 oz. cream cheese
1 c. sugar

1 small ctn. Cool Whip
1 large pkg. strawberries
1 small can crushed pineapple
2 c. boiling water

Mix first 3 ingredients and press in 9 x 13 x 1½ inch pan. Bake 7 minutes at 400°. Cool.

Mix 8 ounces cream cheese and 1 cup sugar. Add small carton Cool Whip. Put over pretzels. Refrigerate to cool. Mix Jell-O and water; dissolve. Add strawberries and pineapple. Chill until thick. Pour over cream cheese mixture. Refrigerate until ready to serve. *Umm good.*

Joye Robinson, Georgetown Evening Lions Club
Georgetown, Texas, Williamson County, USA

PRETZEL SALAD

2 c. crushed pretzels
1½ sticks oleo, melted
¼ c. sugar
1 (8 oz.) cream cheese, softened
1 c. sugar

12 oz. Cool Whip
2 (3 oz.) pkg. strawberry gelatin
2 c. hot pineapple juice
2 (10 oz.) pkg. frozen strawberries
and juice

Mix pretzels, melted oleo, and sugar. Bake at 350° for 10 minutes in 9x13 inch pan. Cool. Mix cream cheese, 1 cup sugar, and Cool Whip. Spread on pretzel layer. Dissolve jello in hot juice. Add strawberries with juice to jello. Refrigerate till partially set. Spread over top of cream cheese layer. Refrigerate 4 hours. Cut in squares to serve.

This is so good, it can double as a dessert. It is requested at all family functions.

Mrs. Lester (Linda) Lee, Elburn Lions Club
Elburn, Illinois, USA

❧

The best remedy for a short temper is a long walk.

PRETZEL SALAD

1 c. crushed pretzels
6 Tbsp. melted butter
⅓ c. sugar
8 oz. cream cheese

⅓ c. sugar
20 oz. crushed pineapple, drained
8 oz. Cool Whip

Mix pretzels, butter, and sugar together. Put in jelly roll pan and bake 6 minutes at 400°. Cool.

Mix together cream cheese and sugar. Add pineapple. Fold in Cool Whip. Chill.

Mix pretzel mixture with cheese mixture. Put in serving bowl. *Enjoy!*

"Speak when angry and it will be the best speech you'll ever regret."
Jeanette Olson, Siren Lions Club
Siren, Wisconsin, USA

TANGY CRANBERRY SALAD

2 oranges
1 lb. fresh cranberries
1 c. sugar
2 pkg. lemon jello

2½ c. hot water
1 c. chopped celery
1 c. chopped nuts

Wash, peel, seed, and cut up oranges. Chop oranges and cranberries in food processor. Add sugar; let stand for 2 hours. Dissolve jello in water; let cool. Combine cranberry mixture with jello; add celery and nuts. Turn into mold; chill until set. Serves 15.

Mrs. Lion Robert (Margaret) Logan, Canton Lions Club
Canton, Georgia, USA

CRANBERRY SALAD

1 pkg. fresh cranberries
4 red apples
1 pkg. small marshmallows
Dash of vanilla

1 c. whipping cream
1 c. chopped walnuts
1½ c. sugar
3 to 4 Tbsp. sugar

Grind cranberries coarsely in meat grinder or food processor. Chop apples and mix with cranberries. Add marshmallows and sugar. Mix well. Let stand while whipping cream. Whip cream. Add dash of vanilla and 3 to 4 tablespoons sugar. Stir nuts into whipped cream, then cranberry mixture and mix well. Chill before serving.

As a man grows older and wiser, he talks less and says more.
Betty Arnold, Rock Hill Lions Club
Rock Hill, South Carolina, USA

APPLE-CRANBERRY SALAD

2 c. raw cranberries, coarse
   ground
1 c. apples, cut in small pieces
1 small can crushed pineapple,
   drained
1 scant c. hot water
1 c. chopped walnuts
1 pkg. red jello
1½ c. sugar
Dash of nutmeg

Dissolve jello in hot water. Add sugar while hot. Cool, then add other ingredients. Cool until set.

Evelyn Steele, Lyman Lions Club
Lyman, Wyoming, USA

GRANDMA'S CRANBERRY SALAD

1 lb. cranberries, ground
1 c. sugar
8 oz. crushed pineapple, drained
1 small container Cool Whip
¾ c. chopped nuts
1 small bag miniature
   marshmallows

Mix ground cranberries and sugar. Refrigerate overnight. Next morning, remove from refrigerator and add rest of ingredients. Mix well. Return to refrigerator until ready to serve.

My grandmother first made this in 1952. We've had it every Thanksgiving since then.

Patti O'Brien, Sundowners Lions Club
Emporia, Kansas, USA

CONGEALED CRANBERRY SALAD

2 (3 oz.) boxes sugar free cherry
   gelatin
2 c. hot water
1 can whole cranberry sauce
1 (15¼ oz.) can crushed
   pineapple, drained
1 c. celery, chopped
1 c. pecans, chopped

Dissolve gelatin in boiling water in large serving bowl. Add whole cranberry sauce, broken apart and mashed. Blend in crushed pineapple that has been drained. Stir in pecans and celery. Can be put in 9x13 inch dish. Refrigerate to congeal. Serves 8 to 10. This is a good salad for diabetics.

Some people eat to live - others live to eat.
Leola C. Jurrens, Downtown Bartlesville Lions Club
Bartlesville, Oklahoma, USA

❧

Every obstacle is an opportunity - and a test.

RAW CRANBERRY SALAD

1 lb. raw cranberries
4 apples
1 orange
2 c. sugar

2 pkg. strawberry jello (use ½
   amount water hot)
½ c. chopped nuts
1 small can crushed pineapple

Grind or chop the first 3 ingredients. Mix together with sugar; set aside. Mix the 2 packages of jello together with ½ amount of hot water. Let cool. Add the chopped to the first mixture. Stir in the jello and the small can crushed pineapple. Refrigerate.

Dan Steffan, Independence Eastview Lions Club
Independence, Missouri, USA

CRANBERRY SALAD

1 pkg. fresh cranberries
1 c. sugar
1 small can crushed pineapple
   (not drained)

12 oz. Cool Whip
1½ c. small marshmallows
1 c. nuts

Put cranberries in a blender and chop in small pieces. Mix cranberries, sugar, and pineapple together; let set overnight. Add rest of ingredients and mix well. Keep in refrigerator until ready to serve.

Faye Blount, Levelland Lioness Club
Levelland, Texas, USA

BLEU CHEESE DRESSING

⅓ c. vinegar
½ c. sugar
1 tsp. Worcestershire sauce
¼ c. ketchup
½ tsp. salt
1 c. Wesson oil
1 small onion, grated

Garlic (optional)
1 small pkg. cream cheese (room
   temperature)
½ or 1 (4 oz.) pkg. Bleu cheese
   (depending on desired
   taste)

Mix together first 8 ingredients with a mixer. Add cream cheese and Bleu cheese and mix together.

Mrs. Susan Sanders, Lion, Hedgesville Lions Club
Hedgesville, West Virginia, USA

Doing what you love is the basis of having abundance in your life.

FETA CHEESE SALAD DRESSING

⅓ c. olive oil
1 clove garlic, minced
½ tsp. dry oregano
2 Tbsp. white wine vinegar

¾ tsp. dry basil
1 tsp. Worcestershire sauce
½ c. crumbled Feta cheese

Combine in jar and shake. Chill. Pour over greens or cucumbers or tomatoes. Serves 4 to 6.

Has a short refrigerator life of about 4 to 5 days.

Sarah Wehling, Bothell Lions Club
Bothell, Washington, USA

MR. MAC'S SALAD DRESSING

2 c. safflower oil
1 c. lemon juice
1 tsp. seasoned pepper (black)
1 tsp. salt
½ tsp. dry mustard

1 tsp. fresh pepper
1 Tbsp. Worcestershire sauce
Dash of Tabasco
¼ c. minced onion
1 hard cooked egg, minced

Put all ingredients in a blender. Process. Refrigerate overnight. Serve over mixed salad greens or spinach and mushroom salad. Makes 3½ cups.

Sarah Wehling, Bothell Lions Club
Bothell, Washington, USA

POPPY SEED DRESSING

1½ c. sugar
2 tsp. dry mustard
2 tsp. salt
⅔ c. white or wine vinegar

3 Tbsp. onion juice
2 c. salad oil
3 Tbsp. poppy seeds

Mix sugar, mustard, salt, and vinegar in a deep, narrow bowl. Add onion juice and stir. Slowly add oil, beating constantly until thickened. Stir in poppy seeds and store in refrigerator until ready to use. Yield: 3½ cups.

Mrs. Lion Robert (Margaret) Logan, Canton Lions Club
Canton, Georgia, USA

OLD WAREHOUSE SALAD DRESSING

1 medium grated onion
1 tsp. prepared mustard
1 tsp. salt
1 tsp. whole celery seed

⅓ c. white vinegar
1 c. salad oil
⅔ c. sugar

Mix all ingredients well and store in refrigerator. Shake well before serving. Can be made in blender. Very good sweet/sour dressing.

Verna Ball, Sherrodsville Lions Club
Sherrodsville, Ohio, USA

DIET FRENCH SALAD DRESSING

1 tsp. oil
1 Tbsp. vinegar
1 tsp. paprika
1 pkg. sugar substitute

Salt to taste
Dill weed and chives to taste
Parsley and celery seed to taste

Combine oil, vinegar, paprika, and sugar substitute in small bowl. Whisk until sugar substitute dissolves. Add salt, dill weed, chives, parsley, and celery seed. Mix well. Sprinkle over salad greens and other vegetables. Toss to mix. You may double or triple to make enough salad dressing for desired number of servings.

Approximately per serving: 42 calories, 0 g protein, 1 g carbohydrates, 0 g fiber, 5 g TFat, 0 mg cholesterol, and less than 1 mg sodium.

If you want to really lose weight, try this.

F.L. Godwin, East Lake Lions Club
Birmingham, Alabama, USA

HOT BACON DRESSING

4 slices bacon
¼ c. sugar
½ tsp. salt
1 Tbsp. flour
¼ c. water

1 egg (whole)
¾ c. water
¼ c. vinegar
2 hard cooked eggs

Fry bacon. Cut in small pieces and fry till crisp. Drain off excess fat. Mix sugar, salt, flour, and ¼ cup water together; mix well. Add this to bacon in pan and cook ingredients to desired thickness.

Claude H. Ohlinger, Blandon Lions Club
Blandon, Pennsylvania, USA

HOT BACON DRESSING

1 egg
½ c. sugar

¼ c. vinegar

Mix in blender. Fry 4 slices bacon. Dice up 4 slices of bacon and fry crisp. Do not pour any grease off, but pour blender mix in pan. Stir and cook about 1 minute until it gets shiny. Pour over lettuce or any greens.

Always use twice as much sugar as vinegar.

Grace Stuffle, Silver Run-Union Mills Lions Club
Westminster, Maryland, USA

Every place along the way is somewhere you had to be to be here.

BOILED BACON DRESSING

4 slices bacon
½ c. sugar
½ tsp. salt
1 Tbsp. cornstarch

1 beaten egg
¼ c. vinegar
1 c. water

Microwave bacon in 4 cup glass dish after cutting into chunks. Put bacon on paper towel to drain. Add water, vinegar, egg, salt, sugar, and cornstarch to grease in dish. Whisk with wire whisk. Cook on HIGH in microwave at 1 minute and 30 second intervals, whisking well after each till thick. Add bacon. Serve warm over lettuce or spinach or dandelion. (Add chopped hard cooked eggs to lettuce for flavor.)

Bonnie Kreamer (Mrs. Kent), Silver Run-Union Mills Lions Club
Westminster, Maryland, USA

PINEAPPLE FRUIT DRESSING

1¼ c. pineapple juice
2 Tbsp. plain flour
6 Tbsp. sugar
1 c. marshmallows

2 eggs
¼ tsp. salt
2 Tbsp. butter

Mix all together, except marshmallows, and heat on low, stirring constantly until slightly thickened. Remove from heat and add marshmallows. Stir and let cool. Pour over cut up fresh fruit. Serve after chilled.

Mrs. Charlotte M. Garner, Pascagoula Evening Lions Club
Pascagoula, Mississippi, USA

❧

The best Preacher is the heart; the best teacher is time;
the best book is the world; the best friend is God.

❦ ❦ ❦

Instant availability without continuous presence
is probably the best role a mother can play.

Notes

A skeptic is a person who, when he sees the handwriting on the wall, claims it is a forgery.

Vegetables

TO QUICK-FREEZE VEGETABLES

Vegetables for freezing are prepared as for cooking, then blanched (scalded) and packed dry or with the brine. The dry pack is less trouble and is satisfactory for all vegetables except green peppers.

Blanching vegetables is important because it minimizes loss of flavor and color. To blanch in boiling water, put about one pound of vegetables in a fine-mesh wire basket with a wire cover to hold food under the water and lower into rapidly boiling water, enough to cover food. Cover the kettle and then COUNT THE TIME RECOMMENDED FOR EACH vegetable. After blanching, chill quickly and thoroughly, plunge the vegetables into ice water, or hold under cold running water. When completely chilled, remove and drain, and PACK AT ONCE.

VEGETABLE	HOW PREPARED	BLANCHING
ASPARAGUS	Wash, cut, sort into groups according to thickness of stalk. Blanch, chill, pack.	3 to 4 minutes in boiling water, depending on size.
BEANS, GREEN AND WAX	Wash, stem, slice, cut or leave whole. Blanch, chill, pack.	Cut: 2 minutes in boiling water. Whole: 2½ minutes in boiling water.
BEANS, LIMA	Shell, wash, blanch, chill. Remove white beans, which may be used for cooking. Pack.	1 to 2 minutes in boiling water, depending on size.
CARROTS	Remove tops, wash, scrape. Slice lengthwise or crosswise as preferred, or leave small carrots whole.	Whole: 4½ minutes in boiling water. Sliced: 3 minutes in boiling water.
CAULIFLOWER	Break heads into flowerets about 1 inch across. Wash, blanch, chill, pack.	3 to 4 minutes in boiling water.
CORN, ON COB	Husk, trim away silk and spots. Wash, blanch, chill, pack.	7 minutes in boiling water for slender ears, 9 for medium, 11 for large.
CORN, KERNELS	Same as corn on cob. After chilling, cut off kernels and pack.	
GREENS Beet, Chard, Kale, Mustard, Spinach, Collards, etc.	Wash, discard bad leaves, tough stems. Blanch, chill, pack.	2 minutes in boiling water.
PEAS	Shell, sort, blanch, chill, pack.	1 to 2 minutes in boiling water, depending on size.
PEPPERS, GREEN	Wash, cut away seeds, slice. Blanch, pack in brine of 1 tsp. salt to 1 c. cold water.	3 minutes in boiling water.

VEGETABLES

STUFFED ARTICHOKES WITH LEMON SAUCE

6 fresh artichokes
4 Tbsp. lemon juice
1 Tbsp. butter
2 onions, chopped
4 tomatoes, chopped

Salt and pepper
250 g minced mutton
½ c. rice
2 egg yolks
1 Tbsp. lemon juice

Trim and wash artichokes. Remove the leaves and sprinkle with lemon juice. Place in a saucepan with boiling water and cook for 20 minutes. Add lemon. Leave for 5 minutes and drain.

Melt butter and braise the onions until soft. Add the chopped tomatoes, minced mutton, and rice. Adjust seasoning and braise for 15 minutes. Stuff the artichokes and put in a greased roasting tin.

Mix 2 egg yolks, 1 tablespoon lemon juice, and 4 tablespoons water; sprinkle the stuffed artichokes. Cook for about 30 minutes at 170°C. Serve hot.

Yiannoula Christodoulidou, Nicosia Cosmopolitan Lions Club
Nicosia, Cyprus

ESCALLOPED ASPARAGUS

2 cans asparagus
3 hard-boiled eggs
1 c. Parmesan cheese
½ tsp. salt

1 can cream of mushroom soup
½ c. fine bread crumbs
1 tsp. paprika

Drain asparagus and save ⅓ cup of liquid. Oil a large casserole dish and arrange asparagus on bottom. Add finely chopped eggs. Sprinkle with cheese and asparagus liquid. Salt to taste. Spread undiluted soup over asparagus. Top with crumbs and dust with paprika. Bake 40 minutes at 350°.

Naomi C. Reid, Rock Hill Lions Club
Rock Hill, South Carolina, USA

❦

If you push yourself you will go farther than if you are pulled.

ASPARAGUS LUNCHEON BAKE

2 (10 oz.) pkg. frozen chopped
   asparagus
1 (10 oz.) can condensed cream of
   mushroom soup (undiluted)
¼ c. milk
1 can water chestnuts, drained
   and sliced

2 (3 oz.) cans sliced mushrooms,
   drained
4 hard cooked eggs, sliced
½ tsp. salt
Dash of pepper
1 (3½ oz.) can French fried onion
   rings

Cook asparagus according to package directions; drain. Place asparagus in greased 7x11 inch baking pan. Put on top asparagus, water chestnuts, mushrooms, and eggs. Combine soup, milk, salt, and pepper. Pour mixture over asparagus. Sprinkle onion rings on top. Bake, uncovered, in a 350° oven for 20 minutes. Serves 6.

ROASTED ASPARAGUS

1½ lb. asparagus spears

2 tsp. vegetable oil

Preheat oven to 400°F. Trim asparagus and arrange in single layer in baking pan. Drizzle with oil. Bake about 18 minutes or until tender.

Ruby Fleming, Otter Valley Lions Club
Otterville, Ontario, Canada

ASPARAGUS HOT DISH

2 c. chopped celery
1 green pepper, chopped
1 (6 oz.) can tuna
1 can cream of mushroom soup
1 can cream of chicken soup

1 c. mayonnaise
1 lb. or more cooked asparagus
1 c. grated Cheddar cheese
1 small can mushrooms
8 oz. cooked noodles

Mix all together. Bake in buttered pan or dish in 350° oven for 1 hour. A handful of cashews may be placed on top if you wish.

This dish freezes well before you bake it. Very good hot dish. Yummy.

This is one of my Aunt Delores Fehlen's favorite recipes from Wisconsin. I love it, too.

Elsie Louise Hall, Silver Run-Union Mills Lions Club
Westminster, Maryland, USA

❧

Many people are <u>expecting</u> a miracle instead of <u>being</u> a miracle.

CROCKERY COOKER BAKED BEANS

1 lb. dry pinto beans
6 c. water
1½ tsp. salt
1 tsp. dry mustard
½ tsp. pepper

½ c. chopped onion
½ c. molasses
½ c. brown sugar
½ lb. bacon, chopped

Place beans in boiling water (enough to cover) and simmer for 10 minutes. Combine beans, water, and cooked bacon in crock. Cover and cook on LOW for about 12 hours. Drain beans, reserving liquid. Combine beans with remaining ingredients and add enough bean liquid to cover beans. Cover and cook on LOW for another 6 hours. Yield: 6 to 8 servings.

BAKED BEANS

8 lb. baby lima beans
½ c. salt
4 qt. water

4 c. molasses
2 lb. light brown sugar
2 lb. bacon, cut up

Soak lima beans in water overnight (cover well). Drain. Add 4 quarts water and salt. Cook until about half cooked. Add molasses, brown sugar, and bacon, fried crisp with drippings. Cook for about an hour. This amount fits in electric roaster. Cook beans at about 400°, then add ingredients. Turn to 250°. Stir several times and scrape sides. This amount fits in an electric roaster. Temperature may vary.

This recipe has been used by the Club for their chicken barbecue for about 40 years.

Harleysville Lions Club, 14R
Harleysville, Pennsylvania, USA

FRED'S BAKED BEANS

6 (16 oz.) cans pork and beans,
    drained
2 Tbsp. Worcestershire sauce
1 medium onion, chopped
    (reserve 2 slices as
    garnish)*

2 tsp. prepared mustard
4 medium sweet pickles, chopped
1 (20 oz.) pineapple chunks,
    drained
4 to 6 Tbsp. heavy sour cream
2 c. brown sugar

Preheat oven to 350°F. Mix all ingredients in pot. Put into oven and bake until hot and bubbly. Top with sliced onion. Bake for 15 minutes.

* Optional.

Fred W. Plummer, Saginaw, Texas, Lions Club
Saginaw, Texas, Tarrant County, USA

BAKED BEANS

2 lb. navy beans
1½ c. white sugar
1 c. catsup
½ c. Karo syrup
1 tsp. mustard

1 large onion, chopped
¼ c. molasses
½ lb. bacon
½ tsp. salt

Soak beans all day. Bring to boil and simmer 20 minutes. Do not drain. Add the rest of the ingredients. Put in a roaster. Cover and bake overnight at 250°F.

When you take these beans to a potluck, they don't last very long.
Lion Beverly Wilkens, Plato Lions Club
Plato, Minnesota, USA

DRUNKEN BEANS

¾ lb. bacon, chopped
3 large onions, chopped
6 (15 oz.) pinto beans, drained
3 (12 oz.) dark beer
3 c. beef broth

3 large tomatoes, chopped
1½ c. chopped cilantro
3 jalapeno chilies, chopped fine
1 Tbsp. sugar

Cook bacon in pot until crisp. Add onions to pot and cook to tender, about 15 minutes. Add bacon, beans, beef stock, tomatoes, cilantro, chilies, and sugar. Season to taste with salt and pepper. Bring to boil. Reduce heat and simmer until thickened, stirring occasionally, about 1½ hours. This dish is really like a soup.
Lion Ray Wayte, Caruthers Lions Club
Caruthers, California, USA

SETTLER'S BEANS

½ lb. hamburger
½ lb. bacon
1 small onion
1 can pork and beans with sauce
1 can kidney beans, drained
1 can butter beans, drained

1 c. ketchup
½ c. white sugar
½ c. brown sugar
½ tsp. dry mustard
2 Tbsp. baking molasses

Brown hamburger, bacon, and onion together. Put in baking dish. Combine rest of ingredients and put into meat mixture. Bake at 350° for 1½ to 2 hours.

Crock pot directions: Brown meats and onion; put in crock pot. Add rest of ingredients. Cook on LOW for 8 to 10 hours or HIGH for 4 to 5 hours. Serves 6.

❦

Being bored is a choice.

SEVEN-BEAN CASSEROLE

½ lb. bulk sausage (mild), mixed
   with ½ lb. bulk sausage
   (hot)
2 medium onions, chopped
1 can green beans
1 can yellow beans
1 can lima beans
1 can kidney beans

1 can butter beans
1 can chili beans (with juice)
1 can pork and beans
1 can tomato soup
3 Tbsp. catsup
1 c. brown sugar
2 Tbsp. mustard
Strips of bacon

Saute onions. Roll sausage into small meatballs and brown. Mix chili and kidney and pork and beans in a large bowl. Drain remaining beans. Add and toss gently.

Combine tomato soup, catsup, sugar, mustard, and onions. Carefully mix with beans. Fold in sausage. Place strips of bacon on top. Bake at 350° for 1 hour, uncovered, in deep 9x13 inch pan or a large casserole dish.

HUSBAND PLEASING BEANS

1 lb. ground beef
2 medium onions, chopped
½ stick margarine
5 cans (16 oz.) pork and beans

¼ c. yellow mustard
¼ c. maple syrup
½ c. brown sugar
1 c. catsup

Brown ground beef and onions in margarine. Mix with remaining ingredients. Put in baking dish and refrigerate overnight. Bake at 300° for 1½ hours.

Intelligence is like a river, the deeper it flows the less noise it makes.
Peggy Alewine, Rock Hill Lions Club
Rock Hill, South Carolina, USA

FOUR BEAN CASSEROLE

½ lb. bacon
1 lb. hamburger
1 medium onion
1 can kidney beans
1 can green limas

1 can butter beans
1 can pork and beans
½ c. catsup
¾ c. brown sugar

Brown bacon and drain fat; crumble. Brown hamburger with onion. Add the 4 cans of beans (don't drain liquid), catsup, brown sugar, and crumbled bacon. Mix and put in baking dish. Bake at 350° for 1½ hours. Serves 8.

❦

You are the sum of all your choices up until this moment.

REFRIED BEANS

3 c. dried pinto beans
1 medium onion
1 clove garlic
¼ to ½ tsp. ground comino

1 tsp. sugar
Salt and pepper to taste
Water

Wash beans. Beans are more flavorful if soaked overnight, but may be cooked right away. Put beans in pan with large amount of water. Add whole peeled onion, whole garlic clove, and all seasonings. Simmer for at least 2 hours or until beans are soft. Add water, as needed, during cooking. When beans are done, remove onion and garlic.

Mash beans. Add touch of garlic powder and 1 to 2 tablespoons bacon drippings. Salt to taste. Heat until all of bacon drippings are absorbed.

Use on the side with Colorado Chile and Mexican Rice or use in burritos.

RANCH BEANS

2 Tbsp. butter
1 lb. chuck ground beef
1 env. Lipton's onion soup
2 (1 lb.) cans beans in tomato
  sauce

1 lb. kidney beans, drained
1 c. ketchup
½ c. cold water
2 Tbsp. prepared mustard
2 tsp. cider vinegar

Bake in 350° oven for 35 to 40 minutes. Brown beef in butter. Add soup mix. Add all other ingredients.

Dave Bernier, Westbrook Lions Club
Westbrook, Maine, USA

COLD WATER BEANS

1 lb. cooked pinto beans
1 onion, chopped
1 (4 oz.) can chillies
1 (4 oz.) can taco sauce
2 garlic cloves, chopped

1 tsp. chili powder
1 can stewed tomatoes
1 lb. hamburger meat, browned
  and drained

Cook pinto beans until almost done, then add the rest of ingredients and simmer until beans and onions are done. This, served with salad and corn bread, makes a great meal and easy to prepare.

Shirley Ward, Levelland Lions Club
Levelland, Texas, USA

Think about it - are you part of the problem or part of the solution?

CALICO BEANS

1 lb. ground beef
½ lb. bacon
¾ c. brown sugar
½ c. catsup
2 tsp. vinegar
1 tsp. mustard
Salt and pepper
1 (16 oz.) can lima beans, drained

1 (16 oz.) can kidney beans
1 (16 oz.) can butter beans,
   drained
1 (16 oz.) can Northern beans,
   drained
1 (16 oz.) can baked beans with
   pork

Brown ground beef and drain. Lightly cook bacon and cut into pieces. Mix all in casserole. Bake 2 hours at 275°.

Lion Lynne Harvey, Biloxi Lions Club
Biloxi, Mississippi, USA

HOBO BEANS

1 lb. lean ground beef
½ pkg. onion soup mix
¾ c. ketchup
½ c. cold water

2 Tbsp. prepared mustard
2 tsp. vinegar
1 Tbsp. brown sugar
1 large can pork and beans

Brown ground beef. Add remaining ingredients and place in a casserole. Bake at 350° for 1½ hours, uncovered. Serves 6 to 8.

HO BO BEANS

1 lb. ground beef
1 medium onion, chopped
½ c. water
2 Tbsp. brown sugar
1 c. catsup

2 tsp. vinegar
2 tsp. mustard
2 (16 oz.) cans pork and beans
1 (16 oz.) can kidney beans

Brown meat and drain. Mix all ingredients together and bake 30 minutes, uncovered, at 400° in a 2½ quart dish. (Also can be frozen.)

Lion Carol Van Scyoc, Graysville/Proctor Lions Club
Glen Easton, West Virginia, USA

You can't turn the clock back, but you can rewind it.

RED BEANS AND RICE

1 lb. pinto beans
1 pkg. German sausage
1 c. chopped onion
1 can Ro-Tel tomatoes or picante
sauce

1 can tomatoes
Salt to taste
1 tsp. garlic powder
1 c. rice (uncooked)

Wash and soak beans, then boil with the German sausage (cut in small pieces) for approximately 45 minutes. Add the chopped onion, canned tomatoes, and Ro-Tel or picante sauce, salt, garlic powder, and also some of the Cajun spice mix if you have it. Simmer for at least an hour, or until tender. Add the cup of dry rice and continue to cook slowly (the rice will absorb a lot of liquid so be sure there is plenty of bean juice).

This is a very good, filling meal all by itself! This is another of my "trial and error" recipes - just keep adding till it tastes right!

Frances Cantrell, Bowie Evening Lions Club
Bowie, Texas, USA

SANTA MARIA BBQ BEANS

1 lb. small pink beans
1 strip bacon, diced
½ c. diced ham
1 small garlic clove, minced
¾ c. tomato puree

¼ c. red chili sauce
1 tsp. salt
1 tsp. dry mustard
1 tsp. sugar

Pick over the beans to remove dirt and small stones; cover with water and let soak overnight in a large container. Drain, cover with fresh water, and simmer 2 hours, or until tender. Saute bacon and ham until lightly browned; add garlic and saute a minute or two longer, then add tomato puree, chili sauce, sugar, salt, and mustard. Drain most of the liquid off beans and stir in sauce. Keep hot over low heat until ready to serve.

Great served with Tri Tip.

Lion Dan Rodrigues, Caruthers Lions Club
Caruthers, California, USA

Set your goals out of reach, not out of sight.

BLACK BEANS AND RICE

1 Tbsp. vegetable oil
1 medium yellow onion, chopped
  fine
1 small sweet red pepper, seeded
  and chopped fine
2 cloves garlic, minced
1¾ c. cooked, drained black
  beans

½ c. long-grain rice
1½ c. low-sodium chicken broth
¼ tsp. red pepper flakes
¼ tsp. dried thyme, crumbled
1 bay leaf
½ c. shredded Cheddar cheese (2
  oz.)

In a large heavy saucepan, heat the vegetable oil over moderate heat for 1 minute. Add the onion and red pepper; cook, stirring for 5 minutes or until the onion is soft. Add the garlic, black beans, rice, chicken broth, red pepper flakes, thyme, and bay leaf. Bring to a boil. Adjust the heat so that the mixture bubbles gently. Cover and simmer for 20 minutes or until the rice is tender. Remove the bay leaf. Spoon the rice and beans onto 4 heated plates and sprinkle with the cheese. Makes 4 servings.

THREE-BEAN BAKE
(Microwave)

1 (31 oz.) can pork and beans in
  tomato sauce
1 (16 oz.) can cut green beans,
  drained
1 (15 oz.) can garbanzo beans or
  chickpeas, drained

1 small onion, chopped
3 Tbsp. brown sugar
1 Tbsp. prepared mustard
¼ c. catsup
3 slices bacon, cut into pieces

Combine all ingredients, except bacon, in 2 quart glass casserole. Top with bacon. Microwave, covered, for 14 to 16 minutes or until heated through.

QUICK CHILI BEANS

Have on hand 1 large can pinto beans.

Add:

1 chopped onion
1 large can Ortega whole chili
½ lb. stick linguica

3 strips bacon, cooked
1 can stewed tomatoes
1 chili block

Combine all ingredients. Bring to a boil and simmer for 20 minutes. Serves 6. Very easy to make.

Lion Alfred Duran, Caruthers Lions Club
Caruthers, California, USA

BEET RUSSE

2 c. hot cubed beets
½ c. French dressing

1 c. sour cream, whipped
½ c. minced green onion

Mix beets with dressing. Place in a serving dish. Top with sour cream. Sprinkle with minced onion. A very good side dish. Quick and easy to make.

Mrs. Olwen Curphey, Eagleville Trooper Lions Club
Norristown, Pennsylvania, USA

BORSCH

Place equal amounts of the following in fry pan with large amounts of butter:

4 or 5 beets
4 or 5 carrots
1 large head cabbage
4 or 5 medium onions

Dill
1 c. tomatoes
4 or 5 potatoes
Cream

Add any other vegetables that suit your fancy. Fry until well blended and soft. Add can of tomatoes and boil together in water. Add equal amounts of potatoes. When done, add cream and serve.

Terry Pister, Prince Albert Downtown Lioness Club
Prince Albert Saskatchewan, Canada

BROCCOLI-EGG CASSEROLE

1 (10 oz.) pkg. frozen, chopped
    broccoli
2 Tbsp. all-purpose flour
2 Tbsp. margarine
Salt and pepper to taste

1 c. milk
2 slices American cheese
2 hard cooked eggs, diced
Ritz cracker crumbs

Cook broccoli as directed on box. Melt margarine in saucepan over medium heat. Add flour and seasonings; stir for 2 to 3 minutes. Add milk and continue stirring until thickened. Melt cheese slices in sauce. Combine sauce, eggs, and broccoli in 1 quart casserole; top with crumbs. Bake at 350° for 20 minutes or until bubbling. Makes 6 servings.

Mrs. Lion Robert (Margaret) Logan, Canton Lions Club
Canton, Georgia, USA

Get even with those people who have helped you.

BROCCOLINI

1 lb. thin spaghetti
1 (10 oz.) frozen chopped broccoli
1 stick margarine

1 Tbsp. garlic Season-All salt
⅔ c. Parmesan cheese

While cooking the spaghetti, prepare the broccoli according to package directions; set aside. Drain spaghetti. Return it to the pot with 1 stick margarine. Keep heat on stove at low while stirring margarine through spaghetti. Sprinkle 1 tablespoon of the garlic Season-All salt and toss it through the pasta. Add the Parmesan cheese and broccoli, working it evenly into the spaghetti. Note: You may want to add garlic salt and cheese more or less to taste. Fresh cooked broccoli can be substituted.

Nicki Florentine, Silver Run-Union Mills Lions Club
Westminster, Maryland, USA

MARINATED BROCCOLI

3 or 4 stalks broccoli (use mostly
   top part)
1 zucchini, sliced
1 medium size head cauliflower
Fresh mushrooms (as many as
   you like)

1 medium onion, cut up
1 green pepper, cut or diced
3 medium carrots, sliced thin
1 can black olives, sliced
Celery, sliced (as much as you
   like)

Dressing:

1 c. oil
4 Tbsp. sugar
1 c. red wine vinegar
2 Tbsp. MSG seasoning

1 Tbsp. dill weed
1 Tbsp. garlic powder
1 Tbsp. salt
1 tsp. pepper (coarse)

Cut all fresh vegetables into small bit size pieces and wash well. Mix all dressing ingredients together in blender. Refrigerate dressing overnight. Pour dressing over vegetables and toss lightly to coat. Let marinate for about 2 to 4 hours before serving. Makes large bowl of salad.

BROCCOLI WITH TANGY SAUCE

2 Tbsp. mayonnaise
2 Tbsp. light cream
1 pkg. frozen broccoli, cooked

1 Tbsp. lemon juice
⅛ tsp. salt

In a small pan, combine all ingredients, except broccoli. Heat, stirring over low heat. Serve over hot broccoli.

Paula Burns, Lyman Lions Club
Lyman, Wyoming, USA

BROCCOLI DRESSING CASSEROLE

2 pkg. chopped broccoli
1 can cream of mushroom soup

1 box Stove Top dressing
Velveeta cheese

Put frozen broccoli in bottom of casserole dish. Put cream of mushroom soup on top of that. Fix Stove Top according to directions. Put on top of soup. Put slices of cheese on top. Bake at 350° for 20 to 30 minutes.

Mrs. William (Candy) McCartney, Elburn Lions Club
Elburn, Illinois, USA

BROCCOLI CASSEROLE

2 boxes broccoli, cooked in salt
   water
1 can mushroom soup
1 can celery soup

3 eggs, beaten slightly
1 c. mayonnaise
1 c. grated cheese
¼ c. butter

Mix and cover with 1½ cups cracker crumbs. Cook 40 minutes at 350°.

Even President George Bush would like this!!

Esther P. Redd, East Lake Lions Club
Birmingham, Alabama, USA

BROCCOLI CASSEROLE

1 c. celery, chopped
1 c. onion, chopped
1 stick butter or margarine
1 large pkg. broccoli
1 c. Minute rice

1 (8 oz.) Cheez Whiz
1 can cream of mushroom soup
1 small jar sliced mushrooms,
   drained

Cook broccoli in water 3 minutes. Simmer all ingredients. Add broccoli. Put in casserole dish, 9x13 inches. Bake 30 minutes at 350°.

Mrs. Rich (Doris) Hall, Elburn Lions Club
Elburn, Illinois, USA

CHEESY BROCCOLI AND RICE CASSEROLE

2 (10 oz.) pkg. frozen broccoli
1 c. Minute rice
1 can cream of mushroom soup
1 can cream of chicken soup

1 small jar Cheez Whiz
½ c. chopped onion
½ c. chopped celery

Thaw broccoli until you can break it apart. Mix all ingredients together in large casserole dish. Bake at 350° for 30 minutes, uncovered.

Toni Krueger, Onekama Lions Club
Onekama, Michigan, USA

BROCCOLI RICE CASSEROLE

1 stick butter
1 c. Minute rice
1 c. boiling water
½ c. chopped celery
8 oz. Cheez Whiz

¼ to ½ c. chopped onion
1 can mushroom soup (not
 diluted)
1 pkg. chopped broccoli, thawed

Melt butter in baking dish. Mix the Cheez Whiz with boiling water. Mix balance of ingredients together well and add Cheez Whiz mixture. Bake at 350° for 1 hour.

Katharine Dutterer (Mrs. John), Silver Run-Union Mills Lions Club
Westminster, Maryland, USA

BROCCOLI-RICE CASSEROLE

1 pkg. frozen broccoli
1 onion, chopped
1 c. celery, chopped
1 stick butter

1 can mushrooms
2 c. Minute rice
1 small jar Cheez Whiz
1 tsp. salt

Cook broccoli and drain. Saute onion and celery; combine all ingredients and mix well. Pour into greased dish. Bake at 350° for 20 to 30 minutes.

Linda Hartley, President, Lyman Lions Club
Lyman, Wyoming, USA

COMPANY'S FAVORITE SIDE DISH

1 pkg. long grain and wild rice mix,
 cooked
10 oz. broccoli, cooked
1 can sliced water chestnuts,
 drained

1 (8 oz.) jar Cheez Whiz
1 (4 oz.) can mushrooms, drained
1 can cream of mushroom soup
1 (6 oz.) pkg. onion garlic croutons
4 Tbsp. butter

Place cooked rice in bottom of casserole. Top with broccoli, mushrooms, and water chestnuts. Mix Cheez Whiz and undiluted mushroom soup; pour over. Top with croutons that have been tossed with melted butter. Bake at 350° for 30 minutes. Makes 8 to 10 servings.

To feel rich, count all the things you have that money can't buy.

BROCCOLI AND RICE CASSEROLE

1 (10 oz.) pkg. chopped frozen
broccoli
1 small jar Cheez Whiz

Rice
1 small sour cream
1 can cream of mushroom soup

Bring 1½ cups water to boil. Add 1½ cups rice. Cover. Remove from heat. Let stand for 15 minutes. Place rice in casserole dish. Bring broccoli to boil in ¼ cup water. Cook until all liquid is gone. Mix above remaining ingredients together in bowl. Add broccoli to ingredients in bowl. Mix well. Pour on top of rice. Heat in microwave or in 350° oven approximately 15 minutes or until hot.

Anne Davis, Saginaw, Texas, Lions Club
Saginaw, Texas, USA

BROCCOLI, RICE, AND CHEESE

1 can cream of mushroom soup
1 small jar Cheez Whiz
1 small pkg. frozen chopped
broccoli

½ c. chopped onions
1½ c. rice

Cook broccoli and rice to directions. Mix all ingredients. Bake at 350° for 30 minutes.

Pauline Sammons
Waldo, Arkansas, USA

BROCCOLI-CAULIFLOWER CASSEROLE

2 pkg. broccoli spears, thawed
and drained
1 pkg. cauliflower, thawed and
drained
1 can dried onion rings

1 jar sliced mushrooms, drained
1 can cream of celery soup
1 can cream of mushroom soup
1 can sliced water chestnuts
1 (8 oz.) jar Cheez Whiz

Heat soups; stir in Cheez Whiz until melted. Chop broccoli and cauliflower; place in bottom of 9x13 inch dish. Sprinkle mushrooms and water chestnuts on top. Cover with soup mixture. Top with onion rings. Bake at 350° for 30 to 45 minutes (until bubbly). Serves 10.

This is a wonderful casserole to take to any function. It always gets many compliments!

Mrs. Lion George (Dianne) Murphy, Canton Lions Club
Canton, Georgia, USA

❦

Nothing you can imagine in your mind is impossible.

BROCCOLI AND CAULIFLOWER HOT DISH

1 large pkg. frozen broccoli and
   cauliflower
1 c. instant rice (not cooked)
1 (8 oz.) jar Cheez Whiz

1 can cream of chicken soup
1 small onion, diced
½ c. milk
2 Tbsp. melted butter

Mix rice, Cheez Whiz, soup, onion, milk, and butter. Add frozen broccoli and cauliflower. Put into a sprayed 9x13 inch glass baking pan. Bake at 350° for 45 minutes.

May use other varieties of frozen packaged vegetables.

William Groskreutz, Jr., Wells Lions Club
Wells, Minnesota, USA

BROCCOLI AND CAULIFLOWER CASSEROLE
(Dan's Ozark Casserole)

1 head cauliflower, chopped
1 (16 oz.) pkg. frozen broccoli
8 oz. fresh mushrooms, chopped
   (or 2 cans stems and pieces,
   drained)
3 cloves garlic, crushed
1 can cream of mushroom soup
   (do not dilute)

1 can celery soup (do not dilute)
1 can green beans, drained
6 to 8 oz. ham, chopped or cubed
2 c. shredded Cheddar cheese
1 c. sour cream
Salt and pepper to taste
1 large onion, chopped
1 bell pepper, chopped

Mix all ingredients in a large casserole dish or pan. Save 1 cup of Cheddar cheese for topping. Bake at 350° for approximately 1 hour. Remove from oven. Sprinkle with remaining cheese and place back in oven for 10 minutes so cheese can melt. Makes 10 to 12 servings or more.

Dan Steffan, Independence Eastview Lions Club
Independence, Missouri, USA

❦

Middle age begins the day you become more interested
in how long a car will last rather than how fast it goes.

BRUSSELS SPROUTS WITH ALMONDS

Crunchy almonds and just a spritz of lemon juice dress up an autumn favorite. When shopping for Brussels sprouts, look for tightly packed heads with a bright green color. Choose smaller ones for a sweeter, more delicate flavor.

10 oz. Brussels sprouts
3 Tbsp. butter
¼ c. sliced almonds

Salt and pepper
1 tsp. lemon juice

Trim the bottom of the Brussels sprouts. Pull off any withered leaves and cut the Brussels sprouts in halves. In a pot filled with about 2 inches boiling salted water, steam the Brussels sprouts until tender, about 10 minutes. Drain.

In a frying pan, melt the butter. Add the almonds and cook until the nuts are browned, about 5 minutes. Add 1 teaspoon salt, ¼ teaspoon pepper, the lemon juice, and the Brussels sprouts; toss to coat. Taste for seasoning and add salt and pepper if needed. Makes 4 servings.

John J. Hess for Mrs. Joanne Brownell, Clarence Center Lions Club
Clarence Center, New York, USA

RALPH'S FAVORITE CABBAGE

1 head shredded cabbage
1 medium onion, diced
½ small bell pepper, diced
1 tsp. paprika
Salt and pepper to taste

1 (No. 2) can tomatoes
6 slices crisp bacon, crumbled
1 clove garlic, crushed
½ tsp. sugar
1 c. water

Combine in saucepan the cabbage, onion, bell pepper, paprika, salt, pepper, sugar, garlic, bacon, and drippings. Add water and simmer until well done. Add tomatoes and cook until thick. Serve on nest of mashed potatoes. Polish sausage can be substituted for bacon. Serves 4. For a spicier dish, use tomatoes with green chilies.

Lion Dorothy Glandon, Petrolia Lions Club
Petrolia, Texas, USA

FRIED CABBAGE

Coarsely chop or slice 1 medium head of cabbage. Place in skillet to which ½ cup of margarine has been melted. Toss and fry a few minutes.

Add:

1 c. milk
1 tsp. salt

1 tsp. sugar

Cover and steam about 20 minutes. Do not overcook. This dish has a distinct, different taste from plain boiled cabbage.

Even people who "hate" cabbage will change their minds after trying this!
Frances Cantrell, Bowie Evening Lions Club
Bowie, Texas, USA

CABBAGE AU GRATIN

White Sauce:

4 Tbsp. flour
2 c. milk
6 Tbsp. oleo

½ tsp. salt
Dash of pepper
½ c. shredded cheese

Parboil 1 medium size head cabbage, coarsely shredded, in salted water for 15 minutes. Drain well. Mix thoroughly (but gently) with White Sauce. Put in buttered baking dish. Top with buttered bread crumbs. Bake 1 hour at 300°.

White Sauce: Melt butter; add flour and other ingredients. Mix well. Add milk and cook until thick.

Donna S. Reitz, Sykesville Lions Club
Sykesville, Pennsylvania, USA

SWEET-SOUR CABBAGE

Step 1:

2 Tbsp. water
2 Tbsp. vinegar or lemon juice
½ tsp. salt

5 c. finely shredded cabbage (1¼ lb.)

Step 2: Use 4 slices bacon.

Step 3:

¼ c. packed brown sugar
2 Tbsp. flour
½ c. water
¼ c. vinegar

1 tsp. salt
1 small onion, diced
⅛ tsp. pepper

Step 1: Mix water, vinegar, and salt. Add cabbage. Cover tightly and simmer till cabbage is tender. Drain off liquid.

Step 2: Fry bacon crisp. Break in small pieces. Reserve the grease.

Step 3: Mix all ingredients. Heat till the mixture is thick. Add the bacon and grease. Combine with cabbage. Serve with sour cream (optional). This recipe can be frozen.

Louise Brooks (Mrs. Russell), Silver Run-Union Lions Club
Mt. Lake Park, Maryland, USA

Wrinkles are receipts for living.

HOT FRUITED CABBAGE

2 apples, chopped
1 onion, chopped
2 Tbsp. butter or margarine
½ medium size cabbage, chopped
1 c. water

⅓ c. brown sugar
½ c. vinegar
1 Tbsp. butter or margarine
½ tsp. salt
Pepper to taste

Saute apple and onion in butter or margarine for 10 minutes. Add cabbage and water. Cover and steam for 20 minutes. When tender, add the brown sugar and vinegar. Just before serving, add the 1 tablespoon butter or margarine, salt, and pepper. Serves 6.

RED CABBAGE AND APPLES

1 medium head red cabbage
2 medium cooking apples
1½ c. water
¼ c. vinegar (cider)

¼ c. butter
¼ c. sugar
½ tsp. salt

Shred cabbage; peel, core, and chop apples. Combine all ingredients in a 3 quart saucepan over medium heat, covered. *Simmer* for about 1 hour, stirring often. Add water if needed.

Walter E. Loomis, North Jackson Lions Club
Jackson, Michigan, USA

BAKED CARROTS

4 c. carrots, cooked and mashed
3 beaten eggs
1 c. cracker crumbs (30 two inches
   square)
1 c. milk

¼ c. grated onion
Salt and pepper
¾ c. grated sharp cheese
2 Tbsp. butter or margarine

Mix thoroughly and pour into 1¼ to 2 quart pan. Dot with butter and bake for 40 minutes. You can also use a medium butternut squash instead of carrots. Serves 6 to 8.

Rebecca Mergaert, North Jackson Lions Club
Sault Ste. Marie, Ontario, Canada

Patience is a virtue that carries a lot of "wait."

COPPER CARROTS

2 lb. carrots, peeled, sliced, and
  cooked until slightly tender,
  about 5 minutes.
1 large onion, peeled, sliced, and
  separated into rings

1 large bell pepper, chopped
1 tsp. salt

Sauce:

½ c. sugar
½ c. vinegar
1 tsp. Worcestershire sauce
¼ c. oil

1 tsp. prepared mustard
1 can tomato soup
Pepper to taste

Mix together the sauce, using a wire whisk to thoroughly mix. Pour sauce over vegetables. Marinate overnight. This is a good keeper - keeps well for at least a week in the refrigerator. Can be used as a vegetable side dish or a salad served in a lettuce cup. Makes 16 servings.

Mrs. Lion Robert (Margaret) Logan, Canton Lions Club
Canton, Georgia, USA

MY FAVORITE CARROTS
(A side dish)

4 to 5 large, raw carrots, pared and
  sliced in small julienne thin
  strips

Margarine
Dill weed
Salt and pepper

In saucepan, saute carrots in margarine until fully cooked. Add dill weed, salt, and pepper to taste.

We fight for these later, if by chance there are any left over.

Lion Sarah Wehling, Bothell Lions Club
Bothell, Washington, USA

ORANGE-GLAZED CARROTS

10 oz. pkg. frozen carrots (or
  canned)
1 Tbsp. margarine

1 Tbsp. orange marmalade
2 Tbsp. chopped pecans

Cook carrots; drain. Stir in margarine, orange marmalade, and pecans. Serves 4. I've made this recipe in large quantities using "institutional size" canned carrots for "potlucks."

Rosemary Kish, Downriver Pride Lions Club
Lincoln Park, Michigan, USA

TOM'S MARINATED CARROTS

5 c. sliced carrots, cooked and
    drained
1 large onion, chopped
1 green pepper, chopped
1 c. sugar
1 c. oil

¾ c. white vinegar
1 tsp. salt
Dash of pepper to taste
1 can condensed tomato soup (as
    is, no water)

Mix last 6 ingredients and pour over the carrots, onions, and peppers.

Thomas H. Crooks, South Lansing Lions Club
Lansing, Michigan, USA

CELERY CASSEROLE
(Out of this world)

4 c. celery, sliced
1 (10¾ oz.) can cream of chicken
    soup
½ c. milk
1 tsp. onion salt
1 tsp. curry powder

1 c. slivered almonds
1 (8½ oz.) can water chestnuts,
    chopped and drained
2 Tbsp. margarine
3 Tbsp. flour

Parboil celery until tender crisp (about 10 minutes). Combine cream of chicken soup, milk, onion salt, curry powder, almonds, and water chestnuts in bowl. Melt margarine in saucepan; sprinkle flour over it and mix with wire whisk until thick. Add to chicken soup mixture and stir until blended.

In buttered 2 quart casserole, alternate layers of celery and sauce, ending with sauce. Sprinkle bread crumbs on top. Bake in a 350° oven for 35 minutes. Yield: 8 servings.

CORN CASSEROLE

2 (16½ oz.) cans yellow cream
    style corn
2 c. (8 oz.) shredded Cheddar
    cheese
1 (4 oz.) chopped green chilies,
    drained

½ c. finely chopped onions
1 c. milk
2 large eggs
1 c. yellow corn meal
1½ tsp. garlic salt
½ tsp. baking soda

Combine first 6 ingredients in large bowl, then combine corn meal and remaining ingredients. Stir into corn mixture. Pour in lightly greased 11 x 7 x 1½ inch baking dish. Bake at 350° for 50 minutes or until knife inserted comes out clean. Makes 8 servings.

Pauline Sammons
Waldo, Arkansas, USA

CHEESY CORN CASSEROLE

1 can whole kernel corn	2 eggs
1 can creamed corn	2 c. grated Cheddar cheese
1 stick butter or margarine, melted	1 box Jiffy corn muffin mix
1 c. sour cream	

Mix together whole kernel corn, creamed corn, corn bread mix, melted butter, sour cream, eggs, and 1 cup grated cheese. Pour into a 9x13 inch casserole dish. Add another cup of cheese on top. Bake 45 minutes at 350°. Serves 8.

John Payne, Bloomington Lions Club
Bloomington, Illinois, USA

SCALLOPED CORN AND CARROT CASSEROLE

⅓ c. butter	1 c. liquid (from corn and carrots)
1 c. chopped onion	1 c. corn
2 to 4 Tbsp. flour	1 c. slightly cooked carrots
½ to 1 tsp. curry powder	1 Tbsp. butter
1 tsp. salt	1 c. bread crumbs
1 tsp. sugar	

Melt butter. Add onion and cook till tender. Add flour, curry powder, sugar, and salt; make a roux. Add liquid to make a sauce. Mix in corn and carrots. Place in ovenproof dish. Cover with bread crumbs and dab with 1 tablespoon butter. Bake, uncovered, at 375° for 30 minutes. Very good with ham and fish.

Very tasty with baked ham or bar-b-q fish. A lot of people have asked for this recipe, as I take it to a lot of potlucks.

Heather Greer, Jasper Mountain Lions Club
Jasper, Alberta, Canada

THREE CORN CASSEROLE

1 can whole kernel corn (undrained)	2 eggs, beaten
1 can cream style corn	1 box Jiffy corn bread mix
1 (8 oz.) ctn. onion soup dip (dairy section)	

Mix all ingredients well. Pour into a Pam sprayed casserole. Bake 35 to 45 minutes at 350°. Serve.

Sara Cummins, Kosciusko Lions Club
Kosciusko, Mississippi, Attala, USA

Make moments worth remembering.

VIVIAN'S CORN BAKE

1 can creamed corn
1 can whole corn kernels, drained
2 eggs, beaten

1 c. sour cream
1 pkg. Jiffy corn bread mix
½ c. margarine, melted

Mix all ingredients together and bake in 9x13 inch greased pan at 350° for 1 hour. I add ¼ cup sugar to ingredients and ¼ cup drained pimentos to above ingredients.

Ruth E. Little, Hedgesville Lions Club
Berkeley Springs, West Virginia, USA

OLD-FASHIONED CORN PUDDING

2 Tbsp. sugar
1½ Tbsp. cornstarch
1 c. milk
3 eggs
1 can cream style corn

1 Tbsp. melted butter
½ tsp. salt
Dash of nutmeg
1½ c. frozen corn

Mix together sugar and cornstarch. Add to creamed corn. Add milk gradually, stirring until smooth. Add frozen corn and mix lightly. Add eggs, butter, and salt. Mix well. Turn into a greased 1 quart baking dish. Sprinkle with nutmeg. Place baking dish in a pan of hot water. Bake at 300° for 1¾ hours or until custard sets.

Margaret Yingling (Mrs. Preston), Silver Run-Union Mills Lions Club
Westminster, Maryland, USA

FROZEN CORN

Cut 6 cups of tender sweet corn from cob.

Add:

1 c. water
1½ tsp. salt

3 Tbsp. sugar

Cook for 1 minute after it starts bubbling. Remove from heat and set pan in ice water to cool. Pack in containers and freeze. Add butter or margarine when heating for use.

PDG Lloyd E. Wright, Georgetown Lions Club
Georgetown, Ohio, USA

Whatever you are, be a good one.

BAKED EGGPLANT

1 lb. eggplant
½ lb. dried bread crumbs
1 (5 oz.) can evaporated milk
½ c. milk
¼ c. onions, chopped
¼ c. celery, chopped
¼ c. green pepper, chopped

¼ c. margarine
1 tsp. salt
½ tsp. sage
½ tsp. pepper
1 Tbsp. pimento
2 eggs
1 c. grated cheese (any kind)

Peel and cut eggplant into 1 inch pieces. Soak in salted water 6 hours. Drain, cover with water, and simmer until tender.

Meanwhile, soak bread crumbs in combined milk. Saute onions, bell peppers, and celery in ¼ cup margarine until tender. Combine drained eggplant, soaked bread crumbs, onions, green peppers, celery, salt, pepper, sage, pimento, and slightly beaten eggs. Pour into greased oblong baking dish. Sprinkle top with cheese. Heat in oven for 15 to 20 minutes at 350°. Do not brown cheese. Serves 6.

GREEN BEAN SCANDIA

1 (No. 2) can cut green beans
1 Tbsp. chicken broth base
2 Tbsp. oleo
1½ Tbsp. vinegar
1½ Tbsp. water
1 Tbsp. sugar

½ tsp. whole dill seed
Dash of pepper
1 Tbsp. cornstarch
1 Tbsp. cold water
2 c. packed, chopped cabbage

Drain liquid from beans. Add next 7 ingredients and bring to boiling, stirring. Stir cornstarch mixed with water. Cook and stir until mixture thickens and is clear (about 5 minutes). Add cabbage and heat to boiling! Simmer, covered, for 35 minutes (do not boil). Drain green beans. Add to mixture and serve at once.

I run the vacuum cleaner often ... not to clean, but to drown out the kids.

GREEN BEANS WITH LIME AND DILL

Dill's distinctive flavor adds a lively touch to green beans. Be sure to mix in the lime juice and butter just before serving, so the acid in the juice doesn't fade the bright green color of the beans.

1 lb. green beans	2 Tbsp. butter
Salt and pepper	2 tsp. chopped fresh dill
1 lime	

Trim the green beans. In a pot of about 2 inches boiling salted water, steam the green beans until tender, about 10 minutes.

Meanwhile, grate 1 teaspoon of the green zest from the lime and squeeze 1 tablespoon juice. In a large frying pan, melt the butter. Add the green beans and ½ teaspoon salt; toss until the beans are heated through. Stir in the lime zest and juice; sprinkle with the chopped dill. Taste the beans for seasoning and add salt and pepper if needed. Makes 4 servings.

John J. Hess for Mrs. Joanne Brownell, Clarence Center Lions Club
Clarence Center, New York, USA

LIMAS BAKED IN SOUR CREAM

1 lb. dried limas	1 Tbsp. dry mustard
¾ c. brown sugar	1 Tbsp. Karo syrup (light or dark)
½ c. butter	½ pt. sour cream
2 tsp. salt	

Soak beans overnight; drain and cook until almost tender in salt water. Drain and rinse. Place in casserole and add remaining ingredients. Mix well. Bake at 300° for 2 hours. May substitute margarine for butter and plain yogurt for sour cream.

Betty Groft (Mrs. Cyril), Silver Run-Union Mills Lions Club
Westminster, Maryland, USA

BAKED LIMA BEANS

3 cans Seaside lima beans, slightly drained	½ c. chili sauce
2 handfuls brown sugar	Salt/pepper to taste

Mix the above ingredients together. Place in a baking dish. Lay bacon strips over top. Bake at 325° for approximately 2 hours. Note: Make sure you do not overbake them, or they will be too dry.

Eileen Peck, Rootstown Lions Club
Rootstown Township, Rootstown, Ohio, USA

❦

Delight in the moment!

VIDALIA ONION CASSEROLE

5 *large* Vidalia onions
2 sticks butter or margarine

24 Ritz crackers, crumbled
Parmesan cheese

Peel onions and slice into thin rings. Saute onions in butter for 15 to 20 minutes, until clear. Put half of onions into a casserole. Top with half of the crumbs and sprinkle with cheese. Repeat layers, ending with cheese. Bake, uncovered, in 325° oven about 30 minutes. To dress up casserole, top with canned French fried onion rings at the last moment.

Estelle C. Turner, Riverdale Lions Club
Riverdale, Georgia, USA

SAUTEED PEPPERS

This vivid combination of garlicky peppers gets a spark of heat from fresh jalapeno. Add more or leave it out, according to your taste.

2 cloves garlic
1 onion
2 green peppers
1 red pepper

3 Tbsp. oil
Salt and pepper
2 tsp. minced jalapeno pepper

Mince garlic. Cut the onion into quarters. Slice peppers. In a large frying pan, heat oil over medium-low heat. Add onion. Cook, stirring occasionally, until tender, 8 to 10 minutes. Stir in the garlic, peppers, and 1 teaspoon salt. Cover and cook 5 minutes. Stir in ¼ teaspoon pepper and the minced jalapeno. Cover and continue cooking until peppers are tender, 3 to 5 minutes. Taste for seasoning and add salt and pepper if needed. Makes 4 servings.

John J. Hess for Mrs. Joanne Brownell, Clarence Center Lions Club
Clarence Center, New York, USA

MAKE AHEAD POTATOES

12 large potatoes
1 tsp. onion powder
Salt to suit taste
Paprika

8 oz. cream cheese
8 oz. sour cream
¼ c. melted butter or oleo

Boil potatoes until done; drain water. Combine potatoes, cream cheese, and sour cream; mash and whip until fluffy. Add a small amount of water, if needed, and the onion powder. Mix well. Spread in 9x13 inch pan and refrigerate or freeze until needed.

When ready to use, drizzle oleo over top and sprinkle with paprika. Bake at 350° for 1 hour. Bake, uncovered, for the last 15 minutes.

POTATO STUFFING

3 lb. cooked white potatoes
3 Tbsp. butter
½ stalk celery, diced
½ c. tomato sauce
¼ tsp. thyme
3 to 4 Tbsp. brown sugar
¼ c. raisins
1 hot pepper, minced

6 Tbsp. oil
2 medium onions, chopped
¼ sweet pepper, minced
    (medium)
2 tsp. chopped parsley
Dash of black pepper
¼ c. milk
4 eggs

Mash potatoes. Heat oil and butter in a frying pan on low heat. Be careful not to burn them. Add onions, celery, and sweet pepper; cook over low flame until tender. Add tomato sauce, parsley, thyme, black pepper, and brown sugar. Cook for 5 minutes. Add seasoning (sauce mixture) to mashed potatoes and mix thoroughly. Add milk, raisins, eggs, and hot pepper. Mix well. Bake in greased, shallow baking dish at 325° for about 1 hour. Serve hot with any main course you desire.

Mrs. Inger E. Francis, Charlotte Amalie Lions Club
St. Thomas, U.S. Virgin Islands

CHIPPED POTATOES

4 potatoes (unpeeled)
1 Tbsp. onion, grated
⅛ tsp. salt
1 Tbsp. parsley

½ tsp. thyme
1½ c. Cheddar cheese, grated
¼ c. margarine

Scrub potatoes, but do not peel. Microwave potatoes on HIGH 14 minutes. Cool, then slice into microwave dish. Add onions. Brush potatoes with melted margarine. Add salt, parsley, and thyme. Put cheese over all and microwave on HIGH 2 minutes till cheese is melted. Serves 4 to 6.

1. *Keep your temper - no one wants it.*

2. *Each day is worth living if you take time to love, laugh, and pray.*
Margaret A. Dutterer (Mrs. Alvin), Silver Run-Union Mills Lions Club
Westminster, Maryland, USA

POTATOES AND GREEN CHILIES

6 potatoes
1 pt. sour cream
1 large or small can green chilies

½ lb. Monterey Jack cheese,
    broken in pieces
Salt and pepper

Boil potatoes in jackets and slice thin. Mix with remaining ingredients and place in casserole. Bake at 350° for 45 minutes.

CRUNCH-TOP POTATOES

⅓ c. butter
4 large potatoes
¾ c. crushed corn flakes

1½ c. shredded Cheddar cheese
2 tsp. salt
1½ tsp. paprika

Melt butter in large pan. Add single layer of sliced ½ inch potatoes. Turn once in butter. Mix remaining ingredients and sprinkle over. Bake for 45 minutes or until done and tops are crisp.

MASHED POTATO CASSEROLE

Mashed potatoes
Cabbage
Onions
Celery

Cheese (any kind)
Salt and pepper
Paprika

Use your own imagination as to how much of each you like.

Mash potatoes. Fry cabbage, onions, and celery. Add salt, pepper, and paprika. Mix everything together. Cover with cheese. Bake at 350° for ½ hour. Serve with ham or any kind of meat you like.

You can use vinegar for scratches on furniture.
Grace Balliet (William E. Balliet), Gouldsboro Lions Club
Gouldsboro, Pennsylvania, USA

REFRIGERATED MASHED POTATOES

5 lb. potatoes, pared and
   quartered
2 (3 oz.) pkg. cream cheese
1 c. dairy sour cream

2 tsp. onion salt
1 tsp. pepper
2 Tbsp. butter
1 Tbsp. chives (optional)

Cook potatoes in boiling water until tender; drain well. Mash until smooth. Add cream cheese, sour cream, onion salt, salt, pepper, and butter. Beat with potato masher until smooth and fluffy. Place in refrigerator container. Cool, then cover. Recommended storage time is 2 weeks. Place desired amount of potatoes in greased casserole. Dot with butter and microwave until heated through. If using full amount, heat in 2 quart casserole. Makes 8 cups.

A make ahead recipe that makes potatoes taste like a million. This can be doubled for a large group.

❧

Life is meant to be lived.

POTATO LOAF

5 lb. potatoes, peeled, cooked,
  and diced
3 Tbsp. flour

1 medium onion, diced
1 stick butter or margarine, melted
Salt and pepper to taste

Cook potatoes until tender, but firm. Drain and coat with flour. Add onion, salt, and pepper. Pour melted butter or margarine over and toss to coat. Pack into loaf pan and press down firmly. Bake 1½ to 2 hours or until golden brown. Loosen with knife and turn out on platter.

Lion Ada Ahrens, Royalton Hills Lions Club
North Royalton, Ohio, USA

TWICE BAKED POTATOES

10 large baking potatoes
1 lb. butter
1 c. milk
1 tsp. Cajun seasoning

1 tsp. salt
1 tsp. black pepper
Slices of American cheese

Bake potatoes at 350° for 1 hour and 20 minutes, then cool. Cut potatoes in halves and scoop out center, leaving shells. In bowl, mix potato mixture, butter, milk, Cajun seasoning, salt, and pepper. Fill potato shells with this mixture. Place on sheet pan. Heat at 350° for 25 minutes, then cover each with ⅓ slice of cheese. Heat for 10 minutes, then serve. Leftovers can be frozen and reheated in a microwave up to 3 weeks.

Pat Lamb, Moweaqua Lions Club
Moweaqua, Illinois, USA

STUFFED BAKED POTATOES

4 (6 oz.) baked potatoes
2 Tbsp. butter or margarine
¾ c. milk
1 egg, slightly beaten

Salt and pepper to taste
½ c. shredded Cheddar cheese
Paprika

Allow potatoes to stand at room temperature 2 to 3 minutes after baking. Cut a thin slice from the top of each potato. Caution: Potato will be hot. With a spoon, remove the potato pulp from each potato, leaving a thin shell. Mash potato pulp with a fork or potato masher.

Add butter, milk, egg, salt, pepper, and cheese. Whip potato mixture with a rotary beater or electric mixer until light and fluffy. Spoon mixture into shells and sprinkle with paprika. Heat potatoes, uncovered, on FULL power for 5 minutes.

If desired, after cooking in microwave oven, potatoes may be placed under the broiler unit of a conventional oven to brown for a few minutes. Be sure to use a broilerproof dish.

Lee Seybold, Moweaqua Lions Club
Moweaqua, Illinois, USA

CHEESY POTATOES

6 potatoes, pared and cut into thin slices
3 Tbsp. butter or margarine
⅓ c. sliced onion
3 Tbsp. flour
1 c. milk
½ c. heavy cream

2 tsp. Dijon mustard
¼ tsp. salt
⅛ tsp. ground pepper
Dash of nutmeg
1 c. shredded Gruyere cheese, divided

Grease a 1½ quart shallow baking dish. Cook potatoes in boiling salted water for 7 to 10 minutes. Meanwhile, preheat oven to 350°. In another medium saucepan, melt butter over medium heat. Add sliced onion; cook, stirring, 4 minutes or until soft. Add flour and cook 1 minute, stirring constantly. Gradually add milk, cream, mustard, salt, pepper, and nutmeg. Cook, stirring constantly, until slightly thickened. Remove from heat. Stir in ⅔ cup of the cheese until melted. Drain potatoes well. Layer potatoes in baking dish. Pour cheese mixture over potatoes. Sprinkle with the remaining ⅓ cup cheese. Bake for 20 minutes, then place under broiler and broil for 2 minutes, or until lightly browned. The type of cheese used is personal preference. Sharp Cheddar is excellent.

Eunice Murphy, Carver (33-S) Lions Club
Carver, Massachusetts, USA

HASH BROWN POTATO DISH

2 lb. frozen hash brown potatoes
½ c. melted oleo
1 tsp. salt
¼ tsp. pepper

½ c. chopped onions
1 c. sour cream
2 c. grated Cheddar cheese
1 c. cream of chicken soup

Mix all together. Pour into 9x13 inch pan with Pam. Top with 2 cups crushed corn flakes and ¼ cup melted oleo. You can put in smaller pans and freeze one.

THOSE POTATOES

1 bag frozen hash browns
1 large onion, chopped
2 cans cream of mushroom soup

1 (16 oz.) container sour cream
2 c. grated Cheddar cheese
1 c. corn flakes

Saute onion in oil or butter. Add potatoes, soup, and sour cream. Put in large cake pan. Sprinkle top with cheese. Bake at 350° until very light golden. Sprinkle top with corn flakes. Continue baking until bubbly and golden brown.

Coni Phelps, Lyman Lions Club
Lyman, Wyoming, USA

❦

Desire change and you will welcome risk.

HASH BROWN POTATO CASSEROLE

1 (2 lb.) bag frozen hash brown
   potatoes, thawed
2 c. shredded Cheddar cheese
1 pt. sour cream
2 Tbsp. chopped green onion

1 can cream of celery soup
½ c. melted butter
1¼ c. crushed corn flakes or
   potato chips

Mash hash browns, cheese, sour cream, chopped onion, and soup. Melt margarine or butter. Put ½ in potato mix and the other ½ in the corn flakes; toss. Sprinkle corn flake mix on top of potato mixture. Bake 1 hour at 350°. Serves 12.

May be frozen. Use 9x13 inch pan or a 3 quart casserole for baking. Rich and delicious.

Vivian M. Turner, Ponderosa Lions Club
Prather, California, Fresno County, USA

GRATER TATER CASSEROLE

2 lb. frozen hash browns, thawed
1 can cream of potato soup
1 can celery soup
1 c. sour cream

½ c. chopped onion
1 can mushrooms
1 c. grated cheese

Combine potatoes, soup, sour cream, onion, mushrooms, and ½ of cheese. Pour into buttered 9x13 inch baking dish. Top with remaining cheese. Bake for 1 hour at 350°.

Rexie Martin, Rock Hill Lions Club
Rock Hill, South Carolina, USA

ITALIAN POTATO CASSEROLE

Peel and slice 6 potatoes; put in bottom of pan (9x13 inches). Mix 1 can Cheddar cheese soup and ½ soup can water. Pour over potatoes. Brown hamburger with onion and 1 taco seasoning. Add it to pan. Mix 1 can Italian tomato soup and ½ can water. Pour on top. Pat pepperoni on top (optional). Sprinkle with sage, salt, and pepper. Bake until potatoes are done (1 to 1½ hours). Top with Cheddar cheese. Return to oven until cheese is melted.

Elaine Dahlke, Brownton Lions Club
Brownton, Minnesota, USA

Go where there is no path and leave a trail.

POTATO CASSEROLE

1 (32 oz.) pkg. frozen hash brown
   potatoes, thawed
1 can cream of chicken soup
1 (8 oz.) ctn. sour cream

2 Tbsp. onion flakes or 1 small
   chopped onion
12 oz. grated sharp cheese
1 tsp. salt

Mix together all ingredients and pour into 9x12 inch casserole which has been lightly greased. Crush 2 cups corn flakes and mix with ½ cup melted butter. (I sometimes use potato chip crumbs without additional butter.) Crumble this over the potato mixture. Bake at 350° for 30 minutes covered, then bake 15 minutes uncovered. Yield: 10 to 12 servings.

Mrs. Lion Robert (Margaret) Logan, Canton Lions Club
Canton, Georgia, USA

POTATO CASSEROLE

1 large bag hash browns (frozen)
8 oz. sour cream
2 cans potato soup

8 oz. sharp cheese, grated
½ tsp. garlic salt
½ c. Parmesan cheese

Layer hash browns in buttered casserole. Mix sour cream, potato soup, grated cheese, and garlic salt. Pour over potatoes and sprinkle with Parmesan cheese. Dot with butter and bake 1 hour at 350°.

Mrs. Tom Raad (Jamie), Rock Hill Lions Club
Rock Hill, South Carolina, USA

GOURMET POTATOES

6 medium size potatoes
2 c. shredded Cheddar cheese
¼ c. butter
1½ c. sour cream
⅓ c. chopped onions

1 tsp. salt
¼ tsp. pepper
2 Tbsp. butter
Paprika

Cook potatoes in skins. Cool. Peel and shred coarsely. In a saucepan over low heat, combine cheese and ¼ cup butter. Stir until almost melted. Remove from heat and blend in sour cream, onion, salt, and pepper. Fold in potatoes and put in a greased casserole. Top with butter and paprika. Bake at 350° for 30 minutes.

This has been a family favorite, especially when served with brisket. It also goes well with pork.

Norma M. Klein, Emporia Noon Lions Club
Emporia, Kansas, USA

❧

Each day comes just once in a lifetime.

HOLIDAY POTATO DISH

4 lb. frozen hash browns
1 c. chopped onion
1 c. chopped celery
¼ c. butter
1 can cream of mushroom or
  cream of chicken soup

1 pt. sour cream
1½ c. shredded Cheddar cheese
½ c. crushed corn flakes or
  crackers
3 Tbsp. melted butter

Cut up potatoes. Saute onion and celery in ¼ cup butter. Remove from heat. Stir in soup and sour cream. Mix together potatoes and cheese; place in greased 9x13 inch pan. Pour soup mixture over all and mix well. Cover and refrigerate overnight. (Do not cover with aluminum foil.)

Next day, sprinkle with corn flake or cracker crumbs; drizzle with 3 table-spoons melted butter. Bake at 350° for 1 hour. Makes 12 servings.

CHEESY SCALLOPED POTATOES

½ lb. Cheddar cheese
¼ c. butter or margarine
4 Tbsp. flour
2 c. milk

1 tsp. salt
½ tsp. pepper
2 small yellow onions
5 medium potatoes (or more)

Preheat oven to 350°F. Shred cheese. In 2 quart saucepan, melt butter over low heat. Blend in flour. Add milk all at once. Cook, stirring constantly, until thickened. Add shredded cheese, salt, and pepper. Continue stirring and cooking until cheese melts. Remove from heat. Spread ½ cheese sauce in bottom of shallow 2½ quart baking dish. Slice potatoes and onions. Arrange over cheese sauce layer. Top with remaining cheese sauce, spreading evenly. Bake at 350°F. for 1 hour or until potatoes are done. Makes 6 to 8 servings.

This dish is a big hit at the Lions meetings steak dinners. Dave is Lion Tamer and fills in as Chef.

Lion Dave Shabino, Rootstown Lions Club
Rootstown Township, Rootstown, Ohio, USA

Occupy a small place in a great way.

POTATOES ELEGANTE

9 medium potatoes
¼ c. butter
1 can cream of chicken soup
⅓ c. diced onions

1 pt. sour cream
1½ c. Cheddar cheese, grated
4 Tbsp. crushed corn flakes
4 Tbsp. melted butter

Cook potatoes with skins on until almost done. Cool. Peel and grate potatoes. Heat ¼ cup butter in cream of chicken soup. Blend in sour cream, onions, and cheese in soup mixture. Stir in grated potatoes. Place in buttered casserole. Mix 4 tablespoons crushed corn flakes with 4 tablespoons melted butter. Sprinkle over casserole. Bake 45 minutes at 350°. Serves 6 to 8.

Richard T. Hoffler, Lower Allen Lions Club
Mechanicsburg, Pennsylvania, USA

SPANISH RICE

1 tsp. cooking oil
1 c. rice (regular, not instant)
¼ onion, diced
2 or 3 garlic cloves, mashed

3 slices bell pepper
1 or 2 beef bouillon cubes
3 c. water

Brown the rice in the oil. Dissolve the bouillon cube in 1 cup of the water. Add the rest of the ingredients and cook, covered, 15 minutes.

Janie Fox, Saginaw, Texas, Lions Club
Saginaw, Texas, USA

BAKED RICE

1 c. Uncle Ben's converted rice
1 can Campbell's French onion
  soup

1 can Campbell's beef consomme
  soup
½ stick margarine

Combine all ingredients in casserole dish with top. Bake at 350° for 1 hour. Stir and serve.

Lioness Phyllis Club, Lawrenceville Lioness Club
Lawrenceville, Virginia, USA

❦

Few people are fast enough to keep up with their good intentions.

SPINACH BUREK FROM YUGOSLAVIA

1 (10 oz.) pkg. frozen spinach
⅔ c. finely minced white or yellow onion
2 Tbsp. finely minced parsley
4 Tbsp. butter
2 tsp. dried dill

1 c. Feta cheese, crumbled
1 c. small curd cottage cheese
2 eggs, lightly beaten
1 pkg. filo leaves
¼ lb. unsalted butter (to brush on filo leaves)

One pound of Feta will make 10 to 12 of the pastry wrapped "sausages." Unfold 2 filo leaves. Cover the remaining filo with damp towel. Lay the 2 sheets vertically (short side facing you) on wax paper or dry towel. Lay one sheet directly on top of the other. Use a pastry brush. Quickly spread butter on entire surface. Brush from edges to center. Mix spinach, cheeses, onion, parsley, dill, and eggs together. Spread ⅓ cup of filling in a line along the edge toward you, leaving 1 inch at the bottom and both sides. Lift up towel or waxed paper to begin filo roll. After 1 roll, stop and fold in 1 inch margins, brushing them with butter. Continue rolling by lifting towel or paper until burek is completely rolled. Place burek seam side down on lightly greased baking sheet. Slash burek diagonally on surface, 3 inches apart. Brush liberally with butter and sprinkle sparingly with water. Bake at 375° for 15 to 20 minutes or until golden brown. Cut along slashes and serve sizzling hot.

Funny how people don't have time to do it right, but they find time to do it over.

Mary Kathleen Meeker, Ponderosa Lions Club
Auberry, California, USA

SPINACH SQUARES

2 Tbsp. butter or margarine
3 eggs
1 c. unsifted flour
1 tsp. salt
1 tsp. baking powder
1 c. milk

1 lb. shredded Cheddar cheese
2 (10 oz.) pkg. frozen chopped spinach, thawed and thoroughly drained by squeezing in hands
Paprika

Preheat oven to 350°. Melt butter in a 9x13 inch pan as the oven preheats. When melted, remove from oven and tilt the pan to thoroughly coat the bottom. Let stand at room temperature as you prepare the following.

In a large bowl, beat eggs thoroughly. Add flour, salt, and baking powder. Mix well. Thoroughly mix in milk, cheese, and spinach. Spread mixture evenly in the buttered dish. Sprinkle with paprika.

Bake for about 30 minutes, or until slightly browned on top and knife inserted comes out clean. Remove from oven. Let stand at room temperature for about 30 minutes. Cut into 1 inch squares.

Can be frozen, defrosted, and reheated in a moderate oven.

SUMMER SQUASH CASSEROLE

2 lb. or 6 c. summer squash, sliced
¼ c. onion, chopped
1 c. condensed cream soup
½ c. butter, melted

1 c. dairy sour cream
1 c. shredded carrots
1 (8 oz.) pkg. herb seasoned
    stuffing mix

In pan, cook sliced squash and chopped onion in boiling salted water; drain. Combine stuffing mix and butter. Spread half of stuffing mixture in bottom of 12 x 7½ x 2 inch baking dish. Combine balance ingredients with squash and spoon on top of stuffing mixture. Sprinkle remaining stuffing mixture over vegetables. Bake in a 350° oven for 25 to 30 minutes or until heated through.

Katharine Dutterer (Mrs. John), Silver Run-Union Mills Lions Club
Westminster, Maryland, USA

SPINACH STRUDEL

2 (10 oz.) pkg. frozen spinach,
    thawed and drained
    thoroughly
6 slices bacon
1 medium onion, chopped (about
    ½ c.)
1 large clove garlic, finely
    chopped
1 (8 oz.) can water chestnuts,
    drained and chopped

1 Tbsp. lemon juice
1 tsp. salt
½ tsp. prepared horseradish
6 frozen phyllo (thin frozen pastry)
    sheets, thawed
¼ c. margarine, melted
1 tsp. sesame seeds

Fry bacon in 10 inch skillet until crisp. Remove from skillet and drain; crumble and reserve. Pour off all but 1 tablespoon bacon drippings. Cook and stir onion and garlic in drippings, until onion is tender, about 5 minutes. Stir reserved bacon, water chestnuts, lemon juice, salt, and horseradish into onion mixture. Mix with spinach.

Unfold phyllo sheets; carefully separate 1 phyllo sheet and place on un-greased cookie sheet. Cover remaining sheets with damp towel to prevent them from drying out. Brush phyllo sheets with margarine. Layer remaining sheets, brushing each sheet with margarine. Spread spinach mixture within 2 inches of edge; fold 2 inch edges on long sides over filling. Roll up, beginning at a narrow end. Move to center of cookie sheet, placing seam side down. Brush margarine; sprinkle with sesame seeds. Bake in a 375° oven until light brown, about 45 minutes. Cut into 1 inch slices. Yields 6 servings.

Lion Nora Gauer, Rootstown Lions Club
Rootstown, Ohio, USA

❦

Create tomorrow's memories today.

SQUASH CASSEROLE

1 onion, chopped
1 bell pepper, chopped
3 c. cooked yellow squash
1 stick butter or oleo
1/8 tsp. cinnamon (or a little less)

1 (10¾ oz.) can mushroom soup
4 eggs, beaten
1/3 box Waverly wafers, crushed
  (no substitute)
Salt and pepper to taste

Saute onion and bell pepper in butter. Combine all ingredients, except crackers. Pour in a greased casserole dish. Cover with the crushed crackers. Dot with butter. Bake at 350°F. for 25 minutes. Serves 8 to 10.

Mrs. Charlotte M. Garner, Pascagoula Evening Lions Club
Pascagoula, Mississippi, USA

SWEET POTATOES

1 large can sweet potatoes
Apples (2 or 3)
1 c. brown sugar
3 Tbsp. maple syrup
2 tsp. lemon juice

½ tsp. cinnamon
¼ tsp. ginger
3 Tbsp. butter
¼ c. apple cider

Peel and cut apples ¼ inch thick. In a small saucepan, melt your butter, apple cider, and syrup. Add sugar, lemon juice, cinnamon, and ginger. Bring to a boil. Lower heat and let mixture cook at a slow boil for 10 minutes. Arrange sweet potatoes and apples in a 2 quart casserole. Pour sauce over all. Bake at 325° for 25 to 30 minutes or until apples are tender. Baste several times while baking. Note: Baking may take longer, depending on the variety of apple used.

Mary Bankert (Mrs. Harvey), Silver Run-Union Mills Lions Club
Westminster, Maryland, USA

PINEAPPLE BOURBON SWEET POTATOES

3 (1 lb. 2 oz.) cans sweet potatoes
1 (1 lb. 4 oz.) can crushed
  pineapple
1 c. brown sugar

1/3 c. bourbon
½ c. butter
½ tsp. vanilla extract
2½ c. miniature marshmallows

Drain liquid off sweet potatoes and pour into a 2½ quart baking dish. Mash sweet potatoes. Add drained pineapple, brown sugar, bourbon, butter, and vanilla. Mix until well blended. Heat mixture in baking dish in microwave, stirring frequently. Once mixture is thoroughly heated, sprinkle a layer of miniature marshmallows over the top. Bake in preheated 350° oven, uncovered, until marshmallows are golden brown, about 30 minutes. Serves 8.

Believe you can and you're halfway there.

SWEET POTATOES WITH PECANS

4 large sweet potatoes
½ stick (¼ c.) butter or margarine, softened
¾ c. sugar
⅛ tsp. salt
¼ c. Jack Daniels whiskey
½ c. pecans, coarsely chopped

Place the sweet potatoes in a large saucepan and add enough water to cover completely. Bring the water to a boil, cover, and cook the potatoes until tender, about 35 minutes. Drain.

When the potatoes are cool enough to handle, peel off the skins. Place the potatoes in a mixing bowl and mash with the butter or margarine. Beat in the sugar, salt, and Jack Daniels.

Spread half the potato mixture in a greased 1½ quart round casserole and sprinkle with half the pecans. Repeat layers. Bake the casserole in a 325° oven until hot and the pecans turn light brown, about 30 minutes. Yield: 6 to 8 servings. Yams make this casserole even richer.

Ann Cude, Huffman Lions Club
Huffman, Texas, USA

SWEET POTATO CASSEROLE

4 lb. sweet potatoes (unpeeled)
6 medium bananas (about 2½ lb.)
¼ c. orange juice
2 tsp. Grand Marnier (orange liqueur)
½ c. firmly packed brown sugar, divided
½ tsp. ground cinnamon
Dash of salt
¼ c. unsalted butter, divided

Cook sweet potatoes in boiling water to cover 30 to 35 minutes or until tender; drain and let cool slightly. Peel and cut crosswise into ¼ inch slices; set aside. Slice bananas into ¼ inch slices. Combine orange juice, Grand Marnier, ¼ cup brown sugar, cinnamon, and salt in a large bowl; stir well. Add banana slices, tossing gently to coat.

Arrange ⅓ of sweet potato slices in a lightly greased 3 quart casserole; top with half of banana slices. Sprinkle with 1 tablespoon brown sugar; dot with 2 tablespoons butter. Repeat layers once, ending with sweet potato slices. Sprinkle with remaining 2 tablespoons brown sugar; dot with remaining 2 tablespoons butter. Bake at 375° for 45 minutes or until bubbly. Yield: 12 servings.

Ed Hohmann, Huffman Lions Club
Huffman, Texas, USA

❦

Tomorrow belongs to those who fully use today.

SWEET POTATO CASSEROLE

3 c. cooked mashed sweet
    potatoes
1 c. sugar
2 eggs

½ c. margarine
1 tsp. vanilla
1 small can crushed pineapple

Topping:

1 c. brown sugar
⅓ c. flour

⅓ c. melted butter or margarine
1 c. nuts

Preheat oven to 350°. Mix together potatoes, sugar, eggs, margarine, pineapple (do not drain), and vanilla. Pour into a buttered baking dish. Mix flour and sugar; add chopped nuts. Pour in melted margarine. Mix together and pour over potatoes. Bake for 30 minutes at 350°.

Lioness Sue P. Wright, Lawrenceville Lioness Club
Lawrenceville, Virginia, USA

SWEET POTATO CASSEROLE

1 large can sweet potatoes
½ c. milk
2 Tbsp. butter
1 tsp. vanilla
1 Tbsp. sugar

Salt
1 c. brown sugar
⅓ c. flour
1 c. chopped pecans or walnuts
⅓ stick margarine

Beat first 6 ingredients together. Spread in 9x13 inch casserole dish. Mix remaining 4 items together and spread on top of potatoes. Bake at 300° for 45 minutes.

Lion Mike Bradley, Rootstown Lions Club
Rootstown, Ohio, USA

SWEET POTATO CASSEROLE

3 c. sweet potatoes
2 Tbsp. butter
½ c. cream
½ c. brown sugar

1 egg, beaten
1 tsp. salt
1 c. small marshmallows
½ c. chopped pecans

Cook potatoes with jackets on; peel and mash. Add butter, cream, brown sugar, egg, and salt; mix well. Add nuts and put in greased 1 quart baking dish and top with marshmallows. Bake in 350° oven for 35 minutes or until golden brown.

PDG Lloyd E. Wright, Georgetown Lions Club
Georgetown, Ohio, USA

If we all did the things we are capable of, we would astound ourselves.

SWEET POTATO CASSEROLE

2½ c. cooked sweet potatoes, mashed
1 stick softened margarine
1 c. Pet milk

¾ c. sugar
2 eggs, beaten
1 tsp. vanilla
Dash of cinnamon

Topping:

1 stick margarine
1 c. brown sugar

½ c. self-rising flour
1 c. chopped pecans

Mix all ingredients well. Pour into casserole dish. Bake at 350° for 30 minutes. Add topping; bake 15 minutes longer.

For topping, mix margarine, sugar, and flour. Cook over low heat until thick. (If too thick, add a little milk.) Pour over potatoes and sprinkle pecans over top.

Kathy Parker, Rock Hill Lions Club
Rock Hill, South Carolina, USA

YAM-YAM SWEET POTATOES

3 c. sweet potatoes, mashed
½ c. butter
2 eggs

1 c. sugar
1 Tbsp. vanilla

Topping:

1 c. brown sugar, packed
⅓ c. flour

1 c. chopped nuts
⅓ c. butter

Mix and pour in buttered casserole dish. To prepare topping, mix all ingredients with fork until crumbly. Sprinkle on top of potatoes. Bake at 350° for 20 minutes.

Phyllis Hillis, McMinnville Lions Club
McMinnville, Tennessee, USA

FRIED GREEN TOMATOES

Have on hand 4 large green tomatoes. Remove stem end and cut into thick slices. Dip one slice at a time into milk, then into corn meal. Fry in ½ inch deep hot oil over medium heat until golden brown on each side. Blot on paper towel, salt lightly, and enjoy!

This is from a Lone Star Gas Co. recipe pamphlet from 1948. These are very good for a change from the same old vegetables.

Frances Cantrell, Bowie Evening Lions Club
Bowie, Texas, USA

Dare to dream great dreams.

SCALLOPED TOMATO AND ARTICHOKES

1 (28 oz.) can plum tomatoes
1 (14 oz.) can artichoke hearts (or
  1 pkg. frozen, prepared and
    drained)
⅛ lb. butter (½ stick)

2 Tbsp. chopped shallots
½ tsp. basil
⅓ c. finely chopped onion
2 Tbsp. sugar (optional)
Salt and pepper to taste

Pierce tomatoes and drain well. Prepare artichoke hearts. Saute onion and shallot in butter. Add all ingredients, tossing carefully. Turn into greased casserole dish. Bake 15 minutes at 325°F. If prepared ahead and chilled as I do, double baking time. Whole button sauteed mushrooms are a nice addition to this dish.

Expensive, but so impressive and well liked by all.

Vivian Quinlan, Mathews Lions Club
Mathews, Virginia, USA

MACARONI AND TOMATOES

1½ c. macaroni or egg noodles
1 (No. 2) can chopped tomatoes

½ pt. whipping cream
Salt and pepper to taste

Cook macaroni until done. Pour off water. Add tomatoes with juice and cream. Bring to a boil. Ready to serve.

Lots of calories, but very good.

Roger Gage, Decatur Lions Club
Decatur, Texas, USA

STUFFED TOMATOES

¼ c. orzo*
4 medium tomatoes
1 onion
¼ c. grated Parmesan
½ tsp. salt
2 Tbsp. oil

1 clove garlic
½ tsp. oregano
½ c. shredded Mozzarella
¼ c. chopped parsley (fresh)
¼ tsp. sugar
¼ tsp. pepper (white)

Boil orzo until tender (8 to 10 minutes). Slice off top of tomatoes. Scoop out pulp; chop and drain. Set shells aside. Heat oil and saute onion and garlic. Add oregano. Remove from heat and combine all ingredients, except shells. Stuff shell with mixture and place in cake pan or casserole. Cover and bake at 375° for 12 to 15 minutes. Uncover and bake for about 5 more minutes or until brown.

This is a great dish, even house husbands can make it.

* Bulgur wheat or rice can be substituted.

Walter E. Loomis, North Jackson Lions Club
Jackson, Michigan, USA

HOLIDAY YAM CASSEROLE

5 or 6 medium uncooked yams or
    sweet potatoes
¾ c. white sugar
½ c. brown sugar
¼ c. dark syrup
¾ c. butter or margarine
2 or 3 tsp. cinnamon
2 tsp. nutmeg

Pinch of ginger
½ c. orange juice
¼ c. pineapple juice or crushed
    pineapple
Slivered nuts (pecans or walnuts
    as desired or tiny
    marshmallows)

Heat oven to 300° to 350°. Boil uncooked potatoes until tender. Melt butter and stir in both kinds of white and brown sugars and condiments. Add liquid or orange and pineapple juices or crushed pineapple to preceding mixture. Set aside the preceding ingredients until later.

Lightly grease the casserole dish with margarine or butter. Slice cooked potatoes round or lengthwise and place in dish. Pour the complete mixture over layers of yams or sweet potatoes. Top with slivered nuts as desired. Cook for 25 or 30 minutes.

HAWAIIAN YAMS

4 large sweet potatoes, cooked
    and mashed
1 c. sugar
1 tsp. vanilla

1 c. evaporated milk
¾ c. coconut
½ tsp. salt
1 egg

    Topping:

1 (20 oz.) can crushed pineapple
    (undrained)
1 large jar maraschino cherries
    and juice

1 c. sugar
3 Tbsp. cornstarch

Mix first 7 ingredients together and place in buttered baking dish. Bake at 350° for 30 minutes. Meanwhile, combine the 4 topping ingredients in a saucepan and cook until thick and glossy. Pour over baked sweet potato mixture and serve. This makes a large casserole.

Mrs. Boyd Bradley (Frances), Rock Hill Lions Club
Rock Hill, South Carolina, USA

❧

There is nothing better than the encouragement of a good friend.

SUGARY SAM YAMS

Yam ingredients:

3 c. canned yams, drained
½ c. milk
2 eggs

1 stick margarine
½ c. sugar
1 tsp. vanilla

Mix yam ingredients with electric mixer. Pour into oblong casserole, 12x7 or 13x9 inches.

Topping ingredients:

1 c. brown sugar, lightly packed
2 Tbsp. flour
1 tsp. vanilla

⅓ c. margarine, softened
1 c. Grape-Nuts

Mix topping with fork. Spread over potato mixture. Bake till bubbly and golden brown for 45 minutes at 350°.

BREADED ZUCCHINI

¾ c. dry bread crumbs
1 tsp. dried leaf oregano
1 tsp. dried leaf parsley
2 Tbsp. grated Parmesan cheese

3 to 4 medium size zucchini, cut in
    ¼ inch slices
3 egg whites, beaten until foamy
Dash of pepper

1. Preheat oven to 325°F. (165°C.). Mix bread crumbs, oregano, parsley, and cheese in a flat dish.
2. Dip zucchini slices in egg whites, then in bread crumbs; spray with no stick cooking spray.
3. Spread a baking sheet with no stick cooking spray. Arrange coated zucchini on sprayed baking sheet. Bake 5 to 7 minutes; turn. Spray zucchini again. Bake another 5 to 7 minutes or until golden brown.
4. Serve hot. Makes 6 servings.

Variation: Substitute cauliflower, whole mushrooms or whole green beans for zucchini.

Nutritional breakdown (3 or 4 pieces): 71 calories, 4 g protein, 11 g carbohydrates, trace of fat, 137 mg sodium, and 1 mg cholesterol.

Maria Specht, President, Prince Albert Downtown Lioness Club
Prince Albert, Saskatchewan, Canada

There is no possession more valuable than a good and faithful friend.

ZUCCHINI AND CAULIFLOWER SKILLET

¼ c. chopped onion
1 clove garlic, minced
2 Tbsp. cooking oil
1 (7½ oz.) can tomatoes, cut up
1 Tbsp. snipped parsley
1 Tbsp. tomato paste
½ tsp. salt

½ tsp. dried crushed oregano
¼ tsp. pepper
2 medium sliced zucchini (½ inch thick)
2 c. cauliflowerets
½ c. water
1 c. shredded Mozzarella cheese

In saucepan, cook onion and garlic in oil till onion is tender. Stir in undrained tomatoes, tomato paste, salt, oregano, and pepper. Boil gently, uncovered, for 10 to 15 minutes or until slightly thickened, stirring occasionally.

Meanwhile, in a 10 inch skillet, cook zucchini and cauliflowerets in water over medium heat about 5 minutes or until crisp-tender. Drain.

Pour tomato mixture over vegetables. Cover and cook for 4 to 5 minutes or until heated through. Sprinkle with Mozzarella cheese. Cook, covered, about 3 minutes longer or until cheese is melted. Sprinkle with parsley if desired. Makes 4 to 6 servings.

Adults and children both enjoy this recipe, with children renaming the recipe "Pizza Vegetables."

Shirley Leonardi, Jasper Mountain Lions Club
Jasper, Alberta, Canada

ZUCCHINI FRITTERS

2 c. zucchini
1 tsp. salt
1 grated carrot
1 medium onion, minced
1 egg

½ c. flour
Dash of pepper
2 Tbsp. parsley (fresh - may use dry accordingly)

Sprinkle salt on zucchini and let set 15 minutes. Squeeze out excess water and mix together with remaining ingredients. Drop by tablespoon in ¼ inch hot oil in heavy fry pan. Brown on both sides.

Dorothy Wimmer, Rock Falls Lions Club
Sterling, Illinois, USA

Save for old age by putting away a few pleasant thoughts.

VEGETABLE PAELLA

2 c. sliced onions
1 garlic clove, crushed
1½ c. chicken stock
1 c. uncooked white rice
½ tsp. ground turmeric
Dash of pepper
1½ c. cold water
4 medium size carrots, diced

1 large red bell pepper, diced
1 (10 oz.) pkg. frozen green beans, thawed
1½ c. boiling water
2 tomatoes, cut in eighths
Grated Parmesan cheese (optional)

1. Saute onions and garlic in a small amount of stock in a 6 quart Dutch oven.

2. When onions and garlic are softened, add rice, turmeric, and pepper. Mix well. Add remaining broth and cold water. Bring to a boil, reduce heat, and simmer, covered, 20 minutes.

3. Combine carrots, bell pepper, and peas with boiling water in a large skillet. Simmer until carrots are tender. Add cooked rice to vegetable mixture. Cover with tomatoes and simmer, covered, 5 minutes. Place in a serving dish. Sprinkle with Parmesan cheese if desired. Makes 8 servings.

Variation: Serve over cooked kashka or couscous.

Nutritional breakdown (per serving): 99 calories, 4 g protein, 19 g carbohydrates, trace of fat, 118 mg sodium, and 0 mg cholesterol.

Maria Specht, President, Price Albert Downtown Lioness Club
Prince Albert, Saskatchewan, Canada

RATATOUILLA FROM MISSISSIPPI

¼ c. olive oil
¼ c. lowfat margarine
1 clove minced garlic
1½ tsp. salt
½ tsp. basil leaves
½ tsp. oregano leaves

⅛ tsp. pepper
3 small zucchini, cubed
1 medium eggplant, cubed
2 medium tomatoes, chopped
1 small green pepper, chopped
1 medium onion, chopped

Melt margarine. Add oil, garlic, salt, basil, oregano, and pepper. Mix all vegetables in a large casserole and cover the seasonings over the top. Cover and bake at 325° for 1 hour. Uncover and cook an additional 30 minutes.

Lion Arlene Wall, Biloxi, Mississippi, Lions Club
Biloxi, Mississippi, Harrison County, USA

Give generously, for your gifts will return to you later.

BUREK
(A delightful vegetarian dish from Yugoslavia)

2 c. large curd cottage cheese
2 c. Feta cheese, crumbled
3 Tbsp. sour cream
2 egg yolks, lightly beaten

2 Tbsp. parsley, finely minced
1 pkg. filo leaves
¼ lb. butter, melted (to brush on
  filo)

Prepare burek. One pound of Feta to make 10 to 12 of the pastry wrapped (sausages). Unwrap 2 filo sheets. Cover remaining filo with damp towel. Lay the 2 sheets vertically (short side facing you). On wax paper or dry towel, lay one sheet directly on top of the other. Using a pastry brush, quickly spread butter on entire surface. Brush from edges to center. Mix cheeses, sour cream, egg yolks, and parsley together. Spread ⅓ cup filling in a line along the edge toward you, leaving 1 inch margins at the bottom and both sides. Lift up towel or wax paper to begin filo roll. After one roll, stop and fold in 1 inch side margins, brushing them with butter. Continue rolling by lifting towel or paper until burek is completely rolled. Place burek on lightly greased baking sheet. Slice burek diagonally on surface, 1 inch apart for hors d'oeuvres, 3 inches apart for dinner burek. After baking burek will cut easily along the slashes. Brush liberally with butter and sprinkle sparingly with water. Bake at 375° for 15 to 20 minutes or until golden brown.

Mary K. Meeker, Ponderosa Lions Club
Auberry, California, USA

CRUNCHY VEGETABLE CASSEROLE

1 can French style green beans
1 can shoe peg corn
¼ c. chopped onion
½ c. chopped celery
¼ c. chopped green pepper
  (optional)
1 stick butter, melted

1 c. sour cream
½ c. grated sharp cheese
1 can cream of celery soup
¼ c. slivered almonds
Ritz crackers (enough to cover
  well)

Drain green beans and corn. Mix with other ingredients, except almonds and cracker crumbs. Pour into a 2 quart greased casserole dish and top with sauteed crushed cracker crumbs. Add almonds last 5 minutes of baking time as they burn easily. Bake at 350° for 45 minutes.

"Opened by mistake" applies more often to mouths than it does to mail.
Mildred Wolfe, Rock Hill Lions Club
Rock Hill, South Carolina, USA

Live your life as an exclamation!

KENTUCKY VEGETABLE CASSEROLE

2 (10 oz.) pkg. mixed vegetables (frozen)
1 c. grated sharp cheese

1 can mushroom soup
1 (5 oz.) can evaporated milk
1 (2.8 oz.) can onion rings

Cook vegetables in cup of water 4 minutes; drain well. Place in a 2 quart casserole. Mix the remaining ingredients (except onion rings). Pour over vegetables. Bake 25 minutes at 350°. Remove from oven and top with can of onion rings. Return to oven and bake 8 to 10 minutes or until golden brown. Serves 8 to 10.

Howard Cook, Shively Lions Club
Louisville, Kentucky, USA

MIXED VEGETABLES WITH WHITE SAUCE

½ small cauliflower, cut in small florets
6 to 8 small broccoli florets
2 to 3 small courgettes, cut into 1 inch slices

1 tin or a small bag of corn (frozen)
Salt and pepper
½ c. walnuts, cut in halves
6 olives

White Sauce:

⅓ c. vegetable oil or 1 Tbsp. butter
2 level Tbsp. flour
2 c. milk

Salt and pepper
1 Tbsp. Parmesan cheese

Cook vegetables in boiling water (but do not overcook). Cook courgettes for 7 to 8 minutes, cauliflower for 5 minutes, and broccoli for 3 minutes; strain corn. Put the above mixture of vegetables in an ovenware dish and sprinkle with walnuts. Place prepared ingredients in a bowl. Dice the Feta cheese and put on top with the olives.

White Sauce: Put oil or butter in a small pan, heat and add flour. Stir well. Add milk and bring to a boil, stirring continuously till it thickens. Cover vegetables with sauce. Sprinkle with Parmesan cheese. Put in a medium hot oven for 15 to 20 minutes. Serve hot.

Nitsa Pashouli, Nicosia Leda Lions Club
Nicosia, Cyprus

❧

You will never become dizzy doing good turns.

VEGETABLE CASSEROLE

½ loaf Swedish limpa bread, cut in
   1 inch cubes
2 small zucchini, sliced
2 green peppers, sliced
1 doz. mushrooms, sliced

1 bunch broccoli, chunked
½ head cauliflower, chunked
2 carrots, sliced
4 to 6 large tomatoes
1 to 2 c. grated Cheddar cheese

In a large baking casserole, place bread on the bottom and the rest of the vegetables on top, ending with tomatoes and cheese. Any other vegetable can be added or any subtracted. The tomatoes on top drip the juice through to the bread and the cheese covering (heavy) seals it. Bake for 1 hour at 350°.

SWISS VEGETABLE MEDLEY

1 (16 oz.) pkg. frozen California
   Blend vegetables (broccoli,
   cauliflower, and carrots),
   thawed and drained
1 (10 oz.) can cream of mushroom
   soup

1 c. Swiss cheese, shredded
⅓ c. sour cream
1 c. Durkee French fried onions

Combine vegetables, soup, ½ cup of the cheese, the sour cream, and ½ of the onions in a large mixing bowl. Bake at 325°, covered, in a 2 quart glass casserole for 35 minutes. Uncover. Sprinkle the remainder of the cheese and onions over the top. Bake for 5 to 10 more minutes, uncovered, until the cheese is melted.

This dish has received many raves at potlucks and family gatherings.
Kimberly A. Klepec, Bloomington Lions Club
Bloomington, Illinois, USA

GRIT PIE

4 c. water
1 c. quick grits
1 (4 oz.) stick butter or margarine

1 (8 oz.) roll garlic cheese
2 eggs

Bring water to boil in 4 quart saucepan. Add grits and cook about 5 minutes. Add cheese and stir until melted. Beat eggs. Add to mixture. Stir until blended. Pour into 10 inch greased Pyrex pie plate. Top with crushed corn flakes. Bake 45 minutes at 350° in preheated oven. Serve warm as a casserole.

This recipe won second prize in a national natural foods contest and I still enjoy the prize, a clock radio. This is the first time it's been shared in 20 years.
Lee Woods, PDG, Interlachen Lions Club
Interlachen, Floriday, USA

Notes

Blessed is the person who is too busy to worry in the daytime and too sleepy to worry at night.

Entrees

MEAT ROASTING GUIDE

Cut	Weight Pounds	Approx. Time (Hours) (325° oven)	Internal Temperature
BEEF			
Standing rib roast			
(10 inch) ribs	4	1¾	140° (rare)
(If using shorter cut (8-inch)		2	160° (medium)
ribs, allow 30 min. longer)		2½	170° (well done)
	8	2½	140° (rare)
		3	160° (medium)
		4½	170° (well done)
Rolled ribs	4	2	140° (rare)
		2½	160° (medium)
		3	170° (well done)
	6	3	140° (rare)
		3¼	160° (medium)
		4	170° (well done)
Rolled rump	5	2¼	140° (rare)
(Roast only if high quality.	3	160° (medium)	
Otherwise, braise.)		3¼	170° (well done)
Sirloin tip	3	1½	140° (rare)
(Roast only if high quality.		2	160° (medium)
Otherwise, braise.)		2¼	170° (well done)
LAMB			
Leg	6	3	175° (medium)
		3½	180° (well done)
	8	4	175° (medium)
		4½	180° (well done)
VEAL			
Leg (piece)	5	2½ to 3	170° (well done)
Shoulder	6	3½	170° (well done)
Rolled shoulder	3 to 5	3 to 3½	170° (well done)

POULTRY ROASTING GUIDE

Type of Poultry	Ready-To-Cook Weight	Oven Temperature	Approx. Total Roasting Time
TURKEY	6 to 8 lb.	325°	2½ to 3 hr.
	8 to 12 lb.	325°	3 to 3½ hr.
	12 to 16 lb.	325°	3½ to 4 hr.
	16 to 20 lb.	325°	4 to 4½ hr.
	20 to 24 lb.	300°	5 to 6 hr.
CHICKEN (Unstuffed)	2 to 2½ lb.	400°	1 to 1½ hr.
	2½ to 4 lb.	400°	1½ to 2½ hr.
	4 to 8 lb.	325°	3 to 5 hr.
DUCK (Unstuffed)	3 to 5 lb.	325°	2½ to 3 hr.

NOTE: Small chickens are roasted at 400° so that they brown well in the short cooking time. They may also be done at 325° but will take longer and will not be as brown. Increase cooking time 15 to 20 minutes for stuffed chicken and duck.

ENTREES
ENTREES - BEEF

BEEF INTERNATIONAL

2 cans beef consomme
3 sprigs parsley
2 tsp. celery flakes
Dash of Tabasco
4 peppercorns
3 medium onions, halved
1 tsp. Accent
2 garlic cloves

1 bay leaf
1 tsp. oregano
2 tsp. salt
1 tsp. sugar
1 (12 oz.) can beer
6 to 7 lb. boned and rolled beef
   roast

Combine all ingredients in a Dutch oven and bring to a boil. Add meat. Cook at very low heat (325°), covered, in oven for at least 3 hours or until tender.

Horseradish Sauce (serve with roast-gravy):

3 c. broth in which meat was
   cooked
6 Tbsp. butter

6 Tbsp. flour
1 c. sour cream
¼ c. horseradish

Strain broth. Melt butter; blend in flour. Add to broth to make a gravy. Thicken over low heat. Stir in sour cream slowly, then add horseradish before serving.

MEXICAN FLANK STEAK

2 (1 lb.) flank steaks
Salt and pepper
Garlic salt
1 (15 oz.) can tamales
1 beef bouillon cube

¼ c. boiling water
1 (8 oz.) can tomato sauce
¼ tsp. ground cumin
½ tsp. chili powder

Trim steaks of fat and pound on both sides with meat tenderizer. Season with salt, pepper, and garlic salt. In small bowl, break tamales (with paper removed) into pieces and toss with sauce from can. Spread tamales over surface of steaks. Roll steaks lengthwise. Tie with string and place in 9x13 inch pan.

Dissolve bouillon cube in boiling water and stir into tomato sauce, ground cumin, and chili powder. Spoon sauce over meat. Bake, uncovered, at 350° for 1¼ to 1½ hours, basting occasionally. Serves 8.

If you don't need both steak rolls for one meal, make them both and freeze one.

ROULADEN MIT SPAETZLE

Hot spicy mustard
6 breakfast steaks
1 onion, chopped
4 Tbsp. parsley
6 slices bacon, partially
   precooked

6 dill pickle spears
2 cans beefy mushroom soup
2 cans mushrooms

Saute onion and parsley in a small amount of butter or margarine. Spread mustard on meat with onion and parsley. Place pickle and bacon slice on one end of meat and roll up. Secure with pick. Roll in flour and brown in skillet on all sides. Add a little water, mushrooms, and both cans of soup. Simmer very slow for 2 to 3 hours in electric skillet or bake at 250°, covered. Uncover the last 30 minutes, turning meat once.

Can also be cooked in crock pot on LOW all day or for 5 hours on HIGH. Serve with Spaetzle (or egg noodles).

Spaetzle:

2¾ c. flour
1 tsp. salt
⅛ tsp. nutmeg

⅛ tsp. paprika
4 eggs
¾ c. water or part milk and water

Stir together flour, salt, nutmeg, and paprika. Add eggs and water. Beat until thick and smooth. Press into boiling water with spaetzle maker or spread dough very thin with spatula. Cut into small strips (dip spatula in water several times during cutting) and drop into large kettle of boiling, salted water. If noodles do not keep their shape, add a little flour to dough. Boil gently for about 5 minutes. Remove with slotted spoon. Drain well and add a little butter. Continue with remaining dough. Serve hot.

SPICY ORIENTAL CARAMELIZED BEEF

¼ c. light brown sugar
2 Tbsp. soy sauce
1 Tbsp. cornstarch
1 tsp. garlic powder
½ tsp. ground red pepper

1 lb. boneless sirloin steak, cut in
   thin strips
Cooking oil
3 sliced scallions

In large shallow glass baking dish, blend brown sugar, soy sauce, cornstarch, garlic powder, and pepper. Add beef and turn to coat. In large skillet, heat ½ inch oil to 350°. Fry beef until brown. Remove with slotted spoon. Drain on paper toweling. Garnish with scallions and crushed red pepper. Serve over rice.

Catherine Walsh, Westbrook Lions Club
Westbrook, Maine, USA

POLYNESIAN ROAST

3 lb. roast
¼ c. flour
¼ c. vegetable oil
1 c. pineapple slices
3 Tbsp. lemon juice
2 Tbsp. finely packed brown sugar

¼ c. soy sauce
1 clove minced garlic
½ Tbsp. dried basil, crushed
2 Tbsp. cornstarch
¼ c. cold water

Preheat oven to 350°. Cook roast on all sides with flour, then brown in oil. Drain pineapple and reserve juice. Combine juice, lemon juice, brown sugar, soy sauce, garlic, and basil. Mix well. Pour over meat. Bake at 350° for 2 hours or until tender. Top with pineapple slices and bake 10 minutes more.

Combine cornstarch and water. Remove roast to platter. Add ½ to 1 cup water to drippings. Bring to a boil, then add cornstarch. Cook and stir until sauce thickens. Serve sauce over meat. Makes approximately 6 servings.

Lion Eula Johnson, Graysville/Proctor Lions Club
Glen Dale, West Virginia, USA

CARIBBEAN PICADILLO

5 lb. lean ground beef
2 to 3 Tbsp. vegetable oil
5 c. onions, chopped
4 large garlic cloves, minced
5 green bell peppers, chopped
4 c. canned or fresh tomatoes,
   peeled and chopped

1½ tsp. salt
½ tsp. freshly ground pepper
1 c. sliced pimento stuffed olives
½ c. capers with a few drops of
   juice
Hot cooked rice

Cook beef in oil in large skillet until meat loses red color. Crumble with long handled fork while cooking. Add onions and garlic; cook, stirring, until onions are translucent. Pour off fat. Stir in green peppers, tomatoes, salt, and pepper. Simmer, uncovered, for 10 minutes or until most of the liquid is evaporated. Stir now and then while cooking. Add olives and capers. Simmer for 2 minutes to blend flavors. Serve hot on rice.

Picadillo can be prepared ahead, refrigerated or frozen, and reheated in large skillet. Makes 18 to 20 servings, but is easy to divide or multiply. Two double recipes will serve 100 with salad, rice, and bread.

❧

Most smiles are started by another smile.

ITALIAN BEEF

4 lb. roast beef
1 Tbsp. oregano
3 bay leaves
2 Tbsp. vinegar
2 tsp. caraway seed
2 medium onions, cut up

½ tsp. garlic powder
½ c. water
2 tsp. fennel seeds
4 green peppers, cut in strips
3 beef bouillon cubes

Salt and pepper roast. Place in Dutch oven. Add all other ingredients, except peppers and bouillon cubes. Cover and place on low heat. Simmer for 3 hours, adding more water, if necessary, to keep meat from sticking. Take out meat. Add to sauce, green peppers, 3 bouillon cubes, and 3 cups water; simmer for ½ hour. Slice or shred meat and return to Dutch oven with peppers. Cover and cook for ½ hour longer or until desired tenderness. Serve on French bread. (Take out bay leaves.)

THAI BEEF WITH NOODLES

1 lb. boneless beef top sirloin, cut
   1 inch thick
¼ c. dry sherry
1½ Tbsp. reduced-sodium soy
   sauce
1 tsp. grated fresh ginger
1 tsp. minced garlic
1 tsp. oriental dark roasted
   sesame oil

¼ to ½ tsp. crushed red pepper
   pods
2 c. cooked Ramen noodles or
   linguine
¼ c. chopped green onion tops or
   fresh cilantro

Combine sherry, soy sauce, ginger, garlic, sesame oil, and pepper pods. Place beef steak in plastic bag; add marinade. Close bag securely and marinate 15 minutes. Pour off marinade; reserve. Heat nonstick skillet over medium heat 5 minutes. Add steak and cook 12 to 15 minutes for rare (140°F.) to medium (160°F.), turning once. Remove steak; keep warm. Dissolve 2 teaspoons cornstarch in reserved marinade and ¼ cup water; add to skillet. Bring to a boil, stirring constantly. Stir in noodles. Carve steak into thin slices and serve over noodles. Sprinkle with green onion. Makes 4 servings.

John J. Hess for Mrs. Joanne Brownell, Clarence Center Lions Club
Clarence Center, New York, USA

❦

Time is nature's way of preventing everything from happening at once.

BEEF BURGUNDY

3 lb. beef stew meat
1 c. red wine or enough to cover meat
2 cans golden mushroom soup

1 pkg. dry onion soup mix
Pepper to taste and a little salt if needed

Soak meat in wine for at least 1 hour. Combine all ingredients and bake in 325°F. oven for 3 to 3½ hours, covered, for about 2 hours. Serve over cooked noodles or rice. Serves 6 generously.

OVEN BEEF BURGUNDY

4 lb. round steak, cubed
1 c. burgundy wine
2 cans cream of celery soup

1 can cream of mushroom soup
1 env. onion soup mix
4 to 6 c. sliced mushrooms

Marinate meat in wine for ½ hour at room temperature. In a 5 quart casserole, mix remaining ingredients and add meat mixture. Bake at 275° for 4 hours. Serve over noodles or rice. Serves 6 to 8 people.

BAKED SWISS

2 lb. round steak, cut
1 env. dry onion soup
1 (10 oz.) can sliced mushrooms, drained
½ c. celery

1 (14 oz.) can canned tomatoes
1 Tbsp. bottled steak sauce
1 Tbsp. Minute tapioca
1 tsp. parsley flakes

Cut steak in serving size pieces. Arrange in 2 quart casserole. Sprinkle dry soup over. Spread mushrooms on top. Sprinkle celery over all. In small bowl, stir tomatoes, sauce, tapioca, and parsley. Pour over steak. Cover and bake in 350° oven for 2 hours until tender. Serves 6.

Mrs. Laurie Kovach, Brandon Crocus Lions Club
Brandon, Manitoba, Canada

Your candle loses nothing by lighting another's candle.

SIMPLE SALISBURY STEAK

1 can Campbell's cream of
   mushroom soup (divided)
1 lb. ground beef
½ c. dry bread crumbs

1 egg, beaten
¼ c. finely chopped onion
1½ c. sliced mushrooms

In bowl, mix thoroughly ¼ cup of the soup, beef, bread crumbs, egg, and onion. Shape firmly into 6 patties. In skillet over medium-high heat, cook patties, a few at a time, until browned on both sides. Spoon off fat. Stir in remaining soup and mushrooms; return patties to skillet. Reduce heat to low. Cover and simmer 20 minutes or until done, turning patties occasionally.

Alvah Coe, Onekama Lions Club
Onekama, Michigan, USA

LEAN BEEF AND VEGETABLE POT ROAST

2½ to 3 lb. rump roast*
1 c. boiling water
½ c. red wine
4 onions, cut in wedges
8 to 10 carrots, cut in 2 to 3 inch
   pieces

Vegetable oil cooking spray
2 beef bouillon cubes (low-
   sodium if preferred)
4 cloves garlic, minced
4 to 5 white potatoes, halved

Preheat oven to 325°. Trim fat from roast. Spray a roasting pan with nonstick spray. Using medium heat, slowly brown the roast on all sides, turning it often. Pour off any drippings. Dissolve the bouillon cubes in 1 cup boiling water and add to meat along with the wine. Add onions and garlic. Cover and cook at 325° for 2 hours. Add the potatoes and carrots; cook, covered, for another 30 minutes or until the meat and vegetables are fork-tender. Skim any fat from the juice in the pan and serve juice over the sliced meat. Serves 8 to 10.

* You can also use shoulder roast or bottom round roast.

Michael Hadeed, Alexandria Evening Lions Club
Alexandria, Virginia, USA

Life is what you make it.

MORCON - BEEF ROLL

1½ lb. beef flank steak
2 Tbsp. soy sauce
1 tsp. Worcestershire sauce

1 tsp. lemon juice
1 tsp. white wine or beer
1 tsp. white sugar

Filling:

2 pieces Vienna sausage
1 small pack raisins (optional)
6 strips pork liver (optional)
6 strips carrots
2 pieces hard-boiled eggs
2 strips chorizo de bilbao or 1 strip
   chenise sausage

4 strips canned pimiento or fresh
   green pepper
6 strips pork back fat
4 strips pickles
Dash of ground pepper
5 c. water

    Spread beef flank steak. Arrange all the ingredients alternately. Roll and tie. Put in a pressure cooker or casserole. Boil until tender (pressure cook for 40 minutes), then fry a little.

Sauce:

½ lb. beef liver, dissolved in 1 c.
   water
⅓ c. butter
⅓ c. chopped red onion
½ tsp. minced garlic

3 Tbsp. tomato paste
1 Tbsp. Worcestershire sauce
3 Tbsp. white sugar
2 Tbsp. cooking oil
½ tsp. fine salt

    Broil liver until half cooked. Pound, then squeeze out the juice. Set aside. Heat pan. Pour oil. Fry garlic. Saute onion. Add butter, tomato paste, Worcestershire sauce, and all the seasonings. Add liver. Stir. Let it boil, then add sauce from Morcon. When boiling, add the Morcon and cook until the sauce is thick.

Leticia Alves, Rizal Lions Club
Sacramento, California, USA

❦

If you could kick the person most responsible for most of your troubles,
you wouldn't be able to sit down.

MAMIE'S MEAT PIE

Have on hand two 9 inch pie crusts.

Saute:

1 lb. ground chuck
¼ c. chopped onion

¼ c. chopped green pepper

Add:

1 small can tomato sauce
1 small can mushrooms
Salt and pepper

Dash of catsup
Dash of Worcestershire sauce

Put in pie crust.

Place on top:

1 can sliced mushrooms
1 jar green olives

Grated cheese to cover

Add top crust and bake at 350° until crust is brown (about 30 minutes). Freezes beautifully.

Lion Jane Price, Canton Lions Club
Canton, Georgia, USA

MIGAS MIGAS

1 medium onion, chopped fine
1 bell pepper, chopped
1 lb. ground beef
1 (No. 2) can (approx. 2½ c.)
　　tomatoes or juice
½ c. catsup

1 tsp. chili powder
Dash of Tabasco (optional)
1 tsp. salt
½ lb. cheese, grated
Fritos (small bag)

Saute onion and pepper in oil until tender, not brown. Add ground beef and cook until meat is well done, not brown. Drain excess grease. Add tomatoes (tomato juice), catsup, chili powder, Tabasco, and salt. Simmer for 10 minutes. Pour into greased (Pam) baking dish. Cover with Fritos, pushing down into meat mixture. Cover with grated cheese. Bake at 300° until cheese melts and is lightly browned. I use Pam to keep from sticking instead of a greased dish.

Anna Hillis, McMinnville Lions Club
McMinnville, Tennessee, USA

To be loved, love.

STEAK ROLLS

1 lb. round steak or 6 minute
   steaks
½ c. diced celery
½ c. mushroom stems and pieces
2 Tbsp. shortening

1 env. onion soup mix
½ c. catsup
¼ tsp. Worcestershire sauce
¼ tsp. garlic powder
1½ c. water

Pound meat thin. Combine celery and mushrooms. Place 2 tablespoons mixture in center of each piece of meat and roll, fastening with toothpicks. In medium size skillet, melt shortening and brown rolls.

Combine onion soup, catsup, Worcestershire sauce, garlic powder, and water. Pour into skillet. Simmer, covered, for 1½ hours.

STEAK 'N GRAVY

1½ lb. round or sirloin steak
1 can Campbell's French onion
   soup

1 can Campbell's golden
   mushroom soup

Preheat oven to 350°. Place meat in 9x12 inch pan. Add soups and *no* water. Cover with foil. Bake for 1½ hours. Makes its own gravy. Put foil-wrapped potatoes with meat dish for 1½ hours and make a salad and you're ready for dinner.

Mary Tharp, Cuba Lions Club
Cuba, Illinois, USA

BAKED CHUCK AND MUSHROOM SAUCE

2½ lb. boneless chuck
1 (10½ oz.) can cream of
   mushroom soup
1 can water (use soup can)
1 small bay leaf
½ tsp. Worcestershire sauce

1 garlic button, sliced
1 onion, sliced
1½ tsp. salt
¼ tsp. pepper
3 Tbsp. shortening

Cut chuck in serving pieces. Roll in flour and brown in skillet with shortening. Remove browned meat to baking dish. If desired, brown onion and garlic; add mushroom soup and water to shortening (drippings in skillet) and bring to a boil. Stir to blend. Add seasonings and pour over browned meat. Cover and bake in a 350° oven for about 2 hours. Uncover and bake for ½ hour longer. (Add more water if needed.) Serve over cooked noodles.

❦

A friend is a gift you give yourself.

SWEET SOUR SPARERIBS

Several lb. spareribs or country
   style ribs
½ c. sliced green onion
½ c. sliced celery
½ c. green pepper, cut in pieces
½ c. chili sauce
½ c. pineapple juice

Salt and pepper to taste
¼ c. lemon juice
¼ c. brown sugar
2 Tbsp. butter
2 Tbsp. cornstarch
Celery salt
Garlic salt

Mix in a bowl the onions, celery, green pepper, chili sauce, pineapple juice, and sugar. Sprinkle in celery salt, garlic salt, salt, and pepper. Mix 2 tablespoons of cornstarch and ¼ cup lemon juice. Add to mixture. Brown ribs in butter on both sides. Place ribs in covered roaster and pour sauce mixture over them. Bake at 350° for 2 hours or until tender.

Mary Tirpak, Moweaqua Lions Club
Moweaqua, Illinois, USA

CHICKEN FRIED STEAK AND GRAVY

1 lb. top round steak (½ inch thick)
1 tsp. salt
½ tsp. pepper
¾ c. flour

¼ c. milk
1 egg, beaten
¼ c. shortening

   Gravy:

¼ c. oleo
¼ c. flour
1 tsp. salt

¼ to ½ tsp. pepper
2 c. milk

Divide steak into 4 pieces. Score ⅛ inch deep on each side. Pound to ¼ inch thickness. Combine salt, pepper, and flour; set aside. Combine milk and beaten egg. Dredge steaks in flour mixture. Dip in milk mixture; dredge again in flour. Heat shortening in skillet on medium high. Fry steaks about 2 to 3 minutes on each side until golden brown. Remove and keep warm.

Gravy: Melt butter (oleo) in skillet with drippings. Add flour, salt, and pepper. Cook slowly on medium, stirring until bubbly. Add the milk to flour in skillet. Cook gravy on low until thickness desired. To serve, pour over fried steak.

Men love this with biscuits and rice. (Can also substitute venison steaks.)
Terry Jones, Kosciusko Lions Club
Kosciusko, Mississippi, USA

❦

There is nothing that cannot happen today.

GOURMET SIRLOIN TIPS

1½ lb. sirloin tips
2 Tbsp. oil
1 clove garlic, minced
1 c. ketchup
3 Tbsp. Worcestershire sauce

½ c. melted margarine or butter
1 Tbsp. lemon juice
½ tsp. salt
⅛ tsp. pepper

Saute garlic in hot oil. Add meat and brown on all sides over medium heat. Mix remaining ingredients and add to meat. Cover and simmer over low heat on top of range or bake in 350° oven for 1 hour, or until meat is tender. Serve over hot fluffy rice. Serves 4.

Ursula J. Harrington, Westbrook Lions Club
Westbrook, Maine, USA

BEEF OR LAMB SHISH KABOBS

2 lb. sirloin, cut into 1¼ inch cubes
½ c. sherry wine
1 tsp. seasoned salt
1 tsp. garlic powder
1 tsp. coarse black pepper
3 tsp. fresh parsley, minced
1 onion, chopped
2 Tbsp. Worcestershire sauce

½ tsp. basil leaves
¼ c. Wesson oil
16 mushroom caps
4 tomatoes, quartered
2 green bell peppers, cut into large
 squares
1 red onion, cut into eighths

For Lamb Shish Kabob - Add:

1 squeezed lemon juice
½ tsp. margarine

¼ c. olive oil instead of Wesson
 oil

Combine oil, wine, salt, pepper, garlic powder, chopped onions, parsley, basil leaves, and Worcestershire sauce for marinade. Marinate for 6 hours or longer. Skew meat and vegetables; broil over BBQ grill or broiler. Serves 4. Excellent tasting shish kabob.

Lion Francis Correia, Caruthers Lions Club
Caruthers, California, USA

❧

The most precious gifts are wrapped in love.

STANDING RIB ROAST

Have on hand 2 to 3 rib beef rib roast (small end - 4 to 6 pounds).

Salt   Accent (optional)
Pepper   Sherry wine
Garlic powder

1. Sprinkle with ½ teaspoon salt, ½ teaspoon pepper, ½ teaspoon garlic powder, ½ teaspoon Accent, and ¼ cup sherry.
2. Use meat thermometer into thickest part of meat.
3. Roast in 325°F. oven until internal temperature reaches 140°F. for rare (1¾ to 2¼ hours), 160°F. for medium (2¼ to 3½ hours, and 170°F. well done (2¾ to 4 hours).

When roast is done, allow to stand at room temperature 15 minutes for easy carving.

This is what our club served for District Governor Visitation Night.
Lion Jerry Chow, Caruthers Lions Club
Caruthers, California, USA

MEXICAN ROAST

3 lb. roast   1 can tomatoes
3 Tbsp. chili powder   1 large onion, chopped
1 Tbsp. garlic salt   1 lb. dry pinto beans (don't soak)
1 can Ro-Tel tomatoes

Put all ingredients in large roaster pan and cover with water. Make sure all ingredients are well covered with water. Bake in 250° oven for about 12 hours.
Arvella James, White Deer Lions Club
White Deer, Texas, USA

The time to look down on your neighbor
is when you stoop over him to give him a lift.

CHATEAUBRIAND

Season 1 whole filet mignon with soy sauce, sherry wine, and garlic powder. Roast in oven 1½ hours at 250°F.

Make sauce:

1 cube butter	**2 Tbsp. flour**
½ basket mushrooms	**1 c. beef broth**
1 tsp. salt	**½ c. sherry wine**

Melt butter in skillet. Saute mushrooms until golden brown. Sprinkle with salt and flour. Add beef broth and bring to a boil. Add sherry wine and simmer 5 or 6 minutes.

To serve Chateaubriand, slice diagonally in ¼ inch slices. Pour sauce over and serve.

This is best of the best.

Lion Doug Steiner, Caruthers Lions Club
Caruthers, California, USA

❦

Good teachers are the ones who are able to challenge young minds without losing their own.

❦ ❦ ❦

There is nothing to worry about. Either you have control or you do not. If you do, then take control, if you don't, then dismiss it. Don't waste your energy worrying.

❦ ❦ ❦

It is a funny thing about life; if you refuse to accept anything but the best, you very often get it.

GOVERNORS SAUERBRATEN

Marinade:

2 c. vinegar
1 c. red wine
1 c. water
2 Tbsp. sugar
½ tsp. whole black peppers

4 bay leaves
3 sliced onions
12 whole cloves
1 tsp. mustard seeds
2 tsp. salt

Additional ingredients:

4 to 5 lb. rolled pot roast
2 Tbsp. flour
½ tsp. mustard seed
1½ tsp. salt
6 whole cloves
Speck of pepper

½ tsp. whole black pepper
¼ c. fat
⅓ c. ginger snap crumbs
1 sliced onion
½ c. sour cream
Salt and pepper

Soak meat in marinade 2 to 4 days, turning daily. Remove meat, reserving marinade. Dry meat well in paper towels. Combine flour, ½ teaspoon salt, and pepper (to taste). Use to coat meat on all sides. Brown meat well in hot fat in Dutch oven. Add ¾ cup marinade, 1 sliced onion, ½ teaspoon mustard seeds, 6 cloves, and ½ teaspoon whole peppers. Simmer, covered, approximately 3½ to 4 hours or until fork tender, adding ¼ cup marinade if needed. Remove meat and keep warm. Strain drippings into glass measuring cup. Let stand 2 minutes to settle. Pour off all except bottom ⅓ cup of drippings. Return this to Dutch oven. Stir in crumbs. Slowly stir in 2 cups of strained reserved marinade (add water if needed). Cook, stirring, until thickened. Stir in sour cream. Heat, but do not boil. Season if necessary. The meat can be top or bottom round, depending on choice. It can be marinated as long as 7 days which enhances the flavor quite a bit. A cheap wine does very well.

Steve Naples, D.G., Middletown Twp. Lions Club
Middletown Township, New Jersey, USA

Never tell people how to do things.
Tell them what to do, and they will surprise you with their ingenuity.

SAUERBRATEN - MARINATED BEEF

4 lb. pot roast (any beef pot roast)
2 c. vinegar
2 c. water
1 large onion
¼ c. sugar
2 tsp. salt

10 peppercorns
3 whole cloves
2 bay leaves
1 lemon, rinsed and cut into ¼
    inch slices

Wipe the roast clean and place it in a 3 to 4 quart bowl; set aside. Combine the rest of the ingredients (except the lemon) into a saucepan and heat it without boiling. Pour the hot mixture over the meat in the bowl and allow to cool. Add the sliced lemon. Cover and set in refrigerator. Marinate for 4 days, turning meat once each day.

When ready to cook the meat, remove it from the marinade; drain and heat the meat in a kettle over low heat, using 2 to 3 tablespoons of butter. Brown the meat slowly on all sides over medium heat. Add 2 cups of the marinade (keep the rest for making gravy).

Bring liquid to a boil; reduce heat and cover the kettle tightly. Simmer for 2½ to 3 hours, or until meat is tender when pierced with a fork. Add more marinade if necessary.

For gravy, melt ¼ cup butter and blend in ¼ cup flour; gradually add 3 cups of the reserved marinade, stirring constantly. Bring to a boil; cook until mixture thickens. One-half cup of thick sour cream may be added. Serve the meat and gravy with potato pancakes.

❧

The best way to wake up with a smile on your face
is to go to bed with one already there.

❧ ❧ ❧

Show me a man who is a good loser
and I'll show you a man who is playing golf with his boss.

SAUERBRATEN

4 lb. beef rump (eye of round is best)
2 beef bouillon cubes (optional)
6 bay leaves
8 whole cloves
1 large onion
1 Tbsp. sugar

Salt and pepper to taste
1 small bottle catsup (or slightly more)
1 full c. vinegar
3 stalks celery, cut up
3 c. water

Put all in a roasting pan with the meat and roast in oven slowly. Put in at about 400°. Turn down in 20 minutes and keep at 325° for about 2½ to 3 hours.

When the meat is done, take out and cool. Strain gravy and thicken with browned flour. Cut the cooled meat in slices and return to finished gravy. Ready to serve.

It is best served with noodles fried (if preferred) as a part of the meal. We usually keep the finished product in the refrigerator overnight and then the next day reheat and serve. We like a lot of gravy, so we double the bay leaves, cloves, onions, catsup, and water. Also, use 1½ cups vinegar rather than 1 cup. (Use 1 additional cup water for each bouillon cube.

A German recipe handed down and very good and simple to prepare. As a vegetable, we serve carrots.

Mrs. George E. Ducar (Anna N.), East Syracuse Lions Club
East Syracuse, New York, USA

MEAT MARINADE

1 tsp. Worcestershire sauce
⅔ c. ketchup
1 clove garlic
½ small onion, chopped

Dash of pepper
¼ tsp. salt
3 tsp. sherry
1 London broil or other beef

Blend all ingredients, except the beef, in a blender and pour over the beef. Allow to sit for several hours. Bake in oven as for the beef or place in a smoker to smoke for 3½ to 4 hours. May also be grilled to taste.

William M. Davidson, IV, Statesboro Lions Club
Statesboro, Georgia, USA

The heart sees what is invisible to the eye.

MARINATED STEAK

1½ c. salad oil
¾ c. soy sauce
⅓ c. fresh lemon juice
½ c. garlic flavored wine vinegar
½ c. Worcestershire sauce
2 Tbsp. dry mustard

1½ tsp. parsley flakes
2¼ tsp. salt
1 Tbsp. pepper
1 lb. sirloin steak, cut into 3 inch
    pieces

Mix all ingredients well. Drop pieces of sirloin steak into mixture and soak overnight.

Sauce can be kept in refrigerator for 1 week or frozen.

PEPPERED BEEF TENDERLOIN
WITH MUSTARD AND HORSERADISH SAUCE

2 tsp. whole black peppercorns,
    coarsely ground
2 tsp. whole white peppercorns,
    coarsely ground
2 tsp. whole green peppercorns,
    coarsely ground

2 tsp. coarse salt
3 Tbsp. Dijon mustard
2 Tbsp. butter (room temperature)
1 c. loosely packed fresh parsley,
    chopped
2 lb. beef tenderloin

Sauce:

1 c. sour cream
3 Tbsp. Dijon mustard

2 Tbsp. prepared horseradish

Mix sauce ingredients in small bowl. Cover and refrigerate until ready to serve. Can be prepared up to 2 days ahead. Put peppercorns in bowl. Mix in salt. Whisk mustard, butter, and 1 cup chopped parsley in medium bowl to blend. Rub mixture all over tenderloin. Roll tenderloin in peppercorn mixture, coating completely. This can be done up to one day ahead. Cover and refrigerate.

Preheat oven to 450°. Place tenderloin on rack set in a shallow baking pan. Roast until meat thermometer inserted into center registers 130° for rare, about 35 minutes. Transfer roast to platter and let stand 10 minutes. Cut in slices, surround with parsley, and serve with sauce. Serves 6.

Lion Pat Demian, Royalton Hills Lions Club
North Royalton, Ohio, USA

There's a lot of thanks in giving.

PEPPER STEAK

1 lb. lean boneless sirloin steak, trimmed
1 clove garlic, crushed
1 tsp. ground ginger
1 tsp. salt
½ tsp. pepper
2 Tbsp. oil
3 large green peppers, cut into strips
2 large onions, thinly sliced
½ tsp. sugar
¾ c. beef broth
¼ c. soy sauce
6 oz. water chestnuts, sliced
1 Tbsp. cornstarch, dissolved in ¼ c. cold water

Place steak in freezer for 1 hour to firm for easier slicing. Cut across grain into ⅛ inch thick slices. Saute garlic, ginger, salt, and pepper in oil in skillet till garlic is golden. Add steak slices and brown lightly, about 2 minutes. Remove meat. Add green peppers and onions; cook for 3 minutes. Return meat to skillet along with sugar, broth, soy sauce, water chestnuts, and cornstarch, dissolved in water. Simmer for about 2 minutes or until sauce thickens. Serve plain or over hot cooked rice.

BBQ BEEF RIBS

Boil 1 rack beef back ribs (about 7 to 8 pounds) for 20 minutes. Remove ribs from water; drain. Place in *glass baking dish*. Cover and refrigerate for 4 to 8 hours. Place ribs, bone side down, on grill, 3 inches from medium coals; cook 20 minutes. Turn and cook about 20 minutes longer and until beef is as done as desired. Baste frequently with sauce while ribs are cooking. Makes 8 servings.

BBQ Sauce - Use commercial BBQ sauce *or*:

1 Tbsp. vegetable oil
1 onion, chopped
1 (16 oz.) can tomato sauce
¼ c. cider vinegar
¼ c. honey
2 Tbsp. lemon juice
1 Tbsp. chili powder
2 Tbsp. Worcestershire sauce

In a 2 quart saucepan, heat oil. Add onions and cook until soft. Stir in the remaining ingredients. Cook over low heat. Stir for 20 minutes. Cool to room temperature. Makes 3 cups.

Taste the flavor of the west.

Lion John Barcellos, Caruthers Lions Club
Caruthers, California, USA

Years wrinkle the skin, but lack of enthusiasm wrinkles the soul.

BBQ SPARERIBS, CHINESE STYLE

3 to 4 lb. spareribs
Salt
Sugar

½ c. honey
1 tsp. soy sauce

Soy Sauce Marinade:

½ c. soy sauce
1 clove garlic, crushed (or garlic
    powder, coarse grind)
3 slices fresh ginger root, crushed

¼ c. dark brown sugar
2 Tbsp. sherry wine
½ c. hoisin sauce (optional)
¼ c. honey

Before marinating, the ribs may be rubbed with sage and salt and left for 1 hour.

To prepare the marinade, combine the crushed garlic and ginger with the soy sauce, sugar, sherry, hoisin sauce. Marinate for 2 to 4 hours. Save extra marinade.

Preheat oven to 375°F. Place ribs on metal rack over a roasting pan filled with water. Roast for 45 minutes, basting frequently with extra marinade. Halfway through the cooking, the ribs may be glazed with the combination of honey and soy sauce mixture. During last 3 minutes, turn heat up to 450° to crisp the ribs.

Finger licking good.

Lion Rod Chow, Caruthers Lions Club
Caruthers, California, USA

BEEF BRISKET BARBECUE

2½ lb. boned fresh beef brisket
1½ tsp. salt
½ c. finely chopped onions
½ c. catsup
¼ c. vinegar

1 Tbsp. Worcestershire sauce
1½ tsp. liquid smoke
¼ tsp. pepper
1 bay leaf, crumbled

Sprinkle beef with salt. Place in ungreased 9x13 inch baking dish. Mix remaining ingredients and pour over beef. Cover and cook in 325° oven until beef is tender, about 2 hours. Makes 10 servings.

❦

Reach deep and find the wonder inside yourself.

SANTA MARIA BBQ TRI TIP

Charcoal
1 top sirloin steak or tri tip (about
   3 inches thick)

1 Tbsp. salt
½ tsp. pepper
½ tsp. garlic

Prepare a hot fire in your barbecue grill. Santa Maria-style is best done on a grill with an adjustable grate so the distance between the meat and the heat can be altered. If all you have available to you is a covered cooker, you will need to make some minor adjustments in technique, such as spreading out the coals to lower the temperature, or perhaps removing the meat for a few minutes after searing to allow the coals to cool slightly. *Do not cover.* Let the wood or charcoal burn down to red-hot coals. If you are using oak chips and charcoal, soak the oak chips in water and add them to the hot charcoal just before the meat goes on.

Combine the salt, pepper, and garlic salt; rub the mixture over the surface of the meat. Put the meat on the grill and adjust the grate so the meat is only 2 or 3 inches from the coals. To seal in the juices, sear one side 5 to 8 minutes; turn and sear the second side, then lower the grate (or raise the grill) so that the meat is 6 to 8 inches from the hot coals. Continue cooking 20 to 30 minutes, turning every 7 or 8 minutes until the beef is cooked to the desired degree of doneness, 130° for rare. Slice and serve with crispy toasted French bread to sop up the meat juices.

This is the rave of central California.

Lion Herluf Hansen, Caruthers Lions Club
Caruthers, California, USA

CARUTHERS BBQ TRI-TIP

5 lb. beef tri-tip roast
1 Tbsp. salt
½ tsp. black pepper
½ tsp. garlic powder

½ tsp. monosodium glutamate
   (Accent)
½ c. sherry wine

Let marinate for 2 hours. To oven roast (375°), cook 45 minutes for rare, 60 minutes for medium, and 75 to 90 minutes for well done. Place meat, fat side up, on rack in open roasting pan.

To BBQ, cooking time (per side) is 20 minutes for rare, 30 minutes for medium, and 40 minutes for well done. To serve: Slice across grain of meat and serve with green salad, corn on the cob, and buttered garlic.

Secret recipe from our BBQ Master.

Lion Jack Christensen, Caruthers Lions Club
Caruthers, California, USA

❦

Make yourself necessary to somebody.

BUTTER BALL STEAK BARBEQUE

3 to 4 lb. butterball steak or thick
    top sirloin
4 Tbsp. softened butter
1½ tsp. salt
1½ tsp. ground black pepper

2 Tbsp. dry mustard
2 tsp. paprika
2 Tbsp. olive oil
1 tsp. Worcestershire sauce

Make a paste of butter, salt, pepper, mustard, and paprika. Rub both sides with 3 tablespoons of seasoned butter. Let steak marinate for 2 hours. When ready to barbecue, combine olive oil and Worcestershire sauce. Place steak on barbeque and grill 8 to 10 minutes on one side. Turn and baste meat lightly with olive oil mixture, then grill 8 to 10 minutes on the other side. Turn and baste again. Continue grilling until done to your satisfaction. Serve steak smeared with remaining butter and sprinkle with parsley.

It is butterly delicious.

Lion Frank Cattuzzo, Caruthers Lions Club
Caruthers, California, USA

KOREAN BARBEQUE BEEF BY CECILE PARK

2 lb. "super thin" sliced beef
2 Tbsp. sesame oil
⅛ c. soy sauce (more or less)
¼ c. sugar
1 tsp. chopped garlic

2 Tbsp. green onion
1 tsp. roasted sesame seeds
Splash of sherry or wine
Sesame oil

Combine all ingredients and allow to marinate in refrigerator 30 minutes minimum ("overnight" okay). Use nonstick skillet over medium high heat. Stir-fry in small batches until liquid evaporates, using 1 teaspoon oil with each batch. Transfer to warm plate. Serve along with hot steamed rice accompanied by Kimchee.

This was passed on to me by Cecile Park, Chesterfield, Virginia. "Use milk-peanuts (peanut butter) or sugar to cool the heat of Thai peppers in your mouth. Peanuts "clear the breath" of hot peppers.

Our wonderful neighbors introduced us to this dish and we often while away the evening dining on this lovely meal.

Lion Vivian Quinlan, Mathews Lions Club
Mathews, Virginia, USA

When we are conscious of the treasure in us, we are fully alive.

BBQ CUPS

1 lb. ground beef
½ c. BBQ sauce
1 Tbsp. minced onion

1½ Tbsp. brown sugar
8 oz. can biscuits
¾ c. shredded Cheddar cheese

Brown meat. Stir in sauce, onion, and brown sugar. Press biscuits into greased muffin cups. Spoon meat mixture into cups. Top with cheese and bake at 400° for 10 minutes.

Beverly Ryan, Decatur Lions Club
Decatur, Texas, USA

EASY SLOPPY JOES

1 lb. hamburger
½ c. chopped onion
1 can chicken gumbo soup

½ can water
2 Tbsp. catsup
1 Tbsp. prepared mustard

Brown hamburger and onion in skillet. Drain grease after hamburger and onion are done. Add remaining ingredients and simmer for about 15 minutes. Serve on buns.

MEAT BARBECUE

2 c. cooked roast, chopped (pork, beef, or venison)
½ c. ketchup
½ c. water

2 Tbsp. brown sugar
1 Tbsp. dry mustard
1 Tbsp. Worcestershire sauce
1 tsp. chopped onion

Mix together all ingredients, except meat. Simmer over low heat 5 to 10 minutes, until ingredients are blended well and mixture has cooked down some. Add meat and simmer 5 to 10 minutes more. Breaking up the chunks by pressing them against the side of the pan helps make this less "soupy."

Lynn Sommerville, Craigsville Lions Club
Craigsville, West Virginia, USA

BARBEQUE BEEF

2 c. water
1 (14 oz.) bottle catsup
1½ tsp. chile powder
1 large onion, chopped

1½ tsp. salt
½ tsp. dry mustard
3 lb. ground beef (do not brown)

Bring to a boil and add ground beef; simmer for 3 hours. Serves about 30.

Lion Beverly Wilkens, Plato Lions Club
Plato, Minnesota, USA

LIONS BARBECUE RECIPE

1½ lb. boneless beef chuck roast
2 carrots, cooked first
1 big onion
2 medium mangos (bell peppers)
3 Tbsp. vinegar
3 Tbsp. table sugar

1 Tbsp. Worcestershire sauce
1 medium size (14 oz.) bottle
  ketchup
1 Tbsp. chili powder
Salt to taste
Pepper to taste

Boil roast and cut up or tear up. Add ingredients. Let all cook or simmer for 45 minutes or until everything is done. This recipe is finger licking good.

Lion Sharon Madison, Latonia Lions Club
Covington, Kentucky, USA

"QUICK AND EASY" BARBECUED BURGERS

2 lb. ground pork or lean ground
  chuck steak
1 tsp. finely chopped onion
Salt and pepper to taste
½ c. cold water

½ c. catsup
1 Tbsp. brown sugar
2 tsp. dry mustard
1 tsp. chili powder

Brown together the meat, onion, salt, and pepper. Meanwhile, make a sauce of the remaining ingredients. Cook together until all is dissolved and slightly thickened. Add to the browned meat. Simmer either in the oven or on top of stove. Serve on buns.

Kenneth Strohbehn, Gladbrook, Iowa, Lions Club
Gladbrook, Iowa, USA

TERIYAKI BURGERS

2½ lb. ground beef
⅔ c. water chestnuts, finely
  chopped
⅓ c. soy sauce
⅓ c. dry sherry or orange juice
2 tsp. molasses or packed brown
  sugar

½ tsp. ground ginger
2 cloves garlic, finely chopped or
  pressed
10 hamburger buns

Mix ground beef and water chestnuts. Shape into 10 patties, about ¾ inch thick. Place in ungreased glass or plastic container. Mix remaining ingredients and pour over patties. Cover and refrigerate at least 3 hours. Turn once. Remove from marinade, saving marinade. Broil or grill patties 4 inches from heat 10 to 15 minutes or until desired doneness, brushing often with marinade and turning once. Easier method, though a bit moist to work with, combine all ingredients and grill. Saves time and effort and even possibly tastes better.

Paul E. Rohde, Woodbury Lions Club
Woodbury, Minnesota, USA

POLISH HAMBURGERS

1¼ lb. lean ground beef
1 medium onion, chopped fine
Dash of pepper
1 can cream of celery soup
  (undiluted)

½ can French fried onions
3 cans Pillsbury crescent rolls

Brown meat and onions; drain fat. Add pepper and celery soup. Crumble onions in mixture. Mix well. Separate crescent rolls. Put 1 heaping tablespoon of meat mixture on large end of crescent roll. Roll from large end as you would crescent rolls. Bake at 375° until nice and brown.

Mary Murphy, Rock Hill Lions Club
Rock Hill, South Carolina, USA

EASY MEAT LOAF

1½ c. herb-seasoned stuffing mix
½ c. warm water
1 env. onion soup mix
1 (8 oz.) can tomato sauce

1 egg
1 lb. ground beef
½ lb. seasoned Italian sausage

Moisten stuffing mix with water. Stir in all other ingredients. Put into baking pan. Form into a loaf and bake at 350° for 50 or 60 minutes. Serves 4. Best D Meatloaf you ever had!

Lion Lee Pirolozzi, Rootstown Lions Club
Rootstown Township, Rootstown, Ohio, USA

MEAT LOAF ROLL

1 (10 oz.) pkg. frozen chopped
  broccoli, spinach or French
  style green beans
2 lb. hamburger
2 eggs
¾ c. soft bread crumbs
¼ c. catsup
¼ c. milk

½ tsp. salt
¼ tsp. pepper
¼ tsp. dried oregano
1 tsp. salt
1 (3 oz.) pkg. sliced ham
3 slices Mozzarella or Swiss
  cheese, cut diagonally into
  halves

Rinse frozen vegetables under cold running water to separate; drain. Mix hamburger, eggs, bread crumbs, catsup, milk, ½ teaspoon salt, pepper, and oregano. Pat hamburger mixture into rectangle, 12x10 inches, on piece of aluminum foil, 18x15 inches.

Arrange vegetables on hamburger mixture to within ½ inch of edges; sprinkle with 1 teaspoon salt. Arrange ham on vegetables. Roll up rectangle carefully, beginning at 10 inch side and using foil to lift. Press edges and ends of roll to seal. Place on rack in shallow roasting pan. Bake, uncovered, in a 350° oven for 1¼ hours. Overlap cheese on top. Bake just until cheese begins to melt, about 1 minute longer. Garnish with celery leaves if desired. Serves 8.

SWEET 'N' SOUR MEAT LOAF

1 small onion, minced	¼ tsp. pepper
1 c. canned tomatoes	1 tsp. salt
¼ c. brown sugar	1 egg
¼ c. vinegar	2 lb. hamburger
¼ c. crushed crackers	1 tsp. prepared mustard

In small bowl, mix onion, tomatoes, sugar, and vinegar enough to break up tomatoes. In another large bowl, mix together crackers, mustard, egg, meat, salt, and pepper. Add half of tomato sauce mix; press into 1¼ quart casserole or loaf pan. Pour over remaining tomato sauce. Bake at 400°F. for 45 minutes. This has a good sweet 'n' sour flavor.

Mrs. Laurie Kovach, Brandon Crocus Lions Club
Brandon, Manitoba, Canada

BARBEQUE BEEF LOAVES

1½ lb. ground beef	4 slices finely diced stale bread
¼ lemon juice	(or ½ c. rolled oats)
½ c. water	¼ c. chopped onion
1 egg, slightly beaten	2 tsp. salt

Mix and shape into loaves. Put in oblong greased pan.

Topping:

½ c. catsup	¼ tsp. ground cloves
⅓ c. brown sugar	¼ tsp. allspice
1 tsp. dry mustard	

Mix all together. Bake loaves at 350° for 15 minutes. Cover top with topping and place lemon slices on each. Continue baking 30 minutes.

Elaine B. Wymer, Rootstown Lions Club
Rootstown Township, Rootstown, Ohio, USA

KANSAS STYLE BAR-B-Q MEAT LOAF

1 c. barbecue sauce (Hunt's thick)	¾ c. quick oatmeal (uncooked)
1 egg, beaten	¼ c. onion, chopped
¼ c. green pepper, chopped	1 tsp. salt
¼ tsp. black pepper	1½ lb. ground beef (lean)

Preheat oven to 350°. Combine all ingredients, except beef. Mix well. Add beef and mix lightly, but thoroughly. Press into 4x8 inch loaf pan. Bake 1 hour. Let stand before slicing. Serves 8.

Geneva Gee, Mt. Airy Foothills Lions Club
Mt. Airy, North Carolina, USA

PRETZEL MEATLOAF

1 c. evaporated milk
1 egg
1½ lb. ground beef
1 c. pretzel crumbs (I use rolling pin)
1 medium onion, finely chopped
1 (4 oz.) can mushrooms (optional)

¾ tsp. salt
1¼ tsp. Accent
⅛ tsp. thyme
⅛ tsp. savory
⅛ tsp. marjoram (optional)

Beat evaporated milk and egg in mixing bowl. Add ground beef and mix well. Add pretzel crumbs and remaining ingredients, mixing with fork until blended. Form into a loaf in greased shallow baking pan. Bake in a moderate oven about 1 hour. Yield: 6 servings.

A 4 ounce can of tomato sauce poured over loaf about 15 minutes before it is finished baking may be added.

Betty Moll, wife of Lion Norman Moll, South Whitehall Lions Club
Schnecksville, Pennsylvania, USA

MEAT LOAF WELLINGTON

1 can cream of mushroom soup
1½ lb. ground beef
1 c. bread crumbs
1 slightly beaten egg

¾ c. minced onion
½ tsp. salt
Dash of pepper
1 pkg. crescent dinner rolls

Combine ¼ cup soup with beef, bread crumbs, egg, onion, salt, and pepper. Mix thoroughly. (May use more soup if needed.) Shape firmly into loaf. Bake at 375° for 55 minutes in a shallow baking pan. Separate rolls. Place crosswise over top and down sides of meat loaf, overlapping slightly. Bake 15 minutes. Remove from pan. Drain grease. Add remaining soup to drippings. Simmer a few minutes and serve as gravy over meat loaf.

Patricia Samuel, Kathleen Ann Gooley, Chesterfield Bay Lions Club
Mt. Clemens, Minnesota, USA

LITTLE CHEDDAR LOAF

1½ lb. ground beef
¾ c. oats
1 tsp. salt (optional)
½ c. grated Cheddar cheese
¼ c. chopped onions

1 egg
¾ c. milk
1 Tbsp. brown sugar
1 Tbsp. mustard
⅓ c. catsup

Combine ground beef, oats, salts, cheese, onions, egg, and milk. Shape into 6 loaves. Place in a shallow baking pan. Combine brown sugar, mustard, and catsup; spread over each loaf. Bake at 350° for 35 minutes.

Lion Connie Cunningham, Graysville/Proctor Lions Club
Glen Easton, West Virginia, USA

GOURMET MEAT BALLS

1 lb. ground beef
1 egg
¼ c. milk

½ c. Quick Quaker Oats
1 small onion, chopped
Salt, pepper

Mix well.

1 pkg. brown gravy mix

2 Tbsp. Miracle Whip dressing

Make meat balls the size of walnuts. Cook them. Make brown gravy mix. Add Miracle Whip. Pour over cooked meat balls.

Jeanne Wait, Whitestown Lions Club
Whitestown, Indiana, USA

MEAT BALLS STROGANOFF

1 lb. ground beef
1 small onion, grated
1 tsp. salt
¼ tsp. nutmeg
¼ tsp. ground cloves
Dash of pepper
2 Tbsp. flour

1½ tsp. dry mustard
1 env. instant beef broth or 1 beef
    flavored bouillon cube
1 c. water
1 c. dairy sour cream
2 Tbsp. chopped parsley

1. Mix ground beef lightly with onion, salt, nutmeg, cloves, and pepper. Shape into small balls.

2. Brown balls. Pour off drippings and remove balls from pan.

3. Mix flour and mustard; stir in instant beef broth or bouillon cube and water. Cook, stirring constantly, until sauce thickens.

MEAT BALLS

4 lb. ground beef
1 tsp. onion powder
1 tsp. garlic powder
4 eggs
½ c. milk

2 c. bread crumbs
8 oz. Heinz chili sauce
16 oz. jar grape jelly
1 c. burgundy wine

Mix ground beef, onion powder, eggs, bread crumbs, and milk well. Make into 1 inch balls and brown in skillet. Drain off any fat.

Mix chili sauce, grape jelly, wine, and garlic powder. Stir and heat for 20 minutes. Add meat balls to this mixture and simmer a short time before serving.

Betty Arnold, Rock Hill Lions Club
Rock Hill, South Carolina, USA

LIONS PICNIC MEATBALLS AND SAUSAGE

1 lb. ground beef
1 c. bread crumbs
1 egg
½ tsp. salt
1 lb. sweet Italian sausage, cut
   into 1½ inch pieces
1 lb. kielbasa, cut into 1½ inch
   pieces

1 green pepper, cut in strips
1 red pepper, cut in strips
1 yellow pepper, cut in strips
1 onion (large), cut in strips
1 qt. spaghetti sauce
½ c. grape jelly

Mix first 4 ingredients. Form into 1½ inch meat balls. Brown in small amount of oil in skillet until done. Remove and set aside. Brown sausage and kielbasa in same skillet. Remove and set aside. Lightly brown peppers and onions. Drain oil. Melt jelly in microwave-safe dish 1 minute or until melted. Blend with spaghetti sauce in 2 quart crock-pot or slow cooker. Add meats and vegetables in alternate layers to the top. Heat on LOW for 1 hour. The secret ingredient is the grape jelly.

This dish won first prize at the 1993 Annual Lions Picnic.
Lion Shirley Riemenschneider, Rootstown Lions Club
Rootstown Township, Rootstown, Ohio, USA

CHILI AND MEATBALL CASSEROLE MEATBALLS

1 lb. ground chuck
1 lb. ground pork
¼ c. bread crumbs
1 clove garlic, crushed
¼ tsp. pepper
2 eggs, slightly beaten
½ c. milk

1 tsp. oregano
½ tsp. basil
¼ c. chopped parsley
2 Tbsp. grated Parmesan cheese
2 tsp. salt
2 Tbsp. salad oil

1. Make meatballs in bowl; combine meats, bread crumbs, garlic, pepper, eggs, milk, oregano, basil, parsley, Parmesan, and salt. Mix well. With moistened hands, shape into 24 (1½ inch) meatballs.
2. Preheat oven to 350°. In hot oil in large skillet, brown meatballs well. Remove as browned to 3 quart casserole.
3. Make chili and discard all but 2 tablespoons drippings. In hot drippings, saute onions and garlic about 5 minutes.
4. Add tomatoes, sauce, chili powder, salt, oregano, basil, and ¼ cup water; bring to boil. Pour over meatballs.
5. Bake, covered, for 1 hour. Combine flour with wine and stir into casserole along with beans. Bake, covered, for 20 minutes longer.

Dave Bernier, Westbrook Lions Club
Westbrook, Maine, USA

Love doesn't try to see through others, but to see others through.

PORCUPINE MEATBALLS

1 lb. ground beef or pork (or more)
½ c. uncooked rice
½ c. finely chopped onion
½ c. finely chopped celery
½ c. finely chopped green pepper
1 egg

1 Tbsp. Worcestershire sauce
2 tsp. prepared mustard
1 tsp. salt
¼ tsp. pepper
¼ tsp. garlic powder

Make in 1½ inch balls. Place in 2½ quart casserole.

Sauce:

1 can cream of mushroom soup   **¼ c. ketchup**
½ c. water

Boil and pour over balls. Cover and bake at 350° for 1 hour.

Optional: Put ⅓ cup cheese on last few minutes.

RICEBALLS

1 lb. ground beef
1 c. Minute rice
½ c. tomato juice

1 egg
1 tsp. salt
1 onion, chopped

Sauce:

2 c. tomato juice   **½ c. sugar**

Mix ingredients together and form into balls. Mix sauce ingredients together and pour over meat mixture. Simmer for 20 minutes.

For any jello salad, mix jello and water together night before and leave on counter top all night. Next morning, it will be slightly jelled and ready for fruit.
Carol Morgan, Moweaqua Lions Club
Moweaqua Illinois, USA

BARBEQUE MEATBALLS

1 lb. hamburger
1 small onion
½ c. bread crumbs
1 egg
2 Tbsp. oil
¾ tsp. salt

¼ tsp. pepper
¾ c. ketchup
2 Tbsp. Dijon mustard
2 Tbsp. brown sugar
1 tsp. Worcestershire sauce

Mince onion. Combine beef, onion, bread crumbs, salt, pepper, egg, and a little milk. Make into balls and cook in oil. Remove meatballs with slotted spoon. Add ketchup, ⅓ cup water, mustard, brown sugar, and Worcestershire sauce to pan; bring to boil. Return meatballs to pan and simmer until hot.
Kathy Gallant, Westbrook Lions Club
Westbrook, Maine, USA

ORIENTAL MEATBALLS

16 oz. hamburger
1 egg
1 small onion, grated

1 tsp. dry mustard
Salt and pepper
Pinch of Italian seasoning

Sauce:

¼ c. soy sauce
½ c. tomato juice (or V-8 juice)

1 pkg. Sweet 'N Low

Mix first 6 ingredients and form small balls. Pour sauce ingredients into pan. Add meatballs. Cover and simmer for ½ hour. Let cool in refrigerator. Skim off fat. Reheat.

Mary Levesque, Westbrook Lions Club
Westbrook, Maine, USA

SWEET AND SOUR MEATBALLS

1 (12 oz.) jar chili sauce
1 (6 oz.) jar grape jelly
1 lb. extra-lean ground beef
2 green onions, finely chopped, or
   2 Tbsp. minced onion

3 Tbsp. bread crumbs
Salt and pepper to taste
Oregano to taste

Preheat oven to 350°. In medium saucepan over low heat, combine chili sauce and jelly; stir occasionally until jelly melts. Or, in a microwave-safe bowl, combine chili sauce and jelly. Stirring occasionally, microwave on HIGH until jelly melts, 1 to 2 minutes. Set sauce aside.

In large bowl, combine beef, onions, bread crumbs, salt, pepper, and oregano to taste; mix thoroughly. Form into small balls and place in deep baking dish. Pour sauce over meatballs, making sure all are covered. Bake in preheated oven 35 minutes. Makes 25 servings. Nutrients per serving: 75 calories, 2 grams fat (24 percent total calories), 9 milligrams cholesterol, and 254 milligrams sodium.

Evelyn W. Carpenter, Lawrenceville Lions Club
Lawrenceville, Virginia, Brunswick County, USA

How good it feels when others believe in you. Believe in yourself!

SWEET AND SOUR MEATBALLS

1 lb. ground round beef
Small onion, chopped
Dash of pepper
12 oz. Smucker's apricot
  preserves

½ lb. sausage
1 egg
Dash of salt
½ c. Heinz bar-b-que sauce

Mix and shape into meatballs. Brown either in frying pan or can brown in microwave. If using microwave, in 700 watt microwave, cover with wax paper and cook on HIGH 4 minutes. Rearrange meatballs and turn over; cover with wax paper again and cook on HIGH 4 minutes. Move meatballs to another dish and pour mixture (12 ounces Smucker's apricot preserves mixed with ½ cup Heinz bar-b-que sauce) over meatballs. Cover with tin foil and cook at 350° for 30 minutes in regular oven. Serve with rice or use for meatball sandwiches.

Robert Blake, Mt. Airy Foothills Lions Club
Mt. Airy, North Carolina, USA

🍏

There really is no stress in the world -
only people thinking stressful thoughts.

🍏 🍏 🍏

The best and most beautiful things in the world cannot be seen
or even touched. They must be felt with the heart.

Helen Keller

🍏 🍏 🍏

Rare is the person who can weigh the faults of others
without putting his thumb on the scales.

ENTREES - POULTRY

ISRAELI CHICKEN

1 Tbsp. and 1 tsp. vegetable oil
1 whole chicken, cut into 8 to 12
   pieces and skinned
2 c. onions, thinly sliced
1 c. orange juice (no sugar added)
2 Tbsp. honey
1 tsp. salt
1 tsp. paprika

1 tsp. ground ginger
1 tsp. ground nutmeg
8 large pitted black olives, sliced
1 Tbsp. water
2 tsp. cornstarch
1 c. canned mandarin orange
   sections (no sugar added)

Preheat oven to 350°F. In 10 inch nonstick skillet, heat oil. Brown chicken on all sides. Spread onion slices on bottom of shallow 3 quart casserole. Place chicken on top of onions. Combine juice, honey, and seasonings. Pour mixture evenly over chicken and top chicken with olives. Cover casserole and bake until chicken is tender, about 45 minutes.

Transfer chicken and olives to serving platter and keep warm. Scrape onions and pan juices into 1 quart saucepan; bring to a boil. In small cup, combine water and cornstarch, stirring to dissolve cornstarch. Stir into onion mixture.

Reduce heat and simmer, stirring constantly, until mixture thickens. Pour over chicken. Serve garnished with orange sections. Makes 4 servings.

MEXICAN CHICKEN

1 can cream of chicken soup
1 can cream of mushroom soup
½ can Ro-Tel tomatoes and green
   chilies
1½ c. chicken broth

½ onion
1 pkg. Doritos
1 c. grated cheese
1 whole chicken or 6 chicken
   breasts

Boil chicken and remove bone. Mix the 2 soups, Ro-Tel tomatoes and green chilies, onions, and broth in large bowl. Mix well. Layer Doritos, layer chicken, and layer the soup mixture, until all is used. Bake 1 hour at 350°. Five minutes before cooking is up, add cheese on top and let melt. Serve. Bake in 13x9x2 inch pan.

Pauline Sammons
Waldo, Arkansas, USA

Think big thoughts, but enjoy small pleasures.

HAWAIIAN CHICKEN

2 frying chickens, cut into serving
   pieces
1 c. flour

Salt and pepper
2 cans cream of chicken soup
1 c. crushed pineapple

Put flour, salt, and pepper in bag. Add pieces of chicken, 2 at a time, and shake to coat. Brown in fry pan. Combine soup and pineapple. Place chicken in casserole. Pour soup mixture over. Bake at 350° for 45 minutes.

Denture cleaning tablets will take coffee, tea, and juice stains out of tea cups. So will vinegar and most other bleaches.

Dianne Crayston, Jasper Mountain Lions Club
Jasper, Alberta, Canada

CHICKEN HAWAIIAN

1 tsp. freshly grated ginger root
3 garlic cloves, minced
2 shallots, minced
1 c. chicken stock
¾ c. chopped onion
6 oz. unsweetened pineapple juice
14 oz. chicken breasts, skinned,
   boned, and cubed
1 c. fresh pineapple, cubed

¼ tsp. poultry seasoning
1 Tbsp. low-sodium soy sauce or
   tamari
¼ c. tomato puree
¾ c. sliced red bell pepper
¾ c. sliced green bell pepper
1 Tbsp. cornstarch or arrowroot
¼ c. water
1 Tbsp. apple juice concentrate

1. Combine ginger root, garlic, shallots, and stock in a large nonstick saucepan. Simmer 10 minutes.

2. Add the onion and cook 5 minutes. Add the pineapple juice. Simmer 1 minute.

3. Add the chicken, pineapple, seasoning, soy sauce, tomato puree, and bell peppers. Simmer 15 minutes or until chicken is tender.

4. Dissolve the cornstarch in the water and apple juice concentrate in a small bowl. Blend into the chicken mixture. Cook, stirring constantly, until thickened and clear. Cook 2 minutes more. Makes 6 servings.

Variation: Serve over cooked brown rice or pasta.

Nutritional breakdown (per serving without rice or pasta): 146 calories, 18 g protein, 17 g carbohydrates, 0.5 g fat, 178 mg sodium, and 30 mg cholesterol.

Maria Specht, President, Prince Albert Downtown Lioness Club
Prince Albert, Saskatchewan, Canada

Never underestimate the power of a kind word.

LUAU CHICKEN
(Hawaiian recipe)

1 (1 lb.) can peaches, sliced
1/3 c. ketchup
2 Tbsp. soy sauce
2 Tbsp. brown sugar

1/4 tsp. garlic powder
1 tsp. ginger
2 lb. chicken breast, cooked
1 Tbsp. vegetable oil

Mash peaches and juice with fork in small bowl. Mix in ketchup, soy sauce, brown sugar, garlic, and ginger. Cut meat into bite-size pieces. Brown meat in oil in frying pan. Pour sauce over meat. Cover and cook over low heat 40 to 60 minutes.

This recipe is a 4-H dish which is very good!
Sandra Scott (Greg Scott, member), Bascom Lions Club
Fostoria, Ohio, USA

CASABLANCA CHICKEN

2 Tbsp. lowfat yogurt
1/2 tsp. ground cumin
1/2 tsp. ground cinnamon
2 chicken breasts, skinned,
  boned, and pounded thin
1 large eggplant

1/4 c. chicken stock
3 garlic cloves, finely minced
3 large shallots, finely chopped
12 cherry tomatoes
3/4 tsp. dried leaf oregano

1. Blend yogurt, cumin, and cinnamon in a small bowl.

2. Rub 1/2 of the yogurt mixture all over chicken; cover with plastic wrap and marinate in refrigerator 2 hours or overnight.

3. Prick eggplant skin; steam until tender. Peel and chop.

4. Spray a medium size skillet with no stick cooking spray. Add stock and saute garlic and shallots until soft. Add eggplant and stir 2 minutes. Remove from heat; add remaining yogurt mixture and blend well. Keep warm.

5. Spray another medium size nonstick skillet. Add chicken breasts; cook 3 to 4 minutes on each side, constantly turning so as not to burn or stick.

6. Add tomatoes, chicken, and oregano to eggplant mixture. Serve on brown rice. Makes 4 servings.

Nutritional breakdown (per serving without rice): 175 calories, 28 g protein, 5 g carbohydrates, 3 g fat, 70 mg sodium, and 75 mg cholesterol.

Maria Specht, President, Prince Albert Downtown Lioness Club
Prince Albert, Saskatchewan, Canada

You can't build a reputation on what you plan to do.

KOTOPOULO ME BAMYES - CHICKEN WITH OKRA

1 chicken (about 2 kg)
¼ c. corn oil
1 onion, finely chopped

1 glove garlic, crushed
1½ c. chopped, peeled tomatoes
500 g okra, prepared as in method

Cut chicken into serving pieces and wipe dry. Heat oil in a heavy saucepan or flameproof casserole and brown chicken on all sides. Remove to a plate when browned. Reduce heat; add onion, garlic, and tomatoes. Cover and simmer for 20 minutes. Add chicken and continue for 20 minutes.

Preparation of okra: Wash well. Trim stem end, without cutting pod, removing a thin layer. Dry okra well in a cloth or spread out and leave until dry. Fry in ½ cup corn oil for 5 minutes, tossing gently with wooden spoon. Add okra to the chicken; sprinkle with 2 to 3 tablespoons of vinegar and some water if needed (about ½ cup). Cover and continue cooking on a low heat for 30 minutes. Serve with rice pilaff.

Chrystalleni Louca, Famagusta Arsinoe Lions Club
Limassol, Cyprus

ORIENTAL CHICKEN

¼ c. vegetable oil
1 pkg. boneless chicken thighs
1 can sliced water chestnuts
1 (16 oz.) pkg. frozen oriental
  vegetables (or frozen baby
  vegetables)
2 cans (10½ oz.) chicken gravy
  (Franco-American)

Small dash of Worcestershire
  sauce
Dash of garlic powder
4 to 5 splashes soy sauce
½ c. water
1 can Chinese noodles
Wok or equivalent pan

Clean and cut up chicken into bite-size pieces. Put oil in wok and heat until hot. Put chicken into hot oil and cook until all sides are firm. Add frozen vegetables right from package. Add water chestnuts.

In a separate container, mix gravy, garlic powder, Worcestershire sauce, soy sauce, and water. Mix well together. Pour mixture into wok with chicken. Mix. Cover. Cook till chicken and vegetables are tender, approximately 20 to 30 minutes. Serve over rice and top with Chinese noodles. Boneless chicken breasts may be substituted, however, thighs come out more tender.

Theresa Wrinkle, Chesterfield Bay Lions Club
Mt. Clemens, Michigan, USA

❦

Lord, grant that I may always desire more than I can accomplish

CAJUN GUMBO FILE

2 Tbsp. vegetable oil
2 Tbsp. flour
1 large chicken, cut up
Water to cover chicken
Canned chicken broth (to add to
    broth from chicken to make
    4 c.)
½ lb. Brown and Serve sausage
1 lb. small frozen, peeled shrimp
½ c. finely chopped shallot (if
    available)

2 c. finely chopped onion
2 c. okra, cut into ½ inch pieces
    (or 2 c. canned, drained)
1 large can tomatoes (with juice)
2 pods pressed garlic
Salt and pepper to taste
¼ tsp. Tabasco
1 bay leaf
4 c. water
File powder to taste

Stew chicken; remove skin, fat, and bones. Cut up into bite-size. Set aside. Measure broth. Add canned chicken broth to make 4 cups. In large, heavy pot, heat vegetable oil. Add flour, stirring constantly to make a dark brown roux.

In separate skillet, brown sausage. Drain and slice into ¼ inch rounds. Prepare shrimp if necessary. Saute shallot, onion, and okra, if raw. (If canned, add with other vegetables.) To pot containing roux, add broken up tomatoes and juice, garlic, salt, pepper, Tabasco, bay leaf, 4 cups chicken broth, 4 cups water, chicken, and sausage. Cover and simmer gently for at least an hour, stirring occasionally. Add shrimp. Heat until pink. Remove bay leaf. Sprinkle on file at very last. Serve over prepared rice (or with oyster crackers).

❧

*Of all the deathbed regrets ever given, not one of them has been,
"I wish I had spent more time at the office."*

❧ ❧ ❧

*If people concentrated on the really important things in life,
there'd be a shortage of fishing poles.*

CAJUN CHICKEN WITH A TWIST

2½ tsp. Cajun Magic
4 boneless, skinless chicken
    breast halves
4 Tbsp. margarine
¼ c. all-purpose flour
1 c. chopped onion
½ c. chopped celery

½ c. fresh squeezed orange juice
3 Tbsp. dark brown sugar
1 Tbsp. grated fresh orange peel
1 c. basic chicken stock or water
1 tsp. cornstarch, dissolved in 1
    Tbsp. water
Hot cooked rice

Sprinkle 1½ teaspoons of Cajun Magic evenly over both sides of chicken. In 10 inch skillet, melt 2 tablespoons of margarine over high heat until it comes to a hard sizzle. Coat seasoned chicken pieces with flour. Shake off excess flour and lay in skillet. Cook approximately 3 minutes or until lightly browned. Remove from skillet and reserve. Reduce heat to medium and add remaining margarine to skillet to deglaze pan. Stir and scrape bottom to get up the browned bits. Add the onions, celery, and the remaining Cajun Magic. Stir frequently to keep from sticking.

Cook approximately 7½ minutes or until vegetables are browned and soft. Stir in orange juice and increase heat to high. Continue to stir and scrape pan bottom and sides to well incorporate browned bits. Add brown sugar, orange peel, and stock. Cook about 3 minutes or until boiling. Whisk in dissolved cornstarch. Cook 1 minute. Return chicken to pan, reduce heat to low, and simmer 10 minutes. Serve over hot rice. Unboned chicken parts may be used, but allow longer cooking time.

Louise Brooks (Mrs. Russell), Silver Run-Union Mills Lions Club
Mt. Lake Park, Maryland, USA

ITALIAN CHICKEN

1 green pepper
1 medium onion, minced
1 clove garlic or ½ tsp. garlic salt
3 (8 oz.) cans tomato sauce
1 (8 oz.) can mushrooms and
    liquid

1 (8 oz.) can English peas, drained
2 tsp. Worcestershire sauce
12 large chicken breasts
8 oz. pkg. noodles
Salt and pepper to taste

Cover chicken with water; add salt and cook till done. Remove bones, cut into bite-size pieces. Save broth to cook noodles (about 10 minutes). Drain and add to above. Mix green pepper, onion, garlic, and oil. Cook on medium heat till clear. Add tomato sauce, bite-size chicken, mushrooms, peas, and Worcestershire sauce. Reheat. Serves 8 to 10.

No virtue is ever so strong that it is beyond temptation.

Kathy Parker, Rock Hill Lions Club
Rock Hill, South Carolina, USA

❦

In a child's lunch box are a mother's thoughts.

CHINESE STYLE OVEN ROASTED CHICKEN

1 whole body fryer
¼ c. sherry wine
2 Tbsp. soy sauce

1 tsp. garlic powder (coarse)
1 tsp. salt, black pepper, green
onions

Sprinkle with wine on chicken and inside cavity. Rub with soy sauce. Sprinkle with garlic, salt, and black pepper. Stuff green onion in body cavity. Roast in oven at 325°F. for 1½ hours until done. The chicken will be juicy and tender.

Lion Stanley Silva, Caruthers Lions Club
Caruthers, California, USA

GREEK CHICKEN AND TOMATO CASSEROLE

1 lemon (juice)
Pinch of ground cloves
½ tsp. ground cinnamon
Pepper
1 large skinned chicken, cut up

1 tsp. olive oil
6 tomatoes, peeled and chopped
2 Tbsp. tomato paste
2½ c. hot water

Mix together the lemon juice, cloves, cinnamon, and pepper. Rub mixture well into chicken pieces. Heat oil in large, nonstick saucepan. "Fry" chicken in oil until golden brown. Remove chicken and keep it hot while stirring tomatoes and tomato paste into the drippings. Gradually stir in hot water. Cook over gentle heat until tomatoes are mushy and sauce is thick. Return chicken pieces to pan, turning pieces to coat them with sauce. Cover pan and cook over very low heat for about 45 minutes, until chicken begins to fall off the bones. Serve with plain boiled rice. Makes 6 servings. Contains 208 calories, 9 g fat, and 72 mg cholesterol per serving.

Mrs. Charlotte M. Garner, Pascagoula Evening Lions Club
Pascagoula, Mississippi, USA

RO-TEL CHICKEN

1 whole chicken, boiled and meat
removed from bone
1 (11 oz.) can cream of mushroom
soup
1 (11 oz.) can cream of chicken
soup

1 (11 oz.) can Cheddar cheese
soup
1 can Ro-Tel tomatoes
1 large onion, grated
1 large (14½ oz.) bag Doritos
2 c. grated Cheddar cheese

Mix together the soups, onions, and Ro-Tel tomatoes. Grease a 9x13x2 inch casserole dish and put a third of tomato and soup mixture on bottom a layer of chicken, next ⅓ of Doritos. Start with another layer of soup mixture and continue with each layer, ending with chicken and soup mixture last; sprinkle a little cheese on top. Be sure to layer cheese between the layers. Bake at 350° for 30 minutes till it is good and bubbly.

Mrs. Charlotte M. Garner, Pascagoula Evening Lions Club
Pascagoula, Mississippi, USA

STUFFED CHICKEN BREAST

1 sweet red pepper
1 sweet green pepper
1 yellow pepper
Salt and pepper to taste
4 boneless chicken breasts

½ tsp. thyme
2 Tbsp. oleo or butter
1 tsp. Dijon mustard
2 oz. white wine

Clean pepper and cut into ⅜ to ½ inch strips. Saute in 1 tablespoon oleo and seasonings (¼ teaspoon each). Cool. Flatten breasts, then roll pepper strips up in the breast (with skin side out). Close with toothpicks (I use washed, shiny nails.) Mix other half of seasonings with 1 tablespoon oleo, Dijon mustard, and wine. Use for basting while cooking on bar-b-q grill or pan-fry if desired. (Your favorite marinade can be substituted for basting.)

Walter E. Loomis, North Jackson Lions Club
Jackson, Michigan, USA

RANCH CHICKEN

2 c. pineapple juice
2 pkg. milk recipe Hidden Valley
   Ranch dressing

8 boneless chicken breasts
2 Tbsp. cornstarch

Mix juice and dressing mix. Marinate chicken in ½ juice mixture in 9x13 inch pan for 2 to 24 hours. Bake at 350° for 45 to 60 minutes until tender. Combine cornstarch with remaining juice. Heat to thicken. Brush chicken with sauce.

❦

If you find yourself believing that you must always be
the way you have always been before, you are arguing against growth.

❦ ❦ ❦

By the time a man realizes that maybe his father was right,
he usually has a son who thinks he's wrong.

STUFFED CHICKEN BREAST WITH THREE CHEESES

4 whole boneless chicken breasts
¼ tsp. pepper
4 Tbsp. butter or margarine
2 oz. (¼ c.) goat cheese, crumbled
2 oz. (¼ c.) shredded Gouda
   cheese
2 oz. (¼ oz.) shredded Port salad
   cheese

6 medium tomatoes, peeled,
   seeded, and chopped
¼ c. Chablis or dry white wine
1 Tbsp. fresh or 1 tsp. dried basil
½ tsp. salt
¼ c. all-purpose flour
1 Tbsp. chopped shallots

Lay chicken breasts flat and lightly pound to an even thickness. Sprinkle with salt and pepper. Combine cheeses and divide evenly among breasts, placing cheeses in the center. Fold breasts over completely enclosing cheeses. Secure with toothpicks. Dredge chicken breasts in flour. Melt butter in a large fry pan; saute chicken until golden brown on both sides. Transfer chicken to an 8x10 inch oblong baking dish. Bake in a preheated 400° oven for 15 to 20 minutes or until juices run clear.

Meanwhile, remove all but 3 tablespoons of pan drippings from fry pan. Saute shallots until tender, about 1 minute. Stir in tomatoes, wine, and basil. Cook over medium high heat until reduced to 3 cups. To serve, place breasts on a warm plate. Top with sauce.

Dave Bernier, Westbrook Lions Club
Westbrook, Maine, USA

CHICKEN BREASTS DIANE

4 large boneless chicken breast
   halves (or 8 small)
½ tsp. salt
¼ to ½ tsp. black pepper
2 Tbsp. olive or salad oil
3 Tbsp. chopped fresh chives or
   green onions

2 Tbsp. butter or margarine
Juice of ½ lime or lemon
2 Tbsp. brandy or cognac
   (optional)
3 Tbsp. chopped parsley
2 tsp. Dijon style mustard
¼ c. chicken broth

Place chicken breast halves between sheets of waxed paper or plastic wrap. Pound slightly with mallet. Sprinkle with salt and pepper. Heat 1 tablespoon each of oil and butter in large skillet. Cook chicken over high heat for 4 minutes on each side. Do not cook longer or they will be overcooked and dry. Transfer to warm serving platter. Add chives or green onion, lime/lemon juice, and brandy/cognac, if used, parsley, and mustard to pan. Cook 15 seconds, whisking constantly. Whisk in broth. Stir until sauce is smooth. Whisk in remaining butter and oil. Pour sauce over chicken. Serve immediately.

Eric E. Steen, Merritt Island Lions Club
Merritt Island, Florida, USA

NUTTY CHICKEN BREAST

6 boneless skinless chicken
   breast halves
¼ lb. cholesterol free oleo
½ c. walnuts or pecans
Lemon pepper

Garlic powder
Ginger
White cooking wine
1 c. flour

Melt oleo in 10 inch saute pan and heat to fry temperature. Sprinkle lemon pepper generously onto chicken breast. Sprinkle garlic powder and ginger to taste; let set for 10 minutes. Roll in flour, then place chicken into saute pan and cook 5 minutes on each side or until golden brown. Grate nuts onto chicken and into liquid, scraping pan regularly. Add ⅔ cup wine. Lower heat and simmer, covered, for 5 minutes. Serve on plate, covering meat with nut wine sauce. If fluid is skimpy in pan, add ½ cup water. Serve with pasta or chicken flavored Rice-A-Roni and favorite vegetable. Salt and pepper can be added to suit taste - some like to sprinkle a small amount of sugar onto chicken as the nuts are added.

R. Hilton McCrory, Alexandria Lions Club
Alexandria, Louisiana, USA

PENNE WITH CHICKEN, SUN-DRIED TOMATOES, AND ONIONS

1¾ c. chicken broth
½ c. sun-dried tomatoes
1 Tbsp. olive oil
1½ lb. onions, thinly sliced

1 lb. boneless, skinless chicken
   breasts
½ lb. penne

1. Heat broth to a boil; pour over sun-dried tomatoes and leave until softened, about 30 minutes.

2. Meanwhile, in large, nonstick frying pan heat oil over low heat. Add onions. Cook, covered, stirring occasionally, until very soft, about 20 minutes. Uncover, raise heat to medium, and cook, stirring often, until dark golden brown, about 10 minutes longer.

3. In a frying pan, pour water to a depth of ¼ inch. Add chicken and bring to a boil. Cover, reduce heat, and simmer, turning the chicken once, until cooked through, about 8 minutes. Cool, then cut in ¼ inch diagonal slices.

4. Drain the tomatoes, reserving their liquid, and chop.

5. Add the reserved liquid, tomatoes, and chicken to the onions and reheat.

6. In a large pot of boiling salted water, cook the penne. Drain, return to pot, and toss with chicken mixture to coat. Makes 6 servings.

John J. Hess for Mrs. Joanne Brownell, Clarence Center Lions Club
Clarence Center, New York, USA

❦

Be glad you had the moment.

MARINATED CHICKEN BREASTS

4 boneless, skinless chicken
   breasts

⅔ c. Worcestershire sauce
⅔ c. red wine vinegar

Place chicken breasts in a flat pan. Mix vinegar and Worcestershire sauce in a 2 cup measuring cup. Pour over chicken breasts and let marinate for at least 30 minutes in refrigerator. Remove from marinade with food tongs, allowing excess to drip back into pan. Place on hot grill, griddle or skillet. Cook until done in center over *medium* heat. May also be baked in metal pan in a 350° oven for 1 hour or until done.

Frances B. Blount, Saginaw Lions Club
Saginaw, Texas, Tarrant Co., USA

CHICKEN BREAST IN WINE

4 breasts, skinned and salted
1 can cream of chicken soup

2 cans cream of celery soup
½ can sherry wine

Put breasts in a 9x12 inch pan, bone side up. Spoon soup mixture on top of chicken. Sprinkle little paprika on top. Bake at 275° for 3 hours. Last 5 minutes, put some shredded sharp cheese on each breast. The soup makes your gravy good on wild rice. It's good!

Nita Konrade, Offerle Lions Club
Offerle, Kansas, USA

CHICKEN BREAST IN HEAVY CREAM
AND SPICY MUSTARD

4 chicken breasts (boneless/
   skinless)
4 Tbsp. spicy mustard
3 Tbsp. butter

¼ c. flour
1 pt. heavy cream
Salt and pepper to taste

Coat chicken breasts with mustard (probably 2 tablespoons). Salt and pepper each piece; flour each piece and saute in butter for 5 minutes on each side. Remove from pan. Add heavy cream and 2 tablespoons mustard to frying pan. Return chicken breast to pan and cook another 5 to 10 minutes.

This is the recipe which makes guests think you are a gourmet cook.
Rev. Fred Gilbert, Dannemora, New York, Lions Club
Dannemora, New York, USA

He is happiest who finds peace in his home.

CHICKEN DELITE

3 chicken breasts
1 c. celery, diced
1 c. mushrooms, sliced
1 c. water chestnuts, sliced
1 stick margarine

1 can mushroom soup
1½ c. sour cream
1 pkg. stuffing mix
1 c. broth

Boil chicken breasts and cut up. Saute lightly in ½ stick margarine the celery, mushrooms, and water chestnuts, then mix the mushroom soup (do not add water) with the sour cream. Mix in chicken pieces. Pour into slightly greased 9x13 inch pan. Mix together 1 package stuffing mix, broth, and ½ stick margarine. Spread over chicken mixture. Bake for 45 minutes at 350°. (It can serve 15.)

To be contented with what one possesses is great riches.
Leola C. Jurrens, Downtown Bartlesville Lions Club
Bartlesville, Oklahoma, USA

CHICKEN MARSALA

6 to 8 pieces, boned chicken
   breast
1 c. chicken broth
1 c. Marsala wine
1 small onion, chopped

1 pkg. mushroom soup mix
½ stick butter
6 Tbsp. olive oil
1 c. flour
Salt and pepper to taste

Pound the chicken breast. Salt and pepper to taste. Dredge in the flour. Heat olive oil and butter in skillet or wok and saute the chicken breast until done. Remove to a shallow dish. Add the chicken broth, wine, soup mix, and onions to the remaining liquid. Cook until the mixture is about 1 cup. Thicken if necessary and pour over the chicken. Serve with buttered noodles or twice baked potatoes and favorite side dish.

William M. Davidson, IV, Statesboro Lions Club
Statesboro, Georgia, USA

CHICKEN WITH PECANS

4 to 6 chicken breasts, boned
2 c. chopped pecans or other nuts
2 eggs, beaten

Salt and pepper to taste
Nature's Seasoning (if desired)

Salt and pepper chicken breast as desired. Sprinkle with Nature's Seasoning. Dredge in flour and dip in the eggs. Roll chicken breast in the crushed nuts and place in a greased baking dish. Bake at 375° for 45 to 50 minutes or until done. Serve immediately with favorite side dishes.

William M. Davidson, IV, Statesboro Lions Club
Statesboro, Georgia, USA

CHICKEN DIABLO

4 chicken breasts (or cut up
   chicken parts)
½ stick butter (or margarine)
½ c. honey

¼ c. prepared mustard
1 tsp. salt
1 tsp. curry powder

Wash chicken; pat dry and, if desired, remove skin. Melt butter in shallow baking pan and stir in remaining ingredients. Roll chicken in butter mixture to coat both sides and arrange, meaty side up, in a single layer pan. Bake at 375°, uncovered, until tender and highly glazed. Goes great with rice and fried bananas. If you like food from India, you will like this recipe.

Suzanne Mooneyham, Cheyenne Mountain Lions Club
Colorado Springs, Colorado, USA

CHICKEN DISH

8 to 10 chicken breasts, skinned
   and boned
1 pkg. dry onion soup mix

1 (6 to 8 oz.) jar apricot preserves
1 (6 oz.) bottle Thousand Island
   dressing

Roll chicken breasts. Place rolled side down in greased casserole. Mix together the soup, preserves, and dressing; pour over chicken. Bake at 350° approximately an hour, basting occasionally. Serve over plain rice or seasoned rice, spooning sauce on the chicken and rice. Good luncheon or dinner.

Hugh Duncan, East Lake Lions Club
Birmingham, Alabama, USA

CHICKEN WINGS

1 c. oil
3 lb. chicken wings
2 tsp. finely chopped garlic
1 inch square fresh ginger, thinly
   sliced

⅓ c. white wine (Chinese cooking
   wine is preferred)
¼ c. sugar
⅓ c. soy sauce
⅓ c. white vinegar

Heat oil in a wok or deep frying pan until a drop of water sizzles on the oil. Cook one half of the chicken wings. Fry the chicken wings, turning the pieces frequently to allow for even cooking. Cook until golden brown. Remove the chicken wings and drain on a paper towel. Cook the remaining chicken wings in like manner.

Remove the meat and drain the pan's oil, reserving 1 tablespoon. To the remaining oil, add garlic, ginger slices, white wine, sugar, soy sauce, and vinegar.

Return the cooked chicken wings to the soy sauce mixture. Cover with a lid and simmer for 10 to 15 minutes. Stir the chicken wings frequently to coat and monitor the liquid because it burns easily. Add water if the liquid boils low. Serves 4.

CHICKEN WINGS

3 lb. chicken wings
1 c. soy sauce

¼ c. water
¾ c. sugar

Cut off tips. Pour mixture over wings. Add chopped onion over wings. Cover and cook 20 minutes. Uncover and cook about 1½ hours on medium heat. You save time when you don't have to marinate.

Lion Beverly Wilkens, Plato Lions Club
Plato, Minnesota, USA

CHICKEN DRUMETTES

3 to 4 lb. chicken wings
1½ c. orange juice
¼ c. soy sauce

Garlic powder to taste
Bread crumbs or crushed corn
flakes

Disjoint the wings. Save the tips to make chicken broth for other recipes. Place the wings in a covered dish with the orange juice, soy sauce, and garlic. Marinate for 4 to 6 hours in the refrigerator. Remove the wings from the marinade and roll in bread crumbs or corn flakes. Place on cookie sheet and bake 35 to 40 minutes at 350°.

William M. Davidson, IV, Statesboro Lions Club
Statesboro, Georgia, USA

LEMONY HERB DRUMSTICKS

A trio of savory herbs finds an ally in the fresh taste of lemon. Make the zesty marinade in just 5 minutes, then cook the chicken whenever you're ready.

3 lemons
3 Tbsp. oil
Salt
1 tsp. dried thyme

1 tsp. dried oregano
1 tsp. dried marjoram
8 chicken drumsticks

Grate 2 teaspoons yellow zest from lemons and squeeze ⅓ cup juice. In a stainless steel or glass dish, combine lemon juice and zest, oil, 1 teaspoon salt, thyme, oregano, marjoram, and drumsticks. Cover and refrigerate, turning occasionally, at least 1 hour or overnight. Heat the grill. Cook the drumsticks directly over medium-hot coals, turning once and basting occasionally with the lemon-herb marinade, until cooked through, 30 to 40 minutes. Makes 4 servings.

John J. Hess for Mrs. Joanne Brownell, Clarence Center Lions Club
Clarence Center, New York, USA

Unshared joy is an unlighted candle.

SWEET AND SOUR DRUMSTICKS

Apricot preserves add just the right amount of sweetness to these tempting legs. Ginger and a pinch of red pepper flakes give them zip.

1 clove garlic, minced
½ c. apricot preserves
2 Tbsp. soy sauce
2 Tbsp. rice-wine vinegar

2 Tbsp. brown sugar
1 tsp. grated fresh ginger
¼ tsp. crushed red pepper flakes
8 chicken drumsticks

Heat broiler. Combine garlic, preserves, soy sauce, vinegar, brown sugar, ginger, and red pepper flakes. Put drumsticks on rack on broiler pan. Brush with some of the soy sauce mixture. Broil about 6 inches from source of heat, turning and brushing occasionally with soy sauce mixture, until done, about 20 minutes.

John J. Hess for Mrs. Joanne Brownell, Clarence Center Lions Club
Clarence Center, New York, USA

CRISP BAKED DRUMSTICKS

Crunchy on the outside and juicy underneath, these legs deliver fried-chicken flavor without the fat and mess.

½ c. flour
Salt
½ tsp. nutmeg
¼ tsp. cayenne
1 egg

2 Tbsp. milk
8 chicken drumsticks
⅓ c. dry bread crumbs
2 Tbsp. oil

Heat oven to 375°. In a plastic bag, combine the flour, 2 teaspoons salt, the nutmeg, and cayenne. Beat together the egg and the milk. Put the drumsticks in the bag, one at a time, with the flour mixture and shake well to coat. After all the legs are coated, add the bread crumbs to the remaining flour mixture. Dip the drumsticks in the egg mixture, then return them to the bag to coat with the bread crumb mixture. Put the drumsticks on an ungreased cookie sheet and drizzle them with the oil. Bake, turning often until the drumsticks are golden and crisp, about 40 minutes.

John J. Hess for Mrs. Joanne Brownell, Clarence Center Lions Club
Clarence Center, New York, USA

Make the world a better place by being all you are.

BAKED PINEAPPLE CHICKEN

1 (20 oz.) can Dole pineapple
    slices
1 clove garlic, crushed
2 tsp. cornstarch
2 tsp. Worcestershire sauce

2 tsp. Dijon mustard
1 tsp. rosemary, crushed
6 half chicken breasts, boned
1 lemon, thinly sliced

Drain pineapple; reserve juice. Combine reserved juice with garlic, cornstarch, Worcestershire sauce, mustard, and rosemary. Arrange chicken in shallow baking pan or broiler-proof dish, skin side up. Broil until browned. Stir sauce; pour over chicken. Bake at 400°F. for 30 minutes. Arrange lemon and pineapple slices around chicken. Spoon sauce from baking pan over all; continue baking 5 minutes. Garnish with fresh rosemary or parsley if desired.

John J. Hess, Clarence Center Lions Club
Clarence Center, New York, USA

PRETTY GOOD CHICKEN

¼ c. olive oil
1 medium onion, chopped
1 small green pepper, chopped
    (optional)
¼ to ½ tsp. minced garlic (to taste)
3 lb. chicken pieces (thighs,
    drumsticks, and wings),
    skinned and fat removed
2 cans ready cut tomatoes (3 large
    fresh)

½ tsp. oregano
½ tsp. thyme
½ tsp. parsley flakes or equal
    fresh
3 tsp. chicken bouillon crystals
2 qt. water
Salt (to taste)
1 small red bell pepper, chopped
    (optional)
Parmesan cheese (to taste)

This recipe works well in a slow cooker. In ¼ cup olive oil, soften chopped onion, green pepper, red bell pepper, and the minced garlic. Add chicken pieces. Add 2 cans tomatoes (or fresh). Stir in oregano, thyme, and parsley flakes. Add chicken bouillon, water, and salt (to taste). Cook on medium heat for 1 hour or until chicken is done and falls easily from bone. (Or, cook all day in slow cooker for 4 to 6 hours). Serve on a bed of rice. Garnish with parsley and sprinkle lightly with grated Parmesan cheese.

Herb Rice (as much as needed):

1 tsp. minced onion
Rice
½ tsp. parsley flakes

1 Tbsp. oil
¼ tsp. chicken bouillon crystals

Cook rice (2 parts water to 1 part rice) to yield as much as you need. Add rice to boiling salted water. Stir in minced onion, parsley flakes, and oil, also ¼ teaspoon bouillon. Boil rice, uncovered, for 10 minutes, stirring occasionally. Cover tightly and turn off heat. Let set for 10 minutes.

The next day, combine leftover rice with leftover chicken liquid for a fantastic soup.

CHICKEN CACCIATORE

Chicken
1 small can tomato sauce
1 onion, chopped

1 green pepper, chopped
1 can mushrooms
1 small pkg. Mozzarella

Brown chicken in oven. Add tomato sauce, onion, pepper, and mushrooms. Bake for about 45 minutes. Add Mozzarella last 10 minutes.

CHICKEN A-LA-BEE

2 whole chickens, cut up
3 Tbsp. minced garlic
2 Tbsp. minced onions
1 tsp. fresh ginger, minced
Salt and pepper to taste
1 Tbsp. browning sauce (Kitchen
  Bouquet)

2 to 3 Tbsp. cooking oil
1 small can concentrate orange
  juice
½ c. vodka
½ c. tomato paste
1 lime
½ c. vinegar

Skin and clean chicken with vinegar and lime. Season chicken with the spices (garlic, onions, ginger, salt, and pepper) and refrigerate overnight. To prepare: Place chicken in hot skillet with cooking oil. Cover and let cook under a slow fire for 20 minutes. Add orange juice, vodka, tomato paste, and browning sauce, poured over the chicken; stir and cover. Cook until tender. Serve on a bed of rice and garnish with orange slices.

Lion Bernice E. Hodge, Charlotte Amalie Lions Club
St. Thomas, U.S. Virgin Islands

CHICKEN WITH OLIVES

3½ lb. boneless, skinless chicken
  breasts
3 Tbsp. olive oil
5 cloves garlic, chopped
3 yellow onions, peeled and
  chopped
3 c. tomatoes (very ripe), coarsely
  chopped

1 (6 oz.) jar salad olives
1 Tbsp. oregano
1 c. dry red wine
Salt to taste
Black pepper (freshly ground) to
  taste

Brown chicken in olive oil in large skillet. Do not try to do the entire batch of chicken at one time. Remove chicken from pan and drain most of the oil. Saute the garlic and onion until limp. Add tomatoes and olives; saute until tomatoes are soft. Add pepper, oregano, wine, and chicken. Cover and simmer until the chicken is tender, about 30 minutes. Taste for salt. You may use very little as the olives are salty. Serves 6.

Lion Brenda Mudry, Royalton Hills Lions Club
North Royalton, Ohio, USA

CHICKEN FETAAZINI

1 chicken, boiled and boned
1 lb. pkg. cut spaghetti
1 can chopped pimentos
1 small can chopped ripe olives
1 small jar stuffed olives, quartered
2 cans cream of mushroom soup
8 oz. sharp cheese, shredded

Cook spaghetti and toss everything together, including ½ of cheese. Spoon into 9x13 inch cake pan. Sprinkle rest of cheese over top. Bake 45 minutes at 350°.

Char Harvey, Otis Lions Club
Otis, Colorado, USA

BRAZILIAN HOLIDAY CHICKEN

3 c. chopped chicken (1 inch pieces)
1 large onion, sliced
1½ green bell peppers, diced
1 red bell pepper, diced
3 garlic cloves, chopped
½ bay leaf
1 tsp. garlic powder
¼ tsp. ground cumin (or to taste)
¼ tsp. dried leaf oregano
2 (15 oz.) cans no-salt added tomato sauce
1 (15 oz.) can filled with water
1 Tbsp. fresh lemon juice
5 c. chopped celery

1. Mix all ingredients, except celery, in a large saucepan. Cook 1 hour and 20 minutes.

2. Add celery and cook 20 to 25 minutes more, until celery is crisp-tender. Makes 6 servings.

Variation: Serve with cooked brown rice.

Nutritional breakdown (per serving without rice): 233 calories, 32 g protein, 17 g carbohydrates, 4 g fat, 126 mg sodium, and 77 mg cholesterol.

Maria Specht, President, Prince Albert Downtown Lioness Club
Prince Albert, Saskatchewan, Canada

CHICKEN TETRAZZINI

½ c. chopped onion
1 can cream of mushroom soup
1 can sliced water chestnuts
¼ c. white wine
2 c. cooked chicken
8 oz. cooked spaghetti
2 Tbsp. oleo
½ soup can milk
½ c. Parmesan cheese
⅓ c. sliced green olives
½ tsp. salt
⅛ tsp. nutmeg

Saute onion in oleo. Add soup, milk, water chestnuts, ¼ cup cheese, wine, olives, chicken, and spices. Mix with cooked spaghetti and pour into 2 quart casserole dish. Top with remaining cheese. Bake at 375° for 25 minutes.

Jackie Broaddus, Westbrook Lions Club
Westbrook, Maine, USA

SWEET-AND-SOUR CHICKEN

2 Tbsp. soy sauce
1 Tbsp. cornstarch
2 whole chicken breasts, halved,
   skinned, boned, and cut
   into bite-size cubes
1 Tbsp. vegetable oil
1 cucumber, scored lengthwise
   with tines of fork and cut
   into bite-size cubes

½ cantaloupe, seeded, rinded,
   and cut into bite-size pieces
1 sweet red pepper (or green
   pepper), cubed

Combine soy sauce and cornstarch. Coat chicken pieces thoroughly. Heat oil in large frypan (or wok). Stir-fry chicken for 3 to 4 minutes. Add cucumber, cantaloupe, and pepper.

Sweet-and-Sour Sauce:

2 Tbsp. brown sugar
2 Tbsp. vinegar
½ c. pineapple juice
   (unsweetened)

1 Tbsp. cornstarch in 2 Tbsp. cold
   water
3 oz. blanched whole almonds

Mix together sauce ingredients and add to chicken mixture. Heat, stirring often, until sauce boils and ingredients are heated through. Add almonds. Yield: 4 servings.

SWEET AND SOUR CHICKEN

¼ c. corn oil
1 (8 oz.) bottle Russian salad
   dressing
1 env. dry onion soup mix

1 (10 oz.) jar apricot preserves
1 tsp. salt
3 lb. chicken, cut into serving
   pieces

Combine all ingredients, except chicken. Mix until thoroughly blended. Place chicken in a single layer in shallow baking pan. Pour preserve mixture over chicken and bake for 1 hour or until done at 350°. Baste occasionally with pan drippings. Serve hot with plain rice and sauce from the drippings.

Louise Hoglund, Westbrook Lions Club
Westbrook, Maine, USA

Delight yourself in the surprises of today!

CHICKEN ALMONDINE

2 c. diced cooked chicken
2 c. cooked rice
1 can cream of chicken soup

1 c. diced, cooked celery
½ c. chopped onion
¾ c. Hellmann's mayonnaise

Mix together and spread in 9x13 inch pan. Scatter 2 cups crushed corn flakes and ½ cup slivered almonds on top. Bake at 350° for ½ hour. You can also use turkey instead of chicken.

Peg Turner, Rootstown Lions Club
Rootstown, Ohio, USA

ORANGE-A-TANGY GOURMET CHICKEN

4 boneless chicken breasts,
  halved
½ tsp. pepper
⅓ c. oat bran
3 Tbsp. safflower oil
1½ c. orange juice
¼ c. finely diced onion

¼ c. finely diced green pepper
1 carrot, finely diced
Few broccoli flowerets
2 bay leaves
1 clove garlic, minced
⅛ tsp. paprika
2 Tbsp. slivered almonds

Remove skin from chicken. In paper bag, mix pepper and bran. Shake each chicken breast in a bag to coat with mixture. Brown chicken breast in safflower oil. Use large skillet.

Add 1½ cups orange juice, onion, green pepper, bay leaves, garlic, carrots, and broccoli flowerets. Bring to a boil on high heat. Turn heat down to low. Sprinkle chicken with paprika. Simmer, *uncovered,* for 45 minutes or until tender. (Note: If too much juice evaporates, add ½ cup more. You should end up with about 1 cup of orange sauce in the skillet from juice.)

To serve, spoon sauce over chicken. Sprinkle with almonds. Yield: 4 servings.

Good recipe from California (chicken, orange juice, vegetables, and almonds plentiful).

Have fun doing something, and success will follow.

FOIL BAKED CHICKEN
(Main dish or cubed as appetizer)

¼ c. water
3 Tbsp. catsup
3 Tbsp. vinegar
2 Tbsp. Worcestershire sauce
1 Tbsp. lemon juice
3 Tbsp. brown sugar
2 Tbsp. margarine

1 tsp. salt
1 tsp. paprika
1 tsp. chili powder
1 tsp. dry mustard
⅛ tsp. cayenne (red pepper)
1 (2½ to 3½ lb.) chicken, cut up

Heat sauce to a boil. Put the chicken into a large piece of foil. Put the foil into a large baking dish. Pour all the sauce over the chicken. Close and seal the foil. Allow air space in foil for the steaming. Bake in a 350°F. oven for 50 to 60 minutes, then open the foil for 15 minutes. Baste once. If you don't baste, the skin gets crispy, which some prefer.

Sarah Wehling, Bothell Lions Club
Bothell, Washington, USA

OVEN BUTTERED FRIED CHICKEN

⅓ c. flour
⅓ c. corn starch

Season flour and corn starch with salt and pepper.

½ c. melted butter
1 cube butter to grease bottom of
   pan
1 fryer, cut up

Dip pieces in ½ cup melted butter. Roll in flour and corn starch mixture. Place pieces of chicken, *skin side up*, in greased pan. Sprinkle with remaining butter and flour. Bake at 375°F. about 1 hour or until done. Do not turn. Makes 4 servings.

Chicken that is finger licking good.

Lion Cliff Hunter, Caruthers Lions Club
Caruthers, California, USA

Great achievements begin with small opportunities.

MONTEREY CHICKEN

This recipe can be made in advance for dozens of guests and is easy to transport.

8 large (7 or 8 oz.) whole chicken breasts, skinned and boned
1 (7 oz.) can chopped mild green chilies
½ lb. Monterey Jack cheese, cut into 8 strips
½ c. fine dry bread crumbs
¼ c. freshly grated Parmesan cheese

1 to 3 tsp. chili powder
½ tsp. salt
¼ tsp. ground cumin
¼ tsp. freshly ground black pepper
6 Tbsp. butter, melted
Tomato Sauce (recipe follows)

Garnish:

Sour cream   **Fresh limes**

Pound the chicken breasts between 2 sheets of waxed paper until thin. Spread each breast with 1 tablespoon of the green chilies. Place 1 cheese strip on top of each portion of chilies. Roll up each chicken breast and tuck ends under.

Combine the bread crumbs, Parmesan cheese, chili powder, salt, cumin, and pepper in a shallow dish. Dip each stuffed breast into the melted butter and roll in the bread crumb mixture. Place the breasts in a baking dish, seam side down. Drizzle with remaining butter. Cover and chill for at least 4 hours or overnight. Preheat the oven to 400°F. Bake for 25 to 40 minutes, or until done. Serve with the Tomato Sauce and garnish with sour cream and fresh limes. Serves 8.

EVERYDAY BROCCOLI CHEESE CHICKEN

1 Tbsp. margarine
4 skinless, boneless chicken breast halves
1 can Campbell's new broccoli cheese soup

⅓ c. milk
⅛ tsp. salt
2 c. broccoli flowerets

In skillet over medium heat, in hot margarine, cook chicken 10 minutes or until browned on both sides. Spoon off fat. Stir in soup, milk, and pepper. Heat to boiling. Add broccoli. Reduce heat to low. Cover and simmer 10 minutes or until chicken is fork-tender and broccoli is done, stirring occasionally. Makes 4 servings.

Anita Neibert, Whittemore Lioness Club
Whittemore, Michigan, USA

When it is dark enough, you can see the stars.

MANDARIN CHICKEN

Frying chicken, cut in serving
  pieces
½ c. oil
1 Tbsp. Lawry's seasoned salt
2 tsp. paprika
1 tsp. black pepper
½ tsp. garlic salt
1½ c. water, combined with 2
  chicken bouillon cubes

Juice from 2 medium oranges
1 orange rind, grated
3 Tbsp. brown sugar
3 Tbsp. cornstarch, mixed with ½
  c. cold water
6 to 8 green onions, slivered
½ c. slivered almonds

Dry chicken pieces well. Combine oil, seasoned salt, pepper, garlic salt, and paprika. Rub pieces of chicken well with oil mixture. Place chicken pieces on a cookie sheet with an edge of 1 inch. Bake in a 375° oven for 15 minutes. Lower oven temperature to 350°. Continue to cook until tender (about 45 minutes).

Combine orange juice, sugar, bouillon water, and orange rind. Allow mixture to come to a boil. Thicken with cornstarch and water mixture. Sprinkle chicken with slivered green onions and almonds. Pour sauce over all. Serve with rice and a vegetable.

CHICKEN TETRAZZINI

Meat from cooked hen or turkey
  (hen size 5 lb.)
4 cans cream of mushroom soup
1 pkg. noodles, cooked

About 15 to 18 slices American
  cheese
½ to ¾ lb. buttered cracker
  crumbs

I take the mushrooms and add chicken broth to make 2 quarts. Layer the chicken and noodles. Top with cheese slice. Pour the soup and broth over the top; top off with crumbs. Bake at 350° until golden brown and bubbling, about 1 hour.

This can be prepared a day ahead and refrigerated or even stored in deep freeze. Use extra-large oblong pan.

Wilber McClaughry, Cuba Lions Club
Cuba, Illinois, Fulton, USA

Your greatest asset is yourself. Share it with others.

CHICKEN NAPOLEON

2½ to 3½ lb. cut up chicken
4 large tomatoes
Cooking oil

Garlic
½ c. white wine
¼ c. crumbled bread

Brown chicken in cooking oil and cook until nearly done. Remove chicken; dip 4 large tomatoes in boiling water. Take out seeds, peel, and cut in large pieces. Add 2 tablespoons sliced garlic. Add ½ cup white wine. Add crumbled bread. Drain oil from pan chicken was cooked in. Place tomatoes, garlic, bread, and wine under chicken. Simmer slow for 15 minutes.

Catherine Walsh, Westbrook Lions Club
Westbrook, Maine, USA

POPPY SEED CHICKEN

2 c. boiled and boned chicken
   breast
1 c. sour cream
2 (10¾ oz.) cans cream of chicken
   soup

1 stick butter, melted
2 Tbsp. poppy seed
1½ stacks Ritz crackers, crushed

Place chicken chunks in baking dish. Combine sour cream and chicken soup. Pour over chicken. Sprinkle Ritz crackers over soup mixture. Melt butter and pour over crackers. Sprinkle with poppy seed. Bake 30 to 40 minutes in 350° oven.

Beverly Foster, East Lake Lions Club
Birmingham, Alabama, USA

POPPY SEED CHICKEN

1 Tbsp. butter or margarine
8 oz. sliced fresh mushrooms
5 c. cubed cooked chicken
1 can cream of chicken soup
   (undiluted)

1 c. sour cream
1 (2 oz.) jar pimento, drained and
   diced

Topping:

½ c. margarine, melted
1⅓ c. finely crushed butter
   flavored crackers

2 tsp. poppy seeds

In a skillet, melt butter. Saute mushrooms until tender. Stir in chicken soup, sour cream, and pimento. Mix well. Spoon mixture into a greased 2 quart casserole. In a small bowl, combine all topping ingredients. Sprinkle over the chicken. Bake at 350° for 20 minutes. Makes 6 servings.

CHICKEN DIVAN

2 (10 oz.) chopped, frozen
    broccoli, cooked
2 c. cooked, cut up chicken
3 c. medium white sauce (hot)
½ c. lite cream

½ tsp. Worcestershire sauce
1 c. shredded Parmesan cheese
4 tsp. dry mustard
2 Tbsp. chopped onion
1 jigger of sherry

Place cooked, drained broccoli in bottom of 9 inch square pan. On top, place bite-size chicken pieces. To cooked, hot white sauce, add cream, Worcestershire sauce, mustard, sherry, onion, salt, and pepper. Stir over low heat until cheese is melted. Pour over chicken layer. When ready to serve, bake for 30 minutes at 400°.

Double for 13x9x2 inch pan. Serves 12. Do not add extra sherry (optional).
Conant Homestead, Westbrook Lions Club
Westbrook, Maine, USA

PAPRIKA CHICKEN

1 Tbsp. low cholesterol margarine
    and corn oil (to cover
    bottom of skillet)
1 to 2 lb. skinless chicken breast
    in strips
Lawry's chicken seasoning
Paprika

Warm water
Green pepper slices (desired
    amount)
Onion strips (desired amount)
Chopped celery (desired amount)*
Dash of minced garlic

Add chicken strips to oil/margarine in skillet. Sprinkle with chicken seasoning. Cook for about 2 minutes on each side. Should be slightly browned, then sprinkle paprika on each side. Add pepper, onion, celery, and garlic. Add warm water to cover bottom of skillet.

When water starts to boil, lower heat and cover with lid. Cook until tender, about 15 to 20 minutes. Add more water if necessary.

Use as a meat dish or chop into bite-size pieces and put on rice.

* Can use celery seed for chopped celery.

Become the most positive and enthusiastic person you know.

BAKED CHICKEN WITH WINE

2 to 3 lb. boned chicken breast
¼ c. butter, margarine or oil
1 medium onion, chopped (½ c.)
½ lb. fresh mushrooms
1 can mushroom soup
¾ c. dry sherry

1 Tbsp. parsley
1 tsp. salt
1 tsp. paprika
Dash of pepper
1 or 2 lemon slices

Brown chicken slowly in butter. Remove from skillet and place in single layer in 11x7 inch shallow baking dish. Add mushrooms and onions to butter remaining in skillet and cook until tender, but not brown. Add soup, sherry, seasonings, and lemon slices; blend thoroughly. Pour over chicken. Bake, uncovered, at 350° for 1 hour or until chicken is tender. Serves 4.

John W. Kline, Reno Plumb Lane Lions Club
Reno, Nevada, Washoe, USA

CHICKEN COOKED IN WINE

3 to 4 lb. chicken pieces, washed
    and patted dry (remove
    skin)
Salt and pepper to taste
2 cloves garlic, chopped

1 tsp. rosemary
¾ c. red wine (burgundy or any
    inexpensive red wine)
½ tsp. vinegar
¼ c. water

Salt and pepper chicken. Add chopped garlic to pan. Brown chicken pieces well on one side. Turn and sprinkle rosemary on all pieces. Brown well. After browned well, transfer chicken and garlic to a roasting pan. Add wine, vinegar, and water. Cover with foil and bake at 325° for about 1 hour. Uncover and bake ½ hour more. Turn occasionally and baste.

This recipe was my grandmother's; it's about 75 to 85 years old!

Rita M. Granitz, South Whitehall Lions Club
Allentown, Pennsylvania, USA

Some people find fault like there was a reward for it.

CHICKEN KORMA

2 (2½ to 3 lb.) chickens, skinned
 and cut in small pieces
2 c. lowfat yogurt
2 garlic cloves, minced
2 medium size onions, chopped
1 tsp. ground paprika
2 tsp. finely chopped ginger root
Dash of pepper
2 Tbsp. chicken stock

2 tsp. ground coriander
½ tsp. ground chile
1 tsp. ground cumin
Small amount of peeled
 cardamom pods
1 tsp. poppy seeds
1 Tbsp. ground turmeric
1 bay leaf
2 Tbsp. chopped cilantro

1. Place chicken in a large bowl. Add yogurt, 1 garlic clove, ½ onion, paprika, ginger root, and pepper. Cover and refrigerate a few hours.

2. Spray a large heavy saucepan with no stick cooking spray. Add remaining onions and garlic and 2 tablespoons stock; cook until soft.

3. Add coriander, chile, cumin, cardamom seeds, poppy seeds, and turmeric. Saute 2 to 3 minutes. Add chicken and enough water to cover; add any remaining marinade. Add bay leaf. Simmer about 45 minutes or until chicken is tender. Sprinkle with cilantro. Serve over rice. Makes 8 servings.

Nutritional breakdown (per serving without rice): 175 calories, 27 g protein, 0 carbohydrates, 9 g fat, 99 mg sodium, and 61 mg cholesterol.

Marie Specht, President, Prince Albert Downtown Lioness Club
Prince Albert, Saskatchewan, Canada

LEMON-GARLIC ROAST CHICKEN

2 lemons
1 (3 lb.) chicken
1 small garlic bulb

3 Tbsp. olive oil
Chopped fresh parsley

Cut up 1 lemon into 8 pieces. Rub the outside of the chicken with peel side of the pieces and then put the lemon pieces inside the chicken with the whole garlic bulb. Pour the olive oil on top and inside of the chicken. Roast for 1½ hours in a preheated 325°F. oven.

Half an hour before taking the chicken out of the oven, pour freshly squeezed juice from the second lemon over top and sprinkle with parsley. Discard lemon pieces and garlic before serving. Serves 4.

The opportunity you are waiting for is already here.

CURRIED CHICKEN CASSEROLE

4 chopped and cooked chicken
    breasts
2 cans cream of chicken soup
2 pkg. frozen broccoli

¾ c. Miracle Whip
1 tsp. curry powder
4 oz. Cheddar cheese
½ c. seasoned bread crumbs

Mix soup, Miracle Whip, and curry powder. Spread over chicken and broccoli (9x12 inch baking pan). Top with Cheddar cheese and sprinkle with bread crumbs. Dot with butter. Bake at 350° for 45 minutes.

Stephen Hepner, Saginaw Lions Club
Saginaw, Texas, USA

SAUTEEN BREAST OF CHICKEN IN CURRY SAUCE

½ c. chicken breasts, boned
⅓ c. flour
6 chicken breasts, boned
6 Tbsp. butter
1 apple, cored and chopped
1 stalk celery, chopped
1 leek, chopped
1 medium onion, chopped
4 c. chicken stock

½ c. white wine
1 c. heavy cream
Salt and pepper
¾ c. shredded coconut
2 bananas, peeled and sliced
6 peach halves
¼ c. mango chutney
Rice pilaf

Combine curry powder and flour; dredge chicken, reserving excess flour mixture. In a 3 inch deep fry pan, saute chicken in butter until golden. Remove and reserve. Saute apple, celery, leek, and onion until tender; stir in reserved flour mixture until smooth. Add chicken stock and wine; bring to a boil. Reduce heat and add chicken. Simmer, covered, for 20 to 25 minutes or until chicken is done. Remove chicken to a heated platter. Strain sauce and return to fry pan. Bring sauce to a boil. Reduce heat and stir in cream until heated. Season to taste with salt and pepper.

Dave Bernier, Westbrook Lions Club
Westbrook, Maine, USA

CURRIED CHICKEN

½ c. honey
¼ c. mustard
1 Tbsp. curry

4 to 6 Tbsp. butter
4 to 8 chicken thighs

Melt honey and butter together; add mustard and curry. Wash and dry thighs. Roll thighs in big bowl with sauce until covered. Put in baking pan. Bake for 40 minutes at 350°.

Rebecca Mergaert, North Jackson Lions Club
Sault Ste. Marie, Ontario, Canada

CHICKEN PENNY

1 whole chicken, baked
2 cans spaghetti
1 jar pimento
1 bell pepper, chopped

1 can cream of chicken soup
1 (8 oz.) block American cheese,
  grated

Debone chicken; cut in pieces and add other ingredients with cheese over top. Cook at 350° for 20 to 25 minutes or until bubbly.

There has never been, nor will there ever be, a right way to do a wrong thing!

Kathy Parker, Rock Hill Lions Club
Rock Hill, South Carolina, USA

CHICKEN DISH

10 boned chicken breasts
1 small jar chipped beef
1 can mushroom soup

1 small ctn. sour cream
5 strips bacon (uncooked)

Place the chipped beef on the bottom of a 9x12 inch casserole. Wrap ½ strip bacon around each chicken breast. Fasten with a toothpick. Place in casserole on top of beef. Mix sour cream and soup together; pour over meat. Bake, covered, for 2 hours in a 325° oven. Uncover and cook ½ hour.

Husband Nelson Prewitt, Secretary-Treasurer of Midway Lions for about 25 years.

Nelson Prewitt, Midway Lions Club
Midway, Kentucky, Woodford, USA

CHICKEN PIE

4 chicken breasts
1 can celery soup
1 can cream of chicken soup
2 c. chicken broth

1 c. self-rising flour
1 c. buttermilk
1 stick oleo

Cook chicken in water until tender. Pull from bone and cut in bite-size pieces. Place in bottom of 13x9 inch pan. Boil soups and broth together; pour over chicken. Melt oleo and pour over chicken-soup mix. Mix flour and buttermilk; pour over chicken-soup mixture. Bake at 350° till brown.

Ramsay Harless, East Lake Lions Club
Birmingham, Alabama, USA

Happiness is a thing to be practiced.

CHICKEN DISH

1 chicken fryer
1 c. cream of chicken soup
1 c. cream of celery soup
1 c. sweet milk

1 pkg. Pepperidge Farm herb
   stuffing
1½ c. chicken broth
1 stick oleo

1. Stew and bone chicken. Put in 9x13 inch dish.
2. Heat soups and milk; pour over chicken.
3. Heat chicken broth and oleo; mix with dressing.
4. Spoon dressing mix on top of chicken and bake 35 or 40 minutes at 350°.

Joe Heath, East Lake Lions Club
Birmingham, Alabama, USA

PARMESAN CHICKEN AND WILD RICE

½ c. melted butter
4 c. cooked chicken
1 can cream of mushroom soup
1 can cream of celery soup
1 can cream of chicken soup

½ can water
¼ c. grated Parmesan
1½ c. wild rice (uncooked)
1 small onion, chopped
Salt and pepper to taste

Pour melted butter in 9x13 inch pan. Top with raw rice, diced chicken, onion, salt, and pepper. Combine soups with water. Pour over chicken. Sprinkle with cheese. Bake for 45 to 50 minutes at 350°, or until rice is done.

"If you like your job, why not let your face know it!"

Jeanette Olson, Siren Lions Club
Siren, Wisconsin, USA

CHICKEN BOGG

1 chicken
1 lb. sausage
2 c. uncooked rice

1 medium onion, chopped
Salt and pepper to taste

Boil the chicken until it begins to fall off the bone. Remove from the stock. Chop this chicken and the sausage into small pieces; return both to the stock. Also, add the chopped onion and the rice. Make sure that there is at least 4 cups of liquid for the rice. Simmer for 25 to 30 minutes until the rice is done. Serve with favorite side dish.

Note: May use country ham or other meats as well.

LaGail H. Davidson (Mrs. W.M.D., IV), Statesboro Lions Club
Statesboro, Georgia, USA

❦

Be kind. Remember everyone you meet is fighting a hard battle.

CHICKEN AND RICE

4 chicken hind quarters
1 chopped onion
¼ tsp. salt, pepper, and garlic
   powder

1 c. long grain rice
1 (14½ oz.) can clear chicken
   broth

Heat oven to 350°. Bake chicken that has been seasoned with salt, pepper, and garlic powder approximately 40 minutes. Remove the chicken from the pan and add chopped onion, rice, and chicken to the pan. Cover with the can of broth. Continue baking until the rice has absorbed the broth and the chicken is brown. Serve immediately with a salad. It is delicious.

Sally Weinschenk, Ponderosa Lions Club
Auberry, California, USA

CHICKEN CASSEROLE

2 c. cooked chicken (bite-size
   pieces)
2 to 3 c. cooked rice
½ c. chopped celery
¼ c. chopped onion
1 can cream of chicken soup

1 can cream of mushroom soup
2 Tbsp. lemon juice
½ c. mayonnaise
Slivered almonds
Pepperidge Farm herb seasoned
   stuffing mix

Mix first 8 ingredients together; pour into buttered casserole dish. Top with almonds or either the Pepperidge Farm herb seasoned stuffing mix and dot with butter. Bake at 350° for 25 to 30 minutes.

I take this dish to our covered dish dinners and always have requests to bring it to the next dinner.

Lioness Mary Ogletree, Fort Walton Beach Lioness Club
Destin, Florida, USA

CHICKEN AND RICE

1 (3 to 4 lb.) frying chicken, cut up
5 medium size carrots
5 stalks celery

1 medium onion
1 c. Uncle Ben's converted rice
Salt and pepper

Chop carrots, celery, and onion into 1 inch pieces. Put all ingredients, including cut up chicken, into large kettle. Put enough water to cover ingredients - be generous with water (about 2 inches from top of kettle). Bring to boil. Turn down to simmer for 2 hours. After 2 hours, remove chicken from kettle, set chicken aside, and when cool enough to handle, remove skin from chicken. Pour chicken stock through strainer into another pot. While still warm, chop vegetables into ¼ inch pieces. From chicken stock, take 2 cups and bring to boil. Add 1 cup rice and simmer for 20 minutes. Remove from heat and let set for 5 to 7 minutes until all water is absorbed by rice. Add vegetables, salt, and pepper. Use remaining chicken stock for chicken soup, adding your choice of ingredients. Peel chicken from bone and lay on top of rice. Serves 4.

SIMPLE SUNDAY CHICKEN

1½ c. instant rice
1 large cut up fryer-broiler chicken
1 can cream of chicken soup

1 can cream of celery soup
2 cans water
1 pkg. dried onion soup

Spray 9x13 inch pan with no-stick surface. Pour rice into pan evenly. Place chicken on top of rice, skin side up. Mix the 2 cans of soup with the water and pour evenly over chicken. Spread onion soup over the top. Cover the pan with foil. Bake at 325° for 2 hours or until chicken is done. Serves 6. Pork chops may be used instead of chicken.

CHICKEN CASSEROLE

1 can cream of celery soup
1 can cream of chicken soup
1 can cream of mushroom soup

3 c. water
1½ c. uncooked rice
2 to 3 lb. chicken

Mix soups with water; set aside. Grease 9x13 inch baking dish. Sprinkle rice in bottom of pan. Add ½ of soup mixture. Lay raw chicken (salted) on this. Pour rest of soup over chicken. Bake 1½ hours at 325°. I use breasts and/or thighs. I like this better baked 2 hours.

Delia P. Krueger, Emporia Sundowners Lions Club
Emporia, Kansas, USA

HERBED CHICKEN CASSEROLE

3 large chicken breasts, cut in
    halves, or 1 cut up chicken
½ tsp. salt

⅛ tsp. pepper
¼ c. butter or margarine

Browning Time:

1 can condensed cream of
    chicken soup
¾ c. sauterne wine (dry)
1 (5 oz.) can water chestnuts,
    drained and sliced
1 (No. 303) can broiled, sliced, and
    drained mushrooms

2 Tbsp. minced onion or 3 thinly
    sliced scallions (including
    some green)
¼ tsp. thyme

Season chicken with salt and pepper. In large skillet, heat butter and chicken; brown well on all sides. Arrange browned chicken, skin side up, in a shallow roasting pan or casserole.

Combine soup with pan drippings; slowly add wine, stirring until smooth. Add remaining ingredients and heat to boiling point. Pour sauce over chicken and cover with foil. Bake at 350° until chicken is almost cooked (about 40 minutes). Uncover and continue baking until fork tender. Serve with hot fluffy rice.

CHICKEN AND SWISS CHEESE CASSEROLE

4 to 5 chicken breasts, skinned
   and boned, or use leftover
   chicken
1 can cream of chicken soup

⅓ can water
Pepperidge Farm or Stove Top
   dressing

Skin and bone chicken. Arrange chicken in greased baking dish. Cover with slices of Swiss cheese. Pour over 1 can cream of chicken soup and ⅓ can water. Top with dressing made from ½ package of Pepperidge Farm mixed according to directions on bag or use Stove Top. Bake 45 minutes at 350°. Do not cover.

Toni Krueger, Onekama Lions Club
Onekama, Michigan, USA

COUNTRY CLUB-STYLE HOT CHICKEN SALAD

4 c. chopped cooked chicken
2 c. chopped celery
4 hard cooked eggs, chopped
1 (2 oz.) jar diced pimiento,
   drained
1 Tbsp. finely chopped onion

1 c. mayonnaise
2 Tbsp. lemon juice
¾ tsp. salt
1 c. (4 oz.) shredded Cheddar
   cheese
⅔ c. sliced almonds, toasted

Combine chicken, celery, eggs, pimiento, onion, mayonnaise, lemon juice, and salt; mix well. Spoon into a lightly greased 12x8x2 inch baking dish; cover and bake at 350° for 20 minutes. Sprinkle cheese over casserole. Top with almonds. Bake, uncovered, an additional 3 minutes or until cheese melts. Yield: 6 to 8 servings.

Mrs. Lion Robert (Margaret) Logan, Canton Lions Club
Canton, Georgia, USA

THANKSGIVING STUFFING

1 lb. seasoned bread cubes
¾ lb. Bob Evans pork sausage
2 sticks margarine
3 chicken bouillon cubes
3 c. hot water

1 lb. fresh mushrooms, sliced
1 c. finely chopped onion
1 c. finely chopped celery
Poultry seasoning
Sage

Brown sausage. Saute mushrooms, onions, and celery in margarine separately. Combine mushrooms, onions, celery, and sausage with bread cubes. Dissolve chicken bouillon cubes and 1 stick margarine into hot water; mix into bread cube mixture. Add poultry seasoning and sage to taste. Stuff turkey or chicken and roast according to size of turkey. Can be baked alone wrapped in foil and put into baking dish at 350° for 1 hour. Onions and celery are best chopped very fine in food processor. Amount of ingredients can be adjusted to taste. Add more water if moister stuffing is preferred and less water if drier stuffing is preferred.

Kathleen Meister, Onekama Lions Club
Onekama, Michigan, USA

CROCK POT DRESSING

1 c. oleo
1 c. chopped onion
1 c. chopped celery
1½ tsp. salt
1½ tsp. sage

½ tsp. pepper
12 to 13 c. dry bread cubes
3½ to 4½ c. broth and/or milk
2 well beaten eggs

Pack lightly in crock pot. Cover and set on HIGH for 45 minutes, then on LOW for 4 to 8 hours.

SAUSAGE STUFFING

8 c. bread crumbs
1 medium onion, cut fine
2 stalks celery, cut fine
½ tsp. salt

¼ tsp. pepper
1 lb. sausage meat
½ tsp. sage
1 egg

Mix bread crumbs, onions, celery, salt, pepper, and sage. Beat egg; add to mixture with hot water to desired consistency. Break sausage into small pieces. Add to bread mixture. Stuff bird or put in pan and bake at 300° for 45 minutes.

Dave Bernier, Westbrook Lions Club
Westbrook, Maine, USA

OLD-FASHIONED BREAD STUFFING

1½ doz. 5-day-old (dry) hot dog or
    hamburg buns (12 c.)
1 c. butter or margarine
3 onions, chopped (1½ c.)
3 c. chopped celery with leaves

1½ tsp. salt
½ tsp. pepper
2 to 3 Tbsp. leaf sage, crumbled
2 chicken bouillon cubes
2 c. boiling water

Crumble buns into a large bowl. Melt butter in a large skillet. Add onions and celery; saute slowly until tender (about 15 minutes). Add to buns with salt, pepper, and sage. Add bouillon cubes to boiling water and stir into bun mixture enough to make a moist mixture.

Stuff turkey cavity lightly. Spoon extra into a buttered casserole. Spoon a little extra chicken broth over top and bake, covered, with turkey during last 45 minutes of roasting.

Excellent recipe to use when large quantity of stuffing (dressing) is needed for a community turkey supper.

Ruby Fleming, Otter Valley Lions Club
Otterville, Ontario, Canada

❦

The time to be happy is now; the place to be happy is here.

HERB-SMOKED TURKEY

1 (8 to 14 lb.) turkey, thawed,
    cleaned and patted dry
½ c. butter or margarine, melted
2 garlic spears, minced
½ tsp. marjoram
½ tsp. dried thyme
½ tsp. rosemary
½ tsp. basil
¼ tsp. sage

2 Tbsp. parsley, chopped
½ tsp. salt
½ tsp. coarsely ground pepper
2 c. white wine (at room
    temperature)
Hickory chunks, soaked
Charcoal
Metal or foil drip pan (cake size)

Note: This recipe will not work on a gas grill, only a barbeque grill such as a kettle style. It is excellent served with cheese and crackers.

Build a charcoal fire around the drip pan. Pour wine into drip pan and add enough water to fill half full. When coals are glowing and ashy gray (30 to 40 minutes), add soaked wood chunks. Replace grill. Fold wings under back of turkey and place (breast side up) on grill over the drip pan. Do not allow to cook too fast.

Baste several times with a mixture of the butter and spices. Cook for 15 minutes per pound, adding more briquets and wood chips to the fire after 45 to 60 minutes to maintain a constant temperature. Let bird stand on platter or carving board for 10 to 20 minutes before slicing. The meat under the skin will be a pink color due to the smoking.

SWEDISH MEATBALLS WITH SOUR CREAM SAUCE

1 lb. ground turkey
½ c. dry bread crumbs
¼ c. egg substitute
⅔ c. skim milk

1 tsp. minced onion
⅛ tsp. pepper
⅛ tsp. nutmeg
1 Tbsp. sugar

Sour Cream Sauce:

1 can lowfat cream of mushroom
    soup (undiluted)
1 (4 oz.) can mushrooms with
    liquid

½ pt. nonfat sour cream

Combine all ingredients for meatballs and mix. Let it set for 3 to 4 minutes. Make into small balls. Brown meatballs in electric frying pan at 300°. Reduce heat to 220° and simmer for 20 minutes. Combine ingredients for Sour Cream Sauce in a pan and heat through. Pour sauce over meatballs and serve.

Kathy Gallant, Westbrook Lions Club
Westbrook, Maine, USA

All glory comes from daring to begin.

TURKEY MEAT LOAF

1 lb. ground turkey (lean)
1 lb. turkey sausage (mild or hot)
¾ c. Quaker Oats (uncooked) or
  bread crumbs
1 egg or egg white or egg
  substitute

1 c. tomato juice (mild or spicy)
¼ c. chopped onion
1 pkg. Lipton Recipe soup mix
  (any flavor)
¼ tsp. pepper
¼ to ½ tsp. salt (optional)

Heat oven to 350°F. Combine ground turkey and turkey sausage; set aside. Combine all other ingredients and mix well, then add turkey and mix thoroughly. Press into loaf pan. Bake 1½ hours. Drain. Let stand 5 minutes. Slice and serve.

Lion Ron Jones, Golden Triangle Lions Club
Milpitas, California, USA

TURKEY MEAT LOAF WITH HERBS

2 lb. ground turkey
1 c. dry bread crumbs
2 egg whites
1 c. tomato sauce
½ c. fine chopped onions
½ c. fine chopped fresh green
  peppers

1½ tsp. salt
½ tsp. crushed Italian seasoning
⅛ tsp. ground thyme
Dash of pepper

Combine the ground turkey, bread crumbs, egg whites, tomato sauce, onions, green peppers, salt, thyme, oregano, and Italian seasoning. Mix thoroughly. Form into a loaf and place it into a shallow pan. Bake the loaf in a preheated moderate oven (350°) for 1½ hours or until lightly browned. (*Tip:* Grease pan with Pam.)

This is a heartwise meat dish.

Shirley E. Curtis, North Jackson Lions Club
Jackson, Michigan, USA

GENO'S ITALIAN TURKEY SAUSAGE

2 lb. ground lowfat turkey
2 Tbsp. fennel
2 bay leaves, crushed
1 Tbsp. dried parsley
3 to 6 cloves garlic, minced
1 to 2 Tbsp. red pepper flakes
2 tsp. salt

½ tsp. black pepper
½ to 1 tsp. onion powder
1 tsp. paprika
1 tsp. sweet basil leaves
½ tsp. oregano powder
4 Tbsp. water

Mix all ingredients together very well. Make into patties for grilling or meat balls for baking. This is excellent baked in your favorite pasta sauce.

Lion Gene Domanico, Spokane Central Lions Club
Spokane, Washington, USA

BOMBAY TURKEY

4 Tbsp. butter or margarine
2 to 3 tsp. curry powder
½ c. chopped onion
3 Tbsp. all-purpose flour
¼ tsp. salt
Dash of pepper

1½ c. chicken broth
2 c. diced cooked turkey
1 tsp. shredded lemon peel
⅔ c. long-grain rice
¼ c. chopped cashew nuts
2 Tbsp. chopped canned pimiento

In medium skillet, melt butter. Add curry and heat 2 to 3 minutes. Stir in onion and cook till tender, but not brown. Blend in flour, salt, and pepper, stirring well. Add chicken broth all at once. Cook and stir till boiling; cook 2 minutes longer. Add cooked turkey and shredded lemon peel; heat mixture to boiling. Cook rice according to package directions. Stir in cashew nuts and pimiento. Serve turkey mixture over rice. Makes 4 to 6 servings.

If you are tired of the same leftover recipes, this one is special and easy.
Lion Evenly Tautrim, Chino Valley Lions Club
Chino Valley, Arizona, USA

CORNISH GAME HEN AND WILD RICE SUPREME

4 fresh or frozen Cornish game
    hens
2 Tbsp. butter or margarine,
    melted
1 (16 oz.) long grain and wild rice
    mix
1 (10¾ oz.) can chicken broth

2 Tbsp. butter or margarine
1 bunch green onions, sliced
6 large mushrooms, sliced, or 1
    (4.5 oz.) jar sliced
    mushrooms
½ c. dry white wine
2 bay leaves

Thaw hens if frozen. Remove giblets. Rinse hens and pat dry. Brush inside and out with melted butter. Remove seasoning packet from rice mix. Use 1 teaspoon seasoning per hen and rub inside and out. Pour chicken broth and ½ cup water into a shallow roasting pan. Bake, breast side up, for 15 minutes at 450°.

Meanwhile, melt 2 tablespoons butter in a skillet. Add green onions, mushrooms, and rice packet from mix. Saute, stirring frequently. Slowly add 1¼ cups water, remaining seasonings from packet, wine, and bay leaves. Bring to a boil. Pour rice mixture into roasting pan. Make sure rice does not rest on top of hens. Brush hens with remaining butter. Cover loosely with foil. Reduce heat to 350° and bake for an additional 45 minutes or until all liquid is absorbed. Serve hens on a bed of rice. Makes 4 servings.

We are shaped and fashioned by what we love.

CORNISH HENS WITH WILD RICE

1 (6 oz.) pkg. mixed long grain wild rice
1¼ c. water
½ stick (4 Tbsp.) butter
1 medium onion, finely chopped
2 c. chicken broth

1 pkg. frozen green peas, thawed
2 Cornish hens, halved
Fresh ground pepper
Butter
Salt
Dry mustard

Preheat oven to 325°. Combine rice (minus packaged seasonings) and water in 2 quart saucepan. Cover and cook for 12 minutes or until water is absorbed. Melt butter in 3 quart Corning Ware casserole (moderate heat). Add onion and cook for 3 minutes. Sprinkle in flour; stir. Gradually add broth and heat to boiling point. Gently stir in rice and peas. Rub hens with butter, salt, pepper, and mustard. Arrange on rice mixture; cover and bake for 45 minutes or until rice and hens are tender. Serves 4.

Catherine Walsh, Westbrook Lions Club
Westbrook, Maine, USA

❧

The more value you attach to those things outside of yourself,
the more you give those things the power to control you.

❧ ❧ ❧

Maybe the kids would eat better
if you installed a drive-up window off the kitchen
and handed them dinner in a bag.

❧ ❧ ❧

Kind words can be short and easy to speak,
but their echoes are truly endless.

ENTREES - SEAFOOD

SCALLOPED OYSTERS

1 pt. oysters
2 c. soft bread crumbs
¼ c. milk

6 Tbsp. butter or other fat
Salt and pepper

Oil a bake dish. Put in a layer of crumbs, then a layer of oysters, butter or other fat in little pieces. Salt and pepper. Repeat, ending with a layer of bread crumbs, with small pieces of fat dotted over them. Do not have more than 2 layers of oysters. Moisten with milk and oyster liquor mixed together. Bake in moderate oven (350°F. to 400°F.) until brown, about half hour, and serve in same dish.

This recipe has fooled so many people that said they didn't eat oysters. I say this is our family favorite dish.

Maude E. Mason, Hedgesville Lions Club
Hedgesville, West Virginia, USA

HADDOCK-SHRIMP BAKE

2 lb. fresh haddock
1 can cream of shrimp soup
1 small bag frozen appetizer baby
   shrimp
¼ c. melted margarine

1 tsp. minced onion
½ tsp. Worcestershire sauce
¼ tsp. garlic salt
1¼ c. crushed Ritz crackers

Preheat oven to 375°F. Slightly thaw fillets, if frozen, and baby shrimp. Place in a greased, shallow 13x9x2 inch baking dish. Mix baby shrimp in cream of shrimp soup. Spread fish evenly with soup. Bake for 20 minutes. Combine remaining ingredients and sprinkle over fish. Continue baking for 15 minutes or until fish easily flakes.

Mrs. Jeff Crosby, Exeter Township Lions Club
Exeter, Pennsylvania, USA

SHRIMP RUMALDE

2 green onions
8 Tbsp. Creole mustard
1 Tbsp. mayonnaise
3 tsp. horseradish
2 Tbsp. lemon juice
2 cloves garlic
1 hard-boiled egg

¾ c. olive oil
¼ c. wine vinegar
½ c. ketchup
2 Tbsp. Worcestershire sauce
2 Tbsp. dry mustard
3 tsp. paprika
3 lb. shrimp, cooked and peeled

Place the shrimp on a bed of lettuce. Place the remaining ingredients in a blender and blend well. Pour sauce over the shrimp and serve.

LaGail H. Davidson (Mrs. W.M.D., IV), Statesboro Lions Club
Statesboro, Georgia, USA

MAINE JEMBALAYAK

2 c. shrimp
½ c. ham
2½ c. tomatoes
1½ c. water
1 onion, chopped
1 Tbsp. flour
1 green pepper

½ clove garlic
1 Tbsp. parsley
¾ c. uncooked rice
Salt
Pepper
2 Tbsp. butter

Preheat electric skillet to 350°. Melt butter; stir in flour. Add diced green pepper and cooked ham, coarsely chopped. Cook, stirring, for 5 minutes. Add tomatoes (canned), water, onion, garlic, salt, pepper, and parsley. Bring to boil. Add rice. Reduce heat to 200° to 225°. Simmer for 30 minutes or until rice is tender. Add cooked Maine shrimp just before done.

Joyce Bolton, Westbrook Lions Club
Westbrook, Maine, USA

BARBECUED SHRIMP

2 cloves garlic, minced
Hot sauce to taste
Paprika
Salt and pepper
1 lemon, squeezed
Dash of oregano

1 Tbsp. chili sauce
1 c. sherry wine
1 lb. shrimp (16 to 20 size)
1½ tsp. Worcestershire sauce
3 sticks melted butter

To prepare shrimp, remove sand veins by running knife down the back of shrimp. Leave shell and tail on. Marinate for 1 hour or more in sauce made from the above ingredients. Broil shrimp over charcoals, turning and basting often until done, 4 to 5 minutes. Do not overcook. Can be cooked by frying in the skillet. Coat skillet with butter and pan-fry until done, 4 to 5 minutes, when shrimp change to pink. Very good for appetizer.

Great for a cookout!

Lion Manuel Medeiros, Caruthers Lions Club
Caruthers, California, USA

Add to your joy by counting your blessings.

SCAMPI MARINARA

1 lb. raw large shrimp
1 c. water
¼ c. butter
2 Tbsp. minced onion
3 cloves garlic, minced
2 Tbsp. brandy

1 Tbsp. lemon juice
1 tsp. salt
Dash of cayenne pepper
1 c. whipping cream
1 Tbsp. corn starch
Parsley sprigs

Shell and devein shrimp. Reserve shells and place in small skillet. Add water and boil 5 minutes or until liquid is reduced to ¼ cup. Strain. Reserve broth; discard shells. Melt butter in skillet or electric fry pan at 375°. Add onions and garlic; saute 1 minute. Add shrimp and saute 2 minutes. Add brandy; ignite and shake pan until flame subsides. Stir in reserved broth, lemon juice, salt, and cayenne pepper. Combine corn starch and cream. Reduce heat and stir until thickened. Serve over fresh pasta noodles. Garnish with parsley sprigs.

This is a very rich and special recipe that I like to make for very special people (my family).

Pat Boardrow, South Benton Lions Club
Monroe, Oregon, USA

CURRIED SHRIMP AND CHICKEN BREAST
WITH ZUCCHINI AND CARROTS

1 lb. shrimp, cleaned, deveined,
   and cooked
1 lb. chicken breast (boneless),
   cooked
½ c. onion, chopped (optional)
½ c. celery, chopped (optional)
2 lb. zucchini squash (1 inch
   cubes)

1 lb. carrots, peeled and sliced ¼
   inch thick
1 can cream of shrimp soup
1 can cream of chicken soup
½ c. mayonnaise
1 tsp. lemon juice
2 tsp. curry powder
Parmesan cheese

Shrimp and chicken may be stir-fried just until tender, but I prefer shrimp boiled briefly (2 minutes) and chicken breast steamed just until tender. Grease casserole dish. Boil or steam vegetables until done. Do not overcook them. Drain well. Spread in casserole. Put chicken breast and shrimp on top of vegetables. Combine soups with remaining ingredients and spread on top. Shake grated cheese over top. Bake 40 to 45 minutes or until heated through in 350° oven.

The best casserole I've ever eaten, created by taking the best from 2 recipes in my files.

Lion Vivian Quinlan, Mathews Lions Club
Mathews, Virginia, USA

A caress is better than a career.

ANGEL HAIR SCALLOPS AND SHRIMP

1 pkg. angel hair pasta
3 Tbsp. olive oil
3 cloves garlic, minced
½ lb. scallops, shelled
½ lb. medium shrimp, shelled
½ c. white wine
1 medium can crushed tomatoes

1 can chicken broth
¼ tsp. oregano
¼ tsp. basil
¼ tsp. black pepper
Pinch of red pepper flakes
2 Tbsp. chopped fresh parsley

In heavy pan, saute garlic. Add shrimp and scallops; cook till opaque. Add wine, tomatoes, broth, oregano, basil, and both peppers. Simmer sauce 10 minutes only. Cook angel hair pasta as directed. Drain. Toss with sauce. Sprinkle with fresh parsley.

Bunny Creo, Merritt Island Lions Club
Merritt Island, Florida, USA

ASIAN SHRIMP, VEGETABLES, AND NOODLES

4 oz. thin Chinese egg noodles or
   capellini (angel hair)
2 Tbsp. oil
1 carrot, cut into thin diagonal
   slices
¾ lb. bok choy (about 5 c. diced)
¼ lb. mushrooms, thinly sliced
3 scallions, cut into ¼ inch slices
2 cloves garlic, minced

1¾ c. chicken broth
1 Tbsp. soy sauce
½ lb. medium shrimp, peeled and
   deveined
4 oz. fresh mung-bean sprouts
1 tsp. grated fresh ginger
2 Tbsp. rice-wine vinegar
1 Tbsp. sesame oil (optional)

1. In a large pot of boiling salted water, cook the noodles. Drain and set aside.

2. In a large frying pan, heat the oil over medium-high heat. Add the carrot, bok choy, mushrooms, scallions, and garlic; cook, stirring occasionally, until the vegetables are tender, about 5 minutes.

3. Add the chicken broth, soy sauce, and ½ cup water. Bring the mixture to a boil.

4. Stir in the shrimp, bean sprouts, and fresh ginger. Return to boil and cook until the shrimp are firm, about 2 minutes.

5. Stir in rice-wine vinegar, noodles, and sesame oil. Serve immediately.

(Mrs. Joanne Brownell) by John J. Hess, Clarence Center Lions Club
Clarence Center, New York, USA

❦

Find happiness in today - it is there for the taking.

SHRIMP AND TORTELLINI

1 lb. medium size shrimp
   (unpeeled)
1 (9 oz.) pkg. cheese tortellini
⅓ c. butter or margarine

1 shallot, minced
2 Tbsp. fresh basil, chopped, or 2
   tsp. dried basil
½ c. Parmesan cheese, grated

Peel and devein shrimp; set aside. Cook pasta according to package directions. Drain and set aside. Melt margarine in skillet; add shrimp, shallot, and basil. Cook about 5 minutes, stirring constantly. Add pasta and cheese. Toss gently. Serve. Serves 4.

Lion Margaret Morton, Royalton Hills Lions Club
North Royalton, Ohio, USA

SHRIMP SCAMPI

1 lb. shrimp (16 to 20 size)
2 oz. butter
1 tsp. chopped garlic
1 whole lemon

Pinch of chopped parsley
Salt and pepper to taste
1 Tbsp. brandy
1 tsp. white wine

Clean shrimp and devein. Melt butter in saute pan with garlic. Add shrimp. When shrimp start to turn pink, add lemon, parsley, salt, pepper, brandy, and white wine. Saute for about 4 to 6 minutes. Makes 6 servings. Per serving: 256 calories, 16 grams fat, 262 milligrams cholesterol, and 288 milligrams sodium.

Wendell Walker, Charlotte Amalie Lions Club
St. Thomas, U.S. Virgin Islands

SPICY CAJUN SHRIMP

1 tsp. ground red pepper
1 tsp. dried basil, crumbled
½ tsp. dried oregano, crumbled
½ tsp. dried thyme leaves,
   crumbled
½ tsp. crushed red pepper
½ tsp. salt
½ tsp. black pepper

⅓ c. butter or margarine
1½ tsp. minced garlic
1 tsp. Worcestershire sauce
2 doz. large shrimp, peeled
1 large tomato, coarsely chopped
¼ c. beer (at room temperature)
3 c. hot cooked rice

Combine ground red peppers, basil, oregano, thyme, crushed red pepper, salt, and pepper in cup. Combine butter, garlic, Worcestershire sauce, and seasoning in large skillet. Heat butter over high heat just until butter melts. Stir in shrimp and tomato. Cook 2 minutes, stirring constantly. Stir in beer; cover and cook 1 minute longer or until shrimp is bright pink and meat is firm and opaque. Serve over rice. Makes 4 servings.

Lion Ed Johnson, Graysville/Proctor Lions Club
Glen Dale, West Virginia, USA

CRAB AND SHRIMP BAKE

1 medium size green pepper,
  chopped
1 medium size onion, chopped
1 c. celery, chopped
1 (6½ oz.) can crabmeat
1 (6½ oz.) can shrimp or equal
  amount of cooked shrimp

½ tsp. salt
⅛ tsp. pepper
1 tsp. Worcestershire sauce
1 c. mayonnaise
1 c. buttered crumbs

Combine ingredients, except crumbs. Place in casserole and sprinkle with buttered bread crumbs. Bake at 350° for 30 minutes. Serves 8.

SHRIMP JAMBALAYA

2 c. fully cooked ham
¾ c. chopped onion
½ tsp. garlic powder
2 Tbsp. margarine or butter
2 (15 oz.) cans tomato sauce with
  bits
1 (10½ oz.) can beef broth
1 c. uncooked long grain rice
1 bay leaf

1 tsp. sugar
½ tsp. ground thyme
¼ tsp. chili powder
Dash of freshly ground pepper
1 lb. cooked shrimp
¼ c. sliced pitted olives
1 medium green pepper, cut in ¾
  inch squares

In large saucepan, cook ham and onion in butter till onion is tender. Add garlic powder, tomato sauce, beef broth, 1 cup water, rice, bay leaf, sugar, thyme, chili powder, and pepper. Cover and simmer until rice is tender, about 15 minutes.

Add shrimp, olives, and green pepper squares. Simmer, uncovered, to desired consistency. Do not overcook shrimp! Five minutes should be sufficient. Cover and let set for another 5 minutes. Makes 4 to 6 servings.

MARYLAND LADY CRAB CAKES

1 c. Italian bread crumbs
1 egg
¼ c. mayonnaise
½ tsp. salt
¼ tsp. pepper

1 tsp. Worcestershire sauce
1 tsp. dry mustard
1 lb. crabmeat
Oil for frying

Mix bread crumbs, egg, mayonnaise, and seasonings. Add crabmeat. Mix gently but thoroughly. If mixture is too dry, add a little more mayonnaise. Shape into 6 cakes. Cook cakes in fry pan in just enough oil to prevent sticking until browned, about 5 minutes each side. Imitation crabmeat works well.

CRAB DELIGHT

½ lb. crabmeat
1 medium onion, chopped
½ c. sour cream
½ c. mayonnaise
2 eggs, beaten

1 can Cheddar cheese soup
½ tsp. Old Bay seasoning
Butter
Crushed corn flakes

Mix all ingredients together, except the last 2. Place in a greased baking dish. Cover with the corn flakes and dot with the butter. Bake 45 minutes at 350°. Serves 4 to 5 people. Serve with favorite side dishes.

William M. Davidson, IV, Statesboro Lions Club
Statesboro, Georgia, USA

CRAB BURGERS

1 large can crab
1 small jar green olives, sliced
1 small can hot tomato sauce

1 c. sharp Cheddar cheese, cubed
¾ c. mayonnaise

1. You can use imitation crab (costs a little less), but canned is better and fresh crab is great! Break crab down into small pieces.
2. Mix all the above together and place on open face hamburger buns.
3. Broil until the bits of cheese start to melt. Watch so you don't let them burn.

Eleanor Jacobs, Spokane Central Lions Club
Spokane, Washington, USA

LANDLUBBER'S CRABMEAT SPREAD

1 lb. fully cooked imitation or real
    crabmeat, thawed
16 oz. cream cheese
½ c. mayonnaise
Dash of cayenne or Tabasco

1 tsp. lemon juice
1 medium onion, chopped
1 celery rib, finely chopped
Salt and pepper to taste

Chop crabmeat in food processor or by hand. Mix all ingredients in a double boiler and heat through, stirring occasionally. Serve warm or cold with crackers or French bread. May be served cold as a sandwich filling. Makes 3 cups.

Lois Gnuse, Arlington Lions Club
Arlington, Nebraska, USA

The delights of self-discovery are always available.

MAGGIE'S CLAM CAKES

1 tsp. baking soda
½ c. boiling water
1 c. flour, sprinkled with Accent
    for flavor
2 lb. minced clams

2 lb. boxes unsalted crackers,
    ground up
6 to 8 eggs
1 bottle clam juice

Mix together; keep some cracker crumbs to use in forming the clam cakes so they won't stick together. Fry in deep fat at about 300°. Makes about 40 to 50 clam cakes, depending on the size.

Maggie Harnois, Westbrook Lions Club
Westbrook, Maine, USA

WHITE CLAM SAUCE LINGUINE

2 c. chopped clams
2 medium zucchini, sliced
1 box fresh mushrooms, sliced

1 onion, chopped (optional)
2 sticks margarine
½ c. half & half

Saute clams, zucchini, mushrooms, and onions in margarine. Reduce heat and slowly add half & half. Season to taste. Pour over cooked linguine noodles.

Kelly Brown, Lyman Lions Club
Lyman, Wyoming, USA

DEEP-FRIED COUNTRY-STYLE PRAWNS

1 lb. shrimp
1 Tbsp. wine sherry
2 Tbsp. cornstarch
5 c. oil

1½ tsp. salt
½ tsp. Accent (optional)
½ tsp. black pepper

1. Clean shrimp. Remove sand vein in center of shrimp. Marinate in 1 tablespoon wine for 15 minutes, then coat with 2 tablespoons cornstarch.

2. Heat 5 cups oil. Deep-fry shrimp over high heat for 1½ minutes. Remove and drain dry.

3. Heat wok or pan until very hot. Stir-fry shrimp and use left hand to slowly sprinkle in seasoning. Stop stirring when all the seasoning has been mixed. Remove to serving plate.

Flavored and spiced just right.

Lion Paul Rasmussen, Caruthers Lions Club
Caruthers, California, USA

❧

Live that your memories will be a part of your happiness.

SALMON PIE

2 (15½ oz.) cans salmon, boned
2 large onions
2 Tbsp. butter
8 large potatoes, peeled and
   cooked

1 c. milk
Salt and pepper to taste
Biscuit mix
Pastry for 2 double crust 9 inch
   pies

Combine salmon, onions, and butter. Mix thoroughly. Add potatoes and mash. Stir in milk and whip until smooth. Spread mixture in prepared pastry shells. Top with crust and crimp edges to seal. Bake at 350° for 20 minutes.

Dave Bernier, Westbrook Lions Club
Westbrook, Maine, USA

SALMON PIE

16 oz. can red Alaska salmon
1 onion
Salt and pepper

4 potatoes
Pie crust

In large kettle, cook and boil 4 potatoes, onion, and salt until done. Roll out pie dough. Place in bottom of pie plate. When potatoes are cooked, drain and add salmon, including bones, skin, juice, and all. Mash together well until consistency of soft mashed potatoes. Add milk if needed. Place top crust on top of mixture. Brush crust with milk. Bake at 450° for 10 minutes and at 350° for 30 minutes or until golden.

Grace P. Curtis, Westbrook Lions Club
Westbrook, Maine, USA

SALMON LOAF

1 can salmon
½ c. bread or cracker crumbs
2 well beaten eggs

¼ tsp. salt
1 Tbsp. flour
1 c. milk

Stir all together. Shape in a loaf pan. Put a pat of butter on top and bake 30 minutes at 350°.

Andrea Juhl, Otis Lions Club
Otis Colorado, USA

When it rains, look for the rainbow!

POACHED SALMON ALA DISHWASHER

1 (3 lb.) whole salmon (head and
    tail removed)
Salt
Freshly ground pepper
2 Tbsp. butter, cut into pieces
1 small onion, sliced
1 small lemon, sliced
½ c. white wine
Watercress or parsley sprigs
Lemon wedges

Rinse salmon thoroughly. Pat dry. Sprinkle liberally with salt and pepper inside and out. Place on piece of foil large enough to wrap fish completely. Arrange butter, onion, and lemon slices in cavity. Sprinkle with wine. Fold foil around fish, making a water tight package. Wrap several more layers of foil to seal completely. Place fish on top rack of dishwasher. *Do not* add detergent. Set washer for full cycle, including drying cycle.

When cycle is finished, remove fish package and unwrap. Discard onion and lemon slices. Carefully lift out backbone and smaller bones. (They should come out in one piece.) Scrape off any discolored spots. Remove fins. Serve warm or chilled on bed of watercress or parsley. Garnish with lemon wedges. Serve with favorite seafood sauce.

OUTDOOR GRILLED SALMON

3 to 4 lb. boneless, skinless
    salmon fillets, chilled
Thin sliced white onion
Season salt
Dill flakes
Ground basil
¼ lb. softened butter
Fresh squeezed lemon juice
Clam shell grill basket
Pastry brush

Lay salmon fillets on open basket. Season up side lightly with season salt, dill, and basil. Mix butter and lemon juice; paint fish liberally. Layer onion rings on buttered fish to flavor and moisten and keep fish from sticking to basket. Close basket and turn over. Open basket and repeat above to other side of fish. Cook over charcoal or rocks at 350° for 15 to 20 minutes, depending on thickness of fish, then turn grill basket over for about 10 minutes more. Baste first cooked side with any butter/lemon that's left. A little butter smoke flavors. Feeds 3 to 5.

John Martuch, Onekama Lions Club
Onekama, Michigan, USA

❦

What we see depends on what we're looking for. Expect the best.

BERING SEA BAKED SALMON

1 medium size salmon, scaled and
   cleaned
1 lemon, sliced into 6 sections
½ tsp. garlic salt
½ tsp. fresh or dried dill

Dash of pepper
1 small onion, sliced
½ c. diced celery
½ to 1 c. tomato sauce or ketchup

Preheat oven to 350°. Take one medium salmon; scale, clean, and rinse in cold water. If preferred, fillet fish. Place cleaned salmon in a large greased shallow baking dish. Season with garlic salt, pepper, and dill. Arrange onions, celery, and lemon slices inside the salmon or on top of one fillet. If your salmon is filleted, place the second piece on top. Take remaining lemon slices and arrange them over the fish, then pour your tomato sauce or ketchup over the complete fish. Bake in a covered dish at 350° for approximately 1 to 1½ hours or until the salmon flakes easily with a fork. Makes 8 to 10 servings. Serve with mashed potatoes or rice and cole slaw.

Marie L. Reader, Bering Sea Lions Club
Nome, Alaska, USA

CHEESY SALMON CHOWDER

2 lb. fish filets
2 c. potatoes
1 c. celery
1 c. carrots
½ c. onions

1 lb. Velveeta cheese
1 (12 oz.) can Pet milk
1 Tbsp. salt
Pepper to taste

Bring 4 cups water to boil. Add fish and boil for 5 minutes. Remove fish to dry paper towel; cool, then flake and remove bones. To water, add carrots, celery, and onions; cook until done. Drain ½ water off; add Pet milk, diced potatoes, salt, pepper, and fish. Mix well. Put cheese on top and simmer until potatoes are done and cheese is melted. Other fish species can be used. Lite cheese and Pet milk can be used.

Lion Frank English, Onekama Lions Club
Onekama, Michigan, USA

When a friend asks, there is no tomorrow.

ROUGHY ROLL-UPS

2 (10 oz.) pkg. frozen broccoli
spears
4 to 8 fillets orange roughy
1 (10½ oz.) can cream of
mushroom or celery soup
(choice)

¾ c. low-cal mayo or Miracle Whip
1 lemon

Cook broccoli and drain. Divide broccoli among the fish fillets; place on each and roll up. Secure with a toothpick. Mix soup with the mayonnaise and the juice of the lemon. Pour over the fillets and bake for 35 to 40 minutes at 350°. Garnish with lemon twists and serve with a bit of parsley for color. Super best, simple, easy, and quick to make.

Lou Wierichs, Jr., Appleton Evening Lions Club
Appleton, Wisconsin, USA

MERMAID FISH FILLET

Mixture:

8 oz. *orange roughy*, patted dry
(skin side up - 4 to 5 oz.
fillets)
Lemon pepper

1 lb. imitation crabmeat
1 small bunch green onions
Mayonnaise (approx. 3 Tbsp.)

Pat fillets dry and sprinkle with lemon pepper. Chop 12 ounces to 1 pound imitation crabmeat (or use canned crab), small bunch of green onions (chopped also, use some tops), and 1 teaspoon lemon pepper. Mix enough mayonnaise to hold together (3 tablespoons). Spread mixture on fillets and roll up fillets from head to tail. Arrange on Pyrex baking plate.

Topping:

2 egg whites
1 tsp. lemon juice
4 Tbsp. mayonnaise

1 tsp. French's mustard
2 Tbsp. fresh dill or 2 tsp. dried dill

Garnish:

Radish roses
Parsley

Lemon wedges

Whip 2 egg whites and 1 teaspoon lemon juice stiff. Fold in mayonnaise, French's mustard, and fresh dill or dried dill. Mix and spoon over rolled fillets. Place dish on aluminum foil and shape up around edge of plate for sides. Bake at 425° for 20 to 25 minutes. Garnish with radish roses, parsley, and lemon wedges.

How old would you be if you didn't know how old you were?

QUICK AND ELEGANT ORANGE ROUGHY
(Microwave)

1 to 1½ lb. orange roughy fillets
⅓ c. sliced mushrooms
¼ c. chopped onions
1 tsp. salt
½ tsp. pepper
1 tsp. marjoram

¼ c. dry white wine
2 tsp. lemon juice
¼ c. grated Monterey Jack cheese
¼ c. bread crumbs or dry stuffing
   mix
½ c. melted butter

Sprinkle onions and mushrooms over the bottom of an oblong glass dish. Arrange fillets over vegetables, overlapping only the thin part of the fillets. Season the fish with salt, pepper, and marjoram. Sprinkle the wine and lemon juice over all. Top with cheese and bread crumbs; pour butter over all. Cover with wax paper and microwave for 5 to 7 minutes on HIGH or until flaky.

Note: This may be baked in a conventional oven at 400° for 7 minutes, covered, and for 5 minutes more, uncovered.

CATFISH PARMESAN

⅔ c. Parmesan cheese
¼ c. flour
½ tsp. salt
¼ tsp. black pepper
1 tsp. paprika

1 egg, beaten
¼ c. milk
5 to 6 small (2 lb.) catfish fillets
¼ c. margarine, melted
⅓ c. sliced almonds

Combine first 5 ingredients. Stir well. Combine egg and milk; dip fillets in egg mixture, then dredge in flour mixture. Arrange in a lightly greased (spray with Pam) 13x9x2 inch baking dish. Drizzle with margarine. Sprinkle almonds over top. Bake at 350° for 35 to 40 minutes until fish flakes easily when tested with fork. Makes 6 servings.

After stewing a chicken for diced meat for casseroles, etc., let cool in broth before cutting into chunks. It will have twice the flavor.
Mrs. Charlotte M. Garner, Pascagoula Evening Lions Club
Pascagoula, Mississippi, USA

❦

Laughing at yourself gives you a lot to smile about.

BAKED GREEK FISH

2 lb. haddock or whitefish
2 c. cooked carrots
2 large onions
2 green peppers

1 can tomato soup
1 Tbsp. poultry seasoning
2 Tbsp. olive oil

Fry peppers and onions that have been sliced thin in olive oil until tender. Cook carrots and set aside. Combine carrots, onions, peppers, and poultry seasoning to tomato soup. Mix well and pour over raw fish that has been placed flat in a 13x9 inch pan. Bake at 350° about 30 to 45 minutes or until done.

Pamela Barrows (Mary Nanos), Westbrook Lions Club
Westbrook, Maine, USA

HADDOCK

1 lb. haddock
½ pkg. Coon cheese or extra
  sharp
½ pkg. Ritz crackers

3 Tbsp. margarine
Dash of onion juice
Dash of Worcestershire sauce

Butter baking dish. Arrange haddock. Melt margarine. Add crushed Ritz crackers, onion juice, Worcestershire sauce, and lemon juice. Mix and add topping to fish. Bake in preheated 400° oven for 10 minutes or until crumbs are lightly browned. Precut fish in serving size pieces.

Connie Levecque, Westbrook Lions Club
Westbrook, Maine, USA

BAKED FISH

1 lb. fish (cod or haddock)
2 cans Campbell's cream of
  shrimp soup
Ritz crackers

Butter
Salt
Pepper

Lay fish in a baking dish. Season with salt and pepper. Spread soup over fish (undiluted). Crumble Ritz crackers (as many as you like) on top of soup. Dot with butter. Bake at 350°F. for 30 minutes.

You'll think you're in heaven when you eat this.

Nancy Goureia, Berkley Lions Club
Berkley, Massachusetts, USA

❦

People live up to what you believe of them.

SEAFOOD STUFFED SHELLS

½ lb. jumbo shells
4 Tbsp. butter
1 carrot, diced
1 rib celery, diced
1 onion, diced
2 cloves garlic, minced
1 lb. medium shrimp, peeled and
    coarsely chopped
1 lb. cod or other whitefish fillets,
    cut in ¾ inch chunks

¾ tsp. dried thyme
1½ tsp. salt
½ tsp. black pepper
2 Tbsp. chopped parsley
3 c. milk
3 Tbsp. flour
2 oz. Gruyere cheese, shredded
    (about ⅔ c.)

1. In large pot of boiling salted water, cook shells until almost done. Drain and set aside.

2. Heat oven to 350°. Butter a 3 quart baking dish.

3. In large frying pan over medium-low heat, melt 1 tablespoon of butter. Add carrot, celery, onion, and garlic. Cover and cook, stirring occasionally, until vegetables are soft, about 7 minutes.

4. Add shrimp, cod, thyme, ¾ teaspoon salt, and ¼ teaspoon pepper. Raise heat to medium and cook until shrimp are pink and cod looks white, about 5 minutes more. Stir in parsley and set aside.

5. In small saucepan, heat 2½ cups of the milk just to a boil.

6. In a saucepan over medium heat, melt remaining 3 tablespoons butter. Whisk in the flour and cook, whisking, until it foams, 1 to 2 minutes. Add hot milk, whisking constantly. Return mixture to a slow boil and cook until thickened, about 3 minutes. Whisk in the remaining salt and pepper.

7. Stir ¾ cup of this white sauce into fish mixture. Thin remaining white sauce with ½ cup milk.

8. Stuff shells and arrange in a baking dish. Pour remaining white sauce over shells. Sprinkle cheese over shells, cover with foil, and bake for ½ hour. Uncover the dish and bake 15 minutes longer. Makes 8 servings.

(Mrs. Joanne Brownell) by John J. Hess, Clarence Center Lions Club
Clarence Center, New York, USA

BAKED FISH

2 lb. fish fillets or steaks
1 tsp. salt
½ tsp. pepper
2 Tbsp. lemon juice
1 tsp. chopped onion

1 clove garlic, chopped
1 tsp. melted margarine or 1 tsp.
    olive oil
Paprika

Cut fish into serving pieces. Sprinkle both sides with salt and pepper. Add lemon juice, onion, and garlic to the melted margarine. Dip each piece of fish into this mixture and place in a greased baking dish. Pour rest of mixture over fish. Bake in a moderate oven at 350°F. for 30 to 40 minutes or until fish flakes easily with a fork. Sprinkle with paprika. Serve immediately. Serves 5.

Ava Brathwaite, Charlotte Amalie Lions Club
St. Thomas, U.S. Virgin Islands

HALIBUT SOUFFLE

1 lb. halibut	3 to 4 eggs
2 c. milk	Crumbs
Cheese	Onion

Cook 1 pound fresh halibut in salted water to cover and 2 slices onion. Cook for 20 minutes or until fish flakes. Drain and discard onion. Make thin white sauce. Add enough sharp cheese to desired taste. Cool slightly. Add 3 to 4 well beaten eggs. Butter 1½ quart casserole. Layer fish and sauce; end with sauce. Cover top with buttered crumbs, chips, etc.

Joyce Bolton, Westbrook Lions Club
Westbrook, Maine, USA

HALIBUT CASSEROLE

2 lb. halibut, cut in 1 inch cubes	1 c. half & half
4 slices bacon, cut in 1 inch pieces	1 Tbsp. lemon juice
¾ c. onion, chopped	3 Tbsp. flour
3 medium potatoes, diced	2 Tbsp. sherry wine
3 c. milk	Parsley
1 Tbsp. salt	Pepper
3 Tbsp. butter	Water

Cook bacon in pan until half done. Add onions and continue cooking until onions are translucent. Add potatoes and enough water to cover; cook until potatoes are tender. Add halibut, milk, salt, and pepper. Simmer for 6 to 8 minutes.

Meanwhile, make a roux by melting 3 tablespoons butter in saucepan over low heat. Blend in flour; stir in half & half with wire whisk and continue beating until thick. Slowly stir roux into potatoes and halibut until it is well blended and just bubbles. Add sherry and lemon juice. Pour into serving dish. Sprinkle with parsley. Serves 8.

Earl L. Drake, Reno Plumb Lane Lions Club
Reno, Nevada, USA

❦

Optimism is having 3 teen-agers and only one car.

ENTREES - PORK

LION LARRY'S ROAST SUCKLING PIG

1 suckling pig (2 weeks old),
    opened and cleaned (about
    10 lb.)
2 bay leaves
1 sprig parsley
2 cloves garlic
1 small onion

1 sprig thyme
½ lb. lard or shortening
Salt
Paprika
White wine
Water

Put the suckling pig, spread flat, open side up, in a roasting pan. Chop and sprinkle with the bay leaves, parsley, garlic, onion, and thyme. Rub with shortening. Season with salt and paprika. Pour into the pan 1 glass of white wine and 3 glasses of water. Put in the oven at 350°. After 45 minutes, remove from the pan the excess juice and fat. Cook another 45 minutes, then turn, skin side up, and brush the skin with the pan juice. Cook until the skin is golden brown color and crispy (another 30 to 45 minutes). Serve garnished with baked potatoes or salad.

Lion Larry Roesch, Elmhurst Noon Lions Club
Elmhurst, Illinois, USA

B-B-Q PORK RIBS

4 to 4½ lb. country style ribs or
    spareribs
½ c. catsup
½ c. chili sauce
2 Tbsp. brown sugar
¼ c. chopped onions

½ tsp. salt
⅛ tsp. garlic powder
2 tsp. mustard
1 Tbsp. Worcestershire sauce
Dash of Tabasco sauce
½ lemon or 1 Tbsp. lemon juice

In large saucepan, cover ribs with water. Salt to taste. Simmer for 1 hour over medium heat. For BBQ sauce, combine all ingredients. Mix well.

To barbecue, place on grill 4 to 6 inches from hot coals. Cook about 30 to 45 minutes until brown. Brush with sauce. Serves 6 to 8.

Finger licking good!

Lion Ray Loflin, Caruthers Lions Club
Caruthers, California, USA

Every person you meet is an opportunity for kindness.

MANDARIN PORK AND VEGETABLES

2 Tbsp. cornstarch
1¼ c. water
⅓ c. soy sauce
⅓ c. corn syrup
¼ to ½ tsp. crushed dried red
    peppers
1 lb. boneless pork, cut in thin
    strips (can also use chicken
    or beef)

2 garlic cloves, minced
2 c. broccoli, cut up
2 onions, sliced
1 carrot, cut in thin strips
½ lb. mushrooms
Vegetable oil

Make sauce. Mix cornstarch and water till smooth. Stir in soy sauce, corn syrup, and red peppers; set aside.

In large skillet or wok, heat 2 tablespoons oil. Add meat and garlic. Stir-fry for 5 minutes or till tender. Remove from skillet. Heat 2 tablespoons oil. Add broccoli, onions, and carrot. Stir-fry for 2 minutes; add mushrooms. Stir-fry for 1 minute more till vegetables are tender crisp. Return meat to pan. Stir in sauce and stir till hot. Serve over rice.

PORK TENDERLOIN WITH CINNAMON

2 lb. pork tenderloin
4 Tbsp. sugar
¼ tsp. salt
4 Tbsp. soy sauce
1½ tsp. cinnamon

2 Tbsp. sherry
1 tsp. ginger
2 tsp. dry mustard
2 tsp. lemon juice

Preheat oven to 325°. Put pork in roasting pan. Combine all other ingredients and pour over pork. Bake 1 hour, basting frequently with sauce.

Joanne Wetzler, Clarence Center Lions Club
Clarence Center, New York, USA

SWEET AND SOUR PORK

1 c. water
⅔ c. vinegar
½ c. brown sugar
4 Tbsp. corn starch
1 tsp. salt

2 Tbsp. soy sauce
2 c. pineapple
3 lb. lean pork, diced and browned
    in bacon fat

Cook first 7 ingredients until clear and thick. Add pork and cook 1 hour, covered. A few minutes before serving, add thinly sliced green pepper and onion, also pineapple chunks. Heat thoroughly. I make sure there is no fat left.

Shirley Canterbury, Eastmont Lions Club
East Wenatchee, Washington, USA

SAUERKRAUT MEATBALLS

½ lb. pork sausage
½ c. chopped onion
14 oz. sauerkraut, snipped,
    drained, and squeezed
2 Tbsp. fine bread crumbs

4 oz. cream cheese
2 Tbsp. parsley
1 tsp. mustard
¼ tsp. garlic salt
⅛ tsp. pepper

Sauce for dipping:

Mustard   **Mayonnaise**

Brown pork sausage with onion. Add sauerkraut and bread crumbs. Combine cream cheese, parsley, mustard, garlic salt, and pepper; mix all together and chill. Form small balls and roll into flour, then egg and milk and fine cracker crumbs. Fondue or deep-fry.

HONEY-BAKED HAM

1 (3 to 4 lb.) boneless ham
1 c. dark brown sugar
½ c. prepared mustard

4 oz. honey
Whole cloves

Blend sugar, mustard, and honey together. Score ham and stud ham with cloves. Coat ham with mixture. Bake slowly at 325° for 1½ hours (18 to 20 minutes per pound).

This is a holiday favorite.

Lion President Ed Gomes, Caruthers Lions Club
Caruthers, California, USA

HAM LOAF

2 lb. ground ham
1¼ lb. ground pork
1½ c. bread crumbs

2 eggs
1 c. milk

Sauce:

1 c. brown sugar
½ tsp. dry mustard

½ c. vinegar, diluted with water

Mix well the meat mixture and shape into loaf. Mix sauce ingredients and pour over ham loaf. Baste often while baking. Bake at 350° for 1 to 1½ hours.

Success lies not in being the best but in doing your best.

Louise J. Eshleman, Middletown Lions Club
Middletown, Pennsylvania, USA

HAM LOAF

1 lb. ground smoked ham
1 lb. ground lean pork
3 c. *Wheaties*
2 eggs, beaten

1 c. milk
½ tsp. salt
⅛ tsp. pepper

Mix preceding ingredients thoroughly. Pack into greased 9x5x3 inch loaf pan.

For catsup topped loaf, spread 3 tablespoons catsup over top before baking. Bake at 350° (moderate oven) for 1½ hours. Unmold. Makes 8 servings.

HAM BALLS

1½ lb. ground ham
½ lb. ground pork
2 lb. ground beef *or* 4 lb.
  purchased ham loaf

2 eggs
1 can evaporated milk
2 c. graham cracker crumbs

Topping:

1 (10½ oz.) can tomato soup or V-
  8 juice
½ c. vinegar

1½ c. brown sugar, packed
1½ tsp. dry mustard

Combine above ingredients and make into balls. Bake ham balls 15 to 20 minutes and drain. Pour topping over ham balls and bake at 325° for 1 hour. Yields 30 balls. This can be made into cocktail size balls and used as an appetizer.

Topping: Combine and pour over balls.

Quinter J. Herring, Bloomington Lions Club
Bloomington, Illinois, USA

HAM BALLS

1 lb. ground ham
2 c. bread crumbs
1 c. milk
2 tsp. dry mustard
1 c. water

1½ lb. ground pork
2 eggs, well beaten
2 c. brown sugar
1 c. vinegar

Combine ham and pork, bread crumbs, eggs, and milk. Mix thoroughly. Shape into ¾ inch balls and place in 9x13 inch pan. Blend brown sugar, dry mustard, vinegar, and water in a saucepan. Heat and pour over balls. Bake 1 hour in a 325° oven. Baste frequently or roll balls over in the sauce. Serve hot. If sauce gets thick, add water. Watch sauce does not burn. Balls can be frozen and warmed to serve later. Makes 50 to 60 balls.

Lion Connie Sample, Royalton Hills Lions Club
North Royalton, Ohio, USA

SICILIAN MEAT ROLL

2 eggs, beaten
¾ c. soft bread crumbs
½ c. tomato juice
2 Tbsp. parsley
½ tsp. dried oregano
1 clove garlic

2 lb. ground beef
8 slices boiled ham
1½ c. Mozzarella cheese,
  shredded
3 slices Mozzarella cheese

Combine first 6 ingredients, ¼ teaspoon salt, and ¼ teaspoon pepper. Add beef and mix well. On wax paper, pat meat to 12x10 inch rectangle; arrange ham on top, then shredded cheese. Starting from one end, roll meat, using paper to lift; seal edge and ends. Place, seam side down, in a 13x9x2 inch pan. Bake at 350° for 1¼ hours. Center will be pink. Halve cheese slices and place on top. Return to oven until melted.

Dan Bernier, Westbrook Lions Club
Westbrook, Maine, USA

PORK CHOPS WITH APPLES AND ONIONS

4 center-cut pork loin chops, cut
  ½ inch thick
Vegetable oil cooking spray
1 medium onion, sliced and
  separated into rings
2 apples, cored and cut into thin
  wedges

½ tsp. dried sage, crushed
1 c. apple juice
1 tsp. brown sugar
1 Tbsp. cold water
2 tsp. cornstarch

Trim fat from chops. Rub sage onto both sides of meat. Spray 12 inch skillet with vegetable oil cooking spray. Preheat skillet. Cook chops for 5 minutes; turn. Add onion to skillet. Cook mixture for 5 to 7 minutes more or until no pink remains in chops. Remove chops and keep warm, leaving onion in skillet.

For sauce, in same skillet with onions, stir in apple wedges, juice, and brown sugar. Bring to boil; reduce heat. Simmer, covered, for 3 to 5 minutes or until apples are crisp-tender. Combine water and cornstarch. Add to skillet. Cook and stir until bubbly. Cook 2 minutes more. Serve chops with apple mixture.

Michael Hadeed, Alexandria Evening Lions Club
Alexandria, Virginia, USA

❦

Whatever you do, do it with all the might that is in you!

PORK CHOPS AND POTATOES

6 pork chops (½ inch thick)
1 Tbsp. cooking oil
5 c. sliced potatoes
6 (1 oz.) slices American cheese
1 tsp. salt

¼ tsp. pepper
½ c. chopped green onion
½ can (10½ oz.) cream of celery
   soup
1¼ c. milk

Brown pork chops in cooking oil. While pork chops are cooking, slice potatoes and arrange in 13x9 inch pan. Mix remaining ingredients together and pour over potatoes. Cover with the cheese slices and pork chops. Cover with foil. Bake 1 hour, then uncover and bake ½ hour longer or until tender. You may add garlic if like.

Ruth Wright, Moweaqua Lions Club
Moweaqua, Illinois, USA

PORK CHOP AND POTATO CASSEROLE

5 to 8 pork chops
8 to 10 medium potatoes
1½ to 2 c. Colby cheese
½ c. chopped bell pepper
½ c. onion
1 can cream of mushroom soup

1 can cream of chicken soup
1 small can mushrooms
¾ c. milk
½ tsp. garlic powder
Salt and pepper

While peeling and slicing potatoes, brown pork chops in small amount of oil. After browned, remove from heat. Mix soups and milk together; set aside. Put cheese, drained mushrooms, seasonings, bell pepper, and onion in with potatoes and ¾ of soup mixture. Stir together.

In a 9x13 inch oblong pan (greased), put potato mixture in. Put browned pork chops on top of potato mixture. Spoon rest of soup mixture on top of pork chops and bake at 350° until potatoes are tender.

If grease or pie filling boils over, pour salt on it and it will stop the smoking.
Judy Carey, Huffman Lions Club
Huffman, Texas, USA

PORK CHOP AND RICE CASSEROLE

4 to 5 pork chops, trimmed of fat
½ stick butter
Seasoning salt to taste

1 can cream of mushroom soup
1 can milk
1 c. Minute rice

Brown pork chops in butter (seasoned). In bowl, mix rice, soup, and milk. Pour over pork chops in casserole dish or roasting pan. Bake at 350° for 1 hour (½ hour with lid on and ½ hour with lid off).

Mrs. Steve (Pam) Hall, Elburn Lions Club
Elburn, Illinois, USA

DIFFERENT PORK CHOPS

4 (½ to ¾ inch) pork chops
4 onion slices

4 pepper rings (may use chopped)
1 can tomato soup

In ovenproof skillet, brown pork chops. Place onion slice and pepper ring on each chop. Pour tomato soup (undiluted) over all. Cover. Bake at 350° for 1 hour. These are easy to make and very good.

Gloria Bonager, East Prospect Lions Club
East Prospect, Pennsylvania, York County, USA

HAWAIIAN GRILLED PORK CHOPS

1 (20 oz.) can pineapple slices
   (undrained)
6 (1 inch thick) pork chops
½ c. soy sauce

⅓ c. vegetable oil
¼ c. minced onion
1 clove garlic, minced
1 Tbsp. brown sugar

Drain pineapple, reserving ¼ cup juice. Set pineapple aside. Place chops in a large shallow dish. Combine reserved pineapple juice and next 5 ingredients, mixing well. Pour over chops. Cover. Let marinate at least 2 hours, turning occasionally. Place chops on grill and brush with remainder of marinade as they cook. When chops are almost done, place slice of pineapple on each and brush with marinade. Serves 6.

This is my husband's absolute favorite dish.

Mrs. Lion Tommy (Lynda) McFarland, Canton Lions Club
Canton, Georgia, USA

Everything you know about yourself
corresponds to a belief you are holding.

❧ ❧ ❧

I'd rather be a failure at something I enjoy
than be a success at something I hate.

MOM MICHAUD'S NEW YEAR RAGOUT

5 lb. lean, fat trimmed pork chops
5 lb. extra-lean beef or turkey
    hamburg
2 to 3 medium chopped onions
2 c. flour

4 to 5 qt. water for pot
½ c. water for paste
Salt, pepper
Cinnamon, cloves (powdered)

1. Brown the flour in skillet. *Cool.*
2. In large pot, add water and chopped onions to taste along with the fat-trimmed pork chops. Cook until well done.
3. While pork chops are cooking, make meatballs with onions to taste and hamburger meats. Add salt and pepper to taste.
4. When pork chops are cooked, remove from the pot, retaining the broth.
5. To broth, add readied meatballs and cook till done.
6. While meatballs are cooking, chip the cooked pork chops and add to the cooked meatball stew. Add water to enhance content of stew.
7. Heat stew on *low* heat.
8. While stew continues to cook, make a paste of the browned flour until manageable. Use *cold* water to make.
9. Add the paste *slowly* to low heat, cooking stew until desired consistency is achieved.
10. Add cinnamon and cloves to taste. Serve with pickled beets and whole, cooked potatoes. Serve with French bread. Serves 15 to 20.

Well worth the wait! Absolutely delicious!
Doris Robidoux, Blackstone Valley Women's Club
Manville, Rhode Island, USA

When you find out that you have some kind of physical affliction, you can either prepare to suffer or prepare to heal.

A pessimist is someone who feels bad about feeling good because he is afraid he will feel worse when he feels better.

ENTREES - MISCELLANEOUS

VENISON STROGANOFF

2 lb. venison, cut in cubes
¼ tsp. garlic powder
2 bay leaves
1 onion, diced
1½ c. ketchup

12 oz. sour cream
1 Tbsp. beef base
1½ c. water
Flour to coat meat
Oil for cooking meat

Coat venison with flour. Brown venison cubes in oil. After browning, place venison in Dutch oven. Add bay leaves, garlic powder, onion, ketchup, beef base, and water. Simmer 2 hours on low heat. Just before serving, add sour cream and heat through. May be served over cooked egg noodles or rice.

Lion Connie Nagengast, Columbus Noon Lions Club
Columbus, Nebraska, USA

HUNTER'S STEW - BOURGUIGNON

10 lb. venison
2 carrots
2 onions (1 onion in marinade)
1 celery (½ in marinade)
1 bunch parsley
1 qt. beef stock (not in marinade)
1 qt. red wine
2 tsp. salt

2 bay leaves
2 cloves
12 whole black peppers, crushed
1 qt. vinegar
Pinch of thyme
Pinch of rosemary
Pinch of marjoram

Marinate venison with above ingredients (except stock) for 2 days. Cut venison into 1 inch cubes. Brown in hot pan with a pinch of oil (your choice). Deglaze pan with 1 diced onion, 2 cloves garlic (crushed), and 2 cups red wine. Place ingredients into stock pot. Add stock and 4 ounces tomato paste. Simmer till tender, about 1 to 1½ hours. Thicken with about 4 to 5 ounces of roux. Season with salt, Maggi, Tabasco, and Worcestershire (about 2 to 3 pinches). Serve with jardineire of carrots, celery, diced potatoes, all branch, and chopped parsley. When browning meat, do it in small amounts. Will take several times, but the flavor is great.

Lion Dwayne Alshanski, Carpenters Lions Club
Carpentersville, Illinois, USA

❧

Do your best - not because your work is worth it, but because you are.

BARBECUED VENISON MEAT BALLS

2 lb. ground venison
1 pkg. onion soup mix

1 egg
¼ c. bread crumbs

Combine venison, dry soup mix, egg, and bread crumbs. Shape into walnut size balls and brown, either in saute pan or arrange on cookie sheet and put under broiler till brown. Transfer to Dutch oven, casserole, or crock pot. Add the sauce and simmer for about 30 to 40 minutes (crock pot on LOW for 1½ hours).

Sauce:

1 (14 oz.) bottle or can pizza sauce
1 (14 oz.) bottle catsup

1 (10 oz.) currant or apple jelly

Combine pizza sauce, catsup, and jelly in blender till smooth. (Must use blender.)

Can be made in advance and frozen.

FLAT ROAST LEG OF LAMB

Have on hand 1 bone-in leg of lamb, split lengthwise.

Baste ingredients:

⅓ c. olive oil or salad oil
3 Tbsp. lemon juice
½ tsp. onion
½ tsp. dry rosemary

¼ tsp. sugar
¼ tsp. pepper
1 clove garlic, minced or pressed

Bar-beque 4 to 5 inches from coals; sear both sides (10 minutes each). Baste, cover, and cook 60 minutes longer. Turn roast every 15 to 20 minutes and baste.

W.C. Behrcus, Reno Plumb Lane Lions Club
Reno, Nevada, USA

Take a tip from nature ... your ears can't shut, but your mouth can.

LAMB STEW

2 lb. boneless lamb
1 crushed large garlic clove
1 c. (8 oz. can) tomato sauce
½ c. water
½ tsp. ground allspice
½ tsp. paprika
4 c. hot cooked rice

2 c. coarsely chopped onion
¼ c. olive oil
½ c. white wine
½ tsp. salt
½ tsp. cumin
¼ c. chopped parsley

Cut lamb into 1 inch cubes. Brown lamb, onion, and garlic in olive oil in large skillet or saucepan. Drain off excess fat. Add remaining ingredients. Reduce heat and boil gently, covered, 1 hour or until lamb is tender. (Add more water during cooking if necessary.) Serve with rice. Serves 8.

Michael Hadeed, Alexandria Evening Lions Club
Alexandria, Virginia, USA

BASIL VEAL AND PASTA

1 lb. veal cutlets
1 tsp. basil leaves
¼ tsp. salt
⅛ tsp. crushed red pepper
1 Tbsp. olive oil
1 small red pepper, cut in strips

½ c. chopped onion
1½ c. mushrooms
½ tsp. cornstarch
⅓ c. white wine
2 c. cooked linguine

Pound veal to ⅛ inch thick. Cut into strips; stir basil, salt, pepper, and oil. Heat 1 teaspoon of this oil in a 10 inch skillet over medium heat. Stir-fry bell peppers and onion for 1 minute. Add mushrooms. Stir for 2 minutes until crisp; set aside. In rest of oil, stir-fry veal strips half at a time for 1 to 2 minutes, just until cooked. Stir wine and cornstarch until smooth. Cook over high heat about 30 seconds until thick. Return veal and vegetables; heat through. Serve over pasta.

Dave Bernier, Westbrook Lions Club
Westbrook, Maine, USA

❦

If you can imagine it, you can achieve it.
If you can dream it, you can become it.

HOUDAH CURRY OF VEAL

¼ c. butter
1 c. chopped onion
2 Tbsp. minced garlic
1½ lb. veal, cut into 1 inch cubes
4 c. beef stock
1½ tsp. chicken base concentrate
Mango chutney
2 c. crushed pineapple
Salt and pepper
Toasted shredded coconut

Chopped macadamia nuts
Raisins
¼ c. vegetable oil
½ c. chopped shallots
½ c. curry powder
2 c. applesauce
Deep-fried onions
Shrimp chips
Rice pilaf

In a large Dutch oven, heat butter and oil until butter is melted. Add onions, shallots, and garlic; saute until light brown. Add veal and saute for 5 minutes. Stir in curry powder, beef stock, chicken base, pineapple, and applesauce. Bake, uncovered, at 450° for 1 to 1¼ hours. Season to taste with salt and pepper; garnish with a combination of coconut, chutney, macadamia nuts, onions, raisins, and shrimp chips. Serve with rice pilaf. Serves 6 people.

Dave Bernier, Westbrook Lions Club
Westbrook, Maine, USA

SUPER DOGS

1 lb. wieners
2 Tbsp. sugar
1 tsp. salt
2 Tbsp. shortening
¾ c. milk

1 c. flour
1½ tsp. baking powder
⅔ c. corn meal
1 slightly beaten egg

Combine all but the wieners and dip them into the mixture, coating thoroughly. Drop into deep fat, frying until golden brown.

Janie Fox, Saginaw Lions Club
Saginaw, Texas, USA

❦

Judgment means that you view the world as you are,
rather than as it is.

FRANKS IN A LOAF

Heat oven to 400°.

6 frankfurters	1 c. Bisquick baking mix
6 julienne strips Cheddar or	¼ c. milk
American cheese or 2 Tbsp.	1 tsp. parsley flakes
sweet relish or catsup	1 egg

Grease loaf pan, 9x5x3 inches. Split frankfurters lengthwise, not cutting completely through. Fill each with a strip of cheese or about 1 teaspoon relish or catsup.

Mix remaining ingredients with fork; beat vigorously 30 seconds. Spread in pan. Arrange frankfurters crosswise on dough in pan, curving slightly and pressing to fit pan. Press into dough slightly. Bake until bread is light brown, about 20 minutes. To serve, cut bread between frankfurters. Makes 6 servings.

High altitude directions (3500 to 6500 feet): Heat oven to 425°. Bake until bread is light brown, 15 to 20 minutes.

IRISH CORNED BEEF AND CABBAGE

5 lb. lean corned beef brisket	½ tsp. rosemary leaves
1 large onion, sliced	1 (2 lb.) head cabbage, cut into
1 large carrot, peeled and sliced	quarters

In a 10 to 12 quart pan, cover beef with water. Boil for 5 minutes. Discard water. Add more water to cover meat, onion, carrot, and rosemary. Cover and simmer until meat is very tender when pierced (3½ to 4 hours). Lift out the meat. Keep warm on a platter. Bring stock to boiling. Add cabbage and cook, uncovered, until tender crisp when pierced. Reserve stock for Emerald Sauce. Slice meat across grain. Serve with sauce.

Emerald Sauce:

3 Tbsp. butter or margarine	1½ to 2 Tbsp. horseradish
3 Tbsp. all-purpose flour	¼ c. sour cream
1¾ c. corned beef stock	½ c. chopped parsley

In 1 to 2 quart pan, melt butter. Add flour. Stir till bubbly. Add stock and stir to boiling. Add rest of ingredients. Stir till hot. Serves 6 to 8.

❦

The past cannot be changed, but the future is still in your power.

BRATWURST

1 to 2 chopped onions
⅛ c. brown sugar
¼ c. vinegar
4 oz. ketchup
2 Tbsp. mustard

2 to 3 shakes of soy sauce
2 to 3 shakes of Worcestershire
  sauce
Cheap beer
Bratwursts

Add preceding mix to enough cheap beer to soak bratwurst in a kettle. Soak for 20 minutes. Bring mix to slow boil for 5 to 10 minutes. Finish them by browning them on a grill.

BUFFALO STEAK BBQ

3 lb. buffalo rib-eye steak (2
  inches thick - beef may also
  be used)
4 Tbsp. softened butter
1½ tsp. salt

1½ tsp. ground black pepper
2 Tbsp. dry mustard
2 tsp. paprika
2 Tbsp. olive oil
1 tsp. Worcestershire sauce

Make a paste of butter, salt, pepper, mustard, and paprika. Rub both sides with 3 tablespoons of seasoned butter. Let steak marinate for 2 hours.

When ready to BBQ, combine olive oil and Worcestershire sauce. Place steak on BBQ and grill 8 to 10 minutes on one side. Turn and baste meat lightly with olive oil mixture, then grill 8 to 10 minutes on the other side. Turn and baste again. Continue grilling until done to your taste. Serve steak smeared with remaining butter and sprinkle with parsley.

Best in the west!

Lion Mae Segovia, Caruthers Lions Club
Caruthers, California, USA

BARBECUE DEER

Deer meat (any amount)
Butter (enough to cook in)

Barbecue sauce (to cover)

Take some deer lion and cut thin. Put in skillet and add water to cover. Parboil 3 minutes. Rinse and drain. Put back in skillet. Add butter. Cook and stir. Cover with butter for 3 more minutes, then add barbecue sauce to cover and simmer until done.

You can use pork or beef and lamb. Use any amount, depending on how many people to be served.

Lion Roger Van Scyoc, Graysville/Proctor Lions Club
Glen Easton, West Virginia, USA

DEER MEAT IN SAUCE

3 lb. deer meat, cubed
3 medium onions, sliced
1 large pepper
1 large can tomato sauce *or* chili sauce
1 large can whole tomatoes
Salt and pepper to taste

1 clove garlic
¼ tsp. oregano
½ c. brown sugar *or* ¼ c. honey
1 Tbsp. Worcestershire sauce
Basil and parsley flakes (if desired)

Sear meat in melted Crisco in skillet. Put remaining ingredients in crock pot or Dutch oven. Drain meat and add to sauce. Bring meat and sauce just to a slight boil; reduce heat and simmer for approximately 3 hours, or until meat is tender.

Mrs. Susan Sanders, Lion, Hedgesville Lions Club
Hedgesville, West Virginia, USA

SMALL GAME GOULASH

1 rabbit or pheasant
2 c. flour
1 Tbsp. Lawry's seasoning salt
1 Tbsp. black pepper
1 tsp. onion salt

3 to 4 shakes of garlic powder
3 Tbsp. margarine
1 to 2 cans cream of mushroom soup

Cut meat into small chunks. Roll in flour seasoned with salts, pepper, and garlic powder. Brown in margarine in a frying pan. Transfer browned meat cubes into a larger pan. Add cream of mushroom soup (1 or 2 cans, depending on amount of meat). Warm and stir together (about 10 minutes). Although this recipe tastes particularly fantastic with rabbit or pheasant, it also tastes great with squirrel, venison, grouse, duck, or even chicken or beef.

Charles Cleaver, Roseville 11-A2 Lions Club
Roseville, Michigan, USA

SALAMI

5 lb. hamburger (not chuck)
4 Tbsp. Tender Quick salt (less salt)
2½ tsp. liquid hickory smoke
2½ tsp. coarse black pepper

1 tsp. garlic powder
2½ tsp. mustard seed
Hot pepper (red), crushed (optional)

Mix well and refrigerate 24 hours. Form into 6 rolls, about 3 inches in diameter and 7 inches long. Place rolls on rack in roasting pan. Bake at 170° for 8 hours. Turn rolls often. This can also be made in smaller rolls. Good as a snack with crackers.

Verna Ball, Sherrodsville Lions Club
Sherrodsville, Ohio, USA

LEG OF LAMB, BONED

¾ c. olive oil
¼ c. red wine vinegar
1 medium onion, chopped
2 cloves garlic, crushed
2 tsp. mustard
2 tsp. salt

2 tsp. oregano
½ tsp. basil
2 bay leaves, crushed
¼ tsp. pepper
1 leg of lamb

Mix all of the ingredients together and set aside. Bone the lamb (known as butterfly the lamb). Place lamb and marinade in a covered dish or plastic bag and refrigerate it for 24 to 36 hours, turning occasionally. Remove and place on cooking pan with the fat side up. Broil for about 10 minutes 4 inches from the heat. Turn meat over, brush with marinade, and broil another 10 minutes. Decrease heat to 400° and continue to cook for about 10 more minutes. Serve with mint jelly and favorite side dishes.

William M. Davidson, IV, Statesboro Lions Club
Statesboro, Georgia, USA

Anything you must have owns you.
When you release it, you will start getting more of it.

❦ ❦ ❦

Thirty days hath September, April, June, and November.
All the rest have 31, except January and February,
which seems to have 80.

❦ ❦ ❦

Good instincts usually tell you what to do
long before your head has figured it out.

Notes

🍂

*The most important thing a father can do for his children
is to love their mother.*

Casseroles
and
Main Dishes

FREEZING CASSEROLES

Casserole cookery can mean carefree cooking when the dish can be prepared in large batches for more than one use. This will also be quite economical since you will be able to take advantage of less expensive vegetables when they are at peak seasons and meats on special sale.

Since many casseroles require time-consuming chopping and measuring, it is wise to fix an extra portion that can be cooked and frozen — to be used in the future when there isn't enough time to prepare a family meal or when unexpected guests arrive.

If you feel that you can't spare having the casserole dish in the freezer and out of daily use, just line the dish with heavy duty aluminum foil. Pour the mixture into the foil-lined dish and freeze solid. After the food is frozen, remove the foil from the casserole dish, peel off the food, wrap in freezer paper, fold tightly, seal with freezer tape and return to freezer.

DOs & DON'Ts

* DO label each container with the contents and the date it was put into the freezer. Always use frozen cooked foods within one to two months.

* DO avoid freezing a large recipe of casserole mixture until you try freezing a small amount. Some flavors tend to change during freezing.

* DO cook large turkeys and roasts. Remove large portions of meat from the bone and freeze for casseroles.

* DON'T overcook foods that are to be frozen. Food will finish cooking while being reheated.

* DON'T use too much salt and other seasonings. Some flavors tend to fade while others get stronger. It is better to add more seasonings later if necessary.

* DON'T freeze spaghetti, macaroni, or noodle mixtures. These tend to lose texture and become too soft when reheated.

* DON'T freeze potatoes. Don't freeze fried poultry or meats. Don't freeze cooked egg white.

* DON'T re-freeze thawed meats and poultry. Use thawed meat or poultry within twenty-four hours.

CASSEROLES AND MAIN DISHES

TURKEY-CHEDDAR PIE

1 (9 inch) pie crust, refrigerated
  (unbaked)
1 lb. ground turkey
2 c. frozen mixed vegetables
½ c. chopped onions
1 beaten egg white

1 Tbsp. water
1 (11 oz.) condensed Cheddar
  cheese soup
1 (5 oz.) can (⅔ c.) evaporated milk
½ tsp. dried thyme

Let pie crust stand at room temperature according to package directions. In a 3 quart saucepan, brown turkey. Drain off any fat. Stir in vegetables, chopped onions, soup, milk, and thyme. Bring to boil; reduce heat. Simmer 5 minutes. Spoon into 8 inch round baking dish.

Unfold cut slits in crust so steam can escape. Place crust on top of dish. Turn edge under; flute. Combine egg white and water; brush over crust. Bake at 400° for 25 to 30 minutes or till golden. Let stand 5 minutes. Makes 4 to 5 servings.

Quick and economical.

Joyce E. Steen, Merritt Island Lions Club
Merritt Island, Florida, USA

TURKEY DINNER PIE

Pastry for 9 inch 2 crust pie (can
  use frozen)
2 Tbsp. butter or margarine
2 Tbsp. flour
1 tsp. salt
⅛ tsp. pepper
⅛ tsp. thyme

½ c. chicken broth
½ c. light cream (can use milk)
2 Tbsp. dried minced onion
2 c. cubed cooked chicken or
  turkey
1 (1 lb.) can peas and carrots,
  drained

Melt butter in large saucepan over low heat. Blend in flour, salt, pepper, and thyme. Cook over low heat, stirring until mixture is smooth and bubbly. Remove from heat. Stir in chicken broth, cream, and dried onions. Heat to boiling, stirring constantly. Boil and stir 1 minute. Stir in chicken and vegetables.

Pour into pastry lined pie pan. Place strips of pastry across filling. Trim; turn edge of bottom crust over strips. Seal and flute. Cover edge with 2 to 3 inch strips of aluminum foil to prevent excessive browning; remove foil last 15 minutes of baking. Heat oven to 425°. Bake 35 to 40 minutes or until golden brown. I use frozen crust, laying the second on top of mixture, fluting and cutting slits in it.

Phyllis Hills, McMinnville Lions Club
McMinnville, Tennessee, USA

TURKEY-WILD RICE CASSEROLE

Cook 1 cup wild rice.

Saute until tender:

½ c. onion   ½ c. butter

Remove from heat.

Combine:

⅔ to ¾ c. flour   1½ c. milk
Juice from 1 (6 oz.) can
   mushrooms and chicken broth
   to make 1½ c.

Cook until thick. Add rice, mushrooms, 3 cups turkey or chicken (cubed), ¼ cup pimento, 2 teaspoons parsley (preferably fresh), and salt and pepper to taste. Put into 2 quart dish. Cover with ½ cup blanched, slivered almonds. Place in 350° oven for 30 to 45 minutes until almonds are toasted. Serves 10.

CHICKEN AND DRESSING CASSEROLE

¼ c. oleo   1 can chicken rice soup
1 medium onion   3 to 4 c. cubed chicken, cooked
5 c. cubed bread   1 pkg. mixed vegetables or carrots
1 tsp. poultry seasoning   or peas

Melt oleo. Add chopped onion. Cook until clear. Add bread cubes and seasoning, then add chicken rice soup. Alternately layer chicken, dressing mix, and vegetables. Bake in covered casserole for 1 hour at 350°. Makes a good all around casserole.

No one can create anger or stress in you -
only you can do that by virtue of how you look at your world.

CHICKEN CASSEROLE

3 c. cooked chicken breasts (or 1
    whole), diced
1 can cream of chicken soup
2 c. celery, thinly sliced
½ to 1 c. almonds, slivered
¼ c. pimento or green pepper
¾ c. mayonnaise

2 Tbsp. lemon juice
3 Tbsp. grated onion
3 hard-boiled eggs, chopped
1 tsp. salt
¼ tsp. pepper
½ c. Cheddar cheese, grated
1 c. potato chips, crushed

Preheat oven to 450°. Combine chicken (some broth if desired) and rest of ingredients in greased casserole dish (9x12 inches). Sprinkle with cheese, then chips on top. Bake, covered, 15 minutes at 450°. Reduce heat to 350° and bake another 20 to 30 minutes.

We first had this recipe at a family reunion (brought by Lynda O'Shea). I make it at home quite often, but somebody always checks to see if it will show up at the reunion.

Pam Sedlar, Onekama Lions Club
Onekama, Michigan, USA

CHICKEN CASSEROLE

1 (6 oz.) box stuffing (if desired,
    use your own stuffing)
1 (16 oz.) can green beans (French
    style), partially drained
1 c. (or more) chicken or turkey

Water chestnuts or almonds
    (optional)
1 can cream of mushroom or
    celery soup and milk (as can
    directs)

Prepare stuffing according to directions on the box. Set aside 1⅓ cups of stuffing (about half of mixture). Place the rest of the stuffing in the bottom of a small roaster or casserole. Spread green beans over the stuffing. Place the chicken over the green beans. Add chestnuts or almonds if desired. Top with set aside stuffing. Over this, add the soup and milk which have been mixed together. Bake at 400° for 30 to 40 minutes. Serves 8 to 12.

A pessimist has no starter, but an optimist has no brakes.

CHICKEN CASSEROLE

1 c. elbow macaroni
½ c. diced celery
¾ c. chicken broth
1 (10½ oz.) can condensed cream
    of celery soup
1 (3 or 4 oz.) can mushrooms

2 c. cut-up chicken or turkey
½ c. minced parsley
½ tsp. Worcestershire sauce
¾ c. soft bread cubes
2 Tbsp. butter or margarine

Cook macaroni according to directions on package. Drain. Cook celery in chicken broth (or use a chicken flavored bouillon cube plus ¾ cup water) for 5 minutes. Combine cooked macaroni, celery, broth, celery soup, mushrooms, chicken (or turkey), parsley, and Worcestershire sauce. Add salt if needed. Pour into greased 2 quart casserole. Sprinkle with bread cubes; dot with butter. Bake in oven at 350° for 30 to 40 minutes. Makes 8 servings.

Patsy Gagnon (Mrs. Charles), Silver Run-Union Mills Lions Club
Westminster, Maryland, USA

QUICK CHICKEN CASSEROLE

3 (3 oz.) cans chicken, drained
2 cans cream of mushroom soup
    (undiluted)
½ c. skim milk

1 c. dry casserole onions
1 (5 oz.) can water chestnuts,
    sliced thin
3 oz. can chow mein noodles

Combine ingredients and pour into a greased 9x13 inch casserole. Bake, uncovered, at 325° for 45 minutes.

You do not get much done by starting tomorrow.

Jean Roddey, Rock Hill Lions Club
Rock Hill, South Carolina, USA

Make it a personal commitment to do what you love
and love what you do. Today.

CHICKEN POT PIE

1 fryer, cooked and deboned
1 can cream of chicken soup or
   thickened broth from
   boiling chicken (2 c.)

4 eggs, boiled and chopped
   (optional)
1 lb. mixed vegetables
Salt and pepper to taste

Cook mixed vegetables (you may add more if desired). Add cooked vegetables to chicken and broth. Add eggs. Salt and pepper to taste and simmer until vegetables are tender.

Topping:

1 c. self-rising flour
1 c. sweet milk (evaporated milk
   preferred)

½ stick plus 1 Tbsp. margarine

Mix all ingredients. Put chicken and vegetables into baking dish, then evenly spread or pour on topping. *Do not stir.* Bake at 350° for 45 minutes or when top is brown.

Variations: Use beef, turkey instead of chicken and you have a different pot pie.

Bertha Smith, Parkway Lions Club
Panama City, Florida, USA

CHICKEN AND BROCCOLI WITH MUSHROOM SAUCE

1 (10 oz.) pkg. salt free frozen
   broccoli
3 Tbsp. margarine
3 Tbsp. flour
1 c. low-salt chicken broth

1 (4 oz.) can mushrooms and
   liquid
1 lb. skinned, sliced chicken
2 Tbsp. chopped parsley
2 Tbsp. bread crumbs

Preheat oven to 375°. Cook broccoli to directions on box. Mix margarine and flour in saucepan. Cook over medium heat. Blend in chicken broth, stirring until smooth. Stir in mushrooms with liquid. Season to taste, if you like. Place broccoli in shallow baking dish. Cover with sliced chicken. Pour mushroom sauce over entire dish. Top with bread crumbs and parsley. Bake, uncovered, for 20 to 25 minutes. Serves 4.

To love and be loved is the greatest happiness of existence.

CHICKEN AND RICE SUPREME

1 (6 oz.) box long grain wild rice
¼ c. melted margarine
⅓ c. chopped onion
2 to 3 c. diced chicken
⅓ c. flour
1 c. milk
1 c. chicken broth

1 tsp. salt
¼ tsp. pepper
⅓ c. chopped pimento
¼ c. chopped parsley
¼ c. slivered almonds
1 c. frozen peas (need not be
    cooked)

Cook rice as directed on package. Saute onion in melted margarine. Blend in flour, salt, and pepper; gradually add liquids to make a white sauce. Cook till thickened as a creamed gravy. Add chicken, rice, pimento, parsley, almonds, and peas. Transfer to a 2 quart casserole dish. Bake at 425° for 30 minutes.

RICE AND CHICKEN CASSEROLE

2 c. cooked rice or Minute rice to
    make 2 c.
1 whole chicken, boiled and cut
    off bone

2 cans cream of chicken soup
1 small can mushrooms, chopped
¼ tsp. curry powder
Salt and pepper to taste

Cook chicken and rice. Mix together and put in buttered casserole with crumbled potato chips on top. Bake at 350° for 30 minutes or until bubbly.

I sometimes use 1 can cream of mushroom soup and 1 can cream of chicken soup.

Phyllis Rockers, Emporia Sundowners Lions Club
Emporia, Kansas, USA

You may not always be able to control what goes on outside,
but you can always control what goes on inside.

HOT CHINESE CHICKEN

8 broiler fryer chicken thighs, skinned, boned, and cut in 1 inch pieces
¼ c. cornstarch
¼ c. oil
⅛ tsp. garlic powder or salt
1 large tomato, cut in chunks
1 (4 oz.) can mushrooms or 1 pkg. fresh mushrooms, sliced

1 c. chopped green onions
1 tsp. Accent
⅓ c. sliced water chestnuts
1 c. chopped celery
¼ c. soy sauce (or to taste preferred)
2 c. shredded iceberg lettuce

Recipe for the rice (Minute rice):

4½ c. rice
4½ c. water

5 beef bouillon cubes
½ c. onion

Roll chicken in cornstarch. Heat oil in wok over medium high heat. Add chicken and quickly brown. Sprinkle with garlic powder and garlic salt. Add tomato, water chestnuts, mushrooms, onion, and celery. Sprinkle with Accent and stir. Stir in the soy sauce. Now, cover and reduce heat to low; simmer for 5 minutes. Remove from heat.

When cooking the rice, add the onions and beef bouillon cubes right in with it.

After the Chinese chicken and rice are prepared, you can either put the lettuce under everything to eat it, or you can toss it in with the Chinese chicken after it is prepared.

HARVEST SUPPER CHICKEN CASSEROLE

2 (3 to 4 lb.) chickens
1 c. flour
1½ c. half & half

3 c. broth
Salt

Boil chicken and bone. Cut into small pieces. Make gravy using flour, half & half, broth, and salt. Put layer of chicken in casserole, then layer of gravy. Repeat till chicken and gravy are used. Put buttered crushed corn flakes on top. Bake at 350° until hot and bubbly. (Use a 9x13 inch casserole.) I sometimes use leftover turkey.

Lion Ellen Olson, Plattsmouth Lions Club
Plattsmouth, Nebraska, USA

Love is the greatest refreshment in life.

CHICKEN CASSEROLE

1½ sticks butter
4 boiled chicken breasts
1 c. diced celery
1 can celery soup

1 can mushroom soup
1 (8 oz.) can evaporated milk
⅓ c. onion flakes
1 pkg. Pepperidge Farm dressing

Brown dressing and butter in skillet. In casserole, dice chicken breasts. Add celery, onion flakes, soup, and milk. Top with dressing mix. Bake in 350° oven for 30 minutes covered and 15 minutes uncovered.

Bob Hummer, Hodgenville Lions Club
Hodgenville, Kentucky, USA

CHICKEN CASSEROLE

1 large chicken, boned
1 doz. tortillas
1 large onion, cut up
2 c. grated cheese
1 can cream of chicken soup

1 can cream of mushroom soup
1 can Ro-Tel tomatoes and
  peppers
1½ c. chicken broth (off of boiled
  chicken)

Boil chicken and bone. Blend soups, tomatoes and peppers, and chicken broth until smooth. Place in 3 quart pan ½ of tortillas, ½ of soup and onions, and ½ half of cheese, then repeat. Bake ½ hour covered and ½ hour uncovered at 350°.

Nancy Dean, Stamps Lions Club
Stamps, Arkansas, USA

The only one who never makes mistakes
is the one who never does anything.

❦ ❦ ❦

In the long run, pessimists may be proven right,
but the optimist has a better time along the way.

COW PLOPPES WITH SALAD

2 pkg. crescent rolls
2 c. cooked chicken
3 oz. cream cheese
½ to ¾ c. sour cream

1 Tbsp. onion, minced
2 Tbsp. butter or oleo
Pepper to taste

Mix all ingredients, except rolls, and place on dough. Pinch 2 rolls together. Place about 2 tablespoons filling on each ploppe (rolls). Pinch edges together in center. Bake on ungreased cookie sheet. Bake at 350° for 25 minutes.

Salad:

2 (1 lb.) frozen mixed vegetables,
   cooked and drained
1 onion, minced

½ c. celery, chopped
1 green pepper, chopped
1 can kidney beans, drained

Dressing:

¾ c. sugar
1½ Tbsp. flour
½ c. cider vinegar

½ tsp. salt
1 Tbsp. dry mustard

Mix cooked and drained vegetables, onion, celery, green pepper, and kidney beans. Cook dressing until thick and clear. Pour over vegetables while hot. Mix and refrigerate 24 hours. Serve with ploppes.

John Hasser, Isle Lions Club
Wahkon, Minnesota, USA

VEGETABLE AND CHICKEN POT PIE

1 Tbsp. margarine or butter
1 c. chopped celery
1 (10¼ oz.) can cream of chicken
   soup
½ c. milk
½ tsp. onion powder
¼ tsp. thyme
⅛ tsp. pepper

1 (16 oz.) bag frozen vegetables
   (combination of broccoli,
   cauliflower, and carrots),
   thawed
¾ c. frozen peas
1½ c. cooked cubed chicken
1 (10 oz.) can Hungry Jack flaky
   biscuits

In large skillet, melt margarine. Add celery and stir over medium high heat until crisp tender. Stir in soup, milk, onion powder, thyme, and pepper. Mix well. Stir in veggies and chicken; heat through. Spoon into a 12x8 inch baking dish. Heat oven to 375°. Separate biscuits. Cut each biscuit into 4 pieces. Arrange over hot filling. Bake at 375° for 20 to 25 minutes or until biscuits are golden brown and filling is bubbly. Makes 6 servings. I cook my own broccoli, cauliflower, and carrots for the frozen veggies accordingly.

Dorothy Wimmer, Rock Falls Lions Club
Sterling, Illinois, USA

HOT CHICKEN CASSEROLE

1 medium chicken, cooked, deboned, and cut up
1 (16 oz.) container sour cream
1 can mushroom soup
1 bag frozen broccoli, cooked
Salt and pepper to taste
1 box Pepperidge Farm croutons

In mixing bowl, add chicken, sour cream, soup, broccoli, salt, and pepper. Grease a 9x13 inch pan. Pour mixture into this. Bake at 350° about 30 minutes or until hot and bubbles. Serves 10 to 12.

HOT CHICKEN SALAD CASSEROLE

4 large chicken breasts, cooked
3 hard-boiled eggs, sliced
½ can cream of chicken soup
2 c. celery, finely cut
1 c. mayonnaise
1 c. sour cream
1 (8 oz.) can water chestnuts, drained and sliced
½ c. slivered almonds
2 Tbsp. onions, minced
2 Tbsp. lemon juice
1 tsp. salt
¼ tsp. pepper
1 c. Cheddar cheese, grated
1 small can fried onion rings, crushed
1 (4 oz.) can mushroom pieces, drained

Discard skin of chicken; cut into 1 inch pieces. Mix chicken with remaining ingredients, except cheese and onion rings. Turn into 13x9x2 inch pan or casserole. Top with cheese. Bake at 350° for 30 minutes. Sprinkle onions over all. Bake 15 minutes longer. Delicious!

Marjorie M. Schales, Moweaqua Lions Club
Moweaqua, Illinois, USA

CHICKEN NOODLE CASSEROLE

1 lb. chicken strips, cut into 1 inch pieces
1 (16 oz.) bag egg noodles
Frozen broccoli
Frozen cauliflower
Velveeta cheese
1 pt. light cream
Bread crumbs

1. Parboil chicken pieces.
2. Boil egg noodles for 5 minutes, then add broccoli and cauliflower to water and cook for 3 more minutes.
3. Layer a large casserole dish with above ingredients, beginning with noodle layer, then chicken, then cheese until all ingredients are added.
4. Pour cream over dish, then sprinkle bread crumbs. Bake at 350° for 30 minutes.

Stacey Anderson, Westbrook Lions Club
Westbrook, Maine, USA

KING RANCH CHICKEN CASSEROLE

1 can cream of chicken soup
1 can cream of mushroom soup
2 c. chicken broth
1 (10 oz.) can Ro-Tel tomatoes and
   chilies

1 (3 to 4 lb.) chicken, cooked and
   cut into bite-size pieces
1 large onion, chopped
2 c. grated American cheese

Combine soups, broth, and tomatoes; set aside. Oil a 3 quart casserole. Layer half of tortilla pieces, half of chicken, half of onion, and half of cheese in the casserole. Pour half of chicken broth mixture over layers. Repeat layers of tortillas, chicken, and onion, then pour remaining chicken broth mixture over. Top with remaining cheese. Bake at 350° for 45 to 60 minutes. Serves 8.

CHICKEN AND CRESCENT ROLL CREATION

2 (8 oz.) cans crescent dinner rolls
16 oz. pkg. cut broccoli, thawed
   and drained
4 to 5 c. chopped cooked chicken

8 oz. Cheddar cheese, shredded
¼ c. chopped onion
½ tsp. poultry seasoning
1 can cream of chicken soup

Heat oven to 375°. Separate dough into 4 long rectangles. Press 2 rectangles into bottom and ¼ inch up side of ungreased 15x10 inch jelly roll pan. Bake for 6 to 8 minutes until golden brown.

In bowl, combine broccoli, chicken, cheese, onion, and seasoning. Spoon chicken mixture over crust. Seal perforations of remaining 2 rectangles; cut each lengthwise into 5 strips. Bake for 18 to 23 minutes. Makes 8 servings.

Excellent for company. Serve with garden salad and fresh fruit.

Jean Lancaster, Moweaqua Lions Club
Moweaqua, Illinois, USA

❦

Whoever can be trusted with small things
can also be trusted with large things.

CHICKEN STRATA

8 slices day-old bread
2 c. diced cooked chicken
½ c. chopped onion
½ c. chopped green pepper
½ c. finely chopped celery
½ c. mayonnaise

¾ tsp. salt
2 slightly beaten eggs
1½ c. milk
1 can condensed cream of
    mushroom soup
½ c. grated sharp Cheddar cheese

Butter 2 slices bread; cut in ½ inch cubes and set aside. Cut remaining bread in 1 inch cubes; place half of unbuttered bread cubes in bottom of 8x8x2 inch baking dish.

Combine chicken, vegetables, mayonnaise, salt, and dash of pepper; spoon over bread cubes. Place remaining unbuttered bread cubes over chicken mixture.

Combine eggs and milk; pour over all. Cover and chill 1 hour or overnight. Spoon soup over top, then sprinkle with buttered bread cubes. Bake in slow oven (325°F.) for 50 minutes or till set. Sprinkle cheese over top during last few minutes of baking. Serves 6.

W. Harold Arnett, Reno Plumb Lane Lions Club
Reno, Nevada, USA

CHICKEN POT PIE

1 (2½ to 3 lb.) chicken
1 stick butter (¼ lb.)
¼ tsp. salt
½ tsp. black or white pepper
1 c. milk (skim, 1% or 2% or whole)
1 c. flour

3 tsp. baking powder
1 can condensed cream of celery
    soup
1 can chicken broth (14½ oz. by
    weight) or 1¾ c. broth from
    cooked chicken

Cook chicken with enough water to barely cover, adding the salt and pepper. Cook until tender. Remove chicken from the pot and reserve the broth. Bone chicken; remove skin and discard. Place chicken in a 7x13 inch Pyrex baking dish. Melt butter and pour over chicken. Sift flour with baking powder and blend in milk, stirring until smooth. Spread over the chicken.

In a saucepan, blend condensed soup with broth and heat to boiling. Pour the soup mixture over the flour mixture and chicken. Bake at 400°F. till lightly browned (45 minutes to an hour). Yield: 6 to 8 servings.

Note: Chicken may be left in large pieces or cut into 1 inch cubes as desired.

Old Indian Proverb: "To give dignity to a person (man) is above all things."
A.J. and Wanda Groenendale, Fort Collins Lions Club
Fort Collins, Colorado, USA

❦

Love is perhaps the only glimpse we are permitted of eternity.

EASY CASSEROLE

2 to 3 c. chicken or turkey
1 can cream of mushroom soup
1 can cream of celery soup
1 pkg. Pepperidge Farm stuffing
  mix

2 cans broth from turkey or
  chicken

Cut poultry into bit-size pieces. In casserole dish, 9x12 inches or about that size, layer stuffing mix on greased or Pammed casserole dish, then layer of soup, then a layer of poultry, then a layer of stuffing mix. Repeat until all items are used. Finish with layer of stuffing mix. Pour in the 2 cans of broth. Bake in 350° oven for 30 minutes or until hot through and through.

This is good for leftover Thanksgiving or Christmas turkey.
Glenn E. Bunch, Jr., PDG 31-H, Snow Hill Lions Club
Snow Hill, North Carolina, USA

POWDERHOUSE CASSEROLE

½ stick butter
1 can cream of mushroom soup
1 can cream of chicken soup
1 can cream of celery soup

1 c. uncooked rice (not Minute
  type)
1⅓ c. water
About 6 pieces chicken

Season chicken parts with salt and pepper. Melt butter. Combine butter and remaining ingredients, except chicken. Place in casserole dish. Put chicken pieces on top. Cover and bake at 300° for 3 hours or at 350° for 1½ hours. Serves 4.

If a recipe calls for sour milk and none is on hand, just mix 1 cup sweet milk into 1 tablespoon vinegar or lemon juice.
Carolyn Cashin, Berlin Lions Club
Berlin, Massachusetts, USA

❦

Love doesn't make the world go round.
Love is what makes the ride worthwhile.

CHICKEN CHEESE PIES

Chicken Base:

2 Tbsp. butter, melted
¼ c. flour
1 tsp. salt
1 tsp. sage
1 c. water
1 c. milk

1 chicken bouillon cube
2 c. chopped, cooked chicken
1 (10 oz.) pkg. frozen mixed
    vegetables, thawed
½ c. sliced celery
¼ c. chopped onion

Biscuit Topping:

¾ c. buttermilk baking mix
½ c. shredded Cheddar cheese

¼ c. milk

Melt butter over low heat. Stir in flour and seasonings. Cook until smooth, stirring constantly. Remove from heat. Gradually stir in water, milk, and bouillon cube. Bring to a boil over medium heat, stirring constantly. Boil and stir until thickened. Add chicken and vegetables. Cover and simmer for 15 minutes or until vegetables are crisp tender. Spoon mixture into 4 buttered 2 cup individual casseroles or 1 large casserole.

Combine baking mix and cheese. Add milk, stirring only until moistened. Drop biscuit dough by tablespoonfuls over hot chicken mixture. Bake in preheated 375°F. oven for 14 to 16 minutes or until biscuits are lightly browned. Makes 4 servings.

TALARINI

1 to 2 lb. hamburger, cooked and
    ½ grease drained
1 medium onion, chopped
1 green bell pepper, chopped
1 can corn with liquid
2 cans stewed tomatoes with
    liquid

1 (8 oz.) pkg. egg noodles
    (uncooked)
2 cans sliced black olives with
    liquid
1 lb. sharp Cheddar cheese,
    grated

Brown hamburger with onion and bell pepper. Season to taste with favorite seasoned salt or spice. Blend all but 1 can of black olives and ¼ of the cheese. Place in large baking pan and cover with foil. Bake 45 minutes at 325° to 350°. Remove foil and add drained can of black olives and remainder of cheese. Bake an additional 15 minutes, uncovered. It's fast, easy to prepare, and always a crowd pleaser.

Toni Kett, Laughlin Lions Club
Laughlin, Nevada, USA

Miracles happen to those who believe in them.

TALGARINI

Brown:

1 lb. sausage
1 lb. ground beef

1 green pepper, chopped
1 onion, chopped

Add:

2 cans tomato soup

1 can tomato paste

Simmer ½ hour.

Add:

1 can shoe peg corn
1 jar pimentos
1 lb. grated cheese
1 can mushrooms

½ lb. cooked shell macaroni
Salt and pepper to taste
Garlic salt to taste

Good with tossed salad, garlic bread, ambrosia fruit salad. Serves 12.

Lion Jane Price, Canton Lions Club
Canton, Georgia, USA

DUTCH NOODLES

1 small onion, chopped
1 lb. sausage or ground beef
6 Tbsp. water

Salt and pepper (to taste)
1 small head cabbage, shredded
½ pkg. (8 oz.) Kluski noodles

Cook meat and onion in skillet until well browned. Drain and save 4 tablespoons drippings. Add drippings, water, and shredded cabbage to meat; sprinkle with salt and pepper. Cover and steam for 15 minutes.

Meanwhile, cook Kluski noodles as directed. Drain noodles. Add noodles to cabbage mixture and toss. Cook, uncovered, for 8 to 10 minutes. Serves 4.

Aidele Miller, Manistique Lakes Area Lioness Club
Curtis, Michigan, USA

❦

Eyestrain has never been caused by looking on the bright side of life.

CHOP SUEY

6 c. dark meat turkey
7 c. turkey broth
10 c. celery, sliced
5 c. chopped onion
3 Tbsp. brown gravy
3 Tbsp. molasses
2 to 4 dashes of garlic powder
4 dashes of grated horseradish
4 dashes or 1 tsp. paprika

1 large or 2 small cans
  mushrooms
2 cans water chestnuts
2 cans bamboo shoots
4 cans bean sprouts
10 Tbsp. or more cornstarch,
  mixed with cold water to
  thicken gravy

Cover 3 drumsticks or 1 large thigh of turkey with water. Add 4 beef and 3 chicken bouillon cubes. Cook till meat is tender. Bone. Use about 6 cups turkey and 7 cups broth. Put in large kettle. Add cut celery and onions. Cook 10 minutes, adding gravy mix and seasonings. Add remaining ingredients. Cook another 10 minutes after it comes to a boil. Mix cornstarch in ½ to ¾ cup water. Stir in gradually. Cook 2 to 3 minutes. Ready to serve over chow mein noodles or cooked rice. Good for lunch or dinner. Skin turkey before cooking to comply with no or lowfat diet. Skim broth also. Chill it if necessary.

Iris S. Dian, Dolly Madison of Greensboro Lions Club
Greensboro, North Carolina, USA

AMERICAN CHOP SUEY

3 cans tomato soup
Onion

Green pepper

Use to taste or preference.

1 lb. hamburger
1 c. macaroni, cooked (can use
  more if you like)

Brown green pepper and onion in a bit of margarine. Add hamburger and brown. Add tomato soup and simmer. Cook macaroni and combine with meat mixture.

Linda MacLeod, Westbrook Lions Club
Westbrook, Maine, USA

❦

Love is space and time measured by the heart.

PASTITSIO - A GREEK MACARONI CASSEROLE

1½ lb. ground beef
2 medium onions, chopped
2 (6 oz.) cans or 1 (12 oz.) can
   tomato paste
1½ c. water
2 tsp. salt
½ tsp. pepper
¼ tsp. cinnamon

¼ tsp. nutmeg
1 (7¼ oz.) pkg. macaroni and
   cheese dinner
2 c. milk
3 eggs, slightly beaten
½ c. grated Parmesan cheese
4 slices American cheese, cut in
   halves diagonally

Brown beef and onions in a skillet; drain excess fat. Stir in tomato paste, water, salt, pepper, cinnamon, and nutmeg. Cover and simmer for 20 minutes.

Cook macaroni according to package directions; drain. Mix the cheese in package with milk in a saucepan; cook over low heat, stirring until sauce is slightly thickened and creamy. Place half of cooked macaroni in bottom of greased 9x13x2 inch baking dish; sprinkle with all of the Parmesan cheese. Cover with meat mixture, then remaining macaroni. Pour sauce over the top. Bake at 325° for 40 minutes or until custard sets. Arrange cheese halves, overlapping, on top. Bake about 5 minutes longer. Makes 8 good size servings.

Ellen Ostrand, Lady Lions of Rohnert Park Lions Club
Rohnert Park, California, USA

MARCETI

2 lb. ground beef
1 onion, chopped
1 c. celery, chopped
3 cans tomato soup, mixed well
   with 1½ cans water

¼ lb. Longhorn cheese, cut in
   small pieces
1 lb. pkg. noodles
1 large can mushrooms
Salt and pepper to taste

Fry beef, then add onion, celery, mushrooms, and cheese. Add cooked noodles and tomato soup. Salt and pepper to taste. Bake at 350° for 1 hour.

Verna Ball, Sherrodsville Lions Club
Sherrodsville, Ohio, USA

❦

A smile is a wrinkle you don't want to remove.

LUMPIA

1 lb. hamburger, browned
½ c. chopped onions
2 ribs celery, chopped fine
2 carrots, chopped fine

½ green pepper
1 pkg. rice, won ton or egg roll
   wrappers

1. Simmer with hamburger until tender.
2. Cool.
3. Roll ingredients into wrappers.
4. Brown in skillet or deep-fry.
5. Serve hot with side of sweet-sour sauce.

I enjoyed this recipe while stationed on Guam with the U.S. Navy.
Lion Scott Long, South Whitehall Township, Inc., Lions Club
Allentown, Pennsylvania, USA

LITTLE TOSTADA TARTS

Heat oven to 475°.

1½ c. Bisquick baking mix
¼ c. chili powder
¼ c. cold water
1 lb. ground beef
1 (1¼ oz.) pkg. taco seasoning mix
1 c. water
½ c. shredded Cheddar cheese (2
   oz.)

⅓ c. shredded lettuce
¾ c. dairy sour cream
½ c. chopped tomato
2 Tbsp. sliced green onion
8 Bugles Nacho cheese snack

Grease eight 6 ounce custard cups. Mix baking mix and chili powder; stir in ¼ cup water until a dough forms. Divide dough into 8 parts. Press each part in custard cup. Place custard cups in jelly roll pan, 15½ x 10½ x 1 inch. Bake until light golden brown, 8 to 10 minutes; cool completely. Loosen tarts with knife; remove from custard cups.

Brown ground beef in 2 quart saucepan; drain. Stir in seasoning mix (dry) and 1 cup water. Heat to boiling over medium-high heat, stirring occasionally; reduce heat. Simmer over low heat, stirring occasionally, 15 minutes. Spoon into tarts. Top with remaining ingredients. Makes 8 servings.

Remember when pies were set out on the windowsill to cool, not to thaw?

CHICKEN CHALUPAS

1 (8 oz.) bag Nacho cheese Doritos
4 cooked chicken breasts, cubed
   into ½ inch pieces
1 can cream of chicken soup
1 can cream of mushroom soup

½ c. chicken broth
1 c. lite sour cream
1 (4 oz.) can green chilies, diced
1 c. grated Cheddar cheese

Grease 9x13 inch glass baking dish. Line with Doritos chips. Spread chicken on top of chips. Place cream of chicken soup, cream of mushroom soup, chicken broth, sour cream, and green chilies in blender. Blend until creamy smooth. Pour mixture over chicken. Sprinkle cheese on top. Bake in a 350°F. oven for 40 minutes. Serves 4 to 6.

CHALUPAS

2 medium soft avocados (2 large
   or 3 small)
1 onion
Salt and pepper
1 tomato
1 small clove garlic or garlic
   powder

1 pkg. tortillas (about 15)
1 lb. cooked red beans (pinto)
1 to 2 tsp. mayonnaise
1 lb. sharp cheese, grated
2 c. chopped lettuce and tomatoes

Put avocados, tomato, onion, and garlic through the meat grinder or food processor (be careful not to overprocess). Mix well with salt, pepper, and mayonnaise. Put in the refrigerator, covered tightly, until ready to use. Put cooked beans in an iron skillet and mash thoroughly. (These are also called refried beans.) Fry the tortillas in deep oil till crisp; drain well. To make chalupa: Take 1 tortilla, spread on refried beans. Add some avocado salad. Add some chopped lettuce, tomato, and teaspoon of grated cheese. (We prefer garlic powder - not as strong as garlic.)
Reece Anderson, Saginaw Lions Club
Saginaw, Texas, USA

❦

Take care of the minutes and the hours,
and the years will take care of themselves.

MONTEREY STYLE ENCHILADAS

1 medium onion
1 crushed garlic clove or 1 tsp.
  garlic powder
2 c. tomato puree
2 chopped canned green chilies
2 c. cooked chopped chicken

1 doz. tortillas
6 bouillon cubes
3 c. cream
½ lb. grated Monterey Jack
  cheese

Saute chopped onion until soft in 2 tablespoons oil. Add crushed garlic clove (or garlic powder), 2 cups tomato puree, canned green chilies, and cooked chopped chicken. Season with salt to taste. Simmer until hot. Fry tortillas in ¼ inch hot oil just until soft. (Do not let them get crisp.) Dissolve 6 chicken bouillon cubes in hot cream. Dip each tortilla in this. Place in baking dish. Add chicken filling and roll up.

Pour remaining cream mixture over enchiladas. Top with cheese. Bake at 350° for 30 minutes. May garnish with avocado, chopped green or black olives, etc. Sprinkle paprika on top. This recipe is to die for! You'll love it!

Janine K. Cox, Bakersfield Pioneer Lions Club
Bakersfield, California, USA

GREEN ENCHILADAS

Cheese Sauce:

½ lb. Velveeta cheese
1 small can evaporated milk

1 can cream of chicken soup
1 small can green chiles, chopped

Filling:

1 lb. ground meat
¼ to ½ c. chopped onions
½ lb. Cheddar cheese, shredded

Salt and pepper to taste
1 doz. corn tortillas

In double boiler, heat Velveeta cheese, milk, soup, and green chiles until cheese melts. In skillet, brown meat and saute onions. Add Cheddar cheese and stir. In another skillet, fry tortillas in hot oil until limber. Fill tortillas with meat mixture and roll. Place rolled tortillas in baking pan. Pour cheese sauce over tortillas. Bake 30 minutes at 350°.

Violet M. Heslep, Huffman Lioness Club
Huffman, Texas, USA

Grandma's cookies didn't need preservatives - they never lasted that long.

SOUR CREAM CHICKEN ENCHILADAS

1 chicken (whole or chicken parts)
2 cans cream of chicken soup
1 can diced green chilies
16 oz. sour cream

½ c. diced onion
1 c. Pace picante sauce
2 c. Cheddar cheese, shredded
Flour tortillas

Boil chicken in salted water; drain, reserving broth. Cool and remove chicken from bones. Chop in small pieces. Refrigerate broth until grease hardens. Lift off and discard; reserve remaining broth.

Mix soup, sour cream, picante sauce, green chilies, onions, and 1 cup broth. Reserve 1½ cups of this mixture. To remaining mixture, add the diced chicken and 1 cup of the shredded cheese. Wrap flour tortillas in damp towel and place in microwave for about 1 minute (to warm enough to separate). Spoon about 2 tablespoons of mixture onto each tortilla. Roll and place in baking dish with rolled edge on bottom. When dish is filled, spread reserved mixture over top; cover and bake at 350° for approximately 40 minutes. Uncover and sprinkle the remainder of cheese over top. Return to oven until melted, about 5 minutes.

This is one of my pre-health-conscious creations. It's loaded with calories, but we all deserve to break our diets occasionally and this is a good way to do it!

I've yet to find anyone who doesn't love these enchiladas!
Frances Cantrell, Bowie Evening Lions Club
Bowie, Texas, USA

LAYERED CHICKEN ENCHILADA BAKE

1 medium onion, chopped
2 or 3 Tbsp. butter or margarine
1 can cream of chicken soup
1 can cream of mushroom soup
2 or 3 lb. chicken, cooked and
  boned

1 can chicken broth
1 pkg. corn tortillas (or flour)
1 lb. shredded Longhorn cheese
1 small can chopped green chilies
1 (7 oz.) can enchilada sauce
  (optional)

Brown onion in butter. Combine with soups, broth, and chili peppers. Add chicken. Drop tortillas, one at a time, into about ½ inch of hot fat in skillet. Cook until soft and limp. This goes quick. Also I use the enchilada sauce instead of oil.

Grease a large baking dish, 10x13x2 inches. Add a layer of the chicken mix and a layer of cheese; repeat with another layer. Cover with a third layer of the tortillas. Sprinkle with the remainder of cheese. Pour the remaining enchilada sauce over the entire pan. Bake 30 minutes at 350°. Enjoy!!!! I use chicken leg and thigh quarters, boiling them in a large kettle with salt and seasoning, and use some of the broth instead of canned. The remaining broth will keep in fridge. Great to cook rice in.

Dan Steffan, Independence Eastview Lions Club
Independence, Missouri, USA

CHEESE 'N CHICKEN ENCHILADAS

1 medium onion, chopped
2 Tbsp. margarine
1½ c. shredded cooked chicken or turkey
1 (12 oz.) jar picante sauce, divided

1 (3 oz.) pkg. cream cheese, cubed
1 tsp. ground cumin
2 c. (8 oz.) shredded extra sharp Cheddar cheese, divided
8 (6 inch) flour tortillas

Heat oven to 350°F. Cook and stir onion in margarine in large skillet until tender. Stir in chicken, ¼ cup picante sauce, cream cheese, and cumin; cook until thoroughly heated. Stir in 1 cup cheese. Spoon about ⅓ cup chicken mixture in center of each tortilla; roll up. Place, seam side down, in 12x7 inch baking dish. Top with remaining picante sauce and cheese. Bake 15 minutes. Makes 4 to 6 servings.

Mrs. Kristen Thompson, Hedgesville Lions Club
Hedgesville, West Virginia, USA

CHICKEN ENCHILADAS

1 c. Ricotta cheese (made with part-skim milk)
½ c. chopped green onions
2 Tbsp. Weight Watchers whipped salad dressing
4 oz. chopped cooked chicken

4 flour tortillas
1 c. picante sauce
½ c. plain yogurt
3 Tbsp. sour cream
4 oz. grated cheese

Combine first 4 ingredients and mix well. Divide the mixture between the 4 tortillas. Roll up and place in a 1 quart casserole dish. Pour the picante sauce over rolled, filled tortillas. Next, combine the yogurt and sour cream; spoon over tortillas. Sprinkle the grated cheese atop. Bake at 350° for 25 to 30 minutes. Makes 4 generous servings.

If you meet someone too tired to smile, give one of yours; nobody needs a smile as much as those who have none to give.

Bettie Patterson, Kosciusko Lions Club
Kosciusko, Mississippi, USA

Real discipline is when you can pick strawberries without eating any.

TURKEY ENCHILADAS

1½ c. shredded or chopped,
    cooked turkey
1½ c. picante sauce
1 (3 oz.) pkg. cream cheese
½ c. sliced green onion
¾ tsp. ground cumin

1½ c. shredded Monterey Jack or
    Colby cheese (I mix mine)
10 (6 to 7 inch) flour tortillas
Shredded lettuce
Radishes
Ripe olive slices

Combine turkey, ½ cup picante sauce, cream cheese, green onion, and cumin in skillet. Place over low heat until cheese is melted, stirring occasionally. Stir in ½ cup shredded cheese. Spoon scant ⅓ cup of the turkey mixture down center of each tortilla; roll up and place, seam down, in lightly greased 9x12 inch baking pan.

Spoon remaining picante sauce over enchiladas. Cover with remaining cheese. Bake at 350° for 20 minutes or until heated through. Garnish with lettuce, radishes, and olives. Serve with additional picante sauce.

MEXICAN GOULASH

1 lb. hamburger
1 qt. canned tomatoes or paste
½ c. chopped onions
½ c. chopped green peppers

1 tsp. chili powder
1 (8 oz.) box sea shell macaroni
1 c. buttermilk

Brown hamburger with onions and green peppers. Add tomatoes (I put mine in the blender because we don't like hunks of tomatoes). Cook for about 40 minutes on medium heat, stirring often. Cover. Cook sea shells and drain. Pour into hamburger mixture. Add buttermilk and let simmer for awhile. Add salt, pepper, and chili powder. Cook for about 5 minutes more.

This is a meal in one. Add a salad or cole slaw. This freezes well for future meals. This recipe goes to a lot of family reunions and block parties.

Dora T. Poythress, Lawrenceville Lioness Club
Lawrenceville, Virginia (Brunswick), USA

Man cannot live on bread alone. He needs peanut butter, too.

SUPER NACHOS

1 lb. ground beef
1 large onion, chopped
2 (1 lb.) can refried beans
1 (4 oz.) can green chilies
3 c. shredded Monterey Jack
    cheese

1 jar taco sauce
Corn or flour tortillas
Sour cream (optional)

Brown the ground beef and chopped onion in a skillet; drain off excess liquids. In a 9x13 inch pan, spread the refried beans. Top the beans with the meat and onion mixture, then a layer of the green chilies. Next, layer the 3 cups of shredded cheese. Top this layer with taco sauce. Bake in 400° oven for 25 minutes.

To serve: Warm either corn or flour tortillas. Place 2 tablespoons of hot mixture on tortilla, then add a spoon of sour cream. Roll up and eat.

Janie Fox, Saginaw Lions Club
Saginaw, Texas, USA

TICO-TACO

1 lb. ground beef
1 packet low-salt taco seasoning
    mix
½ head lettuce, shredded
2 tomatoes, chopped
1 small onion, chopped

1½ c. grated Cheddar cheese
1 (16 oz.) can black beans
½ c. sliced black olives
½ c. sour cream
½ c. salsa (medium)
1 small bag corn chips

In skillet, brown ground beef and drain. Add taco seasoning mix and prepare according to package directions. While beef is cooking, prepare individual bowls of fresh ingredients: Lettuce, tomatoes, onion, and cheese. Also arrange bowls of drained and heated black beans, black olives, sour cream, and salsa. Arrange layer of crushed corn chips on plate. Top with seasoned beef. Continue to layer other ingredients. Serves 4.

Faith sees the invisible, believes the incredible,
and receives the impossible.

MEXICAN HASH CASSEROLE

1 Tbsp. oil
1 lb. ground beef
1 medium onion
½ tsp. salt
½ tsp. pepper
½ tsp. cumin
1 clove garlic

1 (500 ml) jar mild enchilada or
   taco sauce
12 crisp taco or tostada shells or
   corn chips
¼ lb. Cheddar cheese
Sour cream for garnish

In a medium skillet, heat the oil. Brown the meat. Add the onion and fry until softened. Add salt, pepper, cumin, garlic, and sauce. Cook for 20 to 30 minutes.

In a greased 9x9 inch baking dish, arrange alternate layers of tacos, meat, and cheese. Bake at 350° for 30 to 40 minutes, or until bubbling through. Top each serving with a generous dollop of sour cream.

Rebecca Mergaert, North Jackson Lions Club
Sault Ste. Marie, Ontario, Canada

MEXICAN SKILLET SPAGHETTI

1 lb. ground beef
1 (15 oz.) can tomato sauce
4¾ c. water (2½ tomato sauce
   cans)
2 (1¼ oz.) pkg. taco mix

2 Tbsp. instant minced onion
½ tsp. salt
8 oz. uncooked spaghetti
½ c. shredded natural Cheddar
   cheese

In 12 inch skillet, brown the ground beef (electric skillet at 350°). Add tomato sauce, water, taco mix, minced onion, and salt. Bring mixture to boiling; add spaghetti. Reduce heat to 220°. Simmer, covered, until the spaghetti is tender, stirring frequently, about 25 to 30 minutes. Sprinkle with shredded cheese. Serves 6.

Lion Karen Stowers, Amarillo North Lions Club
Amarillo, Texas, USA

*There is not enough darkness in all the world
to put out the light of one small candle.*

BLUE RIBBON COMPANY CASSEROLE

1 (6 oz.) pkg. wild rice, cooked
2 pkg. (10 oz.) frozen chopped
   broccoli, defrosted
1½ c. cubed cooked ham
1 c. (4 oz.) shredded Cheddar
   cheese
1 (4 oz.) can sliced drained
   mushrooms

1½ c. cubed cooked chicken
1 c. mayonnaise
1 tsp. prepared mustard
½ tsp. curry powder
1 (10¾ oz.) can cream of
   mushroom soup (undiluted)
¼ c. grated Parmesan cheese

In greased 2 quart casserole, layer first 6 ingredients in order listed. Combine mayonnaise, mustard, curry, and soup. Spread over casserole. Sprinkle with Parmesan cheese. Bake at 350° for 45 to 60 minutes or till top is light golden brown. Yield: 8 servings.

This is easier than it looks and a wonderful one-dish filling meal.
Vic Creo, President, Merritt Island Lions Club
Merritt Island, Florida, USA

COUNTRY HAM CASSEROLE

1 lb. Velveeta pasteurized cheese
   spread, cubed
1 c. milk
½ c. Miracle Whip salad dressing
2 c. chopped, cooked ham

1 (10 oz.) pkg. frozen chopped
   broccoli, cooked and well
   drained
1 tsp. chopped chives
5 oz. cooked spaghetti

Heat process cheese spread, milk, and salad dressing over low heat. Stir until sauce is smooth. Add remaining ingredients and mix well. Pour into 2 quart casserole dish and bake at 350° for 35 to 40 minutes or until hot. Makes 6 to 8 servings.

HAM AND CHEESE CASSEROLE

8 slices stale bread, crust trimmed
   and cubed
6 eggs
1 tsp. dry mustard

2 c. milk
½ lb. ham, chopped
2 c. shredded Cheddar cheese

Arrange bread cubes in greased rectangular baking dish. Beat eggs in mixer bowl until foamy. Add mustard, milk, ham, and cheese; mix well. Pour over bread cubes. Chill for 7 hours or overnight. Bake at 350° for 1 hour or until firm. Let stand 10 to 15 minutes before serving. Yields 8 servings.

Lion Ethel D. Parr, Mt. Holly Springs Lions Club
Gardners, Pennsylvania, USA

HAM AND NOODLE CASSEROLE

2 c. ground ham (raw or cooked)
½ lb. American cheese
½ green pepper
1 c. chopped celery

2 (6 oz.) pkg. fine noodles
¼ lb. (1 c.) sliced mushrooms
1 can condensed tomato soup

Cut cheese into small pieces and mince green pepper. Mix all ingredients, including soup (diluted with an equal amount of water), with noodles which have been cooked in boiling salted water until tender and drained. Bake in casserole in a moderate oven (350°) for 1 hour. Serves 8.

BROCCOLI AND HAM CASSEROLE

12 slices white or wheat bread
¾ lb. sliced cheese
1 (10 oz.) pkg. frozen chopped
    broccoli
6 eggs

3½ c. milk
2 Tbsp. minced onion
½ tsp. salt
¼ tsp. dry mustard

Cut bread with a donut cutter, reserving scraps. Arrange scraps in a 9x13 inch buttered pan. Layer cheese, broccoli, and ham over the bread scraps. Top with bread donuts. Combine remaining ingredients in blender. Blend. Pour over the top. Bake, uncovered, at 325° for 55 to 60 minutes. Let stand for 10 minutes. Cut into squares to serve. Makes 8 nice servings or 12 small.

Mrs. Richard E. Borkosky (member, Richard Borkosky),
Bascom Lions Club
Fostoria, Ohio, USA

PORK CHOP AND POTATO BAKE

6 pork chops, browned
1 can cream of celery soup
½ c. milk
½ c. sour cream

24 oz. frozen hash browns,
    thawed
1 c. shredded Cheddar cheese
Onion rings

Mix together soup, milk, and sour cream with thawed hash browns. Put into 9x13 inch pan. Put chops on top. Cover with cheese and onion rings. Bake 40 minutes at 350°. Remove from oven and put more cheese and onion rings on top. Bake 5 minutes more.

Elaine Dahlke, Brownton Lions Club
Brownton, Minnesota, USA

❦

Originality is simply a pair of fresh eyes.

CRAB CASSEROLE

1 full (1 to 2 lb.) Dungeness crab, cleaned, shelled, and flaked
1 pkg. frozen spinach, thawed and drained
3 oz. fresh, grated Parmesan cheese
10 fresh mushrooms, sliced and cleaned (brushed, not washed)
1 Tbsp. parsley, minced
2 Tbsp. flour
2 Tbsp. butter
3 Tbsp. whipping cream
½ c. milk

Melt butter in small saucepan. Add flour and beat with a whisk. Slowly add milk. Melt cheese in this mixture. Add unwhipped whipping cream. Add parsley. In deep baking dish, layer mushrooms, crab, and spinach. Pour sauce over layers. Bake at 350°F. for 35 or more minutes or until bubbling.

Sarah Wehling, Bothell Lions Club
Bothell, Washington, USA

TUNA BISCUIT BRAID

2 cans tuna, drained
¼ c. mayonnaise
2 Tbsp. chopped parsley
1 Tbsp. minced onion
½ tsp. salt
⅔ c. milk
2 c. Bisquick
2 c. frozen peas (add to sauce below)

Medium Cream Sauce:

2 Tbsp. butter
2 Tbsp. flour
Salt and pepper
1 c. milk

Heat oven to 425°. Mix tuna, mayonnaise, parsley, onion, and salt. Make Bisquick dough: Add milk all at once to Bisquick and stir with fork into soft dough. Beat 15 strokes; turn onto floured board. Knead 8 to 10 times. Roll into rectangle, 12x10 inches. Put on baking sheet.

Spread tuna mixture down center of dough. Make slits down each side from edge of dough to tuna filling. Brush strips over from side to side over filling. Seal ends. Bake 15 to 20 minutes. Serve with creamed peas. See sauce above.

Great for a hot lunch or quick supper.

Mrs. Larry (Nancy) Wilkison, Elburn Lions Club
Elburn, Illinois, USA

Peace is when time doesn't matter as it passes by.

EASY FRIDAY CASSEROLE

1 (8 to 10 oz.) noodles
1 (6 oz.) can tuna fish
1 small chopped onion
1 small chopped green pepper

1 can cream of mushroom soup
1/3 c. sweet milk
Grated Cheddar cheese (enough
  to cover top)

Cook noodles until almost tender. In greased 3 quart baking dish, alternate layers of cooked noodles, tuna, pepper, onion, and soup mixed with milk. Top with grated cheese and cover. Bake at 325° for 45 minutes.

Bertha Smith, Parkway Lions Club
Panama City, Florida, USA

SHRIMP AND HAM JAMBALAYA

1 1/3 c. uncooked Minute rice
2 c. cooked shrimp
1 c. cooked ham
2 stalks celery, cut up
3 or 4 slices cooked and crumbled
  bacon
1/2 chopped onion (medium)

1 can cream of celery soup
1/2 c. mustard or chili sauce
1 Tbsp. parsley
1 Tbsp. chopped green pepper
1/2 to 1 c. grated American cheese
1/2 c. skim milk

Cook rice. Combine all ingredients and bake at 400° for 15 minutes, then at 375° for 15 to 20 minutes.

June and Jean Pierce, Moweaqua Lions Club
Moweaqua, Illinois, USA

BROWN RICE CHEESE

2 1/2 c. cooked brown rice
3 green onions with tops, diced
1 c. lowfat cottage cheese, lightly
  drained

1 tsp. dried dill weed
1/4 c. grated Parmesan cheese
2 Tbsp. skim milk
1 tsp. low-sodium soy sauce

1. Preheat oven to 350°F. (175°C.). Spray a 1 quart baking dish with no stick cooking spray. Combine all ingredients in a medium size bowl.
2. Pour into sprayed baking dish. Bake 20 minutes. Makes 6 servings.

Variation: Substitute cooked ditalini or other small pasta for rice.

Maria Specht, President, Prince Albert Downtown Lioness Club
Prince Albert, Saskatchewan, Canada

❦

Now is the best time of life.

RED BEANS AND RICE

1 lb. red beans	2 c. onions, chopped
2 qt. water	1 bell pepper, chopped
1 meaty ham bone (or cubes of ham)	2 stalks celery, chopped
	Salt and pepper to taste
1 lb. hot sausage	

Rinse beans. Cover with water and set on medium heat. Bring to boil. Add all other ingredients. Lower heat to simmer. Cook several hours. Use wooden spoon to mash some beans on pot to produce creamy smooth texture. Serve over cooked rice.

From a friend in New Orleans.

Barbara Allison, Moweaqua Lions Club
Moweaqua, Illinois, USA

TOASTED RICE AND PASTA PILAF

1 Tbsp. vegetable oil	½ bay leaf
¾ c. white long grain rice	¼ c. chopped parsley
2 oz. thin spaghetti, broken	1 c. chicken broth
1 small onion	

Heat oil in heavy medium size saucepan over medium heat. Add rice and spaghetti. Cool, stirring constantly, until golden brown (3 to 5 minutes). Add onion and cook, stirring, 3 minutes longer. Carefully add broth and bay leaf. Reduce heat and bring to a boil. Cover and simmer until rice and spaghetti are tender and broth is absorbed. Remove from heat and discard bay leaf. Fluff with fork and serve.

Lion Paul Neely, Graysville/Proctor Lions Club
Proctor, West Virginia, USA

SPANISH RICE

1 lb. ground beef	2 c. water
¼ c. green peppers, chopped	¼ c. catsup
1 medium onion, chopped	1 Tbsp. Worcestershire sauce
1 to 1½ stalks celery, chopped	16 oz. (2 c.) tomatoes (undrained), cut up
1 c. uncooked white or brown rice	
1 tsp. salt	Cheddar cheese
⅛ tsp. pepper	

Brown beef, onion, green peppers, and celery. Drain off fat. Add remaining ingredients, except for cheese. Simmer, covered, for 30 to 40 minutes or until rice is tender and liquid is absorbed. Top with cheese. Return liquid and let stand till cheese is melted. Serves 5 to 6 people.

A Dutch oven works really well with this recipe.

FRIED RICE

2 c. precooked white rice
¼ lb. frozen peas
3 strips bacon
½ onion (yellow), chopped
Leftover (other) meat
2 scrambled eggs
Green onion

1 Tbsp. Worcestershire sauce
1 Tbsp. soy sauce
Dash of pepper
Dash of garlic powder
½ tsp. sesame oil
Dash of monosodium glutamate
(MSG)

Cut bacon into 1 inch squares. Fry bacon in wok (or large frying pan) at medium-high heat. Add in other leftover meats, such as ham, steak, chicken, etc. Chop onion and fry with meats.

Turn down heat and mix in rice. (Rice should have been cooked the day before and stored in refrigerator.) Fry gently. Add Worcestershire sauce (to taste), soy sauce, MSG, garlic powder, and sesame oil. Mix in frozen peas. Once thawed, add to rice the scrambled eggs and stir in rice. Add green onions and turn down heat.

This is a good way to get rid of leftovers. Cooking time is minimal. Chopping and preparing ingredients takes the most time.

Eugene Pei, S.W. Denver Lions Club
Denver, Colorado, USA

SAUSAGE AND RICE CASSEROLE

1 lb. bulk pork sausage
1 onion, chopped
1 c. rice (uncooked)
1 c. celery

2 cans cream of chicken soup
1 can water
1 can sliced mushrooms

Fry pork and drain. Add all other ingredients and bake in oven at 350° for 50 minutes.

Happy is the man who knows what to remember of the past, what to enjoy in the present, and what to plan for the future.

SPECIAL PIZZA

1 c. corn meal
1 c. all-purpose flour
½ tsp. salt
½ c. soft shortening
⅓ c. water
1 jar Chef Boyardee pizza sauce

1 (15 oz.) can southwestern black
   beans, drained
1 lb. turkey sausage, precooked
   and drained
1 medium green pepper, chopped
½ c. black olives, chopped

Sift flour and salt into mixing bowl. Cut in shortening until it resembles crumbs. Add water slowly; toss with fork until it all holds together. (Add small amounts of water if needed.) Knead gently a few seconds. Place in middle of jelly roll pan. Roll out even to edges of pan. Prick with fork. Bake at 425° for 10 to 12 minutes in preheated oven. Stir together drained turkey sausage, drained black beans, and pizza sauce. When crust is baked, spread on sausage mixture. Spread on olives and peppers. Return to oven for 10 to 12 minutes or until bubbly. Cheese can be added.

"PISSALADIERE A L'APPEL" - FRENCH PIZZA

1 (10 oz.) pkg. frozen patty shells
1 Tbsp. butter or margarine
¼ c. chopped green onion
⅓ c. spaghetti sauce
½ tsp. oregano leaf, crushed
1 egg yolk

1 tsp. water
16 thin slices pepperoni
1 (6 oz.) pkg. cooked ham
1 (6 oz.) pkg. Mozzarella cheese,
   sliced

Allow frozen patty shells to thaw at room temperature. Place in slightly overlapping rows. Roll out to a 9x16 inch rectangle. Cut lengthwise into 2 strips, one 16x4 and one 16x5 inches. Place both on a large cookie sheet and chill. Saute onion in butter or margarine until soft. Stir in spaghetti sauce and oregano, stirring often until sauce is thick, about 5 minutes. Beat egg yolk in water slightly. Brush edges of the 4 inch strip with egg mixture. Spoon sauce down the center of strip, leaving a 1 inch border where the egg yolk is spread. Cut pepperoni slices in halves. Arrange on top of sauce. Cut ham and cheese into 2 inch strips and arrange on top of pepperoni, allowing ham and cheese to cover. Carefully place the 5 inch strip over the top, pressing the edges together with a fork. Brush top with egg yolk and cut 4 slits in dough with a sharp knife. Do not cut all the way through to the filling. Bake at 425° for 25 minutes until pastry is puffed and golden brown. Put on cutting board. Cut in 1 inch strips. Garnish with cherry tomatoes and parsley (optional).

Dan Steffan, Independence Eastview Lions Club
Independence, Missouri, USA

Stop and let the world go on without you once in a while.

QUICK PIZZA

Dough:

2 c. flour
½ Tbsp. baking powder
1 tsp. salt

¼ c. oil or shortening
1 c. water

1. Stir together and dump on large oiled cookie sheet.
2. Oil hands and press out to edges.
3. Spread on 1 large can spaghetti sauce (any flavor).
4. Use your imagination for toppings - anything you like or have leftover, i.e., green onions, olives, pineapple, sausage, bacon, etc.
5. Top with 8 ounces white cheese and 8 ounces yellow cheese (grated) or any mixture of cheeses.
6. Bake at 375° for 30 to 45 minutes. Take spatula and lift edges to see if brown.

Jack and Ruth Graham, Lyman Lions Club
Lyman, Wyoming, USA

POPOVER PIZZA

Heat oven to 400°.

1 lb. ground beef
1 (15 oz.) can tomato sauce
½ c. chopped green pepper
2 Tbsp. Bisquick baking mix
1 Tbsp. snipped parsley
½ tsp. pepper
2 c. shredded Cheddar cheese (8 oz.)

¾ c. water
¼ c. margarine or butter
1 c. Bisquick baking mix
4 eggs
¼ c. chopped green onions

Brown ground beef in 10 inch skillet; drain. Stir in tomato sauce, green pepper, 2 tablespoons baking mix, the parsley, and pepper. Heat to boiling. Boil and stir 1 minute. Pour into ungreased rectangular pan, 13x9x2 inches. Sprinkle with cheese.

Heat water and margarine to rolling boil in 3 quart saucepan. Add 1 cup baking mix all at once. Stir vigorously over low heat until mixture forms a ball, about 1½ minutes. Remove from heat. Beat in eggs, one at a time; continue beating until smooth. Spread over beef mixture. Sprinkle with onions. Bake until puffy and golden brown, 25 to 30 minutes. Serve immediately. Makes 6 servings.

❧

Tomorrow doesn't matter, for I have lived today.

HOMEMADE PIZZA

Dough:

2 Tbsp. yeast	1 Tbsp. honey
1¼ c. warm water	2 c. wheat flour

Dissolve yeast in warm water. Add honey and wheat flour. Let rise.

Add:

¼ c. olive oil	1½ c. wheat flour or white flour
1 tsp. salt	

Mix and push onto 2 round pizza pans. Add sauce (recipe follows) and top with 8 ounces Mozzarella per pizza and ¼ cup Parmesan per pizza. Add whatever veggies or meats you want. Bake at 425° for 20 minutes.

Pizza Sauce:

1 c. onions	3 Tbsp. olive oil

Saute onions in olive oil. Add 1 tablespoon minced garlic and cook 2 minutes.

Add:

4 c. canned tomatoes	1 Tbsp. basil
1 c. tomato paste	1 bay leaf
1 Tbsp. oregano	1 Tbsp. salt
1 Tbsp. honey	

Bring to boil. Turn down and simmer 1 hour. Very good for pizza sauce or spaghetti.

Jan Wheeler, Sundowners Lions Club
Emporia, Kansas, USA

SPAGHETTI WITH WALNUTS AND PARMESAN

12 oz. spaghetti	½ c. finely chopped walnuts
6 Tbsp. olive oil	¼ c. grated Parmesan cheese
1 garlic clove, crushed	3 Tbsp. finely chopped parsley

Cook the spaghetti in plenty of boiling salted water until firm to the bite, about 7 to 10 minutes; drain. Heat oil in small skillet; stir in garlic. Saute 1 minute. Add walnuts; saute 2 minutes. Toss the walnut sauce, spaghetti, cheese, and parsley together. Serve immediately. Makes 4 servings.

❦

We're in charge of the effort. God will handle the results.

SAUSAGE SPAGHETTI

1 lb. smoked sausage
2 green peppers, diced
2 medium onions, diced
2 (15 oz.) cans tomato sauce
1 (6 oz.) can tomato paste
1 can sliced mushrooms

1 Tbsp. Worcestershire sauce
1 tsp. basil leaves
1 tsp. salt
¼ tsp. pepper
⅛ tsp. garlic powder
1 lb. spaghetti

Cut sausage in slices and fry till almost brown. Add peppers and onions; cook till tender. Stir in remaining ingredients and simmer, uncovered, for 20 minutes. Cook spaghetti. Pour sauce over drained spaghetti.

"Put a little sugar in what you say, and salt in what you hear."
Jeanette Olson, Siren Lions Club
Siren, Wisconsin, USA

AWESOME SPAGHETTI

1 to 1½ lb. ground beef
½ c. onion
½ to 1 green pepper
1 tomato
1 small can tomato sauce

Pepperoni
Smoked sausage
Salt and pepper to taste
Cooked spaghetti

Brown ground beef; drain off fat. Chop onion and green pepper; add to ground beef. Cut pepperoni and sausage into small pieces; add to beef mixture. Add tomato sauce and chopped tomato. Simmer. Cook spaghetti as directed on package. Drain. Top with meat sauce.

Carolyn Lemon, Emporia Sundowners Lions Club
Emporia, Kansas, USA

A mother ... one who can take the place of all others,
but whose place no one else can take.

983-94

SPAGHETTI BAKE

2 lb. ground beef
1 c. chopped onion
1 (28 oz.) can tomatoes with juice,
    cut up
1 (15 oz.) can tomato sauce
1 (6 oz.) can tomato paste
¾ c. water
1 (4 oz.) can mushroom pieces,
    drained
2 tsp. sugar

1 tsp. dried oregano
1 tsp. Italian seasoning
1 tsp. salt
½ tsp. garlic powder
1 (8 oz.) box spaghetti (little more),
    broken, cooked, and
    drained
1 to 2 c. shredded Mozzarella
    cheese
⅓ c. Parmesan cheese

Cook beef and onion until browned. Drain fat. Stir in tomatoes, sauce, paste, water, mushrooms, sugar, oregano, and remaining seasonings. Bring to boil, then simmer, uncovered, 20 minutes, stirring occasionally. Remove from heat. Stir together meat sauce and drained spaghetti. Place half of spaghetti in 15x9 inch baking dish. Sprinkle with Mozzarella cheese. Top with remaining spaghetti. Sprinkle with any remaining Mozzarella cheese and the Parmesan cheese. Bake at 375° for 30 minutes. This can be made in advance and refrigerated, baking when ready to serve.

Ruth Wright, Moweaqua Lions Club
Moweaqua, Illinois, USA

HOBO SPAGHETTI

1 medium onion
3 cans Franco-American
    spaghetti

1 lb. lean ground beef
Salt and pepper to taste
Garlic to taste

Saute onion until translucent; add ground beef and cook until brown. Pour off excess fat. Add spaghetti and heat until warmed through.

Myron Phelps, Lyman Lions Club
Lyman, Wyoming, USA

May life's greatest gifts always be yours -
happiness, memories, and dreams.

CHICKEN SPAGHETTI

1 fat hen
1 (12 oz.) pkg. spaghetti
¼ lb. butter
1 green pepper, chopped
1 onion, chopped
2 cloves garlic

1 can sliced mushrooms
¼ lb. grated Cheddar cheese
1 (4 oz.) can tomato sauce
1 can Ro-Tel tomatoes
Salt and pepper to taste

Stew and bone the hen. Boil spaghetti in chicken broth. In butter, saute until tender the green pepper, onion, garlic, and mushrooms. Remove from heat and stir in grated cheese, tomato sauce, and Ro-Tel tomatoes. Add salt and pepper to taste. In large casserole, combine chicken, spaghetti, and sauce. Bake 45 minutes at low temperature (250°).

Christa Wade (Mrs. J.W.), Georgetown Evening Lions Club
Georgetown, Texas, USA

CHICKEN SPAGHETTI

1 fryer or 2 bags leg quarters
1 large onion, chopped
1 lb. Velveeta cheese
1 lb. spaghetti

1 small jar pimentos, chopped
1 bell pepper, chopped
1 can Ro-Tel tomatoes
2 qt. water for cooking chicken

1. Cook and debone chicken, reserving broth. Chop into pieces.
2. Cook bell pepper and onion in broth until tender.
3. Add broken spaghetti. Cook until done.
4. Combine Ro-Tel, pimento, and cubed Velveeta and chicken.
5. Stir until cheese melts.
6. Pour into greased casserole and bake at 350° for 30 minutes, covered.

Excellent for freezer. Freeze before baking.

Terry Jones, Kosciusko Lions Club
Kosciusko, Mississippi, USA

Faith is building on what you know is here
so you can reach what you know is there.

SPAGHETTI WITH MEAT BALLS

1 lb. ground beef
½ tsp. salt
¼ chopped onion
1 egg, slightly beaten
½ c. bread crumbs
2 Tbsp. cooking oil
¼ c. chopped green pepper
¼ c. chopped celery
2 (10½ oz.) cans condensed
 tomato soup
1 c. water
½ lb. spaghetti
Parmesan cheese

Combine beef, salt, onion, egg, and bread crumbs; form into balls, about 8 or 10. Brown meat balls in cooking oil; remove from skillet. Cook green peppers and celery in oil until tender. Add tomato soup and water, stirring well. Simmer 15 minutes. Place meat balls in sauce. Simmer 30 minutes longer, stirring occasionally. Cook spaghetti according to package directions. Drain. Pour sauce and meat balls over spaghetti. Makes 4 generous servings.

This recipe has been used by the Wolfe family for 30 plus years.
Hazel Wolfe, Otis, Colorado, Lions Club
Otis, Colorado, USA

JENNY'S SPAGHETTI

3 cloves garlic
1 Tbsp. olive oil
1 medium onion, chopped
1 lb. lean hamburger
1 lb. Italian sausage
3 Tbsp. oregano
1 (16 oz.) can plum tomatoes
1 (4 oz.) can tomato sauce
1 (2 oz.) can tomato paste
1 cube beef flavoring
1 bay leaf
1 green pepper, diced
½ c. Parmesan cheese
1 (1 lb.) box spaghetti noodles

In a large pot, cook onion and garlic in olive oil until onions are translucent. Add sausage, hamburger, and oregano. Cook until browned. Cut plum tomatoes and add. Add sauce and paste. Add beef cube and bay leaf. Add green pepper and Parmesan cheese. Bring to a boil, then simmer at least 4 hours. Bring pot of water to a boil. Cook spaghetti 4 minutes and drain. Add to pot of meat sauce and continue simmering 1 hour. The longer you cook it, the better it tastes.
Kathy Skolak, Whitestown Lions Club
Whitestown, Indiana, USA

Character is like the foundation of a house - it's below the surface.

SICILIAN-STYLE SPAGHETTI WITH TUNA

1 Tbsp. olive oil
1 medium onion, chopped
2 ribs celery, chopped
14½ oz. can tomatoes in their juice
3 Tbsp. raisins

¼ c. red wine vinegar
1 Tbsp. sugar
6⅛ oz. can chunk light tuna
   packed in water
½ lb. spaghetti

    1. In a frying pan, heat oil over medium heat. Add onion and celery; cook until soft, about 5 minutes. Add tomatoes with juice, crushing them with a fork. Stir in raisins and simmer, uncovered, stirring occasionally, until thick, about 15 minutes.

    2. Stir in vinegar, sugar, and ¼ cup water. Cook to a thick sauce, 15 minutes more.

    3. Add tuna and heat through. Season to taste with salt and pepper.

    4. Meanwhile, in a large pot of boiling salted water, cook spaghetti. Drain and toss with sauce. Makes 4 servings.

John J. Hess for Mrs. Joanne Brownell, Clarence Center Lions Club
Clarence Center, New York, USA

CLAM SPAGHETTI

1 lb. spaghetti
1 (10 oz.) pkg. frozen broccoli
2 (6½ oz.) cans chopped clams

¾ tsp. garlic powder
½ c. grated Parmesan cheese

Cook spaghetti as directed on package; drain and set aside. Cook broccoli according to package instructions. Drain liquid. Set aside. Heat canned clams in juice until hot. Add garlic powder to clams and juice. Put spaghetti in microwaveable dish. Pour clams and juice plus cooked broccoli over top. Mix all together, tossing to blend ingredients. Sprinkle ½ cup grated Parmesan cheese into ingredients. Toss again. Heat in microwave, covered, about 5 minutes until warmed or heat in oven, covered, 15 minutes at 325°.

AMERICAN SPAGHETTI

¾ lb. spaghetti, cooked and
   drained
½ green pepper

1 onion, medium
2 lb. ground beef

    Brown all.

3 ribs celery
1 qt. tomatoes
1 jar Ragu chunky country style
1 bay leaf
⅛ tsp. garlic powder

1 tsp. oregano
⅓ c. sugar
Salt and pepper
Mushrooms

    Mix all together and cook.

Lillian Kataja, Onekama Lions Club
Onekama, Michigan, USA

LAZY DAY LASAGNA

1 lb. ground beef
1 (14½ oz.) can tomatoes
   (undrained)
1 (6 oz.) can tomato paste
1½ tsp. salt
1½ tsp. basil leaves
½ tsp. oregano leaves
⅛ tsp. garlic powder

½ c. water
2 c. cottage cheese
¼ c. Parmesan cheese
1 egg
1 Tbsp. parsley flakes
8 uncooked lasagna noodles
2 c. (8 oz.) shredded Mozzarella
   cheese

1. Crumble ground beef into 1½ quart glass casserole.
2. Microwave (HIGH), uncovered 5 to 6 minutes or until no longer pink, stirring once. Stir to break meat into pieces. Drain. Stir in tomatoes, tomato paste, salt, basil, oregano, garlic powder, and water. Cover with casserole lid.
3. Microwave (HIGH) 4 to 5 minutes or until mixture boils. Combine cottage cheese, Parmesan cheese, egg, and parsley; mix well.
4. Pour 1½ cups tomato sauce mixture into 12x8 inch glass baking dish. Spread evenly in dish. Place 4 uncooked noodles evenly over sauce. (They may overlap slightly.)
5. Top with half the cottage cheese mixture, spreading evenly. Sprinkle with half the Mozzarella cheese. Spoon 1 cup sauce evenly over cheese. Place 4 or more noodles on sauce. Top with even layers of remaining cottage cheese mixture, Mozzarella cheese, and tomato sauce. Cover with plastic wrap.
6. Microwave (HIGH) 15 minutes. Rotate dish.
7. Microwave (MEDIUM - 50%) for 15 to 20 minutes or until noodles are tender. Remove plastic wrap. Sprinkle lasagna with an additional 2 tablespoons Parmesan cheese.
8. Microwave (HIGH), uncovered, 1½ to 2 minutes or until cheese is melted. Let stand about 10 minutes before cutting into squares for serving. Makes about 6 servings.

Tips: With FULL power in steps 6 and 7, microwave (HIGH) 15 minutes; let stand 5 minutes, then microwave (HIGH) 5 minutes. Let stand 5 minutes. Add Parmesan cheese and microwave as directed in step 8.

Casserole can be assembled ahead through step 5. If refrigerated, increase time in step 7 to 20 to 25 minutes.

Lion Betty Conley, Lyerly, Chapter President, Mt. Airy Foothills Lions Club
Mt. Airy, North Carolina, USA

❧

Life is short. Eat dessert first.

TUNA LASAGNA

9 lasagna noodles
20 oz. mixed frozen vegetables
2 cans condensed cream of
  mushroom soup
2 cans tuna fish, flaked and
  drained

½ soup can milk
Sliced cheese (American, sharp,
  etc. - any type)

Grease lasagna pan. Cook noodles as package directs. Cook mixed vegetables as directed and drain. In medium saucepan, heat 2 cans of mushroom soup and ½ can of milk until blended. Add the 2 cans of tuna fish (drained) and cooked mixed vegetables until heated. Layer noodles 3 across lasagna pan and cover with ½ of soup mixture. Top with cheese slices. Repeat this step until last of noodles are used. Top last layer with soup mixture only. Bake at 350° for ½ hour. Let sit 15 minutes before serving. Reheat leftovers in microwave, adding few drops of water.

Lion Karen Bateman, South Whitehall Lions Club
Orefield, Pennsylvania, USA

LASAGNA ROLLS

6 lasagna noodles
1 lb. ground beef

1 jar spaghetti sauce
8 oz. shredded Mozzarella cheese

Cook lasagna noodles according to package directions. In a skillet, brown beef and drain excess fat. Stir in spaghetti sauce. Simmer 5 minutes. Drain noodles. Spread ¼ cup meat sauce on each noodle; top with 1 to 2 tablespoons cheese. Carefully roll up each noodle and place in a 9x9 inch baking dish, seam side down. Spoon remaining sauce over each roll and sprinkle with remaining cheese. Bake at 400° for 10 to 15 minutes or until heated through.

Lynn Sommerville, Craigsville Lions Club
Craigsville, West Virginia, USA

May we always have something to do, something to love,
and something to hope for.

LASAGNE

1 lb. ground beef
2 (6 oz.) cans tomato paste
10 oz. lasagne noodles
1 (3 oz.) cream cheese
2 tsp. salt
2 beaten eggs
1 lb. can tomatoes

Garlic
Salt and pepper
1 large ctn. cottage cheese
1 tsp. pepper
6 oz. American cheese
6 oz. Swiss cheese
6 oz. Mozzarella cheese

Brown and then drain the ground beef. Add tomatoes and tomato paste with seasonings and simmer, uncovered, for 30 minutes. Cook noodles; drain and rinse. Combine cottage cheese, cream cheese, salt, pepper, and eggs in separate bowl. Grate the other 3 cups cheeses. In a 9x13 inch Pyrex dish, which may be sprayed with Pam to prevent sticking, layer noodles, cottage cheese mixture, grated cheese, and meat sauce; repeat. Top with Parmesan cheese. Bake at 375° for 30 minutes. Let stand 10 minutes, then cut in squares to serve.

Beverly Ryan, Decatur Lions Club
Decatur, Texas, USA

ZUCCHINI LASAGNA

1 lb. ground beef
¼ c. chopped onion
1 can tomato sauce
½ tsp. salt
½ tsp. dried oregano
½ tsp. dried basil
¼ tsp. ground pepper

4 medium zucchini (1¼ lb.)
1 c. creamed cottage cheese
1 egg, beaten
3 Tbsp. flour
1 c. (4 oz.) shredded Mozzarella
cheese

In large skillet, brown beef and onion over medium heat. Drain. Add tomato sauce and seasonings. Bring to boil. Simmer 5 minutes.

Meanwhile, slice zucchini crosswise into ¼ inch slices. In small bowl, combine cottage cheese and egg. In a greased 12x8x2 inch baking pan, place half the zucchini and sprinkle with half the flour. Top with cottage cheese mixture and half the meat mixture. Repeat layer of zucchini and flour. Sprinkle with Mozzarella cheese and remaining meat mixture. Bake at 375° for about 40 minutes or until heated through. Remove from oven and sprinkle with additional cheese if desired. To cut more easily, let stand 10 minutes before serving. Makes 6 to 8 servings.

To obtain maximum attention, it's hard to beat a good big mistake.

CABBAGE LASAGNA

2 lb. lean ground beef
1 medium onion, chopped
1 green pepper, chopped
1 medium cabbage, shredded

½ tsp. oregano
1 tsp. salt
1 (18 oz.) can tomato paste
8 oz. Mozzarella cheese

Saute ground beef, onion, and pepper until meat is brown. Boil cabbage until tender. Save 2 cups of liquid and drain off whatever liquid remains. Combine 2 cups of the reserved cabbage liquid, salt, and tomato paste; simmer over low heat for 5 minutes. Add meat, onions, and green pepper to tomato mixture into a 9x13 inch pan. Layer cabbage, then remaining tomato mixture. Top with slices of cheese to cover. Bake at 400° until cheese is browned, about 35 to 40 minutes.

Joyce Stober, Baroness Stiegel Lioness Club
Akron, Pennsylvania, USA

GREEK LASAGNA

1 lb. chopped meat
1 medium onion
1 can tomatoes
8 oz. Mozzarella cheese

6 to 8 medium potatoes
Salt and pepper to taste
Pinch of basil

Brown meat. Add onion, then tomatoes. Layer meat/tomato mixture, potatoes, and cheese until casserole is full. Bake at 350°, covered, for 1 hour.

Toni Bell, Merritt Island Lions Club
Merritt Island, Florida, USA

❦

Most of us will never do great things,
but we can do small things in a great way.

❦ ❦ ❦

Most people are willing to change -
not because they see the light, but because they feel the heat!

SPINACH LASAGNA

7 Tbsp. butter
2 cloves garlic, minced
1 medium onion, chopped
2 (10 oz.) pkg. frozen spinach,
    thawed and drained
½ tsp. pepper
15 oz. Ricotta cheese
2 eggs
1 tsp. oregano
1 tsp. salt

¼ c. flour
⅛ tsp. grated nutmeg
2½ c. milk
3 oz. grated Parmesan cheese
    (about 6 Tbsp.)
9 cooked broad lasagna noodles
    (about 7 oz.)
8 oz. Mozzarella cheese, shredded
    (about 2 c.)

Heat oven to 350°. Use 1 tablespoon of the butter to grease 9x13 inch baking pan.

2. In a frying pan, melt 4 tablespoons butter. Add garlic and onion; cook until tender, about 5 minutes. Add spinach and pepper; toss to blend. Remove from heat.

3. In a bowl, mix together the Ricotta, eggs, oregano, and ½ teaspoon of salt.

4. In small saucepan, melt remaining 2 tablespoons butter. Stir in flour, nutmeg, and the other ½ teaspoon salt, mixing until smooth. Add milk and cook, stirring constantly, until sauce thickens and just comes to a boil. Remove from heat. Stir in 4 tablespoons Parmesan.

5. Spread ½ the cream sauce over bottom of pan. Top with 3 noodles. Spread half the Ricotta mixture over noodles, then half the vegetables and half the Mozzarella. Top with another 3 noodles, then the rest of the Ricotta, vegetables, and Mozzarella. Top with last 3 noodles and the remaining cream sauce. Sprinkle with remaining Parmesan and bake until hot and bubbly, 40 to 45 minutes. If desired, set under broiler to lightly brown top, 3 to 5 minutes. Let stand 10 minutes before serving. Makes 8 servings.

John J. Hess for Mrs. Joanne Brownell, Clarence Center Lions Club
Clarence Center, New York, USA

LASAGNE

1½ lb. ground meat
1 medium onion, chopped
¼ c. celery
1 clove garlic, chopped
2 (16 oz.) cans tomatoes
1 (6 oz.) can tomato paste
2 tsp. salt
½ tsp. oregano

¼ tsp. cayenne pepper
1 bay leaf
6 oz. Mozzarella cheese
⅓ c. grated Parmesan cheese or
    Romano
6 oz. Ricotta or cottage cheese
1 (8 oz.) pkg. lasagne noodles

Cook meat, onion, celery, and garlic, then add the rest of the ingredients, except the cheeses. Cook for 20 minutes and remove bay leaf. Cook noodles and drain. Layer noodles, meat sauce, and cheeses. Bake at 350° for 30 minutes.

Barb Allison, Moweaqua Lions Club
Moweaqua, Illinois, USA

CRAFTY CRESCENT LASAGNE

Meat Filling:

½ lb. ground sausage
½ lb. ground beef
¾ c. chopped onion
½ clove garlic, minced (optional)
1 Tbsp. parsley flakes

½ tsp. leaf basil (optional)
½ tsp. leaf oregano
½ tsp. salt
Dash of pepper
1 (6⅓ oz.) can tomato paste

Brown meats and drain. Add remaining ingredients. Simmer for 5 minutes. May be made ahead and refrigerated.

Cheese Filling:

½ to 1 c. cottage cheese
1 egg

¼ c. Parmesan cheese

Combine all ingredients.

Crust:

2 cans crescent rolls
2 (7x4 inch) slices Mozzarella
cheese

1 Tbsp. milk (optional)
1 Tbsp. sesame seeds (optional)

Unroll crescents into 8 rectangles. Place on ungreased cooky sheet, overlapping edges (15x13 inches). Press edges together. Spread half of meat down center of dough to within 1 inch of 13 inch end. Top meat with Cheese Filling. Put on remaining meat. Place cheese slices on top. Fold 1 inch edges over filling. Pull sides over filling. Pinch edges to seal. Brush with milk and sprinkle on seeds. Bake at 375° for 20 to 25 minutes until golden brown.

Tip: May be prepared ahead of time, covered with plastic wrap, and refrigerated for 2 to 3 hours before baking. Bake for 25 to 30 minutes.

A happy home is more than a roof over your head -
it's a foundation under your feet.

LASAGNA

1 lb. Italian sausage
1 lb. ground beef
1 large can tomato sauce or 1 (16 oz.) can tomatoes, pureed
2 (6 oz.) cans tomato paste
10 oz. lasagne or wide noodles
3 c. fresh Ricotta or creamy cottage cheese

½ c. grated Parmesan or Romano cheese
2 Tbsp. parsley flakes
2 beaten eggs
1 lb. Mozzarella cheese, sliced very thin

Brown meat slowly and spoon off excess fat. Add tomato sauce and tomato paste. Simmer, uncovered, for 20 minutes, stirring occasionally. Cook noodles in large amount of boiling, salted water till tender; drain and rinse. Combine remaining ingredients, except Mozzarella cheese.

Place half of the noodles in 13x9x2 inch baking dish. Spread with half of the cottage cheese filling. Add half of the Mozzarella cheese and half the meat sauce. Repeat layers. Bake at 375° for 30 minutes. Let stand for 10 minutes before cutting into squares. Filling will set slightly. Makes 12 servings.

Or, assemble early and refrigerate. Be sure to allow 15 minutes longer in the oven.

CLASSIC LASAGNA

½ pkg. (16 oz.) lasagna noodles
1 lb. lean ground beef
1 lb. Italian sausage (mild or hot)
1 medium onion, chopped
1 rib celery, chopped
½ green pepper, chopped
¼ tsp. garlic powder
Salt and pepper to taste
1 tsp. oregano

1 can tomato soup
1 (6 oz.) can tomato paste
1 (8 oz.) can tomato sauce
1½ c. water
¾ lb. Mozzarella cheese
Parmesan cheese
1 (12 oz.) container Ricotta cheese (optional)

Cook lasagna noodles according to package directions. Brown meat and sausage. Drain off liquid. Add tomato soup, sauce, and paste. Add spices and water, celery, green pepper, and onion. Mix well and cook for 1 hour.

To assemble, pour ½ cup sauce on bottom of a 9x13 inch pan. Layer lasagna noodles, slices of Mozzarella cheese, and sauce. Sprinkle with Parmesan cheese. Repeat layers, ending with Mozzarella cheese and sauce. Sprinkle with Parmesan cheese. (You can fill one layer with Ricotta cheese if you like.) Bake in a 375° oven for 40 minutes. Let stand for 10 minutes before cutting.

Every man's work is a portrait of himself.

LINGUINI WITH ESCAROLE AND CHICKPEAS

2 tsp. olive oil
1 head escarole (about 1½ lb.), cut
    into 1½ inch wide shreds
4 cloves garlic, minced
½ c. chicken broth

1 c. canned chickpeas, drained
½ tsp. salt
¼ tsp. pepper
½ lb. linguini
Parmesan cheese (optional)

    1. In large frying pan, heat oil over medium-high heat. Add escarole and garlic. Cover and cook, stirring occasionally, until escarole wilts, about 5 minutes.
    2. Add chicken broth, chickpeas, salt, and pepper; bring to a boil.
    3. Meanwhile, in large pot of boiling salted water, cook linguini. Drain.
    4. Add escarole mixture to pasta; toss and serve. Pass grated Parmesan cheese if desired. Makes 4 servings.

John J. Hess for Mrs. Joanne Brownell, Clarence Center Lions Club
Clarence Center, New York, USA

EASY FETTUCCINE ALFREDO

1 (8 oz.) pkg. Philadelphia cream
    cheese
¾ c. grated Parmesan cheese

½ c. margarine
½ c. milk
8 oz. box fettuccine

    In large pan, stir together cream cheese, Parmesan cheese, margarine, and milk over low heat until smooth. Cook fettuccine noodles while preparing sauce. Drain noodles and add sauce. Serve with salad and soft bread sticks.

Lion Ron Wilson, Graysville/Proctor Lions Club
Proctor, West Virginia, USA

Three essentials: a faith to live by, a self to live with,
and a purpose to live for.

Worry wastes today's time to stifle tomorrow's opportunities
with yesterday's problems.

CHEESE AND SAUSAGE MANICOTTI

1 Tbsp. olive oil
1 onion, chopped
3 cloves garlic, minced
28 oz. can whole tomatoes
1 tsp. dried oregano
½ tsp. dried thyme
1½ tsp. salt
½ tsp. pepper
12 manicotti shells
½ lb. sweet Italian sausage,
    casing removed

3 c. Ricotta cheese
1 oz. grated Parmesan cheese
    (about ⅓ c.)
3 eggs
¼ c. chopped parsley
⅛ tsp. cayenne pepper (more to
    taste)
4 oz. Mozzarella cheese, shredded
    (about 1 c.)

1. Heat oven to 375°. In large frying pan, heat oil over medium heat. Add onion and garlic; cook until soft, 3 to 5 minutes. Stir in tomatoes with their juice and crush them with a fork. Add oregano, thyme, ¾ teaspoon salt, and ¼ teaspoon pepper. Boil over medium-high heat until thickened, about 15 minutes. Transfer tomato sauce to a bowl. Wipe out frying pan.

2. Meanwhile, in large pot of boiling salted water, cook manicotti shells. Drain and set aside.

3. Heat frying pan over medium-high heat. Add sausage and cook, breaking it up with a spoon, until brown, about 5 minutes. With slotted spoon, transfer meat to paper towels and drain.

4. In a large bowl, combine the sausage, meat, Ricotta, Parmesan, eggs, parsley, cayenne, and the remaining salt and pepper; stir to combine. Stuff the shells with sausage mixture.

6. Spread 1 cup tomato sauce on the bottom of a 3 quart baking dish. Arrange the shells in one layer; pour remaining sauce over and sprinkle with Mozzarella. Cover with foil and bake 20 minutes.

6. Uncover and bake until cheese is melted and bubbling, about 15 minutes. Cool slightly before serving. Makes 6 servings.

John J. Hess for Mrs. Joanne Brownell, Clarence Center Lions Club
Clarence Center, New York, USA

SOUR CREAM NOODLE BAKE

1 (8 oz.) pkg. noodles
1 c. sour cream
6 large green onions
¾ c. shredded sharp cheese
1 can tomato soup

2 Tbsp. butter
1 tsp. salt
½ tsp. pepper
¼ tsp. garlic powder
1 lb. ground beef

Cook and drain noodles. Combine cheese, sour cream, onions, and noodles. Brown meat; add salt, pepper, garlic powder, and tomato soup. Alternate layers of noodles and meat; begin with noodles and end with meat. Top with cheese. Bake at 350° for 20 to 25 minutes. Very good.

"Lori" Kelsey, Mitchell Lions Club
Mitchell, South Dakota, USA

SWISS NOODLES

1 (8 oz.) pkg. medium noodles, cooked and drained
½ lb. Swiss cheese, grated
1 Tbsp. Worcestershire sauce
¼ c. butter, melted
½ tsp. salt
¼ tsp. pepper
2 c. sour cream

Add cheese to hot noodles. Stir in all other ingredients, except sour cream. Cool slightly. Add sour cream and toss slightly. Place in buttered 2 quart casserole and bake for 1 hour in a 350° oven. Serves 6.

Lion Eve Kolbus, Royalton Hills Lions Club
North Royalton, Ohio, USA

SAUSAGE AND MACARONI CASSEROLE

1½ lb. link pork sausage
1 onion (large), chopped
1 (8 oz.) jar sliced mushrooms
1 (8 oz.) jar sliced pimentos
1 bell pepper (large), chopped
1 (31 oz.) can whole tomatoes
Butter
1 lb. elbow macaroni

Cut sausage into 1 inch pieces. Fry and drain. Saute onion, mushrooms, pimentos, and pepper in butter. Cook, drain, and cool macaroni. Break tomatoes into pieces with hands. Mix together in a large bowl and pour in a 9x13 inch (3 quart) baking dish. Bake at 350° for 45 minutes.

Phyllis Hillis, McMinnville Lions Club
McMinnville, Tennessee, USA

MACARONI AND CHEESE

1½ or 2 c. uncooked macaroni
1 pkg. extra sharp or Coon cheese
1 small onion, chopped fine
1 can cream of mushroom soup
Margarine
1 can water
Pepper

I use bread crumbs for topping. Butter casserole. Cook macaroni according to directions on package. Melt cheese in double boiler. Add soup, water, and pepper. I use frozen chopped onion. Heat and mix well. Pour this over macaroni in casserole. Cook at 350° in a preheated oven for 35 minutes or until bubbly.

Connie Levecque, Westbrook Lions Club
Westbrook, Maine, USA

❦

What the new year brings depends on what we bring the new year.

MISS MARIA'S MACARONI CASSEROLE

1 (8 oz.) box elbow macaroni
1 can tomatoes, chopped
1 medium onion, chopped
½ green pepper, chopped
2 c. grated Cheddar cheese

¼ c. butter
4 Tbsp. flour
2 c. milk
Salt and pepper to taste
½ tsp. dry mustard (if desired)

Cook macaroni according to package directions. Combine vegetables and simmer until tender, but crisp. While this is being done, make a sauce of the butter, flour, and milk. When thickened, add cheese and seasoning. Combine all ingredients, correct seasoning, and pour into a large buttered casserole. Sprinkle with buttered bread crumbs and bake in a moderate (350°) oven until topping is lightly browned. To vary this recipe, mayonnaise and/or Worcestershire sauce may be added.

Lion Owen has been a local Lions Club member since 1935, and during his long lifetime, enjoyed his mother-in-law's (Marie Garwood Rudasill) good cooking for many years. One of his favorite dishes was her Macaroni Casserole and his wife still serves it to him frequently.

Mrs. Lion Ralph (Frances) Owen, Canton Lions Club
Canton, Georgia, USA

TEX-MEX MACARONI AND CHEESE

12 oz. ruote (wagon wheel) pasta
4 Tbsp. butter
1 medium onion, minced
3 small hot green chile peppers,
   minced
¼ c. flour
1 tsp. chili powder
½ tsp. salt

½ tsp. cumin
¼ tsp. pepper
2½ c. milk
½ lb. Cheddar cheese, shredded
   (about 2 c.)
½ lb. Monterey Jack cheese,
   shredded (about 2 c.)

1. Heat the oven to 350°. Butter a 2 quart casserole.
2. In a large pot of boiling salted water, cook pasta until softened. Drain and set aside.
3. In large saucepan over medium heat, melt butter. Add onion and chile peppers; cook until tender, about 5 minutes.
4. Stir in the flour, chili powder, salt, cumin, and pepper; cook 1 minute.
5. Stir in milk and cook, stirring constantly, until sauce thickens. Remove from heat and stir in cheeses until melted. Stir in pasta, tossing to coat.
6. Put in prepared casserole dish and bake until pasta is hot and bubbly, about 25 minutes. Makes 6 servings.

John J. Hess for Mrs. Joanne Brownell, Clarence Center Lions Club
Clarence Center, New York, USA

PIEROGI CASSEROLE

12 lasagne noodles
8 to 10 potatoes
1 tsp. salt
1 lb. Velveeta or ½ Velveeta and ½
    sharp cheese (any
    combination - must be grated)

2 onions
2 sticks butter

Cook noodles. Boil potatoes. Saute onions and butter while potatoes are cooking. Mash potatoes and cheese together. Add ¾ butter and onions to potatoes. Mix well. In 9x13 inch pan: Layer noodles and potatoes, ending with noodles. Pour remaining onions and butter over top. Bake at 350° for 15 to 20 minutes.

Marie Ohlinger, Blandon Lioness Club
Blandon, Pennsylvania, USA

HOMEMADE RAVIOLI

There are 3 steps to this recipe. You have 3 things to make - the noodle dough, the filling, and the sauce.

Noodles:

4 eggs, well beaten with dash of
    salt

4 c. flour

Filling:

6 slices bread, soaked in milk
3 lb. hamburger
Garlic salt (to taste)

2 eggs
1 small can grated cheese
Salt and pepper (to taste)

Sauce:

2 Tbsp. shortening
2 medium onions, finely cut
1 bunch celery, finely cut
1 large can tomato juice

2 lb. hamburger
Garlic salt (to taste)
Salt and pepper (to taste)

Noodle dough: Make dough tender, but not sticky. Roll out on board and cut into squares. Place ball of meat mixture in center. Fold over and press down edges with fork. Boil in salt water until tender, about 20 minutes.

Sauce: Put shortening in skillet with onion and celery; simmer until brown, then add hamburger and fry until brown. Season to taste and add tomato juice. Let simmer while you make the ravioli noodles.

Everyone comments how good the raviolis are - better than boughten ones or restaurant ones.

Mrs. Edward (Lioness Lucille) Yann, St. Jacob Lions Club
St. Jacob, Illinois, USA

RATATOUILLE

1 lb. Italian sausage, cut into 1½
   inch pieces
2 medium onions, sliced
1 medium green pepper, cut into
   strips
2 lb. zucchini, sliced

1 tsp. salt
¼ tsp. pepper
½ c. shredded Cheddar cheese
2 cloves garlic, sliced
3 medium tomatoes
Cooking oil

Fry sausage; set aside. Discard drippings. Put cooking oil in pan. Cook onion, green pepper, and garlic. Add zucchini and cook about 10 more minutes. Add tomatoes, peeled, seeded, and cut into chunks. Add salt and pepper. Add sausage and cook about 15 minutes, stirring occasionally, then add cheese. Cook until cheese is melted on top.

Catherine Walsh, Westbrook Lions Club
Westbrook, Maine, USA

GOULASH

8 oz. macaroni
4 c. water
½ c. chopped onion
½ c. chopped green pepper

1 (15 oz.) can tomatoes
1 tsp. oregano
1 lb. lean ground beef
Salt and pepper to taste

Cook macaroni in boiling water for 15 minutes. Drain. Saute onion and green pepper in oiled skillet until soft. Add beef and cook until browned. Add tomatoes. Mix with macaroni and heat through; serve.

This has been a family meal we have enjoyed since 1954.

Marvin and Bert Clifton, Dumas Noon Lions Club
Dumas, Texas, USA

BUSY DAY GOULASH

1 lb. ground beef or turkey
½ c. celery, bell pepper, onions
2 cloves garlic, chopped
Fresh mushrooms (or 1 small can)
1 can mushroom, celery or cream
   of chicken soup

1 c. chicken broth and ½ c. wine
Dash of hot sauce
1½ c. macaroni
½ c. Parmesan cheese
½ c. bread

Brown ground meat in 1 tablespoon fat; drain off fat. Place in a 2 quart casserole that has been sprayed with oil. Saute vegetables in 2 tablespoons white wine or broth. Add to meat mixture. Cook macaroni; drain and add remaining ingredients. Sprinkle bread crumbs and cheese on top. Bake 30 minutes in a 325° oven. Cube leftover bread and dry for 30 minutes in 325° oven. Bag and keep in freezer. Use for croutons, bread crumbs.

Joann Geist, Fallbrook Lioness Club
Fallbrook, California, USA

VEGETABLE CASSEROLE

2 (16 oz.) cans French cut green
  beans, drained
1 (10¾ oz.) can cream of celery
  soup (no liquid)
1 (16 oz.) can white shoe peg corn,
  drained

1 c. sharp Cheddar cheese, grated
1 small onion, chopped
1 small jar pimento, chopped and
  drained
½ c. sour cream

Topping:

1 stick margarine, melted
35 Ritz crackers, crushed

½ c. almonds, slivered

Mix green beans, soup, shoe peg corn, Cheddar cheese, grated onion, pimento, and sour cream. Now pour this mixture into a 9x13 inch Pyrex dish. Mix melted butter and crackers; cover casserole. Bake at 350° for 45 minutes.

Swallow your pride occasionally, it's non-fattening.
Leola C. Jurrens, Downtown Bartlesville Lions Club
Bartlesville, Oklahoma, USA

MEATLESS MOUSSAKA

1 eggplant (about 1¼ lb.), peeled
  and cut in ¼ inch slices
3 egg whites
1 c. cooked brown rice
2 c. lowfat cottage cheese

½ c. instant nonfat milk powder
½ c. finely chopped onion
¼ tsp. crushed or ground sage
1¾ c. marinara sauce
3 Tbsp. grated Parmesan cheese

1. Preheat oven to 375°F. (190°C.). Drop eggplant in unsalted boiling water 4 minutes. Drain on paper towels.

2. Lightly beat egg whites. Add rice, cottage cheese, milk, onion, and sage. Mix well.

3. Spread ½ cup sauce on bottom of an 11x7 inch baking dish. Alternate layers of eggplant, cottage cheese mixture, and sauce until all is used.

4. Finish with sauce and cover with cheese. Bake 30 to 40 minutes, until bubbly. Makes 5 servings.

Nutritional breakdown (per serving): 226 calories, 18 g protein, 34 g carbohydrates, 2 g fat, 500 mg sodium, and 5 mg cholesterol.
Maria Specht, President, Prince Albert Downtown Lioness Club
Prince Albert, Saskatchewan, Canada

❦

Be great in little things.

BROCCOLI-LIMA CASSEROLE

1 (10 oz.) box frozen broccoli
1 (10 oz.) box frozen lima beans
1 can mushroom soup
1 pkg. onion soup mix

1 (8 oz.) sour cream
1 stick oleo
3 c. Rice Krispies

Cook broccoli and lima beans until tender. Mix with soup, onion soup mix, and sour cream. Pour into casserole. Melt oleo and stir in Rice Krispies. Spread over casserole. Bake at 350° for 30 minutes.

Put small pat of oleo in pan of boiling potatoes so they won't boil over.
Lynette Cutler, Moweaqua Lions Club
Moweaqua, Illinois, Shelby County, USA

MOUTCHENTRA - LENTIL WITH RICE

2 c. lentils
1 c. rice
1 large onion

½ c. corn oil for frying
Salt to taste

Put lentils in a pan with water and cook until almost tender. Cooking time may vary. Add more water if necessary. When nearly cooked, strain liquid, then add back 2 cups. Add salt and rice. Cook until all liquid has been absorbed. Peel and slice onion into rings. Fry into a small pan with the corn oil and add to the lentil and rice mixture; mix well with a wooden spoon. Serve in a plate with a fried egg on top, as main meal.

Dinos Mitsides, Nicosia Within the Walls Lions Club
Nicosia, Cyprus

IMPOSSIBLE ZUCCHINI-TOMATO PIE

2 c. zucchini, chopped
1 c. fresh tomato, chopped
½ c. onion, chopped
⅓ c. Parmesan cheese, grated
1½ c. milk

¾ c. Bisquick
3 eggs
½ tsp. salt
¼ tsp. pepper

Grease 9 inch pie plate or quiche dish. Sprinkle zucchini, tomato, onion, and cheese in pan. Beat remaining ingredients in blender until smooth on high speed, about 15 seconds. Pour into pan over zucchini mixture. Bake in 400° oven until knife inserted in center comes out clean, about 30 minutes. Cool for 5 minutes before serving. Serves 6.

Lion Kyle Dickard, Royalton Hills Lions Club
North Royalton, Ohio, USA

A man is happy so long as he chooses to be happy.

GREEN CHILI CASSEROLE

1 large can whole green chiles (or more)
6 eggs, well beaten
2 Tbsp. flour

4 oz. of 3 different cheeses, grated
1 small can chopped black olives (optional)
1 bunch green onions, chopped

Layer chiles, eggs and flour mixture, and cheeses. Sprinkle top with onions and olives. Bake until eggs set or about 30 to 45 minutes at 350°.

Jack and Ruth Graham, Lyman Lions Club
Lyman, Wyoming, USA

KASH VARNISHKAS

¼ lb. farfelle pasta
2 Tbsp. butter
1 medium onion, chopped
1 stalk celery, chopped
1 egg

½ c. medium buckwheat groats
1 c. chicken broth
½ tsp. salt
¼ tsp. pepper

1. In large pot of boiling salted water, cook the pasta. Drain and set aside.
2. In a frying pan over medium heat, melt butter. Add onion and celery; cook until soft, about 5 minutes. Raise heat to high.
3. Beat egg. Add groats to pan and stir to mix. Add egg and stir constantly about 2 minutes to coat groats and vegetables. Work quickly to blend egg into mixture and avoid having raw egg come in contact with pan.
4. Add the chicken broth, salt, and pepper. Cover pan and reduce heat to low. Cook mixture until stock has evaporated and groats are fluffy, 3 to 5 minutes.
5. In a large bowl, combine pasta with the buckwheat mixture and toss gently to blend. Makes 4 servings.

John J. Hess for Mrs. Joanne Brownell, Clarence Center Lions Club
Clarence Center, New York, USA

ZUCCHINI CASSEROLE

4 lb. zucchini (about 3 good size)
¼ c. melted butter or margarine
1 small onion
2 c. grated Cheddar cheese
1 tsp. paprika

8 soda crackers, crushed (large squares)
1 c. sour cream
Salt and pepper

Boil zucchini until tender, whole. Cool. Split lengthwise and scoop out the center of each. Place the shells in a shallow baking dish which has been buttered. Combine the remaining ingredients in a bowl and fill the shells with this combination. Bake for 25 minutes at 350°.

Ellen Ostrand, Lady Lions of Rohnert Park Lions Club
Rohnert Park, California, USA

BARBECUED SAUERKRAUT

1 large can sauerkraut
2 c. tomato juice or tomatoes

1 c. brown sugar
1 lb. ground chuck (beef)

Drain sauerkraut well. Do not rinse. Brown ground beef with a little onion, salt, pepper, garlic powder, and Worcestershire sauce. Combine all ingredients in casserole and bake 1 hour at 350°. Spaghetti sauce may also be used as well.

Donna S. Reitz, Sykesville Lions Club
Sykesville, Pennsylvania, USA

UNSTUFFED CABBAGE ROLLS

2 Tbsp. margarine or butter
1¼ c. uncooked rice
1 head cabbage, shredded
1½ lb. uncooked ground beef

2 (14 oz.) cans crushed tomatoes
   or 2½ c. fresh stewed
   tomatoes

Melt margarine in 3 to 5 quart casserole. Layer uncooked cabbage followed by uncooked rice, then uncooked ground beef, crumbled. Pour tomatoes on top. Cover with lid or foil and bake 60 minutes in a 375° oven. Do not uncover while cooking. Quick and easy. Ten minute preparation time. Serves 6 to 8.

Cynthia Dowd, Chesterfield Bay Lions Club
Chesterfield, Michigan, USA

❦

The world is round and the place which may seem like the end may also be the beginning.

❧ ❧ ❧

If you treat every situation as a life-and-death matter, you will die many times.

POLISH STUFFED CABBAGE - GOLABKI

1 (3 lb.) head green cabbage
¼ c. butter or margarine
1 small onion, chopped
1 lb. lean ground beef
1½ lb. lean ground pork
1½ c. cooked long grain white rice

1 tsp. salt
¼ tsp. freshly ground black
   pepper
3½ c. beef broth (bouillon broth)
1 (6 oz.) can tomato paste
2 Tbsp. all-purpose flour

With a sharp knife, remove core from cabbage. Carefully remove wilted or decayed outer cabbage leaves; discard. In a large saucepan, boil enough salted water to cover cabbage. Immerse cabbage in boiling water. Cook over medium high heat for 5 to 7 minutes. With fork or tongs, gently remove leaves as they become tender. Drain well. Let cool.

Preheat oven to 325°F. (165°C.). Trim main leaf stems. Melt 1 tablespoon butter or margarine in a small skillet. Add onion; saute over medium heat until golden brown.

In a large bowl, combine sauteed onion, beef, pork, rice, salt, and pepper. Spread a cabbage leaf flat. Depending on leaf size, place 2 tablespoons filling on cabbage leaf near base. Fold bottom of leaf over filling, then fold sides toward center. Roll tightly. Repeat with remaining filling and cabbage leaves.

Heat 1 tablespoon butter or margarine in a large skillet. Place filled cabbage leaves, seam down, in skillet. Cook over medium heat until browned, 8 to 10 minutes, turning once with a spatula. Arrange cabbage rolls, seam side down, in a medium roasting pan. Add 3 cups broth or bouillon.

In a small bowl, combine ½ cup broth or bouillon and tomato paste. Pour over stuffed cabbage. Cover and bake for 40 minutes or until fork tender. In a small skillet, melt remaining 2 tablespoons butter or margarine. Stir flour into butter or margarine until smooth. Cook over medium heat, stirring, until golden brown. Ladle 1 cup broth or bouillon from stuffed cabbage into flour mixture; blend. Pour mixture over stuffed cabbage. Cook, uncovered, until liquid bubbles and thickens slightly. Place stuffed cabbage on a large platter. Pour pan juices into a serving bowl. Serve hot with pan juices. Makes 10 to 12 servings.

We do not remember days, we remember moments.

MEXICAN CABBAGE

1 lb. hamburger meat
2 c. water
1½ c. tomatoes
1 small onion, cut up
2 cloves garlic

1 pod hot pepper, cut up
½ tsp. coarse ground pepper
1 medium size head cabbage, cut up
Salt to taste

Brown meat in skillet and put in saucepan, then add rest of ingredients. Cover and simmer for about 30 to 45 minutes. Take the lid off and boil for awhile to cook down.

This is good for those on a diet. My kids like it with corn bread or Mexican corn bread.

Faye Blount, Levelland Lioness Club
Levelland, Texas, USA

CABBAGE AND BEEF CASSEROLE

1 lb. ground beef
1 c. chopped onion
1 medium head cabbage
½ c. uncooked rice
1 large can tomato soup

1 can water
2 Tbsp. sugar
1 Tbsp. vinegar
Salt to taste

Brown beef with onion until beef loses its red color and onion is transparent. When beef is brown, stir in raw rice. While beef is cooking, shred cabbage more coarsely than for slaw. Place in a greased baking dish or shallow casserole. Place beef mixture in a layer over the cabbage. Mix soup, water, sugar, and vinegar together. Pour over beef and cabbage layers. Cover with lid or foil. Bake at 350° for 1 hour.

HAMBURGER CABBAGE CASSEROLE

1 large head cabbage
1 lb. lean ground beef
1 large onion

2 cans Campbell's cream of
tomato soup
1 stick butter

Take 2 tablespoons of butter to grease a large roasting pan with cover. Cut cabbage in half and then in half again. Core and discard core. Chop cabbage coarsely and place in roasting pan. Saute hamburger and chopped onion in rest of butter until red is out of the hamburger. Put hamburger and onion on top of the cabbage in pan. Pour 2 cans of undiluted soup over all ingredients. Put lid on and bake at 350° for about a half hour. Stir and continue baking and stirring every 20 minutes until cabbage is soft, about 2 hours. Salt and pepper to taste.

Gennie Leiser, Plainfield Township Lions Club
Nazareth, Pennsylvania, USA

TATER TOPPED CASSEROLE

1 lb. ground beef
½ c. onions
Salt and pepper

1 can condensed cream of celery
    soup
Tater tots

Preheat oven to 400°. Grease a shallow 2 quart baking dish. Brown ground beef and onions in a skillet over medium heat. Spoon off fat. Salt and pepper to taste. Spread mixture in baking dish; pour soup over everything. Top with a layer of tater tots. Bake 45 minutes or until bubbly. Serves 5.

TATER TOTS CASSEROLE

1 lb. ground beef
1 can cream of celery or
    mushroom soup
1 small onion, chopped
⅔ can water in the soup can

Salt and pepper to taste
1 bag mixed frozen vegetables
American cheese
1 small bag tater tots

Brown ground beef and onion; drain off grease. Steam frozen vegetables until almost done. Drain off water. Add salt and pepper to taste. Mix ground beef and vegetables with 1 can of soup and ⅔ can of water; pour this mixture into baking dish. Cover with grated American cheese and top with tater tots. Bake at 350° for 1 hour.

TATER TOT CASSEROLE

2½ lb. lean ground beef
1 pkg. dry onion soup mix
1 can peas, drained

2 cans mushroom soup
    (undiluted)
1 pkg. tater tots

Press ground beef into cake pan. Layer remaining ingredients. Bake in a 350° oven for 1 hour or until done.

Valerie Borecky, Lyman Lions Club
Lyman, Wyoming, USA

❦

Friendships will last if they are put first.

TATER-TOPPED CHILI BEEF

1 lb. ground beef
1 medium onion, chopped
2 Tbsp. fat or oil
2 to 3 Tbsp. chili powder
1 can corn, drained

1 can condensed tomato soup
1 lb. frozen French fries
1 c. (4 oz.) shredded process
  cheese

Brown beef and onions in fat. Mix in chili powder. Add corn. Stir in soup. Spoon beef mixture into large shallow baking dish. Put frozen French fries on top. Bake at 400° for 10 minutes. Sprinkle cheese over potatoes and bake 10 minutes longer.

Can fix this the day before, then add potatoes and cook.

Dorothy V. Wipreed, Bothell Lions Club
Bothell, Washington, USA

FRANKFURTER SCALLOP

4 large potatoes, sliced
1 tsp. salt
¼ tsp. pepper
½ lb. wieners, sliced
½ c. grated Cheddar cheese
2 medium onions, sliced

⅓ c. celery leaves
⅓ c. minced parsley
2 large tomatoes, sliced
½ can (or more) mushroom soup
1 small can mushrooms (stems
  and pieces)

In a large skillet, put a layer of potatoes, seasoned with salt and pepper. Add wiener layer and sprinkle with grated cheese. Next, put the layer of onions and sprinkle on the celery and parsley leaves. Now, add the layer of sliced tomatoes and drop by teaspoonfuls the mushroom soup over top. Lastly, add mushrooms and a little more parsley if desired. Cover pan with lid and bake slowly at 300° to 325° for 1 hour or until potatoes are tender. Serves 6.

IMPOSSIBLE CHEESEBURGER PIE

1 lb. ground beef
1½ c. chopped onion
½ tsp. salt
¼ tsp. pepper

1 c. shredded Cheddar cheese
1½ c. milk
¾ c. Bisquick
3 eggs

Note: For 9 inch pie, decrease milk to 1 cup, Bisquick to ½ cup, and 1 egg.

Heat oven to 400°. Lightly grease 10 inch pie plate. Cook and stir the beef and onion until brown. Drain. Add salt and pepper. Spread beef mixture in plate. Sprinkle with cheese. Beat rest of ingredients until smooth. Pour into pie plate and bake about 30 minutes until golden brown. Let stand for 5 minutes.

Warren Gilman, Westbrook Lions Club
Westbrook, Maine, USA

MOUSSAKA

1 lb. lean ground beef	½ tsp. oregano
1 medium onion, chopped	½ tsp. rosemary
1 large eggplant, peeled and cubed	¼ tsp. cinnamon
1 (8 oz.) can tomatoes, cut up	¼ tsp. salt
1 can mushrooms, drained	¼ tsp. pepper
¼ c. chopped parsley	2 eggs
1 clove garlic, minced	1 (8 oz.) Neufchatel cheese
	1 c. plain yogurt

In skillet, cook beef and onion until brown. Drain. Stir in vegetables, mushrooms, herbs, and seasoning. Cook, uncovered, for 15 minutes, stirring occasionally. Turn in rectangular baking dish. Use electric mixer to blend eggs, cheese, yogurt, and dash of salt until smooth. Pour over meat. Bake at 350° for 15 to 20 minutes. Serves 8.

HAMBURGER PIE

1 lb. hamburger meat	1 can whole kernel corn
1 can tomato soup	1 onion, cut up
1 can tomato sauce	1 c. cheese
1 can green beans	

Brown hamburger, meat, and onion. Drain. Add tomato soup and sauce. Drain green beans and drain corn. Cream potatoes. Put mixture in long pan. Top with mashed potatoes and cheese. Bake until cheese melts.

Nancy Dean, Stamps Lions Club
Stamps, Arkansas, USA

Laugh a lot and when you are older,
all your wrinkles will be in the right places!

COUNTRY COTTAGE CASSEROLE

1 lb. ground beef (lean)
1 (16 oz.) can Veg-All (mixed
    vegetables)
1 pkg. frozen crescent rolls
1 Tbsp. dried minced onions
½ tsp. salt
¼ tsp. seasoned pepper

¼ tsp. ground nutmeg
2 Tbsp. cornstarch
Reserved liquid from the canned
    vegetables
4 slices Velveeta cheese, cut into
    8 triangles

Brown ground meat in a frying pan. Season with the salt, minced onion, seasoned pepper, and nutmeg. Drain liquid from the Veg-All. Stir Veg-All into meat. Stir the cornstarch in the reserved liquid. Add to meat mixture and stir until thickened.

Preheat oven to 375°F. Line a lightly greased 7x11 inch baking pan with the crescent rolls. Overlap edges to form a crust up the sides of the pan. Pour meat mixture into the crust. Spread evenly. Bake for 10 minutes. Cut Velveeta into thin triangles. Lay over top to form a nice pattern. Bake for an additional 5 minutes or till crust is browned.

DYNAMITE

3 large onions
1 bunch celery
3 large green peppers
¼ lb. butter
1 hot cherry pepper

1 lb. ground beef
Salt and pepper
1 large can crushed tomatoes
1 can tomato sauce

Cut all vegetables in small pieces. Cook celery until soft in water to cover. Add balance of vegetables. Cook slowly until tender. Add large can crushed tomatoes and 1 can tomato sauce; let simmer for 15 minutes. Brown hamburger in separate skillet. Add to vegetable mixture. Refrigerate overnight. Heat and serve on hot dog roll (steamed). Salt and pepper to taste. Crushed cherry pepper is optional (I like it hot).

Newt Curtis, Westbrook Lions Club
Westbrook, Maine, USA

❧

A man is not old until regrets take the place of dreams.

HAMBURGER CASSEROLE

1¼ lb. ground beef
½ c. chopped onion
¼ c. green pepper, chopped
2 tsp. chilli powder
½ tsp. garlic salt

1 c. tomato sauce
½ c. sour cream
1 egg, beaten
1½ c. shredded Cheddar cheese
1 can refrigerator biscuits

Brown beef and add next 5 ingredients. Mix sour cream, egg, and ½ of the cheese in a small bowl. Mix beef mixture and sour cream mixture together. Arrange ½ biscuits in bottom of greased 8x8x2 inch pan (flatten biscuits a little). Pour beef mixture over biscuits and top with remaining biscuits; top with cheese. Bake at 375° for 25 to 30 minutes. I use a slightly larger pan than is called for so as not to run over in the oven.

Ruth Wright, Moweaqua Lions Club
Moweaqua, Illinois, USA

IMPOSSIBLE BLT PIE

Heat oven to 400°.

12 slices bacon, crisply cooked
    and crumbled
1 c. shredded Swiss cheese (4 oz.)
1½ c. milk
½ c. mayonnaise or salad
    dressing

4 eggs
1 c. Bisquick baking mix
⅛ tsp. salt
⅛ tsp. pepper
Coarsely shredded lettuce
Thinly sliced tomatoes

Grease pie plate, 10 x 1½ inches. Layer bacon and cheese in plate. Beat remaining ingredients, except lettuce and tomatoes, until smooth, 15 seconds in blender on high or 1 minute with hand beater. Pour into plate. Bake until top is golden brown and knife inserted in center comes out clean, 30 to 35 minutes. Cool 5 minutes.

Garnish with lettuce and tomatoes, and if desired, crisply cooked and crumbled bacon and mayonnaise or salad dressing. Makes 6 servings.

🌱

Time has a wonderful way of showing us what really matters.

CHEESEBURGER PIE

1 lb. ground beef
½ c. evaporated milk
½ c. ketchup
⅓ c. fine dry bread crumbs
¾ tsp. salt
¼ c. chopped onion
½ tsp. oregano

⅛ tsp. pepper
1 (9 or 10 inch) unbaked pastry
  shell
4 oz. process American cheese,
  shredded
1 tsp. Worcestershire sauce

Combine beef, milk, ketchup, bread crumbs, onion, salt, pepper, and oregano. Mix thoroughly. Spread in the unbaked pastry shell. Bake in a 350° oven for 35 to 40 minutes. Toss together cheese and Worcestershire sauce; spread atop the meat. Bake for 10 minutes more. Remove from oven and let stand for 10 minutes before serving.

Ursula J. Harrington, Westbrook Lions Club
Westbrook, Maine, USA

CHILI SQUARES

½ c. flour
1 tsp. baking powder
½ tsp. salt
10 eggs, beaten
¼ c. margarine, melted
2 c. small curd cottage cheese

1 lb. shredded cheese (Cheddar
  and Mozzarella)
1 small can green chili peppers,
  chopped
1 lb. sausage, crumbled and fried
  (I use hot and extra sage)

Crumble sausage and brown in skillet; drain grease. Combine first 3 ingredients, then mix with eggs. Mix margarine, cheeses, green chilies, and sausage. Pour into a 9x13 inch pan and bake at 400° for 15 minutes, then reduce to 350° for 30 to 40 minutes or until golden brown.

This is very good for a brunch, breakfast or supper on a cold winter day. I got this recipe at Spring Fling '91 at the Texas 4-H Center in Brownwood - they served it to about 200 hungry campers.

Frances Cantrell, Bowie Evening Lions Club
Bowie, Texas, USA

❦

It's a big thing to do a little thing well.

ONE DISH CONNELLY RECIPE

From the Denver Post, Friday, October 2, 1953.

1 lb. lean ground beef (uncooked - ground turkey can be used)
½ finely cut green pepper
1½ c. green beans
½ c. sliced carrots
1 can tomato soup or 1 can cream of chicken soup (not both)

½ tsp. salt
Few grains of pepper
Finely diced onion (optional)
½ c. grated cheese

Use a casserole. Arrange the ingredients in layers and cover with soup. Sprinkle with cheese and bake at 350°F. for ¾ to 1 hour. When serving hot, add more cheese.

P.S. Any leftover meat and other vegetables may be substituted. (Mrs. Ila Mae Hobson, Homemaking Co-ordinator at Opportunity School, Denver, Colorado, first gave the recipe at a late afternoon meeting in 1948. Mr. Connelly liked it so well that he has eaten it approximately 2,500 times in 5 years.) You can use fresh vegetables or canned.

Lion Kathleen Schatz Dague, Aurora Eastgate Lions Club
Aurora, Colorado, USA

HAMBURGER DRESSING HOT DISH

1½ lb. hamburger
1 small onion
1 box croutons
1 tsp. pepper
1½ c. diced celery

½ c. diced onion
1 can cream of celery soup
1 can cream of mushroom soup
1 can evaporated milk

Mix together hamburger, small diced onion, and pepper. Pat into a 9x12 inch pan. Layer on top the celery, croutons, and onions. Mix together in blender the cream of celery, chicken, and mushroom soups. Add evaporated milk and blend. Pour over hamburger mixture. Bake at 375°F. for about 1½ hours. Makes 8 to 10 servings.

ONE POT DINNER

½ to 1 lb. ground beef
¾ lb. bacon, cut in small pieces
1 c. chopped onion
2 (1 lb. 15 oz.) cans pork and beans
1 (1 lb.) can kidney beans, drained
1 (1 lb.) can lima beans, drained

1 c. ketchup
¼ c. brown sugar
3 Tbsp. white vinegar
1 Tbsp. liquid smoke
Salt
Pepper

Brown ground beef in skillet; drain off fat and put beef in crock pot. Brown bacon and onion; drain off fat. Add bacon, onion, and remaining ingredients to crock pot. Stir together well. Cover and cook on LOW for 4 to 9 hours.

CALICO BEANS AND-OR CORN

1 lb. ground beef
½ c. catsup
¾ c. brown sugar
1 tsp. dry mustard
2 Tbsp. vinegar

1 tsp. salt
1 can pork and beans
1 can red kidney beans
1 can green beans
1 can lima beans or 1 can corn

Brown and drain fat from ground beef, discarding fat. Add next 5 ingredients and mix. Add pork and beans. Drain and add ingredients from the next 3 cans. Bake 40 minutes at 350°.

Lion Howard Stringham, North Jackson Lions Club
Jackson, Michigan, USA

HAMBURGER AND BEAN CASSEROLE

1 lb. hamburger
1 small onion, chopped
1 large green pepper, chopped
3 large celery stalks, chopped
3 tsp. Worcestershire sauce
½ tsp. salt
¼ tsp. pepper
½ c. ketchup

2 tsp. mustard
¾ c. brown sugar
¼ c. molasses
1 tsp. lemon juice
Garlic (if you wish)
2 large cans pork and beans,
    drained

Saute hamburger, onion, green pepper, and celery stalks. Drain off grease. Add remaining ingredients and simmer. Heat thoroughly. Bake 1½ hours at 350°. Tastes better prepared the day before serving (bake the next day).

Mrs. Rich (Doris) Hall, Elburn Lions Club
Elburn, Illinois, USA

BEEF AND BEAN BARBEQUE

½ c. celery
¼ c. green pepper
½ c. brown sugar
½ c. vinegar
1 (No. 2½) can pork and beans

1 small can tomato sauce
1 small can water
1 Tbsp. thyme
1 Tbsp. dry mustard
2 tsp. garlic powder

Brown 1 pound of hamburger. Add other ingredients and cook 10 minutes. Place beans in casserole dish. Pour topping over beans. Bake at 375° for 45 to 55 minutes.

Donna J. Boyer, Reno Plumb Lane Lions Club
Reno, Nevada, USA

Make the most of the best and the least of the worst.

FRENCH CANADIAN TOURTIERE

1 lb. ground beef and pork, mixed
2 onions (medium)

4 potatoes
Pie crust for 2 crust pie

Stir and cook meat and 1 onion, chopped, for about 1 hour in large kettle. Salt and pepper while cooking. Boil potatoes and 1 onion separately. When cooked, add to meat mixture after draining and mash together with hand masher until smooth. Salt and pepper to taste. Add ½ teaspoon cinnamon and ¼ teaspoon ground clove (more or less). Place in pie crust and cover with top crust. Bake at 425° for 10 minutes and at 350° for 30 minutes until golden brown. Swish milk on top crust before baking.

Grace P. Curtis, Westbrook Lions Club
Westbrook, Maine, USA

GROUND BEEF-VEGETABLE CASSEROLE

2 lb. ground chuck
3 or 4 large potatoes, sliced
5 carrots, sliced
2 large onions, sliced

1 can peas (reserve juice)
1 can tomato soup
Salt and pepper

Brown meat just so all red color is gone. Drain. Spray 2 quart baking dish with Pam. Layer vegetables in baking dish with potatoes, then carrots, onions, and salt and pepper to taste. Add peas, then ground beef. Mix reserved juice from peas with soup and pour over meat. Cover with foil and bake at 350° for 1½ hours or until potatoes and carrots are done.

Variation by E. Krist: May use one 10 ounce package frozen peas. Add ½ cup water to tomato soup.

HAMBURGER AND POTATO CASSEROLE

1 lb. ground beef
4 c. thinly sliced potatoes
1 (10½ oz.) can vegetable beef
soup

½ tsp. salt
1 (3 oz.) can French fried onion
rings

Crumble ground beef in a 12x8 inch glass baking dish. Microwave at HIGH 4 to 6 minutes or until meat loses most of its pink color. Break up and drain. Stir in sliced potatoes, soup, and salt. Cover with plastic wrap. Microwave on HIGH 14 to 18 minutes, or until potatoes are tender. Stir halfway through cooking time. Stir mixture. Sprinkle onion rings on top. Microwave, uncovered, at HIGH for 1½ to 3 minutes or until heated through. Serves 4 to 6.

"Good and easy."

P.D.G. Paul E. Peck, Rootstown Lions Club
Rootstown Township, Rootstown, Ohio, USA

CORNISH PASTIES

Crust mixture for 4 pasties:

4 c. flour
1⅓ c. Crisco

1½ tsp. salt
½ c. plus 2 Tbsp. ice water

Filling for 4 pasties:

4 large potatoes, peeled and thinly sliced (chipped) ⅛ inch thick and ½ inch square
1¾ lb. stew meat, cut in thin slices

Onions to make 8 heaping Tbsp. sliced thin
Veggie to make 8 tsp., sliced thin
4 tsp. butter

Mix crust mixture as for pie crust, cutting in the shortening and adding ice water all at once. Stir with fork to form a ball. Divide in 4 pieces. Roll each ball in a 9 inch circle. On ½ of pastry, put 1 cup chipped potatoes, ½ cup meat packed down and rounded top, 2 heaping tablespoons onion, 2 teaspoons veggie, salt and pepper to taste, and 1 teaspoon butter. Fold remainder of dough over this mixture and crimp together to close. Brush a little milk on each pastie to give a nice brown color to crust. Put on a cookie sheet and bake 1 hour in a 400° oven. Serve with a cabbage salad and rice pudding for dessert.

When the men worked in the mines, this was a favorite - they had their meat/ potatoes and vegetables all wrapped up in a crust. They held them in their hands to eat.

Russell E. Larson, Hurley Lions Club
Hurley, Wisconsin, USA

FINNISH PASTY

Prepare pie crust for 10 inch pie. Roll pie crust dough into 1 large circle to enable dough to fold over to middle of pie.

Before folding, fill crust with alternating layers of the following:

1 to 2 lb. hamburger (raw)
1 small onion, chopped
3 medium potatoes, sliced in medium chunks

1 can diced rutabagas (or you may prepare fresh rutabaga - use juice)
Cabbage (optional)

Fold edges of crust towards middle of pie. Bake at 350° for 1 to 1½ hours or until crust is brown. Serve with catsup.

This is an old family recipe which is loved by children and adults alike.

Janice Hinds, North Maplewood Lioness Club
Maplewood, Minnesota, Ramsey County, USA

You can become the person you want to be.

HUNGRY JACK CASSEROLE

1 lb. ground beef
1 tsp. salt
¾ c. bbq sauce
2 Tbsp. brown sugar

1 Tbsp. instant onion
1 can Hungry Jack biscuits
1 c. shredded cheese
1 (16 oz.) can pork and beans

Brown beef and drain; stir in salt, bbq sauce, pork and beans, brown sugar, and onion. Reheat above and pour in casserole dish. Cut biscuits in halves and place, cut side down, over mixture. Sprinkle cheese over top. Bake 25 minutes at 350° or until brown on top.

Pat Lamb, Moweaqua Lions Club
Moweaqua, Illinois, USA

VERY HOT BANGERS AND MASH

4 large potatoes
6 hot Italian sausage (about 6
   inches long each)
1 large purple onion
6 cloves garlic

20 slices jalapeno peppers
2 Tbsp. finely ground cayenne
   pepper
1 orange

Boil 4 large potatoes until soft. Take off skins; mash and sprinkle with salt and pepper to taste. You may add butter and milk if you desire. Cook the hot Italian sausage either by frying in a pan or baking as you like. Cut the purple onion into small pieces and set aside for late in the process. Peel the orange and discard the inside. Keep the peel. Cut the peel into narrow strips about 4 inches long. Peel the garlic and chop fine. Spread the mashed potatoes on a serving dish. Mix onion and garlic; spread over the potatoes. Arrange 4 sausages around the outside of the serving plate. Cut two sausages in half and take these four sections and make a cross in the middle of the plate. Arrange the orange peels in half moon shapes. Put a slice of jalapeno peppers just under the orange slice. Sprinkle the cayenne pepper over the entire area. Serve water, ice tea, or cold beer.

William J. Eakin, Reno Plumb Lane Lions Club
Reno, Nevada, USA

You have to face the music before you can lead the band.

MEATBALL CASSEROLE

1 lb. hamburger
1 onion, diced
1 clove garlic, pressed
2 slices bread, shredded

4 large potatoes
1 can corn
8 oz. sour cream

Mix hamburger, onion, garlic, and bread thoroughly. Form into meatballs and brown. Peel potatoes and cut into strips. Parboil potatoes. In a casserole dish, put meatballs, potatoes, and corn. In skillet, mix grease from meatballs, corn juice, and potato juice. Add sour cream. After sour cream is dissolved, add flour to thicken. Pour mixture over meat and vegetables. Bake at 350° for 30 minutes.

This is one of my husband's favorite meals. It reheats great too!

Faith Spivey, Manteno Lions Club
Manteno, Illinois, USA

SOUPER MEAT 'N POTATOES PIE

1 can cream of mushroom soup
1 lb. ground beef
¼ c. finely chopped onion
1 egg, slightly beaten
¼ c. fine dry bread crumbs
2 Tbsp. chopped parsley

¼ tsp. salt
Dash of pepper
2 c. mashed potatoes
¼ c. shredded mild or sharp
   cheese

Mix thoroughly ½ cup soup, beef, onion, egg, bread crumbs, parsley, and seasonings. Press firmly into 9 inch pie plate. Bake at 350° for 30 minutes; spoon off fat. Frost with potatoes. Top with remaining soup and cheese. Bake 10 minutes more or until done. Garnish with cooked sliced bacon if desired. Makes one 9 inch meat pie. I always use instant potatoes; nice short cut after a long day at the office.

Janice Baynard, Dolley Madison Lions Club
Greensboro, North Carolina, USA

NUTTY NOODLE CASSEROLE

6 oz. pkg. noodles
1½ lb. ground beef
1 Tbsp. Worcestershire sauce
⅛ tsp. garlic powder
Thyme to taste

2 Tbsp. minced onion
½ c. sliced green olives
1 can mushroom soup
½ lb. grated American or Cheddar
   cheese

Boil noodles. Brown meat. Add olives, seasonings, onion, and sour milk, then blend. Drain noodles. Add to meat. Put layer of mixture in 1½ quart casserole. Add layer of cheese, then meat, etc. Bake at 350° for 30 minutes.

Claire Perry, Westbrook Lions Club
Westbrook, Maine, USA

WATSON GOULASH

1 lb. lean ground beef
1 onion, chopped
1 clove garlic, minced
1 lb. cooked elbow macaroni
1 can tomato soup
1 (4 oz.) can tomato sauce

1 (4 oz.) can mushroom pieces
1 can whole kernel corn, drained
1 can peas, drained
1 lb. Cheddar cheese, shredded
1 tsp. chili powder
Salt and pepper to taste

Saute ground beef, garlic, and onions; drain excess grease. Mix all ingredients. Place in ovenproof casserole dish. Bake at 350° for approximately 35 minutes or until hot. Serves 12 very hungry people.

Hint: Refrigeration for a few hours or overnight enhances flavor.

My family calls this "Watson Goulash" but a relative obtained the recipe from a U.S.O. volunteer during World War II.

Lion Pat Ballard, Milpitas Host Lions Club
Milpitas, California, USA

HAMBURGER NOODLE CASSEROLE

9 oz. pkg. noodles
1 lb. ground beef
1 can cream of mushroom soup

1 can chicken rice soup
Bread crumbs

Cook and drain noodles according to package directions. Saute ground beef. Combine cooked noodles, ground beef, and soups. Mix and pour into a buttered baking dish. Sprinkle with bread crumbs. Bake 30 minutes. Serves 6 to 8 people. Serve with hot garlic bread, tossed salad, and light dessert. I often do this in my electric skillet, omitting bread crumbs and not baking at all if I'm in a hurry or unexpected company arrives.

Delia P. Krueger, Emporia Sundowners Lions Club
Emporia, Kansas, USA

HAMBURGER AND MACARONI CASSEROLE

2 c. macaroni
1 lb. ground beef
1 (10 oz.) can tomato soup
1 (10 oz.) can cream of mushroom
  soup

1 medium green pepper, diced
¼ c. chopped pimiento (optional)
2 c. cubed Colby cheese
1 can French fried onions

Prepare macaroni according to package directions. Drain. Brown ground beef; drain. Add soups, green pepper, pimiento, and cooked macaroni. Place half the mixture in a greased 2½ quart casserole. Sprinkle with half the cheese and half the onions, then add the remaining meat and macaroni mixture. Top with remaining cheese. Bake at 350° for 25 minutes. Top with remaining onions and bake 5 minutes longer.

Mrs. Mike (Shirley) Stoffa, Elburn Lions Club
Elburn, Illinois, USA

MARZETTI

1½ lb. ground beef
½ lb. ground pork
1 lb. onion, chopped
2 bell peppers, chopped
1 stalk celery, chopped
½ tsp. chili powder

2 cans tomato sauce
1 can tomato soup
1 can mushroom soup
Sliced cheese
3 pkg. wide noodles

Cook meat, onions, pepper, and celery in about 3 tablespoons of bacon fat. Cook noodles according to directions. Mix all ingredients with noodles (add ½ cup chopped black olives and ½ cup chopped mushrooms if desired). After everything is mixed, pour in baking dish and cover with sliced cheese. Bake 1 hour in 350° oven. Serves 14.

It is easy to have a balanced personality. Just forget your troubles as easily as you forget your blessings.

Carole Choate, Rock Hill Lions Club
Rock Hill, South Carolina, USA

BEEF STROGANOFF AND RICE CASSEROLE

Beef Stroganoff:

3 lb. sirloin tip steak strips or
  cubes
2 cans cream of mushroom soup

1 env. Lipton onion soup
¾ c. sherry

Bake for 1½ hours at 350° covered and 1½ hours uncovered. Last hour of baking, add 4 ounce jar of mushrooms. Just before serving, add ½ pint sour cream. Serve over rice or noodles.

Rice Casserole:

1 (14 oz.) pkg. Minute rice
1 Tbsp. salt

½ c. butter
5½ c. boiling water

Put rice in casserole with butter, cut in pieces. Add salt. Pour boiling water over. Cover and bake at 450° for 20 minutes.

Better than counting your years is making all your years count.

VEGETABLES WITH BEEF OVER RICE

1 lb. extra lean ground beef
1½ c. chopped green bell pepper
2 yellow Hungarian hot peppers,
  diced
1 c. chopped onion
5 c. chopped fully ripe tomatoes

2 c. okra, cut in ½ inch pieces
½ tsp. salt
¼ tsp. freshly ground black
  pepper
6 c. cooked rice
Freshly grated Parmesan cheese

Brown the beef in a preheated 10 inch iron skillet. Remove the beef from skillet and set aside. Add oil, peppers, and onions; saute until just tender. Add okra, salt, and black pepper; saute 10 minutes. Add tomatoes and simmer, stirring frequently until tomatoes cook down slightly, about 20 minutes. *(Do not overcook.)* Moments before serving, stir the beef into the vegetables and ladle over bowls of hot rice. Sprinkle generously with the grated cheese. Serves 6. If possible, use home grown, straight from the garden, vegetables. Fresh or sourdough bread goes well with this entree.

Jerald V. Parsell, Sr., Sec., MJF, Alexandria Evening Lions Club
Alexandria, Virginia, USA

HAMBURGER AND MINUTE RICE CASSEROLE

1 c. Minute rice
1½ to 2 lb. lean hamburger,
  browned and drained

1 can cream of mushroom soup
1 can stewed tomatoes
Dash of salt

Mix all these ingredients together and put into greased casserole. Cover top with grated cheese. Bake in 350° oven for 20 to 30 minutes.

This was my mother's recipe. It's easy and fast - just add a salad.
Glen Cox, Lyon Noon Lions Club
Emporia, Kansas, Lyon County, USA

❦

It is better to have thirty minutes of wonderful
than a lifetime of nothing special.

BURGER CASSEROLE

1 (8 oz.) pkg. noodles, cooked in salted water

1 lb. ground beef, browned
2 Tbsp. butter

Add:

2 (8 oz.) cans tomato sauce
1 tsp. salt

1 Tbsp. Worcestershire sauce

Combine:

1 c. cottage cheese
¼ c. sour cream
1 (8 oz.) pkg. cream cheese

¼ c. onion or onion flakes
2 Tbsp. green pepper, chopped

Use 2½ quart casserole, greased with butter. Spread ½ of noodles in casserole. Cover with cheese mixture, then remaining noodles. Pour 2 tablespoons melted butter over noodles. Cover with meat sauce. Garnish with parsley flakes. Bake at 350° for 35 to 40 minutes. Serve hot with salad and rolls for a complete meal. Serves 6 to 8.

❣

Learn from the mistakes of others.
You don't have enough time to make them all yourself!

❣ ❣ ❣

The problem with owning your own home
is that no matter where you sit,
you see something you should be doing.

❣ ❣ ❣

A bad habit never disappears miraculously;
it's an undo-it-yourself project.

Breads

EQUIVALENT CHART

3 tsp..................................1 Tbsp.	¼ lb. crumbled Bleu cheese....................1 c.
2 Tbsp...................................⅛ c.	1 lemon......................... 3 Tbsp. juice
4 Tbsp...................................¼ c.	1 orange........................⅓ c. juice
8 Tbsp...................................½ c.	1 lb. unshelled walnuts.... 1½ to 1¾ c. shelled
16 Tbsp..................................1 c.	2 c. fat.................................1 lb.
5 Tbsp. + 1 tsp.........................⅓ c.	1 lb. butter.................. 2 c. or 4 sticks
12 Tbsp..................................¾ c.	2 c. granulated sugar....................1 lb.
4 oz......................................½ c.	3½-4 c. unsifted powdered sugar.............1 lb.
8 oz......................................1 c.	2¼ c. packed brown sugar.................1 lb.
16 oz....................................1 lb.	4 c. sifted flour........................1 lb.
1 oz.....................2 Tbsp. fat or liquid	4½ c. cake flour........................1 lb.
2 c...................................... 1 pt.	3½ c. unsifted whole wheat flour............1 lb.
2 pt...................................... 1 qt.	4 oz. (1 to 1¼ c.) uncooked
1 qt.......................................4 c.	macaroni................... 2¼ c. cooked
⅝ c. ....½ c. + 2 Tbsp.	7 oz. spaghetti................ 4 c. cooked
⅞ c. ....¾ c. + 2 Tbsp.	4 oz. (1½ to 2 c.) uncooked
1 jigger.......................1½ fl. oz. (3 Tbsp.)	noodles................... 2 c. cooked
8 to 10 egg whites.......................1 c.	28 saltine crackers....................... 1 c. crumbs
12 to 14 egg yolks.......................1 c.	4 slices bread........................ 1 c. crumbs
1 c. unwhipped cream.................2 c. whipped	14 square graham crackers.......... 1 c. crumbs
1 lb. shredded American cheese...............4 c.	22 vanilla wafers .... 1 c. crumbs

SUBSTITUTIONS FOR A MISSING INGREDIENT

1 square **chocolate** (1 ounce) = 3 or 4 tablespoons cocoa plus ½ tablespoon fat

1 tablespoon **cornstarch** (for thickening) = 2 tablespoons flour

1 cup sifted **all-purpose flour** = 1 cup plus 2 tablespoons sifted cake flour

1 cup sifted **cake flour** = 1 cup minus 2 tablespoons sifted all-purpose flour

1 teaspoon **baking powder** = ¼ teaspoon baking soda plus ½ teaspoon cream of tartar

1 cup **sour milk** = 1 cup sweet milk into which 1 tablespoon vinegar or lemon juice has been stirred

1 cup **sweet milk** = 1 cup sour milk or buttermilk plus ½ teaspoon baking soda

¾ cup **cracker crumbs** = 1 cup bread crumbs

1 cup **cream, sour, heavy** = ⅓ cup butter and ⅔ cup milk in any sour milk recipe

1 teaspoon **dried herbs** = 1 tablespoon fresh herbs

1 cup **whole milk** = ½ cup evaporated milk and ½ cup water or 1 cup reconstituted nonfat dry milk and 1 tablespoon butter

2 ounces **compressed yeast** = 3 (¼ ounce) packets of dry yeast

1 tablespoon **instant minced onion, rehydrated** = 1 small fresh onion

1 tablespoon **prepared mustard** = 1 teaspoon dry mustard

⅛ teaspoon **garlic powder** = 1 small pressed clove of garlic

1 lb. **whole dates** = 1½ cups, pitted and cut

3 medium **bananas** = 1 cup mashed

3 cups **dry corn flakes** = 1 cup crushed

10 **miniature marshmallows** = 1 large marshmallow

GENERAL OVEN CHART

Very slow oven .... 250° to 300°F.
Slow oven .... 300° to 325°F.
Moderate oven .... 325° to 375°F.
Medium hot oven .... 375° to 400°F.
Hot oven .... 400° to 450°F.
Very hot oven .... 450° to 500°F.

CONTENTS OF CANS

Of the different sizes of cans used by commercial canners, the most common are:

Size:	Average Contents
8 oz...1 cup
Picnic... 1¼ cups
No. 300 .... 1¾ cups
No. 1 tall ....2 cups
No. 303 ....2 cups
No. 2 .... 2½ cups
No. 2½ .... 3½ cups
No. 3 .... 4 cups
No. 10 .... 12 to 13 cups

BREADS

NEVER-FAIL BUNS

To 3 cups of lukewarm water, add:

½ c. white sugar　　　　　　　**1½ tsp. salt**
2 pkg. yeast

When yeast rises to top, add:

4 eggs, well beaten　　　　　　**10 c. flour**
½ c. vegetable oil

Mix and knead well. Let rise to double in size, about 2 hours. Punch down and let rise again. Make into buns. Place on greased pan and let rise for 1 hour or until light. Bake at 375° for 20 minutes (I bake mine longer). When removed from oven, brush tops with melted butter. When thoroughly cool, store in plastic bags. Freeze well.

DELICIOUS ROLL DOUGH

2 pkg. yeast　　　　　　　　　**1 c. butter**
½ c. warm water　　　　　　　**1 Tbsp. salt**
1 c. scalded milk　　　　　　　**3 eggs, beaten**
1 Tbsp. sugar　　　　　　　　**2 c. scalded milk**
2 c. flour　　　　　　　　　　**9 c. flour**
1 c. sugar

Crumble 2 packages of yeast in ½ cup warm water. Let stand while scalding 1 cup milk. Cool the milk, then add 1 tablespoon sugar, 2 cups flour, and yeast. Stir and then let stand until it is double in bulk. This is called sponge.

Cream 1 cup sugar, 1 cup butter, 1 tablespoon salt, 3 beaten eggs, and 2 cups scalded milk (cooled), then add the sponge. Add 9 or more cups of flour to stiffen. This should not be real stiff. Cover and let rise until it is doubled in bulk. Shape into rolls, braids, cinnamon rolls, or whatever you like. Let rise. Bake at 375° until light brown, 10 to 15 minutes according to your oven.

❦

No day is complete until you've heard the laughter of a child.

BASIC ROLL DOUGH

2 pkg. active dry yeast
½ c. warm water
2 c. milk, scalded
½ c. sugar

½ c. shortening
2 tsp. salt
7 c. sifted all-purpose flour
2 eggs

Soften yeast in warm water (110°). Combine milk, sugar, shortening, and salt. Cool to lukewarm. Add 1½ cups of flour and beat well. Beat in yeast and eggs. Gradually add remaining flour to form soft dough, beating well. Place in greased bowl, turning over to grease surface. Cover and let rise until double (1½ to 2 hours). Roll out, shape into rolls, and bake at 350° until brown.

Bertha Smith, Parkway Lions Club
Panama City, Florida, USA

SEMMEL - HARD ROLL

12 c. flour
5 c. lukewarm water (5½ to 6 in winter)

2 pkg. yeast (2 scant tsp.)
2 Tbsp. salt

Dissolve the yeast with water in a large bowl (6 quart or larger). Add salt and flour; beat with a large wooden spoon until dough begins to form blisters on surface and dough is shiny and smooth. Cover and allow to rise till double, or place in the refrigerator overnight. Lightly stir down and drop by large spoonfuls onto a well greased cookie sheet (12x15 inches), 6 Semmel per sheet.

Bake in a 425° to 450° oven for about 15 minutes or until nicely browned. Serve hot with butter and honey or jam or make sandwiches with cheese or meat. Slice rolls horizontally with a table knife. This recipe is fine for a family of 5 or 6. Extra batter can be kept in the refrigerator for several days, baking as needed.

DINNER ROLLS

½ c. warm water
2 pkg. dry yeast
1 c. milk
¼ c. sugar

1 tsp. salt
¼ c. margarine
2 eggs, well beaten
5¼ c. flour

Scald milk and let cool to lukewarm. Add sugar, salt, and margarine. In large bowl, dissolve yeast in water. Add milk mixture, eggs, and 2 cups flour. Beat till smooth and add enough remaining flour to make smooth and elastic.

Put in greased bowl and let rise till double. Shape into desired rolls and let rise again. Bake 15 to 20 minutes at 400°.

Gayle Nash, Otis Lions Club
Otis, Colorado, USA

378

HALF-TIME SPOON ROLLS

1 pkg. dry yeast
¼ c. warm water
¼ c. sugar
⅓ c. shortening

1 tsp. salt
¾ c. scalded milk, cooled
1 egg, beaten
3½ c. flour

Dissolve yeast in water. Combine sugar, shortening, salt, and cooled milk in a large bowl. Blend in the dissolved yeast and egg. Add flour and mix until well blended. Place in a greased bowl and cover. Let rise until doubled in bulk (45 to 60 minutes). Stir down and spoon into well greased muffin tins, filling half full. Let rise again about 45 minutes. Bake in oven preheated to 400° about 15 minutes. Makes 18 medium rolls.

EDNA'S ROLLS

1 yeast cake
1 c. scalded milk
1½ tsp. salt
3½ to 4 c. flour (plain or bread)

½ c. lukewarm water
3 Tbsp. shortening
3 Tbsp. sugar

Pour hot milk over shortening, salt, and 2 tablespoons sugar. Let cool. Add the yeast and other sugar to lukewarm water; let stand until foamy, about 15 minutes. Add this to the milk and stir in half the flour. Beat well. Add balance of flour. Beat and knead well. Roll out. Put in roll shapes. Brush rolls with butter. Place in greased pan. Let set to rise and leave for 2 hours. Bake in 350° oven for 20 minutes. Brush with butter.

Glenn E. Bunch, Jr., Snow Hill Lions Club
Snow Hill, North Carolina, USA

SWEET POTATO ROLLS

3 c. whole wheat flour
3 c. all-purpose flour
2 pkg. dry yeast
1½ c. warm water (105° to 115°)
⅓ c. firmly packed brown sugar

1¼ tsp. salt
½ c. butter or margarine, softened
2 eggs
1 (9 oz.) can sweet potatoes
    (undrained)

Combine flours, mixing well. Combine yeast and warm water in blender; process to dissolve yeast. Add sugar, salt, butter, eggs, sweet potatoes, and 1 cup flour to yeast mixture. Blend until smooth. Place remaining flour in large bowl. Add yeast mixture, mixing to make a soft dough. Turn dough out on a lightly floured board. Knead 5 minutes or until smooth and elastic. Place in a greased bowl; turn over. Cover with plastic wrap and refrigerate 6 hours or overnight. Before baking, divide dough in half. On floured surface, roll each half into a 16 inch circle, ¼ inch thick. Cut each circle into 16 wedges. Roll up each wedge, starting at widest edge. Place wedges on greased baking sheets with point on bottom. Cover and let rise in warm place 30 minutes. Bake at 350° for 15 minutes. Yield: 32 rolls.

ICEBOX ROLLS

1 pkg. dry yeast
½ c. warm water
½ c. shortening
½ c. sugar

2 c. warm water
1½ tsp. salt
8 c. flour
7 eggs, beaten

Dissolve the yeast in the ½ cup water. Cream the shortening and sugar. Add the beaten egg, water, salt, and yeast. Add the flour and mix well. Put in large greased bowl and grease the top of dough. Cover and place in the refrigerator. When ready to use, take as much dough as needed, shape the rolls, and place in greased pan. Let rise 3 hours and bake in hot oven (400°) for 12 to 15 minutes.

Edna Bunch, Snow Hill Lions Club
Snow Hill, North Carolina, USA

OATMEAL ROLLS

2 c. water
1 c. dry rolled oats
3 Tbsp. butter
⅓ c. water
2 pkg. active dry yeast

⅔ c. packed brown sugar
1 Tbsp. white sugar
1 tsp. salt
5 to 5¾ c. all-purpose flour,
    divided in half

In a saucepan, bring 2 cups water to a boil. Add oatmeal and butter; simmer 1 minute. Remove to a large mixing bowl and let cool to 120° to 130°. Heat the remaining water to 120° to 130°; add yeast. To the oatmeal mixture, add brown and white sugars, salt, yeast mixture, and half of the flour. Mix well. Add enough of the remaining flour to make a soft dough. Turn out onto a floured board; knead 6 to 8 minutes or until smooth and elastic. Add additional flour if necessary. Place dough in a greased bowl, turning once to grease top. Cover and let rise until doubled, about 1 hour. Punch dough down; divide in half and shape each half into 12 balls. Place 1 inch apart on 2 greased 13x9 inch pans. Cover and let rise until doubled, about 45 to 60 minutes. Bake at 350° for 20 to 30 minutes. Yield: 24 rolls.

The real measure of our wealth is how much we'd be worth
if we lost all our money.

INSTANT MIRACLE ROLLS

3 pkg. dry yeast
5 c. unsifted self-rising flour
1 tsp. soda
2 c. lukewarm buttermilk

½ c. warm water
¼ c. sugar
1 c. shortening

Dissolve yeast in warm water and set aside. Mix flour, sugar, and soda; cut in shortening. Add buttermilk and yeast, then mix. Place desired amount of dough on floured cloth; pat out and cut with biscuit cutter. Let warm to room temperature. Bake in 350° oven 10 to 15 minutes.

May be placed in oven immediately or taken from refrigerator and placed in oven without being allowed to rise. Mixture can be stored in covered bowl in refrigerator and used as needed because it keeps for several weeks.

Adran Groves, Mt. Airy Foothills Lions Club
Mt. Airy, North Carolina, USA

HOT ROLLS (REFRIGERATED)

½ c. sugar
½ c. shortening (Crisco)
2 c. milk
1 pkg. yeast
1 egg, beaten

Flour
1 Tbsp. salt
½ tsp. baking powder
½ tsp. soda

Put first 3 ingredients in saucepan and bring almost to a boil, then cool. When this is lukewarm, add yeast and beaten egg. Add enough flour (2 to 3 cups) for a soft dough. Let stand 1 hour or double its size. Add salt, baking powder, and soda. Be sure to mix well. Add enough flour to make a dough stiff to handle. Cover with foil and let rise once. Punch down and put in refrigerator overnight before using any dough. Use as needed and let rise before baking. Dough will last 2 weeks in refrigerator. Bake at 375° until brown.

Eloise Stewart, Moweaqua Lions Club
Moweaqua, Illinois, USA

❧

Change is a process, not an event.

QUICK AND EASY ROLLS

2 c. whole wheat flour
2 to 2½ c. unbleached white flour
2 pkg. yeast
1 tsp. salt
½ tsp. soda

1 c. plain yogurt
¾ c. water
½ c. butter or margarine
¼ c. honey

Combine whole wheat flour, yeast, salt, and soda in mixing bowl. Stir together yogurt, water, butter or margarine, and honey. Warm over low heat or in microwave until very warm. Add to yeast mixture and mix until blended, then beat on medium speed for 2 minutes. Add remaining flour (enough to make a soft dough). Knead for several minutes or use dough hooks on mixer for 2 minutes.

Cover with plastic wrap and a towel; let rise for 20 minutes in a warm place. Uncover and punch dough down. Divide in half. Shape rolls to fit 2 greased 8 inch pans. Cover and let rise for 20 minutes. Bake at 400° for 15 to 20 minutes.

Note: This recipe makes very good communion bread if baked in 2 round loaves instead of rolls.

FRENCH BREAD STICKS

3½ to 4 c. all-purpose flour,
　divided
2 tsp. salt
2 tsp. sugar
1 pkg. dry yeast
1¼ c. warm water (105° to 115°)

Corn meal
2 egg whites
2 Tbsp. water
Poppy seeds
Sesame seeds

Combine 1¼ cups flour, salt, sugar, and yeast in large bowl. Add 1¼ cups water and beat on low speed to combine. Beat for 3 minutes at high speed. Add remaining flour and mix or knead until dough is smooth and elastic. Place dough in lightly greased bowl and turn to coat all sides. Cover and let rise (85°), free from drafts, until double in bulk. Punch down. Cover and let rise again until double. Punch down; knead until smooth. Divide into 36 equal pieces. Roll each into 8 x ½ inch sticks. Place sticks 1 inch apart on well greased baking dish. Sprinkle with corn meal.

Combine egg whites and 2 tablespoons water; beat lightly. Brush sticks with mixture. Let rise for about 50 minutes until double. Brush again; sprinkle with poppy or sesame seeds. Bake in oven at 400° and put pan of water on bottom shelf for 15 minutes. Brush again and bake for 10 to 12 minutes more, or until golden brown. Makes 3 dozen.

❧

That I am here is a wonderful mystery to which I will respond with joy.

HONEY DEW BISCUITS

1 c. butter, whipped
1 c. strained honey
2 c. flour
1 c. sugar

1 c. sour cream
1 tsp. baking soda
½ tsp. salt
1 egg

Mix well all ingredients and bake in greased and floured muffin pans. Bake at 375°F. for 10 to 12 minutes.

Bonita K. Blakey, Moweaqua Lions Club
Moweaqua, Illinois, USA

BETTER ANGEL BISCUITS

Step 1:

1 c. whole wheat flour
2 c. plain flour
1 tsp. baking soda

1 c. Crisco (frozen between 2
   sheets of waxed paper and
   rolled ¼ inch thick)

Step 2:

2 c. plain flour
1 tsp. salt
¼ c. sugar

2 env. yeast
2 c. warmed buttermilk (125°F.)
1 whole egg

Egg Wash:

1 egg, beaten
1 Tbsp. oil

2 Tbsp. milk or sour cream

Step 1: Sift flours and soda. Cut in Crisco until resembles small pea sized lumps. Keep cold while preparing step 2.

Step 2: In large bowl of mixer, combine dry ingredients (flour, salt, sugar, and yeast). Add buttermilk and egg. Beat about 2 minutes. Let rest while you grease baking sheets and combine egg wash ingredients in small dish. Fold Crisco mix into yeast mix and stir until it firms up. Turn out onto floured surface and knead about 10 turns. Roll ½ inch thick. Cut with biscuit cutter. Brush with egg wash. Let rise 20 minutes at room temperature. Bake at 400°F. until light brown. This method is more complicated, but definitely worth the trouble.

Lion Vivian Quinlan, Mathews Lions Club
Mathews, Virginia, USA

❦

How come the person who snores always falls asleep first?

MAGIC BISCUITS

Note: These biscuits can be prepared in a large quantity ahead of time and then baked as few or as many as desired when needed.

5 c. flour	4 Tbsp. sugar
1 tsp. soda	1 c. vegetable shortening
1 tsp. salt	2 pkg. RadidRise yeast
4 tsp. baking powder	2 c. buttermilk

Dissolve yeast in ¼ cup warm (not hot) water. Sift flour, soda, salt, baking powder, and sugar together. Cut in shortening with a blender or 2 knives or a fork. Add yeast and milk to dry mixture. Mix to stiff dough. Knead 10 to 12 strokes on floured board or table. Pinch off biscuits or roll and cut out. Allow to rise 10 minutes and bake.

The dough can be stored several days in the refrigerator. Make into biscuits as desired and allow to rise 15 to 20 minutes before baking. For even greater convenience, the dough can be rolled, cut, placed on a baking sheet, and frozen. The frozen biscuits are placed in the oven as soon as it is turned on. They will thaw as the oven heats.

Nancy Dean, Stamps Lions Club
Stamps, Arkansas, USA

BISCUITS
(Risen buttermilk biscuits)

2 c. flour	1 tsp. salt
2 Tbsp. any kind liquid, lard, etc.	1 pkg. yeast
2 Tbsp. honey (Tupelo or wildflower)	

Place in a mixing bowl (Tupperware with top is suitable) 1 cup of flour. Add buttermilk and yeast. Mix well and add the rest of the ingredients. Mix well, then add the rest of the flour plus enough to make soft dough that can be kneaded. Knead 10 or 15 times until it is "silky" and allow to stand in bowl with top covered (to keep from drying out) until doubled in size, then divide into 4 equal parts and roll out 3 biscuits from each part. Flatten to ½ inch thickness. Place on greased pan, edges slightly touching, and allow to rise for 40 minutes. After they have doubled in size, bake in a 400° oven for 10 to 12 minutes. Turn out upside down on racks to cool for crispy bottoms. *Rising is best accomplished in a warm (not hot) place.*

A 1992 blue ribbon winner at the Bay County Fair.

J. Gordon King, Parkway Lions Club
Panama City, Florida, USA

Angels can fly because they take themselves lightly.

LUCY'S BISCUITS

2 c. self-rising flour
1½ sticks margarine, melted
8 oz. sour cream (room
    temperature)

Ungreased miniature muffin pan

    Mix all ingredients together. Drop by teaspoonful into muffin pan. Bake at 450° for 10 to 12 minutes. Yield: About 36 small biscuits.

    These are great with vegetables or salads. Be prepared, they will all disappear!

Mrs. Lion George (Dianne) Murphy, Canton Lions Club
Canton, Georgia, USA

7-UP BISCUITS

4 c. Pioneer original biscuit mix
1 can 7-Up

4 oz. sour cream

    Roll out thick. Melt 1 stick of butter in pan. Turn biscuits over in butter and bake at 425° until brown.

Nancy Dean, Stamps Lions Club
Stamps, Arkansas, USA

ALASKA BREAD

1 pkg. dry yeast
½ c. warm water
⅛ tsp. ginger
1 Tbsp. sugar
2 Tbsp. sugar

1 large can evaporated milk
2 Tbsp. vegetable oil
1 tsp. salt
4 c. flour

    This recipe freezes well and is good toasted.

    Combine first 4 ingredients; set bowl in warm place until bubbly (about 10 minutes). Add rest of ingredients and mix with mixer until stiff. If you can't mix all the flour in with the mixer, add remaining flour with a wooden spoon. Put into two 1 pound greased coffee cans. Spray lids with Pam and place on top. Set in warm place to rise and when lids pop off, bake in preheated 350° oven for 30 minutes or until tops are brown.

The only things kids wear out faster than shoes are parents and teachers.

BARBADOS BREAD

6 oz. flour
6 oz. potato
4 oz. margarine
1 tsp. baking powder
1 tsp. vanilla essence

2 eggs
3 oz. cherries
1 tsp. ground spice
¾ c. milk

Cook sweet potato and cream smoothly. Prepare fruit and dust with flour. Cream margarine and sugar. Sift flour and baking powder. Add creamed potato and creamed sugar and margarine together. Beat eggs, adding flour alternately with milk and flour the last addition. Add fruit and fold in lightly, being careful to retain the air. Put into greased loaf tins dusted with flour. Decorate with cherries and sprinkle with granulated sugar. Bake in a moderate oven.

Joan Jordan, East Barbados Lions Club
Belleville, St. Michael Barbados

BEER BREAD

3 c. self-rising flour
1 (12 oz.) can warm beer

3 Tbsp. sugar

Mix together and pour into two 9x5 inch pans. Let stand 20 minutes before baking. Bake at 350° for 1 hour. Put on wire rack to cool.

Lois Gnuse, Arlington Lions Club
Arlington, Nebraska, USA

BROCCOLI BREAD

1 box Jiffy corn bread mix
1 (10 oz.) pkg. frozen chopped
    broccoli, thawed and
    drained
1 large onion, chopped

6 oz. cottage cheese
½ c. margarine, melted
4 beaten eggs
1 tsp. salt

Mix all ingredients, except corn meal mix. Add it last. Pour into greased 9x13 inch Pyrex dish. Bake 25 minutes at 400°. Serve hot.

P.D.G. Lion Dr. Wilford Lyerly, Mt. Airy Foothills Lions Club
Mt. Airy, North Carolina, USA

For most kids, cleanliness isn't next to godliness - it's next to impossible.

CHEDDAR, BACON, AND OLIVE BREAD

2½ c. flour
2½ Tbsp. sugar
2 tsp. baking powder
½ tsp. baking soda
1 tsp. salt
1 tsp. dry mustard
Generous pinch of cayenne
   powder

¼ c. margarine
1 c. shredded Cheddar cheese
1 egg
1 c. buttermilk
1 tsp. Worcestershire sauce
5 slices bacon
1 c. pitted black olives

Mix together flour, sugar, baking powder, baking soda, salt, mustard, and cayenne powder. Cut in margarine with a fork until mixture resembles coarse meal. Stir in cheese. In a small bowl, combine egg, buttermilk, and Worcestershire sauce.

Make a well in flour mixture and pour in liquid. Mix just until moistened. Cook bacon until crispy and crumbly. Coarsely chop black olives. Stir in bacon and olives. Turn batter into a greased loaf pan. Bake at 375° for 30 to 40 minutes. Turn out of pan and cool on rack.

To make muffins: Divide batter among 12 well-greased muffin pans. Bake at 375° for 20 to 25 minutes. Makes 1 loaf or 12 muffins.

HOT MEXICAN CORN BREAD

2 eggs
1½ c. corn meal
1 can cream style corn
½ green bell pepper, chopped
1 bunch green onions, chopped
1 tsp. salt

2 tsp. baking powder
1 (8 oz.) sour cream
⅔ c. Wesson oil
3 or 4 jalapeno peppers, seeds
   removed and chopped
1½ c. grated cheese

Mix all ingredients, except cheese. Grease and flour pan. Pour half of mixture in pan. Spread ½ of cheese, then rest of mixture, then the rest of cheese. Bake at 350° for 30 minutes. Continue baking at 400°F. for 15 minutes.

Mrs. Charlotte M. Garner, Pascagoula Evening Lions Club
Pascagoula, Mississippi, USA

❧

Nostalgia: Life in the past lane.

BROCCOLI CORN BREAD

2 pkg. Jiffy corn muffin mix
1 c. small curd cottage cheese
4 eggs
½ c. chopped onions
2 pkg. frozen broccoli, chopped
1 stick margarine, melted

Set oven to 400°. In large mixing bowl, mix together the muffin mix, cottage cheese, eggs, chopped onions, chopped broccoli, and margarine. Bake in a well greased 9x13 inch pan at 400° for 25 to 30 minutes or until golden brown.

Experience is a wonderful thing. It enables you to recognize a mistake when you make it again.

Genice Woods, Craigsville Lions Club
Craigsville, West Virginia, Nicholas, USA

DILLY BREAD

1 pkg. dry yeast, dissolved in ¼ c.
warm water
1 c. cottage cheese, heated to
lukewarm
2 Tbsp. sugar
1 Tbsp. instant onion
1 egg
1 Tbsp. butter
2 tsp. dill seed
2½ c. flour
1 tsp. salt
¼ tsp. baking powder

Combine all ingrdients. May have to add additional flour to make stiff dough. Cover and let rise until double in bulk, about 50 to 60 minutes. Stir down and turn into greased 1½ quart casserole or bread pan. Let rise for 30 to 40 minutes. Bake at 350° for 40 to 50 minutes or until golden brown. Brush with butter. Serve warm.

GRAPE-NUTS BREAD

2 c. milk, scalded
1 c. Grape-Nuts cereal
3 c. sifted self-rising flour
4 tsp. baking powder
1 tsp. salt
½ c. sugar
1 egg, beaten
3 tsp. butter

Pour hot milk over Grape-Nuts. Cool. Sift flour, then measure. Add salt and baking powder; add egg and melted butter to Grape-Nuts mixture. Mix well. Add flour and mix well again. Pour into greased loaf pan. Let stand 20 minutes. Bake 1 hour and 20 minutes at 350° or until done.

Note: Cream cheese is great on this.

Bertha Smith, Parkway Lions Club
Panama City, Florida, USA

❦

Wish not so much to live long but to live well.

ONION HARVEST BREAD - ZWIEBELKUCHEN

1 (1 lb.) loaf frozen bread dough,
   thawed
5 medium onions, thinly sliced
3 Tbsp. butter or margarine

2 eggs
¾ c. half & half (light cream)
Salt and pepper to taste
½ to ¾ c. fine diced ham

While bread dough is thawing, cook onions in butter in a large skillet over medium heat, stirring occasionally, until they are soft and limp and beginning to brown, 20 to 30 minutes. Beat eggs with half & half and salt; stir in onions. Roll out dough into a large rectangle, then pat dough evenly into a greased 10x15 inch jelly roll pan, pressing the dough up onto the sides and ends of the pan. Pour in the onion mixture, spreading it evenly over the dough. Sprinkle with diced ham. Bake in 400° oven for 25 to 30 minutes, until dough is well browned and the filling is set. Serve warm, cut in strips. Makes 8 to 10 servings as first course or appetizer.

Served warm, this creamy onion-topped bread is a favorite German snack.
Dan Steffan, Independence Eastview Lions Club
Independence, Missouri, USA

POPPY SEED BREAD

3 c. flour, sifted
1½ tsp. salt
1½ tsp. baking powder
2½ c. sugar
3 eggs
1½ c. milk

1 c. + 2 Tbsp. salad oil
3 Tbsp. poppy seed
1½ tsp. vanilla
1½ tsp. almond flavoring
1½ tsp. butter flavoring

Glaze:

3 c. powdered sugar
¼ c. fresh orange juice
½ tsp. vanilla

½ tsp. almond flavoring
½ tsp. butter flavoring

Add ingredients into mixer bowl in the order given. Beat for 2 minutes. Bake in 2 large loaf pans or 4 smaller ones. Use a 350° oven and watch carefully for 55 minutes; may take less time for small pans. Do not overbake.

Mix glaze while bread bakes. Remove bread from pans and immediately glaze. As they cool, reapply glaze.

❦

Happiness is found along the way, not at the end of the road.

PORK AND BEAN BREAD

1 c. raisins
1 c. boiling water
3 eggs
1 c. oil
2 c. sugar
1 (16 oz.) can pork and beans
1 tsp. cinnamon

1 tsp. soda
½ tsp. salt
½ tsp. baking powder
1 tsp. vanilla
1 c. nuts
2 c. flour

Mix raisins with boiling water. Stir and set aside. Beat eggs, oil, sugar, and pork and beans till all beans are broken up. Add dry ingredients. Add nuts and vanilla. Drain raisins and add to mixture. Stir in well. Pour into 2 well greased loaf pans. Bake at 325° for 50 to 60 minutes. (I use 3 small loaf pans and bake 50 minutes.)

Phyllis Rockers, Emporia Sundowners Lions Club
Emporia, Kansas, USA

SALT RISING BREAD

Starter:

3 medium potatoes, peeled and
  sliced
3 Tbsp. white corn meal

1 tsp. salt
1 tsp. sugar
4 c. boiling water

Dough:

1 c. warm water
½ tsp. baking soda
1 c. undiluted evaporated milk
  (room temperature)

4 c. all-purpose flour
2 Tbsp. soft butter
½ tsp. salt
10 c. all-purpose flour

Never let ingredients get cold. Use 2 quart heavy plastic or earthenware bowls.

Put potatoes in warmed bowl; sprinkle corn meal, salt, and sugar over them. Add boiling water. Stir to mix. Cover and place in boiling water in larger bowl. Cover all tightly with foil, then 3 bath towels to keep as warm as possible. Set in warm place. Let stand 24 hours. Potato mixture should have a covering of foam ½ to 1 inch thick. Keep water at 100°.

Pour off liquid from potato mixture into a very large bowl. Rinse potatoes with warm water; reserve the water and add soda. (Discard potatoes.) Add to large bowl. Stir in milk and 4 cups flour; beat until smooth. Stir in butter and salt; mix in remaining flour until a stiff dough forms. Save 1 cup of flour to put on breadboard. Knead 10 minutes. Grease 5 bread pans. Let rise in pan. Bake at 350° for 45 to 50 minutes until lightly browned. Cool, stir, and freeze.

An old recipe of great-aunt.

Emilie I. Dubuy, Reno Plumb Lane Lions Club
Reno, Nevada, USA

SHEPHERD'S BREAD

7 c. flour
¼ c. honey
1 c. milk
¼ c. butter

1 Tbsp. salt
2 pkg. dry yeast
1½ c. warm water

Mix flour, salt, honey, and yeast. Combine the milk, water, and butter. Heat over low heat until warm. Gradually add liquid mixture to dry ingredients and beat with electric mixer on medium speed for 2 minutes. If still sticky, add additional flour to make soft dough. Knead on lightly floured board for 8 to 10 minutes or until smooth and rubbery to the touch.

Shape into large ball and place into greased bowl. Cover and let rise until double in bulk. Punch down and let rise again, 15 minutes. Divide dough. Shape into 2 round balls. Place on baking sheet. Let rise again until double in bulk and bake at 400° for 30 minutes.

STUFFED SPINACH-CHEESE BREAD

1 large loaf unsliced French bread
1 stick butter (margarine)
¼ c. olive oil
10 cloves garlic, coarsely
   chopped
1 pkg. frozen chopped spinach,
   thawed and squeezed dry

1 c. grated Swiss cheese
½ c. grated Mozzarella cheese
½ tsp. dried basil
½ tsp. thyme
½ tsp. garlic salt
¼ tsp. coarse black pepper

Cut top from bread; carefully scoop out bread from both halves, leaving crust intact. In large mixing bowl, tear inside bread into small pieces and combine with spinach. Heat butter and olive oil together in skillet until slightly bubbly. Add garlic and stir over heat for 30 seconds.

Remove from heat and add to bread mixture, stirring until well combined. Add cheeses and seasoning; mix well. Mound mixture in bottom crust. Replace top crust and wrap loaf lightly in foil. Bake for 35 minutes at 350°. Serve warm.

For cookout, bake ahead, leave wrapped, and reheat on grill rack for about 15 minutes just before serving.

Life is like an exciting book, and every year starts a new chapter.

SPOON BREAD

1 c. yellow corn meal
2 c. boiling water
3 Tbsp. butter

1 tsp. salt
3 large eggs, well beaten
1 c. milk

Slowly add corn meal to the boiling water, stirring constantly, until thick and smooth. Add butter and salt; cool to lukewarm, then add eggs and milk. Beat for 2 minutes; pour into greased casserole. Bake in preheated 375° oven for 40 to 50 minutes or until golden brown. Spoon out while piping hot and pass more butter! Great served with a rice dish. This recipe comes out of traditional southern cooking.

Rev. Fred Gilbert, Dannemora, New York, Lions Club
Dannemora, New York, USA

SOURDOUGH WHITE BREAD

2 c. warm water
2 c. warm milk
¼ c. Tupelo honey (or wildflower)
1 Tbsp. butter
2 Tbsp. sugar

2 tsp. salt
1 pkg. yeast
2 tsp. soda (mix with 1 Tbsp.
   water)

Starter:

2 pkg. yeast
2 c. water

2 c. flour

Starter: Mix well and let stand overnight. Replenish with equal parts water and flour after using. Keep in refrigerator in glass casserole bowl with top. Don't allow metal to touch the starter. Use a wooden spoon to mix together and allow to sit before storing in the refrigerator.

With 1 cup of starter, mix the following ingredients: Mix 2½ cups of the flour and 2 cups water. Allow to stand in a warm (not hot) place overnight. Next morning, mix butter with the milk and stir in the yeast (don't get the milk too hot or it will kill the yeast). Add the honey and mix thoroughly, then add 2 more cups of flour and cracked wheat. Sprinkle sugar, salt, and soda mixture on top and mix in well. Allow to stand for 50 minutes, or until mixture is bubbly, then add flour until dough cannot be stirred, then place on floured board and knead 100 times or until "silky" mixture is developed. Cover and allow to rise in a warm place until double in bulk. Punch down and form into 4 loaves. Place into well greased pans and let rise again until double in bulk. Bake at 400° for 20 minutes. Reduce heat to 325° and bake 20 minutes longer or until done. (Tap with a spoon and a hollow sound indicates they are done.) Empty out on racks to cool. Rub with butter to prevent too much crustiness. This recipe is a fail-safe method to bake sourdough bread. This recipe can be used without the 1 package of yeast but 4 or more hours are required in rising.

J. Gordon King, Parkway Lions Club
Panama City, Florida, USA

HOMEMADE WHITE BREAD

2 c. warm water
2 Tbsp. sugar
1 Tbsp. salt

2 Tbsp. shortening
1 pkg. yeast
6 to 6¼ c. flour

Mix together water, sugar, salt, and shortening until dissolved. Stir in yeast. Mix by hand the flour until dough is easy to handle. Place in greased bowl, turning to grease both sides. Cover and let rise 1½ hours. Punch down and divide into 2 parts. Flatten dough, knead, and shape into loaves. Place in greased bread pans. Cover with damp cloth and let rise until sides of dough have reached top of pans, about 1½ hours. Bake for 15 minutes at 450°, then lower oven temperature to 375° and continue baking for 25 more minutes. Coat top of loaves with butter while still hot. Makes 2 loaves.

WHITE BREAD

2 Tbsp. honey
2 Tbsp. crisco
1 Tbsp. salt
1 c. boiling water

1 yeast cake
8 c. white flour
1 c. canned milk
1⅓ c. lukewarm water

Add honey and Crisco to boiling water; stir to melt. Add canned milk. When lukewarm, add crumbled yeast cake. Add 4 cups flour and beat well with spoon, then add remaining flour. Let rise twice. Bake 1 hour. (Add lukewarm water after crumbled yeast cake.) Makes 2 loaves.

Evelyn Steele, Lyman Lions Club
Lyman, Wyoming, USA

DANISH ROLLS

1 pkg. active dry yeast
¼ c. warm water
1 c. milk
1 tsp. salt
¼ c. sugar
¼ c. butter
¼ tsp. nutmeg

¼ tsp. lemon extract
⅛ tsp. almond extract
1 egg
1⅔ c. flour
3 c. flour
½ c. firm butter

Dissolve yeast in ¼ cup warm water. Scald milk. Add salt, sugar, and ¼ cup butter. Cool to lukewarm. Add yeast mixture, spices, egg, and 1⅔ cups flour. Beat until smooth. Gradually add about 3 cups flour to make soft dough. Knead until smooth. Place in greased bowl. Cover and let rise till double. Roll into rectangle, ½ inch thick. Mark in 3 parts. Dot center ⅓ with ½ cup butter. Fold ends over center, pinching edges closed. Roll out to ½ inch. Fold in half and roll again. Repeat 3 times. Roll into rectangle. Roll into long snack. Cut into ½ inch coils. Place on greased sheets. Cover and let rise until light. Bake at 450° for 8 to 10 minutes. You may need to cool dough between rolling out the 3 times.

B. Allison, Moweaqua Lions Club
Moweaqua, Illinois, USA

BUNDT CARAMEL ROLLS

1 pkg. Rhode's bread rolls
1 pkg. dry butterscotch pudding
   (not instant)
½ c. oleo

¾ c. brown sugar
¾ tsp. cinnamon
2 c. pecans

Butter a Bundt or 9x13 inch pan. Put pecans on buttered pan. Put in frozen bread rolls. Sprinkle dry butterscotch pudding over rolls. Pour melted oleo over top. Mix cinnamon and brown sugar together. Sprinkle over rolls. Set out on counter, uncovered, overnight. Bake at 350° for 20 to 25 minutes. Take out of oven and let set 5 minutes, then flip over on waxed paper cookie sheet.

This is so easy and very good.

Janice Bender, Baugo Lions Club
Elkhart, Indiana, USA

Dream of the person you would like to be,
but don't waste the person you are.

It is possible to own too much.
A person with one watch knows what time it is;
a person with two watches is never sure.

Frustration is when the same snow that covers the ski slopes
makes the roads to them impossible.

CARAMEL-CREAM CHEESE CINNAMON ROLLS

Filling:

1 c. brown sugar	**¼ c. flour**
1 c. sugar	**1½ Tbsp. cinnamon**
½ c. butter	**½ c. chopped nuts**

Dough:

¾ c. milk	**⅓ c. warm water**
½ c. butter	**3 eggs (room temperature)**
2 pkg. dry yeast	**5½ to 6½ c. flour**

Caramel-Cream Cheese Topping:

1 (8 oz.) pkg. cream cheese	**1 tsp. vanilla**
½ c. brown sugar	

Mix filling ingredients with beater for 1 minute. Set aside while preparing dough.

Combine first 4 dough ingredients in saucepan. Heat at low temperature until butter melts and sugar dissolves. Cool to lukewarm. Dissolve yeast in warm water in warmed bowl. Add lukewarm milk mixture, eggs, and 5 cups flour. Mix for 3 minutes with beater at low speed. Continue mixing at low speed while adding remaining flour, ½ cup at a time, until dough clings to beater; knead 3 to 5 minutes longer.

Place in greased bowl and cover with clean towel. Let rise in warm place, free from draft, about 1 hour or until double in size. Punch down and roll to 10 x 30 x ¼ inch rectangle. Spread filling ingredients on dough. Roll dough tightly from long side to form 30 inch roll. Cut into 21 (1½ inch) slices. Place 7 rolls each in 3 greased 8 x 1½ inch cake pans. Cover and let rise for 1 hour more or until double in size. Bake at 350° for about 20 minutes. Remove from pans immediately.

Mix all 3 topping ingredients with beater for 5 minutes or until well creamed. Top rolls with Caramel-Cream Cheese Topping. Serve warm for melt-in-your-mouth cinnamon rolls! Makes 21 rolls.

❦

It is better to look ahead and prepare than to look back and regret.

OLD-FASHIONED CINNAMON ROLLS

½ c. sugar
½ tsp. salt
1 pkg. dry yeast
4 c. flour (about)
1 c. milk
Butter or margarine

1 egg
½ c. packed light brown sugar
½ c. chopped walnuts
½ c. raisins
1½ tsp. cinnamon
Sugar Glaze (recipe follows)

In bowl, combine sugar, salt, yeast, and 1 cup flour. In saucepan, heat milk and ¼ cup butter until warm (120° to 130°). Butter or margarine does not need to melt completely. With mixer at low speed, beat liquid into dry ingredients. Add medium speed, beat 2 minutes. Beat in egg and 1 cup flour; beat 2 minutes. Stir in 1½ cups flour.

On floured surface, knead dough until smooth, about 10 minutes, adding more flour (about ¼ cup) while kneading. Shape dough into ball and place in greased container. Cover and let rise in warm place, away from draft, until doubled, about 1 hour.

Punch down dough; turn onto floured surface. Cover and let rest 15 minutes. Meanwhile, combine brown sugar, walnuts, raisins, and cinnamon. Grease 13x9 inch baking pan. Melt ¼ cup butter. On floured surface, roll dough into 18x12 inch rectangle. Brush with melted butter; sprinkle on sugar mixture. Starting with 18 inch side, roll dough jellyroll fashion; pinch seam to seal. With seam side down, cut roll crosswise into 18 slices; place in pan, cut side down. Cover and let rise until double, about 40 minutes.

Preheat oven to 400° and bake 20 minutes. Cool slightly; brush with Sugar Glaze. Makes 18 rolls.

Sugar Glaze:

1 c. powdered sugar
4 tsp. water

½ tsp. vanilla

In small bowl, stir powdered sugar and water until smooth; add vanilla. Spread on rolls.

PDG Lloyd E. Wright, Georgetown Lions Club
Georgetown, Ohio, USA

God adds to the beauty of His world by creating true friends.

GOOD CINNAMON ROLLS

1 tsp. salt
2 c. boiling water
4 Tbsp. Crisco
½ c. sugar

2 eggs
½ c. cold water
1 cake yeast (1 pkg.)

Dissolve yeast in ¼ cup water. Add Crisco to boiling water to melt. Add sugar and salt after cools. Some add slightly beaten eggs. Add flour to make dough. Put in refrigerator overnight to rise. Roll out dough. Top with brown sugar, butter, and cinnamon. Roll up and cut for rolls. Let rise and bake at 350° for 25 to 30 minutes. After they cool, drizzle powdered sugar icing on rolls.

Icing: Mix powdered sugar and milk together.

Lion Elizabeth Riggenbach, Graysville/Proctor Lions Club
Proctor, West Virginia, USA

DANISH PUFF

½ c. butter or margarine, softened
1 c. Gold Medal flour
2 Tbsp. water
½ c. butter or margarine

1 c. water
1 tsp. almond extract
1 c. Gold Medal flour
3 eggs

Heat oven to 350°. Cut ½ cup butter into 1 cup flour. Sprinkle 2 tablespoons water over mixture; mix. Round into ball and divide in half. On ungreased baking sheet, pat each half into strip, 12x3 inches. Strips should be about 3 inches apart.

Heat ½ cup butter and 1 cup water to rolling boil in medium saucepan. Remove from heat and quickly stir in almond extract and 1 cup flour. Stir vigorously over low heat until mixture forms a ball, about 1 minute. Remove from heat. Beat in eggs (all at once) until smooth and glossy.

Divide in half. Spread each half evenly over strips. Bake for about 60 minutes or until topping is crisp and brown. Cool. (Topping will shrink and fall, forming the custardy top of this puff.) Frost with sugar glaze and sprinkle generously with nuts.

Confectioners Sugar Glaze:

1½ c. confectioners sugar
2 Tbsp. butter or margarine,
  softened

1½ tsp. vanilla
1 to 2 Tbsp. warm water
Chopped nuts

Mix confectioners sugar, butter, vanilla, and warm water until smooth and of spreading consistency.

Laughter is a tranquilizer with no side effects.

SANDBAKKLSE

1 c. butter or oleo
½ c. sugar
1 egg, beaten
3 c. flour
¼ tsp. salt (optional)
½ lb. (about 28) light colored
    candy caramels
¼ c. evaporated milk

¼ c. butter or margarine
1 c. sifted powdered sugar
6 oz. (1 c.) chocolate chips
⅓ c. evaporated milk
2 Tbsp. butter or margarine
1 tsp. vanilla
½ c. sifted powdered sugar

Cream 1 cup butter or margarine with sugar; add egg. Add flour with salt. Press into tart tins. Bake 10 minutes at 350° to 375°. Should be light colored.

Caramel filling: Combine caramels and evaporated milk in top of double boiler. Heat until caramels melt, stirring occasionally. Remove from heat and stir in ¼ cup butter and 1 cup sifted powdered sugar.

Icing: Melt chocolate chips with ⅓ cup evaporated milk over low heat. Remove from heat. Stir in 2 tablespoons butter, vanilla, and ½ cup powdered sugar. Makes 35 to 70, depending on the tin size. Shells may also be served plain or filled with fruit, jellies, etc.

❦

Those who bring sunshine to the lives of others
cannot keep it from themselves.

❦ ❦ ❦

I'm not going to worry -
until the animals start lining up two by two for the next space shuttle!

BOHEMIAN KOLACHES

¾ c. lard or butter
¾ c. sugar
3 eggs
1 oz. yeast

1 tsp. salt
2 c. water or scalded milk (milk
    takes longer to rise)
5½ to 6 c. flour

Pour hot milk (or water) over lard, sugar, and salt. Crumble yeast in a little water. Cool milk to lukewarm, then add eggs and yeast. Beat with electric beater with 3 cups flour, about 3 minutes. Add remainder of flour; stir with a spoon. This will be very soft dough. Let rise in warm place until double. With buttered hands, form small balls (size of walnut or golf ball). Place on greased baking sheet. When double in size, make a depression in center and fill with either of the following fillings. Makes 5 dozen.

Filling recipes for Kolaches -

Poppy Seed Filling:

1 can Solo poppy seed filling
1 egg, beaten
2 Tbsp. milk
1 graham cracker, crushed

1 Tbsp. vanilla
2 Tbsp. butter
3 Tbsp. brown sugar

Let come to boil in Teflon pan. Stir all the time. Makes enough filling for ½ recipe.

Prune Filling:

1 lb. pitted prunes, cooked and
    mashed or ground
1 tsp. cinnamon

1 c. sugar
½ tsp. salt

Cottage Cheese (to be used with Prune Filling):

1 ctn. cottage cheese
½ c. sugar
1 egg, beaten

Pinch of salt
1 Tbsp. corn starch

Cook until thick, stirring constantly. Put 1 teaspoon in center of Prune Filling. Bake at 375° for 15 to 18 minutes.

❧

It is great to be great, but it is greater to be human.

PATE'S ELEPHANT EARS

1 pkg. dry yeast
¼ c. warm water
2 c. all-purpose flour
1½ Tbsp. sugar
½ tsp. salt
1 c. butter or oleo
½ c. scalded milk

1 egg yolk
2 Tbsp. oleo, melted
2 c. sugar
1 Tbsp. + ½ tsp. cinnamon, mixed
¼ c. butter, melted
½ c. pecans, chopped

Dissolve yeast in ¼ cup warm water; let stand 5 minutes. Combine flour, 1½ tablespoons sugar, and salt in large bowl; cut oleo into flour mixture with a pastry blender until mixture looks like coarse meal. Combine milk, egg yolk, and yeast mixture; add to flour mixture, mixing well. Chill dough 2 hours.

Turn dough onto floured surface; knead 1 to 2 minutes. Cover and let stand for 10 minutes. Roll dough into 18x10 inch rectangle on a lightly floured surface. Brush with 2 tablespoons melted oleo. Combine sugar and cinnamon; sprinkle 1 cup of mixture over dough. (You may not need to use the whole cup of sugar, just so dough is covered.)

Roll up jelly roll fashion, starting at long side. Cut into 18 (1 inch) slices. Sprinkle remaining cinnamon mixture lightly over wax paper. Transfer slices to ungreased baking sheet; spread with remaining oleo and sprinkle with cinnamon, sugar, and pecans. Bake at 375° for 10 minutes or until lightly browned. Cool on wire rack.

Lion President Nancy L. Philip, Elmhurst Noon Lions Club
Elmhurst, Illinois, USA

❦

Some people eat from the three basic food groups -
canned, frozen, and takeout.

❦ ❦ ❦

Mid-life crisis:
When the mortgage and the tuition payments
add up to more than you make.

PEANUT BUTTER TEA RING

1 Tbsp. dry yeast	2 eggs, beaten
½ c. warm water	½ c. sugar (scant)
1 Tbsp. sugar	⅓ c. oil or shortening
1 c. milk, scalded and cooled some	1 tsp. salt
	3½ to 4 c. flour

Filling:

1 c. cream style peanut butter	Raisins (optional)
¼ c. sugar	

Topping:

Powdered sugar frosting	Chopped peanuts

Soak yeast in the warm water and sugar in mixing bowl for 5 minutes. Stir in a little of the flour to make a paste. Add warm milk, beaten eggs, and remaining ingredients. Mix by hand until blended. Knead on floured board until elastic. Put in buttered bowl and let rise for 1 hour in a warm place.

Roll dough into rectangle, ¼ inch thick. Spread with peanut butter. Sprinkle with sugar and raisins. Roll up lengthwise and place on buttered cookie sheet, joining ends to form a circle. With scissors, cut through the roll within an inch of the bottom. Let rise for about 45 minutes. Bake at 350° for 30 to 35 minutes.

While warm, spread the top only with powdered sugar frosting, allowing it to trickle down sides. Sprinkle with chopped peanuts. Serve warm. *Enjoy!*

EASY MONKEY BREAD

3 cans (10 count) buttermilk biscuits	¼ c. milk
½ c. chopped pecans	1 stick butter or margarine
½ c. brown sugar	1 c. sugar
	1 tsp. cinnamon

Mix brown sugar, pecans, and milk; heat in saucepan until sugar is melted. Pour into Bundt or tube pan. Melt butter and pour into bowl. Mix sugar and cinnamon; put in another bowl. Dip each biscuit in butter, then into sugar-cinnamon mix. Place biscuits on a plate until all biscuits are ready. Place in tube pan with other mixture to form ring. Cook 30 minutes at 350°. Let set at least 3 minutes before turning out of pan.

Glenn E. Bunch, Jr., PDG 31-H, Snow Hill Lions Club
Snow Hill, North Carolina, USA

❦

Give yourself the moment. Let it happen.

STOLLEN OR CHRISTMAS LOAF

2 pkg. dry yeast or 1½ cakes
  compressed yeast
1½ c. water or milk, scalded and
  cooled
6 c. all-purpose flour, sifted before
  measuring
½ lb. raisins
½ lb. blanched, chopped almonds
½ c. chopped candied citron (red
  and green or other candied
  fruit)

¾ c. sugar, sifted
1½ c. butter, softened
3 eggs
¾ tsp. salt
¾ tsp. grated lemon rind
2 Tbsp. brandy or rum (or several
  drops of rum extract)
Melted butter

Have all ingredients at about 75°F. Dissolve yeast in lukewarm (85°F.) water or milk, about 10 minutes. Add 1 cup of the flour. Permit this sponge to rise in a warm place until doubled in bulk. Sprinkle a little of the sifted flour over the nuts and fruits. Set aside. Beat the butter in a large bowl until very soft. Add the sugar gradually, blending until light and creamy. Beat the eggs in one at a time. Add the salt, lemon rind, and brandy or extract.

Add the sponge and remaining flour. Knead the dough until smooth and elastic. Permit it to rise until almost doubled in bulk. Toss it onto a floured board and knead in the fruits and nuts.

Divide into 2 loaves and place them in greased pans. Brush tops with melted butter. Let the loaves rise, covered, until they again almost double in bulk. Preheat oven to 350°F. Bake the loaves for about 45 minutes. When cool, they may be dusted with confectioners sugar or iced with confectioners sugar icing.

You're only young once.
After that, you have to make up some other excuse for your actions.

POPPY SEED STOLLEN OR ALMOND TEA RING

4¾ c. flour
1 c. scalded milk
¼ c. butter
½ c. sugar
1 tsp. salt

2 yeast cakes or 2 pkg. dried yeast
2 eggs
1 can Solo almond filling or 1 can
    Solo poppy seed

Pour hot milk over butter, sugar, and salt; stir well. Crumble yeast into lukewarm water (115°) and dissolve. Cool milk to lukewarm; add yeast and well beaten eggs. Gradually pour this into the flour to make a soft dough. Put on floured board and knead. Form into ball and place in greased bowl. Cover and let rise until double in bulk.

When yeast dough is light, roll into rectangular square, about ½ inch thick. Brush lightly with melted butter; spread around and then spread the filling. Roll into jelly roll style and place on greased cookie sheet. Form into a ring and cut almost through with scissors at 1 inch intervals, then twist slices. Cover and let rise until double in bulk. Bake at 350° for 30 minutes.

Butter Frosting:

1 c. confectioners sugar, sifted
2 Tbsp. milk

2 Tbsp. melted butter
¼ tsp. vanilla

Blend sugar and butter. Add milk and vanilla. Beat until smooth. Spread over stollen. Sprinkle with ground nuts and halved maraschino cherries or halved walnuts and the cherries.

A small town is a place where no one panics
when the police department takes his vacation.

There is hope for anyone who can still look in a mirror
and laugh at what he sees.

WHODONITS

1 cake yeast or 1 pkg. yeast	½ c. lukewarm water
½ tsp. sugar	½ c. sugar
½ c. shortening	1 egg
1 c. milk	2 tsp. salt
1 c. hot water	Cinnamon and sugar mixture
7 to 7½ c. flour	Tiny marshmallows

Dissolve 1 cake of yeast or 1 package of yeast in ½ cup lukewarm water; add ½ teaspoon sugar. Let stand for 30 to 45 minutes. Cream together ½ cup sugar and ½ cup shortening; add yeast and 1 egg. Beat. To this, add 1 cup milk poured into 1 cup hot water and 2 teaspoons salt. Cool to lukewarm and add yeast mixture. Stir well and add enough flour to make a soft dough; knead until smooth. It takes about 7 to 7½ cups of flour. Cover and let rise in a warm place until doubled.

Prepare tiny marshmallows by coating the marshmallows with melted oleo and then a mix of cinnamon-sugar. Roll in the mixture. Take a small amount of bread dough and wrap around the 2 marshmallows; seal thoroughly, then roll each prepared ball in oleo and cinnamon-sugar mix. Place in prepared pans (use the tiny tart pans or make into a Bundt cake, layering approximately 3 layers). Singles should bake for about 12 minutes and Bundt cake for approximately 1 hour. After 45 minutes of baking at 325°, covered with foil, remove and bake for 15 minutes. Cool upside down to let all of the cinnamon-sugar mixture run down the sides. Cool for approximately 30 minutes and remove from the pan. Cool thoroughly before freezing, or cut while still warm.

SPICE BREAD-IN-A-JAR

⅔ c. shortening	⅔ c. water
2 c. applesauce	3⅓ c. flour (plain)
4 eggs	½ tsp. baking powder
2 tsp. soda	1 tsp. cinnamon
1½ tsp. salt	1 c. pecans or walnuts
1 tsp. cloves	1 c. raisins
2⅔ c. sugar	

Cream shortening with sugar in mixer bowl until light and fluffy. Add applesauce, water, and eggs; mix well. Add mixture of flour, soda, baking powder, salt, and spices; mix well. Stir in nuts and raisins. Spray 7 widemouthed 1 pint jars with Pam. Fill jars ⅔ full. Bake at 325° for exactly 45 minutes. Remove jars from oven 1 at a time and seal quickly with 2 piece lids, pressing bread down if necessary. Let stand until cool. Give as gifts. Use only jars suitable for canning. Contains 120 cal, 1.6 g pro., 19.7 g carb, 4.3 g T Fat, 19.6 mg chol., 50.8 mg potas., and 3.6 mg sod.

Barbara Lane, Mt. Airy Foothills Lions Club
Mt. Airy, North Carolina, USA

TRINITY EASTER BREAD

4 to 4½ c. all-purpose flour
2 pkg. Red Star Instant Blend (dry yeast)
⅓ c. sugar
½ tsp. salt
½ c. water
⅓ c. milk
⅓ c. butter or margarine
2 Tbsp. grated lemon rind
2 eggs
1 (10 oz.) jar maraschino cherries, well drained and halved (about 1 c.)

Heat oven to 375°. In large mixer bowl, combine 1½ cups flour, yeast, sugar, and salt. Mix well. In saucepan, heat water, milk, and butter until warm (120° to 130°). Butter does not have to melt. Add to flour mixture. Add eggs. Blend at low speed until moistened; beat at medium speed 3 minutes. By hand, gradually stir in lemon rind, cherries, and enough remaining flour to make a firm dough. Knead on floured board until smooth and elastic, 5 to 8 minutes. Place in greased bowl, turning to grease top. Cover; let rise in warm place until light and doubled, about 1 hour. Punch down dough and divide in 3 parts. Shape each ⅓ into a smooth ball. On large cookie sheet (greased), place 3 balls together in shape of a cloverleaf. Cover and let rise until doubled, about 45 minutes. Bake at 375° for about 30 to 35 minutes.

If too dark, cover loosely with foil, last 5 to 10 minutes of baking. Remove from cookie sheet. Cool. Drizzle with powdered sugar glaze and garnish with chopped nuts and cherries if desired. Makes 1 large coffee bread.

So easy to do because I (the undersigned) never made homemade bread in my life; it came out beautiful. It put it in 9 mini loaf pans.
Lion Ethel D. Parr, Mt. Holly Springs Lions Club
Gardners, Pennsylvania, USA

❧

Never mind trying to remember the seven dwarfs or the eight reindeer
Just remember the Ten Commandments.

STICKY BUNS

2 c. milk
4 to 6 Tbsp. sugar
2 tsp. salt
2/3 c. shortening

2 eggs
2 cakes or pkg. yeast
1/2 c. lukewarm water
6 c. flour

Syrup:

2 c. brown sugar
1 c. molasses

1/4 c. butter
1/3 c. water

In saucepan, place the first 4 ingredients and heat to lukewarm. In mixing bowl, place the eggs, yeast that has been dissolved in lukewarm water, and the mixture from the saucepan. Add flour. Dough should not be too stiff. Put dough on floured board and knead a little. May need 1 more cup flour. Clean bowl and grease. Put dough back into bowl and cover with waxed paper. Let rise until double. Turn on floured board and knead a little. (Cut dough in half to work easier.) Use rolling pin to roll into rectangular shape 1/4 inch thick. Spread dough with melted butter and sprinkle with sugar and cinnamon. Roll jelly roll fashion and cut to preferred size. Place in well greased pans which have the syrup and nuts in, cut side down, and let rise until double in size. Bake at 350° for 15 to 20 minutes. Let stand 5 minutes before removing from pans.

Syrup: Heat ingredients until dissolved. Pour into greased pans. Put in nuts. Top with dough and let rise until doubled. This recipe makes 40 rolls. I cut 10 rolls from each long roll and this fits into one round cake pan. Use 4 round cake pans.

He who sees a need and waits to be asked for help is as unkind as if he had refused it.

Louise J. Eshleman, Middletown Lions Club
Middletown, Pennsylvania, USA

QUICK STICKY BUNS

1/4 c. oleo, melted
1/4 c. firmly packed brown sugar
1 Tbsp. corn syrup
1/4 c. chopped pecans

11 oz. can refrigerated soft bread
  sticks
1 Tbsp. sugar
1/2 tsp. cinnamon

Blend oleo, brown sugar, and syrup in 8 inch round cake pan. (I do mine right on top of stove.) Sprinkle with pecans. Remove dough from can (*do not unroll!!*). In shallow dish, combine sugar and cinnamon; dip rolls (1 side) in mixture. Arrange sugared side down over pecan mixture. Sprinkle with any remaining sugar mixture. Bake at 375° for 19 to 24 minutes. Cool 1 minute. Invert onto serving plate.

Unexpected company for coffee? This is great - *fast and easy.*

Pam Sedler, Onekama Lions Club
Onekama, Michigan, Manistee County, USA

SCANDINAVIAN COFFEE BREAD
(Canadian style)

2 Tbsp. whole cardamon seeds,
   crushed
2 c. milk, scalded and cooled
2 tsp. sugar
2 pkg. dry yeast
¾ c. white sugar

⅔ c. butter or oleo
3 eggs, beaten
1½ tsp. salt
8 c. flour
1 orange (zest and juice)
Sugar (to sprinkle top)*

Scald milk. Cool to warm. Add 2 teaspoons sugar, yeast, and ground carda-mon seed. Let stand 10 minutes. Put in large bowl or pan. Mix in butter and eggs; mix dry ingredients together. Add to bowl. Knead. Add flour to make dough elastic. Put back in bowl. Let rise until double. Punch down and knead. Form into loaves or make into knots (about 6 inches long). Let rise about half, not double. Bake in oven at 350° for 30 minutes. Makes about 20 to 25 for knots. If baking into tie (knots), monitor time so as not to burn.

* Brush top with mixture of 1 egg and 1 tablespoon water; sprinkle with sugar.

Kathleen Mergaert by Walter E. Loomis, North Jackson Lions Club
Jackson, Michigan, USA

SWEDISH COFFEE ROLL

½ c. scalded milk
Salt
½ c. sugar
½ c. oleo
2 eggs

½ cake or 1 pkg. dry yeast,
   dissolved in warm water (½
   c.) with 1 tsp. sugar
3 to 4 c. flour

Pour scalded milk over softened oleo, salt, and sugar. Cool to lukewarm. Add dissolved yeast and beaten eggs. Work in flour (enough to make a soft dough). Knead. Dough should be soft! Let rise till double in bulk. Roll out in a rectangular shape as thin as possible. Spread with oleo, brown sugar, cinnamon, and nuts. Roll from length side. Form in ring on baking sheet. Cut nearly through with scissors and let rise again. Bake in a 350° oven for 25 to 30 minutes (no more). Ice and sprinkle with nuts if desired.

❦

When you get something for a song, watch out for the accompaniment.

PLUM COFFEE CAKE

2 eggs
¾ c. sugar
1½ c. flour
1½ tsp. baking powder
½ tsp. salt
⅓ c. milk

4 Tbsp. melted margarine
½ tsp. lemon extract
½ tsp. vanilla
2 c. plums, well ripened and pitted
⅓ c. sugar
½ tsp. cinnamon

Beat eggs and sugar until well combined. Sift flour, baking powder, and salt. Combine milk, margarine, and extracts. Add flour mixture to egg mixture, alternating with milk mixture. Pour into greased 8 inch round pan.

Put fruit on top and lightly press down. Combine ½ cup sugar and ½ teaspoon cinnamon; sprinkle it on top of fruit. Bake in 350° oven for 35 to 40 minutes.

NORTH TEXAS STATE UNIVERSITY COFFEE CAKE

½ c. shortening
1 c. sugar
1 egg
2 c. flour

2 tsp. baking powder
½ tsp. salt
¾ c. milk
1 tsp. vanilla

Topping:

¼ c. margarine
¾ c. sugar

1½ tsp. cinnamon
¼ c. flour

Heat oven to 350°. Cream shortening, sugar, and egg. Blend in flour, baking powder, and salt, adding milk alternately with dry ingredients. Add vanilla. Pour batter into greased 8x8 inch pan. Spread ⅓ cup melted margarine on top. Crumble topping over all and bake 40 minutes.

Janie Fox, Saginaw Lions Club
Saginaw, Texas, USA

BANANA MUFFINS

2 c. all-purpose flour
½ c. sugar
2 tsp. baking powder
½ tsp. soda
½ tsp. salt

¼ tsp. nutmeg or cinnamon
½ c. mashed banana
½ c. milk
⅓ c. oil
1 egg, slightly beaten

Heat oven to 375°. Line with paper baking cups or grease (not oil) 12 muffin cups. In medium bowl, combine first 6 ingredients. Stir in remaining ingredients just until dry ingredients are moistened. Spoon batter into prepared muffin cups, filling ⅔ full. Bake at 375° for 15 to 20 minutes or until golden brown. Immediately remove from pan. Serve warm. Makes 12 muffins.

BELFAST MUFFINS

1 c. sugar
½ c. margarine

1 c. milk
1 egg

Stir dry ingredients:

1½ c. flour
⅛ tsp. salt
2 tsp. baking powder

¾ c. wheat germ
1 c. blueberries or raspberries

Topping:

⅓ c. brown sugar
⅓ c. nuts, chopped

½ tsp. cinnamon

Mix in order given. Do not stir too much. Bake in greased or lined muffin pans in a 425° oven for 20 to 25 minutes. Makes 16 to 18.

Donna Juhl, Otis Lions Club
Otis, Colorado, USA

MAINE BLUEBERRY MUFFINS

2 eggs
½ c. sugar
½ c. oil
1½ c. milk

3 c. flour
1½ Tbsp. baking powder
1 tsp. salt
1½ c. blueberries

Beat together eggs, sugar, and oil until well blended. Stir in milk. Sift together flour, baking powder, and salt. Add to egg mixture, stirring just until flour is moistened. Fold in blueberries. Fill greased muffin cups ⅔ full. Bake at 400° for about 30 minutes.

A cinnamon-sugar topping can be sprinkled on top of muffins, if desired, before baking.

Mrs. Jeff Crosby, Exeter Township Lions Club
Exeter, Pennsylvania, USA

BLUEBERRY MUFFINS

2 c. flour
½ c. sugar
3 tsp. salt
4 Tbsp. shortening

1 egg
¾ c. milk
¾ c. blueberries

Preheat oven to 400°. Mix all together. Put into greased muffin pan. Bake 15 to 20 minutes.

Gladys Filla, Yakima West Valley Lions Club
Cowiche, Washington, USA

ORANGE BRAN MUFFINS

½ c. raisins
½ c. chopped dried apple slices
½ c. fresh orange juice
1 c. flour
1 Tbsp. baking powder
2 tsp. baking soda
Pinch of salt

¾ c. sugar
½ tsp. cinnamon
¾ c. Bran Flakes cereal
1 egg
½ c. milk
⅓ c. vegetable oil

In small bowl, combine raisins, dried apples, and orange juice (soak for 30 minutes). Preheat oven to 350°. Line two 8 cup muffin tins with paper liners. In a large bowl, sift together flour, baking powder, baking soda, salt, sugar, and cinnamon. Add the bran cereal and mix thoroughly. In another bowl, beat together the egg, milk, and oil. Make a well in center of dry ingredients and pour the egg mixture into it. Add the raisins, apples, and orange juice; stir just until all the ingredients are incorporated. Do not overmix.

Fill each cup about ¾ full with the batter and bake until the muffins are well colored and a toothpick inserted in the center comes out clean, 18 to 20 minutes. Transfer to a rack and allow them to cool.

Mary Sawtelle, Westbrook Lions Club
Westbrook, Maine, USA

RAISIN CARROT MUFFINS

2 c. oat or bran flake cereal
1 c. skim milk
2 egg whites
3 Tbsp. oil
⅓ c. brown sugar
1½ c. flour

3 tsp. baking powder
¼ tsp. salt
1 tsp. vanilla
¼ tsp. cinnamon
1 c. grated carrots
½ c. raisins

Combine first 5 ingredients in medium size bowl and let stand 5 minutes until flakes are softened. Add the flour, baking powder, salt, cinnamon, and vanilla. Stir just until moistened. Fold in the grated carrots and raisins. Do not overstir. Spray 12 muffin cups with nonstick cooking spray and fill with muffin batter. Bake at 350° for 20 minutes. Makes 12 muffins.

❦

Rare indeed is the person who looks for trouble and fails to find it.

DOLE RAISIN PINEAPPLE MUFFINS

½ c. brown sugar, packed
¼ c. margarine
1 egg
¾ c. Dole pineapple juice
1 tsp. grated orange peel
1½ c. all-purpose flour

½ c. whole wheat flour
1½ tsp. baking powder
½ tsp. baking soda
¼ tsp. salt
¼ tsp. ground cinnamon
1 c. Dole raisins

Beat sugar and margarine until light and fluffy. Beat in egg, juice, and orange peel. Combine remaining ingredients; stir into juice mixture until moistened. Spoon batter into 6 muffin cups coated with cooking spray. Bake at 375°F. for 25 minutes. Cool on rack; serve warm.

John J. Hess, Clarence Center Lions Club
Clarence Center, New York, USA

SOUTH PACIFIC MUFFINS

1 (20 oz.) can crushed pineapple
½ c. sliced almonds
2 c. all-purpose flour
1 tsp. baking soda
1 tsp. salt
1 (3 oz.) pkg. cream cheese

1 c. sugar
2 tsp. vanilla
1 egg, beaten
½ c. dairy sour cream
¼ c. coconut

Drain pineapple. Reserve juice. Heavily grease muffin pans and line with almonds. Mix flour with soda and salt. Blend cream cheese, sugar, and vanilla until smooth. Stir in the egg. Add flour mixture alternately with sour cream. Fold in drained pineapple and coconut. Spoon into prepared pans. Bake at 350°F. for 35 minutes, or until golden brown. Let stand in pan for 5 to 10 minutes. Turn out onto wire rack.

Glaze:

1 Tbsp. butter or margarine
1 c. powdered sugar

1 Tbsp. reserved pineapple juice

Blend butter, powdered sugar, and pineapple juice for glaze. Drizzle over warm muffins. Makes about 2 dozen muffins.

There is no great success without great commitment.

SIX WEEK MUFFINS

1 box raisin bran cereal	4 eggs
1 qt. buttermilk	5 c. flour
1 c. oil	5 tsp. baking soda
2½ c. sugar	2 tsp. salt

Combine cereal, buttermilk, oil, sugar, and eggs. Mix well. Add flour, soda, and salt. Cover and refrigerate 6 hours before using. Fill muffin tins with papers or grease. Fill ⅔ full. Bake at 375° for 15 to 20 minutes. Cover batter and store in refrigerator for up to 6 weeks and bake when needed.

Pat Tulloch, Bedford Heights Lions Club
Bedford Heights, Ohio, USA

SUGARLESS FRUIT AND NUT MUFFINS

1 c. chopped dates	2 eggs, beaten
½ c. raisins	1 tsp. vanilla extract
½ c. chopped prunes	1 c. all-purpose flour
1 c. water	1 tsp. baking soda
½ c. margarine, cut into pats	½ c. chopped nuts
¼ tsp. salt	

In a saucepan, combine dates, raisins, prunes, and water. Bring to a boil and boil 5 minutes. Stir in margarine and salt. Set aside to cool. Add remaining ingredients to fruit. Stir just until dry ingredients are moistened. Spoon into greased mini muffin pans. Bake at 350° for 15 minutes. If desired, bake in a greased 11x7x2 inch pan for 30 minutes. Makes 32 muffins.

TINY GEMS

1 c. butter or margarine	2 c. self-rising flour
1 c. sour cream	

Cream butter and sour cream. Add flour and mix well. Bake in mini muffin tins at 350° until brown.

The misfortunes hardest to bear are those which never come.
Mildred Wolfe, Rock Hill Lions Club
Rock Hill, South Carolina, USA

You've reached middle age when all your exercise is caution.

RAW APPLE BREAD

2 c. sugar
2 eggs
2 c. finely chopped raw apples
3 c. flour
½ tsp. nutmeg
2 tsp. soda

½ c. shortening
1 c. cold coffee
1 c. raisins
1 tsp. cinnamon
¼ tsp. cloves
½ tsp. salt

Cream sugar and shortening. Add eggs and coffee. Mix well. Add apples and raisins. Sift the dry ingredients together. Add to creamed mixture. Bake 45 to 60 minutes at 350° in 2 well greased loaf pans.

Lion Mavis Hall, Plattsmouth Lions Club
Plattsmouth, Nebraska, USA

APPLE BREAD

½ c. butter or oleo
1 c. sugar (white)
2 eggs
1 tsp. vanilla
½ tsp. salt

1 tsp. soda, dissolved in 2 Tbsp.
   sour milk
2 c. diced apples
2 c. flour

Topping:

2 Tbsp. butter
2 Tbsp. flour

2 Tbsp. sugar
1 tsp. cinnamon

Cream butter and sugar. Add eggs, vanilla, salt, and soda. Add apples and flour. Turn into 2 small or 1 large greased and floured tins. Mix together and sprinkle on top loaf the topping. Bake for 1 hour at 325°.

BANANA BREAD

1 c. ripe bananas (2 or 3 medium)
1 egg
¾ c. milk
3 Tbsp. salad oil
3½ tsp. baking powder

1 tsp. salt
1 c. sugar
2½ c. flour
1 c. chopped nuts (optional)

Heat oven to 350°. Grease and flour loaf pans. Place peeled bananas in large mixing bowl. Beat until almost a puree. Add ingredients as listed, mixing well after each addition. Pour into pan. Bake loaves for 55 to 65 minutes. Test with wooden pick. Bread is done when tester comes out clean. Bake muffins for 45 to 50 minutes. Remove from pans to cool on wire racks. Makes one 9 x 5 x 3 inch loaf, two 8½ x 4½ x 2½ inch loaves, or 24 muffins.

CREAM CHEESE BANANA BREAD

8 oz. cream cheese, softened
2 c. Bisquick
2 eggs
1 c. sugar
1 c. mashed bananas

Chopped maraschino cherries
   (optional)
Walnuts or sliced almonds
   (optional)

Blend cream cheese and sugar together. Add remaining ingredients and mix well. Bake at 350° approximately 45 minutes or till done. Makes 1 loaf.

Judy Stork, Arlington Lions Club
Arlington, Nebraska, USA

BANANA BREAD SUPREME

3 large bananas
2 c. flour
1 c. sugar
2 eggs
½ c. milk
1 stick butter
1 tsp. vanilla

1 tsp. soda
⅓ tsp. salt
½ c. chocolate chips
1 c. crushed pineapple, drained
½ c. chopped walnuts
½ c. maraschino cherries, cut in
   halves

In a bowl, mash the bananas. Blend in sugar, eggs, milk, and warm butter. Mix in vanilla, salt, and soda. Mix in flour. Add chocolate chips, pineapple, walnuts, and cherries. Grease 2 medium bread pans. Bake at 350° for 40 minutes.

BANANA BREAD

4 eggs
2 c. sugar
1 c. Wesson oil
1 tsp. vanilla

2 c. bananas, mashed
2 tsp. soda
4 c. flour
½ c. nuts, chopped

Mix all ingredients well. Pour into 2 greased and floured loaf pans. Bake at 275° for 1 hour and 20 minutes or until done.

Lion Peggy Nelson, Riverdale Lions Club
Riverdale, Georgia, USA

❦

The future belongs to those who create it.

CRUMB-TOPPED COCOA BANANA BREAD

1½ c. flour
1⅓ c. sugar
6 Tbsp. cocoa
1 tsp. baking soda
¼ tsp. cinnamon

Dash of ginger
2 eggs, beaten
⅓ c. oil
1 c. mashed banana

Crumb Topping:

3 Tbsp. flour
2 Tbsp. sugar
1 Tbsp. margarine

⅛ tsp. baking powder
⅛ tsp. cinnamon

Stir together first 6 ingredients in large mixing bowl. Add eggs, oil, and mashed banana. Mix until well blended. Pour into 9x5 inch loaf pan that has been sprayed with nonstick cooking spray.

For crumb topping, mix flour, sugar, baking powder, and cinnamon together. Cut in the margarine with pastry blender until crumbly. Sprinkle over bread batter in loaf pan. Bake at 350° for 50 to 60 minutes or until toothpick tests clean. Let stand 15 minutes before removing from pan. Wrap in foil. May be stored in refrigerator up to 1 week. Makes 1 loaf.

❦

The difference between a "fine watchdog" and a "ferocious beast"
depends on which side of the fence you're on.

❦ ❦ ❦

One thing you can say about kids -
at least they don't bore you with cute things their parents said.

ITALIAN BUTTER BREAD - CHRISTMAS FRUIT BREAD

⅓ qt. water/milk (use half of each)
1 oz. yeast (4 level tsp. dry yeast)
1½ cubes butter (not margarine)
⅓ lb. sugar
¾ lb. raisins

¼ lb. diced citrus fruit and
  cherries (candied)
2 large eggs
2½ lb. flour*

1. Soften the butter.
2. Soften yeast in ½ cup warm water. Let stand till it starts working.
3. In your mixing bowl, add liquid, sugar, and yeast; stir to dissolve sugar, then add all the rest of the ingredients, except flour. Mix together.
4. Add flour. Mix to fairly stiff dough. (Flour varies so the flour you use may require more or less.)
5. Let rise in a warm area (or in slightly warm oven). Let double in size. Punch down again and let rise to ½ the previous size, then dump out onto counter.
6. Dust the counter with flour first before dumping dough, then dust your dough so you don't get sticky with dough.
7. This mix should get you eight 12 ounce loaves. However, a little loaf is good if you divide your dough into 7 equal parts.
8. Round up each chunk of dough, you know, so it's round like a ball.
9. Have 2 cookie sheets greased or sprayed to prevent sticking. Place your round loaves on greased sheets.
10. Let rise, then just before you put them in the oven, wash the top of each loaf with condensed milk (it gives the top a nice shiny finish when baked - otherwise, your bread may look a little anemic?).
11. After brushing top with milk, take a sharp knife and cut a big cross on top. When baked, it makes a nice look to your bread. There's nothing better than to toast a slice of your bread and spread with butter. It's delicious. Of course, you can serve it at a social, but that would really be a waste of a good thing!! No salt is needed for this recipe since the salt is in the butter.

* Gold Medal makes better bread flour. All-purpose may be used if you don't have the other. May take a little more.

Lion Lowell Jacobs, Spokane Central Lions Club
Spokane, Washington, USA

There is nothing like a bit of experience to upset a theory.

GINGERBREAD

1½ c. dark cane syrup
½ c. sugar
1 c. vegetable oil
2 eggs, well beaten

2 tsp. baking soda
4 tsp. ginger
Flour to make stiff dough

Mix the first 3 ingredients together and cook about 5 minutes. It should not be too thick, just a little thick. Mix the next 3 ingredients together and add to the cooled, cooked ingredients. Blend together well. Mix in flour, beating with dough hooks. Mix until dough can be rolled out with greased rolling pin. Roll until about ¼ inch thick. Bake on greased baking sheet at 350° until done. Makes a large batch.

Bertha Smith, Parkway Lions Club
Panama City, Florida, USA

ORANGE BREAD

Cut orange peel from 2 large or 3 small oranges. Cut into very small strips. Boil in water until tender; drain off water.

Add:

⅓ c. boiling water

1 c. sugar

Cook until spins a thread. Cool.

Add:

3 c. flour
4 tsp. baking powder
½ tsp. salt

1 egg in a cup and fill with milk to make 1 full c.

Mix all ingredients. Put in greased loaf pan. Bake at 375° for 45 to 50 minutes. Makes 1 loaf.

Grandma Krause, Chesterfield Bay Lions Club
Heaven, USA

ORANGE, DATE, AND PECAN BREAD

1 orange
1 c. dates, cut in small pieces
1 c. sugar
2 Tbsp. oleo, melted
1 egg, beaten

2 c. flour
1 tsp. baking powder
1 tsp. soda
¼ tsp. salt
½ c. chopped pecans

Squeeze orange and add water to juice to make 1 cup liquid. Remove orange pulp and put peel through food chopper. Combine with dates, sugar, oleo, egg, and orange liquid. Sift flour, baking powder, soda, and salt. Blend into fruit mixture. Add nuts. Pour into a greased 9x5x3 inch loaf pan. Bake at 350° for 50 to 55 minutes. Serves 2 to 6 people.

PEACH CORIANDER BREAD

1 c. sugar
4 Tbsp. butter
1 egg, beaten
2 c. flour
½ tsp. baking powder
½ tsp. baking soda

½ tsp. salt
2 Tbsp. ground coriander
1 c. mashed ripe peaches
½ tsp. orange or almond extract
2 Tbsp. sour cream
½ c. chopped walnuts

Cream together sugar and butter; beat in egg. Measure dry ingredients. Mix peaches, cream, and extract. Add dry ingredients alternately with peach mixture, beginning and ending with dry ingredients and stirring well after each addition. Blend in nuts. Bake in 3x7 inch loaf pan at 350° for 1 hour. Cool in pan 10 minutes. Remove from pan. Cool. Store in airtight wrap in refrigerator. Let ripen at least 24 hours to enhance flavor.

PERSIMMON BREAD

3½ c. sugar
1 c. vegetable oil
4 eggs
2 c. persimmon puree
3 c. flour
½ tsp. baking powder
2 tsp. baking soda

2 tsp. salt
1 tsp. cloves
1 tsp. cinnamon
1 tsp. nutmeg
1 tsp. allspice
1 c. raisins or nuts (optional)

Mix in order given. Grease and flour pans. Bake 45 to 60 minutes at 350°. Yield: 4 small loaves or 2 regular. Good spread with honey-butter. I fix the puree in the fall and freeze it in 2 cup containers. Can have bread all year long.

Martha Walters, Emporia Noon Lions Club
Emporia, Kansas, USA

PISTACHIO BREAD

18 oz. box yellow cake mix
1 pkg. pistachio pudding
½ c. water
¼ c. cooking oil
1 c. red maraschino cherries,
  diced

2 to 3 drops of green food color
4 eggs
1 c. sour cream
½ c. chopped nuts

Mix cake mix and pudding together. Add other ingredients and mix well. Pour into 2 greased and floured bread pans; bake at 350° for 1 hour (loaf pans).

When you find yourself turning green with envy, you are ripe for trouble.
Mildred Wolfe, Rock Hill Lions Club
Rock Hill, South Carolina, USA

PLUM BREAD

1 c. oil
1½ c. sugar
3 eggs
3 c. flour
1 tsp. soda

1 tsp. baking powder
1 tsp. salt
3 tsp. cinnamon
3 tsp. vanilla
2 c. plum pulp

In large bowl, add oil, sugar, and eggs. Mix well. Add dry ingredients and pulp. Mix. Grease and flour 2 loaf pans. Pour equal amounts in pans. Bake at 350° for about 45 to 60 minutes or until done. Makes 2 loaves.

PUMPKIN SWIRL BREAD

Filling:

1 (8 oz.) pkg. cream cheese,
  softened

¼ c. sugar
1 egg, beaten

Batter:

1¾ c. flour
1½ c. sugar
1 tsp. baking soda
1 tsp. cinnamon
½ tsp. salt

¼ tsp. ground nutmeg
1 c. canned pumpkin
½ c. margarine, melted
1 egg, beaten
⅓ c. water

1. Combine cream cheese, sugar, and egg, mixing until well blended; set aside.

2. Combine dry ingredients. Add combined pumpkin, margarine, egg, and water, mixing just until moistened. Reserve 2 cups pumpkin batter; pour remaining batter into a greased and floured 9x5 inch loaf pan.

3. Pour cream cheese mixture over pumpkin batter; top with reserved pumpkin batter. Cut through batters with knife several times for swirl effect.

4. Bake at 350° for an hour and 10 minutes or until wooden pick inserted in center comes out clean. Cool for 5 minutes; remove from pan.

❦

Worry often gives a small thing a big shadow.

MOTHER'S OATMEAL BREAD

1 c. uncooked rolled oats	1 Tbsp. butter or margarine
2 c. boiling water	2 tsp. salt
1 env. active dry yeast	6 c. sifted all-purpose flour
½ c. light molasses or white Karo	

Day before or early on day: In large bowl, mix oats with boiling water. Let stand ½ to 1 hour. Sprinkle yeast into ¼ cup warm water; stir to dissolve. To rolled oats, add molasses or Karo, salt, butter or margarine, and dissolved yeast. Beat with wooden spoon to mix well. Gradually beat in flour, then beat till dough leaves sides of bowl. Cover bowl with towel. Let rise in warm (80° to 85°) till doubled in bulk, about 1 hour. When double, beat it again, then divide in half into 2 loaf pans. Cover and let rise again till double. Bake 50 minutes at 350°.

Joyce E. Steen, Merritt Island Lions Club
Merritt Island, Florida, USA

SWEDISH OATMEAL BREAD

2 c. quick oatmeal	1 Tbsp. salt
2 c. boiling water	1 pkg. yeast
⅓ c. shortening	1½ c. warm water
½ c. molasses	6 to 7 c. flour (or more)

Combine in large bowl the oats, molasses, shortening, salt, and boiling water. Blend well and cool to lukewarm. Add the yeast which is softened in warm water. Gradually add flour to form a stiff dough. Knead for 10 minutes. Place in greased bowl and let rise until doubled, about 2 hours. Punch down and let rise again for 30 minutes. Place dough on floured board. Divide in 3 parts. Let rise for 15 minutes. Shape into 3 loaves. Let rise until doubled. Bake at 350° for 40 minutes. Makes 3 loaves.

RHUBARB BREAD

1½ c. (packed) brown sugar	1 tsp. vanilla
⅔ c. salad oil	2½ c. flour
1 egg	1½ c. diced rhubarb
1 c. sour milk (I use lowfat milk)	½ c. nuts
1 tsp. salt	½ c. sugar
1 tsp. soda	¼ c. butter (I use 2 Tbsp. oleo)

Mix all ingredients, except sugar and butter, together; place in 2 greased loaf pans. (I use 1 regular pan and 1 small pan.) Mix sugar and butter; sprinkle over loaves. Bake at 325° for 1 hour and 15 minutes.

Mary Levecque, Westbrook Lions Club
Westbrook, Maine, USA

FINNISH CHRISTMAS RYE BREAD OR JOULULIMPPU

2 c. rye flour
1 qt. mashed potatoes
2 c. potato water
1 large cake fresh yeast or 1 oz.
   dry yeast, dissolved in ¼ c.
   water (warm)
1½ c. dark molasses
5 c. warm water

½ c. oil
½ c. sugar
3 Tbsp. salt
1 Tbsp. anise seed
1 c. golden raisins
2 c. rye flour
18 to 20 c. all-purpose flour

In large bowl, combine 2 cups rye flour with the mashed potatoes, potato water, and yeast. Stir and cover. Let stand at room temperature for 2 days. Stir in molasses, warm water, oil, sugar, salt, anise, raisins, and rye flour. Add all-purpose flour to make a stiff dough. Turn out onto floured surface and knead until dough loses its stickiness. Place into greased bowl and let rise in a warm place until doubled. Shape into loaf or round pans. Let rise until doubled. Bake at 375°F. for about 40 to 50 minutes or until loaf sounds hollow when tapped. Makes 9 to 10 loaves.

STRAWBERRY BREAD

3 c. flour
1 tsp. salt
1 c. oil
2 c. sugar
1 Tbsp. cinnamon

1 tsp. soda
3 eggs
2 boxes frozen strawberries,
   thawed

Combine preceding ingredients. Grease small loaf pans with butter. Coat with sugar. Fill pans ½ to ¾ full. Bake at 350° for 1 hour.

ZUCCHINI BREAD

3 eggs, beaten
1 c. oil
2 c. sugar
2 c. shredded zucchini
3 c. flour

1 tsp. baking soda
1 tsp. salt
3 tsp. cinnamon
¼ tsp. baking powder
1 c. chopped nuts (optional)

Combine oil, sugar, and zucchini. Sift flour, soda, salt, cinnamon, and baking powder together. Add eggs and zucchini to dry mixture; blend well. Add nuts. Pour into greased and floured bread pan. Bake at 325° for 1 hour and 15 minutes.

Debbie Abbott, Lyman Lions Club
Lyman, Wyoming, USA

CHOCOLATE ZUCCHINI BREAD

1 c. brown sugar
1 c. sugar
½ c. margarine
½ c. oil
3 eggs
1 tsp. vanilla
¾ c. buttermilk
3 c. flour

1 tsp. cinnamon
½ tsp. salt
2¼ tsp. baking soda
5 Tbsp. cocoa
2½ c. grated zucchini
½ c. milk chocolate chips
½ c. raisins
½ c. chopped nuts (optional)

Beat sugar, oil, and margarine until dissolved. Add eggs, one at a time. Add buttermilk and vanilla. Sift all dry ingredients. Add to batter alternately with zucchini. Fold in chips, raisins, and nuts. Pour into greased 9x13 inch pan. Bake at 350° for 1 hour. *Improves with freezing.*

ZUCCHINI NUT BREAD

1 c. vegetable oil
2 c. sugar
3 eggs
2½ c. grated raw zucchini
3 c. flour

3 tsp. cinnamon
1 tsp. baking soda
½ tsp. baking powder
½ c. chopped walnuts
½ to ¾ c. raisins

Grease and flour 2 loaf pans (8x5 inches). Preheat oven to 350°F. Blend vegetable oil, sugar, eggs (added one at a time), and grated zucchini together in large bowl. In another bowl, sift together flour, cinnamon, baking soda, and baking powder. Add this to first mixture, blending thoroughly. Stir in walnuts and raisins. Pour into loaf pans. Bake for 1 hour at 350°F., or until done. (When inserted toothpick is withdrawn dry, bread can be removed from oven.) Cool for awhile before turning out of pans. This bread freezes well, allowing you to enjoy long after summer growing season ends.

Joanne M. Campbell, Lincoln-Blackstone Valley Lions Club
Lincoln, Rhode Island, USA

Have Character! Don't be one.

ZUCCHINI NUT BREAD

1 c. oil
½ c. honey
2 Tbsp. Sweet 'N Low liquid
   (equivalent of ½ c. sugar)
3 eggs
2 tsp. vanilla
3 c. flour*
1½ tsp. baking powder
1 tsp. soda
½ tsp. allspice
3 tsp. cinnamon
1 tsp. salt
3 c. finely grated, unpeeled
   zucchini
1½ c. finely grated carrots
1 c. raisins
¾ c. chopped nuts
¼ c. chopped sunflower seeds

Beat eggs until foamy. Add oil, honey, Sweet 'N Low, and vanilla. Mix well. Sift together in separate bowl the flour, baking powder, soda, allspice, cinnamon, and salt. Set aside. Measure together in another bowl the zucchini, carrots, raisins, nuts, and seeds. Add dry ingredients, approximately 1 cup at a time, alternately with zucchini mixture to the egg mixture. Stir well after each addition. Pour batter evenly divided into 2 greased and floured loaf pans. Bake for 1 hour at 350°. Remove from pan immediately. Cool and slice or cool slightly and wrap in foil to freeze for later.

* May use ½ cup soy flour and ½ cup whole wheat flour for the third cup.

ZUCCHINI FRUIT BREAD

3 eggs
3½ c. sugar
1 c. salad oil
3 Tbsp. vanilla
1 (8 oz.) can crushed pineapple
1½ c. coarsely chopped
   cranberries
3 c. flour
2 tsp. baking soda
½ tsp. baking powder
1 tsp. salt
2 tsp. cinnamon
1 tsp. nutmeg
1 c. chopped nuts or raisins (I use
   both)

Beat eggs. Add sugar and beat until blended. Stir in pineapple and cranberries. Sift dry ingredients and blend well. Pour into greased bread pans. Bake at 350° for 50 minutes. Cool and chill before serving.

This bread keeps very well.

Lion Kathleen Schatz Dague, Aurora Eastgate Lions Club
Aurora, Colorado, USA

❦

Most people use their hands and feet to drive; a few also use their heads.

PINEAPPLE ZUCCHINI BREAD

3 eggs
1 c. oil
2 c. sugar
2 c. grated zucchini
2 tsp. vanilla
1 (8 oz.) can crushed pineapple
3 c. flour

2 tsp. soda
1 tsp. salt
½ tsp. baking powder
1½ tsp. cinnamon
¾ tsp. nutmeg
1 c. walnuts, chopped
1 c. dates or raisins, chopped

With mixer, beat eggs. Blend in oil, sugar, and vanilla. Continue mixing until thick and foamy. Stir in zucchini and pineapple with spoon. Combine flour, soda, salt, baking powder, nutmeg, chopped nuts, and dates or raisins. Stir gently into zucchini-pineapple mixture until blended.

Divide batter into 2 greased and floured loaf pans. Bake at 350° for 1 to 1¼ hours until wooden pick inserted in center comes out clean. Cool 10 minutes and turn out on racks to cool. I add ¼ teaspoon more nutmeg. It is delicious. Can be frozen.

Floyd N. Johnston, Plumb Lane Lions Club
Reno, Nevada, USA

TOASTED BUTTER PECAN LOAF

1 c. sugar
½ c. milk
1½ tsp. baking powder
½ tsp. salt
½ c. pecans
½ c. butter, cut into 10 pieces

2 eggs
1 tsp. vanilla
1½ c. flour
3 Tbsp. butter
1 c. 10X sugar
2 to 3 tsp. milk

Grease and flour one 9x5 inch loaf pan. Brown 3 tablespoons butter and pecans in small saucepan. Drain nuts and save butter. In food processor, process 1 cup sugar, ½ cup milk, 1½ teaspoons baking powder, ½ teaspoon salt, ½ cup butter, 2 eggs, 1 teaspoon vanilla, and toasted pecans for 30 seconds. Add flour and process for 5 seconds.

Pour into pan and bake at 350° for 50 to 60 minutes. Cool completely. Mix saved butter, 1 cup 10X sugar, and 2 to 3 teaspoons milk. Spread on cake.

The best way to appreciate your job is to imagine yourself without it.

OLD WITCHES MAGIC NUT BREAD

3 eggs
¾ c. vegetable oil
1 lb. can pumpkin
½ c. water
2½ c. flour
2¼ c. sugar

1½ tsp. baking soda
1¼ tsp. salt
¾ tsp. nutmeg
¾ tsp. cinnamon
½ c. chopped nuts
1 c. raisins (optional)

Combine all dry ingredients. Beat eggs, oil, pumpkin, and water. Add to dry ingredients. Mix well. Bake in three 1 pound coffee cans for 1 hour and 15 minutes at 350°. Frost with Cream Cheese Frosting.

Cream Cheese Frosting:

4 oz. cream cheese
3 Tbsp. butter

1 tsp. vanilla
½ box powdered sugar

Sprinkle with chopped nuts.

Or, bake in mini loaf pans. This is great at Christmas because the coffee can looks like a log.

Mrs. Ron (Pat) Henne, Elburn Lions Club
Elburn, Illinois, USA

LEMON NUT BREAD

⅓ c. butter, melted
1 c. sugar
2 eggs
½ tsp. almond extract
1½ c. flour
1 tsp. baking powder

1 tsp. salt
½ c. milk
½ c. chopped walnuts
1 Tbsp. lemon peel
3 Tbsp. fresh lemon juice
¼ c. sugar

Blend butter and sugar together. Beat in eggs, one at a time. Add extract. Sift together flour, baking powder, and salt. Add to egg mixture alternately with milk. Blend just to mix. Fold in nuts and peel. Turn into greased and floured bread pan. Bake at 325° for about 70 minutes or until tests done.

Topping: Mix lemon juice and sugar; immediately spoon over hot loaf. Cool 10 minutes, then remove from pan. Wrap in foil and wait 24 hours to let the flavor distribute. Makes 1 loaf.

People who look for the easy way out seem to have trouble finding an exit.

CRANBERRY NUT BREAD

2 c. flour	2 Tbsp. margarine
1 c. sugar	1 Tbsp. orange peel
1½ tsp. baking powder	1 egg
½ tsp. baking soda	1½ c. fresh cranberries
1 tsp. salt	½ c. chopped nuts
¾ c. orange juice	

preheat oven to 350°F. and grease a 9x5 inch loaf pan. Mix flour, sugar, baking powder, baking soda, and salt together in bowl. Add orange juice, margarine, orange peel, and well beaten egg. Mix well. Chop cranberries in food processor. Stir nuts and cranberries into batter. Batter will be thick. Transfer to loaf pan and bake for 55 minutes.

YORKSHIRE PUDDING

2 eggs	1 c. flour
1 c. milk	1 tsp. salt

Beat eggs until light. Add milk, then add sifted flour and salt. Beat 3 minutes with an electric mixer or 5 minutes by hand mixing. Pour into a hot pan which has 4 tablespoons melted butter. Bake at 350° for 40 minutes in an 8x8 inch pan. Cut into squares and serve hot.

This is a holiday recipe that our family enjoys with roast beef and also with ham. It is a hot bread that is delicious with gravy.
Doris Brewer (Mrs. Guy), Silver Run-Union Mills Lions Club
Westminster, Maryland, USA

HAWAIIAN COCONUT SPREAD

8 oz. soft cream cheese	⅓ c. flaked coconut
2 Tbsp. apricot, pineapple or	
peach preserves	

Combine cream cheese and preserves, mixing until well blended. Add coconut and mix well. Chill. Serve with nut bread slices. Makes 1⅓ cups.

Variations: Add ⅛ teaspoon anise seed. Substitute ¼ cup whole cranberry sauce for preserves.

Life happens to us while we are making plans.

TORTILLAS

2 c. flour
¼ tsp. salt
¼ tsp. baking powder

1 Tbsp. shortening
Water

Mix flour, salt, and baking powder. Add shortening. Mix. Add water, as needed, like making a pie crust. Let set for 10 minutes. Pinch off a ball of dough and roll. Roll only on one side. When cooking, the bottom of the tortilla goes first on the griddle. Cook 10 minutes on one side and turn to the other side for 5 minutes.

Janie Fox, Saginaw Lions Club
Saginaw, Texas, USA

AMERICAN INDIAN BREAD - "BANNOCK"

2½ c. flour
5 tsp. baking powder
½ tsp. salt
3 Tbsp. sugar

3 Tbsp. Crisco or lard
1 egg
1 c. water

Mix flour, baking powder, salt, and sugar. Add Crisco or lard; cut in until crumbly. Mix together egg and water; beat. Add to flour mixture. Stir to form soft dough. Knead on floured board about 10 times. Too much toughens bread. Divide; flatten each ball to about ½ inch thick. Can be cooked 2 ways: Grease iron skillet and bake on top of stove. Turn when brown (covered) on low heat or place on greased baking sheet in a 450° oven for 10 to 15 minutes until golden brown. Serve hot with butter, peanut butter, honey, or jam.

For individual servings: Roll out to ½ inch thick. Cut 2½ inch biscuits. Cook in nonstick skillet about 5 minutes per side on medium heat.

Walter E. Loomis, North Jackson Lions Club
Jackson, Michigan, USA

OLD TIME DUMPLINGS

2 c. flour
1 Tbsp. butter
1¼ tsp. baking powder

¾ tsp. salt
Milk

Sift flour, baking powder, and salt into bowl. Add the butter and work in with pastry blender or finger tips. Add sufficient milk to make a stiff batter.

Turn out on a well-floured board and roll about ½ inch thick. Cut in small squares and drop in hot liquid. Cook for 20 to 25 minutes.

You must have a tight fitting cover or dumplings will be heavy.

BLACK RASPBERRY DUMPLINGS

1 qt. fresh or frozen black
   raspberries
1 c. sugar
1 c. water

3 Tbsp. cornstarch
3 c. Bisquick
1 c. milk
¼ c. sugar

In a 6 quart pan, combine raspberries, 1 cup sugar, water, and cornstarch. Stir to blend. Bring to a boil. Turn heat to low. Combine Bisquick, milk, and ¼ cup sugar. Drop by spoonfuls onto boiling berries. Cook over low heat, uncovered, for 10 minutes. Cover and cook 10 more minutes. Serve warm. Makes 10 servings.

MICROWAVE DUMPLINGS

2½ c. beef or chicken broth
1 c. all-purpose flour
2 tsp. baking powder

½ tsp. salt
½ c. milk
2 Tbsp. vegetable oil

Pour broth into a 3 quart glass casserole. Cover with an all-glass lid or plastic wrap. Heat in the microwave oven to boiling (about 8 minutes at HIGH). Meanwhile, combine flour, baking powder, and salt in a bowl. Combine milk and oil; add to the dry ingredients and stir with a fork just until moistened. Drop dumpling mixture by tablespoonfuls into boiling broth. Cook, covered, in microwave oven 6½ minutes at HIGH. Let stand, covered, 5 minutes before serving. Makes 4 to 6 servings.

"Life is like a coin, you can spend it any way you want to, but you can spend it only once."

Richard L. Berg, Mt. Holly Springs, Pennsylvania, Lions Club
Mt. Holly Springs, Pennsylvania, USA

POPOVERS
(Quick and easy)

½ c. milk
⅓ c. sugar
½ tsp. salt
½ tsp. vanilla
1 tsp. shortening

1 egg
1¼ tsp. baking powder
1⅓ c. flour (unsifted)
2 dashes of nutmeg (optional)

Mix all ingredients together; stir until smooth. Drop from teaspoon into deep hot fat or oil (about 375°). They will pop over by themselves. Fry until they are a golden brown; drain and roll in granulated sugar. Makes 36 to 40 (1 inch) round ball cake type donuts.

Your neighbor is the man who needs you.

CORN CUSTARD CAKE

2 Tbsp. butter
2 eggs
½ c. sugar
1 c. buttermilk
¼ tsp. salt

1 tsp. baking soda
1½ c. corn meal
½ c. flour
2 c. milk

Preheat oven to 350°. Put butter in 9 inch cast iron skillet and place in oven to melt. In a large bowl, combine eggs, sugar, buttermilk, salt, baking soda, corn meal, flour, and 1 cup of the milk. Stir to mix well. When butter is melted, pour batter into middle of frying pan. Do not stir. Melted butter will come up around sides of batter. Pour remaining cup of milk into center of batter; do not stir. Bake at 350° for 30 to 40 minutes. When done, top will be golden brown, but bottom will be moist like custard. Serve with heated refried beans and tossed salad. Serves 8.

BUTTERMILK YEAST BISCUITS

1 c. buttermilk (lukewarm)
1 pkg. dry yeast
¼ c. melted shortening
2 Tbsp. sugar
½ c. warm water

3 to 3½ c. flour
1 tsp. baking powder
¼ tsp. soda
¾ tsp. salt

Dissolve yeast in warm water. Add warm buttermilk, melted shortening, sugar, salt, baking powder, and soda. Stir in flour. Knead on floured surface, then roll out and cut into rounds as for biscuits and place in oiled pan. Let rise for 1 hour, then bake 12 to 15 minutes or until browned at 400°.

Arvelle James, White Deer Lions Club
White Deer, Texas, USA

Closets are something some people hang things in
when they run out of doorknobs.

Notes

Show me a man with head held high,
and I'll show you a man who can't get used to bifocals.

Cakes
and
Frostings

Common Baking Dishes and Pans

Spring Form Pan

Layer Cake or Pie Pan

Ring Mold

Baking or Square Pan

Loaf Pan

Brioche Pan

Angel Cake Pan

Bundt Tube

Equivalent Dishes

4-CUP BAKING DISH
= 9″ pie plate
= 8″ x 1¼″ layer cake pan
= 7⅜″ x 3⅝″ x 2¼″ loaf pan

6-CUP BAKING DISH
= 8″ or 9″ x 1½″ layer cake pan
= 10″ pie pan
= 8½″ x 3⅝″ x 2⅝″ loaf pan

8-CUP BAKING DISH
= 8″ x 8″ x 2″ square pan
= 11″ x 7″ x 1½″ baking pan
= 9″ x 5″ x 3″ loaf pan

10-CUP BAKING DISH
= 9″ x 9″ x 2″ square pan
= 11¾″ x 7½″ x 1¾″ baking pan
= 15″ x 10″ x 1″ flat jelly roll pan

12-CUP BAKING DISH OR MORE
= 13½″ x 8½″ x 2″ glass baking dish
= 13″ x 9″ x 2″ metal baking pan
= 14″ x 10½″ x 2½″ roasting pan

Total Volume of Pans

TUBE PANS

7½″ x 3″ Bundt tube	6 cups
9″ x 3½″ fancy or Bundt tube	9 cups
9″ x 3½″ angel cake pan	12 cups
10″ x 3¾″ Bundt tube	12 cups
9″ x 3½″ fancy tube mold	12 cups
10″ x 4″ fancy tube mold	16 cups
10″ x 4″ angel cake pan	18 cups

SPRING FORM PANS

8″ x 3″ pan	12 cups
9″ x 3″ pan	16 cups

RING MOLDS

8½″ x 2¼″ mold	4½ cups
9¼″ x 2¾″ mold	8 cups

BRIOCHE PAN

9½″ x 3¼″ pan	8 cups

CAKES AND FROSTINGS

DIRT CAKE

20 oz. pkg. Oreo cookies
8 oz. pkg. cream cheese
¼ c. margarine, softened
⅓ c. powdered sugar

2 (3 oz.) pkg. French vanilla
   pudding
12 oz. Cool Whip

Crush cookies in food processor. Make pudding to package directions. Mix cream cheese, margarine, and sugar; add to pudding and mix. Fold in Cool Whip.

Line flower pot with foil. Layer crushed cookies and pudding, ending with crushed cookies. Insert stem of artificial flower into plastic straw and place in center of pot. Use garden trowel to serve. Gummy worms may be used for decorative effect.

Controversial! Very often, not recognized as dessert. Fun food!
Doris Robidoux, Blackstone Valley Lions Club
Manville, Rhode Island, USA

WACKY CAKE

A:

1½ c. flour
1 c. sugar
3 Tbsp. cocoa

1 tsp. soda (baking)
½ tsp. salt

B: Use 1 cup of water.

C:

1 tsp. vanilla
5 Tbsp. butter

1 Tbsp. vinegar (cider)

Sift A ingredients in an ungreased cake pan about 9 inches square and make 3 holes. Place in these holes C. Pour 1 cup water (B) over entire mixture and stir until dissolved. Bake in moderate oven (325°F.) for 30 minutes.

Note: No egg and no milk. It is truly great.
Lion Ralph Fliedner, Jr., Lake Ariel Lions Club
Lake Ariel, Pennsylvania, USA

The darkest hour is only sixty minutes long.

CRAZY CAKE

1½ c. cake flour
1 c. sugar
3 Tbsp. cocoa
6 Tbsp. oil
1 Tbsp. vinegar

1¼ c. cold water
1 tsp. baking soda
½ tsp. salt
1 tsp. vanilla

Sift dry ingredients into ungreased flat pan. Make 3 holes in dry ingredients. Put oil, vinegar, and vanilla in them. Pour water over top. Mix with fork until smooth. Do not beat. Bake in 350° oven for 40 minutes.

Evelyn Steele, Lyman Lions Club
Lyman, Wyoming, USA

CRAZY CAKE

3 c. flour
2 c. sugar
⅓ c. cocoa
2 tsp. soda
1 tsp. salt

1 tsp. vanilla
¾ c. oil
2 c. water
2 tsp. vinegar

Sift together flour, sugar, cocoa, soda, and salt directly into ungreased 9x13 inch pan. Put 3 holes in flour mixture. Put oil in one, vinegar, and vanilla. Put 2 cups water over mixture. Mix well with fork. Bake 35 minutes at 350°.

Frosting:

2 c. powdered sugar
2 large Tbsp. peanut butter
1 Tbsp. butter

½ tsp. salt
1 tsp. vanilla

Cream ingredients.

Elaine Dahlke, Brownton Lions Club
Brownton, Minnesota, USA

Show me a nightingale that forgot its song
and I'll show you a humming bird.

COKE CAKE

Cake:

2 c. sugar
2 c. flour
½ c. margarine
½ c. oil
2 eggs
1½ c. small marshmallows

3 Tbsp. cocoa
1 c. Coke
½ c. buttermilk
1 tsp. baking soda
1 tsp. vanilla

Frosting:

½ c. margarine
3 Tbsp. cocoa
1 tsp. vanilla

1 box powdered sugar
5 Tbsp. Coke
1 c. chopped nuts (optional)

Cake: In a large bowl, mix sugar and flour; set aside. In a medium size saucepan, combine margarine, oil, cocoa, and Coke until mixture boils. Pour over flour and sugar mix. Stir until well blended. Add buttermilk, baking soda, eggs, marshmallows, and vanilla; mix well. Pour into an oblong pan sprayed with Pam or similar product. Bake at 325° for 40 minutes.

Frosting: Cake must be cold to frost. In a medium size saucepan, combine margarine, cocoa, and Coke until mixture boils. Remove and add powdered sugar, vanilla, and chopped nuts (optional). Spread on cold cake while frosting is hot.

Diane Howland, Ft. Lauderdale Lions Club
Ft. Lauderdale, Florida, USA

❧

Your best years are when the kids are old enough to help shovel snow but too young to drive the car.

❧ ❧ ❧

Advice to husbands: Never try to guess your wife's size.
Just buy her anything marked "Petite" and hold on to the receipt.

HICKORY NUT CAKE

Cake:

1½ c. sugar
½ c. shortening
1 c. milk
2 c. sifted flour
2 tsp. baking powder

½ tsp. nutmeg
¼ tsp. salt
1 c. nutmeats, chopped fine
3 egg whites

Creamy Nut Filling and Frosting:

2½ Tbsp. flour
½ c. milk
½ c. butter
½ c. sugar

Pinch of salt
½ tsp. vanilla
½ c. chopped nutmeats
1 c. powdered sugar

Mix sugar, fat, and milk. Add sifted flour and other ingredients (alternate dry with milk). Add nutmeats. Fold in beaten egg whites. Bake in moderate oven (350°) in 2 layer cake pans.

Filling and Frosting: Blend flour and milk. Cook over low heat to a very thick paste (about 10 minutes), stirring constantly. Cook to lukewarm. Meanwhile, cream butter with sugar. Add pinch of salt. Beat with eggbeater until fluffy. Fold in vanilla and chopped nutmeats. Use about ⅓ of this for the filling between the layers. To the remainder, blend in powdered sugar (a small amount at a time). Spread on top and sides of cake. This cake is always a real treat at Christmas and holiday parties.

Stella Pierce, Moweaqua Lions Club
Moweaqua, Illinois, USA

BANANA NUT CAKE

1½ c. sugar
1¾ c. flour
½ c. butter
½ c. nuts
2 bananas

2 eggs
4 tsp. sour milk
1 tsp. soda
1 tsp. vanilla

Icing:

½ stick butter
1 (3 oz.) pkg. cream cheese

2 c. powdered sugar
½ tsp. vanilla

Mix sugar and flour; cream in butter and bananas. Add eggs and nuts. Add sour milk, soda, and vanilla. Mix well. Pour into greased and floured 9x13 inch pan. Bake at 350° until done. Cool and add icing.

Icing: Cream all ingredients together.

ANYTIME BRAN CAKE

Cake:

1¼ c. boiling water	1 c. 100% Bran cereal
½ c. margarine	¼ c. white sugar
½ c. brown sugar	2 egg whites
1 tsp. vanilla	1¼ c. flour
1 tsp. cinnamon	1 tsp. baking soda
¼ tsp. salt	

Topping:

3 Tbsp. melted margarine	¼ c. brown sugar
½ c. chopped walnuts	¼ c. 100% Bran cereal

Combine boiling water and bran. Let stand 2 to 3 minutes. Cream margarine and sugars. Add egg whites, vanilla, and bran mixture. Beat well. Add flour, cinnamon, soda, and salt. Mix well. Pour into greased and floured 9x9 inch pan. Bake at 350° for 30 to 35 minutes.

Combine topping ingredients and spread on hot cake. Broil until bubbly. Serves 8 to 10 people.

"EARTHQUAKE CAKE"

1 small can coconut	1 stick oleo, melted
1½ c. chopped pecans	1 (8 oz.) cream cheese
1 German chocolate cake mix	1 box powdered sugar

Sprinkle the coconut and pecans in bottom of a slightly greased 11x16 inch pan. Prepare cake mix as directed on cake box. Pour over coconut and pecans. Next, beat the last 3 ingredients until creamy. Spoon by big spoonfuls over cake. Bake at 350° for 40 to 45 minutes.

Pauline Sammons
Waldo, Arkansas, USA

These days it takes nerves of steel just to be neurotic.

EDENTON (NORTH CAROLINA) TEA PARTY CAKES

¾ c. butter
2 c. brown sugar
3 eggs
1 tsp. soda

½ tsp. salt
Enough flour to make stiff
1 tsp. vanilla flavoring

Cream together butter and brown sugar. Add eggs and blend. Stir soda into small amount of hot water. Cool slightly. Mix into sugar base with salt and enough flour for stiff dough. Put in flavoring. Chill. Roll out thin and cut with cookie cutters. Bake in hot oven around 400° until done.

The tradition around my home in Edenton is that Penelope Barker and the girls served this at the Tea Party when they were protesting high tea prices from England. The tradition is their Tea Party was before the famous Boston Tea Party. Of course, taxes was the main problem.

Glenn E. Bunch, Jr., PDG 31-H, Snow Hill Lions Club
Snow Hill, North Carolina, USA

VANILLA WAFER CAKE

½ lb. butter
2 c. sugar
6 eggs
1 (12 oz.) pkg. vanilla wafers
7 oz. flaked coconut

1 c. maraschino cherries
1½ c. chopped pecans, slivered
2 Tbsp. vanilla
2 Tbsp. cherry juice

1. Cream butter. Add sugar and beat until smooth.
3. Add eggs, one at a time, beating well after each addition.
3. Add vanilla wafers which have been crushed (make sure batter is smooth).
4. Add coconut, chopped pecans, and slivered cherries (mixing well).
5. Pour batter in greased and floured tube pan.
6. Bake in preheated 275° oven for 2 hours or until done.
7. Cool in pan for at least 6 hours before removing from pan.
8. Dump and eat.

Bon Appetit (enjoy). Delicious.

Emily Larose, Huffman Lioness Club
Huffman, Texas, USA

The most important ability is availability.

CALIFORNIA WINE CAKE

1 lb. 3 oz.) pkg. yellow cake mix*
1 (3¾ oz.) pkg. vanilla instant
   pudding
4 eggs

¾ c. oil
¾ c. California sherry
1 tsp. nutmeg

Combine all ingredients. Mix with an electric beater about 5 minutes at medium speed. Pour batter into greased angel food or Bundt cake pan. Bake in moderate oven (350°) about 45 minutes or until done. Cool in pan about 5 minutes before turning on rack. Sprinkle with powdered sugar.

This cake has a light, spongy, pound-cake texture. Great as a shortcake.

* Can also substitute yellow cake with spice cake. Hold the nutmeg.

Leasa Sukut, Bakersfield Pioneer Lions Club
Bakersfield, California, USA

FRUIT COCKTAIL CAKE

2½ c. sugar
2 eggs, beaten
½ tsp. salt
2 tsp. baking soda
2 c. flour
2 tsp. vanilla
1 (16 oz.) can fruit cocktail
   including juice

1½ c. brown sugar
½ c. nuts
½ c. flaked coconut
1 stick margarine, melted
¾ c. evaporated milk

Mix 1½ cups sugar with eggs. Add salt, flour, and baking soda. Add 1 teaspoon vanilla and fruit cocktail. Beat until fruit cocktail is in small pieces. Put batter in 9x13 inch pan. Mix together brown sugar, nuts, and coconut. Sprinkle over batter. Bake at 350° for 45 minutes. While cake is baking, mix together margarine, 1 teaspoon vanilla, 1 cup sugar, and evaporated milk in saucepan. Bring to a rolling boil and pour on cake immediately on removal from oven. If you're like me and hate coconut, try this cake. There really is an exception to every rule.

Faith Spivey, Manteno Lions Club
Manteno, Illinois, USA

❦

Common sense is just about the most uncommon thing there is.

IRISH CREAM CAKE

1 pkg. white cake mix with
   pudding
1½ c. Irish cream liqueur
1 c. miniature semi-sweet
   chocolate chips

4 large eggs
½ c. vegetable oil
½ c. Irish cream liqueur
1 c. powdered sugar

In large bowl, combine first 5 ingredients. Pour into greased and floured Bundt pan. Bake at 350° for 35 to 45 minutes.

Combine liqueur and powdered sugar. While cake is still warm, poke holes in cake with long pronged fork. Drizzle with mixture until it is all used. Cool completely. Remove from pan. *Enjoy.*

Trish Schultz, Ponderosa Lions Club
Auberry, California, USA

PLUM LEAKE CAKE

2 c. sugar
1 c. oil
3 eggs
2 c. sifted flour
3 jars plum baby food

½ tsp. salt
½ tsp. baking soda
½ tsp. cloves
1 Tbsp. cinnamon
Red food color

Combine dry ingredients. Slowly add liquids. Mix together and bake in 350° oven for 1 hour. The Bundt pan should be greased and floured.

Becky Whitaker, Amarillo Centennial Lions Club
Amarillo, Texas, USA

The older generation thought nothing of getting up at 5:00 a.m.
The younger generation doesn't think much of it either.

WHOOPIE PIE CAKE

3 eggs
1½ c. milk
1⅔ c. sugar
4 oz. sweet cooking chocolate or
   ¾ c. semi-sweet pieces

½ c. butter
1 tsp. vanilla
2½ c. all-purpose flour
1 tsp. baking soda

In a small saucepan, beat 1 egg; add ½ cup milk and ⅔ cup sugar. Cook and stir over low heat for several minutes or until mixture begins to barely coat spoon. Add chocolate and stir until melted and mixture is thickened slightly. Cool to room temperature. In a bowl, cream butter until fluffy; add sugar and cream until light. Add vanilla and remaining eggs. Mix well. Sift together the dry ingredients and add alternately with remaining milk. Stir in mixture.

Spread half of batter into large round circles on a buttered and floured cookie sheet; repeat with remaining batter. Bake at 350° for 20 minutes or until top springs back when lightly touched with a finger. Cool and remove to rack for complete cooling. Place one layer on serving plate and spread with filling; top with other layer.

Whoopie Pie Filling:

1 c. milk
5 Tbsp. all-purpose flour
1 c. sugar
½ tsp. salt

½ c. shortening
½ c. butter or margarine
1 tsp. vanilla

In a saucepan, mix milk and flour. Cook, stirring constantly, until mixture comes to a boil and is thickened. Cool. Beat until fluffy. Add remaining ingredients, beating well after each addition.

Dave Bernier, Westbrook Lions Club
Westbrook, Maine, USA

For some people it's hard to get away from it all
without taking almost all of it with them.

PLACEK

1 Tbsp. milk, warmed   **1 oz. yeast**

Dissolve yeast in warm milk.

Sponge:

½ c. milk, scalded   **6 Tbsp. flour**

Mix flour into milk, making certain there are no lumps. Cool to lukewarm, then add dissolved yeast. Let rise until double.

Batter - Step 1:

6 egg yolks   **½ c. sugar**
3 eggs

Cream egg yolks and eggs with sugar; mix with sponge.

Batter - Step 2:

¾ c. butter, melted   **½ tsp. salt**
2 c. flour

Add butter, flour, and salt to creamed mixture. Knead until smooth. Let rise. Place in pans and let rise again. Cover with crumb topping. Bake about 40 minutes at 325°, or until golden brown.

Crumb Topping:

¾ c. sugar   **½ c. flour**
½ c. butter   **1 tsp. vanilla**

Combine all ingredients together until mixture has consistency of corn meal. Can be left in larger chunks if desired.

This recipe was passed down from my grandmother. It originally was worded "a pinch of ... a handful of ... bake in a warm oven ...."

Joan Blaufuss, Depew Lions Club
Buffalo, New York, USA

Nothing is impossible to the people who do not have to do it themselves.

LANE CAKE

8 egg whites
2 c. sugar
1 c. butter
1 c. sweet milk

3½ c. plain flour
2 tsp. baking powder
2 tsp. vanilla
Filling as follows

Preheat oven to 325°. Beat egg whites until almost stiff but not as for making meringue. Let them peak slightly. Add sugar as you beat egg whites, then add butter, all the while beating on medium speed. Alternate flour and milk as you beat, then add baking powder and vanilla. Beat real well. Use well greased 9 inch round pans. Cover bottom of pans with mix. It should make 5 layers. Bake at 325° until it tests done, but is not brown. Turn onto cloth or wax paper; cool.

Filling:

8 egg yolks
1 c. sugar
½ c. butter or margarine
½ c. dark raisins
½ c. light raisins
1 c. coconut
1 lb. mixed chopped nuts (pecans
    and walnuts)

4 oz. candied red cherries,
    chopped
4 oz. candied green cherries,
    chopped
4 oz. candied pineapple, chopped
½ wine glass good wine

Cook in double boiler until thick over low heat, stirring constantly. Eggs will change color. When finished, stir in raisins, coconut, and mixed nuts, cherries, and pineapple. Stir all real well. When blended, stir in wine. Spread as filling between layers and frost top only.

Note: This is delicious. I seal cake and let stand about 2 or 3 days before cutting. It will last for a while.

This is great for Christmas.

Bertha Smith, Parkway Lions Club
Panama City, Florida, USA

MAYONNAISE CAKE

1 c. salad dressing
1 c. honey
2 tsp. baking soda
2 c. flour

½ c. cocoa
1 egg
3 Tbsp. vanilla
¾ c. water

Mix all ingredients together and bake at 375° for 25 to 30 minutes.

Debbie Abbott, Lyman Lions Club
Lyman, Wyoming, USA

❧

Believe the best of everybody.

TEN EGG CAKE

2 c. flour
2 c. sugar
10 eggs
3 c. flour

1 tsp. salt
1 Tbsp. vanilla
¼ c. canned milk (undiluted)
1 c. chopped pecans (if desired)

Mix 2 cups flour and 2 cups sugar well, then add 10 eggs, one at a time, beating after each addition. Add remaining ingredients. Mix well and bake for 1½ hours at 300° in a deep tube pan. You may glaze or frost with your favorite frosting, but is very good plain and keeps for a long time. This is a very moist cake.

Virginia Tate, Bowie Evening Lions Club
Bowie, Texas, USA

TWINKIE CAKE

Place Twinkie on bottom of a long pan. Put a box of frozen (unthawed) strawberries on top of them, then add a box of vanilla instant pudding mix on top of berries. Slice bananas on top of pudding mix and add Cool Whip on top, then top with nuts.

Nancy Dean, Stamps Lions Club
Stamps, Arkansas, USA

THREE-HOLE CAKE

1½ c. flour
1 tsp. soda
3 Tbsp. cocoa (heaping)
1 tsp. vanilla
5 Tbsp. melted shortening

1 c. cold water
½ tsp. salt
1 c. sugar
1 Tbsp. vinegar

Powdered Sugar Icing (if needed!!):

½ stick oleo
2 Tbsp. cocoa
3 Tbsp. milk

½ lb. powdered sugar
½ tsp. vanilla

Sift the flour, salt, soda, and sugar together 3 times. Make 3 holes out of these ingredients. In one hole, place the vanilla. In second hole, place the vinegar, and in the third hole, place the melted shortening, then over everything, pour your cold water. Beat until blended. Bake 30 minutes at 350°. (I generally doubled this recipe when the children were home, but since it is just the husband and myself, I don't even ice with frosting anymore. You may frost with the powdered sugar icing if desired. (I use one 8 inch cake pan now.)

This recipe has been in my family for generations. I received it 40 years ago from my grandma.

Lois Sanner, Moweaqua Lions Club
Moweaqua, Illinois, USA

HOLIDAY PECAN CAKE

1 lb. butter
1 lb. brown sugar
6 eggs, separated (room
   temperature)
1½ oz. lemon extract
4 c. flour

1 tsp. baking powder
½ lb. candied pineapple, chopped
½ lb. candied cherries, halved (red
   and green for color)
1 lb. pecans, chopped

Cream butter with brown sugar. Add egg yolks, beaten. Stir in lemon extract. Add baking powder to flour. Gradually add flour to creamed mixture alternately with the chopped fruit and pecans. Beat egg whites until stiff. Fold into batter. Grease angel food cake pan well. Cut brown paper to fit sides, funnel, and bottom of cake pan; grease well. Pour batter into pan.

Place in refrigerator overnight. Remove from refrigerator at least an hour before baking at 250° for 3 to 3½ hours or until a toothpick inserted comes out clean. Store cake for 2 weeks in an airtight container or heavy-duty foil in the refrigerator to ripen before cutting and serving for best flavor.

This serves a large number because slices are usually cut relatively thin since it is rich and filling.

UGLY DUCKLING CAKE

1 yellow cake mix
1 (16 oz.) can fruit cocktail with
   syrup
1 c. coconut
2 eggs

½ c. brown sugar
½ c. butter
½ c. evaporated milk
1⅓ c. coconut
½ c. sugar

Mix 1 yellow cake mix, one 16 ounce can fruit cocktail, 1 cup coconut, and 2 eggs. Blend. Beat with electric mixer for 2 minutes. Pour into a greased 9x13 inch pan. Sprinkle with ½ cup brown sugar. Bake at 325° for 45 minutes. Bring ½ cup real butter, ½ cup sugar, and ½ cup evaporated milk to a boil. Boil 2 minutes. Remove and stir in 1⅓ cups coconut. Spoon over hot cake. Serve warm or cool.

Pat Tulloch, Bedford Heights Lions Club
Bedford Heights, Ohio, USA

Courtesy is contagious. This world could do with an epidemic.

CRUMB CAKE

Cake:

¼ lb. margarine
1 c. sugar
1 egg
1 tsp. vanilla

1½ c. flour
1 c. milk
2 tsp. baking powder
¼ tsp. salt

Crumbs:

1½ c. flour
1½ tsp. cinnamon
⅛ tsp. nutmeg

¼ tsp. vanilla
⅔ c. melted margarine

Cake: Cream margarine and sugar. Beat in egg and vanilla. Mix in 1 cup milk. Add baking powder and salt mixed with flour. Put in greased and floured 8 inch pans or a 9x13 inch pan.

Crumbs: Mix flour, cinnamon, and nutmeg. Add vanilla. Mix in melted margarine and form crumbs on top of batter in pans. Bake at 350° for 25 to 30 minutes. When cool, sprinkle with confectionery sugar.

Hint: Do not roll crumbs with fingers too long when forming or they will become tough.

W. Leeman, Gouldsboro Lions Club
Gouldsboro, Pennsylvania, USA

BANANA SPLIT CAKE

2 c. graham crackers
3 sticks butter
2 eggs
2 c. powdered sugar
1 tsp. vanilla
1 large can crushed pineapple,
    drained

5 bananas, sliced long
1 large Cool Whip
Chopped nuts
Cherries

Mix crumbs with 1 stick melted butter. Spread in 9x13 inch pan. Beat sugar, eggs, 2 sticks soft butter, and vanilla. Beat for no less than 15 minutes. Spread on top of crumbs crust. Spread drained pineapple on top of filling. Next, put sliced bananas on top. Top off with Cool Whip. Sprinkle nuts on top. Chill overnight.

You can also add strawberries.

Lion Carol A. Case, Manteno Lions Club
Manteno, Illinois, USA

No man is a failure who is enjoying life.

JAM CAKE

2 c. brown sugar
1 c. butter
1 c. seedless black raspberry jam
1 c. chopped pecans
1 c. chopped black walnuts
1 c. raisins
1 Tbsp. soda

2 c. flour
6 eggs
1 Tbsp. cinnamon
1 Tbsp. cloves
3 Tbsp. water
1 Tbsp. vanilla

Cream butter and sugar; add unbeaten eggs and mix well. Add jam (coat nuts and raisins with small amount of flour). Add and mix well. Sift flour with cinnamon and cloves; add to mixture. Add soda, vanilla, and water last. Bake at 325° at least 1 hour or until done.

This recipe was handed down from my great-grandmother who lived in the hills of Eastern Kentucky. We have it at holidays instead of fruit cake.

Lion Juanita Woods, Interlachen Lions Club
Interlachen, Florida, USA

OLD-FASHIONED JAM CAKE

1 c. raisins
1 (8 oz.) can crushed pineapple
  (undrained)
2½ c. all-purpose flour
1 c. sugar
⅓ c. unsweetened cocoa
1 tsp. baking soda
1 tsp. cinnamon

1 tsp. nutmeg
½ tsp. cloves
1 c. butter, softened
4 eggs
1 c. blackberry jam
⅔ c. buttermilk
1 c. chopped pecans

Caramel Icing:

1 c. margarine
2 c. brown sugar, packed
½ c. milk

3½ to 4 c. sifted confectioners
  sugar

Soak raisins in pineapple for several hours or overnight. Sift together dry ingredients and set aside.

In a large mixing bowl, cream butter. Add eggs, one at a time, beating well after each addition. Add jam and buttermilk. Blend well. Add dry ingredients; mix just until all ingredients are combined. Stir in raisin-pineapple mixture and nuts. Spread into 2 greased and floured 9 inch pans. Bake at 350° for 50 minutes or until cake tests done. Cool 10 minutes before removing from pans to cool on wire racks.

Icing: Melt butter. Stir in sugar and milk. Bring to a boil. Remove from heat. Cool until warm. With electric mixer, beat in enough of confectioners sugar until a spreading consistency is reached. Frost cooled cake. Cake freezes well.

PDG Lloyd E. Wright, Georgetown Lions Club
Georgetown, Ohio, USA

FIVE FLAVOR CAKE

2 sticks butter
½ c. vegetable shortening
3 c. sugar
5 eggs, well beaten
3 c. flour
½ tsp. baking powder

1 c. milk
1 tsp. Watkins coconut flavor
1 tsp. Watkins rum extract
1 tsp. Watkins butter extract
1 tsp. Watkins lemon extract
1 tsp. Watkins vanilla extract

Glaze:

1 c. sugar
½ c. butter
1 tsp. Watkins coconut flavor
1 tsp. Watkins rum extract

1 tsp. Watkins butter extract
1 tsp. Watkins lemon extract
1 tsp. Watkins vanilla extract
1 tsp. almond extract

Cream butter, shortening, and sugar until light and fluffy. Add eggs, which have been beaten until lemon color. Combine flour and baking powder; add to creamed mixture alternately with milk. Stir in flavorings. Spoon mixture into prepared 10 inch tube pan (the Bundt pan must be 10 or 12 inch cups - an angel food pan may also be used) and bake at 325° for 1½ hours or until cake tests done. Add glaze if desired. Cool pan about 10 minutes.

Glaze: Combine ingredients in heavy saucepan. Bring to boil. Stir until sugar is melted. Pour on one half of glaze while cake is in pan. Pour the rest when removed from pan.

Carol A. Case, Manteno Lions Club
Manteno, Illinois, USA

ITALIAN LOVE CAKE

1 box marble cake mix
3 eggs
2 tsp. vanilla

1 c. sugar
1½ lb. Ricotta cheese

Icing:

1 small pkg. instant milk
    chocolate pudding mix

1 c. milk
1 (8 oz.) Cool Whip

Prepare cake mix as directed on box. Transfer to a 13x9 inch greased and floured pan. Beat eggs, vanilla, and sugar. Add the Ricotta cheese and stir well with electric mixer. Spoon Ricotta cheese mixture evenly over cake mix. Bake at 350° for 1 hour. Let cake cool.

Icing: Beat pudding mix and milk with electric mixer. Fold in Cool Whip. Use mixer to blend the Cool Whip and pudding together. Spread evenly over cooled cake. Keep cake refrigerated.

This cake is scrumptious and a surprise to your taste buds.
Nicki Florentine, Silver Run-Union Mills Lions Club
Westminster, Maryland, USA

MEXICAN WEDDING CAKE

2 c. flour
2 eggs
1 c. chopped walnuts
½ c. butter (at room temperature)
1 tsp. vanilla
2 c. sugar

2 tsp. baking soda
1 (20 oz.) can crushed pineapple
   with juice
8 oz. pkg. cream cheese (room
   temperature)
1½ c. powdered sugar

Mix flour, sugar, eggs, baking soda, walnuts, and pineapple in a large mixing bowl, using a fork. Pour in an ungreased 9x13 inch glass baking pan and bake for 35 minutes at 350°. (Bake longer if using a metal baking pan.) Cake will still be very soft. Remove from oven and top with frosting.

Frosting: Blend butter and cream cheese until smooth. Add vanilla and powdered sugar. Mix well. Frost cake and refrigerate. The longer this sits, the better it tastes as the flavors blend together.

Lee Avram, Georgetown Evening Lions Club

SCRIPTURE CAKE

4½ c. (I Kings 4:22) flour
1½ c. (Psalms 55:21) butter
2 c. (Jeremiah 6:20) sugar
2 c. (II Samuel 16:1) raisins
2 c. (Song of Solomon 2:13) figs
2 c. (Numbers 17:8) almonds
2 Tbsp. (Judges 14:18) honey
1 pinch (Luke 14:34) salt

6 (Isaiah 10:14) eggs
½ c. (Judges 4:19) milk
2 tsp. (I Corinthians 5:6) baking
   powder
(II Chronicles 9:9) ½ tsp. nutmeg,
   2 tsp. allspice, 4 tsp.
   cinnamon, 2 tsp. cloves

After following instructions in Proverbs 23:14, pour batter into well-greased loaf pans and bake for 50 minutes at 325°. Cool and slice after a (John 11:9).

PDG Lloyd E. Wright, Georgetown Lions Club
Georgetown, Ohio, USA

CHESS CAKE

2 sticks margarine
1 pkg. light brown sugar
2 c. self-rising flour
4 eggs

½ c. sugar
1 Tbsp. vanilla
1 c. chopped pecans

Mix and melt first 2 ingredients over low heat or in a double boiler. Add other ingredients and mix well. Pour in greased oblong cake pan. Bake at 300° for 45 minutes.

Phyllis Hillis, McMinnville Lions Club
McMinnville, Tennessee, USA

OATMEAL CAKE

1¼ c. boiling water
1 c. quick oats
½ c. butter or margarine
1 c. light brown sugar
1 c. white sugar
2 eggs

¼ tsp. cinnamon
Dash of nutmeg
¼ tsp. salt
1⅓ c. flour
1 tsp. soda

Icing:

4 Tbsp. butter
½ c. brown sugar
1½ c. coconut

1 tsp. vanilla
⅓ c. cream or condensed milk
½ c. chopped pecans

Mix oats with boiling water. Let cool 20 minutes. Mix butter, sugars, eggs, and spices. Add oats mixture. Add flour and soda. Mix lightly. Grease and flour 11x13 inch pan. Bake at 350° for 35 to 40 minutes.

Mix icing over medium heat until butter melts and sugar dissolves. Spread on cake after it is done and place under broiler for ½ minute or until bubbly and light brown.

Barb Allison, Moweaqua Lions Club
Moweaqua, Illinois, USA

ICEBOX KRANTZ - CHRISTMAS CAKE

Dough:

1 c. butter
1 tsp. salt
1 c. milk

3 pkg. dry yeast
¼ c. sugar
4 c. flour

Filling:

1 c. melted butter
Brown sugar
Chopped nuts

Raisins or other candied fruit (to taste)

Mix all dry ingredients. Add butter and mix like pie crust. Have milk lukewarm to dissolve yeast. Mix all together and let stand overnight in the refrigerator, then cut dough into 3 parts. Roll thin and spread with melted butter, brown sugar, and chopped nuts. (Raisins or other candied fruit can be added to taste.) Roll up like a jelly roll and let rise in a warm place for 2 hours. Bake approximately ½ hour at 350°. Frost with butter frosting while still slightly warm.

Can be decorated with candied cherries or other fruit for a festive look at Christmas ... "but" good all the year round!!!!

Dorothy Ridgewell, Independence Eastview Lions Club
Independence, Missouri, USA

BLENDER COCONUT CAKE

2 c. milk
¾ c. sugar
⅔ c. Bisquick
4 eggs

½ c. margarine
¾ c. shredded coconut
Dash of nutmeg

Blend all ingredients for 5 minutes. Grease bottom of 9 inch pie pan. Bake for 45 minutes at 350°.

Ann Violette, Westbrook Lions Club
Westbrook, Maine, USA

PEANUT BUTTER CAKE

1 stick butter
1 c. water
½ c. peanut butter
½ c. cooking oil
2 c. flour

2 c. sugar
2 eggs, slightly beaten
1 tsp. vanilla
½ c. milk
1 tsp. baking soda

Peanut Butter Frosting:

1 stick butter
½ c. peanut butter
⅓ c. milk

1 tsp. vanilla
1 lb. box 10X sugar

Bring first 4 ingredients to a boil in large pan. Turn off heat and add the remaining cake ingredients. Stir until well blended. Pour into greased and floured jelly roll pan. Bake at 400° for 20 minutes.

Frosting: Put butter, peanut butter, and milk in saucepan. Cook until it comes to a boil. Remove from stove; add vanilla and 10X sugar. Stir until well blended. Frost cooled cake.

If you don't enjoy what you have, how could you be happier with more?
Louise J. Eshleman, Middletown Lions Club
Middletown, Pennsylvania, USA

An optimist laughs to forget. The pessimist forgets to laugh.

DIABETIC FRUIT CAKE

½ c. chopped dates   ½ c. chopped prunes
½ c. raisins   1 c. water

Bring to a boil; add 1 stick oleo and let cool. Add 2 eggs.

Sift together:

1 c. flour   1 tsp. baking soda
¼ tsp. salt

Add to fruit mixture and stir well. Stir in ½ cup nuts. Bake in a rectangular Pyrex dish at 350° about 25 minutes. Pyrex dish should be 8x10 inches. Be careful not to overbake. This is a moist cake and very good. It is hard to believe it doesn't have any sugar.

Wilma Claar, LaCygne Lions Club
LaCygne, Kansas, USA

INEXPENSIVE FRUIT CAKE

1½ c. raisins   1 tsp. soda
1½ c. dates   2 tsp. cinnamon
2 c. sugar   1 tsp. cloves
2 c. boiling water   1 tsp. salt
5 Tbsp. shortening   1 c. chopped nuts
3 c. all-purpose flour   1 c. mixed candied fruit

Cut raisins and dates in small pieces. Place raisins, dates, sugar, water, and shortening in pan; simmer gently 20 minutes. Cool. Sift flour once before measuring, then sift flour, soda, cinnamon, cloves, and salt together. Stir into cool mixture, adding nuts and fruit (mixed with a little flour) last. Pour into greased and floured tube pan or 2 loaf pans. Cakes can be baked right after Thanksgiving and stored in foil or tin. Cake gets moister with age.

PRESSED FRUIT CAKE

¾ c. milk   1 pkg. candied pineapple,
1 lb. marshmallows   chopped
15 oz. pkg. golden raisins   4 c. chopped nuts (your choice)
2 pkg. candied cherries, chopped   1 lb. graham crackers, crushed

Scald milk and add marshmallows until melted. Mix in raisins, cherries, pineapple, and nuts. Add graham crackers and mix well. Line 2 to 3 loaf pans with wax paper. Press mixture into pans. Press firmly. Cover and let ripen in refrigerator 24 hours. This no bake fruit cake can be covered tightly and frozen. Just thaw, slice, and enjoy anytime.

Antonia Huffman, Saginaw Lions Club
Saginaw, Texas, USA

ICE CREAM FRUIT CAKE

1 large angel food cake
1 large can fruit cocktail, drained
¾ c. chopped nuts
½ gal. vanilla ice cream

1 small bottle maraschino
   cherries, halved
1 small container whipping cream

Break cake in medium chunks. Fold cake, ice cream, fruit cocktail, cherries, and nuts together. Pour into tube cake pan. Freeze for several hours or overnight. Remove cake from tube pan and place on plate. Mix 1 cup whipping cream, ¼ cup sugar, vanilla to taste, and red food coloring (optional); spread over cake. Cover cake well and freeze until serving time.

This cake is a favorite at Christmas time for our family.
Lion District Governor Signey J. Ogletree, District 35-F,
Fort Walton Beach Lions Club
Destin, Florida, USA

BEST FRUITCAKE EVER

1 c. butter
1 c. sugar
4 large eggs
1 c. dried fruit
1 tsp. baking powder
1 tsp. baking soda

1 tsp. salt
Lemon juice
1 c. brown sugar
Nuts
1 or 2 qt. whiskey

Before you start, sample the whiskey to check for quality. (Good, isn't it?) Now go ahead. Select a large mixing bowl, measuring cup, etc. Check the whiskey again as it must be just right. To be sure the whiskey is of the highest quality, pour 1 level cup into a glass and drink it as fast as you can. Repeat, if needed!

With an electric mixer, beat 1 cup of butter in a large fluffy bowl. Add 1 teaspoon of thugar and beat again.

Meanwhile, make sure that the whiskey is of the finest quality. Cry another tup. Open second quart, if necessary! Add 2 arge leggs, 2 cups fried druit and beat till high. If druit gets stuck in beaters, just pry it loose with a drewscriver. Sample the whiskey again, checking for tonscisticy. Next, sift 3 cups of salt or anything, it really doesn't matter. Sample the whiskey.

Sift ½ pint lemon juice. Fold in chopped butter and strained nuts. Add 1 babblespoon of brown thugar, or whatever color you can find, and wix mel. Grease oven and turn cake pan to 350 gredees. Now pour the whole mess into the coven and ake. Check the whiskey again and bo to ged.

Rev. Fred Gilbert, Dannemora Lions Club
Dannemora, New York, USA

❧

Attempt the impossible today.

MYSTERY FRUIT CAKE BALLS

1 pkg. spice cake mix
1 pkg. fluffy white frosting mix
1 c. red candied cherries, chopped
1 c. green candied cherries, chopped

2 c. golden seedless raisins
5 c. chopped nuts, walnuts or pecans

Prepare and bake cake as directed. Cool. Prepare frosting mix as directed. Crumble cooled cake into large bowl. Add nuts, fruit, and frosting. Toss together until mixture is damp and well blended. Shape in 1 inch balls with buttered hands. Chill in refrigerator for 24 hours. Roll in powdered sugar or leave plain.

FLORIDA'S LIGHTEST ORANGE CAKE

6 whites (room temperature 1 hour)
1¾ c. sifted flour (presift)
½ tsp. salt

1½ c. granulated sugar
6 egg yolks
6 Tbsp. fresh orange juice
1 Tbsp. fresh grated orange peel

With electric mixer, beat whites at medium speed till foamy. Gradually beat in ½ cup sugar, beating after each addition till stiff peaks form. Set aside. Preheat oven to 350°.

In small electric mixer bowl at high speed, beat yolks 3 minutes. Don't underbeat!! Gradually beat in remaining 1 cup sugar till smooth. At low speed, blend flour mixture and juice alternately into yolk mixture. Add peel. Using whisk, under and over motion, fold yolk mixture *gently* into whites. Pour into ungreased tube or Bundt pan. Bake 55 minutes in Bundt pan and 40 minutes in tube pan. Invert over bottle till cooled completely. Use serrated knife to cut gently. Don't use pan with nonstick finish. If needed to, cool upright on rack, will fall slightly. Still absolutely delicious.

Bunny Creo, Merritt Island Lions Club
Merritt Island, Florida, USA

The trouble with experience
is it usually teaches you something you didn't really want to know.

ORANGE LIQUEUR CAKE

1 c. chopped pecans
1 (18.25 oz.) yellow cake mix with
    pudding
3 eggs
½ c. vegetable oil

½ c. orange liqueur flavor
2 tsp. grated orange rind
¼ c. orange juice
¼ c. water

Glaze:

½ c. butter or margarine
¼ c. orange juice
¾ c. sugar

2 tsp. grated orange rind
½ c. orange liqueur

Sprinkle pecans in bottom of greased and floured 10 inch tube pan. Combine ingredients for cake in large mixing bowl. Beat 30 seconds at low speed, then 2 minutes on medium speed. Pour into tube pan. Bake at 325° for 1 hour or until wooden pick comes out clean. Cool in pan for 10 minutes. Remove cooled cake to wire rack. Using a meat fork or wooden pick, pierce cake at 1 inch intervals. Spoon glaze over cake.

Glaze: Melt butter in saucepan. Stir in orange juice and sugar; bring to a boil. Boil 5 minutes, stirring constantly. Remove from heat. Add orange and liqueur.

Mrs. Alberta Hopkins, Silver Run-Union Mills Lions Club
Westminster, Maryland, USA

ORANGE MANDARIN CAKE

1 box yellow cake mix
1 can mandarin oranges

⅔ c. oil
4 eggs

Mix with mixer 3 minutes. Takes 3 round cake pans. Bake at 325° for 25 minutes.

Icing:

1 Cool Whip
1 instant vanilla pudding

1 (20 oz.) can crushed pineapple,
    drained

Mix and spread on cake.

Lion Virginia Van Scyoc, Graysville/Proctor Lions Club
Proctor, West Virginia, USA

❧

Do what you can, with what you have, where you are.

MANDARIN CAKE

1 yellow cake mix
1 can mandarin oranges
1 can pineapple

12 oz. Cool Whip
1 large box Jell-O instant pudding
(vanilla)

Drain oranges and make cake as directed on box. Fold in oranges to cake. Bake at 350° and let cool.

Icing: Drain pineapple. Add to instant pudding mix. Fold in Cool Whip.

Pauline Sammons
Waldo, Arkansas, USA

STRAWBERRY CAKE

1 pkg. strawberry Jell-O
1 pkg. Betty Crocker white cake
   mix
4 eggs

½ c. water
¾ c. Wesson oil (scant)
3 Tbsp. sifted flour with ½ tsp.
   baking powder

Frosting:

1 scant stick oleo (2 slices off)
1 pkg. powdered sugar

½ c. frozen strawberries, thawed

Frosting: Put into refrigerator until cake is ready to ice.

Mix ingredients together. Beat 2 minutes at medium speed. After you have beaten, add ½ cup frozen strawberries (thawed). Beat 1 minute more. Pour in 10x15x2 inch pan or 3 layers. Bake at 350° to start. Reduce to 300° after 20 minutes until toothpick inserted comes out dry.

Glen Cox, Emporia Noon Lions Club
Emporia, Kansas, Lyon County, USA

❦

I want my kids to have all the things I could never afford.
Then I want to move in with them.

STRAWBERRY PECAN CAKE

1 box white cake mix
1 c. cooking oil
4 eggs
1 c. coconut

1 (3 oz.) box strawberry gelatin
¼ c. milk
1 c. strawberries (frozen)
1 c. chopped pecans

Mix dry gelatin and cake mix together. Add the rest of the ingredients, adding eggs, one at a time. Bake in 3 greased layered pans at 350° for 25 to 30 minutes or until cake tests done. Frost with Strawberry Frosting.

Strawberry Frosting:

1 stick margarine
½ c. strawberries, drained
½ c. coconut

1 box confectioners sugar
½ c. pecans

Cream butter and sugar. Add remaining ingredients and spread on cake.

Billie Buchanan, East Lake Lions Club
Birmingham, Alabama, USA

ENGLAND CAKE

1 yellow cake
2 cans Thank You pudding
   (vanilla)

20 oz. strawberries
1 large Cool Whip

Bake cake according to box in a 13x9 inch pan. After cake cools, take a spoon and scrape the top half of the cake off and set aside. Put 1 can pudding over cake. Put a layer of strawberries, then a layer of Cool Whip, then take cake that you set aside and put it on top of Cool Whip (can break it up). Put another can of pudding on another layer of Cool Whip, then put some strawberries on top.

Linda Neibert, Whittemore Lioness Club
Whittemore, Michigan, USA

❦

It's not the number of hours you put in,
but what you put in the hours that count.

APPLE CAKE

2 eggs
2 c. sugar
1 tsp. vanilla
1 tsp. salt
1½ tsp. baking soda
½ c. water

2 c. flour
1 tsp. cinnamon
¼ c. raisins
4 c. diced apples
½ c. chopped nuts

Topping:

3 Tbsp. butter
1 egg
½ c. brown sugar

1 tsp. rum extract
1 (4½ oz.) ctn. whipped topping

Cream together eggs, sugar, vanilla, salt, and baking soda. Add water, flour, cinnamon, and raisins. Beat well. Stir in diced apples and nuts. Pour into a 9x13 inch pan. Bake at 350° for 50 to 60 minutes. Cool.

Topping: Melt butter in small skillet. Beat egg and combine with brown sugar; add to the butter and cook slowly over very low heat until thickened. Add rum extract. Cool and mix with whipped topping. Refrigerate. Frost cake when ready to serve. Keeps well.

Lioness Glendora Hauger, Siren Lioness Club, 27-E-1
Siren, Wisconsin, USA

FRESH APPLE CAKE

3 c. flour
2 c. sugar
1 tsp. baking soda
1 tsp. salt
2 tsp. cinnamon

3 eggs
3 c. chopped apples
1 c. chopped nuts
1 c. Wesson oil

Stir together oil, sugar, and eggs. *Do not overbeat.* Add apples, flour, and rest of ingredients. Bake in greased and floured angel food cake pan. Bake 1 hour in a 350° oven. Cool before removing from pan.

It is a good idea to keep your words soft and sweet, you never know when you may have to eat them.

Leola C. Jurrens, Downtown Bartlesville Lions Club
Bartlesville, Oklahoma, USA

Among the many things money won't buy is what it used to.

FRESH APPLE CAKE

1 egg	¼ tsp. salt
¼ c. salad oil	1 tsp. baking soda
1 c. sugar	1 tsp. cinnamon
1 tsp. vanilla	2 c. apples, peeled and chopped
1 c. flour	1 c. walnuts, chopped

Mix together egg, oil, sugar, and vanilla. Sift together dry ingredients and add to egg mixture. Stir well. Fold in apples and nuts. Pour into greased and floured cake pan. Bake at 350° for 35 to 40 minutes. Cake will be crusty on top and may crack. Serve warm with whipped cream if desired.

This recipe came from my mother and is a family favorite.
Pat Ballard, Milpitas Host Lions Club
Milpitas, California, USA

QUICK APPLE DESSERT WITH SAUCE

Cake:

1 c. sugar	½ tsp. salt
¼ c. oleo	½ tsp. cinnamon
2 eggs, beaten	1 tsp. soda
2 or 3 apples, peeled and grated	1 tsp. nutmeg
1 c. flour	

Sauce:

1 c. sugar	¼ c. oleo
½ c. canned milk	1½ tsp. bourbon or vanilla

Cream sugar and oleo until light and fluffy; add eggs and beat well. Stir in apples. Combine flour, salt, cinnamon, soda, and nutmeg. Mix. Add to apple mixture and stir well. Pour into a lightly greased 8 or 9 inch cake pan. Bake at 350° for 30 minutes.

Sauce: Combine ingredients in a saucepan and cook over low heat, stirring until sugar is dissolved. Cook for 4 or 5 minutes. Makes about 1 cup sauce.

To serve, cut cake into 8 pieces and pour sauce over cake.

This sauce is also delicious over ice cream.
Zeta L. Adams, Craigsville Lions Club
Craigsville, West Virginia, USA

Age is a matter of feelings, not of years.

EASY GERMAN APPLE CAKE

1 Pillsbury German chocolate
   cake mix

2 c. apple pie filling
3 eggs

    Beat eggs first. Add cake mix and apple pie filling. Beat with electric mixer for 2 minutes. Bake 40 to 45 minutes at 350° in 13x9 inch pan. Just 3 ingredients makes this cake delicious and it's so easy.

Katharine Dutterer (Mrs. John), Silver Run-Union Mills Lions Club
Westminster, Maryland, USA

GERMAN APPLE CAKE

2 eggs
½ to 1 c. walnuts
2 c. sifted flour
2 c. sugar
2 tsp. cinnamon

1 tsp. baking soda
1 tsp. vanilla
½ tsp. salt
1 c. oil
4 c. thinly sliced apples

    Mix all ingredients together with a spoon as batter will be stiff. Spread into greased and floured 13x9 inch pan. Bake in 350° oven for 45 to 60 minutes. Serve with Cool Whip or ice cream. Serves 12 to 16.

FRESH APPLE CAKE

Small bowl:

2 eggs
1 c. oil

1 tsp. vanilla

Large bowl:

2 c. sugar
2 c. flour
1 tsp. baking soda
½ tsp. salt

3 c. apples, sliced thin
1 c. nuts
1 c. raisins

    Beat eggs, oil, and vanilla slightly, then add to dry ingredients. Stir with large spoon until thoroughly mixed. Pour into 9x13 inch pan. Bake at 350° for 1 hour.

    A moist cake with fruity flavor. Great for the holiday season. Freezes well.

D. Dee Monroe, Independence Eastview Lions Club
Independence, Missouri, USA

Today is a miniature eternity. Enjoy it!

APPLE CAKE

3 eggs
2 c. sugar
1 c. oil
2 c. flour
2 tsp. cinnamon

1 tsp. soda
½ tsp. salt
1 c. nuts (chopped walnuts)
4 c. sliced apples
1 tsp. vanilla

Beat 3 eggs. Add oil and beat. Add vanilla and sugar to egg mixture, mixing thoroughly. Add dry ingredients; mix well. Stir apples and nuts into rest of ingredients. Grease and flour a 9x13 inch pan or Bundt pan. Bake 45 minutes in 350° oven.

Patsy Gagnon (Mrs. Charles), Silver Run-Union Mills Lions Club
Westminster, Maryland, USA

APPLE NUT CAKE

1¼ c. Wesson oil
2 c. sugar
2 eggs
3 c. flour
1 tsp. salt

1½ tsp. soda
3 c. finely chopped peeled
   Delicious apples
1 c. pecans
1 tsp. vanilla

Mix all ingredients. Pour in greased and floured tube pan. Bake at 325° for 1½ hours. Place under cake lid while still warm. Stays fresh for weeks.

Roger Gage, Decatur Lions Club
Decatur, Texas, USA

APPLE CAKE

1 c. sugar
¼ c. brown sugar
½ c. oleo or butter
2 eggs
1 c. milk
2½ c. flour
1 tsp. soda

1 tsp. baking powder
¼ tsp. salt
1 tsp. cinnamon
2 c. apples, chopped
1 c. walnuts
½ c. brown sugar

Heat oven to 325°. Prepare 9x13 inch pan. Cream sugars and oleo or butter. Add slightly beaten eggs. Sift all dry ingredients together. Add to creamed mixture alternately with milk. Fold in chopped apples. Put in prepared 9x13 inch pan. Sprinkle the ½ cup brown sugar and the walnuts over the dough. Bake for 45 to 60 minutes. This will make 18 generous servings. The flavor will be much better after the cake stands 1 or 2 days and it becomes moister.

❦

A smile is contagious ... start an epidemic!

ROSY APPLE CAKE

1 c. flour
1 tsp. baking powder
¼ tsp. salt
3 Tbsp. butter

1 egg, beaten with 1 Tbsp. milk
4 to 5 medium cooking apples
1 (3 oz.) pkg. red Jell-O
1 to 2 Tbsp. sugar

Topping:

¾ c. sugar
¾ c. flour

¾ stick butter

Mix flour, baking powder, and salt together. Cut in butter. Add egg and milk mixture. Mix thoroughly. Press in bottom and up sides of 8 inch round pan. Peel apples and slice into dough lined pan. Sprinkle dry Jell-O over top of apples. Add 1 to 2 tablespoons sugar depending on tartness of apples. Mix the topping and sprinkle crumbles over apples. Bake at 375° for 45 minutes. Easy, pretty "coffee or tea" cake.

Bunny Creo, Merritt Island Lions Club
Merritt Island, Florida, USA

KING SIZE APPLESAUCE CAKE

1 c. margarine
2 c. sugar
2 eggs
1½ tsp. nutmeg
1 tsp. cinnamon
¼ tsp. cloves
2½ c. applesauce

3 c. sifted flour
3 Tbsp. Karo syrup
½ tsp. salt
2 tsp. soda
1 c. chopped walnuts
1 c. light raisins (or dates)

Cream margarine and sugar. Add eggs, one at a time. Add sifted dry ingredients, applesauce, and syrup. Beat at slow speed. Add nuts and fruit. Pour into large cake pan. Bake at 300° for 1½ hours.

Icing: Put 1 cup brown sugar (packed) in pan. Add a little milk plus 2 tablespoons syrup and 2 tablespoons margarine. Boil 3 minutes. Cool. Add 1 teaspoon vanilla and powdered sugar to thicken. Spread on cake. Can use a 9x13 inch pan plus an 8x8 inch pan. A great cake.

Lioness Fran Wulf, Mitchell Lioness Club
Mitchell, South Dakota, USA

I can keep a secret ... but those I tell it to never can.

EASY LEMON CAKE

1 lemon cake mix	1 (3 oz.) lemon jello
¾ c. oil	¾ c. water
4 eggs	

Beat all together for 3 minutes. Pour into 9x13 inch pan. Bake at 350°F. for 35 to 40 minutes. Remove from oven and poke all over with a fork. Mix the juice of 2 lemons or use lemon juice with 2 cups icing sugar. Pour over cake. Return cake to oven for 1 minute more at the same temperature.

Mrs. Laurie Kovach, Brandon Crocus Lions Club
Brandon, Manitoba, Canada

LEMON MERINGUE CAKE

Prepare 1 package lemon cake mix (Duncan Hines) according to package directions.

Filling:

1 (6 oz.) can frozen lemonade concentrate	1 c. sugar
	¼ tsp. salt (you may leave out)
1¼ c. water	1 lemon (juice and rind)
4 Tbsp. cornstarch	4 eggs

Meringue Frosting:

4 egg whites	⅛ tsp. cream of tartar
1 c. sugar	⅓ c. water

Filling: Combine all ingredients, except egg yolks. Boil, stirring constantly. Beat the egg yolks. Add some of the mixture slowly and beat. Return to the mixture in saucepan and cook 2 minutes, stirring constantly. Cool. Split layers. After cutting cake in halves, spread filling between 3 of the layers, or all of them if you want a very tall cake.

Meringue Frosting: Bring sugar and water to a boil; cook until it forms a soft ball in cold water. Beat egg whites stiffly and add cream of tartar to them, beating well. Add the sugar-water syrup slowly to stiffly beaten whites, beating constantly. Add a little salt and vanilla. Place over entire cake and brown in oven 8 to 10 minutes. You may sprinkle coconut or nuts on top of the cake.

Mrs. Rebecca Allen, Kosciusko, Mississippi, Lions Club
Kosciusko, Mississippi, USA

❧

Grandpa used a tranquilizer, too. He called it work.

LEMON SUPREME CAKE

1 Duncan Hines lemon supreme
   cake mix
1 (4 oz.) pkg. lime Jell-O
2 c. hot water

1 (4 oz.) pkg. instant lemon
   pudding
1½ c. milk
1 small ctn. Cool Whip

Bake cake according to directions. Use 9x13 inch pan. While hot, pour over lime Jell-O made with 2 cups hot water. Let cool. Make lemon pudding with 1½ cups milk. Spread over cooled Jell-O. When set, spread with Cool Whip. Before serving, sprinkle with coconut and green sugar if desired.

Lioness LeNora M. Meyer, Mitchell Lioness Club
Mitchell, South Dakota, USA

"DELICIOUS" LEMON PUDDING CAKE

1 lemon cake mix
1 pkg. instant lemon pudding
4 eggs
¾ c. oil

¾ c. water
⅓ c. frozen orange juice, thawed
2 Tbsp. oleo
2 c. sifted powdered sugar

Mix together cake mix, instant lemon pudding, 4 eggs, oil, and water; beat for 10 minutes. Bake at 350° for about 40 minutes.

While cake is baking, mix together ⅓ cup thawed undiluted frozen orange juice, 2 tablespoons oleo, and 2 cups sifted powdered sugar. Take cake from oven and poke holes all over top of cake with an ice pick. Drizzle orange juice mixture over top of cake (will form a glaze). Even better the second day!

Carolyn Sexton, Independence Eastview Lions Club
Independence, Missouri, USA

LEMON SHORTCAKE

1½ c. white sugar
3 eggs, beaten
4 Tbsp. cornstarch
2 c. hot water
10 to 12 biscuits*

Juice of 6 lemons
Zest of 1 lemon rind, scraped on
   fine grater
¼ lb. oleo or butter

Mix sugar and cornstarch, then add hot water. Bring to boil. Boil until clear. Add butter and lemon rind. Stir. Add lemon juice and beaten eggs, stirring constantly. Bring back to a boil and cook 2 to 3 minutes.

My dad used this recipe for years.

* I use enough Bisquick to make 10 to 12 biscuits (follow directions on package).

Walter E. Loomis, North Jackson Lions Club
Jackson, Michigan, USA

CHERRY-GLAZED SPONGE CAKE

1 c. (½ lb.) butter
1½ c. granulated sugar
4 eggs
1 tsp. almond extract

2 c. all-purpose flour
1 (21 oz.) can cherry pie filling
Powdered sugar

In a large bowl, beat butter and sugar until fluffy. Add eggs, one at a time, beating well. Stir in almond extract and flour until blended. Spread a little butter into a 10x15 inch baking dish, until well-greased. With a knife, score it in a crisscross pattern to create 15 pieces. Spoon pie filling into center of each piece. Bake at 350°F. for 35 to 40 minutes. Toothpick test as you do with a cake. After baking, dust with powdered sugar. Makes 7 to 15 servings.

If you are tempted to leave out the almond extract - don't. It's the secret!
Sarah Wehling, Bothell Lions Club
Bothell, Washington, USA

CHERRY CAKE

1 white cake mix
1 box cherry jello
¾ c. hot water

1 small box Cool Whip
1 can cherry pie filling

Bake cake as directed on box in a long pan. When cake is done, punch hole with a fork all over top. Pour jello, dissolved in ¾ cup of hot water, over top. After cool, top with Cool Whip and then add cherry pie filling.

Nancy Dean, Stamps Lions Club
Stamps, Arkansas, USA

PINEAPPLE CAKE

2 c. flour
2 c. sugar
2 eggs

2 tsp. soda
20 oz. can crushed pineapple (not
    drained)

Icing:

½ stick margarine
1 tsp. vanilla

8 oz. cream cheese
1 (1 lb.) box powdered sugar

Mix all and pour into a sheet pan. Bake 20 minutes at 400°. Cool slightly and ice.

Janie Fox, Saginaw Lions Club
Saginaw, Texas, USA

Family ... the we of me.

PINEAPPLE SHEET CAKE

Cake:

2 c. flour
2 c. sugar
1 tsp. soda
2 eggs

½ c. cooking oil
¾ large can crushed pineapple
   (do not drain)

Frosting:

1 (8 oz.) pkg. cream cheese,
   softened
1 stick margarine

1 Tbsp. vanilla
1 box powdered sugar

Cake: Mix dry ingredients; add oil, eggs, and pineapple. Mix well. Bake in greased and floured 9x13 inch pan at 350° for approximately 30 minutes or until done. Test the center with a toothpick. (Glass pans seem to take longer.)

Cream Cheese Frosting: Cream well the margarine, cream cheese, and vanilla. Add powdered sugar and beat until well mixed. Spread on cooled cake and refrigerate.

Sally McGlone, Noon Lions Club
Emporia, Kansas, USA

❦

A road map will tell us everything we want to know
except how to fold it up again.

❦ ❦ ❦

There is no better exercise for the heart
than to reach down and lift someone up.

COCONUT-PINEAPPLE CAKE

1 c. butter, softened
2 c. sugar
4 eggs
3 c. sifted cake flour
1 Tbsp. baking powder
¼ tsp. salt

1 c. milk
1 tsp. pure vanilla extract
1 tsp. pure almond extract
2 c. grated coconut
Pineapple Filling
Seven-Minute Frosting

Cream butter; add sugar and mix well. Add eggs, one at a time, beating well till fluffy and light in color. Combine flour, baking powder, and salt. Add alternately with milk, beginning and ending with flour mixture. Add flavorings. Pour batter into 3 greased and floured 9 inch round cake pans. Bake at 350° for 25 to 30 minutes. Cool 10 minutes in pan. Spread 1 layer with half of Pineapple Filling. Spread ⅓ cup coconut over filling. Repeat with next layer. Spread Seven-Minute Icing on top and sides of cake. Sprinkle with remaining coconut. Yields one 3 layer cake.

Pineapple Filling:

1 c. sugar
3 Tbsp. all-purpose flour
2 eggs, beaten
1 (8 oz.) can crushed pineapple
(undrained)

2 Tbsp. lemon juice
1 Tbsp. butter or oleo
1 tsp. pure vanilla extract

Seven Minute Frosting:

1½ c. sugar
¼ c. plus 1 Tbsp. cold water
2 egg whites

1 Tbsp. light corn syrup
Dash of salt
1 tsp. pure vanilla extract

Pineapple Filling: Combine sugar and flour in a small saucepan; add remaining ingredients. Cook over medium heat, stirring constantly, until thicken (about 2 minutes). Cool. Yield: 1⅓ cups.

Seven Minute Frosting: Combine all ingredients, except vanilla, in top of a large double boiler. Beat at low speed of an electric mixer 30 seconds or just until blended. Place over boiling water; beat constantly on high speed 7 minutes, or until stiff peaks form. Remove from heat. Add vanilla; beat 2 minutes or until frosting is thick enough to spread. Yield: 4½ cups.

This is to be used on Coconut-Pineapple Cake.

Mrs. Charlotte M. Garner, Pascagoula Evening Lions Club
Pascagoula, Mississippi, USA

Knowledge has no power until it is used.

BEST CAKE

2 c. flour
2 c. sugar
2 eggs
1 c. chopped walnuts (preferably
   black)

2 tsp. baking soda
1 tsp. vanilla
1 large can crushed pineapple

Put all ingredients in large bowl and mix well. Bake at 350° for 30 to 40 minutes in ungreased 13x9 inch pan.

Icing:

1 (8 oz.) cream cheese
½ c. margarine
1 tsp. vanilla

1½ c. powdered sugar, sifted (I
   use 2 c. or more)

Mix with fork and put on cake while warm.

Dorothy Wimmer, Rock Falls Lions Club
Sterling, Illinois, USA

DATE CAKE

2 pkg. dates, chopped

1 c. pecans

Place in large bowl with 2 tablespoons soda. Pour 2 cups boiling water over this. Let cool.

Cream together:

2 c. sugar

1 c. oleo

Add 3 eggs and date mixture; mix well. Add 3 cups flour and 1 tablespoon vanilla. Bake in greased 11x16 inch pan at 350° for 40 to 45 minutes. Put icing on while hot.

Icing:

16 dates, chopped
2 c. sugar

1⅓ c. sweet milk
½ c. pecans, chopped

Cook until thick.

Jane McCune, Huffman Lions Club
Huffman, Texas, USA

Pleasant days are just ordinary days made better by good people.

DATE CAKE

1½ c. boiling water
1 c. chopped dates
1½ tsp. soda
¾ c. Crisco
1 c. white sugar
2 eggs

1¾ c. flour
1 tsp. salt
1 c. chopped nuts
1 (6 oz.) pkg. chocolate chips
½ c. sugar

Pour boiling water over chopped dates and soda. Let cool. Cream shortening and sugar. Add beaten eggs. Mix and then add date mixture. Pour into well greased and floured 9x13 inch pan. Mix nuts, chocolate chips, and ½ cup sugar. Sprinkle over cake batter. Bake at 350° for about 45 minutes. Serves 12 to 15.

MOTHER'S DATE CAKE

1 c. cut up dates

1 tsp. soda

Add soda to dates. Pour over this and mix 1 cup boiling water. Set aside.

Butter (size of an egg - I use ½
    stick or a bit more)

1 c. sugar
1 egg

Cream all together. Add date mixture.

Add:

1½ c. sifted flour
1 tsp. baking powder

½ c. floured nuts, chopped

Put in 2 greased cake pans. Bake at 350° for about 30 minutes. Test with toothpick. Cool before frosting.

Frosting for Date Cake - Butter Frosting:

⅓ c. soft butter
3 Tbsp. cream

3 c. sifted powdered sugar
1½ tsp. vanilla

I like 1 teaspoon vanilla and ½ teaspoon almond. Blend butter and sugar. Stir in cream and flavoring till very smooth. (I use an electric beater.) Frost when cake is cool.

Dorothy V. Wipreed, Bothell Lions Club
Bothell, Washington, USA

Yesterday's nest egg will hardly buy today's birdhouse.

CRANBERRY MINCEMEAT CAKE

½ c. butter
1½ c. sugar
3 eggs
1½ c. mincemeat
1½ c. cranberries

¾ c. milk
3 c. flour
2 tsp. baking powder
1 tsp. baking soda
1 tsp. vanilla

In a bowl, cream butter until fluffy. Beat in sugar and eggs. Stir in milk, mincemeat, and cranberries. Stir in remaining ingredients. Stir until well blended. Spoon dough into a greased 1½ quart mold. Bake at 350° for 1 to 1¼ hours, or until to touch in center. Cool in pan 5 minutes. Tap to loosen. Cool thoroughly. Wrap and store in a cool dry place. (I use 3 cups of cranberries.)

Barbara Gibbons, Onekama Lions Club
Onekama, Michigan, USA

RASPBERRY-ALMOND COFFEE CAKE

2 c. Bisquick original baking mix
¼ c. (½ stick) margarine or butter,
    softened
2 Tbsp. sugar

⅔ c. milk
2 Tbsp. sliced almonds
5 tsp. raspberry preserves

Heat oven to 400°. Lightly grease large cookie sheet or pizza pan. Mix baking mix, margarine, and sugar until crumbly. Stir in milk until dough forms; beat 15 strokes. Spread ⅔ cup of the dough into 5 inch circle on center of cookie sheet; sprinkle with almonds. Drop remaining dough by 10 rounded tablespoonfuls about 1 inch from circle and 1 inch apart. Make a shallow well in center of each with back of spoon. Fill with ½ teaspoon preserves. Make about 15 minutes or until golden brown. While warm, drizzle with glaze. Makes 10 servings.

Glaze: Mix ⅔ cup powdered sugar, 1 tablespoon warm water, and ¼ teaspoon almond extract with spoon until smooth and thin enough to drizzle.

Serve as the centerpiece at a sumptuous Sunday brunch or as the finale to a special family dinner. Serve with coffee at breakfast.

Lena Presogna, Amarillo Downtown Lions Club
Amarillo, Texas, USA

❦

He who speaks sows. He who listens reaps.

RICH CRANBERRY COFFEE CAKE

1 (8 oz.) pkg. cream cheese,
   softened
1 c. butter or margarine
1½ c. sugar
1½ tsp. vanilla
4 eggs
2¼ c. all-purpose flour, divided

1½ tsp. baking powder
½ tsp. salt
2 c. fresh or frozen cranberries,
   patted dry
½ c. chopped pecans or walnuts
Confectioners sugar

In a mixing bowl, beat cream cheese, butter, sugar, and vanilla until smooth. Add eggs, one at a time, mixing well after addition. Combine 2 cups flour, baking powder, and salt; gradually add to butter mixture. Mix remaining flour with cranberries and nuts; fold into batter. Batter will be very thick. Spoon into a greased 10 inch fluted tube pan. Bake at 350° for 65 to 70 minutes or until cake tests done. Let stand 5 minutes before removing from the pan. Cool on a wire rack. Before serving, dust with confectioners sugar. Makes 16 servings.

COFFEE CAKE - RIVEL KUCHA

Base:

1 c. white sugar
1 c. soft margarine
2 c. flour
1 tsp. baking powder

1 egg
Apples
Sugar
Cinnamon

Mix dry ingredients as crumbs and save ¾ cup crumbs for topping. Add 1 egg to first 4 ingredients. In 9x13 inch pan, pat mixture lightly. Top with apples sprinkled with sugar and cinnamon or plums, saskatoons if you're lucky. Sprinkle with remainder of crumbs. Bake at 350° for 30 to 40 minutes.

Terry Pister, Downtown Prince Albert Lioness Club
Prince Albert, Saskatchewan, Canada

BOHEMIAN COFFEE CAKE

2 c. flour
½ c. sugar
1 c. brown sugar
1½ sticks margarine
1 c. buttermilk
1 tsp. baking soda

1 egg
¼ tsp. salt
1 c. dried apricots, cut small with
   scissors
1 c. chopped nuts
1 tsp. vanilla

Mix first 4 items as for a pie crust and put less than 1 cup aside for the topping. To the remainder, add the next 7 items; mix and pour into a greased square pan or a 10 inch pie plate. Cover with reserved crumbs and push down with fingers. Bake 45 minutes in a 375° oven. Don't cut this cake for a couple of days!

Ellen Ostrand, Lady Lions of Rohnert Park Lions Club
Rohnert Park, California, USA

APPLE COFFEE CAKE

4 c. apples, pared and diced
3 tsp. cinnamon
⅓ c. sugar (first amount)
4½ c. stirred but unsifted flour
4 tsp. baking powder
3 c. sugar (second amount)

1 tsp. salt
6 large eggs
1½ c. good quality oil
⅓ c. undiluted fresh frozen orange
   juice

Prepare apples first: Wash, pare, core, and chop apples. Measure 4 cups. To them, add cinnamon and ⅓ cup sugar. Mix well and let stand while you mix the batter.

In a large bowl, mix by hand the flour, baking powder, sugar (second amount), and salt. Add eggs, oil, and orange juice concentrate. Lower beaters and beat until smooth and well blended. (This is a lovely batter.)

Oil a 10 inch angel food cake pan and spoon ⅓ of the batter in. Now thoroughly drain all juice from apples, pressing. Spoon half of the apples unevenly over the batter. Cover with ⅓ of batter. Cover with remaining apples. Top with remaining ⅓ of the batter. Bake at 325°F. for 1½ hours. Be sure not to underbake this lovely cake. Cake can be frozen.

Noella Lazzari, Jasper Mountain Lions Club
Jasper, Alberta, Canada

EASY COFFEE CAKE

1 loaf frozen bread dough
½ c. chopped nuts
1 (3 oz.) pkg. butterscotch
   pudding (cooked mix dry,
   not instant)

½ c. margarine
2 Tbsp. brown sugar
½ c. sugar
1 Tbsp. ground cinnamon
2 Tbsp. water

Thaw bread dough until easy to slice. Cut into 14 to 16 slices. Grease a Bundt pan. Sprinkle nuts on bottom of pan, overlapping slices. Combine remaining ingredients in a saucepan. Cook over medium heat until mixture boils. Pour hot mixture over dough. Cover pan with a towel and let stand overnight. Bake at 350° for 25 to 30 minutes. Cool 10 minutes, then turn out of pan. Yields 6 servings.

Grace Bronson, Whittemore Lioness Club
Whittemore, Michigan, USA

Kind words are short to speak, but their echoes are endless.

HEATH COFFEE CAKE

1 stick butter
½ c. white sugar
1 c. brown sugar
1 egg

1 tsp. soda
2 c. flour
1 tsp. vanilla
1 c. buttermilk

Topping:

¾ c. chopped Heath bars
¼ c. chopped nuts

½ c. mixture (reserved)

Blend flour, sugars, and butter. Take out ½ cup of crumb mixture. To rest of mixture, add buttermilk, soda, egg, and vanilla. Blend well and pour into greased and floured 10x14x2 inch pan. Sprinkle topping mixture on top. Bake at 350° for 30 minutes.

Mrs. Ron (Pat) Henne, Elburn Lions Club
Elburn, Illinois, USA

JEWISH COFFEE CAKE

1 pkg. white or yellow cake mix
1 small ctn. sour cream
½ c. oil

4 eggs
1 pkg. instant pudding mix

Mix all together and beat 5 minutes. Grease and flour a Bundt pan or angel food cake pan. You may use a 9x13 inch pan lined with foil and greased. Pour ½ the batter in pan and sprinkle ½ of the following mixture: Mix together 1 cup sugar, 2 teaspoons cinnamon, 2 teaspoons cocoa, and ⅓ cup chopped nuts. Add remaining batter and sprinkle with remaining sugar mixture. Bake at 350° for 50 to 55 minutes in tube or Bundt pan. Swirl a spatula through a couple of times.

Mrs. Mike (Shirley) Stoffa, Elburn Lions Club
Elburn, Illinois, USA

❧

A small town is a place where the only thing taller than the church is the grain elevator.

PULL APART COFFEE CAKE

1 c. milk, scalded	4 c. all-purpose flour
3 Tbsp. butter	2 eggs
¼ c. sugar	Melted butter
½ tsp. salt	1 c. sugar
1 cake yeast	1 tsp. cinnamon
¼ c. lukewarm water	¾ c. chopped nuts

In large bowl, combine first 4 ingredients. Set aside. to cool. Dissolve yeast in lukewarm water; add to cooled milk mixture. Add 1 cup of the flour. Beat well. Add eggs. Beat again. Mix in remaining flour. Turn out on lightly floured board. Cover and let rest 5 minutes. Knead until smooth. Cover and let rise until doubled. Punch down. Break off small pieces of dough and shape into size of golf balls. Dip in melted butter and then in mixture of sugar and cinnamon. Sprinkle some of chopped nuts in bottom of buttered angel food pan. Arrange rolls in pan, sprinkling more nuts between layers. Sprinkle any remaining melted butter and cinnamon mixture over top. Cover and let rise 1 hour or until doubled. Bake at 375° for 35 to 40 minutes. Let stand 10 minutes, then turn out on a serving plate. Pull apart to serve as a sign of friendship.

Frances Gauer, Rootstown Lions Club
Rootstown Township, Rootstown, Ohio, USA

SOUR CREAM COFFEE CAKE

Cream:

¼ lb. butter or margarine	1 c. sugar

Add 2 eggs, one at a time.

Sift together:

2 c. flour	1 tsp. baking soda
¼ tsp. salt	1 tsp. baking powder

Add to rest with 1 teaspoon vanilla. Add ½ pint sour cream. Put ½ the dough in a greased angel food cake pan, then ½ of topping, then the rest of dough. Add rest of topping to top. Bake at 350° for 40 minutes.

Topping: Mix ½ cup sugar, 2 teaspoons cinnamon, and ½ cup chopped nuts.

John J. Hess, Clarence Center Lions Club
Clarence Center, New York, USA

Look for heaven here on earth. It is all around you.

"EASY" COFFEE CAKE
(Only one pan)

1 white cake mix
1 can pie filling (cherry or
    blueberry)

½ c. cold water
½ c. oil
2 eggs

    Put oil in bottom of 9x13 inch pan and spread. Put cake mix, eggs, and water in pan; stir well. Scrape sides. Batter will be lumpy. Place spoonfuls of pie filling around cake. Pull knife through to marbleize. Bake at 350° for 35 to 40 minutes. Best served with whipped cream (or sprinkle powdered sugar on top).

Pam Sedlar, Onekama Lions Club
Onekama, Michigan, USA

LEMON POPPY SEED CAKE

1 box lemon cake mix
4 whole eggs
¾ c. vegetable oil
1 (5¼ oz.) box instant vanilla
    pudding

1¼ c. water
½ c. poppy seeds
1 (21 oz.) can lemon pie filling
1 pt. Cool Whip

    Combine dry cake mix, eggs, oil, dry pudding, water, and poppy seeds. Mix well with electric mixer for about 4 minutes. Bake at 350° in a 9x13 inch pan. Cool. Spread lemon pie filling on top of cake. Frost with whipped cream. Refrigerate for at least 4 hours before serving. Makes 15 servings.

POPPY SEED CAKE

1 pkg. Duncan Hines yellow cake
    mix (pudding added)
½ c. sugar

4 large eggs
8 oz. sour cream
3 Tbsp. poppy seeds

    Grease Bundt pan or tube pan with margarine and sprinkle with sugar. Mix all ingredients, then beat for 2 minutes with mixer set on medium speed. Pour batter into pan and bake at 325° for 50 minutes.

    Great opportunities to help others come seldom, but small ones surround us daily.

Bettie Patterson, Kosciusko Lions Club
Kosciusko, Mississippi, USA

❦

Happiness is a direction, not a place.

POPPY SEED BREAD (CAKE)

1 yellow cake mix or any cake mix will work
¼ c. oil
4 eggs

1 pkg. instant coconut pudding
1 c. boiling water
¼ c. poppy seed

Mix and bake at 350° for 45 minutes. Makes 2 loaves. You can use any cake mix. I prefer cherry chip the best.

Albert Walton, Jackie Walton, Onekama Lions Club
Onekama, Michigan, USA

COUNTRY POPPY SEED CAKE

¼ c. poppy seeds
1 (5¼ oz.) pkg. instant vanilla pudding mix
1 (18¼ oz.) pkg. white cake mix (without pudding in the mix)
½ c. oil

4 eggs
1 c. water
1 tsp. almond extract
2 Tbsp. sugar
½ tsp. ground cinnamon

Glaze:

½ c. powdered sugar
¼ tsp. vanilla

1 to 2 tsp. milk

In a large mixing bowl, combine poppy seeds, pudding, and cake mix. Add oil, eggs, water, and almond extract. Blend with an electric mixer on low speed until dry ingredients are moistened. Increase speed to medium and mix for 2 minutes. Combine sugar and cinnamon. Sprinkle cinnamon/sugar mixture into a greased fluted tube pan. Pour batter into pan and bake at 325° for about 1 hour or until cake tests done. Allow cake to cool 10 minutes before removing to cooling rack. Combine glaze ingredients and drizzle over cooled cake. Yield: 14 servings.

Forgiveness is when you leave Dad's saw out in the rain
and he says it was rusty anyway.

PUMPKIN CAKE

2 c. plain flour	2 c. sugar
2 tsp. baking soda	1 heaping tsp. cinnamon
1 tsp. baking powder	¼ tsp. nutmeg
4 eggs	1 tsp. salt
1 c. vegetable oil	2 c. canned pumpkin

Icing:

1 stick margarine or butter	1 box powdered sugar
1 (8 oz.) pkg. cream cheese	½ c. pecans (optional)
1 tsp. vanilla	

Mix eggs, vegetable oil, and sugar together. Add everything but the pumpkin and beat with a mixer for about 2 minutes. Add pumpkin and beat for another minute. Place in a greased and floured 12¾ x 9 x 2 inch cake pan. Bake for 1 hour at 350°.

Icing: Butter and cream cheese should be softened. Add the powdered sugar and the vanilla. Sometimes I add a touch of milk to make it spread easily. If you choose to use the nuts, chop and sprinkle over the iced cake. Wonderful for Thanksgiving.

Janice P. Baynard, Dolley Madison Lions Club
Greensboro, North Carolina, USA

PUMPKIN CAKE

1 large can pumpkin	1½ sticks oleo
1 box yellow cake mix	1 c. pecans

Follow the recipe on the can for making pie. Pour the mix into a 13x9 inch pan. Sprinkle 1 box yellow cake mix over the pumpkin. Melt 1½ sticks oleo and pour over cake mix. Sprinkle pecans on top. Bake 1 hour and 15 minutes at 350°. Serve with Cool Whip. Freezes very well.

LaVonne Thompson, Mitchell Lioness Club
Mitchell, South Dakota, USA

Replace a bad habit with a good one.

PUMPKIN CAKE

1 box yellow cake mix
2 eggs
¼ c. water
2 tsp. soda

16 oz. canned pumpkin
2 tsp. pumpkin pie spice*
Confectioners sugar (optional)

Heat oven to 350°. Grease and flour Bundt pan. In large mixing bowl, blend all ingredients, except sugar. Beat 4 minutes on medium speed. Pour batter into pan. Bake 40 to 45 minutes or until wooden toothpick inserted near center comes out clean. Cool 10 minutes; remove from pan. Optional: Sprinkle with confectioners sugar.

* Or, use a combined mix of ground cinnamon, cloves, nutmeg, and allspice to equal 2 teaspoons.

This is a very moist cake and it is a nice alternative to traditional Thanksgiving pumpkin pie.

Rosemary Kish, Downriver Pride Lions Club
Lincoln Park, Michigan, USA

PUMPKIN CHIFFON CAKE

1¾ c. cake flour
1¾ c. sugar
1½ tsp. baking soda
1 tsp. salt
4 tsp. pumpkin pie spice
½ c. salad oil

7 egg yolks
¾ c. pureed pumpkin
½ c. cold water
2 tsp. vanilla
1 c. egg whites
½ tsp. cream of tartar

Sift into large mixing bowl in order given first 5 ingredients. Make a well in center and add in order given (oil, egg yolks, pumpkin, water, and vanilla). Beat by hand until smooth. Set aside. Beat egg whites and cream of tartar until very stiff and dry. Fold batter (using rubber spatula) into egg whites by hand while pouring slowly, folding until no lumps remain. Pour into ungreased tube pan. Bake 65 to 70 minutes in preheated oven at 325°F. Invert immediately to cool on cake rack. Cool completely.

Can't locate pumpkin spice, use 5 parts cinnamon or 5 tablespoons, 2 parts ginger or 2 tablespoons, and 2 parts nutmeg or 2 tablespoons.

This creation, by me, in my kitchen, is my own recipe. I have others, but this one I give to you grudgingly and explaining myself in the style of Billy Crystal and with the same pride as the City Slickers. Cakes are my specialty and I have difficulty turning by own creations loose. This cake "holds its own" but is also nice with whipped cream or soft fudge frosting.

Vivian Quinlan, Mathews Lions Club
Mathews, Virginia, USA

PUMPKIN CAKE ROLL

3 eggs
1 c. sugar
⅔ c. canned pumpkin
1 tsp. lemon juice
¾ c. flour
2 tsp. ground cinnamon

1 tsp. baking powder
1 tsp. ground ginger
½ tsp. salt
½ tsp. ground nutmeg
1 c. finely chopped nuts

Filling:

1 c. sifted powdered sugar
2 (3 oz.) pkg. cream cheese

¼ c. butter or margarine
½ tsp. vanilla

In a large mixer bowl, beat the eggs on high speed for 5 minutes or until thick and lemon colored. Gradually beat in sugar. Stir in pumpkin and lemon juice. Stir together flour, cinnamon, baking powder, ginger, salt, and nutmeg. Fold into pumpkin mixture. Spread in greased and floured 15x10x1 inch baking pan..Sprinkle with nuts. Bake in a 375° oven for 15 minutes. Immediately invert cake onto towel sprinkled with powdered sugar. Roll up cake and towel, jelly roll style, starting from short side. Cool completely. Unroll cake.

For filling: In a small mixer bowl, beat the 1 cup powdered sugar, cream cheese, margarine, and vanilla on medium speed until smooth. Spread over cake. Reroll cake. Cover and chill. To serve, cut cake into 1 inch slices.

CARROT CAKE
(Diabetic)

4 eggs
½ c. vegetable oil
3 tsp. cinnamon
2 tsp. soda
2 tsp. vanilla
1 tsp. salt

2 c. flour
¾ c. frozen unsweetened apple juice concentrate, thawed
3 c. raw carrots, grated
1 c. raisins
1 c. walnuts, chopped

Beat eggs. Add vegetable oil. Sift together dry ingredients. Add to eggs and oil. Add apple juice concentrate. Stir in carrots, raisins, and ½ cup walnuts. Spray with Pam, a nonstick spray, an 8½ x 11 inch baking pan. Pour batter into pan. Sprinkle remaining ½ cup walnuts over top. Bake in preheated oven at 325°F. for 40 to 45 minutes or until done. No frosting needed.

A teaspoon of ginger in dry beans while cooking prevents stomach gas.

Barbara E. Marshall, Cuba Lions Club
Cuba, Illinois, USA

❦

Nothing is impossible to a willing heart.

EASY CARROT CAKE

1 yellow or white 2 egg cake mix
1 (4 serving size) vanilla instant
    pudding mix
4 eggs
¼ c. cold water

¾ c. Mazola oil
1½ c. grated carrots
1 c. raisins
2 tsp. cinnamon

Mix all ingredients in order given in electric mixer. Pour into a greased and floured Bundt cake pan. Bake in a 350°F. oven for 1 hour. When cool enough to handle, turn out of cake pan onto a cake rack under which is a piece of waxed paper. With a pastry brush, paint all over the cake with a glaze made up of ¼ cup of heated lemon juice and 1½ cups of icing sugar.

Annette King-Dyrnaes, Jasper Mountain Lions Club
Jasper, Alberta, Canada

CARROT CAKE

1½ c. oil
2 c. sugar
3 eggs
2¼ c. flour
2 tsp. cinnamon
2 tsp. soda

1 tsp. salt
2 c. shredded carrots
2 c. flaked coconut
1 c. chopped walnuts
1 c. crushed pineapple and juice
2 tsp. vanilla

Combine all ingredients in order given. Bake in 9x13 inch pan at 350° for 50 minutes.

Frosting:

1 (3 oz.) pkg. cream cheese
¼ c. melted butter
2 Tbsp. milk

½ tsp. vanilla
Pinch of salt

Add enough powdered sugar to make frosting. This cake rises nicely and is very good.

Janice Hinds, North Maplewood Lioness Club
Maplewood, Minnesota, USA

A room hung with pictures is a room hung with thoughts.

CARROT CAKE

2 c. grated carrots
2 c. sugar
1½ c. oil
6 eggs
3 c. flour
2½ tsp. baking soda
2½ tsp. baking powder
1 tsp. cinnamon

⅓ c. milk
1 tsp. vanilla essence
½ tsp. almond essence
½ c. raisins
½ c. walnuts
½ jar mincemeat or ½ can
   mincemeat pie filling

Beat together the carrots, sugar, and oil. Sift together the flour, baking soda, baking powder, and cinnamon. Beat the eggs. Add the flour mixture alternately with the eggs to the carrots, sugar, and oil. Add the milk, vanilla, and almond essence, then stir in the raisins, walnuts, and mincemeat. Bake at 250° for an hour or until toothpick inserted comes out clean.

Magarita Frett Raymond-Selkridge, Charlotte Amalie Lions Club
St. Thomas, U.S. Virgin Islands

SUPER DELICIOUS CARROT CAKE

2 c. all-purpose flour
2 tsp. baking soda
1½ tsp. baking powder
1 tsp. salt
2 tsp. ground allspice
1 c. packed light brown sugar
1 c. granulated sugar

1 c. vegetable oil
4 large eggs
2 c. shredded carrots
1 (8 oz.) can crushed pineapple,
   drained
1 c. black walnuts, chopped

Frosting:

1 lb. powdered sugar
1 (8 oz.) pkg. cream cheese

1 stick margarine, softened
2 tsp. vanilla

Heat oven to 375°. Grease and flour 13x9 inch pan. Mix flour, baking soda, baking powder, salt, and all spices in a large bowl. In a medium size bowl, mix sugar, oil, and eggs with wooden spoon for 1 minute. Stir in carrots, pineapple, and nuts until well blended. Pour into prepared pan and bake 30 to 35 minutes or until a pick inserted in center of cake comes out clean. Cool completely in pan on rack. Makes 16 servings. Frost with Cream Cheese Frosting.

Frosting: Blend frosting ingredients well. Spread on cooled cake. This will seem like a large amount of frosting, but use it all. This cake stays fresh for a long time. Keep in the refrigerator or freeze.

❦

Laughter is a noisy smile!

RHUBARB DUMP CAKE

4 c. diced rhubarb
1 c. sugar
1 (3 oz.) pkg. strawberry Jell-O
  (dry)

1 pkg. yellow or white cake mix
  (not with pudding)
⅓ c. melted oleo
2¼ c. water

Grease a 9x13 inch pan. Layer into pan in order given: 4 cups diced rhubarb, 1 cup sugar, one 3 ounce package strawberry Jell-O (dry), 1 package of yellow or white cake mix (not with pudding), ⅓ cup melted oleo, and 2¼ cups water. Bake at 350° for 30 to 40 minutes. Cool and serve with Cool Whip or ice cream.

Delicious!

Nancy M. Miller, Onekama Lions Club
Onekama, Michigan, USA

RHUBARB CUSTARD CAKE

1 qt. cut up rhubarb
2 c. sugar
4 eggs, separated
½ c. flour

1 tsp. vanilla
2 to 3 c. milk (to cover rhubarb)
½ c. sugar
4 egg whites

First make your favorite pie crust. Grease and line bottom and sides of a 10x13x2 inch baking pan. Put the cut up rhubarb in a large bowl. Add ½ cup flour and 2 cups sugar. Stir well. In a separate bowl, beat egg yolks and milk; pour over rhubarb and stir. Pour all in the pan with the crust. Bake at 350° for approximately 1 hour. Beat egg whites until stiff peaks form, gradually adding the ½ cup sugar. Spread this over the top of the cake; return to oven and bake until topping is golden brown.

Dorothy Ridgewell, Independence Eastview Lions Club
Independence, Missouri, USA

FLOSSIE'S PISTACHIO LAYER CAKE

1½ c. flour
¾ c. margarine
3 Tbsp. sugar
⅓ c. chopped walnuts
½ c. Cool Whip

8 oz. cream cheese, softened
⅔ c. powdered sugar
2 small pkg. instant pistachio
  pudding
2½ c. milk

Mix flour, margarine, and sugar together with hands. Press into greased 9x13 inch pan. Bake 15 minutes at 325°. Allow to cool completely. Beat together Cool Whip, cream cheese, and powdered sugar. Spread over cooled crust. Beat pudding and milk together for 2 minutes. Spread on top. Serve very cold. Do not leave at room temperature.

Lorrie Cram, Ft. Lauderdale Lions Club
Ft. Lauderdale, Florida, USA

WEIGHT WATCHERS PISTACHIO CAKE

1 box lite white cake mix
3 egg whites
2½ c. diet 7-Up

1 box Jell-O sugar free pistachio
pudding

Frosting:

8 oz. diet Cool Whip
1 c. diet 7-Up

1 box Jell-O sugar free pistachio
pudding

Beat and bake according to directions on box. Cool cake. Beat ingredients for frosting until creamy.

Mrs. Gary (Marcia) Cook, Baugo Township Lions Club
Elkart, Indiana, USA

RUM CAKE

Yellow cake mix without pudding
   in mix
1 box instant vanilla pudding
4 eggs

½ c. water
½ c. dark rum
½ c. oil
1 c. walnuts, chopped

Glaze:

¼ c. butter
½ c. sugar

½ c. water
⅛ c. dark rum

Mix all ingredients, except nuts. Beat on low until all ingredients are moist. Beat on medium for 2 minutes. Grease and flour a Bundt pan. Spread chopped nuts in bottom of pan. Pour cake batter over nuts. Bake at 350° for 35 to 40 minutes. Cool 5 minutes before removing from pan.

Glaze: Mix glaze ingredients together in heavy saucepan. Bring to a low boil. Keep on low boil for 10 to 15 minutes. Stir occasionally. Remove from heat and cool slightly. While cake is warm, poke it all over once with a fork. Spoon glaze over cake slowly. Serves 10 to 12.

Life is too important to be taken seriously.

BACARDI RUM CAKE

1 c. chopped pecans or walnuts
1 yellow cake mix with pudding
4 eggs

½ c. cold water
½ c. vegetable oil
½ c. Bacardi rum (80 proof)

Glaze:

1 stick butter
¼ c. water

1 c. sugar
½ c. Bacardi dark rum (80 proof)

Preheat oven to 325°. Grease and flour 10 inch tube pan. Sprinkle nuts over bottom of pan. Combine ingredients for cake and mix. Pour over nuts in pan. Bake for 1 hour. Cool and place on a serving plate. Prick cake top. Spoon and brush glaze evenly over top and sides.

Glaze: Melt butter in saucepan. Stir in water and sugar. Boil for 5 minutes. Remove from heat and stir in rum.

Mrs. Alberta Hopkins, Silver Run-Union Mills Lions Club
Westminster, Maryland, USA

CHEESE CAKE

1 angel food cake
1 (8 oz.) pkg. cream cheese

1 tub Cool Whip
1 can pie filling

Crumble the angel food cake into pieces. Mix in the cream cheese so that there are no pieces of recognizable cake. Mix in Cool Whip. Pour into serving dish and top with pie filling. Chill before serving. Incredible. Sure to receive rave reviews. Easy to remember how to prepare.

Rev. Fred Gilbert, Dannemora, New York, Lions Club
Dannemora, New York, USA

ICEBOX JELLO CHEESE CAKE

30 graham crackers, crushed
2 Tbsp. powdered sugar
¼ lb. butter, melted
1 c. hot water
1 pkg. lemon jello

1 large pkg. cream cheese
½ c. sugar
1 can cold Milnot (must be cold)
1 tsp. vanilla

Mix hot water with lemon jello until dissolved. Set aside to cool. Mix together crushed graham crackers, powdered sugar, and melted butter. Line pan with half the mixture. In separate bowl, mix cream cheese and sugar together. In another bowl, whip Milnot until thick. Add cheese mixture and jello. Continue whipping until thick. Add vanilla. Pour mixture into crust. Sprinkle remaining crumbs over top. Put in refrigerator for 24 hours.

This is my grandmother's recipe. It has been a hit at many parties.
Faith Spivey, Manteno Lions Club
Manteno, Illinois, USA

CHEESE CAKE

2 (8 oz.) cream cheese
5 eggs

1 c. sugar
½ tsp. vanilla

Topping:

8 oz. sour cream
½ c. sugar

1 tsp. vanilla

Mix sugar and cream cheese. Add 1 egg at a time. Bake at 350° for 1 hour (but check to see for doneness around 40 minutes).

Topping: Mix all together. Pour over top of cheese cake. Bake for 5 minutes at 350°.

Martha Johnson, Dolley Madison Lions Club
Greensboro, North Carolina, Guilford County, USA

CREAM CHEESE CAKE
(Old Polish receipt)

1½ lb. cream cheese
1 c. sugar
1 tsp. vanilla

4 eggs
1 c. sour cream

Beat cream cheese. Add sugar. Beat until light and feathery, then add eggs, one at a time, beating well after each time. Beat in vanilla and sour cream. Grease a pan, 10x6x3 inches, with butter or margarine and bake in a 350° oven for 30 minutes. Center should be firm. Turn off heat and leave in oven for 40 more minutes with the door closed. Remove and let stand until cool. Refrigerate. Top with fruit. I prefer using a 9x12x2 inch pan for a flatter cake.

Dan Steffan, Independence Eastview Lions Club
Independence, Missouri, USA

CHEESE CAKE

2 (8 oz.) Philadelphia cream
   cheese
¾ c. sugar
3 eggs
1 tsp. vanilla

Cherry pie filling
1 c. sour cream
3 Tbsp. sugar
1 tsp. vanilla

Beat cream cheese, sugar, eggs, and vanilla. Mix ingredients and pour half of batter into greased 10 inch glass pie pan. Drop ½ can of cherry pie filling on top keeping 1 inch from edges. Top with the rest of batter. Bake at 350° for about 27 minutes. Cool for 10 to 12 minutes. Mix sour cream, sugar, and vanilla. Pour on top of pie. Bake again for 10 to 12 minutes. Cool. Refrigerate and serve. Delicious.

Mrs. Ray Lesher, Strausstown 14 P. Lions Club
Strausstown, Pennsylvania, USA

CREAM CHEESE CAKE
(New York)

2 (8 oz.) cream cheese
4 eggs
1 c. milk

1 c. sugar
1 Tbsp. vanilla
2 Tbsp. cornstarch or flour

Put in blender on low. Mix 7 minutes. Grease pan with butter (9x9 inches). Pour blended mixture in pan and sprinkle with cinnamon. Bake 1 hour at 325°. Cool at room temperature. Keep refrigerated. This cream cheese cake makes its own crust.

Dorothy Wimmer, Rock Falls Lions Club
Sterling, Illinois, USA

ANGEL FLAKE CAKE

1 (12 oz.) box vanilla wafers
1 c. butter (2 sticks)
2 c. sugar
6 eggs

¼ c. milk
7 oz. coconut
1 tsp. vanilla
1 c. pecans

In food processor, crush vanilla wafers; set aside. Chop nuts; set aside. Cream butter. Add sugar and process until smooth. Add eggs, one at a time. Combine milk and vanilla, then add to butter mixture alternately with crushed wafers, nuts, and coconut. Pour into a microwave Bundt pan that has been lined with 2 coffee filter "rings" cut to fit pan. Cook on HIGH 13 to 14 minutes. Let cool 10 minutes before inverting onto plate.

LaDonna Farned, South Benton Lions Club
Monroe, Oregon, USA

ANGEL FOOD CAKE

1 c. cake flour
1½ c. powdered sugar
1½ c. egg whites (room
    temperature)
¼ tsp. salt

1½ tsp. cream of tartar
1 c. sugar
1½ tsp. vanilla
½ tsp. almond flavoring

Heat oven to 375°. Use one 10x4 inch ungreased tube pan. Sift flour and powdered sugar together 4 times. Set aside. Beat egg whites until frothy. Add salt and cream of tartar. Beat until stiff peaks hold. Add granulated sugar, 2 tablespoons at a time. Fold in flour mixture by hand, 2 tablespoons at a time. Fold in flavorings. Push batter in tube pan. Cut through batter several times. Bake 30 to 35 minutes. Place pan inverted on a funnel or pop bottle. Let hang until cool.

I've won blue ribbons at the fair with this recipe. I sold 20 to 25 cakes every Saturday at the farmers market for 5 years.

Patti O'Brien, Sundowners Lions Club
Emporia, Kansas, USA

BABY FOOD CAKE

½ c. margarine
1¼ c. all-purpose flour
1 c. sugar
½ c. chopped walnuts
2 tsp. cinnamon
1 tsp. baking soda
½ tsp. salt

1 egg
¼ c. (4¾ oz. jar) strained sweet
   potatoes baby food
8¾ oz. can crushed pineapple
   (undrained)
1 tsp. vanilla
1½ c. Cool Whip

Melt margarine in 8 or 9 inch square pan. Remove from heat. Add remaining ingredients, except Cool Whip. Mix well until smooth. Bake at 325° for 40 to 45 minutes. Cool. Top with Cool Whip. Sprinkle with additional cinnamon and nuts. Keep refrigerated.

High altitude adjustment (5200 feet): Decrease sugar to ¾ cup. Add 2 tablespoons milk. Bake at 350° for 40 to 45 minutes. Can be made ahead of time. Can be doubled for 9x13 inch pan.

Doris and Hiram Brey, Harleysville Lions Club
Harleysville, Pennsylvania, USA

BABY FOOD CAKE

½ c. oleo
1 c. sugar
1¼ c. flour
1 c. chopped nuts
2 tsp. cinnamon
1 tsp. soda
½ tsp. salt

1 egg
1 (4 oz.) jar strained sweet potato
   baby food
8¾ oz. can crushed pineapple
   (undrained)
1 tsp. vanilla

Melt oleo in 9 inch pan. Remove from heat. Add sugar, flour, chopped nuts, cinnamon, soda, salt, egg, baby food sweet potatoes, pineapple (undrained), and vanilla. Mix all together in cake pan with a fork until smooth and well blended. Bake at 325° for 40 to 45 minutes or until it tests done. Cool. Can frost with cream cheese frosting or top with Cool Whip. Umm!

Marge Wilson, Plattsmouth Lions Club
Plattsmouth, Nebraska, USA

Nothing in fine print is ever good news.

BABY FOOD POUND CAKE

2 c. self-rising flour
2 c. sugar
½ tsp. cinnamon
½ tsp. cloves
1 c. vegetable oil

3 to 4 eggs
2 small jars apricots with tapioca
   plum or banana baby food
1 c. chopped pecans

Place all ingredients in medium size mixing bowl in order given. Beat for 3 minutes. Grease and flour a tube pan. Pour into pan. Bake for 1 hour at 350°. May be served warm or cool, with a powdered sugar glaze or sifted powdered sugar on top, or plain.

Frances B. Blount, Saginaw Lions Club
Saginaw, Texas, Tarrant County, USA

NOVA SCOTIA POUND CAKE

1 c. butter
1⅔ c. sugar
5 eggs
1½ Tbsp. lemon juice

1 tsp. almond extract
½ tsp. salt
2 c. flour
1 tsp. soda

Cream sugar and butter. Add eggs, one at a time, beating well after each addition. Add extract and salt. Fold in flour and soda. Bake at 325° in loaf pan for 1 hour and 45 minutes.

Ann Violette, Westbrook Lions Club
Westbrook, Maine, USA

SIMPLE POUND CAKE

2 sticks softened oleo
2 c. flour
2 c. sugar

6 eggs
1 tsp. vanilla

Sift flour and sugar together 3 times. Put flour-sugar mixture in large bowl of mixer with remaining ingredients. Beat and stir from sides of bowl about 10 minutes. Bake in greased tube pan 1 hour at 350°.

Marvin Harless, East Lake Lions Club
Birmingham, Alabama, USA

The reward for work well done is the opportunity to do more.

POUND CAKE
(With milk in it)

3 c. sugar
½ c. shortening
1 c. butter
5 whole eggs

3 c. cake flour
1 c. milk
1 tsp. vanilla

Cream sugar, shortening, and butter. Add eggs, one at a time, beating well after each. Add flour and milk/vanilla, alternating and beginning and ending with flour. Bake in greased and floured tube pan 1 hour at 325°F, then at 350°F. for 30 minutes until it tests done by touching with finger tips to leave no print. Cool 10 to 15 minutes in pan. Invert onto cake rack to finish cooling.

I rejected pound cakes "with milk" as not being pound cakes (using only eggs and butter for moisture is my idea of pound cake. By any name, this is a delicious cake given to me by Annette Robinson in Charlotte, North Carolina.
Lion Vivian Quinlan, Mathews Lions Club
Mathews, Virginia, USA

HEREDITY POUND CAKE

3 c. cake flour
½ tsp. baking powder
1½ c. butter or margarine
2½ c. sugar
1½ c. eggs (6 to 7 eggs)

¼ c. milk
2 tsp. vanilla
½ tsp. orange extract
3 Tbsp. melted butter
3 Tbsp. sugar

Let all ingredients stand at room temperature 15 minutes. (If butter is used, let stand 1 hour.) Sift flour and baking powder together; set aside. Cream butter and sugar until light and fluffy. Reduce speed to low; add 1 egg and beat well. Sprinkle 2 tablespoons flour over mix. Beat well. Repeat process until all eggs have been added. Combine milk and flavorings; add milk mixture and remaining flour alternately to batter, beating well after each addition. Pour into a greased and floured 10 inch tube pan. Bake at 350° for 50 to 60 minutes or until golden or golden crack forms around top of cake. Brush top of cake with melted butter; sprinkle with 3 tablespoons sugar.

This recipe was in Southern Living many years ago and it is foolproof!
Esther P. Redd, East Lake Lions Club
Birmingham, Alabama, USA

❦

The surest way to be late is to have plenty of time.

BUTTERNUT POUND CAKE

1 c. Crisco
2 c. sugar
4 eggs
2½ c. all-purpose flour

½ c. self-rising flour
1 c. sweet milk
1 Tbsp. butternut flavoring

Cream Crisco and sugar until light. Add eggs. Beat for 1 minute at high speed. Add 1 cup of flour, beating for 1 minute. Add rest of flour alternately with milk. Add flavoring. Bake 1 hour at 325°, then turn up heat to 350° for 10 to 20 minutes or until golden brown.

Frosting:

⅔ c. sugar
1 stick butter
⅔ c. whole milk

1 c. coconut
2 egg yolks

Beat egg yolks until smooth. Add sugar, milk, and butter. Cook until thickened, stirring constantly. Cool. Spread on cake. Sprinkle coconut over cake. I use Superior Brand flavoring.

Edith Haga, Craigsville Lions Club
Craigsville, West Virginia, USA

SOUTHERN BUTTERMILK POUND CAKE

1 c. buttermilk
¼ tsp. baking soda
3 c. all-purpose or cake flour with
    pinch of salt
3 c. sugar
6 eggs

2 sticks butter or 1 each oleo and
    1 butter
1 Tbsp. vanilla
1 Tbsp. butter flavor
1 tsp. coconut flavor

Place soda in buttermilk; set aside. Thoroughly cream butter and sugar. Reduce speed of mixer to blend. Add eggs, one at a time. Mix well. Add flour and milk, beginning with flour. Mix well before adding milk, mixing well each time. End with flour. Add flavoring. Beat 2 minutes at 1 bowl cake speed. Pour into Bundt pan. Bake at 285° for 1 hour and 40 minutes or until brown. (Optional: Sprinkle ⅔ cup grated coconut on top of dough for topping before baking or add vanilla flavored glaze.) The Bundt pan should be well greased with oleo and floured.

Serve self by serving others.

R. Hilton McCrory, Alexandria Lions Club
Alexandria, Louisiana, USA

❦

A letter is an unannounced visit.

OLD TIME POUND CAKE

Note: It is very important that all ingredients be at room temperature.

6 eggs
2 c. plain flour
2 c. sugar
2 sticks margarine or butter (I
    prefer Superbrand
    margarine)

½ tsp. vanilla
¼ tsp. lemon flavoring

In mixer bowl, blend margarine and sugar until well blended. Add 3 eggs, one at a time while beating. Slowly add ½ flour. After well beaten, repeat with other 3 eggs and flour. Beat really well on medium speed of mixer. Add flavorings, again beating well.

Heat oven to 350°. Pour into loaf pan that has been well buttered. Cook until brown on top, about 1 hour. Check for doneness by inserting a toothpick. If it comes out clean, it is done. Let cool for about 10 minutes and remove from pan.

Bertha Smith, President, Parkway Lions Club
Panama City, Florida, USA

NO-CHOLESTEROL MILLION DOLLAR POUND CAKE

2½ c. sugar
2 c. tub margarine
Egg substitute equal to 6 eggs
2 tsp. lemon extract
2 tsp. vanilla extract

¼ c. skim milk
3¾ c. flour
½ tsp. salt
1 tsp. baking powder

Cream sugar and margarine for 7 minutes; add extracts, milk, flour, salt, and baking powder, mixing well. Add egg substitute, a small amount at a time, beating well after each addition.

Pour into a prepared Bundt pan and bake in a 325° oven for 85 to 90 minutes. Cool cake in pan 10 minutes before removing. May be glazed with 1½ cups powdered sugar and ¼ cup lemon juice if desired. This is a very good, moist cake and you don't have to feel guilty when you eat it!

Frances Cantrell, Bowie Evening Lions Club
Bowie, Texas, USA

❧

Useless laws weaken the necessary laws.

QUICK BLACK FOREST CAKE

1 pkg. devils food cake mix (with
  pudding in mix)
1 can cherry pie filling
1 Tbsp. almond flavoring or 2
  Tbsp. Amaretto liqueur

3 eggs
1 c. chocolate chips

Glaze:

½ c. chocolate chips
1 Tbsp. butter

2 Tbsp. milk
1 c. icing sugar

Mix eggs. Add cake mix and flavoring; mix well. Stir in pie filling and chocolate chips. Bake 45 to 50 minutes at 350°. Cool, then glaze.

Glaze: Melt chocolate and butter. Add milk and icing sugar. Mix and ice cake.

Nice served with whipped cream.

He who laughs - lives.

Donna Lane, Jasper Mountain Lions Club
Jasper, Alberta, Canada

BLACK BOTTOM CUPCAKES

Filling:

1 (8 oz.) pkg. cream cheese,
  softened
1 egg

⅓ c. sugar
⅛ tsp. salt
1 (6 oz.) pkg. chocolate chips

Cake:

1½ c. sugar
2 c. flour
½ c. cocoa
1½ tsp. baking soda
¾ tsp. salt

1½ c. water
½ c. oil
1½ tsp. vinegar
1½ tsp. vanilla

Blend filling until smooth. Add chocolate chips. Sift together all dry ingredients for cake. Add water, oil, vinegar, and vanilla. Fill small cupcake tins ½ full of cake mixture. Drop ½ teaspoon of cream cheese mixture into cake mixture. Bake at 350° for 10 to 15 minutes. Makes 5 or 6 dozen.

Patsy Gagnon (Mrs. Charles), Silver Run-Union Mills Lions Club
Westminster, Maryland, USA

Life is a voyage that is homeward bound.

ROYAL BLACK CAKE

2 lb. raisins
2 lb. currants
1 lb. prunes
1 lb. candied cherries
1 lb. mixed fruit
1 jar minced meat
1 lb. flour
1 lb. brown sugar
1 c. molasses
1 lb. butter
12 eggs
2 Tbsp. lime juice
½ lb. walnuts or almonds

2 tsp. cinnamon
1 tsp. allspice
½ tsp. nutmeg
¼ tsp. mace
¼ tsp. cloves
1 tsp. baking soda
1 Tbsp. baking powder
1 Tbsp. vanilla essence
1 Tbsp. almond essence
2 c. milk
1 bottle brandy
½ bottle rum or 1 c. Peter Herring

Grind fruits and nuts with coarse blade of meat grinder. Soak fruits in ¾ bottle of brandy *and* 1 cup Peter Herring or ½ bottle rum a week or more ahead. Cream butter and sugar. Add 10 eggs and beat well. Sift in dry ingredients, alternating with the fruits, nuts, essence, molasses, and milk. Add remaining 2 eggs. Mix well. The batter should be stiff. Pour in greased brown paper lined heavy cake pans. Fill pans ¾ full as they rise very little. Bake at 350°. A pan of water should be placed on the bottom shelf. Let cool in pans. Sprinkle with brandy. Turn out of pan the next day.

Magarita Selkridge, Charlotte Amalie Lions Club
St. Thomas, U.S. Virgin Islands

BLACKBERRY CAKE AND ICING

1 c. shortening (part butter)
2 c. sugar
4 egg yolks
1 c. buttermilk
3 c. flour
2 tsp. baking soda
2 tsp. nutmeg

¼ tsp. cloves
½ tsp. allspice
2 tsp. cinnamon
2 c. blackberry jam (I use a little
    less)
4 egg whites, beaten but not dry

Cream shortening, sugar, and well-beaten egg yolks. Dissolve soda in buttermilk and add alternately with dry ingredients. Add jam and fold in egg whites. This makes 3 layers. Bake at 350° about 30 minutes.

Icing:

1½ c. granulated sugar (approx.)
2 Tbsp. flour

½ pt. whipping cream

Cook to soft-ball stage. Add 1 teaspoon lemon extract and let cool a little. Beat with spoon until proper spreading consistency.

PDG Lloyd E. Wright, Georgetown Lions Club
Georgetown, Ohio, USA

RED WALDORF CAKE AND FROSTING

½ c. Crisco
1½ c. sugar
2 eggs
1 tsp. vanilla
2 tsp. cocoa
1 tsp. salt

1½ c. buttermilk
2¼ c. cake flour
1 tsp. soda
2 tsp. baking powder
1 tsp. vinegar
2 oz. or ¼ c. red cake coloring

Cream shortening, sugar, and eggs. Make paste of cocoa and food coloring. Add to creamed mixture. Add salt to buttermilk and add alternately with flour. Add vanilla. Last, add soda and vinegar, mixed together. Bake in layers for 30 minutes at 350°F.

Frosting: Cook 3 rounded teaspoons flour in 1 cup milk until thick. Let cool thoroughly. Cream until fluffy 1 cup butter or ½ pound oleo (margarine), 1 cup sugar (granulated), and 1 teaspoon vanilla. Blend into cooled cream sauce. Beat thoroughly.

If you run out of baking powder unexpectedly, mix carefully some baking soda and cream of tartar in these proportions: ¼ teaspoon baking soda to ½ teaspoon cream of tartar.

Barbara E. Marshall, Cuba Lions Club
Cuba, Illinois, USA

❦

No matter how bad the situation,
you can lose your temper and make it worse.

❦ ❦ ❦

My memory is excellent. There are only three things I can't remember:
faces, names, and now I have forgotten the third thing.

492

RED VELVET CAKE

2 oz. red food coloring
3 Tbsp. dry cocoa powder
½ c. shortening
1½ c. sugar
2 beaten eggs
2¼ c. cake flour

1 tsp. salt
1 c. buttermilk
1 tsp. vanilla
1 tsp. soda
1 Tbsp. vinegar

Mix food coloring with cocoa to form a paste; set aside. Cream shortening and sugar; add beaten eggs, then cocoa-coloring mix. Beat well. Sift flour and salt together 3 times; add alternately with buttermilk (start and end with flour). Beat well. Add vanilla and beat again. Remove beaters. Add soda to vinegar and add immediately to batter. Stir gently with a spoon until blended.

Grease and flour two 9 inch round or three 8 inch round cake pans. Pour in batter. Bake in 350° oven for 30 to 35 minutes.

"Whipped" Cream Icing for Red Velvet Cake:

1 c. milk
4 Tbsp. flour
1 c. granulated sugar

1 c. white Crisco
1 tsp. vanilla
1 c. powdered sugar

Cook until thick 1 cup milk and 4 tablespoons flour; let cool. Beat together 1 cup granulated sugar and 1 cup white Crisco shortening. Beat until fluffy. Add cooked mixture to Crisco mixture, 1 teaspoon at a time, until all is added, beating constantly. This is done with an electric mixer at high speed. Add 1 teaspoon vanilla. Add powdered sugar. It should look like whipped cream. Ice top and sides and between layers of 9 inch or 8 inch cake.

Everyone should have a comfortable bed and comfortable shoes, because you are in one or the other most of your life.

Frances B. Blount, Saginaw Lions Club
Saginaw, Texas, Tarrant County, USA

WHITE CHOCOLATE CAKE

2½ c. flour
2 c. sugar
1 tsp. baking powder
4 eggs, separated
½ c. white chocolate, melted over
   boiling water

1 tsp. vanilla
1 c. buttermilk
1 c. chopped nuts (pecans or
   almonds)
1 c. flaked coconut
1 c. margarine

Cream margarine and sugar. Add egg yolks and beat well. Add melted and cooled chocolate and vanilla. Sift together flour and baking powder. Add flour and buttermilk alternately. Do not overbeat. Beat egg whites and fold in. Stir in nuts and coconut. Pour into three 8 inch cake pans. Bake at 350° for 35 to 40 minutes.

Barb Allison, Moweaqua Lions Club
Moweaqua, Illinois, USA

THE BEST WHITE CHOCOLATE CAKE

¼ lb. white chocolate, grated
1 c. butter
2 c. sugar
4 whole eggs
1 tsp. vanilla

2½ c. cake flour
1 tsp. baking powder
1 c. finely chopped pecans
4 oz. coconut, finely grated

You may melt and cool white chocolate, but since you must grate the other ingredients, this saves a clean up. Grate nuts and coconut in food processor, using metal blade. Remove blade from bowl and insert fine shredding blade. Shred chocolate. Set aside. Cream butter, sugar, eggs, (cooled chocolate too if melted), and vanilla. Sift flour and baking powder. Add dry ingredients, alternating with buttermilk. Begin and end with flour mix. Fold in remaining ingredients. Bake in greased and floured 10 inch tube pan 1 hour or 9 inch cake pans for 30 minutes at 350°F. Cool 10 minutes. Invert onto cake rack. Handle carefully.

Alternate baking instructions if not using frosting: Grease tube pan generously. Coat with mixture of flour, coconut, and nuts blended in food processor. I prefer this method. This cake is wonderful and if stored in closed container, is moist and may be better "next week."

Lion Vivian Quinlan, Mathews Lions Club
Mathews, Virginia, USA

DEVILS FOOD CAKE

1½ c. sugar
1 c. shortening
2 eggs
½ tsp. salt
1 tsp. vanilla

½ c. cocoa
½ c. water
1 c. sour milk + 2 tsp. soda
2 c. flour

Mix sugar, shortening, eggs, salt, and vanilla. Mix cocoa and water; add alternately the milk and flour. Pour into greased and floured cake pan. Bake at 350° approximately 25 to 30 minutes. Check with toothpick.

Marilyn Merrill, Whitestown Lions Club
Whitestown, USA

❦

The shortest distance between two points is under construction.

CHOCOLATE CAKE

2½ c. sugar
1 c. soft butter or oleo
1 c. buttermilk
2½ c. flour
1 c. boiling water

2 eggs
2 level tsp. soda
1 Tbsp. vanilla
Dash of salt

Icing:

1 box powdered sugar
3 Tbsp. cocoa
½ stick soft butter or oleo

Enough Milnot milk for spreading
consistency

Cream sugar and butter. Add eggs and beat well. Add buttermilk. Add soda to boiling water, then add to mixture of all sifted dry ingredients. Add vanilla. Beat well till smooth. Cook 1 hour at 350° in oblong pan that has been sprayed with Baker's Best. Cool slightly and spread on icing. Like dinner on the ground chocolate cake. I do not sift dry ingredients if using presifted flour.

Reece Anderson, Saginaw Lions Club
Saginaw, Texas, USA

CHOCOLATE CAKE AND CHOCOLATE FROSTING

Cake:

3 c. sugar
⅔ c. shortening
4 eggs
1 tsp. salt

½ c. milk
⅔ c. cocoa
2 tsp. soda
1¾ c. boiling water

Mix together sugar, shortening, and eggs; add salt, milk, cocoa, soda, and flour. Beat for 1 to 2 minutes. Gradually add the hot water. Grease pans. This will make a 9x13 inch pan and a 9 inch round pan. Bake at 350° for 40 to 45 minutes.

Frosting:

1 c. sugar
¼ c. margarine

¼ c. milk

Bring to a rolling boil for 1 minute. Put in ½ cup chocolate chips. Stir until spreading consistency. Good to eat without frosting.

PDG Dick and Carol Ziegler, Mitchell Lions Club
Mitchell, South Dakota, USA

Find happiness in everything you do.

CHOCOLATE SHEET CAKE

2 c. sugar   2 c. flour

    Put in bowl.

    Bring to boil:

1 stick oleo   4 Tbsp. cocoa
½ c. shortening   1 c. water

    Add hot mixture to sugar and flour. Mix well.

    Add:

2 eggs   1 tsp. salt
½ c. buttermilk   1 tsp. vanilla
1 tsp. soda

    Bake at 400° for 15 minutes on greased cookie sheet. Frost at once with the following.

    Bring to boil:

1 stick oleo   4 Tbsp. cocoa
6 Tbsp. milk

    Add to:

1 (1 lb.) box powdered sugar   1 tsp. vanilla
Nelta Harder, Emporia Sundowners Lions Club
Emporia, Kansas, USA

FUDGE CAKE

    A:

1 c. margarine or butter   ½ c. cocoa
1 c. water

    B:

2 c. flour   1 tsp. baking soda
2 c. white sugar   ½ tsp. salt

    C:

½ c. sour milk   2 eggs, beaten

    Put A ingredients in cooking pot and bring to a boil. Take off stove and let cool a bit. While cooling, prepare B, then prepare C and add to B. Mix well and put into a well greased and floured cake pan. Bake at 350° for exactly 30 minutes. Let cake completely cool off before eating. This cake stores great in freezer.
Lori Ann Symington, Edmonton Golden Gate Lions Club
Edmonton, Alberta, Canada

AUNT MARTHA'S CHOCOLATE CAKE

1 pkg. German chocolate cake mix
1 c. sweetened condensed milk
1 jar caramel ice cream topping

1 (8 oz.) or more container Cool
 Whip
2 Heath bars

Cook cake according to directions. Pour into greased 9x13 inch pan. When cake is done, use wooden spoon to dig holes in cake. Pour sweetened condensed milk over cake. Top with Cool Whip. Spread Cool Whip over top of cake. Process Heath bars in processor until crumbled. Spread over cake. Refrigerate.

Hugh Duncan, East Lake Lions Club
Birmingham, Alabama, USA

AUNT MARGARET'S CHOCOLATE CAKE

Have on hand 1 box devil's food cake mix (I use Duncan Hines).

Frosting:

2 c. sugar
⅔ c. evaporated milk (1 small can)
6 Tbsp. cocoa

½ c. butter or margarine
1 tsp. vanilla extract

Follow directions on box for cake and bake in 12x9x2 inch pan. While cake is baking, make frosting as follows. Mix all ingredients, except vanilla, and boil for 1 minute. Remove from heat and add vanilla. Stir. After cake is baked and still hot, pour the hot frosting over cake and using a large spoon, poke numerous holes into the cake so that much of the frosting is incorporated into the cake.

W. Harold Arnett, Reno Plumb Lane Lions Club
Reno, Nevada, USA

Nothing is more exhausting
than searching for an easy way to make a living.

GAIL'S CHOCOLATE CAKE

2 oz. Hershey's unsweetened
  baking chocolate
¼ lb. butter
6 oz. (¾ c.) unbleached Pillsbury
  XXXX flour

8 oz. (1 c.) granulated sugar
2 eggs
1 tsp. vanilla
2 tsp. baking powder
4 oz. (½ c.) 2% milk

Heat butter and chocolate in pot until they melt into liquid. Place sugar, flour, eggs, milk, vanilla, and baking powder in mixing bowl. Add melted butter/chocolate. Stir contents of mixing bowl with wooden spoon until entire mixture becomes a thick smooth liquid.

Preheat oven to 350°. Grease sides and bottom of cake pan with butter. Use 8 inch square (1¾ or 2 inches deep) or 9 inch round (1½ inches deep) cake pan. Pour mixture into pan. Use rubber spatula to scrape last drops out of bowl. Place in 350° oven for 30 minutes. Test to see if done by inserting clean toothpicks in cake; if they come out clean, cake is done. If they are not clean, return cake to oven and test every 3 minutes until you are satisfied that cake is done.

Let cake cool for at least 60 minutes before icing it. Use double recipe if you want to create a 2 layer cake with two 9 inch round pans or a larger 1 layer cake in rectangular pan (10x12 inches). Before applying icing, either place cake on plate or leave cake in disposable aluminum foil cake pan, from which it will be served.

Gail's Chocolate Cake Frosting:

8 oz. confectioners 10X powdered
  sugar
2 Tbsp. Hershey's unsweetened
  cocoa

3 Tbsp. light cream (or Rich's
  Coffee Rich)
1 oz. butter

Gail Meyers, Clarence Center Lions Club
Clarence Center, New York, USA

CHOCOLATE CAKE

2 c. flour
2 c. sugar
¾ c. cocoa
1 tsp. baking powder
2 tsp. baking soda
¼ tsp. salt

3 eggs (unbeaten)
½ c. salad oil
1 c. milk
1 tsp. vanilla
1 c. boiling water

Mix dry ingredients together in bowl. Add other ingredients and mix well. Pour into well greased 9x13 inch pan or 2 layers (batter will be thin). Bake at 350° for 35 minutes or until done. Can be used for cupcakes. Makes about 22. Boiling water should be added slowly.

Doris and Hiram Brey, Harleysville Lions Club
Harleysville, Pennsylvania, USA

❧

Information is pretty thin stuff unless mixed with experience.

CHOCOLATE CAKE
(One bowl, one spoon)

2 c. flour	2 tsp. soda
½ tsp. salt	2 c. sugar
½ c. cocoa	1 c. Wesson oil
1 c. buttermilk	2 eggs
1 tsp. vanilla	1 c. hot water

Icing:

3 Tbsp. melted butter	3 to 4 Tbsp. milk
1 tsp. vanilla	Confectioners sugar
2 Tbsp. white Karo syrup	

Combine dry ingredients. Add liquids, saving hot water until last. Mix well. Bake in a 350° oven about 30 minutes. Check for doneness by inserting a toothpick in center of cake. No need to grease or flour 9x13 inch pan.

Icing: Combine melted butter, syrup, vanilla, and milk; gradually add confectioners sugar. Beat until thick. Add the sugar and/or milk to your desired consistency.

Becky Whitaker, Amarillo Centennial Lions Club
Amarillo, Texas, USA

CHOCOLATE SHEET CAKE

1 c. water	2 eggs
4 Tbsp. cocoa	½ c. cooking oil
1 stick margarine	1 tsp. vanilla
2 c. sugar	1 tsp. baking soda
2 c. sifted flour	½ c. buttermilk

Bring water, cocoa, and margarine to boil; remove from heat and add remaining ingredients. Mix well. Pour into greased and floured cookie sheet. Bake 25 minutes at 375°.

Icing: Slowly bring to boil 1 stick margarine, 6 tablespoons milk, and 1 tablespoon cocoa. Remove from heat and add 1 (1 pound) box powdered sugar, 1 cup nuts, and 1 teaspoon vanilla. Pour over hot cake.

Nancy Fausett, Lyman Lions Club
Lyman, Wyoming, USA

❦

The will to win is not nearly as important as the will to prepare to win.

CHOCOLATE KAHLUA CAKE

1 chocolate cake mix
1 large pkg. chocolate instant
   pudding

1 large Cool Whip
2 c. milk
1 c. Kahlua

Make cake according to package directions in two 8 inch round pans. Cool. Take cake out of one pan and layer in a deep bowl. Poke holes in cake with end of wooden spoon. Make pudding, using 2 cups milk and 1 cup Kahlua. Pour one-half of pudding over cake and cover with one-half of Cool Whip. Repeat with second layer of cake, then remaining pudding and Cool Whip. Keep refrigerated until ready to serve. Serves 12 to 16.

Lion LaVerne DeAnna, Royalton Hills Lions Club
North Royalton, Ohio, USA

CHOCOLATE ZUCCHINI CAKE

1 c. brown sugar
½ c. granulated sugar
1 stick butter or margarine
½ c. vegetable oil
3 eggs
1 tsp. vanilla
½ c. buttermilk
2½ c. flour

¼ c. cocoa
2 tsp. baking soda
½ tsp. allspice
½ tsp. cinnamon
½ to 1 c. grated zucchini squash
½ to 1 c. semi-sweet chocolate
   bits
½ to 1 c. chopped nuts

Cream butter and sugar well. Beat in eggs, oil, vanilla, and buttermilk. Set aside. In a large mixing bowl, sift dry ingredients. Make a well in center and put wet ingredients, including squash, in it. Add chocolate bits and the nuts. Stir until well blended. Bake in greased and floured tube pan at 350°F. for 1 hour and 10 minutes. I've written this as I read it from a newspaper and I use the maximum amounts called for in each case.

Wonderful while slightly warm. A granddaughter, Jacki, who hates nuts was allowed to eat the whole cake the first time, then was told about the nuts and squash.

As my children and grandchildren grow older, I automatically answer the question "What's for dinner" with the word "yuck."

Vivian Quinlan, Mathews Lions Club
Mathews, Virginia, USA

Talent is a flame. Genius is a fire.

CHOCOLATE SAUERKRAUT CAKE

1½ c. sugar
½ c. shortening
3 eggs
1 tsp. vanilla extract
2 c. flour
1 tsp. baking soda

1 tsp. baking powder
¼ tsp. salt
½ c. cocoa (dry)
1 c. water
1 (8 oz.) can sauerkraut, rinsed,
    drained, and cut small

Cream sugar and shortening until light and fluffy. Add eggs, one at a time, beating well. Add vanilla. Sift dry ingredients and add water. Stir in sauerkraut. Pour into greased 9x13 inch pan. Bake at 350° for 35 to 40 minutes. Cool. Spread your favorite frosting. *Enjoy.*

Mrs. Donald Wald, Stephen Lions Club
Stephen, Minnesota, USA

CHOCOLATE BANANA CAKE

½ c. butter or lard
2 c. granulated sugar
2 eggs
4 Tbsp. cocoa
Pinch of salt

1 tsp. vanilla
2½ c. flour
2 tsp. baking soda
3 large or 4 small bananas
1 c. sour cream

Cream together butter and sugar. Beat in eggs. Add cocoa dissolved in ½ cup boiling water and mix. Add salt, vanilla, flour, and baking soda. Mix. Mash the bananas and add alternately with the sour cream, adding bananas last. Pour in layer cake or 9x13 inch pan. Bake at 350° for approximately 30 minutes. *Delicious.*

Ann M. Kennedy, Gouldsboro Lions Club
Gouldsboro, Pennsylvania, USA

CHOCOLATE VINEGAR CAKE

¾ c. flour
1½ c. sugar
5 Tbsp. cocoa
2 tsp. soda
1 Tbsp. salt

⅔ c. canola oil
2 Tbsp. vinegar
2½ tsp. vanilla
2¼ c. water

Grease and flour 9x13 inch pan. Preheat oven to 350°. Combine flour, sugar, cocoa, soda, and salt, then add remaining ingredients and mix with electric mixer. Batter will be very thin. Bake 35 to 40 minutes. Test with toothpick. Makes 12 generous servings.

Each day can be the beginning of a wonderful future.

MISSISSIPPI MUD CAKE

2 c. sugar
1 c. soft margarine
4 eggs
1½ c. plain flour
⅓ c. cocoa

2 tsp. vanilla
1 bag small marshmallows
¼ tsp. salt
1 c. chopped nuts

Mix sugar, margarine, and eggs. Blend in other ingredients, except marshmallows. Grease and flour oblong pan. Cook 30 minutes in 300° oven. Remove and spread marshmallows on top. Return to oven for 10 minutes or until marshmallows melt.

Icing:

1 stick margarine
⅓ c. cocoa
1 box confectioners sugar
½ c. evaporated milk

1 tsp. vanilla
Dash of salt
1 c. chopped nuts

Mix margarine, cocoa, and milk. Stir and let boil. Add vanilla and sugar. Pour over warm cake.

Phyllis Hillis, McMinnville Lions Club
McMinnville, Tennessee, USA

FROSTING

½ c. shortening
1 Tbsp. butter
2 c. powdered sugar

1 tsp. milk
1 tsp. vanilla

With electric mixer, beat shortening, sugar, and butter together. Add milk and vanilla. Beat until creamy. Add color if desired.

Good for decorating cakes or cookies.

Donna Juhl, Otis Lions Club
Otis, Colorado, USA

STRAWBERRY ICING

32 oz. pkg. powdered sugar
1 stick margarine

Frozen strawberries

Thaw strawberries. Melt margarine. Mix with ½ cup strawberries. Add gradually powdered sugar to make right consistency. Beat on high. Use approximately ¾ package powdered sugar.

Anne Davis, Saginaw, Texas, Lions Club
Saginaw, Texas, USA

CHOCOLATE FROSTING

1½ c. sugar
6 Tbsp. butter

6 Tbsp. milk

Cook. When starts to bubble, time for 2½ minutes, stirring. Take off stove. Add ½ cup chocolate chips and vanilla to taste. Blend with mixette, then spread on 9x13 inch cake.

Dolores Haggberg, Isle Lioness Club
Isle, Minnesota, USA

CHOCOLATE FUDGE FROSTING

½ c. butter
⅓ c. corn syrup
¼ tsp. salt
½ tsp. vanilla flavoring

½ c. cocoa
⅓ c. milk
1 lb. box powdered sugar, sifted

Cream butter. Add corn syrup, salt, and vanilla. Blend. Stir in cocoa. Add milk and sugar, alternating small amounts. Beat until smooth and creamy after each addition. Add enough milk at end to make good spreading consistency.

Very good and easy to make. Very good over yellow cake layers.

Edna K. Bunch, Snow Hill Lions Club
Snow Hill, North Carolina, USA

VANILLA WAFER CAKE

2 sticks oleo
2 c. sugar
6 eggs
1 (15 oz.) box vanilla wafers,
    crushed

½ c. milk
1 small can coconut
1½ c. chopped pecans

Cream oleo and sugar; add eggs and beat well. Add other ingredients and mix well. Bake in oiled and floured tube pan for 2 hours at 250°. Cool and invert pan to turn cake out.

Arvella James, White Deer Lions Club
White Deer, Texas, USA

❦

Ability will never catch up with the demand for it.

Notes

*The best inheritance a parent can give to his children
is a few minutes of his time each day.*

Pies
and
Pastries

CRUSTS FOR ICE CREAM PIES

No rolling, no shaping. No patching, no baking. The secrets to carefree ice cream pies — a favorite summer dessert. Combining coolness and crunch, these make-ahead creations stimulate all sorts of imaginative combinations. Mix and match complementary crusts and ice cream flavors all summer long. Fun family fare, yet perfect for dinner parties.

The simple preparation steps begin with combining your choice of crumbs with sugar, the optional additions suggested, and the melted margarine in a small bowl. Press the mixture in the bottom and up the side of an 8 or 9-inch pie pan or in the bottom of a 9-inch springform pan. Refrigerate for 10 to 15 minutes before filling with ice cream, then freeze until solid. Wrap carefully and store in the freezer. When ready to serve, remove the pie from the freezer 5 to 10 minutes before serving for easier cutting. Dip the knife into warm water to facilitate serving.

Kind	Amount of Crumbs	Sugar	Optional Additions	Margarine or Butter, Melted
Graham Cracker	1½ cups (21 squares)	¼ cup	½ tsp. cinnamon	⅓ cup
Graham Cracker-Walnut	1 cup (14 squares)	2 Tbsp.	½ cup finely chopped walnuts	¼ cup
Vanilla Wafer	1½ cups (30 wafers)	—	—	¼ cup
Chocolate Wafer	1¼ cups (20 wafers)	¼ cup	—	¼ cup
Creme-filled Choc./Vanilla Cookie	1½ cups (15 cookies)	—	—	¼ cup
Crisp Macaroon Cookie	1½ cups	—	—	¼ cup
Gingersnap Cookie	1½ cups	—	—	¼ cup
Shortbread Cookie	1¼ cups	¼ cup	¼ cup sliced almonds (chopped)	¼ cup
Pretzel *	1¼ cups	¼ cup	—	½ cup
Granola	1½ cups (coarsely crushed)	—	—	¼ cup
Coconut	2 cups	—	—	2 Tbsp.
Popcorn *	7 cups popcorn = 3½ cups coarsely ground popcorn	¼ cup (brown sugar)	⅛ tsp. cinnamon	½ cup

TIP: *For ease in serving, butter pan before preparing crust.

PIES AND PASTRIES

BROWN SUGAR PIE

1 (16 oz.) box light brown sugar
6 eggs
2 tsp. vanilla

1 c. white sugar
1 stick melted margarine
⅛ tsp. salt

Mix all ingredients. Pour into unbaked pie shells for about 30 minutes at 350°. Makes 2 pies.

These pies are delicious. I use these so much for taking to families who are bereaved or having different times of celebrations.

Lioness Dora T. Poythress, Lawrenceville Lioness Club
Lawrenceville, Virginia, Brunswick County, USA

CHESS CAKE PIE

⅔ c. butter
2 c. sugar
4 eggs, beaten
1 c. milk

2 Tbsp. flour
¼ tsp. vanilla
Nutmeg

Cream butter and add sugar gradually. Add beaten eggs; add milk and flour which have been blended together. Add vanilla. Pour into two 8 inch pie crusts, unbaked. Sprinkle with nutmeg if desired. Bake in hot 450° oven for 10 minutes. Reduce heat to 325° and bake until firm, about 20 minutes.

FRENCH CHOCOLATE PIE

2 c. sugar
7 Tbsp. cocoa
Pinch of salt
4 eggs, slightly beaten

1 tall can evaporated milk
¾ stick butter, melted
1 c. nuts
2 unbaked pie shells

Mix sugar, salt, and cocoa together. Add beaten eggs, milk, butter, and nuts. Mix well. Pour into unbaked pie shells (9 inch) and bake in 350° oven about 40 minutes or until set. Good served with Cool Whip or vanilla ice cream.

Naomi C. Reid, Rock Hill Lions Club
Rock Hill, South Carolina, USA

You are a unique person with a unique destiny.

NUTTY CHOCOLATE PIE

3 eggs
1 c. Karo corn syrup
1 c. coarsely chopped pecans
1 c. chocolate chips

½ c. sugar
2 Tbsp. melted margarine
1 tsp. vanilla extract
1 unbaked pie shell

Preheat oven to 350°. In large bowl, beat eggs until well combined. Add Karo, pecans, chocolate chips, sugar, margarine, and vanilla extract. Mix until well blended. Pour evenly into pie shell. Bake for 50 to 60 minutes. Can be topped with a whipped cream.

Toni Bell, Merritt Island Lions Club
Merritt Island, Florida, USA

FUDGE PIE

1 stick margarine (4 oz.)
2 oz. baking chocolate
2 eggs

1 c. sugar
¼ c. flour
2 tsp. vanilla

Melt margarine and chocolate over low heat. Remove from heat and cool. Stir together eggs, sugar, flour, and vanilla. Beat until smooth. Stir in chocolate and butter mixture. Pour into 8 inch standard pastry shell. Bake at 350° for 30 to 40 minutes. Serve warm or room temperature with ice cream or whipped topping.

Won First Prize Baking Contest, Amateur Pie entry - 1992 Chocolate Expo. Rehoboth Beach, Delaware.
Lois Peregoy (Mrs. Jerry), Silver Run-Union Mills Lions Club
Westminster, Maryland, USA

COCONUT PIE

1 stick oleo
1½ c. sugar
3 eggs
1 Tbsp. vinegar

1 tsp. vanilla
1 c. coconut
1 (9 inch) unbaked pie shell

Mix softened oleo, sugar, vanilla, vinegar, coconut, and eggs. Pour in shell. Bake at 325° for 1 hour.

Ramsay Harless, East Lake Lions Club
Birmingham, Alabama, USA

A stumble may prevent a fall.

COCONUT CUSTARD PIES

3 c. sugar
1 lb. coconut
4 eggs, beaten
4 pie shells (frozen type)

1 stick margarine, melted
3 Tbsp. vanilla
2 cans evaporated milk

Beat eggs. Add milk, then melted margarine, to eggs, then beat in sugar. Add vanilla. Finally add coconut. Bake at 350° until slightly firm in middle.

Glenn Bunch, Snow Hill Lions Club
Snow Hill, North Carolina, USA

15-MINUTE CUSTARD PIE

4 eggs, slightly beaten
½ c. sugar
¼ tsp. salt

1 tsp. vanilla
2½ c. scalded milk

Thoroughly mix eggs, sugar, salt, and vanilla. Slowly stir into hot, but not boiling, milk. Pour the mixture at once into an unbaked pie shell. Sprinkle the top with a dash of nutmeg. Bake in a very hot oven (475°) for 5 minutes. Reduce heat to 425° for 10 minutes. I test by placing knife in center. Should come out clean. Place pie shell on 9x13 inch tin cake pan cover before pouring custard mixture into the shell. Easier to put in hot oven. Remove pan cover slowly from under pie before baking.

Ilo Love, Craigsville Lions Club
Craigsville, West Virginia, USA

EXQUISITE PIE

2 c. sugar
5 eggs
1 c. raisins
¼ tsp. cinnamon
2 Tbsp. vinegar

2 sticks butter
1 c. coconut
1 c. nuts
¼ tsp. allspice

Beat sugar and butter. Add beaten eggs, vinegar, spices, coconut, nuts, and raisins. Put in unbaked pie shell and bake about 35 to 45 minutes at 400°. This makes 2 pies.

Lioness Phyllis Clarke, Lawrenceville Lioness Club
Lawrenceville, Virginia, USA

❧

It feels good to do what people say you cannot do.

HERSHEY BAR PIE

6 almond Hershey's bars
¼ c. milk

18 large marshmallows
1 c. whipping cream

Melt in a saucepan the candy, marshmallows, and milk. Beat cream until stiff. Fold cream in cooled chocolate mixture. Pour into baked pie shell or graham cracker crust.

Billy W. Higginbotham, McMinnville Lions Club
McMinnville, Tennessee, USA

JAPANESE FRUIT PIE

1 stick butter, melted
½ c. coconut
1 c. sugar
½ c. raisins

½ c. chopped pecans or walnuts
2 eggs
1 Tbsp. vinegar
1 unbaked pie shell (8 or 9 inch)

Combine the first 7 ingredients. Mix well; pour into pie shell. Bake 40 minutes at 300°F. Serves 6.

Ellen Ostrand, Lady Lions of Rohnert Park Lions Club
Rohnert Park, California, USA

JAPANESE FRUIT PIE

¾ stick margarine
2 eggs
1 tsp. vinegar
½ c. coconut

½ c. raisins
½ c. nuts, chopped
1 c. sugar
1 unbaked pie shell

Mix all ingredients well and pour in unbaked pie shell. Bake at 300° for approximately 45 minutes.

Too much time is wasted by some people telling how busy they are.
Betty Steele, Rock Hill Lions Club
Rock Hill, South Carolina, USA

KENTUCKY PIE

1 c. sugar
½ c. flour
1 stick butter, melted
2 eggs, beaten

1 tsp. vanilla
2 Tbsp. bourbon
1 (6 oz.) pkg. chocolate chips
½ c. nuts, chopped or pieces

Mix sugar and flour. Add remaining ingredients and mix well. Pour into unbaked pie shell. Bake at 325° for 1 hour. Best pie I've ever tasted!

Diane Howland, Ft. Lauderdale Lions Club
Ft. Lauderdale, Florida, USA

LIGHT 'N FRUITY PIE

1 (3 oz.) pkg. Jell-O (any flavor)
⅔ c. boiling water
2 c. ice cubes
1 (8 oz.) container Cool Whip,
    thawed

1 baked 8 or 9 inch graham
    cracker crumb crust, cooled

Dissolve gelatin completely in boiling water, stirring 3 minutes. Add ice cubes and stir constantly until gelatin is thickened, about 2 to 3 minutes. Remove any unmelted ice. Using wire whip, blend in whipped topping and whip until smooth. Chill, if necessary, until mixture will mound. Spoon into pie crust. Garnish with fruit if desired.

Fruit Version: Make as directed above. Fold 1 cup fresh, canned, or thawed frozen fruit, drained and sliced, into gelatin-topping mixture before chilling. Use 9 inch crumb crust. Garnish with additional fruit if desired. I used canned peaches once, but the best was with raspberry. I had some frozen. You don't need 2 cups of ice cubes (1½ cups will do).

Lloyd Bollo, Plumb Lane Lions Club
Reno, Nevada, Washoe, USA

NUT MERINGUE PIE

3 egg whites
½ tsp. baking powder
1 c. sugar

10 soda crackers
1 c. nuts

Beat 3 egg whites stiff. Add ½ teaspoon baking powder and 1 cup sugar gradually while beating. Fold in 10 soda crackers, crushed very fine, and 1 cup nuts. Bake at 350° in greased pie pan for 1 hour. Serve with whipped cream or ice cream.

Vera and Jim Ballou, Ponderosa Lions Club
Prather, California, USA

OUT OF THIS WORLD PIE

1 can cherry pie filling
¾ c. sugar
1 large can crushed pineapple
    with juice
1 Tbsp. cornstarch
1 tsp. red food coloring

1 (3 oz.) box cherry jello
1 c. chopped pecans
4 large bananas
2 baked pie shells
Whipped topping

In saucepan, combine cherry pie filling, sugar, pineapple and juice, cornstarch, and food coloring. Cook until thick. Remove from heat; add jello and allow to cool. Add pecans and bananas. Pour into baked pie shells and top with whipped topping. Chill. I make my own pie crust and put it in a 9x13 inch pan (you don't have to put crust up sides) and make this as a dessert dish rather than pie shaped.

Dorothy Wimmer, Rock Falls Lions Club
Sterling, Illinois, USA

PEANUT STREUSEL PIE

⅓ c. peanut butter
1 (9 inch) baked pie shell
⅓ c. flour
½ c. sugar
¼ tsp. salt

¾ c. powdered sugar
2 c. scalded milk
3 egg yolks, slightly beaten
2 Tbsp. butter or margarine
½ tsp. vanilla

Blend peanut butter and powdered sugar in bowl until mealy; set aside. Scald milk; combine sugar, flour, and salt in top of double boiler. Stir in scalded milk and cook over boiling water until thickened, stirring constantly. Stir a small amount of cooked filling in egg yolks and combine with the remaining hot mixture; cook several minutes longer, then add butter or margarine and vanilla. Pour into baked pie shell where ⅔ cup peanut butter and sugar mixture has been sprinkled. Top with meringue and sprinkle other ⅓ peanut butter mixture on top. Bake for 15 minutes at 350°.

Meringue:

3 egg whites
¼ tsp. cream of tartar

½ c. sugar
1 tsp. cornstarch

Sprinkle cream of tarter over egg whites and beat until stiff; add sugar and cornstarch gradually, then beat until stiff and shiny. Pile on pie.

PDG Lloyd E. Wright, Georgetown Lions Club
Georgetown, Ohio, USA

BEST EVER PIE

2 egg yolks
1 c. sugar
½ tsp. cinnamon
½ tsp. cloves
½ tsp. nutmeg

½ c. pecan (halves)
½ c. raisins
1 Tbsp. melted butter
1 Tbsp. vinegar

Beat egg yolks until light and fluffy. Add 1 cup sugar and other ingredients, except the egg whites and vinegar. Beat egg whites. Fold into the above mixture alternately with vinegar. Pour into 8 inch pie shell. Bake 10 minutes at 450°, then at 250° for 25 minutes. Serve with whipping cream on top.

Annette Handley, East Lake Lions Club
Birmingham, Alabama, USA

❦

If you're yearning for the good old days, just turn off the air conditioning.

PECAN PIE

3 eggs
½ tsp. salt
1 tsp. vanilla
⅔ tsp. maple flavoring
1 c. light Karo syrup

1¼ c. chopped pecans
½ tsp. baking powder
⅓ c. melted butter
1 Tbsp. flour

Heat oven to 325°. Very slightly beat eggs. Add sugar, salt, flavorings, butter, syrup, baking powder, and flour. Mix in pecan halves. Pour into pastry lined 9 inch pie pan. Bake 40 to 50 minutes, or until set and pastry is nicely browned. Let set to firm up before cutting.

Kenneth Strohbehn, Gladbrook, Iowa, Lions Club
Gladbrook, Iowa, USA

PECAN DELIGHT PIE

2 eggs
¼ c. milk
⅔ c. sugar
½ stick butter/margarine

½ tsp. vanilla flavoring
1 c. chopped pecans
¼ c. coconut
1 Tbsp. flour

Beat eggs until light, then add sugar, then add melted margarine/butter and then flour. Add milk, coconut, and pecans. Put in prepared or frozen pie shell. Bake in a 350° oven for 25 to 35 minutes or until firm in the middle.

Glenn E. Bunch, Jr., Snow Hill Lions Club
Snow Hill, North Carolina, USA

❦

There are many ways of going forward,
but there is only one way of standing still.

❦ ❦ ❦

School days can be the happiest days of your life ...
if the children are old enough to go.

SWEET POTATO PECAN PIE

Have on hand pie dough for one 8 inch pie shell (deep).

Potato Filling:

1 c. baked sweet potatoes	1 Tbsp. vanilla
½ c. light brown sugar	1 tsp. salt
2 Tbsp. granulated sugar	⅛ tsp. allspice
1 Tbsp. heavy cream	¼ tsp. ground cinnamon
1 Tbsp. unsalted butter	⅛ tsp. nutmeg

Syrup mixture:

¾ c. sugar	¾ c. pecan halves
¾ c. dark corn syrup	2 tsp. vanilla
2 small eggs	Pinch of salt
1½ Tbsp. unsalted butter	Pinch of cinnamon

1. Combine the ingredients for potato filling and beat at medium speed until smooth (2 to 3 minutes).

2. Combine the ingredients for syrup mixture in a mixing bowl. Beat in mixing bowl for 1 to 2 minutes on low speed. Add pecans and set aside.

3. Line an 8 inch deep pie pan with your pie dough. Spoon potato filling in the lined pan. Pour the syrup mixture over the potato filling. Bake at 325° until a knife inserted in the center comes out clean, about 1¾ hours.

PECAN PIE

3 eggs	1 tsp. vanilla
½ c. sugar	¼ c. butter or margarine, melted
1 c. dark corn syrup	1 c. pecans
½ tsp. salt	1 (9 inch) unbaked pie shell

Preheat oven to 375°. Beat eggs well in medium bowl. Add sugar, corn syrup, salt, and vanilla. Beat until well combined. Stir in butter and pecans, mixing well. Turn into pie shell; bake 45 to 50 minutes or until filling is set in center when pie is gently shaken. Let cool. Makes 6 to 8 servings.

Edna Bunch, Snow Hill Lions Club
Snow Hill, North Carolina, USA

To be upset over what you don't have is to waste what you do have.

PECAN PIE

1 c. sugar
½ c. light corn syrup
¼ c. melted butter
3 eggs, beaten

1 c. pecans, chopped
1 unbaked pie shell
1 tsp. pure vanilla extract

Mix sugar, corn syrup, and butter. Add beaten eggs, chopped pecans, and vanilla. Fill unbaked pie shell with mixture and bake in moderately hot oven (400°F.) for 10 minutes. Reduce heat to 350°F. and continue baking for 30 to 35 minutes. Remove from oven and let cool before you serve at least 2 hours.

Mrs. Charlotte M. Garner, Pascagoula Evening Lions Club
Pascagoula, Mississippi, USA

PECAN PIE DIXIE

1 c. sugar
¾ c. white syrup
½ c. oleo
3 eggs

½ tsp. vanilla
⅛ tsp. salt
1½ c. chopped pecans

Blend sugar, syrup, and oleo in saucepan. Bring to a boil. Beat eggs. Blend hot mixture slowly into eggs. Stir in vanilla, salt, and pecans. Pour into unbaked pie shell. Bake at 350° for 45 minutes.

Happiness is like potato salad - when you share it with others, it's a picnic.
Verla Thompson, Apache Lions Club
Apache, Oklahoma, USA

PECAN PIE

1 c. dark syrup
1 c. brown sugar
3 eggs

3 or 4 Tbsp. butter, melted
1 tsp. vanilla flavoring
1 c. pecans

Mix all ingredients well and pour into a 9 inch pie shell, uncooked. Cook at 350° for about 45 minutes. Crust should be brown.

Bertha Smith, President, Parkway Lions Club
Panama City, Florida, USA

Some folks pay a compliment like they went down in their pocket for it.

DONNA'S PECAN PIE

3 eggs, beaten
½ c. sugar
1 c. dark Karo syrup
¼ tsp. salt

1 tsp. vanilla
¼ c. melted margarine
1 c. broken pecans
1 (9 inch) pie shell

Mix eggs, sugar, syrup, salt, vanilla, and margarine. Spread nuts in bottom of shell. Pour mixture over nuts. Bake at 300° for 1 hour.

This pie is easy to make and a fine example of "Southern" cooking.
Mrs. Lion George (Dianne) Murphy, Canton Lions Club
Canton, Georgia, USA

PEANUT BUTTER-JELLY PIE

1 (9 inch) graham cracker pie shell
1 c. milk
½ c. strawberry jam
1 (8 oz.) tub whipped topping
   (unthawed)

½ c. crunchy peanut butter
1 small box vanilla pudding and
   pie mix

Put 1 cup whipped topping in bottom of pie shell. Spread evenly. Put in freezer until frozen. Spread ½ cup strawberry jam over topping. Mix 1 cup milk and ½ cup peanut butter. Stir well. Put in box of pudding mix and remainder of topping. Blend with mixer at low speed about 2 minutes. Pour in shell and put in freezer.
Cathy Cloukey, Mt. Airy Foothills Lions Club
Mt. Airy, North Carolina, USA

PEANUT BUTTER PIE

3 oz. cream cheese
½ c. powdered sugar
½ c. creamy peanut butter

½ c. milk
8 oz. Cool Whip topping
½ c. nuts, chopped

Beat cheese until soft and fluffy. Beat in sugar and peanut butter. Slowly add milk, blending thoroughly. Fold whipped topping into mixture. Pour into crust. Sprinkle with nuts. Freeze for 3 hours or until firm. Place in cooked pie crust. Purchase nonfat crust.

To cut down on fat, make pie with low or no fat ingredients.
Janet L. Gadsby, Titusville, Pennsylvania, Lioness Club
Titusville, Pennsylvania, USA

❦

Happy is the man whose life is consistent with his conscience.

THE BEST PEANUT BUTTER PIE

1 (9 inch) crust, baked and cooled
¾ c. powdered sugar
½ c. Skippy roasted honey-nut
   super chunk peanut butter
⅔ c. sugar plus 3 Tbsp. divided
⅓ c. cornstarch plus 1 Tbsp.,
   divided

3 eggs, separated
2½ c. milk
2 Tbsp. butter
1 tsp. vanilla
½ c. water

Place powdered sugar in bowl. Cut the peanut butter with pastry blender until crumbly. Set aside 2 tablespoons for garnish. Sprinkle remaining crumbs into the pie crust. In a saucepan, combine ⅔ cup sugar, ⅓ cup cornstarch, egg yolks, and milk. Cook over medium heat until mixture thickens.

Remove from the heat. Add butter and vanilla, stirring until the butter melts. Pour into pie shell. In a small saucepan, combine remaining sugar and cornstarch with water; cook over low heat until thickened. Cool slightly. Beat egg whites stiff. Fold in cornstarch mixture.

Spread meringue over the hot filling, sealing to the edges. Sprinkle reserved peanut butter mixture over top. Bake at 350° for 12 to 15 minutes or until golden brown.

PEANUT BUTTER CUSTARD PIE

1 c. light corn syrup
1 c. sugar
3 eggs

½ tsp. vanilla
⅓ c. peanut butter

Combine all ingredients and pour into unbaked pie shell. Bake at 450° for 10 minutes. Reduce heat to 325° and bake 30 to 40 minutes longer or until knife inserted in center comes out clean.

PDG Lloyd E. Wright, Georgetown Lions Club
Georgetown, Ohio, USA

BETTY'S PEANUT BUTTER PIE

1 c. confectioners sugar
8 oz. cream cheese
3 Tbsp. evaporated milk

½ c. crunchy peanut butter
8 oz. Cool Whip
9 inch graham cracker crust

Mix together first 3 ingredients. Add peanut butter and mix well. Fold in Cool Whip. Pour into graham cracker crust. Let chill.

Lib Howard, Rock Hill Lions Club
Rock Hill, South Carolina, USA

SHOO-FLY PIE

Bottom part:

¾ c. dark molasses   ½ tsp. soda
¾ c. boiling water

Top part:

1½ c. flour   ½ c. brown sugar
¼ c. shortening

Additional ingredient: Pastry for one 9 inch crust.

Dissolve soda in hot water and add molasses. Combine sugar and flour; rub in shortening to make crumbs. Pour one third of the liquid into an unbaked crust. Add one third of the crumb mixture. Continue alternate layers, putting crumbs on top. Bake at 375° for approximately 35 minutes. Makes one 9 inch pie.

If it is to be, it is up to me.

Gloria A. Hershberger, Aurora Eastgate Lions Club
Denver, Colorado, USA

MOIST SHOO-FLY PIE

Crumbs:

1 c. flour   1 Tbsp. Crisco
⅔ c. brown sugar

Liquid:

1 c. molasses   1 tsp. baking soda
¾ c. boiling water   1 beaten egg

Mix crumbs well until crumbly. Set aside, reserving ½ cup for top. Mix liquid ingredients, then add crumbs all but the reserved ½ cup into liquid. Pour into unbaked pie shell. Put remaining crumbs evenly over top. Bake at 375° for 10 minutes, then reduce oven to 350° for 25 or 30 minutes.

We judge ourselves by what we feel capable of doing, while others judge us by what we have already done.

Louise J. Eshleman, Middletown Lions Club
Middletown, Pennsylvania, USA

❦

Fear is the darkroom where negatives are developed.

NOT-SO-DRY SHOO-FLY PIE

Base:

2½ c. boiling water
1 tsp. baking soda
2 c. brown sugar, packed

1 c. molasses
2 eggs

Crumbs:

3 c. all-purpose flour
1 c. brown sugar, packed

⅔ c. butter

Base: After water is boiling, remove from heat. Add baking soda, sugar, and molasses. Let cool for 5 minutes. Beat eggs well and stir in. Pour into 3 pie shells.

Crumbs: Mix flour and sugar. Blend in softened butter until crumbs form. If crumbs are not moist, add more butter. Sprinkle into pies. Bake at 350° for 35 minutes. Cool and serve.

Cas Mort (Mrs. Harold), Silver Run-Union Mills Lions Club
Littlestown, Pennsylvania, USA

UP 'N ADAM PIE

4 large eggs, well beaten
1 c. sugar
¼ c. margarine
1 c. milk
2 Tbsp. flour
1 tsp. vanilla
1 tsp. butter flavoring

1 tsp. maple flavoring
¼ c. dark corn syrup
¼ c. oatmeal (quick or regular, uncooked)
½ c. chopped pecans
½ c. coconut, flaked

Preheat oven to 350°. Roll out pie crust, using your favorite crust or a prepared one and place in a 10 inch or deep dish pie shell. Combine eggs, sugar, margarine, milk, flour, flavorings, and dark corn syrup; beat well, then add oats, pecans, and coconut. Blend into mixture. Pour into unbaked pie shell and bake on the lowest rack in the oven for 45 minutes. Test center of pie with sharp knife. If clean, pie is ready. If not, bake for 5 or 10 minutes longer. Pie resembles a custard on the bottom with the coconut, oats, and pecans forming a crusty topping.

Janie Fox, Saginaw Lions Club
Saginaw, Texas, USA

❧

The man who removes a mountain begins by carrying away small stones.

ZUCCHINI CHERRY PIE

Cut 1 large zucchini in half lengthwise. With a melon baller, scoop out flesh to make about 4 cups "cherries." Avoid seeds.

1 pkg. cherry flavored Kool-Aid
  (unsweetened)
1½ c. water
1½ c. sugar
2 Tbsp. lemon juice

3 Tbsp. cornstarch
¼ c. water
A "tad" of almond extract and red
  food coloring (optional,
  though I think a good touch)

In a saucepan, combine zucchini "cherries," Kool-Aid, sugar, and lemon juice. Bring to a boil and then simmer just till slightly tender (should be still firm). Make a paste of the cornstarch and ¼ cup water. Add to saucepan to thicken cherries.

Let stand in refrigerator overnight to enable the "cherries" to absorb the flavor and color of the Kool-Aid. Spoon into 9 inch unbaked crust. Add top crust; prick vent holes. Bake at 375° for 30 to 35 minutes or till browned.

Rev. Fred Gilbert, Dannemora Lions Club
Dannemora, New York, USA

A bird does not sing because he has an answer.
He sings because he has a song.

This would be a wonderful world
if people showed as much patience in all things
as they do in waiting for fish to bite.

There are no secrets to success.
It is the result of preparation, hard work, learning from failure.

518

"APPLE PIE OH MY"

Crust:

1½ c. flour
¾ tsp. salt

½ c. butter flavored Crisco
3 Tbsp. water

Filling:

¾ c. sugar
2 Tbsp. flour
1 tsp. cinnamon

¼ tsp. nutmeg
1 tsp. vanilla
6 to 7 c. sliced peeled apples

Topping:

½ c. butter or margarine
¾ c. brown sugar

1½ c. flour

Crust: Place first 3 ingredients in food processor till blended. Add water. Process just till ball is formed. Roll out dough between sheets of plastic wrap to fit 10 inch pie pan. Peel off top sheet of wrap and fit into pan. Flute edge.

Filling: Mix first 5 ingredients. Pour over apples into large bowl. Let sit while making topping.

Topping: Process in food processor till crumbly.

To complete pie: Place apples in crust and sprinkle topping ingredients over pie to completely cover. Bake in 400°F. oven for 45 to 50 minutes.

Regarding plastic wrap for pie crust - I use 2 sheets side by side or use extra wide. This pie is a family favorite for sure!

Clark Leedy (Joanne), Reno Plumb Lane Lions Club
Reno, Nevada, USA

PERFECT APPLE PIE

Double crust pie crust
6 thinly sliced and peeled apples
¾ c. sugar
2 Tbsp. flour

¾ tsp. cinnamon
¼ tsp. salt
⅓ tsp. nutmeg
1 Tbsp. lemon juice

Heat oven to 450°. Put bottom crust in 9 inch pie plate. Put all ingredients in large bowl. Toss lightly. Spoon into crust. Add top crust and flute edges. Cut several slits in top. Bake for 10 minutes. Lower to 350° for 30 minutes more.

Neut Curtis, Westbrook Lions Club
Westbrook, Maine, USA

❧

Reach out for everything you want to achieve.

MOM'S APPLE PIE

5 large Golden Delicious apples
1 c. sugar
1 heaping Tbsp. flour

Margarine
Crust for top and bottom

Mix cut up apples with sugar and flour. Let stand for approximately 5 to 10 minutes. Prepare crust. Pour apples into crust (pile up) and top with pats of butter. Put on top crust, piercing so steam can escape. Bake at 350° until crust is brown. While hot, brush with small amount of butter and sprinkle with small amount of sugar.

My mom is famous for her cooking and this pie is the best!

Mrs. Lion George (Dianne) Murphy, Canton Lions Club
Canton, Georgia, USA

CRAZY CRUST APPLE PIE

1 c. flour
1 tsp. baking powder
½ tsp. salt
1 Tbsp. sugar
1 egg
⅔ c. shortening

¾ c. water
1 large can apple pie filling
1 Tbsp. lemon juice
½ tsp. apple pie spice or
    cinnamon

Preheat oven to 425°. In small mixer bowl, combine flour, baking powder, salt, sugar, egg, shortening, and water. Blend well. Beat 2 minutes at medium speed. Pour batter into 9 x 1¼ inch pie pan. Combine pie filling, lemon juice, and spice. Pour into center of batter. Do not stir. Bake for 45 to 50 minutes.

Variation for fresh pie filling: Combine 2¼ cups peeled apples, 1 tablespoon lemon juice with ⅓ cup sugar, 2 tablespoons flour, and ½ teaspoon apple pie spice or cinnamon. Pour into center of batter. Don't stir. Sprinkle filling with 1 to 2 tablespoons brown sugar. Bake at 400° for 35 to 40 minutes. Serves 6.

SUGAR FREE APPLE PIE

12 oz. can frozen apple juice
    (concentrate)
3 Tbsp. cornstarch

1 tsp. cinnamon
4 to 5 apples, pared and sliced
Crust for double crust pie

Peel apples and slice into bottom crust. Cook apple juice, cornstarch, and cinnamon until thickened. Pour over apples. Add top crust and bake at 325° for 40 minutes. This is delicious.

You can live without music; you can live without books; but show me the one who can live without cooks.

Leola C. Jurrens, Downtown Bartlesville Lions Club
Bartlesville, Oklahoma, USA

BLUEBERRY CRUMB PIE

1 unbaked 10 inch pie shell	⅓ c. brown sugar
1 Tbsp. flour	2 Tbsp. flour
1 Tbsp. sugar	1 tsp. cinnamon
7 c. blueberries	

Topping:

½ c. flour	Pinch of salt
⅓ c. brown sugar	1 stick butter, softened
⅓ c. granulated sugar	1 c. chopped pecans
1 Tbsp. cinnamon	

Sprinkle flour mixed with sugar over unbaked crust. Mix remaining ingredients and spoon into crust. Combine flour, sugar, cinnamon, salt, and pecans for topping. Blend in butter and crumble over filling. Bake 15 minutes at 400°. Reduce heat to 325° and bake an additional 30 minutes, or until top is brown.

Mrs. Jeff Crosby, Exeter Township Lions Club
Exeter, Pennsylvania, USA

CRANBERRY PIE

Cranberries	½ tsp. almond extract
1½ c. sugar	¾ c. margarine
½ c. walnuts	1 c. flour

Grease pie pan. Line bottom of pan with cranberries. Sprinkle ½ cup sugar and walnuts over berries. Mix remaining sugar with 1 cup flour, ¾ cup margarine, and almond extract. Pour over berries and bake at 350° for 20 minutes.

You must admit that grumblers are hard workers -
they never take a day off.

LEMON MERINGUE PIE

1 c. sugar
1¼ c. water
1 Tbsp. butter
¼ c. cornstarch
3 Tbsp. cold water

7 Tbsp. lemon juice
2 tsp. lemon peel
3 egg yolks
2 Tbsp. milk
1 (8 inch) baked pie shell

Meringue:

3 egg whites
6 Tbsp. sugar

1 tsp. lemon juice

Combine sugar, water, and butter; heat until sugar dissolves. Add cornstarch blended with cold water. Cook slowly until clear, about 8 minutes. Add lemon juice and peel; cook 2 minutes. Slowly add egg yolks beaten with milk. Bring to boiling. Cool and pour into cool baked shell.

Meringue: Beat egg white stiff but not dry; add sugar gradually. Add lemon juice at the last. Spread over cooled filling, sealing to edges of pastry. Brown in oven at 350° for 13 to 15 minutes.

Tom O'Dell Hodgenville Lions Club
Hodgenville, Kentucky, USA

LEMON SPONGE PIE

1 c. sugar
Butter the size of an egg
Grated lemon rind and juice of 1
   lemon

3 Tbsp. flour
1 c. milk
3 egg yolks
3 egg whites, beaten stiff

Cream first 4 ingredients together, then add flour, milk, and egg yolks. Stir thoroughly. Fold in stiffly beaten egg whites. Pour into a 9 inch pie shell and bake at 350° until done and golden brown. This pie will have a creamlike filling on bottom with a spongelike cake on top.

Delicious - old family recipe.

Zeta L. Adams, Craigsville Lions Club
Craigsville, West Virginia, USA

Getting people to like you is only the other side of liking them.

LEMON VELVET PIE

1⅓ c. sugar
6 Tbsp. cornstarch
¼ tsp. salt
1½ c. boiling water
3 eggs, separated
2 Tbsp. butter or margarine
1 Tbsp. grated lemon peel
⅓ c. strained fresh lemon juice

1 tsp. vanilla
1 env. unflavored gelatin
¼ c. cold water
1 c. light cream
1 baked 10 inch pie shell
1 c. heavy cream, whipped
6 to 8 walnut halves (optional)

In saucepan, thoroughly mix together sugar, cornstarch, and salt; add boiling water, stirring constantly. Bring to boil over medium heat. Continue stirring; boil for 3 to 4 minutes. Beat egg yolks slightly; add some of hot mixture to yolks and blend well. Return mixture to saucepan. Add butter and cook for 2 minutes longer, stirring constantly. Do not boil.

Remove from heat; stir in lemon peel, juice, and vanilla. Remove a generous ½ cup of filling; reserve for topping. Soften gelatin in water; add to hot mixture, stirring until thoroughly dissolved. Blend in light cream. Chill until slightly thickened, but not set.

Beat egg whites until stiff, but not dry. Carefully fold into chilled mixture. Pour into baked pie shell; chill until partially set. Spread reserved filling completely over top of pie; chill until firm. Top with whipped cream. Garnish with walnut halves if desired.

LEMON SOUR CREAM PIE

1 c. sugar
4 Tbsp. cornstarch
Dash of salt
1 c. milk
¼ c. margarine

1 (9 inch) pie shell, baked
1 tsp. lemon peel
¼ c. lemon juice
1 c. sour cream
3 eggs, separated

Meringue:

½ c. sugar
2 Tbsp. sugar

¼ tsp. cream of tartar

Combine 1 cup sugar, cornstarch, and salt. Slowly stir in milk. Cook and stir until boiling and thickened. Beat small amount of hot mixture in well beaten egg yolks. Return to heat all the mixture. Stir 2 minutes. Add butter, lemon juice, and lemon peel. Cover and cool. Fold in sour cream. Pour into baked pie shell.

For meringue: Beat egg whites with cream of tartar. Slowly add ½ cup sugar plus 2 tablespoons. Beat until stiff peaks form. Spread on pie. Bake in 325° oven until brown.

Billy W. Higginbotham, McMinnville Lions Club
McMinnville, Tennessee, USA

LEMON BERRY PIE

4 oz. Philadelphia Brand cream
  cheese, softened
1 (6 oz.) Keebler Ready-Crust
  graham cracker pie crust
1 Tbsp. milk
1 Tbsp. sugar
2 tsp. grated lemon peel
1 Tbsp. lemon juice
1 (8 oz.) tub thawed Cool Whip
  whipped topping

1 pt. strawberries, hulled and
  halved
2 c. cold milk
2 (4 serving size) pkg. Jell-O
  Brand vanilla or lemon
  flavor instant pudding and pie
  filling

Helpful hint: Soften cream cheese in microwave on HIGH for 15 to 20 seconds.

Beat cream cheese, 1 tablespoon milk, and sugar in medium bowl with wire whisk until smooth. Stir in lemon peel and juice. Stir in 1½ cups of the whipped topping. Spread evenly in bottom of crust. Press strawberry halves into cream cheese layer, reserving several for garnish if desired.

Pour 2 cups milk into large bowl. Add pudding mixes. Beat with wire whisk 1 minute. Let stand 1 minute or until thickened. Gently stir in 1 cup of the whipped topping. Spoon over strawberries in crust. Refrigerate 4 hours or until set. Garnish with remaining whipped topping and reserved strawberry halves. Store leftover pie in refrigerator. Makes 8 servings.

To prepare with sugar free Jell-O Brand pudding: Prepare as directed above, using sugar free Jell-O Brand vanilla flavor instant pudding and pie filling and Cool Whip lite whipped topping. Substitute light Philadelphia Brand Neufchatel cheese for the cream cheese.

John J. Hess, Clarence Center Lions Club
Clarence Center, New York, USA

LEMON MILLIONAIRE

1 (16 oz.) can lemon pie filling
1 can sweetened condensed milk
1 (12 oz.) container Cool Whip

1 can mandarin oranges
15 oz. can crushed pineapple

Mix lemon pie filling and sweetened condensed milk. Drain mandarin oranges and crushed pineapple. Fold oranges, pineapple, and Cool Whip into pie filling mixture. Any flavor of pie filling may be substituted. Makes 12 servings.

Begin where you are, but don't stay there.

PRINCESS LEMON PIE

7 Tbsp. corn starch
1½ c. sugar
½ tsp. salt
3 eggs, separated
¼ c. lemon juice

2 Tbsp. butter
1 Tbsp. grated lemon rind
6 Tbsp. sugar
1 (9 inch) pie shell

Combine the corn starch, sugar, and salt. Add 2 cups boiling water. Cook until thick and transparent, stirring constantly. Add 3 egg yolks, slightly beaten into which a little of the hot mixture has been added. Cook 2 minutes longer. Blend in lemon juice, butter, and rind. Cool. Pour into pie shell. Top with meringue made with 3 egg whites and 6 tablespoons sugar. Bake 15 minutes at 350°.

Evelyn Steele, Lyman Lions Club
Lyman, Wyoming, USA

NANTUCKET CRANBERRY PIE

Filling:

2 c. raw cranberries
½ c. sugar

½ c. chopped nuts

Batter:

2 eggs, beaten
1 tsp. melted butter
¾ c. melted mayonnaise

1 c. flour
1 c. sugar

Grease a 10 inch pie plate. Place cranberries on bottom; sprinkle sugar and nuts over the cranberries. For batter, mix sugar and butter. Add the rest of the batter ingredients. Pour batter over cranberries and bake at 325° for 35 to 40 minutes. Serves 6 to 8.

FREEZE-AHEAD PEACH PIE FILLING

3½ c. sugar
¾ c. quick-cooking tapioca
¾ tsp. salt

¼ tsp. lemon juice
4 qt. peeled, sliced fresh peaches

In a large mixing bowl, combine all ingredients. Let stand for 15 minutes. Line four 9 inch pie pans with foil. Add fruit mixture and level; place in freezer until frozen solid. When frozen, close foil, sealing well to prevent freezer burn. Remove from pans and stack in freezer until ready to use. To bake, remove frozen peaches from the foil and place in unbaked pie shell. Cover with top crust and seal. Brush with melted butter and cover crust edges with foil. Bake at 400° for 50 minutes or until bubbly and golden brown.

PDG Lloyd E. Wright, Georgetown Lions Club
Georgetown, Ohio, USA

PINEAPPLE PIE

2 c. sugar
3 eggs
3 Tbsp. flour

¾ stick margarine, melted
1 small can crushed pineapple
1 unbaked 9 inch pie shell

Mix sugar, eggs, flour, margarine, and pineapple together in the order given. Pour into the pie shell. Bake at 350° for 1 hour. Serves 8.

PINEAPPLE CHIFFON PIE

1 pkg. lemon Jell-O
2 eggs
1 large can evaporated milk

1⅔ c. pineapple juice
1 c. sugar

Beat eggs and sugar together. Add juice and boil 3 minutes. Add Jell-O. When cool, fold in 1 large can evaporated milk, whipped stiff. Pour in pie shell and place in refrigerator until set.

Edna K. Bunch, Snow Hill Lions Club
Snow Hill, North Carolina, USA

PINEAPPLE CAKE PIE

1 c. sugar
3 Tbsp. flour
½ tsp. salt
3 eggs, separated

3 tsp. lemon juice
1 tsp. grated lemon rind
½ c. crushed pineapple
1 c. warm milk

Mix sugar, flour, and salt. Beat egg whites until stiff and set aside. Add egg yolks, beaten, into dry ingredients. Mix well. Add lemon juice, grated lemon rind, and pineapple to mixture. Stir in milk and then fold in stiffly beaten egg whites. Pour into uncooked pie crust.

Bake at 400° for 10 minutes, then reduce heat to 350° and bake 45 minutes or until set.

PRUNE PIE

1 c. cooked, pitted, minced prunes
1 c. water
1 lemon
1 Tbsp. flour

½ c. sugar
1 tsp. cinnamon
1 tsp. nutmeg
1 (8 inch) baked pie crust

In mixing bowl, add prunes, water, lemon juice and grated rind, flour, sugar, cinnamon, and nutmeg. Mix well. Put ingredients in pan and cook until thickened. Pour into baked pie shell. Put in refrigerator until set. Serves 8.

PUMPKIN FLUFF PIE
(Diabetics may use)

1 (16 oz.) can pumpkin
1 (12 oz.) evaporated skim milk
2 egg yolks, beaten
½ tsp. ground cinnamon
¼ tsp. ground ginger
⅛ tsp. ground nutmeg
8 packets Equal

1 env. unflavored gelatin
¼ c. cold water
3 egg whites
1 tsp. vanilla
¼ tsp. cream of tartar
1 baked 8 inch pie shell

Beat well in large saucepan the pumpkin, milk, and egg yolks. Stir in spices. Thoroughly heat over medium heat, stirring occasionally. Remove from heat and stir in Equal. Combine gelatin and cold water. Let stand for 1 minute. Cook over low heat for 5 minutes or until gelatin completely dissolves. Stir into pumpkin mix. Cool.

Combine egg whites and cream of tartar at room temperature in medium bowl; beat until soft peaks form. Add vanilla. Beat till stiff peaks form. Fold into pumpkin mix. Spoon into baked pie shell. Chill.

One-eighth pie equals 163 calories, 18 g carbohydrate, 8 g protein, and 7 g fat.

PUMPKIN CHESS PIE

1 c. pumpkin
3 eggs, beaten
1½ c. sugar

1 stick margarine
1 tsp. vanilla extract
1 pie crust (unbaked)

Mix pie ingredients. Pour into pie crust. Bake at 350° about 1 hour or until knife comes out clean. Makes 1 large pie.

Violet M. Heslep, Huffman Lioness Club
Huffman, Texas, USA

❦

Remember back when the only thing rarer
than getting a long-distance phone call was making one?

PARADISE PUMPKIN PIE

1 (9 inch) unbaked pie crust
8 oz. cream cheese, softened
¼ c. sugar
1 tsp. vanilla
2 c. pumpkin
1 (14 oz.) can sweetened
    condensed milk (not
    evaporated milk)

2 eggs
1 tsp. ground cinnamon
½ tsp. ground ginger
½ tsp. nutmeg
½ tsp. salt

In small bowl, combine cream cheese, sugar, and vanilla. Spread evenly on unbaked pie crust. Combine all remaining ingredients in large bowl. Mix well and turn into pie crust on top of cream cheese mixture. Bake 15 minutes at 425°. Reduce oven temperature to 350°. Bake 35 to 40 minutes longer or until knife inserted 1 inch from edge comes out clean. Cool before cutting. Garnish as desired. Refrigerate leftovers.

PUMPKIN PIE CRUNCH

1 yellow cake mix
1 (12 oz.) evaporated milk
1½ c. sugar
½ tsp. salt
1 c. margarine, melted

1 (16 oz.) pumpkin
3 eggs
4 tsp. pumpkin pie spice
1 c. chopped nuts

Grease 13x9x2 inch pan. Combine everything *but* cake mix, nuts, and margarine. Pour into baking dish. Sprinkle cake mix on top. Add nuts and drizzle with melted margarine. Bake at 350° for 50 to 55 minutes or until golden brown. Serve with whipped topping. Serves 16 to 20.

My own version: Omit the evaporated milk and salt. Use only 1 cup sugar. I make by own pumpkin pie spice (1 teaspoon cinnamon, 1 teaspoon nutmeg, and dash of ginger).

Rev. Fred Gilbert, Dannemora Lions Club
Dannemora, New York, USA

GIVE THANKS FOR PIE

6 Tbsp. brown sugar
½ tsp. salt
1 tsp. cinnamon
½ tsp. ginger
½ tsp. cloves

3 eggs
1½ c. milk
½ c. Blue Label dark Karo syrup
1½ c. mashed pumpkin
8 inch unbaked pastry shell

Preheat oven to 450°. In medium bowl, mix brown sugar, salt, spices, then eggs. Beat to mix. At low speed, stir in milk, syrup, and mashed pumpkin. Pour into unbaked pastry shell. Bake at 450° for 15 minutes. Reduce heat to 350° and bake 25 to 30 minutes longer. Makes 8 servings. Serve with whipped cream.

RHUBARB PIE

1 egg, well beaten
¾ c. sugar
1 c. finely sliced rhubarb
½ c. soda cracker crumbs

Dash of salt
¼ c. crushed pineapple
2 Tbsp. melted butter
Pastry for 9 inch double crust pie

Combine sugar and egg. Add rhubarb, crumbs, few grains salt, pineapple, and butter. Mix thoroughly. Pour into pastry lined pie pan. Cover with top crust. Bake in 425°F. oven for about 45 minutes.

Lee Seybold, Moweaqua Lions Club
Moweaqua, Illinois, USA

RHUBARB PAN-PAN

4 c. chopped rhubarb
1 c. sugar
1 (3 oz.) box red Jell-O

1 (9 oz.) box Jiffy yellow cake mix
1 c. water
⅓ c. melted butter

Layer in ungreased 9x13 inch pan as follows: First rhubarb, then sugar, Jell-O, cake mix, water, and butter. No need to stir. Bake at 350° for 45 to 50 minutes. Top with Cool Whip if desired. Serves 8.

RHUBARB CUSTARD PIE

1 c. rhubarb chunks
1 c. sugar
3 Tbsp. flour
3 Tbsp. margarine

2 egg yolks, beaten
1 c. milk
2 egg whites, beaten stiff

Put rhubarb in 9 inch unbaked pie shell. Combine other ingredients, except egg whites. Mix well. Fold in beaten egg whites and pour over rhubarb. Bake at 400° for 15 minutes, then at 350° for 30 minutes.

Etta Holsinger, Baroness Stiegel Lions Club
Lititz, Pennsylvania, USA

STRAWBERRY PIE

1 pt. strawberries, capped and
sweetened
1 (9 oz.) Cool Whip

1 can Eagle Brand milk
⅛ c. lemon juice
½ c. chopped nuts

Mix and fold ingredients together. Put in 2 pie shells of either vanilla wafers or graham cracker crust. Chill. Very good and easy.

Glenn E. Bunch, Jr., Snow Hill Lions Club
Snow Hill, North Carolina, USA

STRAWBERRY PIE

1 recipe pie crust
1 qt. strawberries
1 Tbsp. tapioca

1 c. sugar
Butter

Wash and hull strawberries, but leave the berries whole. Use any pie crust recipe. Roll out dough and line bottom of pie plate. Mix strawberries with cup of sugar and tablespoon tapioca. Pour into crust and dot with butter. Cover with a top crust and bake for 15 to 20 minutes at 425°, then lower temperature to 375° and continue baking about 20 to 25 minutes longer.

Dave Bernier, Westbrook Lions Club
Westbrook, Maine, USA

SUGAR-FREE STRAWBERRY PIE

1 (9 inch) baked pie shell
1 qt. strawberries, hulled and cut
   in halves, or 2 large bags
   frozen unsweetened
   strawberries, thawed
1 c. water
2 Tbsp. corn starch

10 or 12 tsp. or packets fructose
   sweetener
Dash of salt
1 to 2 tsp. red food coloring
1 tsp. almond extract or
   strawberry flavoring
Lite Cool Whip (if desired)

Measure water, fructose, corn starch, salt, and food coloring into a saucepan. Cook over medium heat until thickened and becomes translucent (clear red). Remove from heat. Add flavoring and cool 10 minutes, unless you want the strawberries to be somewhat softened, then add strawberries as soon as you remove. Get glaze from heat. Pour into shell. Cool in refrigerator. Cover top with lite Cool Whip before serving if desired.

Frances B. Blount, Saginaw Lions Club
Saginaw, Texas, Tarrant County, USA

❦

Walking is a popular form of exercise that loses some appeal
when it is done behind a lawn mower.

STRAWBERRY HEAVEN PIE

6 egg whites (room temperature)   2 tsp. vanilla
⅛ tsp. salt   2 tsp. lemon juice
2 c. sugar

Beat egg whites and salt until stiff, but not dry. Gradually add 1 cup sugar, beating well after each addition. Add vanilla and second cup of sugar, alternating with lemon juice. Beat until all sugar is dissolved and the meringue is stiff, approximately 15 minutes. Put the meringue into a well greased and floured 10 inch pie plate. Pile the meringue so it is higher in the middle. Bake 1 hour and 30 minutes in 275° oven. Increase heat to 300° and bake 30 minutes longer. The meringue will puff up while it bakes, then cracks and falls in the middle as it cools. Cool and fill with sliced fresh strawberries and whipped cream that has been sweetened slightly. When filling, start with cream, then berries. Top layer will be whipped cream. Decorate with whole berries and chill before serving.

Husband past president 2 times in last several years.

My family's favorite. I won $150.00 and first prize from state of Kentucky. Beautiful pie.

Mitchell Johnston, Midway Lions Club
Midway, Kentucky, Woodford, USA

STRAWBERRY GLAZE PIE

1 baked and cooled pie crust   1 c. water
1 qt. fresh strawberries, washed   Few drops of red food color
   and hulled   1 c. whipping cream, whipped and
1 c. sugar   sweetened
3 Tbsp. corn starch

Cut up 1 cup of the strawberries. Mix sugar and corn starch in a 2 quart saucepan. Stir in water gradually until smooth. Add cut up berries. Cook and stir over medium heat until thick and clear. Stir in food coloring. Cool. Stir in remaining berries, saving ¼ cup for top of pie. Pour into pie crust. Chill until firm, about 3 hours. Top with whipped cream and reserved berries.

Edna K. Bunch, Snow Hill Lions Club
Snow Hill, North Carolina, USA

FRESH STRAWBERRY PIE

1 c. sugar   1 c. hot water
3 Tbsp. cornstarch   1 pt. strawberries (fresh)
1 (3 oz.) strawberry jello

Mix sugar, cornstarch, jello, and hot water. Stir over medium heat until well blended. Let cool. Wash and dry strawberries; cut in halves. Place berries in cooled baked pie crust; pour mixture over. Chill until set. Serve with whipped topping.

Ms. Nancy Dutterer, Silver Run-Union Mills Lions Club
Thurmont, Maryland, USA

FRESH STRAWBERRY PIE

4 c. fresh sliced strawberries
1½ c. water
¾ c. sugar

2 Tbsp. corn starch
1 (3 oz.) pkg. jello (strawberry)
1 (8 inch) pie crust, baked

Combine water, sugar, corn starch, and jello in saucepan; cook over medium heat, stirring constantly until mixture boils. Boil over low heat for 2 minutes until clear and thickened. Pour mixture while still hot over strawberries layered in pie crust. Chill until set, about 2 hours. Top with whipped cream. Keep in the refrigerator until served - not suitable for outdoor picnics in hot weather.

Cynthia Dowd, Chesterfield Bay Lions Club
Chesterfield Bay, Michigan, USA

DONNA'S OIL PIE CRUST

2¼ c. flour
1 tsp. salt

⅔ c. oil
4 Tbsp. water

In a medium bowl, measure flour. Remove ⅓ cup flour to a small bowl; set aside. To the remaining flour, mix in salt. Add ⅔ cup oil. Mix. To ⅓ cup flour, mix in the water and stir to make a paste. Add paste to flour and oil mixture. Stir. Roll between wax paper. Makes double crust for 9 inch pie.

Keep "smilin'," it makes people wonder what you're up to!
Donna Hoeft, Manistique Lakes Area Lioness Club
Curtis, Michigan, USA

MOM'S PIE CRUST

5 c. flour
2 tsp. salt
3 tsp. sugar
2 tsp. baking powder
2 c. shortening

1 egg yolk
3 tsp. vinegar
1 egg white (for top crust)
Ice water (enough to fill c.)

Combine flour, salt, sugar, and baking powder. Cut shortening into dry ingredients. Put egg yolk in a cup and beat it with a fork. Add vinegar to blended egg yolk. Fill cup with ice water. Sprinkle a small amount of liquid over the flour and shortening mixture; blend it together with a fork to make a soft dough. Continue adding water as needed. The dough will be easier to roll out if the dough rests for an hour. Roll out. Will make 2 or 3 two crust pies.

Blend egg white with 1 teaspoon water and brush it on the top crust. Sprinkle a little sugar on top. Bake at 425° until bubbly and lightly browned. *Yum-yum-good!*

It is good to let a little sunshine out as well as in.

NEVER-FAIL-PIE-CRUST-OR-TURNOVERS

5 c. flour
1 c. oleo
1 c. shortening

1 tsp. salt
2 egg yolks
1 c. milk

Mix first 4 ingredients, then put 2 egg yolks in 1 cup measuring cup. Fill to top with milk. Mix with other ingredients. Dough will be a little moist. Can be rolled out and rerolled - will not get tough.

PIE CRUST

2 c. flour
1 c. shortening
Pinch of salt

7 Tbsp. water
1 Tbsp. vinegar
⅓ c. flour

Mix first 3 ingredients. Shake water, vinegar, and ⅓ cup flour in a shaker, then pour over flour mixture. Sometimes you may need to add a little more water. It all depends upon the shortening. (Mix first 3 ingredients with a pastry blender.) This pie dough will never be tough and will be real flaky.

Lee Seybold, Moweaqua Lions Club
Moweaqua, Illinois, USA

APPLE DANISH

2½ c. flour
¾ tsp. salt
1 c. margarine
2 Tbsp. cornstarch

Apples, sliced
Sugar to taste
Cinnamon to taste
Nutmeg to taste

Blend the flour, salt, and margarine. In a measuring cup, put 1 egg yolk and enough milk to make ¾ of a cup. Add to flour mixture. Divide dough in half and roll out. Sprinkle it with 2 tablespoons cornstarch, then add sliced apples and sprinkle with sugar, cinnamon, and nutmeg. Add remaining dough on top. Bake at 375° for 35 minutes. Use a cookie sheet. Dribble with icing while still warm. Delicious!

Shirley Hagyard, Russell Lions Club
Russell, Manitoba, Canada

❧

We all admire the wisdom of people who come to us for advice.

BLUEBERRY PINWHEEL COBBLER

2 c. sugar
2 c. water
1 tsp. vanilla
1 tsp. lemon juice
2 c. blueberries (or peaches, other
   berries or fruit in season,
   chopped in small pieces)

1 stick margarine
½ c. shortening (Crisco type)
1½ c. self-rising flour
⅓ c. milk

1. Put sugar, water, vanilla, and lemon juice in pan; heat till sugar melts.
2. Dough: Cut shortening into flour as for any pie crust. Knead 4 to 5 times lightly. Roll out to 12x9 inch rectangle.
3. Put 1 stick margarine in baking pan and put in oven to melt.
4. On rolled out dough, spread blueberries (or other fruit). Roll up jelly roll fashion, starting with long side. Slice 12 (1 inch) slices. Place on melted margarine.
5. Carefully pour sugar water over and around slices. Bake at 350° approximately 45 minutes. Nice topped with whipped topping or vanilla ice cream.

Anne Murdock (Mrs. LeRoy), Silver Run-Union Mills Lions Club
Westminster, Maryland, USA

BUTTER TARTS

2½ c. Crisco (*cold*)
2 tsp. salt
6 c. flour
1 c. light brown sugar
1 c. corn syrup
2 Tbsp. oleo

2 tsp. vanilla
1 c. water (cold)
⅛ tsp. salt
3 large eggs
Raisins

Using a large bowl, mix flour and 2 teaspoons salt. Add Crisco and cut in until mixture crumbles. Add cold water until mixture makes a soft ball. Roll into a ball. Place in plastic or bag and chill for an hour. In saucepan, combine sugar, syrup, oleo, vanilla, and ⅛ teaspoon salt. Heat until all ingredients are dissolved and melted (do not allow to boil). Remove from heat and add well beaten eggs. Stir until smooth. Remove dough and make about 20 to 24 balls. Put into muffin tins and form up sides. Fill with mixture, but not up to top. Bake at 350° for 20 to 25 minutes, until brown. Remove and cool on rack.

A Canadian Christmas special treat.

Walter E. Loomis, North Jackson Lions Club
Jackson, Michigan, USA

Yesterday is the tomorrow that got away.

CHEESE ROLL

2 c. flour
½ c. shortening or oleo
1 pkg. dry yeast
½ c. warm milk

3 Tbsp. sugar
2 small eggs
1 tsp. salt

Mix yeast into warm milk. Mix all ingredients together and beat with a wooden spoon till dough is smooth. Chill for 3 to 4 hours or overnight.

Filling:

¾ c. sugar
1 tsp. vanilla

2 small eggs
2 (8 oz.) cream cheese

Put all into mixer bowl and beat till light and creamy. Divide dough in half. Roll each into rectangle and spread filling over dough. Roll and fold edge in. Makes 2 rolls. Place on greased cookie sheet. Bake at 400° for 15 to 20 minutes.

Ann Cude, Huffman Lions Club
Huffman, Texas, USA

CHERRY BERRIES ON A CLOUD

Meringue:

6 egg whites
½ tsp. cream of tartar

¼ tsp. salt
1¾ c. sugar

Beat egg whites until frothy. Add cream of tartar and salt; continue to beat until soft peaks form. Gradually add sugar, 2 tablespoons at a time, beating constantly until stiff and glossy. Draw a circle 10 inches in diameter on a piece of brown paper. Pile meringue lightly in circle, spreading it to fill completely. Place paper backed meringue on cookie sheet and bake at 275° for 1 hour. Turn off oven heat and allow meringue to cool completely, about 8 hours in oven.

Filling:

6 oz. cream cheese, softened
1 c. sugar
1 tsp. vanilla

2 c. whipping cream, whipped
2 c. miniature marshmallows

Topping:

1 can cherry pie filling
½ tsp. lemon juice
2 c. fresh strawberries, sliced and
    sweetened, or 16 oz. frozen
    strawberries

Filling: Mix cream cheese, sugar, and vanilla. Fold in marshmallows, then whipped cream. Pull meringue off of paper and place on torte plate. Pile filling on lightly. Refrigerate for 12 hours.

Note: Meringue may be baked in a buttered 9x13 inch pan if desired.

EGG PASTRY

3 c. flour
1 c. shortening
1 tsp. vinegar

1½ tsp. salt
1 egg, beaten
½ c. ice water

Sift together flour and salt; cut in shortening. Beat egg and add to water and vinegar. Add to dry ingredients just enough liquid to hold flour together. Bake pastry when rolled out and placed in pan at 375° approximately 30 to 45 minutes or until done. Makes 5 pastries and will keep in refrigerator about 1 to 2 weeks.

For pecan pie, pour in unbaked pie shell. Egg Pastry is very easy to handle.
Mrs. Charlotte M. Garner, Pascagoula Evening Lions Club
Pascagoula, Mississippi, USA

"GRANDMA CROSBY'S MOLASSES DOUGHNUTS"

2 eggs
½ c. sugar
¼ tsp. salt
¼ tsp. nutmeg
1 tsp. cinnamon
1 tsp. ginger

2 Tbsp. melted butter
1 c. molasses
1 tsp. baking soda
1 tsp. baking powder
1 c. buttermilk
5 c. sifted flour

Beat the eggs and sugar until light and fluffy. Add buttermilk, melted butter, and molasses; mix well. In a separate bowl, mix salt, nutmeg, cinnamon, ginger, soda, powder, and flour. Gradually add this mixture to other. Roll on a floured board and cut with a doughnut cutter or use a glass and thimble. Fry in hot fat about 350°. Turn and when lightly fried on both sides, remove from fat and drain on a paper towel.

Mrs. Jeff Crosby, Exeter Township Lions Club
Exeter, Pennsylvania, USA

Chickens and people are alike in that the more you give them,
the less likely it is that they'll scratch for themselves.

Cookies,
Bars,
Candies

TEMPERATURE TESTS
FOR CANDY MAKING

There are two different methods of determining when candy has been cooked to the proper consistency. One is by using a candy thermometer in order to record degrees, the other is by using the cold water test. The chart below will prove useful in helping to follow candy recipes:

TYPE OF CANDY	DEGREES	COLD WATER
Fondant, Fudge	234 - 238°	Soft Ball
Divinity, Caramels	245 - 248°	Firm Ball
Taffy	265 - 270°	Hard Ball
Butterscotch	275 - 280°	Light Crack
Peanut Brittle	285 - 290°	Hard Crack
Caramelized Sugar	310 - 321°	Caramelized

In using the cold water test, use a fresh cupful of cold water for each test. When testing, remove the candy from the fire and pour about ½ teaspoon of candy into the cold water. Pick the candy up in the fingers and roll into a ball if possible.

In the SOFT BALL TEST the candy will roll into a soft ball which quickly loses its shape when removed from the water.

In the FIRM BALL TEST the candy will roll into a firm, but not hard ball. It will flatten out a few minutes after being removed from the water.

In the HARD BALL TEST the candy will roll into a hard ball which has lost almost all plasticity and will roll around on a plate on removal from the water.

In the LIGHT CRACK TEST the candy will form brittle threads which will soften on removal from the water.

In the HARD CRACK TEST the candy will form brittle threads in the water which will remain brittle after being removed from the water.

In CARAMELIZING the sugar first melts then becomes a golden brown. It will form a hard brittle ball in cold water.

COOKIES, BARS, CANDIES
COOKIES

CHEWY CHOCOLATE COOKIES

2 c. sugar
½ c. Blue Bonnet spread (or any oil)
4 (1 oz.) sq. unsweetened chocolate, melted
4 eggs

2 tsp. vanilla extract
2 c. all-purpose flour
2 tsp. baking powder
¾ tsp. salt
¾ c. confectioners sugar

In large bowl, blend sugar, spread, and chocolate. Add eggs, one at a time, until well blended. Mix in vanilla. Combine flour, baking powder, and salt. Add gradually to chocolate mixture, mixing well after each addition. Cover and chill 2 hours or overnight.

Drop mixture by rounded teaspoon into confectioners sugar, coating lightly. Shape into balls. Place on greased baking sheets, 2 inches apart. Flatten slightly. Bake at 350°F. for 12 to 14 minutes or until done. Remove from baking sheets onto wire racks to cool.

Jessie Novack, Offerle Lions Club
Offerle, Kansas, USA

GINGER SNAPS

¾ c. oleomargarine
1 c. sugar
1 egg
¼ c. molasses
2 c. flour

2 tsp. baking soda
½ tsp. salt
1 tsp. cinnamon
1 Tbsp. ginger

Beat oleomargarine and sugar together well. Add egg, molasses, and all dry ingredients. Refrigerate dough at least 1 hour. Remove from the refrigerator and roll in 1 inch balls, then roll the balls in sugar. Place approximately 2 inches apart on greased cookie sheet. Bake 10 to 12 minutes at 350°F. Yield: Approximately 4 to 5 dozen.

It should be noted that these cookies keep quite well; of course, this is wholly dependent on the voraciousness of the little "crumb-grabbers."
A.J. and Wanda Groenendale, Fort Collins Lions Club
Fort Collins, Colorado, USA

❦

What sunshine is to flowers, smiles are to humanity.

GINGERSNAPS

1 c. sugar
1 c. shortening
¾ c. molasses
1 egg, beaten
1¼ tsp. vinegar

1½ tsp. soda
1¼ tsp. ginger
¾ tsp. salt
⅛ tsp. pepper
3 c. flour

Cream sugar and shortening. Add molasses, egg, and vinegar; mix well. Add flour sifted with soda, ginger, salt, and pepper. Mix batter well. You need a stiff batter and may want to add a "jiff" more flour. Roll batter thin and cut with cookie cutter. Bake at 350° for 8 to 10 minutes.

Edna K. Bunch, Snow Hill Lions Club
Snow Hill, North Carolina, USA

"PIZZELLES"

6 eggs
3½ to 4 c. flour
1½ c. sugar

1 c. margarine*
4 tsp. baking powder
2 Tbsp. anise

Beat eggs, adding sugar gradually. Beat until smooth. Add cooled melted margarine and anise. Sift flour and baking powder; add to egg mixture. Dough will be sticky enough to be dropped by spoon. Bake until golden brown. Baking time is ½ minute, but will vary slightly with personal preference for browning. Makes 2 at a time. Pizzelle irons can be purchased at Italian specialty stores or kitchen shops.

* Do not use oil as a substitute.

Mrs. Jeff Crosby, Exeter Township Lions Club
Exeter, Pennsylvania, USA

OLEO COOKIE

1 c. butter or oleo
½ c. confectioners sugar

1¾ c. flour
1 tsp. vanilla

Mix ingredients well. Make 2 rolls in wax paper. Chill. Slice ¼ inch thick. Bake (ungreased pan) for 12 minutes at 325°. Do not brown. Sprinkle with confectioners sugar.

Helen Dunbar, Huffman Lioness Club
Huffman, Texas, USA

You are rich when you are content with what you have.

TARTS

2 (8 oz.) cream cheese
¾ c. sugar
2 eggs
1 Tbsp. lemon juice
1 tsp. vanilla

24 tin foil cups
24 vanilla wafers
Cherry pie filling or whatever
   filling you would like

Mix sugar and cream cheese until light and fluffy. Beat eggs, then add lemon juice and vanilla. Add to cream cheese mixture. Put a vanilla wafer in cupcake foil cup, then put 1 tablespoon mixture on top. Bake in 350° oven for 20 minutes. When cool, put filling on top and refrigerate.

Came from a good friend.

Carol A. Case, Manteno Lions Club
Manteno, Illinois, USA

BUTTER COOKIES
(Makes 2 round large cookies)

2¼ sticks butter
2¼ c. flour

1 c. sugar
1 egg, beaten

Soften butter with fork. Add sugar and ¾ of the beaten egg. Add flour and mix well. Form into 2 large balls. Grease 2 pie tins and coat with flour. Place each ball into pie tin and knead out to fit pan. Bake at 375° for 10 to 15 minutes. Spread remaining egg onto top before baking to glaze. Cool and cut wedges before serving.

An old Dutch favorite.

Nel VanWieringen, Chesterfield Bay Lions Club
Chesterfield, Michigan, USA

An old-timer remembers when a union suit was something worn
instead of something filed against someone.

CREAM FILLED CONFETTI COOKIES

Cookies:

1 c. sugar
½ c. margarine
¼ c. shortening
2 eggs

2½ c. flour
1 tsp. baking powder
¾ tsp. salt
⅓ c. multicolored candy sprinkles

Filling:

¾ c. margarine
2 c. powdered sugar
1 tsp. vanilla

1 egg
2 or 3 drops of green or red food
color

In large bowl, combine ½ cup margarine, shortening, 1 teaspoon vanilla, and 2 eggs. Beat well. Add flour, baking powder, and salt; mix well. Stir in sprinkles. Cover and refrigerate at least 1 hour. Roll dough, ⅓ at a time, to ⅛ inch thick. Cut with desired cookie cutters. Place on ungreased sheet. Bake at 400° for 5 to 7 minutes. Remove from sheet and cool completely.

In medium bowl, beat ¾ cup margarine until softened. Gradually add powdered sugar and blend well. Add 1 teaspoon vanilla and 1 egg. Beat until light and fluffy. Add food coloring and blend well. Spread 1 heaping teaspoon of filling between 2 cookies. Repeat until used up. Store filled cookies in refrigerator. Makes approximately 3½ dozen 2½ inch cookies.

Cookie cutters of assorted shapes and sizes can be used. This was a favorite of Kansas Lions State Council meeting our Club hosted.

Patti O'Brien, Sundowners Lions Club
Emporia, Kansas, USA

CHEESECAKE COOKIES

⅓ c. (packed) brown sugar
½ c. chopped walnuts
1 c. flour
⅓ c. butter, melted
¼ c. sugar

1 (8 oz.) pkg. cream cheese
1 egg, beaten
1 Tbsp. lemon juice
2 Tbsp. cream or milk
1 tsp. vanilla

1. Combine brown sugar, walnuts, and flour in large bowl.
2. Stir in butter until crumbly (reserve 1 cup for topping).
3. Place remaining mixture in 8 inch square baking pan; press firmly.
4. Bake at 350° for 12 to 15 minutes.
5. Cream sugar and cream cheese until smooth.
6. Beat in egg, lemon juice, cream, and vanilla.
7. Pour onto crust.
8. Top with reserved mixture. Bake at 350° for 25 minutes.
9. Cool thoroughly. Cut into 2 inch squares.
10. Cover with plastic wrap. Keep refrigerated.

Jack and Ruth Graham, Lyman Lions Club
Lyman, Wyoming, USA

LITTLE ROUND SWEDISH COOKIES

½ c. margarine
½ c. brown sugar

1 egg yolk
1 c. flour

Mix well. Form in small balls; dip in 1 egg, slightly beaten. Roll in finely chopped nuts. Press dent in center. Bake in moderate oven for 8 minutes. Remove and press again. Bake 8 minutes more. Take from oven and cool. Fill center with chocolate frosting. Press nut in center. Makes 25 to 30 cookies.

CRISPIE COOKIES

1 c. brown sugar
1 c. white sugar
1 c. shortening (Crisco)
¾ c. oil
1 egg
3 Tbsp. vanilla
3½ c. flour

1 tsp. soda
1 tsp. salt
1 tsp. cream of tartar
1 c. quick oats
1 c. Rice Krispies
1 c. coconut
1 c. chopped pecans

Cream sugars, egg, shortening, oil, milk, and vanilla. Beat in flour, soda, salt, and cream of tartar. Mix in rest of ingredients. Drop by spoonfuls. Bake at 375° for about 8 minutes. Do not overbake.

DISHPAN COOKIES

3 c. brown sugar
2 c. white sugar
3 tsp. vanilla
4 oz. oleo
1½ c. oil
4 eggs

4 c. flour
2 tsp. baking powder
2 Tbsp. cinnamon
1 tsp. salt
4 c. cereal (corn flakes)*
2 c. oatmeal

In large bowl, mix brown and white sugars, oleo, oil, eggs, and vanilla. Mix well. Add flour, cinnamon, salt, and baking soda. Mix in well. Mix in oatmeal and cereal. Drop by teaspoonful on cookie sheet. Bake at 350° for 10 to 12 minutes. Chips may be added if desired.

* I use Apple and Cinnamon Cheerios. Kids love them.

Walter E. Loomis, North Jackson Lions Club
Jackson, Michigan, USA

❦

Gather the crumbs of happiness to make a loaf of contentment.

SNICKERDOODLES

Put into a big bowl and mix:

1 stick margarine
¾ c. sugar

1 egg

Sift together:

1¼ c. plus 2 Tbsp. flour
½ tsp. baking soda

¼ tsp. salt
1 tsp. cream of tartar

Add flour mixture to sugar mixture. Mix well. Dough should be soft and easy to handle. Add a tablespoon of flour if dough is too sticky.

Combine in a small dish and set aside:

1 Tbsp. sugar

1 tsp. cinnamon

Roll dough into balls the size of a walnut. Roll in sugar-cinnamon mixture. Place on ungreased cookie sheet. Bake 8 to 10 minutes at 400°. Don't overbake! Cookies should be soft and puffy. Cool on rack. Makes 3 dozen.

These cookies wrinkle as they cool. I've been told the original baker's children snickered as the cookies cooled hence the name.
Wilma Claar, LaCygne Lions Club
LaCygne, Kansas, USA

BUCKEYES

1 lb. butter (oleo)
2 lb. peanut butter (crunchy or
   plain)

3 lb. powdered sugar
2 (12 oz.) pkg. chocolate chips
1½ sticks paraffin

Mix butter and peanut butter until smooth. Add powdered sugar, a little at a time, until well mixed and can make a smooth ball. Roll into balls about 1 inch, put a toothpick into each ball, and refrigerate for 2 hours. Melt chocolate and paraffin in double boiler. Dip balls and refrigerate until firm.

For best results, butter and peanut butter should warm and be almost liquid before adding the powdered sugar.
Lion Joyce Raymond, Amarillo North Lions Club
Amarillo, Texas, USA

❦

I know not what the future holds, but I know who holds the future.

WELSH CAKES

4 c. all-purpose flour
1½ c. sugar
1 c. butter
1 Tbsp. baking powder

1 tsp. salt
1 tsp. fresh ground nutmeg
3 eggs
1 c. currants, chilled

Combine dry ingredients; set aside. In large mixer bowl, cream the butter. Gradually add sugar. Add eggs, one at a time, beating well after each. Stir currants into flour mix and add to butter mix, stirring until well blended, but do not beat any longer. Divide dough into 2 balls and chill. Remove 1 from refrigerator. On floured surface, roll out to thickness of currants without pressing too hard. Cut rounds with biscuit cutter. Bake on hot griddle just as you would bake pancakes, about 2 minutes on first side and 1 minute for second side, until light brown. Cool on rack. Makes about 6 dozen.

My husband's mother baked these for her family. She died before we met and years later, he spotted a small plate of them at a church dinner. The recipe was shared (from a 1936 magazine) and the lost tradition began again.
Vivian Quinlan and George Quinlan, Mathews Lions Club
Mathews, Virginia, USA

CORN FLAKE COOKIES

2 c. sifted flour
1 tsp. baking soda
½ tsp. salt
½ tsp. baking powder
1¼ c. shortening
1 c. white sugar

1 c. brown sugar, firmly packed
2 eggs, well beaten
1 tsp. vanilla
2 c. flaked or shredded coconut
2 c. corn flakes

Sift together flour, soda, salt, and baking powder. Cream shortening; add sugars gradually. Beat until light. Add eggs and vanilla. Combine dry ingredients and creamed mixture; add coconut and corn flakes. Drop small teaspoonfuls on greased baking sheet, 1½ inches apart. Bake in moderate oven at 350° for 8 to 10 minutes or until delicately browned. Makes 8 dozen.
Patsy Gagnon (Mrs. Charles), Silver Run-Union Mills Lions Club
Westminster, Maryland, USA

❦

When patterns are broken, new worlds can emerge.

CHRISTMAS SURPRISE BALLS

1 c. butter or margarine
⅔ c. sugar
1 large eggs
1 tsp. vanilla
¼ tsp. salt
2¼ c. flour

36 "surprises" (candied cherries, chocolate kisses, tiny gumdrops, buttermints, or dates)
Sifted powdered sugar

Cream together margarine, sugar, egg, and vanilla. Sift salt and flour together; stir into creamed mixture. Mold dough into balls and hide a surprise in each ball. Bake on ungreased cookie sheet at 350° for 13 to 15 minutes. Cool for 10 minutes, then roll in sifted powdered sugar. When cold, reroll in powdered sugar. Makes 3 dozen cookies.

COLORADO SNOW NEWTONS

1 c. chopped dates
1 small can crushed pineapple
1⅓ c. sugar

1 egg
Large box vanilla wafers
Powdered sugar

Combine dates, pineapple, sugar, and egg in a medium saucepan. Cook over low heat and stir until thick. Allow mixture to cool. Spread on vanilla wafer, adding another wafer to make a sandwich. Roll in powdered sugar. Makes about 60 cookies.

CHRISTMAS MOUNDS

1 lb. flake coconut
1 can sweetened condensed milk
1½ lb. powdered sugar
2 sticks softened butter

2 c. chopped pecans
2 (12 oz.) pkg. chocolate chips
½ stick paraffin

Mix coconut, milk, sugar, butter, and nuts in large bowl. Chill for 2 hours. Roll into 1 inch balls and place on cookie sheet. Chill 2 hours. Melt chocolate and paraffin in double boiler or microwave. Dip balls in chocolate with toothpicks. Allow to cool, then remove toothpicks. Store in tins in cool place. Makes about 5 dozen.

The worst prison would be a closed heart.

PREACHER'S COOKIES

2 c. sugar
3 Tbsp. cocoa
½ c. milk
1 stick margarine

½ c. peanut butter
3 c. oatmeal
1 tsp. vanilla

Mix sugar, cocoa, milk, and margarine in saucepan. Let cook over low heat until mixture bubbles around edge of pan, approximately 1 minute. Add remaining ingredients and stir until blended. Spoon onto waxed paper and allow to cool. Makes about 2½ dozen cookies.

This recipe was given to my family by Mrs. Dorothy Cooke who was the pastor's wife at my home church. Rev. George Cooke was pastor of my home church, Ballard's Bridge Baptist for over 25 years. I guess this is how the name came about.

Glenn Bunch, Snow Hill Lions Club
Snow Hill, North Carolina, USA

"CROSBY'S COWBOY COOKIES"

1 c. shortening
1 c. sugar
1 c. brown sugar
1 tsp. vanilla
2 eggs
2 c. sifted flour

1 tsp. baking soda
½ tsp. baking powder
½ tsp. salt
2 c. quick oats (not instant)
1 c. chocolate chips or raisins

Preheat oven to 350°F. In a medium bowl, combine flour, soda, powder, salt, and oats. Mix well with wire whisk and set aside. In a large bowl, blend shortening, vanilla, sugar, and eggs. Gradually stir in other mixture. Do not overmix. Stir in chocolate chips or raisins. Drop by tablespoons onto ungreased cookie sheet 1½ inches apart. Bake 10 to 12 minutes or until cookies are light golden brown. Transfer cookies with a spatula to a cool flat surface.

Mrs. Jeff Crosby, Exeter Township Lions Club
Exeter, Pennsylvania, USA

Humor is the hole that allows the sawdust out of a stuffed shirt.

CHEWY SKOR TOFFEE BITS COOKIES

2½ c. all-purpose flour
1 tsp. baking soda
½ tsp. salt
1 stick margarine, softened
¾ c. sugar

¾ c. light brown sugar
1 tsp. vanilla
2 eggs
10 oz. pkg. Skor English toffee bits

Heat oven to 350°F. Stir together flour, soda, and salt. In large mixer bowl, beat butter, granulated sugar, brown sugar, and vanilla until well blended. Add eggs; blend thoroughly. Gradually add flour mixture, beating well. Stir in Skor bits. Drop by rounded teaspoonfuls onto lightly greased cookie sheets. Bake 9 to 11 minutes or until lightly browned. Cool slightly; remove from cookie sheet. This recipe makes approximately 4 dozen cookies. Best cookies I have ever eaten!!!!

When you take coffee filters out of a coffee maker, wrap them in wax paper or put into plastic bags before you put them in trash basket or can.

Otto L. Eubank, Emporia Lions Club
Emporia, Kansas, USA

SOUR CREAM COOKIES

4 c. flour
1 tsp. soda
1 c. shortening
2 c. sugar
1 tsp. baking powder

1 tsp. nutmeg
1 c. sour cream
½ tsp. salt
2 eggs

Cream shortening and sugar, then add sour cream and soda. Add seasonings (nutmeg and salt) and beaten eggs. Add baking powder and flour. Add to first mixture. Mix well. Let stand overnight in refrigerator. In morning, roll out on mixing board. Cut in desired shapes. Bake in oven at 350° about 12 minutes. These cookies can be cut for all holidays, frosted for all occasions, and treats for all Lion friends

Denny and Clara Culbert, Scio Lions Club
Scio, New York, USA

❦

How can I be over the hill when I never even got to the top?

SOUR CREAM COOKIES

2 c. sugar
1 c. melted Crisco
1 tsp. vanilla

2 eggs, beaten lightly
1 c. sour cream or 8 oz. ctn.

Cream ingredients above.

Add:

2 tsp. soda
1 tsp. salt

5½ to 5¾ c. flour

Bake on greased cookie sheet for 10 minutes in a 375° oven. Works well to drop or roll out. If rolling out, use 5¾ cups flour. Dip the cookie cutters in flour. Decorate the cookies before baking with candy sprinkles, colored sugars, etc. Or, you may bake, then decorate with frosting.

In memory of Natalie Juhl, by Donna Juhl, Otis Lions Club
Otis, Colorado, USA

SOUTHERN SOUR CREAM JUMBLES
(Cookies)

1⅔ c. flour
¼ tsp. baking soda
1 tsp. baking powder
½ tsp. salt
⅓ c. margarine or butter
⅔ c. sugar

1 egg
½ c. commercial sour cream
½ c. fine cocoanut
¼ tsp. cinnamon
1 Tbsp. sugar

Stir together flour, baking soda, baking powder, and salt. Cream margarine. Mix in ⅔ cup sugar and egg. Mix in flour alternately with sour cream, then add cocoanut. Drop by teaspoonful 2 inches apart on greased cookie sheet. Combine cinnamon and 1 tablespoon sugar; sprinkle a little on each cookie. Bake 10 to 12 minutes in a 350° oven.

A favorite at our hospital cafeteria - made by "Alma."
Donna Lane, Jasper Mountain Lions Club
Jasper, Alberta, Canada

❧

Square meals often make round people.

COCONUT COOKIES

⅓ c. melted butter, cooled
¼ c. oil

1 c. sugar
1 tsp. coconut extract

Add:

1 egg
1 (6½ oz.) box biscuit mix (Martha
    Washington)

1 c. instant potato flakes

    Mix first 4 ingredients. Add remaining items. Drop by teaspoon. Bake at 350° for 12 to 14 minutes. Do not bake brown - they'll get too hard.

Thelma Bankert (Mrs. Melvin), Silver Run-Union Mills Lions Club
Littlestown, Pennsylvania, USA

ALMOND COOKIES

1 c. flour
½ c. shortening
½ tsp. baking powder
Few drops of yellow food coloring

1 tsp. almond extract
1 egg yolk
24 blanched almonds
6 Tbsp. sugar

    1. Cream shortening with sugar and almond extract until light and fluffy.

    2. Add food coloring, then work in flour which has been sifted with salt and baking powder.

    3. Shape in wax paper into roll 1 inch in diameter; chill for 1 hour.

    4. Cut into ¼ inch slices. Place on greased cookie sheets, 1 inch apart, rounding the edges of the dough.

    5. Beat egg yolk and water together, then brush each slice of dough with the mixture. Press an almond well into the center.

    6. Bake in oven preheated to 350° for 20 minutes or at 400° for 10 minutes, until light golden brown. This cookie is light and delicious.

Lion Jerry Vohler, Caruthers Lions Club
Caruthers, California, USA

Even worse than a storm or a riot
is a big bunch of kids who are suddenly quiet.

548

GRANDMA'S SPICE COOKIES

1½ c. sugar
⅔ c. margarine or butter
3 eggs or 6 egg whites
2¾ c. flour
1 tsp. nutmeg
1 tsp. allspice
1¼ tsp. cinnamon
¼ tsp. baking powder

½ tsp. salt
1¼ tsp. soda
½ c. plus 1 Tbsp. buttermilk or
    sour milk
1 c. raisins (seedless)
1 c. nuts, chopped (walnuts)
½ c. water

Bring to boil 1 cup raisins in ½ cup water and set aside to soak. Chop nuts. Cream margarine or butter and sugar until creamy and smooth. Add eggs, one at a time, and cream together with sugar and margarine or butter. Drain water from raisins and save to mix with milk later. Use about ½ to ¾ cup of the flour to mix and coat drained raisins and also nuts. Set floured raisins and nuts aside. Mix soda with buttermilk or sour milk. Add remaining raisin water to this: Mix dry ingredients together with liquid ingredients alternately. Add floured raisins and nuts. Mix. Bake at 300° to 325° for 8 to 11 minutes. If cookie is not a nice brown color, place under broiler for a short moment.

APPLESAUCE COOKIES

2 c. flour
1½ c. whole wheat flour
1 tsp. salt
2 tsp. cinnamon
1 tsp. nutmeg
1 tsp. cloves
2 tsp. baking soda

2 c. sugar
1 c. shortening
2 c. applesauce (sweetened)
2 c. bran
2 c. raisins
2 eggs, beaten

Sift the 2 flours, spices, soda, and salt together. Cream the sugar and shortening. Add the beaten eggs and sweetened applesauce. Add the bran to the dry ingredients, then add the sugar and shortening mixture. Beat in the raisins and mix well. Drop on oiled cookie sheet. Bake at 350° for 15 minutes or until the cookies are brown.

Evelyn Steele, Lyman Lions Club
Lyman, Wyoming, USA

❦

For peace of mind, resign as general manager of the universe.

MOLASSES COOKIES

¾ c. shortening
1 c. sugar
1 tsp. vanilla
1 unbeaten egg
4 Tbsp. molasses
2 c. flour

1 tsp. (rounded) baking soda
1 tsp. cinnamon
1 tsp. ginger
1 tsp. allspice
1 tsp. cloves

Mix shortening, sugar, vanilla, egg, and molasses together; beat well. Add remaining ingredients and mix all together. Make small balls from mixture. Roll in sugar and flatten each on cookie sheet. Bake for 15 minutes in preheated 350° oven.

Beverly Swett, Westbrook Lions Club
Westbrook, Maine, USA

MOLASSES CRINKLES

¾ c. shortening
1 c. brown sugar, packed
1 egg
¼ c. molasses
2¼ c. flour

2 tsp. baking soda
¼ tsp. salt
½ tsp. cloves
1 tsp. cinnamon
1 tsp. ginger

Mix thoroughly the shortening, brown sugar, egg, and molasses. Add remaining ingredients and mix well again. Roll into one half dollar size balls. Roll in sugar. Bake at 375° for 10 to 12 minutes. Makes about 2 dozen cookies.

"OLD-FASHIONED" MOLASSES COOKIES

5¼ c. flour
2 tsp. baking soda
1 tsp. cinnamon
1 tsp. cloves
1 tsp. nutmeg
1 tsp. salt

1 c. shortening
1 c. sugar
2 eggs
1 c. molasses
1 c. water

Cream together the shortening, sugar, eggs, molasses, and water; add dry ingredients and mix well. Drop by well rounded teaspoons onto a greased cookie sheet. Bake 12 minutes at 375°F. You may like to garnish each cookie prior to baking with one or more large raisins. These cookies are especially good when eaten with a large glass of cold milk.

A.J. and Wanda Groenendale, Fort Collins Lions Club
Fort Collins, Colorado, USA

❧

Life is a canvas - you fill in the picture.

RAISIN FILLED COOKIES

2 c. brown sugar
1 c. shortening
3 eggs, beaten
1 tsp. soda, dissolved in 1 Tbsp.
   water

3½ c. flour (or more to make soft
   dough)

Filling:

1 c. raisins
1 c. sugar

2 Tbsp. cornstarch
1 c. water

Cream sugar and shortening together. Add beaten eggs. Add dissolved soda. Add flour to make a soft dough. Roll dough to ¼ inch thick for 1 cookie.

Mix filling ingredients together and boil until thick. Add 1 teaspoon filling and put on top piece of dough and press the edges together. Bake at 275° for 20 minutes. Makes 2 dozen cookies.

RAISIN PUFF COOKIES

1 c. raisins
1 c. golden raisins
1 c. water
1 c. oleo
1½ c. sugar
2 eggs

3½ c. flour
1 tsp. soda
½ tsp. salt
½ tsp. baking powder
2 tsp. vanilla

Cook the raisins and water until water is gone. Cool. Cream oleo, sugar, and eggs. Add flour, soda, salt, and baking powder. Mix well. Add raisins and vanilla. Shape into walnut size balls. Roll in sugar. Bake 12 to 15 minutes on greased cookie sheets at 350°.

Verna Ball, Sherrodsville Lions Club
Sherrodsville, Ohio, USA

❧

The person who stays on the straight and narrow path
won't have many folks trying to pass him.

RAISIN COOKIES

½ box raisins, cooked for 15
    minutes, drained, and
    cooled
1 c. Crisco
1 tsp. salt
2 tsp. vanilla

1½ c. sugar
3 eggs, well beaten
3 c. flour
¾ tsp. baking soda
¾ tsp. baking powder
5 Tbsp. milk

Combine Crisco (creamed), salt, and vanilla; blend. Add sugar gradually and cream well. Add eggs and mix well. Sift flour with soda and baking powder; add to mixture alternately with milk, mixing thoroughly. Add raisins and blend. Drop from teaspoon on Crisco and flour dusted baking sheets. Sprinkle with sugar. Bake at 375° for 12 to 15 minutes.

These cookies are made for campers and meetings.
Camp for the Blind, District 14, Beaccon Lodge
Mt. Union, Pennsylvania, USA

DINGBATS

1½ c. chopped dates
1 c. sugar
½ stick butter
1 egg

1 tsp. vanilla
2½ c. Rice Krispies
Coconut

Mix all together on low heat until nice and soft. Remove from stove; add 1 teaspoon vanilla and 2½ cups Rice Krispies. Cool for 5 minutes. Shape into balls with hands, then roll in coconut or chopped nutmeats.

Dave Bernier, Westbrook Lions Club
Westbrook, Maine, USA

ICEBOX DATE COOKIE

1 c. brown sugar
1 c. white sugar
¾ c. shortening

3 eggs
4 c. flour
1 tsp. baking soda

Filling:

1 pkg. seeded dates
½ c. sugar

½ c. water
⅓ c. chopped nuts

For filling: Cut dates fine. Cook with sugar and water. Let cool. Add nuts.

Mix both brown and white sugars and shortening until creamy. Add eggs and mix well. Sift flour and soda; add to sugar and egg mixture. Roll dough out flat. Spread with date filling. Roll like jelly roll. Let stand overnight in icebox. Slice and bake at 325° to 350° for 10 minutes or until golden.

SURPRISE MERINGUES

2 egg whites
⅛ tsp. cream of tartar
⅛ tsp. salt

¾ c. sugar
6 oz. chocolate chips
1 c. walnuts, chopped

Beat the egg whites until stiff. Add cream of tartar and salt; blend together. Add sugar and beat again until very stiff. Add chocolate chips and nuts. Drop by teaspoonfuls on a foil-covered cookie sheet. Bake at 250° for 25 minutes. Sooo good!

Ellen Ostrand, Lady Lions of Rohnert Park Lions Club
Rohnert Park, California, USA

FORGOTTEN KISSES

2 egg whites (room temperature)
¾ c. sugar
¼ tsp. cream of tartar

⅛ tsp. salt
1 tsp. vanilla
1 pkg. chocolate chips

Preheat oven to 375°. Beat egg whites until foamy; add salt and cream of tartar. Beat in sugar, a tablespoon at a time. Add vanilla before last 2 tablespoons of sugar. Fold in chocolate chips carefully. Drop on ungreased cookie sheet. Put in oven and turn oven off. Leave in oven overnight or at least 5 hours. *Do not peek!*

You may double the recipe. These are nice to color - make some pink, yellow, etc. - with food coloring.

An old family favorite.

John Rosa, Plumb Lane Lions Club
Reno, Nevada, USA

BAKE WHILE YOU SLEEP COOKIES

2 egg whites
Pinch of salt
¼ tsp. cream of tartar
⅔ c. sugar

¼ tsp. vanilla
1 c. chopped nuts
1 c. chocolate chips

Preheat oven to 350°. Beat egg whites until stiff. Add sugar, 2 tablespoons at a time, beating well after each addition. Stir in vanilla, nuts, and chocolate chips. Drop by teaspoon on ungreased, foil-lined cookie sheets. Put into oven and turn off immediately. *Do not open oven door* for at least 8 hours. Makes 40 to 50 cookies.

Sue Hopkins (Mrs. John), Silver Run-Union Mills Lions Club
Westminster, Maryland, USA

If you want to attain greatness, think no little thoughts.

MERINGUE COOKIES
(No fat, no cholesterol)

2 egg whites (large)
⅔ c. powdered sugar
2 c. corn flakes

1 tsp. vanilla
1 tsp. coconut or almond flavor

Beat egg whites till very stiff. Gradually add powdered sugar. Fold in 2 cups corn flakes after adding flavoring. Bake at 350° for 10 minutes. Watch carefully. Remove from cookie sheet to cold tray. When cooled, store in airtight container.

To check adequate stiffness of eggs, turn bowl upside down - eggs stay when they are beaten sufficiently.

Iris S. Dian, Dolley Madison of Greensboro Lions Club
Greensboro, North Carolina, USA

CHOCOLATE MERINGUE COOKIES
(No fat)

2 egg whites (large)
⅔ c. white sugar
2 Tbsp. cocoa

1 tsp. vanilla
1 tsp. chocolate or almond
2 c. corn flakes

Beat egg whites till stiff. Gradually beat in sugar mixed with cocoa. I sift sugar and cocoa together. Gently stir in flavorings. Fold in 2 cups corn flakes. Drop by spoonfuls on Pam sprayed or oiled cookie sheet. Bake 10 minutes at 350° in preheated oven. Watch carefully. They burn easily. Remove to cool tray to cool. Store in airtight container.

This is an original recipe I developed for my husband to comply with his no fat diet.

Iris S. Dian, Dolley Madison of Greensboro Lions Club
Greensboro, North Carolina, USA

NO BAKE COOKIES

2 c. sugar
½ c. milk
¼ lb. butter
¼ c. cocoa

½ c. peanut butter (creamy)
Pinch of salt
3 c. quick-cooking oats
1 Tbsp. vanilla

Mix together on stove the sugar, milk, butter, and cocoa. Bring to a boil. When it comes to a rolling boil, let it boil for exactly 1½ minutes. Remove from heat and add peanut butter, salt, oats, and vanilla. Drop by spoonful onto waxed paper. Allow to cool.

Lisa Milam, Emporia Sundowners Lions Club
Emporia, Kansas, USA

NO BAKE COOKIES

2½ c. sugar
½ c. milk

3 Tbsp. cocoa
1 stick oleo

Cook above to full boil.

Add:

½ c. peanut butter
1 tsp. vanilla

3 c. quick oats

Drop by spoonfuls on wax paper.

Dave Bernier, Westbrook Lions Club
Westbrook, Maine, USA

NO BAKE COCOA AND OATMEAL COOKIES

4 c. sugar
1 c. margarine (soft)
4 Tbsp. cocoa
1 c. milk

6 c. quick cooking oats
1 c. peanut butter
2 Tbsp. vanilla extract

Bring first 4 ingredients to a boil. Cook 1 minute. Remove from heat and stir in oatmeal, peanut butter, and vanilla. Mix well and drop by teaspoonfuls on waxed paper. Refrigerate until firm if room is warm. Crunchy peanut butter can be used for extra crunch.

Phyllis Hillis, McMinnville Lions Club
McMinnville, Tennessee, USA

VINEGAR COOKIES

2½ c. flour
1 c. sugar
1 egg
½ tsp. soda
½ tsp. salt

1 tsp. vanilla
1 tsp. white vinegar
1 c. butter
¼ c. sugar and cinnamon, blended
    together

Preheat oven to 350°. Oil cookie sheet. Blend all ingredients in bowl. Spoon out on cookie sheet a teaspoon at a time. Cross press with a flour coated fork. Sprinkle each cookie with sugar-cinnamon mixture. Bake 10 to 12 minutes or until light brown.

Tastes like a sugar cookie but the name surprises everyone.

Char Powers, Auburn Valley Lions Club
Auburn, Washington, USA

❧

The most important things are not things.

CHOCOLATE OATSIES

2 c. sugar
½ c. milk
¼ c. margarine
⅓ c. cocoa

3 c. quick-cooking oats
½ c. coconut (optional)
½ c. peanut butter (optional)
1 tsp. vanilla

Combine sugar, milk, margarine, and cocoa in saucepan. Boil 2 to 3 minutes. Remove from heat. Mix in rest of ingredients. Drop by teaspoonfuls onto waxed paper. Makes about 30. Cool before eating - if you can wait.

Mrs. Lion Robert (Margaret) Logan, Canton Lions Club
Canton, Georgia, USA

GERMANTOWN OATMEAL COOKIES

2 c. oleo
2 c. white sugar
2 c. brown sugar
4 eggs
2 or 3 c. oatmeal
2 tsp. baking soda

2 tsp. baking powder
1 tsp. salt
5 c. flour
2 c. coconut
2 c. chocolate chips

Cream oleo and sugars. Add eggs and beat well after each addition. Add dry ingredients and mix well. Stir in coconut and chocolate chips. Drop on greased cookie sheets. Bake at 350° for 12 to 15 minutes. Yield: 12 dozen. These cookies freeze well.

Gertrude Hayden, Moweaqua Lions Club
Moweaqua, Illinois, USA

GRAND MA COOKIES

3 c. sugar
1 stick butter
¾ c. milk
3 Tbsp. cocoa

3½ c. 1 minute oats
1 c. peanut butter (creamed or
    nuts)
1 tsp. vanilla

Add sugar, butter, milk, and cocoa; cook for 3 minutes until boiling. Take off stove. Add peanut butter, then add vanilla and oats. Place by teaspoon on waxed paper and cool until they can be picked up by hand. Makes about 3 dozen cookies. Delicious. Be sure to cook for 3 minutes because may not set up. You can also add M&M's to the oats.

When my boys were small, they used to say "Mommie make Grand-Ma Cookies." One is now 36 and the other 32 and they still want Grand-Ma Cookies when they come home.

Melba J. Gray, Eastlake Lions Club
Birmingham, Alabama, USA

BANANA OATMEAL COOKIES

1½ c. flour
1 tsp. baking soda
½ tsp. salt
½ tsp. cinnamon
1 tsp. vanilla
1 egg
½ c. chopped nuts (optional)

½ c. butter or margarine
½ c. white sugar
½ c. brown sugar
2 Tbsp. cream or milk
1½ c. oatmeal (not cooked)
1 c. chocolate bits

Sift together flour, soda, salt, and cinnamon. Set aside. Cream together butter and sugars. Add egg and vanilla; blend well. Mash banana in separate bowl and add cream. Alternately add flour and banana to creamed mixture. Add oatmeal and blend. Add chocolate chips and nuts. Bake in 375° oven for 10 minutes.

Patricia A. Cook, Mt. Clemens Lioness Club
Mt. Clemens, Michigan, USA

APPLESAUCE OATMEAL COOKIES

1½ c. flour
1 c. sugar
¾ tsp. cinnamon
½ tsp. baking soda
¼ tsp. nutmeg

¾ c. margarine
1¾ c. quick-cooking oats
1 c. unsweetened applesauce
1 egg, beaten
½ c. nuts, chopped

Preheat oven to 400°F. Mix together dry ingredients, except oats. Cut in margarine. Add oats, applesauce, egg, and nuts. Mix thoroughly until blended. Drop by teaspoonfuls onto greased baking sheet. Bake 10 to 12 minutes.

KATHLEEN'S FAVORITE OATMEAL COOKIES

¾ c. oleo or vegetable shortening
1 c. brown sugar, packed
½ c. white sugar
1 egg
¼ c. water

1 tsp. vanilla
3 c. quick oats (dry)
1 c. flour
1 tsp. salt
½ tsp. soda

Preheat oven to 350°. Beat together shortening, eggs, sugars, water, and vanilla. Add remaining ingredients and mix well. Drop by teaspoonfuls on greased sheets. Bake for about 12 to 15 minutes. Add cocoanut, chopped nuts, raisins or chips for variety.

Just yummy!!

Kathleen Mergaert by Walter E. Loomis, North Jackson Lions Club
Jackson, Michigan, USA

The longest journey begins with a single step.

LAST MINUTE COOKIES

1 c. crunchy peanut butter   1 egg white
1 c. sugar

Mix well and roll into marble size balls. Slightly flatten cookie with back of fork. Place on ungreased cookie sheet and bake at 300° for 18 minutes. Yield: 20 mini cookies. Easy and tastes great!

Stephen Hepner, Saginaw Lions Club
Saginaw, Texas, USA

PEANUT BUTTER COOKIES WITH A TWIST

2½ c. all-purpose flour   1 c. peanut butter
⅔ c. sesame seeds   2 eggs
½ tsp. baking soda   1 tsp. vanilla
1 c. margarine or butter   ½ tsp. ground nutmeg
2 c. packed brown sugar   1½ to 2 c. toasted wheat germ

In a medium mixing bowl, stir together flour, sesame seed, and baking soda. In a larger mixer bowl, beat margarine or butter with an electric mixer on medium speed for 30 seconds or till softened. Add brown sugar, peanut butter, eggs, vanilla, and nutmeg; beat well on medium speed. Add flour mixture, beating on low speed till combined. Shape into 1 inch balls. Roll in wheat germ. Place 2 inches apart on a greased cookie sheet and gently flatten with the bottom of a glass. Bake in a 375° oven for 8 to 10 minutes or until light brown on the bottom. Remove and cool on a wire rack. Makes about 60 cookies. Crunchy on the outside, chewy on the inside, and delicious. Nutrition information per cookie: 118 cal., 3 g pro., 13 g carbo., 6 g fat, 9 mg chol., and 89 mg sodium.

Stella Pierce, Moweaqua Lions Club
Moweaqua, Illinois, USA

PEANUT BUTTER SWIRLS

½ c. shortening   1¼ c. sifted flour
1 c. sugar   ½ tsp. salt
½ c. chunk-style peanut butter   ½ tsp. soda
1 egg   1 (6 oz.) pkg. semi-sweet
2 Tbsp. milk   chocolate pieces

Cream shortening and sugar till light. Beat in peanut butter, egg, and milk. Sift together flour, salt, and soda; stir into creamed mixture. Place dough on lightly floured waxed paper; roll in 15 x 8 x ¼ inch rectangle. Melt chocolate over hot water. Cool slightly; spread over dough. Roll like jelly roll, lifting waxed paper slightly with each turn. Chill ½ hour. Slice cookies ¼ inch thick. Place on ungreased baking sheet. Bake in moderate oven (375°) for 8 to 10 minutes. Makes 4 dozen.

LaRue Eckroth, South Whitehall Lions Club
Allentown, Pennsylvania, USA

QUICK PEANUT BUTTER COOKIES

1 c. sugar
1 c. peanut butter
1 egg

1 tsp. baking soda
6 oz. chocolate chips (optional)

Preheat oven to 350°. Mix ingredients and roll into walnut size balls. Bake 8 to 10 minutes on ungreased cookie sheet. Cool 2 minutes before removing from pan.

Patricia Samuel and Kathleen Ann Gooley, Chesterfield Bay Lions Club
Mt. Clemens, Michigan, USA

PEANUT BUTTER ICEBOX COOKIES

¼ c. peanut butter
¾ c. butter
2 c. dark corn syrup
1 egg
4½ c. sifted flour

1 tsp. baking powder
1 tsp. baking soda
½ tsp. salt
1 c. chopped peanuts

Cream the peanut butter and butter; add the corn syrup. Beat in 1 egg. Sift flour, baking powder, baking soda, and salt together. Add to creamed mixture; stir in chopped peanuts. Chill. Shape into rolls 1½ inches in diameter. Slice and place on greased cookie sheet. Bake at 375° for 12 minutes.

Evelyn Steele, Lyman Lions Club
Lyman, Wyoming, USA

PEANUT BUTTER KISS COOKIES

1 c. sugar
1 c. brown sugar
1 c. shortening
1 c. peanut butter
2 eggs
1 (11 oz.) pkg. chocolate kisses

¼ c. milk
2 tsp. vanilla
3½ c. flour
2 tsp. baking soda
1 tsp. salt

Cream sugars, shortening, and peanut butter. Add eggs, milk, and vanilla. Beat well. Stir together flour, baking soda, and salt. Add to first mixture. Beat well. Shape into 1 inch balls. Roll in additional sugar. Place on ungreased cookie sheet. Bake for 8 minutes; remove and place candy in center. Return to oven for 3 minutes longer in a 350° oven.

Dave Bernier, Westbrook Lions Club
Westbrook, Maine, USA

You never know what you can do until you try.

CHOCOLATE CHIP COOKIES

2 c. shortening (Crisco, Fluffo)
1½ c. sugar
1½ c. brown sugar, packed
2 tsp. vanilla
1 tsp. water
4 eggs

5¼ c. flour
2 tsp. baking soda
2 tsp. salt
1 c. chopped nuts
12 oz. chocolate chips

Mix together in order listed. Bake at 375°.

Valerie Borecky, Lyman Lions Club
Lyman, Wyoming, USA

CHOCOLATE CHIP COOKIES

1 scant c. shortening
½ c. white sugar
1 c. brown sugar
1 tsp. vanilla
2 eggs, well beaten

2 c. flour
1 tsp. baking soda
1 tsp. salt
1 c. chopped nuts
1 pkg. chocolate chips

Combine shortening, 2 sugars, and vanilla. Add beaten eggs, then add flour, etc.

Dolores Haggberg, Isle Lioness Club
Isle, Minnesota, USA

ART'S CHOCOLATE CHIP COOKIES

2 sticks oleo
2 eggs
1 tsp. vanilla
1 c. brown sugar
1 c. white sugar

2¼ c. flour
1 c. quick oatmeal
1 c. chocolate chips
1 tsp. soda
1 tsp. salt

Mix thoroughly and drop by teaspoon on ungreased cookie sheet. Bake 9 minutes or till brown at 375°. (If batter is too dry, add more melted oleo. If too moist, add more flour.) These are the best chocolate chip cookies I've ever made and don't use any other recipe.

Judy Stork, Arlington Lions Club
Arlington, Nebraska, USA

❤

People who snore always fall asleep first.

CHOCOLATE CHIP COOKIES

1 c. shortening
1 c. brown sugar
½ c. white sugar
1 tsp. vanilla
2 eggs, beaten

2¼ c. flour
1 tsp. soda
1 tsp. salt
1 c. chocolate chips

Cream sugars and shortening. Add vanilla and beaten eggs. Sift flour, soda, and salt. Add to creamed mixture. Fold in chocolate chips. Drop by teaspoonfuls on greased cookie sheet. Bake for 10 minutes at 350°.

Carolyn Lemon, Sundowners Lions Club
Emporia, Kansas, USA

CHOCOLATE CHIP COOKIES
(Chicago style)

3½ c. flour
3 tsp. baking soda
1 tsp. salt
½ c. butter
½ c. margarine
1 c. brown sugar
1 c. white sugar
1 egg

1 Tbsp. milk
2 tsp. vanilla
1 c. corn flakes
1 c. oatmeal
1 (12 oz.) pkg. semi-sweet
    chocolate chips
1 c. vegetable oil

Mix together in large bowl 3½ cups flour, 3 teaspoons baking soda, and 1 teaspoon salt. Mix together in another bowl ½ cup butter, ½ cup margarine, 1 tablespoon brown sugar, 1 cup white sugar, 1 egg, 1 tablespoon milk, and 2 teaspoons vanilla. Place in separate bowl 1 cup corn flakes, 1 cup oatmeal, and one 12 ounce package semi-sweet chocolate chips. Mix ingredients of first 2 bowls together, then add flakes and chips; mix in 1 cup vegetable oil. Mix well and bake cookies at 350° for 10 to 12 minutes. Cookies are best if not baked too long.

Irene Savoie, Crandon Lions Club
Crandon, Wisconsin, USA

You are what you eat ... so I eat only rich foods.

CHOCOLATE CHIP COOKIES

¾ c. brown sugar
¾ c. white sugar
½ c. Crisco
½ c. oleo
1 tsp. vanilla
2 eggs
1 tsp. hot water

2¼ c. flour
½ tsp. salt
1 tsp. soda
6 oz. chocolate chips (preferably milk chocolate)
1 c. chopped nuts

Cream the first 6 ingredients together until creamy. Sift in flour, salt, and soda; mix well. Add chocolate chips and nuts. Mix well. Drop by teaspoon on greased cookie sheet. Bake until brown at 350°.

Alma Lemm, Huffman Lions Club
Huffman, Texas, USA

CHOCOLATE CHIP COOKIES

2¼ c. all-purpose flour
1 tsp. baking soda
½ tsp. salt
1 c. (2 sticks) lowfat margarine
¾ c. firm packed brown sugar
9 pkg. Sweet-One sugar substitute

1 tsp. vanilla
½ c. Egg Beaters
1 c. chopped nuts (optional)
1 (12 oz.) pkg. Baker's semi-sweet chocolate chips
½ c. raisins (optional)

Mix flour with baking soda and salt; set aside. Beat margarine, sugars, vanilla, and eggs until light and fluffy. Blend in flour mixture. Stir in nuts and chips. Drop from teaspoonful 2 inches apart on ungreased baking sheets. Bake at 375° for about 10 minutes or until golden brown. Makes about 6 dozen.

Phyllis Rockers, Emporia Sundowners Lions Club
Emporia, Kansas, USA

M&M'S COOKIES

1 c. Crisco
2 eggs
2 tsp. vanilla
1 tsp. salt
1 c. brown sugar, firmly packed

½ c. granulated sugar
2¼ c. flour
1 tsp. baking soda
1½ c. M&M's

Blend Crisco and sugars in bowl. Beat in vanilla and eggs. Sift dry ingredients together; add to mixture and blend well. Stir in ½ cup M&M's. Drop by teaspoon on ungreased baking sheet. Decorate tops with remaining candy. Bake at 375° for 10 minutes or until golden brown.

Dave Bernier, Westbrook Lions Club
Westbrook, Maine, USA

BUFFALO CHIPS

1 c. shortening
1 c. margarine
2 c. white sugar
4 eggs
2 tsp. vanilla
4 c. flour

2 tsp. baking powder
2 c. oatmeal
2 c. corn flakes
1 c. coconut
12 oz. pkg. chocolate chips
1 c. walnuts

Cream shortening and margarine with white and brown sugars until smooth. Beat eggs in one at a time. Add vanilla. Mix flour, baking powder, and soda gradually. Add to creamed mixture. Add rest of ingredients until blended. Thick and lots. Drop 1 teaspoon on ungreased cookie sheet. Bake at 350° for 10 to 12 minutes.

Patricia K. Samuel, Chesterfield Bay Lions Club
Mt. Clemens, Michigan, USA

OATMEAL, PEANUT BUTTER, CHOCOLATE CHIP COOKIES WITH NUTS

1 c. water
½ c. brown sugar
2 eggs
1 tsp. vanilla
½ c. shortening
¾ c. peanut butter

3 c. oatmeal (dry)
½ tsp. baking soda
1 tsp. salt
1 c. flour
1 c. chopped nuts (your choice)
1 c. chocolate chips

Mix together water, brown sugar, eggs, vanilla, shortening, and peanut butter, then add oatmeal, baking soda, salt, flour, nuts, and chocolate chips. Mix until blended, about 1 minute.

Preheat oven to 350°. Drop dough on greased baking sheet by rounded tablespoonful and flatten slightly. Bake 30 minutes until just firm to the touch. Makes about 3 dozen cookies. Butterscotch chips could be used in place of chocolate chips.

Daniel B. Miller, Petrolia Lions Club
Petrolia, Texas, USA

❧

Use soft words and hard arguments.

DELUXE PECAN CHOCOLATE COOKIES

2¾ c. all-purpose flour
1¼ tsp. baking soda
1 tsp. salt
1½ c. butter, softened
1½ c. firmly packed brown sugar
2 eggs

1 tsp. vanilla
1 (24 oz.) pkg. (4 c.) Nestle Toll
   House semi-sweet
   chocolate morsels
1 c. or more chopped pecans

Preheat oven to 375°. Combine flour, baking soda, and salt; set aside. In bowl, combine butter and brown sugar; beat until creamy. Add eggs and vanilla extract; beat until light and fluffy. Gradually blend in flour mixture. Stir in morsels and pecans. Drop by well rounded tablespoonful onto ungreased cookie sheet. Bake at 375° for 10 to 12 minutes. Allow to stand 2 to 3 minutes before removing from cookie sheet; cool. Makes about 3 dozen or more 2 inch cookies. *Delicious.*

Try it! You will like it!!

Esther P. Redd, East Lake Lions Club
Birmingham, Alabama, USA

CHRISTMAS SUGAR COOKIE LOLLIPOPS

¾ c. shortening
1 c. sugar
2 eggs, slightly beaten
3 c. flour

3 tsp. baking powder
½ tsp. salt
⅓ c. milk
1 tsp. vanilla

Paint:

1 egg yolk
1 tsp. water

1 to 2 drops of food coloring

Cream shortening and sugar. Add eggs and beat until smooth. Sift flour, baking powder, and salt. Add to first mixture alternately with the milk. Stir in vanilla. Chill. Roll out on lightly floured board ⅛ inch thick and cut out into 1 inch circles. Place circles onto ungreased cookie sheets. Paint Christmas designs on half the circles (candy canes, stars, trees, snowflakes, etc.). Bake at 350° for approximately 8 minutes. When cool, frost insides of circles with thick powdered sugar frosting and put together in pairs with small straw in center for the lollipop stick. Makes about 3 dozen lollipops.

❦

If you want truly to understand something, try to change it.

SUGAR COOKIES

2½ c. sifted flour
½ tsp. baking soda
¾ tsp. salt
½ c. margarine
½ c. shortening

1 c. sugar
1 tsp. vanilla
1 egg
2 Tbsp. milk

Cream together margarine, shortening, sugar, and vanilla. Add egg; cream together until mixture is fluffy. Stir in dry ingredients until mixture is smooth. Blend in 2 tablespoons milk. Roll out on sugar. Bake on ungreased cookie sheet at 350° for 8 to 10 minutes.

Linda Hartley, President, Lyman Lions Club
Lyman, Wyoming, USA

SOFT SUGAR COOKIES

4 to 5 c. flour
2 c. sugar
1 c. shortening
2 eggs
1 tsp. nutmeg
1 tsp. salt

1 tsp. vanilla
1 tsp. baking soda
½ tsp. baking powder
1 c. evaporated milk
2 tsp. vinegar

Add vinegar to milk; set aside (milk will sour). Cream shortening, sugar, and eggs until blended well. Add nutmeg, salt, vanilla, soda, and baking powder; mix well. Add flour and milk alternately blending well. Mixture will be soft. Refrigerate 1 hour. Drop by rounded teaspoons on greased cookie sheet. Put a thumbprint in each and fill with jam or jelly. Bake at 375° for 10 to 12 minutes. Cookies should not brown.

Cynthia Dowd, Chesterfield Bay Lions Club
Chesterfield, Michigan, USA

DROP SUGAR COOKIES

2½ c. sifted all-purpose flour
½ tsp. soda
¾ tsp. salt
½ c. margarine
½ c. shortening

1 c. sugar
1 tsp. vanilla
1 egg
2 Tbsp. milk

Have all ingredients at room temperature. Sift together flour, soda, and salt. Cream together margarine, shortening, sugar, and vanilla extract thoroughly. Add egg; cream until mixture is fluffy. Stir in dry ingredients until mixture is smooth. Blend in 2 tablespoons milk. Drop on ungreased cookie sheet. Bake at 400° for 12 minutes. Note: Flatten each cookie with sugar coated glass.

Mrs. Lion John (Helen) Jennings, Canton Lions Club
Canton, Georgia, USA

DROP SUGAR COOKIES

2½ c. flour
¾ tsp. salt
½ tsp. baking soda
½ c. margarine (stick type)
½ c. shortening

1 c. sugar
1 tsp. vanilla
1 egg
2 Tbsp. milk

Cream sugar, shortening, and margarine. Add egg, vanilla, soda, salt, and milk; beat until fluffy. Stir in flour. Drop by full teaspoon on ungreased cookie sheets. Press down with a dipped-in-sugar water glass bottom. Bake about 12 minutes at 400° or until lightly browned on edges.

At Christmas time, dip the glass in red or green sugar. This recipe can be doubled and the cookies freeze very well.

Beauty contests started when the second woman arrived on earth.

"Brooks become crooked from taking the path of least resistance. So do people." Harold E. Kohn

Jeanie Braun, LeCenter Lioness Club
LeCenter, Minnesota, USA

MARY'S SUGAR COOKIE

1½ c. sifted confectioners sugar
1 c. butter or margarine
1 egg
1 tsp. vanilla

2½ c. flour
1 tsp. soda
1 tsp. cream of tartar

Mix sugar and butter; add egg and flavoring. Mix thoroughly. Measure flour by dipping method or by sifting. Stir dry ingredients together and blend in. Refrigerate 2 to 3 hours. Heat oven to 375° (quick medium). Divide dough in half and roll ³⁄₁₆ inch thick on lightly floured pastry cloth. Cut with cooky cutter. Sprinkle with sugar or colored sugar. Place on lightly greased baking sheet. Bake 7 to 8 minutes or until delicately golden. Makes 5 dozen.

So good and chewy - they make lovely Christmas cookies.

Shirley Canterbury, Eastmont Lions Club
East Wenatchee, Washington, USA

Be patient with everyone, but above all with yourself.

AUNT JANE'S SUGAR COOKIES

1 c. Crisco
2 c. sugar
2 eggs, beaten
¼ tsp. soda

1 tsp. salt
4 tsp. baking powder
5 c. flour

Cream Crisco and sugar. Add eggs and other ingredients. Add small amount of milk to make a batter. Drop by spoon on cookie sheet. Bake at 375° for 8 to 10 minutes.

In loving memory of Mary Hamilton.

Lion Susan Winland, Graysville/Proctor Lions Club
Moundsville, West Virginia, USA

❧

Giving is receiving ... receiving is giving.
That's really the secret that lies behind living.

❦ ❦ ❦

The average person was born in the country,
worked hard to live in the city,
then worked even harder to get back to the country.

❦ ❦ ❦

Advice is what we ask for when we already know the answer,
but wish we didn't.

BARS

APPLE BARS

½ c. margarine
1 c. sugar
1 egg, beaten
½ tsp. baking soda

½ tsp. cinnamon
1½ c. flour
2 c. raw apples, chopped

Topping:

½ c. brown sugar
½ tsp. cinnamon

½ c. chopped walnuts

Cream together margarine and sugar. Add beaten egg and dry ingredients, then stir in apples. Put in a 9x12 inch cake pan. Sprinkle with topping. Bake in a 350° oven for 20 to 30 minutes. Cool. Makes 15 squares.

APRICOT BARS

⅔ c. dried apricots
½ c. soft oleo
¼ c. sugar
½ tsp. baking powder
¼ tsp. salt

½ tsp. vanilla
1⅓ c. sifted flour
1 c. brown sugar, packed
2 eggs, well beaten
½ c. chopped almonds or nuts

Cover apricots with water. Simmer for 10 minutes. Drain, cool, and chop. Combine oleo, ¼ cup sugar, and 1 cup flour. Mix until crumbly. Pack into 9 inch square pan. Bake in a 350° oven for 20 minutes. Gradually beat brown sugar into beaten eggs. Sift together remaining flour, baking powder, and salt. Add to egg and brown sugar mixture. Mix well. Add vanilla, ¼ cup almonds or nuts, and apricots.

Spread on baked layer. Sprinkle top with remaining nuts. Bake in 350° oven about 20 minutes. Cool and cut into bars or 1½ inch squares. Dust with powdered sugar. Makes 30 bars.

When you aim for perfection, you discover it's a moving target.

APRICOT M-M-MUMBLES

Filling:

2½ c. chopped *whole* apricots
½ c. sugar
2 Tbsp. cornstarch

¾ c. water
3 Tbsp. *fresh* lemon juice

Crumb Mixture:

¾ c. butter, softened
1 c. packed brown sugar
1¾ c. sifted flour

½ tsp. salt
½ tsp. baking soda
1⅓ c. rolled oats (not instant)

Cook filling, stirring constantly over low heat till thickened (about 5 minutes). Cool.

Mix butter with sugar; add dry ingredients, then oats. Press half crumb mixture into greased pan (13x9x2 inches). Spread on filling. Pat on remaining crumbs. Bake at 400° for 20 to 30 minutes. Cool. Cut into bars.

Margaret Yingling (Mrs. Preston), Silver Run-Union Mills Lions Club
Westminster, Maryland, USA

BAKLAVA

10 thawed phyllo leaves
1 can butter-flavored cooking
   spray
¾ lb. chopped walnuts
1 tsp. cinnamon

2½ c. water
3 c. sugar
1 cinnamon stick
3 whole cloves

Spray roasting pan or lasagna pan or 9x13 inch pan. Keep phyllo under damp towel until ready to use. Spray liberally 5 sheets of phyllo and layer in pan, one at a time. Mix walnuts with cinnamon and spread in pan. Spray remaining phyllo and place over nuts. With sharp knife, cut into small diamonds (through all layers). Bake at 350° for ½ hour until golden brown. Cool thoroughly.

Syrup: Combine last 4 ingredients in saucepan and boil for 20 minutes briskly. Pour hot syrup over cool baklava. Let pan rest on counter for a day or two or until all syrup is absorbed. Serves 10 or more.

A true friend never gets in your way unless you happen to be going down.

BING CHERRY BARS

2 c. sugar
⅔ c. evaporated milk
⅛ tsp. salt
12 large marshmallows
½ c. margarine
1 (6 oz.) pkg. cherry chips

1 tsp. vanilla
1 (12 oz.) pkg. peanuts
¾ c. peanut butter
1 (12 oz.) pkg. chocolate chips
1 Tbsp. margarine

Combine in medium saucepan the sugar, evaporated milk, salt, large marshmallows, and ½ cup margarine. Cook over medium heat and boil 5 minutes. Remove from heat. Add cherry chips and vanilla. Mix together and pour in a 9x13 inch buttered pan. Let cool to room temperature.

Melt 12 ounces of chocolate chips and 1 tablespoon margarine in double boiler. Remove from heat; add 12 ounces of crushed peanuts and peanut butter. Mix together and pour over first layer. Let cool. Cut into 1 inch squares. Makes 90 pieces.

BROWNIES

2 c. sugar
1 c. butter or oleo
4 eggs
1 tsp. vanilla
Pinch of salt

½ c. evaporated milk
1 c. flour and 1 c. cocoa, mixed
    together
1 c. nuts

Cream sugar and butter or oleo together. Add eggs and beat well. Add vanilla, salt, and milk. Mix well. Add flour and cocoa mixture. Mix well and add nuts. Bake in 9x13 inch pan for 15 minutes at 350°, then 30 minutes at 325°.

Alma Lemm, Huffman Lions Club
Huffman, Texas, USA

BLONDE BROWNIES

1 box light brown sugar
3 eggs
1 c. chopped pecans

⅓ c. margarine
1½ c. self-rising flour
1 tsp. vanilla

Blend sugar and shortening; add eggs. Mix well. Add flour, nuts, and vanilla. Spread on greased pan. Bake at 350° for 30 minutes. Cut into squares.

Edna K. Bunch, Snow Hill Lions Club
Snow Hill, North Carolina, USA

A home is a house with a heart inside.

CHOCOLATE CHIP BROWNIES

1½ c. flour
1 tsp. baking powder
1 tsp. salt
2 c. sugar
½ c. cocoa

1¼ c. vegetable oil
4 eggs
2 tsp. vanilla
1 (12 oz.) pkg. chocolate chips
1 c. pecans, chopped

Preheat oven to 350°. Grease 9x13 inch cake pan. Measure all dry ingredients into a large mixing bowl. Add oil, eggs, and vanilla; stir slowly at first, then beat (by hand) well until you have a smooth dark brown batter. Add chocolate chips and chopped nuts; mix into batter. Bake 30 to 35 minutes. It will rise up and the top will be lumpy. Let it cool for 15 to 20 minutes, then cut. No need for a frosting - very moist delicious brownie.

Joan D. Utz, North Jackson Lions Club
Jackson, Michigan, USA

DIABETIC BROWNIES

3 oz. semi-sweet chocolate
  squares
2 c. fine graham cracker crumbs
½ c. chopped walnuts

2 tsp. liquid artificial sweetener
½ tsp. salt
1 c. skim milk

1. Preheat oven to 350°.
2. Melt chocolate in top of double boiler over boiling water.
3. Combine remainder of ingredients; add melted chocolate and stir until blended.
4. Turn into slightly greased pan.
5. Bake 30 minutes.
6. While warm, cut into 16 equal squares by dividing pan, 4x4 inches. Cool before removing from pan.

Terry Pister, Prince Albert Downtown Lioness Club
Prince Albert, Saskatchewan, Canada

❦

Words fall lightly as snow. They are easily, thoughtlessly said.
Yet hard words can enter the heart, and lie there as heavy as lead.

CREME DE MENTHE BROWNIES

Brownie ingredients:

1 c. flour
1 c. sugar
½ c. butter
1 tsp. vanilla

4 eggs, beaten
½ tsp. salt
1 (16 oz.) can Hershey's syrup
½ c. nuts (optional)

Middle layer:

2 c. 10X sugar
½ c. butter, softened

2 Tbsp. creme de menthe

Icing:

1 c. chocolate chips

6 Tbsp. butter

Mix brownie ingredients well and pour into a greased 13x9 inch pan. Bake at 350° for 30 minutes.

Middle: Mix together and spread on cooled brownies.

Icing: Melt together and cool slightly. Spread on brownies. Refrigerate until topping hardens. Cut into 1 inch squares.

Sue Hopkins (Mrs. John), Silver Run-Union Mills Lions Club
Westminster, Maryland, USA

He who has little and wants less is richer
than he who has much and wants more.

Opportunities are often missed
because we are talking when we should be listening.

CREME DE MENTHE BROWNIES

Bottom layer:

1 c. sugar
½ c. butter or margarine
4 beaten eggs
1 c. flour

⅛ tsp. salt
1 (16 oz.) can chocolate syrup
1 tsp. vanilla
½ c. chopped nuts

Mint layer:

2 c. powdered sugar
½ c. melted butter (or a little less)
1 Tbsp. water

Mint extract to taste
Green food color (or use 2 to 4
        Tbsp. creme de menthe)

Chocolate topping:

6 Tbsp. butter or margarine

1 c. chocolate chips

Mix ingredients for bottom layer and bake in 10x13 inch pan, greased, at 350° for 30 minutes. Cool.

Mix ingredients for mint layer and spread on brownie layer. Refrigerate until cold.

Melt chocolate chips and margarine. Pour on top of mint layer to cover completely. Cut before chocolate hardens.

"Wonderful." These are very rich and yummy!
Nancy Poole, Culver Community Lions Club
Culver, Oregon, USA

MOM'S BROWNIES

1⅓ c. flour
2 c. sugar
6 Tbsp. cocoa
½ tsp. salt
4 eggs

½ c. milk
1 tsp. vanilla
½ c. oil
½ c. nuts

Mix all ingredients until well blended. Bake in ungreased 9x13 inch pan at 350° for 25 to 30 minutes.

Nancy Fausett, Lyman Lions Club
Lyman, Wyoming, USA

❧

Information is pretty thin stuff unless mixed with experience.

FAMILY-SIZED BROWNIES

2 c. all-purpose flour
2 c. granulated sugar
½ c. (1 stick) butter or margarine
½ c. shortening
1 c. strong brewed coffee or water

¼ c. dark, unsweetened cocoa
½ c. buttermilk
2 eggs
1 tsp. baking soda
1 tsp. vanilla

Frosting:

½ c. (1 stick) butter or margarine
1 Tbsp. dark cocoa
¼ c. milk

3½ c. unsifted powdered sugar
1 tsp. vanilla

1. In a large mixing bowl, combine the flour and the sugar.

2. In heavy saucepan, combine butter, shortening, coffee or water, and cocoa. Stir and heat to boiling.

3. Pour boiling mixture over the flour and sugar in the bowl. Add the buttermilk, eggs, baking soda, and vanilla.

4. Mix well, using a wooden spoon or high speed on electric mixer.

5. Pour into a well-buttered 17½ x 11 inch jelly roll pan.

6. Bake at 400° for 20 minutes or until brownies test done in the center.

7. While brownies bake, prepare the frosting. In a saucepan, combine the butter, cocoa, and milk. Heat to boiling, stirring.

8. Mix in the powdered sugar and vanilla until frosting is smooth.

9. Pour warm frosting over brownies as soon as you take them out of the oven. Cool, then cut.

If you don't have buttermilk, substitute 2 teaspoons vinegar or lemon juice, mixed into ½ cup milk, or use powdered buttermilk. Mix according to package directions.

Janet Larson, Chesterfield Bay Lions Club
Chesterfield, Michigan, USA

"ALL-IN-A-PAN BROWNIES"

½ c. butter or margarine
½ c. cocoa
2 c. sugar
2 tsp. vanilla

4 eggs
¼ tsp. salt
1½ c. flour
1 c. nuts

In a medium size saucepan, melt butter or margarine. Remove pan from heat. Add sugar, eggs, and vanilla. Stir well. Add flour, salt, and cocoa. Mix until well blended; add nuts. Pour in a 9x13 inch pan that has been greased on the bottom or sprayed with a nonstick spray. Bake at 325° for 22 to 25 minutes. When cool, you may either sprinkle with sifted powdered sugar or frost with a chocolate frosting.

Michelle (Shelly) Robinson, Randall/Cushing Lioness Club
Cushing, Minnesota, USA

BROWNIES

6 sq. (6 oz.) unsweetened
   chocolate
¾ lb. butter
3 c. granulated sugar
½ c. flour (yes ½ c.)

6 whole eggs
3 tsp. vanilla extract
Fine cookie crumbs (vanilla
   wafers are a good choice)

Spray 10x14 inch pan with Pam. Dust with cookie crumbs. Repeat this twice. Set aside. Melt chocolate and butter in double boiler. Combine sugar and flour in mixing bowl. Pour chocolate-butter mix over flour mix and stir well to blend. Add vanilla. Add whole eggs, one at a time, beating well after each. Pour and spread into prepared pan. Bake in preheated oven at 325°F. for 1 hour. Cool several hours before trying to cut. They are even better "next week." If storing, store airtight in refrigerator.

Sent to me as "Industrial Strength Better Than Sex Brownies." I don't like the name, but these (slightly revised by me) are the best I've ever eaten.

Lion Vivian Quinlan, Mathews Lions Club
Mathews, Virginia, USA

CARAMEL-CHOCOLATE SQUARES

1 (14 oz.) pkg. caramels
1 (5 oz.) can evaporated milk
1 pkg. Betty Crocker German
   chocolate cake mix
⅔ c. melted margarine

¾ c. coarsely chopped pecans
1 (6 oz.) pkg. semi-sweet
   chocolate chips
1 c. flaked coconut

Heat oven to 350°. Melt caramels and ¼ cup milk over medium heat, stirring constantly. Keep this mixture warm and stir occasionally. Combine dry cake mix, melted margarine, pecans, and remaining milk. Spread ½ of dough mixture in bottom of ungreased 13x9x2 inch pan. Bake 6 minutes. Sprinkle chocolate chips and then coconut over the baked layer. Drizzle caramel mixture over the chocolate chips and coconut. Drop the remaining dough mixture by teaspoon onto caramel layer. Spread evenly by patting the dough around with your finger tips. Bake until cake mixture is dry to your touch, 15 to 20 minutes. Cool completely and refrigerate until firm. Cut into squares. Use 9x13 inch pan. Bake in 350° oven.

Becky Whitaker, Amarillo Centennial Lions Club
Amarillo, Texas, USA

❦

Do not let what you cannot do interfere with what you can do.

CARROT BARS

4 eggs, beaten
2 c. sugar
1½ c. Crisco oil
3 small jars strained baby carrot food

2½ c. flour
2½ tsp. soda
2 tsp. cinnamon
1 tsp. salt

Beat eggs; add sugar, oil, and carrot baby food. Mix well. Combine flour, soda, salt, and cinnamon; add to mixture. Bake on large cookie sheet at 350° for 20 to 25 minutes. Frost with Cream Cheese Frosting.

Cream Cheese Frosting:

1¾ c. powdered sugar
2 (3 oz.) pkg. cream cheese

6 Tbsp. margarine (soft)
1 tsp. vanilla

Mrs. Ron (Pat) Henne, Elburn Lions Club
Elburn, Illinois, USA

CHOCOLATE DESSERT BARS

1½ c. flour
1½ sticks margarine
¼ c. sugar
1 c. nuts, chopped
1 (8 oz.) pkg. cream cheese

1 c. powdered sugar
2 large Cool Whip
2 small boxes chocolate instant pudding
2½ c. milk

Mix together flour, margarine, sugar, and nuts. When thoroughly mixed (like pie dough), press into 9x13 inch pan and bake at 350° for 10 to 15 minutes. Cool completely. Beat together the cream cheese and 1 cup sugar, then, by hand, fold in 1 large Cool Whip. Spread this mixture on cooled crust. Blend together the 2 boxes of pudding mix and milk; put this on the cheese layer. Top the pudding layer with another container of Cool Whip and refrigerate until serving time.

Effa Maue, Onekama Lions Club
Onekama, Michigan, USA

CHOCOLATE AND OAT BARS

1 c. flour
1 c. quick oats
¾ c. brown sugar
½ c. butter, softened

1 (14 oz.) sweetened condensed milk
1 c. chopped nuts
1 (6 oz.) pkg. chocolate chips

Grease 9x12 inch cake pan. Preheat oven to 350°. Combine flour, oats, sugar, and oleo in bowl. Mix well. Reserve ½ of mixture and save. Press the rest of the mixture into bottom of pan. Bake this 10 minutes. Pour sweetened condensed milk over the baked crust. Sprinkle with nuts and chocolate chips. Top with remaining oat mixture and press it down. Bake 25 minutes until brown. Cool. Store at room temperature. Makes enough for 8 people.

CHOCO-NUT PIZZA

½ c. margarine
½ c. brown sugar
½ c. white sugar
½ c. peanut butter
½ tsp. vanilla

1 egg
1½ c. flour
2 c. miniature marshmallows
1 c. chocolate chips
No stick spray

Preheat oven to 375°. Combine and blend brown and white sugars, margarine, peanut butter, egg, and vanilla. Stir in flour to form dough. Spray 14 inch pizza pan. Any pan of equal size will do. Flatten dough ball in pan with lightly floured hands and press out dough to cover and form a shallow rim. Bake for 10 minutes. Remove from oven and sprinkle evenly with chocolate chips and marshmallows. Bake another 5 minutes. Allow to cool on pan, then cut into wedges. Makes 20 servings.

CONGO BARS

⅔ c. shortening
1 lb. brown sugar
3 eggs
2¾ c. flour
1 tsp. salt

1 c. nuts
1 (6 oz.) pkg. semi-sweet
  chocolate bits
1½ tsp. baking powder

Cream shortening and brown sugar. Add eggs and beat well. Sift together flour, baking powder, and salt; add to creamed mixture, then add the nuts and semi-sweet chocolate bits. Batter is very stiff. Spread on greased pan and bake at 350° for 25 to 30 minutes. Makes about 48 bars.

Edna K. Bunch, Snow Hill Lions Club
Snow Hill, North Carolina, USA

DATE BARS

1 c. flour
½ tsp. baking powder
¼ tsp. salt
⅓ c. butter
1 c. sugar
2 eggs

1 tsp. vanilla
1 tsp. grated orange peel
1 (8 oz.) pkg. pitted dates,
  quartered
½ c. coarsely chopped walnuts
Sugar

Preheat oven to 375°. Grease 9 inch square baking pan. Sift together flour, baking powder, and salt. In medium bowl with electric mixer at medium speed, beat butter with sugar until light and fluffy. Add eggs and vanilla; beat until well blended. At low speed, beat in flour mixture. Add peel, dates, and nuts. Turn batter into prepared pan. Bake for 25 to 30 minutes until golden brown. Remove pan to rack and cut into bars while hot. Sprinkle top with sugar. Cool in pan.

Dave Bernier, Westbrook Lions Club
Westbrook, Maine, USA

DISNEYLAND COOKIES

1 c. crushed graham crackers
½ c. melted butter
1 (7 oz.) can Angel Flake coconut
1 (6 oz.) bag butterscotch chips
1 (6 oz.) bag chocolate chips
1 can Eagle Brand milk
1 c. chopped nuts

Combine graham crackers and butter. Press into a 9x13 inch pan. Layer with coconut, butterscotch chips, and chocolate chips. Pour over Eagle Brand milk and sprinkle with nuts. Bake at 350° for 30 minutes. Very easy!!

Linda Lunn, Bakersfield Pioneer Lions Club
Bakersfield, California, USA

FARMER'S SQUARES

½ c. cocoa
1 c. hot water
¾ c. peanut butter
2½ c. flour
½ tsp. salt
2 c. white sugar
1 tsp. baking soda
2 eggs, beaten
½ c. buttermilk
1 tsp. vanilla
1 c. chopped nuts
1 pkg. miniature marshmallows
1 (12 oz.) pkg. chocolate chips
1 c. peanut butter
3 c. Rice Krispies

Mix together cocoa, hot water, and butter. Set aside to cool. Sift together dry ingredients and add alternately to above mixture with eggs and buttermilk. Fold in nuts. Bake in greased cookie sheet at 375° for 20 minutes. Spread miniature marshmallows on top of baked cake. Return to oven until melted, then cool. Mix together in double boiler chocolate chips and peanut butter. Stir in Rice Krispies and spread on cake.

Claude H. Ohlinger, Blandon Lions Club
Blandon, Pennsylvania, USA

❦

The impersonal hand of government can never replace
the helping hand of a neighbor.

FROSTED CREAM BARS

1 c. oleo
1½ c. sugar
2 eggs
1 tsp. vanilla
1 c. raisins
1 c. warm water which the raisins
   were cooked in

1 tsp. soda
2½ c. flour
1 tsp. salt
1 tsp. cinnamon

Cream oleo. Add sugar gradually and beat in eggs. Add vanilla. Bring raisins to boil in a generous cupful of water. Drain raisins and save the liquid. Measure 1 cup water in which raisins were cooked. While warm, add the soda. Sift dry ingredients and add alternately with raisin liquid. Add raisins. Bake in greased jelly roll pan at 350° for 25 to 30 minutes. Melt 2 tablespoons oleo and a little hot water; blend in 1 to 1½ cups powdered sugar and frost. Cut in bars. Real moist. Can be frozen.

Grace Long, Huffman Lioness Club
Huffman, Texas, USA

FUDGE NUT BARS

1 can Eagle Brand sweetened
   condensed milk
1 (12 oz.) pkg. milk chocolate
   chips
1 Tbsp. butter
½ tsp. salt
1 tsp. vanilla

½ c. nuts
1 c. brown sugar
½ c. butter
1 egg
½ tsp. soda
1½ c. oatmeal
1¼ c. flour

Melt together sweetened condensed milk, chocolate chips, 1 tablespoon butter, and ½ teaspoon salt. When melted, add 1 teaspoon vanilla and ½ cup nuts. Mix together 1 cup brown sugar, ½ cup butter, 1 egg, ½ teaspoon soda, 1½ cups oatmeal, and 1¼ cups flour. Save 1 cup of this mixture. Pat remaining mixture in greased pan. Spread on the chocolate mixture. Take the cup of mixture and dot on top. Bake at 350° for 20 to 25 minutes.

Lion Theresa Hill, Hector Lions Club
Hector, Minnesota, USA

GRANOLA BARS

3½ c. oatmeal
1 c. raisins
⅔ c. lowfat margarine
½ c. brown sugar

1 beaten egg white
½ tsp. vanilla
½ tsp. salt
⅓ c. honey

Toast oatmeal 14 minutes in 350° oven. Combine with remaining ingredients. Press into 10x15 inch jelly roll pan. Bake 20 minutes at 350°. Makes 24 bars.

HEATH BARS

1 pkg. club crackers
1 c. butter

1 c. brown sugar
12 oz. semi-sweet chocolate chips

Boil butter and brown sugar together slowly for 5 minutes. Line jelly roll pan with foil up the sides. Cover with crackers (do not break apart). Pour boiled mixture over crackers; spread evenly. Bake at 400° for 5 minutes. Remove from oven. Pour chips over hot bars. Let melt, then spread evenly. Cool and allow to harden. Serve broken pieces.

Joyce Peterson, Brownton Lions Club
Brownton, Minnesota, USA

HEATH BARS

1 c. butter
1 c. margarine
1 c. sugar

1 bag miniature chocolate chips
½ c. chopped walnuts (optional
   for topping)

Cook butter, margarine, and sugar over medium high heat until mixture is a golden brown. (Mixture will separate, then blend back together.) Pour into 10x7 inch buttered tin pan. Immediately sprinkle chips on top. Spread evenly with a knife. Allow to cool thoroughly.

Stacey Anderson, Westbrook Lions Club
Westbrook, Maine, USA

HELLO DOLLIES

1 stick butter (or margarine)
1 c. graham cracker crumbs
1 small can coconut
1 small (6 oz.) pkg. chocolate
   chips

½ c. pecans
1 can condensed sweetened milk

Melt butter (margarine) in 9 inch pan. Cover with graham cracker crumbs, then with coconut, then with chocolate chips, then pecans. Spread condensed milk evenly over all. Bake at 350° for 35 to 40 minutes.

Anna Hillis, McMinnville Lions Club
McMinnville, Tennessee, USA

❦

You will never find a better sparring partner than adversity.

ANYTIME HOLIDAY BARS

1½ c. sugar
1 c. real butter
4 eggs
2 c. flour

1 Tbsp. lemon juice
1 can Solo filling or pie filling
Powdered sugar

Grease and flour jelly roll pan. Cream butter and sugar. Add eggs and lemon juice. Slowly add flour. Spread in jelly roll pan (batter will be thick). With knife, score 24 squares in batter (4 the long way and 6 the short way). Drop 1 teaspoon filling in center of each square. Bake at 350° for 35 to 40 minutes. Sprinkle with powdered sugar while still warm. This is real easy to make and not time-consuming.

Mrs. Bill (Jan) Callaghan, Elburn Lions Club
Elburn, Illinois, USA

LEMON ANGEL BARS

1 box 1 step angel food cake mix   1 can lemon pie filling

Mix the 2 ingredients together with mixer. Put in ungreased jelly roll pan. Bake at 350° for 25 to 30 minutes. Frost with a glaze. This is such a simple recipe and good.

Judy Stork, Arlington Lions Club
Arlington, Nebraska, USA

LINZER TORTE BARS

½ c. slivered almonds
1 c. all-purpose flour
½ c. regular, instant, or quick
   Cream of Wheat cereal
⅓ c. sugar

½ tsp. baking powder
⅓ c. margarine, melted
1 egg
½ c. seedless raspberry
   preserves

In food processor or electric blender, finely grind almonds. In large bowl, mix almonds, flour, cereal, sugar, and baking powder; stir in margarine and egg until crumbly. Reserve ½ cup dough. Press remaining dough on bottom of 9 x 9 x 2 inch baking pan. Spread raspberry preserves to within 1 inch of dough edges. Crumble remaining dough over preserves. Bake at 375°F. for 25 to 30 minutes or until golden brown. Cool completely on wire rack. Cut into 3 x 1½ inch bars. Very good.

Mary J. Card, Amarillo Downtown Lions Club
Amarillo, Texas, USA

❧

Pleasant thoughts make pleasant lives.

MOLASSES RAISIN BAR

1 c. shortening
2 c. sugar
4 eggs
2 c. molasses
8 c. flour

6 tsp. baking powder
1 tsp. salt
1 tsp. baking soda
2 c. canned milk
4 c. raisins

Cream shortening. Add sugar and beat until light. Add beaten eggs. Mix with dry ingredients and add a little at a time with milk. Add fruits and raisins last. Spread very thin in shallow pan. Bake in moderate oven 15 to 20 minutes.

Evelyn Steele, Lyman Lions Club
Lyman, Wyoming, USA

NUT BARS

¼ lb. (1 stick) margarine
2 c. brown sugar
2 eggs, well beaten
2 c. cake flour

1 tsp. baking powder
1 tsp. vanilla
1 c. nuts

Heat butter and brown sugar; blend well. Set aside. After mixture is cool, add well beaten eggs to mixture. Sift cake flour and baking powder; add to mixture. Add vanilla and blend well. Fold in nuts. Bake 1 hour in slow oven (300°). Roll in confectioners sugar after nut bars cool for about 45 minutes. Cut bars in 2 inch pieces.

Ruth Ann Montgomery, Moweaqua Lions Club
Moweaqua, Illinois, USA

ORANGE ZUCCHINI BARS

1½ c. flour
¾ c. sugar
1 tsp. soda
½ tsp. salt
1 tsp. cinnamon
1 tsp. baking powder

1 egg, lightly beaten
1 Tbsp. grated orange peel
1 c. zucchini, grated and drained
1 (6 oz.) can orange juice
¼ c. oil
½ c. nuts, chopped

Mix together flour, sugar, soda, salt, cinnamon, and baking powder. Set aside. In another bowl, combine the lightly beaten egg, grated orange peel, grated zucchini, orange juice, and oil. Fold in dry ingredients with the nuts. Bake in a greased 9x13 inch pan at 350° for 30 to 35 minutes. Cool and frost with Orange Icing.

Orange Icing:

1½ c. powdered sugar
¼ c. soft margarine
½ tsp. grated orange peel

Enough orange juice to make
spreading consistency

Serves 12 to 16.

PEANUT BUTTER CRISPS

1 c. sugar
¼ tsp. salt
4 c. Rice Krispies cereal

1 c. light corn syrup
2 c. peanut butter

Combine sugar, corn syrup, and salt. Cook and stir until sugar is dissolved. Remove from stove and blend in peanut butter, then stir in cereal. Pat evenly into a foil-lined 15x10x1 inch pan. Let cool.

Icing:

4 Tbsp. margarine
¼ c. packed brown sugar
1 Tbsp. milk

½ tsp. vanilla
1¼ c. powdered sugar

In small saucepan, melt margarine and brown sugar; remove from heat. Add milk, vanilla, and powdered sugar; beat until smooth. Remove cereal mixture from pan onto flat surface; peel off foil. Spread top with frosting. Chill, then cut in bars.

PDG Lloyd E. Wright, Georgetown Lions Club
Georgetown, Ohio, USA

SALTED PEANUT CHEWS

Crust:

1½ c. flour
⅔ c. firmly packed brown sugar
½ tsp. baking powder
½ tsp. salt
¼ tsp. baking soda

½ c. margarine, softened
1 tsp. vanilla
2 egg yolks
3 c. miniature marshmallows

Topping:

⅔ c. corn syrup
¼ c. margarine
2 tsp. vanilla
1 (12 oz.) pkg. (2 c.) peanut butter
    chips

2 c. crisp rice cereal
2 c. salted peanuts

Heat oven to 350°F. Lightly spoon flour into measuring cup; level off. In large bowl, combine all crust ingredients, except marshmallows, on low speed until crumbly. Press firmly in bottom of ungreased 13x9 inch pan. Bake at 350°F. for 12 to 15 minutes or until light golden brown. Immediately sprinkle with marshmallows. Return to oven for 1 to 2 minutes or until marshmallows just begin to puff. Cool while preparing topping.

In large saucepan, heat corn syrup, ¼ cup margarine, 2 teaspoons vanilla, and peanut butter chips just until chips are melted and mixture is smooth, stirring constantly. Remove from heat; stir in cereal and nuts. Immediately spoon warm topping over marshmallows and spread to cover. Cool. Cut into bars. Makes 36 bars.

PEANUT BUTTER FINGERS

½ c. butter or margarine	½ tsp. vanilla flavoring
½ c. sugar	1 c. flour
1 c. brown sugar, packed	1 c. quick cooking oats
1 egg (unbeaten)	1 c. chocolate chips
⅓ c. peanut butter	½ c. powdered sugar
½ tsp. soda	¼ c. peanut butter
¼ tsp. salt	2 to 4 Tbsp. milk

Cream butter and add sugar, creaming well. Blend in egg, peanut butter, soda, salt, and vanilla. Add flour and oats. Mix thoroughly. Spread in greased 13x9 inch pan. Bake at 350° for 20 to 25 minutes until lightly browned. Sprinkle immediately with chocolate chips and let stand 5 minutes.

Combine ½ cup powdered sugar, ¼ cup peanut butter, and 2 to 4 table-spoons milk. Mix well. Spread melted chocolate chips evenly. Drizzle with peanut butter mixture. Cool and cut into squares.

Howard Cook, Snively 43N Lions Club
Louisville, Kentucky, USA

PEANUT BUTTER LOGS

1 c. coconut	1 c. crushed graham crackers
1 box confectioners sugar	1 (12 oz.) bag chocolate semi-
1 c. pecans	sweet morsels
1 c. crunchy peanut butter	1 block paraffin wax
2 sticks margarine, softened	

Mix together well the coconut, confectioners sugar, pecans, peanut butter, margarine, and graham crackers. Put in refrigerator for 5 minutes. Take out and roll in small rolls. Melt the chocolate morsels and the wax in a double boiler. Dip each piece in the chocolate mixture and place on wax paper. Makes several small logs.

Bertha Smith, President, Parkway Lions Club
Panama City, Florida, USA

The easiest way to get a healthy body is to marry one.

TWICE BAKED PECAN SQUARES

½ c. butter or oleo, softened
½ c. firmly packed dark brown
  sugar
1 c. all-purpose flour
2 eggs
1 c. firmly packed light brown
  sugar

1 c. coarsely chopped pecans
½ c. flaked coconut
2 Tbsp. all-purpose flour
1 tsp. vanilla extract
Pinch of salt
Powdered sugar

Combine butter and dark brown sugar, creaming until light and fluffy. Add 1 cup flour and mix well. Press evenly into a 13x9x2 inch pan, greased. Bake at 350° for 20 minutes. Beat eggs until frothy. Gradually add light brown sugar, beating until smooth and thickened. Combine pecans, coconut, and 2 tablespoons flour. Stir well. Combine egg mixture, nut mixture, vanilla, and salt. Mix well and spread evenly over crust. Bake at 350° for 20 minutes or until golden brown. Let cool. Sprinkle lightly with powdered sugar and cut into squares. Makes 3 to 4 dozen.

Pauline Sammons
Waldo, Arkansas, USA

QUICK FORTY-NINERS

4 eggs
1 lb. box brown sugar

2 c. Bisquick mix
2 c. chopped pecans

Beat eggs. Beat in sugar and add Bisquick mix. Stir in pecans. Bake in greased 13x9x2 inch pan 35 minutes at 325°. Loosen from sides of pan while warm. Let cool; cut into 48 squares.

Helen Fullerton, Huffman Lions Club
Huffman, Harris, Texas, USA

RASPBERRY SKOR BARS

2 c. flour
2 Tbsp. sugar
¾ c. butter or margarine
½ c. finely chopped walnuts or
  pecans

⅓ c. orange juice
4 (14 oz.) Skor candy bars
Raspberry preserves

Sift together flour, sugar, and salt. Cut butter or margarine into dry ingredients until mixture resembles fine crumbs. Stir in nuts. Add orange juice and mix until dough forms. Divide into 4 portions. Roll each piece of dough onto lightly floured board into a rectangle about 1 inch longer than length of Skor bar and 4 inches wide. Spoon 2 to 3 teaspoons raspberry preserves on center of each dough portion. Cut Skor bar into chunks and place 1 bar on top of preserves on each portion. Fold over and seal on top and ends. Place on greased cookie sheet with fold down. Bake until dough is lightly browned. Bake at 375° for 20 to 30 minutes. While only slightly warm, cut each roll into 8 or 9 pieces. Yield is approximately 32 to 36 bars, depending on size of cuts.

SPECIAL "K" BARS

1 c. brown sugar
1 c. peanut butter
1 c. white syrup

1 Tbsp. butter or margarine
6 c. Special "K" cereal

Bring first 4 ingredients to a boil over medium heat. Boil for 2 minutes. In large bowl, mix the 6 cups Special "K" cereal and boiled mixture until well blended, then spread mixture in 9x13 inch pan, buttered. Cool.

Optional: Frost with ½ cup chocolate chips and ½ cup peanut butter.

RaNaye Baumgarten, Brownton Lions Club
Brownton, Minnesota, USA

HOMEMADE TRIX CANDY BARS

1 lb. chocolate flavored bark,
   melted in microwave
1 lb. caramels, melted in
   microwave

1 sack pretzel logs, broken into 2
   to 3 inch pieces
Chopped nuts (if desired)

Melt your caramels in the microwave. Break your pretzel logs into 3 pieces (so that they are approximately 2 to 3 inches long). Dip your pretzels into the caramel. Place on buttered wax paper. After the caramel sets, drop into the chocolate flavored bark that has been melted. Place on buttered wax paper. (May roll into the chopped nuts if desired.)

I make these for my student workers and needless to say, they disappear in a hurry. Since I work and go to school, I need short cut recipes, so I make them quite often for my student workers.

Lois Sanner, Moweaqua Lions Club
Moweaqua, Illinois, USA

❦

"Merry" is a word for Christmas. "Happy" is a word for New Year's.
"Thanks" is a word for all year long.

CANDIES

APPLETS CANDY

1 c. applesauce
1 pkg. apple Jell-O
1 c. sugar

½ c. nuts (walnuts)
¼ tsp. vanilla
Powdered sugar

Note: Apricots and apricot Jell-O may be substituted.

Heat applesauce to boiling. Add Jell-O and sugar; stir until dissolved. Add nuts and vanilla. Pour into buttered pan. When set hard, cut and dip pieces in powdered sugar.

Note: Applets candy was developed in the State of Washington.

An apple a day keeps the doctor away.

Lion Kathleen Schatz Dague, Aurora Eastgate Lions Club
Aurora, Colorado, USA

DATE AND NUT CHEWS

2 eggs
¾ tsp. salt
½ tsp. almond extract
½ c. sugar
½ c. Karo syrup

1 c. dates, cut fine
1 c. chopped nutmeats
¾ c. sifted flour
⅓ c. confectioners sugar

Place eggs in a large bowl. Add salt and almond extract. Beat until light. Gradually beat in sugar and Karo syrup. Add dates and nuts; mix well. Fold in flour. Pour into 2 greased 8 inch layer cake pans. Bake in moderate oven at 350° for 20 to 25 minutes. Remove from oven and immediately cool and mix mixture up. Cool only until you can handle dough. Roll in hands into small balls 1 inch or less in size. Roll in confectioners sugar. Makes 3 dozen. These cookies keep remarkably well when stored in a tightly covered can or jar.

Zeta L. Adams, Craigsville Lions Club
Craigsville, West Virginia, USA

STRAWBERRY DIVINITY

3 c. sugar
¾ c. water
¾ c. white corn syrup

2 egg whites
½ pkg. cherry Jell-O
½ c. nuts

Combine sugar, syrup, and water. Bring to boil over low heat. Cook to hard ball (250°). Beat whites stiff. Add Jell-O, 1 tablespoon at a time. Beat until peak forms. Pour syrup in fine stream over beaten eggs. Beat until mixture stands in peak and loses gloss. Add nuts. Drop on wax paper.

Brooksy Stamper, Huffman Lioness Club
Huffman, Texas, USA

STRAWBERRY CHEWS

1 lb. coconut, ground fine in a food processor
¼ lb. ground almonds (do as coconut)
Dash of salt
6 oz. pkg. strawberry Jell-O (less 2 Tbsp.)
1 Tbsp. sugar
1 can sweetened condensed milk
½ tsp. vanilla
3 oz. pkg. strawberry Jell-O for rolling

Can add additional red food coloring if desired.

Add all ingredients, except 3 ounce package of Jell-O. Mix well. Shape into berry shapes with your hand. Roll in the 3 ounce package Jell-O plus the 2 tablespoons of Jell-O from the 6 ounce package. Use a tube of green icing (made for cake decorations to make green leaves and a stem on each berry). I'm not good with cake decorations so I use an almond for the stem. These are out of the world good. Looks so pretty for a tea or reception.

Dora T. Poythress, Lawrenceville Lioness Club
Lawrenceville, Virginia, Brunswick County, USA

BEST CARAMELS EVER

1 c. granulated sugar
¾ c. white Karo syrup
1 dash of salt
1½ c. heavy whipping cream

Cook to firm ball stage. Pour into buttered Pyrex dish. Cool, then cut into small squares and wrap individually with waxed paper.

Lee Seybold, Moweaqua Lions Club
Moweaqua, Illinois, USA

SEAFOAM CANDY

3 c. sugar
1 c. water
½ c. dark syrup
2 egg whites
1 tsp. vanilla
½ c. nuts

Boil to a thread. Pour syrup into 2 egg whites, beaten stiff. Continue beating until mixture begins to get stiff. Add flavoring and nuts. Drop by teaspoons onto greased platter. Cool. This was given to me by Mother's old friend, Mrs. Evelyn S. Bunch of Edenton, North Carolina.

Glenn E. Bunch, Jr., Snow Hill Lions Club
Snow Hill, North Carolina, USA

When embracing opportunity, give it a big hug.

MARSHMALLOW ROLLS

1 egg, well beaten
4 sq. semi-sweet chocolate
25 quartered marshmallows
  (colored)

½ jar cherries, cut up
1 c. icing sugar
2 tsp. margarine
1 c. walnuts

Mix egg, melted chocolate, and margarine. Add sugar, then nuts, cherries, and marshmallows. Roll and put in fridge.

If a wee bit sticky when you cut it, first roll whole roll in fine coconut.

To keep stove front lint free, wipe with rubbing alcohol and lint free cloth.
Dianne Crayston, Jasper Mountain Lions Club
Jasper, Alberta, Canada

CHOCOLATE MARSHMALLOWS

1 can Eagle Brand milk
1 (7 oz.) jar marshmallow creme
3 small pkg. chocolate chips
½ tsp. salt

1 c. chopped pecans
1½ lb. large marshmallows
1 tsp. vanilla

In double boiler, melt chips. Add other ingredients, except marshmallows. Into the warm mixture, dip individual large marshmallows. Dry on oiled waxed paper. Can be put in refrigerator to set.

Janie Fox, Saginaw Lions Club
Saginaw, Texas, USA

CHOCOLATE BALLS

1 cube butter (½ c.)
2 lb. powdered sugar
Pinch of salt
1 can sweetened Eagle Brand milk

1 tsp. vanilla
1 c. chopped nuts, coarsely
  chopped

Sift powdered sugar. Cut in butter (no substitutes). Add rest of ingredients. Mix well (with hands). Refrigerate 3 or 4 hours. Roll into small balls (about size of large hazelnut). Set back in refrigerator 2 hours. Stick toothpick in cream ball and dip in chocolate. Top with nut.

Chocolate: Melt over hot water 2 cups chocolate chips and ¾ bar paraffin wax. *Excellent.*

Bess Jones, South Benton Lions Club
Monroe, Oregano, USA

❧

Today is a once-in-a-lifetime opportunity that comes every day!

CHOCOLATE PEPPERMINT ROLL

6 oz. semi-sweet chocolate
3 Tbsp. water
½ c. sugar
6 eggs, separated
1 tsp. vanilla

¼ c. cocoa
1½ oz. red and white peppermint
   candy (about nine 1 inch
   round candy pieces)
1 large ctn. Cool Whip

Heat oven to 400°. Line an 11x15 inch pan with aluminum foil; grease foil generously. In heavy pan, melt the chocolate in the water over very low heat. Stir in sugar. Off the heat, beat in egg yolks with wooden spoon. Stir in vanilla. Beat egg whites to stiff peaks and stir about ¼ into chocolate mixture. Fold in remaining whites. Gently spread into pan. Bake 8 minutes. Remove and cover with a damp cloth. Let cool 10 minutes. Turn out onto a strip of plastic wrap over the end of the rectangle and roll. Cover loosely with a damp cloth. Cool 15 minutes. Crush candy in food processor and fold into Cool Whip. Unroll and spread with mixture. Roll again. Cover and refrigerate. Cut into 1 inch slices. Serves 8.

O'HENRY'S

1½ c. sugar
1½ c. Karo syrup (light)
12 oz. chunky peanut butter

6 oz. Special K cereal
6 oz. chocolate bits
6 oz. butterscotch bits

Boil syrup and sugar until sugar is melted. Stir in peanut butter. Fold in cereal and spread in a buttered jelly roll pan, using a buttered spatula. Melt bits in top of double boiler. Spread on top of cereal mix, using a buttered spatula. Cut into 1 inch squares, using an axe if you are weak. Fantastic. My granddaughter, Jill, omits the bits altogether.

After sharing a plate of thinly-sliced peeled green mango, which we dipped into a fiery mix of hot Thai peppers, salt, and other mysterious ingredients, with my daughter-in-law, Diethong, from Thailand, she remarked, "I like you Mom. You eat what I make and not say yuck!"

"I've been a cook and at-home caterer most of my life. Now retired, I'm a Lion and so proud of it I could burst."

Vivian Quinlan, Mathews Lions Club
Mathews, Virginia, USA

❦

There are no shortcuts to any place worth going.

ENGLISH TOFFEE

3 c. sugar
1 lb. butter (must be butter)
1½ to 2 c. chopped pecans
3 Tbsp. light corn syrup

3 Tbsp. water
2 (11 oz.) Nestle milk chocolate
  morsels

You must have a candy thermometer. Cook sugar, butter, pecans, corn syrup, and water until it reaches 300° on the thermometer. Grease 2 large cookie sheets with Pam. Spread cooked mixture thinly onto cookie sheets. Melt one bag of morsels and spread over both pans of toffee. Refrigerate until chocolate hardens. Melt second bag of morsels. Turn the candy over and frost. Refrigerate several hours and then break into pieces.

Mrs. Charlotte M. Garner, Pascagoula Evening Lions Club
Pascagoula, Mississippi, USA

ENGLISH TOFFEE

1 c. sugar
1 c. butter
3 Tbsp. water
½ c. finely chopped nuts
  (optional)

1 (7 oz.) chocolate bar
½ c. finely chopped nuts (walnuts
  or pecans)

Combine sugar, butter, and water over medium heat, stirring until mixture reaches hard crack stage (310°). Mix in ½ cup nuts (optional). Pour onto greased cookie sheet. While still hot, place chocolate bar on top and spread. Sprinkle with ½ cup nuts. When cold, break into pieces.

Do not substitute butter!

Barb Allison, Moweaqua Lions Club
Moweaqua, Illinois, USA

PECAN CANDY

1 tsp. vanilla
2 c. sugar
2 Tbsp. corn syrup

⅔ c. sweet milk
1 c. pecans

Cook sugar, corn syrup, and sweet milk until mixture forms a ball instantly in cold water. Add vanilla and pecans. Stir well. Pour into buttered pan or dish. Cool.

Bertha Smith, President, Parkway Lions Club
Panama City, Florida, USA

Every day holds the possibility of miracles.

CHEWY PRALINES

2 c. sugar
2 c. white corn syrup
1 lb. butter

2 c. whipping cream
2 tsp. vanilla
7 c. pecans

Over medium low heat, cook sugar and corn syrup. Cook until candy thermometer reaches 250°. Remove from heat. Add butter. Stir until dissolved. Add whipping cream slowly. Return to heat and cook until heat reaches 242° and remove from heat. Add vanilla and pecans. Put on buttered foil. Wrap in Saran Wrap.

I made this for a Lions meeting and the guys were carrying them out in their pockets and wanting more.

Shirley Ward, Levelland Lions Club
Levelland, Texas, USA

RUM OR BOURBON BALLS

1 (6 oz.) semi-sweet chocolate
   morsels
½ c. sugar
3 Tbsp. light corn syrup

⅓ c. rum or bourbon
2½ c. finely crushed vanilla wafers
1 c. finely chopped walnuts
Confectioners sugar

Melt chocolate over hot, not boiling, water. Remove from water and stir in sugar and syrup. Blend in rum or bourbon. Combine wafers and nuts. Add to chocolate mixture, mixing well. Form into 1 inch balls and roll in confectioners sugar. Let ripen in tightly covered container at least several days. Makes about 4½ dozen.

Dave Bernier, Westbrook Lions Club
Westbrook, Maine, USA

BOURBON BALLS

2 c. vanilla wafer crumbs
2 c. chopped nuts
2 c. sifted 10X sugar

¼ c. cocoa
3 Tbsp. light syrup
¼ c. plus 2 Tbsp. bourbon

Combine together all ingredients. Shape into 1 inch balls. Roll in 10X sugar. Makes about 6 dozen.

Mrs. Alberta Hopkins, Silver Run-Union Mills Lions Club
Westminster, Maryland, USA

❧

The only true gift is a portion of thyself.

PEANUT BUTTER CHEWS

1 c. sugar
1 c. Karo light syrup
1 c. peanut butter

1 Tbsp. butter
6 c. corn flakes

Bring to a boil 1 cup sugar and 1 cup Karo light syrup. Remove from heat. Stir in 1 cup peanut butter and 1 tablespoon butter. Pour over 6 cups corn flakes. Mix and drop by spoonful on a buttered cookie sheets. Cool. Makes approximately 25.

Mrs. Helen Gibiser, South Whitehall, Inc., Lions Club
Allentown, Pennsylvania, USA

PEANUT BUTTER BALLS

2 c. peanut butter
2 c. crushed graham crackers

1½ c. confectioners sugar

Chocolate Mixture:

¼ stick paraffin wax

1 large pkg. chocolate chips

Work this together in a deep bowl with your hands until it sticks together. Form into small balls. Dip into chocolate mixture and place on wax paper. Melt mixture over hot water.

Dave Bernier, Westbrook Lions Club
Westbrook, Maine, USA

PEANUT BUTTER EGGS

½ c. butter or margarine, softened
2 c. confectioners sugar
1 c. peanut butter (can use
    chunky, too)
½ c. ground pecans (this is
    optional)

½ tsp. vanilla
1 (12 oz.) pkg. semi-sweet
    chocolate chips
⅓ bar paraffin

In large bowl, combine butter, sugar, peanut butter, pecans, and vanilla; mix well. Refrigerate until firm, about 1 hour. Shape heaping teaspoons of mixture 1 inch long. Refrigerate about 1 hour. Mix chocolate chips with paraffin in top of double boiler. Dip egg mixture in chocolate carefully. Place on wax paper. Store in airtight container. Can be decorated with a cute flower, etc.

Our Ladies Aux. of the LVFD made these one year for Easter and sold them for a money-making project. A lot of work but it paid off. (Great for grandchildren gifts.)

Lioness Dora T. Poythress, Lawrenceville Lioness Club
Lawrenceville, Virginia (Brunswick County), USA

PEANUT BUTTER CANDY

2 sticks unsalted butter
2 c. graham cracker crumbs
2 c. confectioners sugar

1 c. chunky peanut butter
8 oz. Hershey's milk chocolate

Line an 8 inch square cake pan as follows: Turn pan over. Cover with 12 inch square of aluminum foil, shiny side down. Fold down the sides and corners to shape the foil. Remove the foil. Turn pan over again and place foil in pan, pressing carefully to fit smoothly. Set aside.

Melt butter. In large bowl, with wooden spatula, mix butter with crumbs, sugar, and peanut butter. Turn into lined pan. With bottom of teaspoon, smooth mixture to make an even layer. Let stand at room temperature.

Break up chocolate and place it in the top of a medium size double boiler over hot water over low heat (or use electric chafing dish). Cover with folded paper towel (to absorb steam) and the pot lid. Let stand a few minutes until chocolate is partly melted, then uncover and stir until completely melted and smooth. Remove top of double boiler (dry its underside) and pour chocolate onto the peanut butter layer.

With bottom of teaspoon, smooth the chocolate over the bottom layer, touching the sides of the foil. Refrigerate for at least an hour or until firm. Lift candy, still on foil, on a cutting board. Fold down sides of foil. Let stand 1 hour, then cut into 32 small bars. Serve at room temperature. Makes 32 bars.

PEANUT BUTTER BONBONS

1 (12 oz.) jar peanut butter
1 (2 lb.) bag powdered sugar
3 sticks oleo
1½ bags (12 oz.) butterscotch
   chips

¾ bar paraffin wax
Toothpicks

Combine peanut butter, powdered sugar, and oleo together. When fully mixed, form into little balls (size of quarters). After forming balls, melt butterscotch chips and wax in the top of double boiler, then dip balls into mixture of chips and wax (coat completely) by using toothpicks. Makes approximately 100 bonbons.

Toni Provoast, Whittemore Lions Club
Whittemore, Michigan, USA

❧

Few wishes come true by themselves.

OLD-FASHIONED PEANUT BRITTLE

2 c. sugar
1 c. light corn syrup
½ c. water
¼ c. butter or margarine

2 c. raw peanuts
1 tsp. baking soda
About 2 c. unsweetened ribbon
   coconut (optional)

In 3 quart saucepan, heat together sugar, corn syrup, and water, stirring until sugar dissolves. When syrup boils, blend in butter or margarine. Stir frequently after temperature reaches 230°. Add peanuts when temperature reaches 280°. Stir constantly to hard crack stage, 305°. (Just before the soda is stirred in, the coconut may be mixed in.) Remove from heat. Quickly stir in soda, mixing well. Pour onto 2 buttered cookie sheets. Loosen from pans when candy hardens and cools. Break into pieces. Makes 2½ pounds.

PEANUT BRITTLE

2 c. sugar
1 c. white Karo

½ c. water

Stir together and boil to soft ball stage (without stirring).

Add:

1 tsp. salt
1 tsp. butter

1 lb. raw peanuts

Cook, stirring constantly, until reaches hard crack stage. Remove from heat. Add 1 teaspoon vanilla and 1 teaspoon soda. Stir until mixed well and pour on buttered cooky sheets (2). Thin out with table knife. Cool and break up.

Corky Pedersen
Cuba, Illinois, USA

❧

Though no one can go back and make a new start,
anyone can start from now and make a brand-new end.

DIXIE PEANUT BRITTLE

1½ c. raw shelled Spanish
    peanuts (skins on)
1 c. granulated sugar
½ c. light corn syrup

⅛ tsp. salt
1 tsp. butter
1 tsp. vanilla pure extract
1 tsp. baking soda

Stir together peanuts, sugar, corn syrup, and salt in a 2 quart microwave-safe container. Cook on 100% power (HIGH) for 8 minutes, stirring well after 4 minutes. (Cooking time may vary with ovens.) Stir in butter and vanilla. Cook on HIGH 2 minutes longer. Add baking soda and quickly stir until light and foamy. (For safety's sake, keep in mind that the mixture will dramatically increase in volume and could spill over the sides of the container.) Immediately pour onto lightly greased baking sheet. Spread to ¼ inch thickness. When cool, break into pieces. Store in an airtight container. Makes 1 pound.

Placing aluminum foil under the napkin in your bread basket helps keep rolls warm.

Mrs. Charlotte M. Garner, Pascagoula Evening Lions Club
Pascagoula, Mississippi, USA

SUE'S PEANUT BRITTLE

2 c. raw peanuts
1½ c. sugar
½ c. syrup (Golden Eagle
    preferred)

½ c. water
½ stick margarine
Dash of salt
2 tsp. baking soda

Cook all ingredients (except soda) over medium heat until dissolved and until it begins to boil, slightly stirring same. Reduce heat a little. Set timer for 25 minutes. Stir occasionally. Cook candy until it reaches the fine hair stage.* Remove from heat, stir in soda, pour, and spread in a greased pan. Cool. Break into pieces, eat, and enjoy.

* Fine hair stage: Hold spoon with a little of mixture up over pan. Slowly let roll a little over side of spoon like a fine strand of hair. When the strand holds and forms like a fine hair, it is correct stage.

Bertha Smith, Parkway Lions Club
Panama City, Florida, USA

Every private citizen has a public responsibility.

PEANUT BUTTER BRITTLE

1½ c. granulated sugar	1 tsp. vanilla
1½ c. light corn syrup	1 tsp. soda
¼ c. water	2 tsp. water
2 Tbsp. butter	1½ to 1 c. peanut butter
2 c. salted peanuts	

In 2 quart saucepan, cook syrup, sugar, and water to 275°F. Remove thermometer. Lower heat to medium. Add butter. Stir until dissolved. Add salted nuts all at once and stir constantly for 5 minutes over medium heat, placing thermometer back in candy. Continue to cook until brittle is brown (300°F.). Remove from heat or fire and add 1½ or 2 cups peanut butter. Mix well. Add soda which has been added to the water and vanilla. Pour on well greased marble slab or Formica table top. I warm my peanuts and peanut butter in a oven set on warm and also warm the slab or table top with a hot towel or heating pad.

Shirley Canterbury, Eastmont Lions Club
East Wenatchee, Washington, USA

PEANUT BUTTER FUDGE

2 c. white sugar	½ c. marshmallow fluff
½ c. milk	½ c. peanut butter
Piece of butter (size of walnut)	2 tsp. vanilla

Mix and cook until mixture forms a soft ball when tested in cold water. Remove from heat and add marshmallow fluff, peanut butter, and vanilla. Mix together until ingredients are well mixed. Do not beat!! Turn into buttered pan.

Beverly Swett, Westbrook Lions Club
Westbrook, Maine, USA

PEANUT BUTTER FUDGE

1½ c. milk	8 oz. marshmallow cream
4 c. white sugar	2 c. peanut butter (plain or nutty)
1 c. chopped nuts	2 tsp. vanilla

Using a candy thermometer, cook milk and sugar to 240°. Do not stir. Remove from heat and add rest of ingredients. Mix well and pour into 9x13 inch pan to cool. I use the less expensive kind of peanut butter to keep cost down.

Walter E. Loomis, North Jackson Lions Club
Jackson, Michigan, USA

Be what you wish others to become.

983-94

597

BERNICE'S PEANUT BUTTER FUDGE

1½ c. sugar
¾ c. brown sugar
⅔ c. milk
4 Tbsp. peanut butter

2 Tbsp. butter or margarine
4 Tbsp. marshmallow fluff
½ c. chopped walnuts

Boil sugar, brown sugar, and milk until a soft ball can be formed with the mixture in cold water. Remove from heat. Add butter, peanut butter, and marshmallow. Quickly spoon into greased 8 inch square pan. Simple and delicious. Test the texture often, changes quickly.

Lorrie Cram, Ft. Lauderdale Lions Club
Ft. Lauderdale, Florida, USA

PEANUT BUTTER FUDGE

2 c. granulated sugar
1 lb. light brown sugar

¾ c. milk
½ tsp. salt

Mix in a good size pan. Boil for 5 minutes. Remove from heat. Add 12 ounces peanut butter, 1 (7½ ounce) marshmallow fluff, 1 cup chopped nuts, and 1 teaspoon vanilla. Beat (about 5 minutes). Turn into well buttered pan. Cool and enjoy with a cup of tea.

Grace P. Curtis, Westbrook Lions Club
Westbrook, Maine, USA

THREE MINUTE PEANUT BUTTER FUDGE

2 c. sugar
½ c. milk
1 tsp. vanilla
2½ Tbsp. butter

1 c. peanut butter
2 heaping Tbsp. marshmallow
fluff

Cook milk, sugar, and butter to a boil (on medium heat). Let boil (slowly not brisk) for 3 minutes *(no longer!)*. Remove from burner. Add peanut butter, fluff, and vanilla; stir until it begins to thicken. Turn into greased 9x9 inch pan. Cut before completely cool.

Linda Theriault, Westbrook Lions Club
Westbrook, Maine, USA

❦

Pessimism never won any battle.

PEANUT FUDGE

1 (12 oz.) pkg. peanut butter chips
1 (14 oz.) sweetened condensed
   milk
¼ c. margarine

½ c. chopped peanuts
1 (6 oz.) pkg. semi-sweet
   chocolate chips

In a large saucepan, melt peanut butter chips, 1 cup of the condensed milk, and 2 tablespoons of the margarine, stirring occasionally. Remove from heat and stir in the peanuts. Spread into wax paper lined 8 inch square pan. In small saucepan, melt the chocolate chips and the remaining chocolate mixture on top of the peanut butter mixture and chill 2 hours. Turn fudge onto cutting board. Peel off the paper and cut into squares. Tightly cover the leftovers.

DIVINITY FUDGE

3 c. sugar
½ c. white Karo
½ c. cold water

2 egg whites
1 tsp. vanilla

Mix sugar, syrup, and water. Cook slowly until soft ball. Pour ½ of syrup slowly into beaten egg whites; continue beating while cooking. Slowly add this syrup to syrup mixture with vanilla. Drop into a buttered pan.

Dave Bernier, Westbrook Lions Club
Westbrook, Maine, USA

KAHLUA PECAN FUDGE

1⅓ c. granulated sugar
1 (7 oz.) jar marshmallow creme
⅔ c. evaporated milk
¼ c. butter
¼ c. Kahlua

¼ tsp. salt
2 c. semi-sweet chocolate pieces
1 c. milk chocolate pieces
⅔ c. chopped pecans
1 tsp. vanilla

Line 8x8 inch pan with foil. In a 2 quart saucepan, combine sugar, marshmallow creme, milk, butter, Kahlua, and salt. Bring to rapid boil, stirring constantly for 5 minutes. Remove from heat; add all chocolate. Stir until melted. Add nuts and vanilla. Stir and turn into prepared pan. Refrigerate until firm. Cut in squares and store in refrigerator. Makes 2¾ pounds. Makes 64 (1 inch pieces).

❧

The best cure for insomnia is a Monday morning.

MY FUDGE SPECIAL

2 c. brown sugar
1 c. white sugar
¾ c. milk
1 Tbsp. butter or margarine

2 large Tbsp. marshmallow fluff
1 tsp. vanilla
½ c. walnuts

Combine sugar, milk, and butter in fairly large pan and cook (stirring most of the time so it won't catch on bottom), until it reaches 250° or forms medium hard ball when dropped in cold water. Remove from heat. Add vanilla and briskly stir in the marshmallow fluff until it begins to thicken. Add the nuts and pour in a 9x9 inch square greased pan. After it cools a little, cut in small squares.

Dave Bernier, Westbrook Lions Club
Westbrook, Maine, USA

MAMIE EISENHOWER'S MILLION DOLLAR FUDGE

1 (13 oz.) can evaporated milk
4½ c. sugar
2 Tbsp. butter or margarine
Dash of salt
1 (12 oz.) pkg. chocolate bits (Toll House chocolate chips)

1 (12 oz.) bar Hershey's sweet chocolate, broken into pieces
1 (8 oz.) jar marshmallow whip
2½ c. chopped walnuts

Mix evaporated milk, sugar, butter, and salt in saucepan; bring to boiling. Stir occasionally and boil for 7 minutes. Combine all remaining ingredients in large bowl and mix well. Pour boiling mixture over all. Beat until fudge is creamy. Pour into 2 buttered 8x8 inch pans or a glass cake pan.

Donna Juhl, Otis Lions Club
Otis, Colorado, USA

CAN'T FAIL FUDGE

12 oz. chocolate chips
12 oz. butterscotch chips
14 oz. can Eagle Brand milk

1 tsp. vanilla
1 c. nuts

Melt chips. Mix in milk, vanilla, and nuts. Pour in 9x13 inch pan. Chill and cut. Delicious.

Marian Hegdahl, Mitchell Lioness Club
Mitchell, South Dakota, USA

Your life is what your thoughts make it.

CHOCOLATE FUDGE

2 c. sugar
1 small (5½ oz.) can evaporated
    milk
10 regular marshmallows

¼ lb. butter or oleo
1 (6 oz.) chocolate chips
1 c. chopped walnuts (if desired)
1 tsp. vanilla

Boil the sugar, evaporated milk, and marshmallows slow for 7 minutes. Remove from heat and add the butter, chocolate chips, walnuts, and vanilla. Beat until thickens. Pour into greased pan.

Verna Ball, Sherrodsville Lions Club
Sherrodsville, Ohio, USA

EASY CHOCOLATE FUDGE

12 oz. chocolate chips
12 oz. butterscotch chips

4 oz. peanuts
½ tsp. oleo or butter

Melt chocolate chips and butterscotch chips in a microwave-safe container in the microwave. Add the 4 ounces of peanuts. Pour into an 8x8 inch buttered pan. Refrigerate until solid. Cut into squares. Serve in a fancy dish. Tastes just like old-fashioned fudge! Only takes a few minutes to prepare.

Lion Claire Cloon, Aurora Eastgate Lions Club
Aurora, Colorado, USA

CHOCOLATE FUDGE

4 c. sugar
3 Tbsp. syrup
⅓ c. cocoa or 3 sq. chocolate
2 c. nuts

2 Tbsp. butter
1 tsp. vanilla
1 c. milk

Mix sugar, syrup, chocolate or cocoa, and milk. Cook until forms soft ball in cold water. Stir constantly. Add butter and vanilla. Let cool until slightly stiff. Add nuts and vanilla. Pour in buttered plates. Let cool and cut in squares.

Edna Bunch, Snow Hill Lions Club
Snow Hill, North Carolina, USA

CHEEZY FUDGE

½ lb. oleo
½ lb. grated cheese (American or
    Velveeta)
½ c. cocoa

2 lb. powdered sugar
1 tsp. vanilla
½ c. nuts (optional)

Melt cheese and oleo in microwave for about 4 minutes on MEDIUM heat or in double boiler on stove. Add cocoa and powdered sugar; stir well. Add vanilla and nuts, if desired, and put in 9x9 inch buttered pan. Cool.

Notes

It is easy to take liberty for granted
when you have never had it taken from you.

Desserts

APPLE VARIETIES

NAME	SEASON	COLOR	FLAVOR/ TEXTURE	EATING	PIE
Astrachan	July-Aug	Yellow/ Greenish Red	Sweet	Good	Good
Baldwin	Oct-Jan	Red/ Yellowish	Mellow	Fair	Fair
Cortland	Oct-Jan	Green/Purple	Mild, tender	Excel.	Excel.
Delicious, Red	Sept-June	Scarlet	Sweet, crunchy	Excel.	Good
Delicious, Golden	Sept-May	Yellow	Sweet, semifirm	Excel.	Excel.
Empire	Sept-Nov	Red	Sweet, crisp	Excel.	Good
Fameuse	Sept-Nov	Red	Mild, crisp	Excel.	Fair
Granny Smith	Apr-Jul	Green	Tart, crisp	V. Good	V. Good
Gravenstein	July-Sept	Green w/red stripes	Tart, crisp	Good	Good
Ida Red	Oct	Red	Rich	Good	Good
Jonathan	Sept-Jan	Brilliant red	Tart, tender, crisp	V. Good	V. Good
Macoun	Oct-Nov	Dark red	Tart, juicy, crisp	Excel.	Good
McIntosh	Sept-June	Green to red	Slightly tart, tender, juicy	Excel.	Excel.
Newtown Pippin	Sept-June	Green to red	Slightly tart, firm	V. Good	Excel.
Northern Spy	Oct	Red	Crisp, tart	V. Good	V. Good
Rhode Island Greening	Sept-Nov	Green	Very tart, firm	Poor	Excel.
Rome Beauty	Oct-June	Red	Tart, firm, slightly dry	Good	V. Good
Stayman-Winesap	Oct-Mar	Red	Semifirm, sweet, spicy	V. Good	Good
Winesap	Oct-June	Red	Slightly tart, firm, spicy	Excel.	Good
Yellow Transparent	July-Aug	Yellow	Tart, soft	Poor	Excel.

DESSERTS

ALMOND DELITE

3 pkg. unflavored gelatin
5 c. water
1 c. sugar

1 c. milk
1 tsp. almond extract
1 (15 oz.) can fruit cocktail

Warm 5 cups of water. Pour in gelatin until completely dissolved (no bubbles, no particles). Add sugar and stir until dissolved. Add milk and almond extract. Chill in glass/Pyrex bowl or cake dish (13x9x2 inches). When solidified, cut gelatin into 1 inch cubes. Put fruit cocktail in bowl. Add ½ to 1 cup of water. Serve in dessert cups cold.

This is a light, cooling Chinese dessert for those hot summer days.
Eugene Pei, S.W. Denver Lions Club
Denver, Colorado, USA

ALMOND FLOAT

2 pkg. unflavored gelatin
1 c. milk
¾ c. sugar

1 Tbsp. almond extract
Canned lychee
Canned mandarin oranges

1. Sprinkle 2 packages gelatin in 3 tablespoons cold water.
2. Boil 1 cup water; add gelatin mixture, stirring until dissolved.
3. Add milk, sugar, and extract.
4. Stir well. Pour into small square pan; refrigerate until set.
5. Cut into cubes. Mix canned lychee and syrup with drained mandarin oranges. Serve fruit over cubes. You may add other fruits in season.

Very refreshing and tastes so good.
Lion Tony Campos, Caruthers Lions Club
Caruthers, California, USA

APPLE CRISP

8 c. sliced apples
1½ c. sugar
2 tsp. cinnamon
2 c. flour

2 c. sugar
2 eggs, beaten
1½ c. oleo, melted

Place apples in 9x13 inch pan. Cover with sugar and cinnamon. Sift together flour and sugar. Add eggs and stir with fork until crumbly. Sprinkle over apples. Pour melted oleo over. Bake at 350° for 1 hour. Serve warm with ice cream or Cool Whip. I use Jonathan apples.

Harriett McClaughry, Cuba Lions Club
Cuba, Illinois, USA

APPLE CRISP

Tart apples (enough to fill baking
   dish)
1 c. flour
1½ c. sugar
½ tsp. baking powder

½ tsp. salt
1 egg (unbeaten)
⅓ c. melted butter or margarine
Cinnamon

Preheat oven to 350°. Peel and slice apples to fill baking dish almost to top. In a medium bowl, mix flour, sugar, baking powder, and salt. Stir in egg. Mixture will be crumbly. Sprinkle cinnamon over apples in baking dish. Sprinkle flour mixture over top of apples. Pour melted butter over crumbled flour mixture. Bake 40 minutes at 350°.

For those of you with apple trees, this is a delicious alternative to apple pie.
Faith Spivey, Manteno Lions Club
Manteno, Illinois, USA

APPLE CRISP

8 apples, peeled
½ c. water
1 tsp. cinnamon

1½ c. sifted flour
¾ c. sugar
½ c. butter

Slice apples into baking dish. Add water and cinnamon. Sift flour and sugar together, then cut in butter or other shortening. Spread this crumb mixture over the apples and bake in a moderate oven (350°F.) for 45 minutes, or until apples are tender. Cut into squares. Serve, crisp side up, hot or cold, with whipped cream, hard sauce or vanilla ice cream. Serves 8.

Apple-Raisin Crisp: Add ½ cup raisins, ¼ teaspoon nutmeg, and 1 teaspoon lemon juice to the apples.

"There are two things to aim at in life: first, to get what you want; and, after that, to enjoy it. Only the wisest of humans achieve the second." Logan Smith
Richard L. Berg, Mt. Holly Springs Lions Club
Mt. Holly Springs, Pennsylvania, USA

The ultimate test of a relationship is to disagree, but to hold hands.

APPLE CRISP

2 lb. cooking apples, peeled and
   sliced (5½ c.)
¼ c. water
½ c. granulated sugar
½ c. firmly packed light brown
   sugar

½ tsp. ground nutmeg
½ tsp. cinnamon
¼ tsp. salt
¾ c. all-purpose flour
½ c. butter or margarine

Put apples in shallow greased 2 quart casserole; add water. Combine sugars, nutmeg, cinnamon, salt, and flour. Cut in butter with pastry blender. Spoon evenly over apples. Cover and bake in preheated moderate oven (350°F.) for 30 minutes. Uncover and bake for 30 minutes longer. Makes 6 servings.

Helen Gaither, Moweaqua Lions Club
Moweaqua, Illinois, USA

APPLE CRISP

6 to 8 apples, peeled, cored, and
   sliced
¼ to ½ c. water
2 Tbsp. lemon juice

¾ c. flour
1 c. brown sugar
1 tsp. cinnamon
½ c. butter

Put apples in a shallow 2 quart baking dish. Add water and lemon juice. Mix flour, sugar, and cinnamon in bowl. Cut butter in dry ingredients with pastry blender until crumbly. Sprinkle over apples. Bake at 375° for 30 minutes or until apples are tender. Serves 6.

Mrs. Tom Raad (Jamie), Rock Hill Lions Club
Rock Hill, South Carolina, USA

❦

Mid-life crisis is that moment when you realize
your children and your clothes are about the same age.

FRENCH APPLE DESSERT

Dough:

2½ c. flour
2 Tbsp. sugar
1 tsp. salt

½ tsp. baking powder
1 c. shortening
1 egg yolk plus ¾ c. milk, mixed

Filling:

10 to 12 apples
1 c. sugar plus 1 tsp. cinnamon,
    mixed

Topping: Use 1 egg white (stiffly beaten).

Frosting:

1 c. powdered sugar
1 tsp. vanilla

3 Tbsp. melted butter

Mix dough ingredients and divide into 2 parts. Roll to fit jelly roll pan which has been well greased. Peel and slice apples. Put apples onto bottom crust and sprinkle with sugar and cinnamon mixture. Place top crust on apples and seal edges. Cut slits on top crust. Brush with egg white, stiffly beaten. Bake at 375° for 45 minutes. Mix frosting ingredients and drizzle onto hot crust. Serves 20.

APPLE LOAF

2 c. apples, finely chopped
1 c. sugar
1 c. flour
1 tsp. cinnamon
½ tsp. nutmeg

1 egg, beaten
1 Tbsp. melted butter
1 tsp. baking soda
½ c. chopped nuts

Mix sugar, flour, cinnamon, nutmeg, egg, butter, and soda to the chopped apples, then add nuts. Mix well. This will be fairly thick and stiff. Bake slowly at around 250° until the cake sticks done (around 1 hour). Makes 1 loaf.

Serve with whip cream or plain. Warm or cold, then is a good fall dessert.

You're never a loser until you quit trying.

APPLE SQUARES

2 c. flour
⅔ c. shortening
½ tsp. salt
6 to 8 tart apples

1 egg
¼ c. water
1 Tbsp. lemon juice

Mix flour, salt, shortening, egg, water, and lemon juice like pie crust. Roll ½ dough to fit 9x13x2 inch cake pan. Slice and peel apples; spread on dough. Sprinkle with 1 cup sugar, ½ teaspoon cinnamon, and ½ teaspoon nutmeg. Roll out remaining dough and place on top of apples. Bake at 400° for 30 to 40 minutes. Frost while still warm with vanilla frosting.

Mrs. Bill (Jan) Callaghan, Elburn Lions Club
Elburn, Illinois, USA

APPLE TORTE

2 eggs
1½ c. sugar
3 tsp. vanilla
2 c. chopped apples
¾ c. nuts

⅔ c. flour
3 tsp. baking powder
½ tsp. salt
Whipped topping

Beat eggs. Add remaining ingredients (except for whipped topping). Bake in a 9x12 inch pan at 350° for 40 minutes. Serve with whipped topping.

The closest to perfection a person ever comes
is when he fills out a job application form.

❧ ❧ ❧

Happiness is like jelly ...
you can't spread it without getting some on yourself.

ROSE-BLUSH APPLE TORTE

Crust:

¾ c. butter or margarine
1½ c. flour
1½ Tbsp. sugar

⅛ tsp. salt
1 egg yolk

Mix ingredients for crust together until smooth like rich cooky dough. Press evenly into ungreased 9x13 inch pan, bringing dough up the sides a little. Bake at 350° for about 8 minutes until crust is set and very lightly browned on edges.

Filling:

1 c. sugar
¼ tsp. salt
3 Tbsp. cornstarch
1 c. water

2 drops of red food coloring
1 tsp. vanilla
5 c. thinly sliced, peeled apples

Combine sugar, cornstarch, salt, and water in saucepan for filling. Cook over medium heat until thickened (about 5 minutes), stirring constantly. Remove from heat; add food coloring, vanilla, and apples. Spread over partially baked crust.

Streusel Topping:

⅔ c. flour
⅔ c. sugar

¼ c. butter
⅛ tsp. cinnamon

Cover with topping of flour, sugar, butter, and cinnamon, mixed together with finger tips until small crumbs are formed. Sprinkle evenly over filling and bake at 350° for ½ hour. Serve plain or with ice cream.

BANANAS IN WINE SAUCE

4 bananas, sliced lengthwise
4 Tbsp. butter
2 c. sugar

1½ c. water
½ c. red wine
½ tsp. cinnamon

Peel and slice the bananas. Fry in the butter and remove. Add the remaining ingredients to the frying pan and bring to a boil. When the syrup thickens, add the bananas and serve warm.

William M. Davidson, IV, Statesboro Lions Club
Statesboro, Georgia, USA

If you carry your childhood with you, you never become older.

BANANAS FOSTER

3 to 4 bananas, sliced
½ stick butter
½ to ¾ c. brown sugar

1 oz. banana liqueur
1 oz. brandy or blended whisky
3 to 4 bowls vanilla ice cream

Melt the butter and add the brown sugar. When thoroughly blended and melted, add the bananas and the banana liqueur. Stir for about 15 to 20 seconds and add the brandy. Remove from heat and flame the brandy. When the fire is out, serve over the ice cream. Will serve 3 to 4 people.

William M. Davidson, IV, Statesboro Lions Club
Statesboro, Georgia, USA

BANANA S'MORES

¾ c. graham cracker crumbs
½ c. Bisquick baking mix
2 Tbsp. sugar
¼ c. margarine or butter, melted
2 or 3 medium bananas
3 Tbsp. lemon juice

1⅓ c. milk
1 (3½ oz.) pkg. instant vanilla
   pudding and pie filling
¾ c. miniature marshmallows
16 chocolate stars

Mix cracker crumbs, baking mix, and sugar; stir in margarine until moistened. Press in bottom of square microwaveable dish, 8x8x2 inches. Microwave, uncovered, on HIGH (100%), rotating dish ½ turn every minute, until crust bubbles up slightly and then begins to flatten, 1½ to 3 minutes. Cool 10 minutes on wire rack.

Slice bananas; dip into lemon juice and arrange on crust. Beat milk and pudding and pie filling (dry) until smooth. Stir in marshmallows. Spread pudding mixture over banana slices; press chocolate stars onto pudding mixture. Refrigerate no longer than 1 hour if desired. Makes 16 servings.

BANANA CHIFFON CAKE

2 eggs, separated
1⅓ c. sugar
2 c. flour
1 tsp. baking powder
1 tsp. baking soda
1 tsp. salt

1 tsp. vanilla
⅓ c. oil
1 c. mashed bananas (very ripe)
⅔ c. buttermilk
½ c. chopped nuts

Grease two 8 inch round pans well and dust with flour. Beat egg whites until fluffy. Gradually beat in ⅓ cup sugar. Beat until very stiff and glossy. Sift remaining sugar, flour, baking powder, soda, and salt into another bowl. Add oil, bananas, half of buttermilk, and vanilla. Mix well or 1 minute at medium speed on mixer. Add remaining buttermilk and egg yolks. Beat another minute. Fold in beaten egg whites and nuts. Pour in prepared pans. Bake at 350° for 30 to 35 minutes. Frost with cream cheese frosting. I use a 9x13 inch pan.

Dorothy Wimmer, Rock Falls Lions Club
Sterling, Illinois, USA

BANANA CREAM DESSERT

1 c. flour
½ c. oleo
1½ c. chopped nuts
2 large Cool Whip
1 (8 oz.) cream cheese

1 c. powdered sugar
2 pkg. instant banana pudding
3 c. milk
2 medium bananas

Mix 1 cup flour and ½ cup oleo till crumbly as for pie. Add 1½ cups nuts. Mix in and pat in bottom of 9x13 inch pan. Bake for 10 minutes in a 350° oven.

Beat cream cheese and powdered sugar till smooth. Fold in 1 large Cool Whip. Pour over cooled crust. Beat 2 packages pudding and 3 cups milk for 2 minutes. Pour over cream cheese mixture. Slice up the 2 bananas and put on top of pudding; press down a little. Put in refrigerator to cool and set, about 1 hour. Top with the carton of Cool Whip.

Walter M. Leitner, Isle Lions Club
Isle, Minnesota, Aitkin County, USA

BERRY BAVARIAN CROWN
(Ewing's birthday cake)

1 (3 oz.) pkg. strawberry Jell-O
1 c. hot water
½ c. ice water
2 pkg. (10 oz.) frozen strawberries
    or 2½ c. sliced fresh
    strawberries, sweetened

2 c. whipping cream, whipped
1 (10 inch) angel food cake

Ruby Glaze:

1 c. strawberry juice
1 Tbsp. cornstarch

2 to 3 drops of red food coloring
1 tsp. butter

Dissolve gelatin in hot water. Add ice water and chill until slightly congealed. Beat until light and fluffy. Drain berries and reserve juice for Ruby Glaze. Fold in strawberries and the whipped cream. Tear angel food cake into small to medium pieces. Alternate cake pieces and gelatin mixture in a 10 inch angel food cake pan. Chill until firm. Unmold on serving plate. Drizzle with Ruby Glaze.

Ruby Glaze: Blend cornstarch with a little juice. Gradually add to juice in saucepan. Cook until clear, 3 to 5 minutes. Remove from heat. Add food coloring and butter. Cool. Drizzle over the Bavarian mold. Serve.

When I was young, this was called our special birthday cake.
Joyce E. Steen, Merritt Island Lions Club
Merritt Island, Florida, USA

A small house will hold as much happiness as a mansion.

BLACK BOTTOM CUPCAKES

Filling:

8 oz. cream cheese, softened	⅓ c. sugar
1 egg	6 oz. chocolate chips

Batter:

1½ c. flour	1 c. sugar
½ c. cocoa	1 tsp. baking soda
½ tsp. salt	1 c. water
⅓ c. oil	1 tsp. vinegar
1 tsp. vanilla	

Combine first 3 filling ingredients and beat well. Add chocolate chips; mix and set aside. For batter, sift or stir together all dry ingredients, then add remaining items. Beat well. Fill small muffin cups ⅓ to ½ full with batter. Top each with a spoonful of filling. Bake at 350° for 12 to 15 minutes. Be sure to use the very small muffin pans and papers.

The vinegar is not in error!

Diane Howland, Ft. Lauderdale Lions Club
Ft. Lauderdale, Florida, USA

FRESH BLUEBERRY DESSERT

Crust:

1 pkg. graham crackers	¼ c. sugar
½ c. butter	

Filling:

1 c. milk	1 pkg. marshmallows
1 (8 oz.) pkg. cream cheese	1 ctn. Cool Whip
Fresh blueberries or can use fresh peaches, strawberries	

Mix crust ingredients together. Put in 9x13 inch pan and bake for 5 minutes at 350° (no longer or don't bake). Melt marshmallows and milk in the microwave. Add cream cheese and stir till melted and cooled. Fold in Cool Whip and add fresh fruit; pour over crust. Refrigerate.

Marge Klabunde, Brownton Lions Club
Brownton, Minnesota, USA

What lies behind or ahead of you is not as important as what lies in you.

QUICK AND EASY CAKE DESSERT

1 box cake mix (chocolate)
1 (3 oz.) pkg. cream cheese
1 (8 oz.) pkg. whipped cream

1 (3 oz.) pkg. instant chocolate
  pudding
2 c. milk

Bake cake as directed on package in 13x9 inch pan. When cool, mix pudding, cream cheese, and milk until thick. Spread over cake. Top with whipped cream. Decorate as you wish.

You can make this dessert with any cake and pudding as long as they match (lemon, butter pecan, vanilla). This is quick and easy and goes great for any affair you take it to. I usually have to make 2.

Mickey Farrand, Whittemore Lioness Club
Whittemore, Michigan, USA

CROWN CANTALOUPE WITH BANANA FLAMBE

2 oz. butter
¼ lb. sugar
6 oz. concentrated orange juice
1 oz. Grand Marnier

1 oz. Cointreau
3 bananas, sliced
3 cantaloupes
Ice cream

Combine butter and sugar in a frying pan, occasionally stirring until lightly browned. Add orange juice and liquor. Simmer before adding sliced bananas. This makes the banana flambe mixture. Cut cantaloupes in crown style. Remove seeds. Add ice cream of your choice, then top with banana flambe. Makes 6 servings. Per serving: 365 calories, 11 grams fat, 40 milligrams cholesterol, and 105 milligrams sodium.

Wendell Walker, Charlotte Amalie Lions Club
St. Thomas, U.S. Virgin Islands

CARAMEL DESSERT

1 pt. whipping cream, whipped (or
  large ctn. Cool Whip)
1 can Eagle Brand milk
  (sweetened condensed)

1 pkg. vanilla wafers

Crush vanilla wafers and spread in bottom of 9x13 inch pan (reserve 1 cup for top). Remove label from Eagle Brand milk can. Place can in water to cover and boil for 3 hours. Allow it to cool. (The milk will turn to caramel.) Mix this with the whipped cream. Pour over the wafer crumbs and top with reserved 1 cup of crumbs. Chill.

You will need to watch the can while boiling, so it does not boil dry.
Barbara Allison, Moweaqua Lions Club
Moweaqua, Illinois, USA

CARAMEL DUMPLINGS

2 c. sugar
2½ c. hot water
Pinch of salt
2 Tbsp. butter

1 c. flour
½ c. milk
2 tsp. baking powder

Brown ½ cup sugar in heavy skillet, stirring constantly, over medium heat. Add 2½ cups hot water (have a deep pan), 1 cup sugar, pinch of salt, and lump of butter (approximately 1 tablespoon). Boil 10 minutes. Pour in cake pan, 13½ x 9 inches, and cool.

Cream ½ cup sugar and 1 tablespoon butter. Add ½ cup milk, 1 cup flour, and 2 teaspoons baking powder. Drop spoonfuls into caramel mixture. Bake at 375° for 20 minutes or until lightly browned.

This recipe came from my mother-in-law and was a favorite of the family, so during WW II, she had to save sugar and make it once or twice a year for special occasions.

Lioness Irene Swenson, Mitchell Lioness Club
Mitchell, South Dakota, USA

❦

If it weren't for the fact that the TV set and the refrigerator are so far apart, some of us wouldn't get any exercise at all.

❦ ❦ ❦

*Letting things go in one ear and out the other is bad enough.
But it's worse when things go in one ear,
get all mixed up and come out the mouth.*

❦ ❦ ❦

The difference between the impossible and the possible lies in a person's determination.

CHEESECAKE

Pastry Crust:

1 c. sifted all-purpose flour
¼ c. sugar
1 Tbsp. grated lemon peel
1 egg yolk

½ c. (1 stick) butter (room temperature)
½ tsp. vanilla

Filling:

5 (8 oz.) pkg. cream cheese (room temperature - 2½ lb.)
1¾ c. sugar
3 Tbsp. flour
1½ tsp. grated orange peel
1½ tsp. grated lemon peel

¼ tsp. vanilla
5 eggs
2 egg yolks
¼ c. heavy cream (whipping cream)

Preheat oven to 400°F. Combine flour, sugar, and lemon peel. Make a well in center and drop in egg yolk, butter, and vanilla. Quickly work together until well blended. Wrap in wax paper and chill for 1 hour. Roll out about ⅓ of the dough ⅛ inch thick. Fit over bottom of buttered 9 inch springform pan. Trim and save extra dough. Bake circle of dough for about 8 to 10 minutes or until golden. Cool! Butter sides of pan and place sides over bottom. Turn oven to 500°F. Roll out remaining dough and line pan ¾ of the way up the sides.

Blend together cheese, sugar, flour, grated peels, and vanilla until smooth. Add eggs and yolks, one at a time, mixing well after each addition. Blend in cream thoroughly. Turn cheese mixture into springform pan and bake for 10 to 12 minutes. Reduce heat to 200°F. and bake for 60 to 70 minutes. Cool in draft free place. Top with fresh or canned cherries, blueberries or strawberries. Makes 12 to 14 servings.

PEPPERMINT CHEESECAKE

1 c. chocolate wafer crumbs
1 env. unflavored gelatin
¼ c. cold water
2 (8 oz.) containers soft cream cheese
½ c. sugar

½ c. milk
¼ c. crushed peppermint candy
1 c. whipping cream, whipped
2 (1.45 oz.) milk chocolate candy bars, finely chopped

Combine crumbs and margarine. Press onto bottom of 9 inch spring form pan. Bake at 350° for 10 minutes. Cool. Soften gelatin in water, stirring over low heat until dissolved. Combine cream cheese and sugar, mixing at medium speed on electric mixer until well blended. Gradually add gelatin, milk, and peppermint candy, mixing until blended. Chill until thickened, but not set. Fold in whipped cream and chocolate. Pour over crust. Chill until firm. Garnish with additional whipping cream, whipped, combined with crushed peppermint candy. Makes 10 to 12 servings.

CHOCOLATE AMARETTO CHEESECAKE

6 chocolate wafers, finely crushed
1½ c. lite cream cheese product
1 c. sugar
1 c. 1% lowfat cottage cheese
¼ c. plus 2 Tbsp. unsweetened
   cocoa
¼ c. all-purpose flour

¼ c. mocha-mix Amaretto
   creamer
1 tsp. vanilla extract
¼ tsp. salt
1 egg
2 Tbsp. semi-sweet chocolate
   mini-morsels

Sprinkle chocolate wafer crumbs in bottom of an 8 inch spring form pan. Set aside. Position knife blade in food processor bowl; add cream cheese and next 7 ingredients, processing until smooth. Add egg and process just until blended. Fold in chocolate morsels. Slowly pour mixture over crumbs in pan. Bake at 300° for 45 to 50 minutes or until cheesecake is set. Let cool in pan on wire rack. Cover and chill at least 8 hours. Remove sides of pan and transfer to a serving platter. Garnish with chocolate curls if desired. Yield: 12 servings (about 200 calories per serving).

CHEDDAR CHEESE CAKE

1 c. butter
2 c. sugar
6 eggs, separated
3 c. flour (plain)

5 tsp. baking powder
1 c. milk
1 tsp. vanilla

Cream butter thoroughly. Gradually blend in sugar. Add beaten egg yolks, flour, baking powder, and milk; beat until smooth. Beat egg whites until fluffy. Fold in egg whites and add vanilla to cake mixture, stirring just enough to mix. Put in greased and floured 9 inch cake pans. Should make 4 layers. Bake in moderate oven (375°F.) for 10 to 15 minutes.

Cheddar Cheese Cake Icing:

1 lb. Cheddar cheese (Red Rind or
   Daisy cheese)
2 c. sugar

2 Tbsp. butter
¾ c. water

Grate cheese. In a double boiler pot, add sugar, water, and cheese. Cook, stirring constantly, until a sample of mixture forms a soft ball in a cup of cold tap water. Add butter and remove from heat. Put between each layer and over entire cake.

Lion Philip E. Alexander, Ponchatoula Lions Club
Ponchatoula, Louisiana, USA

❦

You will shrink or expand to the size of your vision.

FROZEN CHERRY DESSERT

36 graham crackers
2 Tbsp. margarine
⅓ c. sugar
1 large pkg. Cool Whip

1 small pkg. miniature
  marshmallows
1 large can cherry pie filling

Crush graham crackers for crust. Add margarine and sugar. Pat ¾ of mixture in bottom of buttered 13x9 inch pan. Put on a layer of Cool Whip and then a layer of miniature marshmallows. Freeze for 1 hour. Remove from freezer and spread pie filling on top. Add rest of cracker crumbs and freeze. Remove from freezer 10 minutes before serving. Serves 12. Blueberries may be used.

CHERRY TORTILLAS

1 (20 oz.) can cherry pie filling
6 flour tortillas
½ c. margarine, melted

1 c. sugar
1 c. water
Ice cream

Preheat oven to 350°. Spoon pie filling on tortillas. Fold sides and ends to enclose filling. Arrange, fold side down, in lightly greased 9 inch square baking dish. Mix margarine, sugar, and water together in bowl. Pour over tortillas. Bake for 40 to 45 minutes or until lightly browned. Serve warm with a scoop of favorite ice cream on top. Yield: 6 servings.

Lion Karen Stowers, Amarillo North Lions Club
Amarillo, Texas, USA

CHOCOLATE CHIP LOAF

1¾ c. sifted flour
1 tsp. baking soda
¼ tsp. salt
¼ tsp. ground mace
1 tsp. cinnamon
½ c. shortening

2 eggs
1 c. sweet applesauce
½ c. seedless raisins
½ c. chopped pecans
6 oz. chocolate chips
1 c. sugar

Sift together dry ingredients. Cream together shortening and sugar. Add eggs, one at a time. Add flour mixture and applesauce alternately to shortening mixture. Stir in raisins, nuts, and half of the chocolate chips. Pour into wax paper lined loaf pan. Sprinkle remaining chips over the top of batter. Bake at 325° about 1 hour and 15 minutes. Cool.

Mrs. Mike (Shirley) Stoffa, Elburn Lions Club
Elburn, Illinois, USA

❧

Everyone has a fair turn to be as great as he pleases.

CHOCOLATE LAYER DESSERT

First layer:

1 c. pecans, chopped   **½ c. margarine**
1 c. flour

Mix well and press in a 9x13 inch pan or baking dish. Bake for 20 minutes in a 325° oven. Cool.

Second layer:

8 oz. Philadelphia cream cheese   **1 c. Cool Whip**
1 c. confectioners sugar

Mix together and layer over first layer after it has cooled.

Third layer:

2 boxes instant chocolate   **3 c. milk**
  pudding

Mix pudding and milk; beat with electric mixer for 2 minutes or until thickened, then pour over second layer.

Fourth layer:

1 c. Cool Whip
Shaved chocolate or chopped
  nuts

Top with Cool Whip. Garnish with shaved chocolate or chopped nuts.

PDG Lloyd E. Wright, Georgetown Lions Club
Georgetown, Ohio, USA

CHOCOLATE CREAM CRUNCH

1 c. self-rising flour   **1 (6 oz.) pkg. instant chocolate**
1 c. finely chopped pecans   **pudding**
½ c. margarine, softened to room   **1 (6 oz.) pkg. instant vanilla**
  temperature   **pudding**
1 c. powdered sugar   **3 c. sweet milk**
1 (8 oz.) pkg. cream cheese   **1 small ctn. Cool Whip**

Crust: Mix flour, margarine, and pecans well. Press into a 9x13 inch pan. Bake 20 minutes at 350°. Cool completely.

Filling: Blend cream cheese and powdered sugar until fluffy. Be sure cream cheese is room temperature. Fold in 1 cup Cool Whip. Blend well. Spread on crust. Chill about 1 hour. Mix chocolate pudding and 1½ cups milk. Spread over cream cheese layer. Repeat with vanilla pudding. Chill for about 1 hour. Frost with rest of Cool Whip. Cut in squares and serve.

Note: You must chill in between each layer to be able to spread evenly.

Bertha Smith, Parkway Lions Club
Panama City, Florida, USA

CREAM PUFFS

½ c. margarine
1 c. boiling water
1 c. flour

¼ tsp. salt
4 eggs (large size only)

Start heating your oven to 450° plus. Melt butter in water. Add flour and salt all at once and stir vigorously until mixture forms ball that doesn't separate. Remove from heat and cool slightly. Add eggs, one at a time, beating vigorously after each addition until mixture is smooth. Drop from teaspoon 2 inches apart onto a greased baking sheet. Bake in hot oven (450°) for 15 minutes, then in a moderate oven at 325° for 25 minutes. At no time, open the oven door. Remove with spatula and cool. Cut off the top and fill with a pudding. Put top on and add Cool Whip.

One recipe makes 12 puffs; ½ recipe makes 6 puffs.

Thinking is one thing no one has ever been able to tax.
Lion Kathleen Schatz Dague, Aurora Eastgate Lions Club
Aurora, Colorado, USA

CREAM PUFFS

½ c. butter or margarine
1 c. boiling water
1 c. sifted all-purpose flour

¼ tsp. salt
4 eggs

Vanilla Filling:

½ c. sugar
⅓ c. all-purpose flour

½ tsp. salt
2 c. milk

Mix and allow to boil.

Add:

3 slightly beaten eggs to boiled mixture

1 tsp. vanilla

To do the puffs, melt butter in boiling water. Add flour and salt all at once; stir vigorously. Cook, stirring constantly, until mixture forms a ball that doesn't separate. Remove from heat and cool slightly. Add eggs, one at a time; beat until smooth. Cook at 450° for 15 minutes, then at 350° for 25 minutes on ungreased cookie sheet 3 inches apart. Remove cream puffs and split. With oven off, allow puffs to dry out. Cool on rack. Fill centers with ice cream or vanilla filling. Drizzle with chocolate sauce.

Elizabeth Doak, Westbrook Lions Club
Westbrook, Maine, USA

❦

We can always live on less when we have more to live for.

CREAM PUFF DESSERT

9x12 inch pan
1 stick margarine (¼ lb.)
1 c. water

1 c. flour
4 eggs

Mix:

3 small pkg. vanilla instant
    pudding
4 c. milk

8 oz. cream cheese
8 oz. Cool Whip
Chocolate syrup (small)

Heat water and 1 stick margarine to a boil. Remove from heat. Add 1 cup flour and stir. Add eggs, one at a time. Beat. Put in greased 9x12 inch pan. Bake at 350° for 35 minutes. Mix pudding with milk. Beat cream cheese and mix together. Top with Cool Whip. Drizzle with syrup.

Mrs. Richard Freed, Strausstown 14P Lions Club
Bethel, Pennsylvania, USA

CRANBERRY SUPREME

1 c. graham cracker crumbs
¼ c. melted margarine
2 c. cranberries
1 c. sugar
½ c. water
¼ c. chopped pecans

1 c. heavy cream, whipped
2 Tbsp. orange marmalade
8 oz. cream cheese
⅓ c. sifted confectioners sugar
1 Tbsp. milk
1 tsp. vanilla

Combine crumbs and margarine; press into an 8 inch square pan. Combine cranberries, sugar, and water; bring to a boil. Simmer 20 minutes. Stir in nuts and marmalade. Chill. Combine softened cream cheese, confectioners sugar, milk, and vanilla. Mix well. Fold in whipped cream. Spoon over crust. Top with cranberry mixture. Chill several hours or overnight. Can be frozen. Serves 8.

Any child can tell you that the sole purpose of a middle name
is so he can tell when he's really in trouble.

CRANBERRY SOUR CREAM COFFEE CAKE

Adjustable to low calorie, low cholesterol. Elegant dessert!

1 stick margarine (low salt)
1 c. sugar
2 eggs (substitute Egg Beaters)
1 tsp. baking powder
1 tsp. baking soda
½ tsp. salt

2 c. flour
½ pt. sour cream (lowfat)
½ tsp. almond flavoring
1 can whole cranberries
½ c. nuts

1. Cream margarine and sugar.
2. Gradually add eggs.
3. Add dry ingredients alternately with sour cream.
4. Add flavoring and nuts.
5. In greased tube pan, layer batter, cranberries, then batter.
6. Bake at 350° for 55 minutes.
7. When cooled completely, drizzle with topping of:

¾ c. confectioners sugar
½ tsp. almond flavoring

2 tsp. warm water

Other jams or jellies may be used. I serve mine plain.

Doris Robidoux, Blackstone Valley Women's Club
Manville, Rhode Island, USA

EASY EGG CUSTARD

3 eggs
1 c. sugar
3 Tbsp. flour

1 large can evaporated milk
1 tsp. vanilla
2 Tbsp. butter

Mix all ingredients well and pour into greased pie plate. Bake at 350° for 30 minutes.

Rosa Brafford, Rock Hill Lions Club
Rock Hill, South Carolina, USA

PANNUKAKKUA - FINNISH CUSTARD

3 c. warm milk (not scalded)
3 eggs
¾ c. flour

¼ c. sugar
½ tsp. salt
½ stick butter or oleo

Place butter in a 9x13 inch pan, then place pan into oven while the oven warms to 400° temperature. Beat eggs. Add sugar and salt. Add warm milk alternately with flour. Batter will be thin. Pour into hot pan with the melted oleo and bake for 30 minutes. Serve with syrup or berries.

DESSERT

Crumble together:

2 c. flour   ½ c. sugar
1 c. oleo

Add:

2 c. coconut   **1 c. chopped pecans**

Stir all together. Bake in 9x13 inch cake pan for 35 minutes at 400°, stirring every 10 minutes. When done, take 1 cup of mixture and set aside for topping. Pat rest of mixture in bottom of cake pan. Let cool. When cool, take 2 large or 4 small boxes of butter pecan pudding, using 6 cups milk, and mix. Pour on top of crust. Top with softened Cool Whip. Sprinkle the 1 cup of mixture set aside on top. Chill for 1 hour.

Helen Anderson, Cuba Lions Club
Cuba, Illinois, USA

ECLAIR CAKE

1 lb. graham crackers   3¼ c. milk
2 pkg. vanilla instant pudding (can   **1 (8 oz.) pkg. Cool Whip**
use sugar free)

Mix milk and instant pudding. Beat until smooth. Pour ½ of filling over crackers (bottom layer). Pour remaining filling over second layer. Cover with third layer of crackers. Refrigerate for 2 hours.

Frosting - Melt in double boiler:

3 Tbsp. milk   **2 tsp. light corn syrup**
2 pkg. Nestle Choco-bake   **2 tsp. vanilla**
unsweetened liquid chocolate   **3 Tbsp. butter**

When melted and blended, add 1½ cups confectioners sugar. Beat until smooth. Spread on cake and refrigerate for 24 hours. This dessert freezes well. Serves 12.

Mildred Noack, Westbrook Lions Club
Westbrook, Maine, USA

❦

Kindness consists of loving people more than they deserve.

CHOCOLATE ECLAIRS

Whole graham crackers
2 pkg. instant vanilla pudding,
  prepared as directed using
  only 1½ c. milk per pkg.

1 large ctn. Cool Whip, stirred
1 can Betty Crocker chocolate
  frosting

Layer ingredients in 9x13 inch pan as follows:

1. Line pan with whole graham crackers.
2. Top with ½ pudding.
3. Cover with Cool Whip.
4. Repeat steps 1 to 3.
5. Top with chocolate frosting.

Chill overnight and cut in squares.

CHOCOLATE ECLAIR DESSERT

1 c. water
1 stick margarine or butter (¼ lb.)
1 c. flour
4 eggs
1 large pkg. instant vanilla
  pudding mix

8 oz. pkg. cream cheese, softened
1 (8 oz.) ctn. Cool Whip
Hershey's chocolate syrup

Preheat oven to 400°. Boil water and margarine or butter together with dash of salt. Add flour all at once. Stir. Cool slightly. Add 4 eggs, one at a time, and beat with whisk. Put in a 9x13 inch greased pan. Spread. Bake at 400° for 30 minutes. Cool.

Prepare pudding mix per instructions on box. Add cream cheese and beat well with mixer until smooth. Pour over cooled cake. Let stand in refrigerator at least 15 minutes. Top with Cool Whip. Drizzle with chocolate syrup just before serving. I like to use Pyrex dish.

Lois Rogers, North Maplewood Lioness Club
St. Paul, Minnesota, USA

Recall it as often a you wish, a happy memory never wears out.

FOUR-LAYER DESSERT

First layer:

2 c. flour   **1 c. chopped walnuts**
1 c. butter or margarine

Mix like pie crust. Press in pan, 9x13 inches. Bake at 350° for 15 to 20 minutes.

Second layer:

2 c. Cool Whip   **2 (8 oz.) cream cheese**
2 c. powdered sugar

Beat until fluffy and spread over cooled crust.

Third layer:

2 large pkg. instant chocolate   **5 c. cold milk**
**   pudding**

Mix as directed on package. Pour over second layer.

Fourth layer: Top with Cool Whip and sliced walnuts. Keeps for 3 days.

FRUIT COBBLER

Have on hand 1 can fruit pie filling.

Topping:

1 egg   **1 tsp. vanilla**
¾ c. sugar   **1 c. flour**
½ c. milk   **2 tsp. baking powder**

Grease an 8x8 inch pan. Pour pie filling in it. In mixing bowl, beat egg, sugar, milk, and vanilla together. Add flour and mix well. Pour topping over pie filling. Bake about 45 minutes at 350°. Makes 6 to 8 servings.

Nothing makes a person more productive than the last minute.

FRUIT JELLO
(Family favorite original)

1 (4 serving size) sugar free Jell-O (strawberry-banana or any other fruit flavored gelatin)
3 oz. Philadelphia cream cheese, softened
2 c. hot boiling water
½ c. Cool Whip
1 c. sliced strawberries, drained
1 (8 oz.) can pineapple tidbits or crushed, drained well
1 small can mandarin oranges, drained and cut up
1 apple, diced
¼ c. (or more) chopped walnuts (optional)

Dissolve gelatin in boiling water. Add Philadelphia cream cheese and blend at medium speed until mixture is completely smooth. Chill until slightly thickened. Add Cool Whip, fruits, and nuts. Pour into individual dishes or a mold. Chill until set.

Suggestions: Use drained pineapple juice or syrup as part or all of the liquid called for in recipe. Lemon or lime flavor gelatin is excellent for pineapple and shredded carrots combination. This does well in a mold and makes a colorful addition to the dining table.

Viola Haines (Mrs. Ray), Silver Run-Union Mills Lions Club
Taneytown, Maryland, USA

FRUIT PIZZA

1 box sugar cookie mix
1 (8 oz.) cream cheese
1 c. sugar
1 large can crushed pineapple
1 can mandarin oranges
1 small jar maraschino cherries
2 large bananas
½ c. chopped pecans

Mix sugar cookie mixture as directed on box. Spread on regular cookie sheet and bake at 350°F. for 8 to 10 minutes. Let cool. Drain pineapple well and save juice. Drain oranges. Slice bananas and soak in pineapple juice for 10 to 15 minutes.

Mix softened cream cheese and sugar until smooth and creamy. Spread mixture on cooled cookie dough like frosting. Top cream cheese with pineapple. Arrange oranges, bananas, and cherries on top of pineapple. Finish by sprinkling with chopped pecans.

Barb Barton, Baugo Lions Club
Elkhart, Indiana, USA

You can't get anywhere unless you start.

FRUIT DELIGHT

2 cans fruit cocktail, drained
1 small can mandarin oranges,
   drained
1 small can pineapple chunks,
   drained

1 small box vanilla pudding
   (cooking kind)
1 c. fruit juice

Mix fruit together in large bowl. Cook pudding mix with the cup fruit juice as directed on box until thick. Pour pudding over fruit while hot. Refrigerate until cool. Before serving, slice 2 bananas and add to mixture.

David Boyd, Jr., Snow Hill Lions Club
Snow Hill, North Carolina, USA

FRUIT CRUNCH

Fruit (apples, blueberries,
   peaches, or any other fruit)
1 c. sugar

1 c. Bisquick
Butter

Put apples, blueberries, peaches, or any other fruit in baking dish. Add water if fresh fruit is used. In separate bowl, mix sugar and Bisquick. Pour mixture over fruit. Dot generously with butter. Bake about 1 hour in a 375° oven.

This was my mother's favorite recipe. She used it often when cooking for her Kentucky farmer husband and her children and grandchildren.

Bernice Naylor Callaway, Elizabeth City Lions Club
Elizabeth City, North Carolina, USA

ICEBOX FRUIT CAKE

1 (½ lb.) pkg. walnuts, chopped
1 (½ lb.) pkg. pecans, chopped
2 c. raisins (I like to use both dark
   and light raisins)
1 can coconut
4 oz. red candied cherries
4 oz. green candied cherries

4 oz. candied pineapple
1 large (1 lb.) box graham
   crackers, crushed
1 large bag marshmallows
1 can evaporated milk
1 stick margarine (at room
   temperature)

Melt margarine, marshmallows, and milk over low heat. When melted, add remaining ingredients. Mix well. You may have to use your hands. Pour into a greased dish. Store in refrigerator, covered. Will last for weeks.

Bertha Smith, Parkway Lions Club
Panama City, Florida, USA

❦

Every day, something is being done that "couldn't be done."

GEORGIA FRUIT COBBLERS

6 to 8 c. peeled and sliced fruit
2 c. sugar
⅓ c. flour
Dash of nutmeg

1 tsp. almond flavoring
½ c. butter
Pastry of your choice (your own
or a commercial variety)

Mix sugar, flour, and nutmeg; combine with fruit. Pour into a 9x13 inch baking pan. Pour any remaining liquid and the flavoring over all. Dot with butter. Cover with pastry strips or solid pastry cover slashed in center to allow for escaping steam. Bake in 400° oven for about 45 minutes.

My husband, Lion Ralph Owen, and I both grew up in Georgia and learned to love Georgia products and southern cooking. Cobbler pies fit both categories and I give a recipe for "Peach Cobbler," since Georgia is commonly known as the "Peach State." For apple or berry cobbler, I omit almond flavoring.

Mrs. Lion Ralph (Frances) Owen, Canton Lions Club
Canton, Georgia, USA

FRUIT COCKTAIL DESSERT

1½ c. flour
1 c. sugar
1 egg, slightly beaten
1 tsp. soda
½ tsp. salt

1 tsp. vanilla
16 oz. can fruit cocktail (do not
drain)
1 c. brown sugar
½ c. chopped pecans (or walnuts)

Put all ingredients (except brown sugar and nuts) in bowl and mix well. Pour into an 8x12 inch baking pan, greased well and floured. Mix brown sugar and nuts together; sprinkle over batter. Bake at 325° approximately 40 to 45 minutes. Serve with ice cream or whipped topping. Bake early in the day for serving at dinner. Flavor improves upon sitting.

Anne Murdock (Mrs. LeRoy), Silver Run-Union Mills Lions Club
Westminster, Maryland, USA

FRUIT COCKTAIL DESSERT

2 c. fruit cocktail, well drained
1 c. sugar
1 c. flour
1 tsp. baking soda

Dash of salt
1 egg, slightly beaten
½ c. brown sugar for topping
½ c. chopped nuts for topping

Add egg to fruit cocktail. Sift dry ingredients. Mix lightly with fruit. Pour into buttered square baking dish. Sprinkle brown sugar and nuts on top. Bake at 375° for 30 to 40 minutes. Check center with toothpick. This can be served warm or cold with whipped cream or Cool Whip.

Eileen Peck
Rootstown, Ohio, USA

GERMAN CHOCOLATE DELIGHT

1 box German chocolate cake mix
1 can Eagle Brand milk
1 jar caramel ice cream topping

1 large Cool Whip
6 Heath bars, crushed

Mix and bake cake as directed on box. After cake is done, punch holes in cake. Drizzle Eagle Brand milk and caramel ice cream topping over cake. Cool. Cover with Cool Whip and sprinkle crushed Heath bars on top. Keep refrigerated. Cake gets better after it has time to soak up the toppings - if you can wait!!

Charles Miller, Hodgenville Lions Club
Hodgenville, Kentucky, USA

GINGERBREAD WITH HOT LEMON SAUCE

2 eggs
¾ c. brown sugar
¾ c. molasses
¾ c. oil
2½ c. flour
2 tsp. baking soda

2 tsp. ginger
1½ tsp. cinnamon
½ tsp. cloves
½ tsp. nutmeg
½ tsp. baking powder
1 c. boiling water

Lemon Sauce:

½ c. sugar
1 Tbsp. corn starch
1 c. boiling water

2 Tbsp. butter
1½ Tbsp. lemon juice
Pinch of salt and nutmeg

Add beaten eggs to sugar, molasses, and oil, then add dry ingredients which have been sifted together. Lastly add the hot water. Beat until thoroughly blended. Pour into a greased 9x13 inch pan and bake at 350°F. for 30 to 40 minutes until toothpick comes out clean.

Lemon Sauce: Mix together sugar and corn starch; add boiling water and cook until thickened. Remove from heat and add remaining ingredients. Serve Gingerbread while still warm bathed in hot Lemon Sauce. Particularly good when the weather is cold, snowy, and crisp.

A.J. and Wanda Groenendale, Fort Collins Lions Club
Fort Collins, Colorado, USA

❧

The time is always right to do what is right.

GRASSHOPPER PIE

24 big marshmallows
¾ c. milk
15 Oreo cookies, finely crushed
2 Tbsp. butter or margarine,
  melted

3 Tbsp. creme de menthe liqueur
3 Tbsp. creme de cacao liqueur
1 c. heavy cream, whipped

Combine marshmallows and milk in top of double boiler and melt. This will take some time. Meanwhile, crush cookies and reserve enough to sprinkle on top of pie. Melt butter. Combine with crushed cookies in bowl, then make crust in a 9 inch pie plate. Chill crust. When marshmallows are melted, remove from heat and cool to lukewarm (10 to 15 minutes). Add creme de menthe and creme de cacao; stir together. Refrigerate until set (not runny). Stir occasionally. Whip cream until it holds peaks. Mix into marshmallow mixture. Pour into crust. Sprinkle reserved crumbs on top. Put waxed paper over top and refrigerate for 12 hours. Crumbs should keep wax paper off pie filling. Makes 8 servings.

LEMONY DESSERT

75 Ritz crackers, crushed
1½ sticks melted butter
¾ c. sugar
1 (13½ oz.) Cool Whip

1 (12 oz.) lemonade concentrate,
  thawed
1 can Eagle Brand milk

Mix crumbs, butter, and sugar; put into a 9x13 inch pan. Save ½ cup for on top. Mix Cool Whip, lemonade, and Eagle Brand milk on low speed with mixer, then spread in pan over the crumbs. Top with the ½ cup crumbs. Freeze. This will keep up to 4 weeks.

Lion Beverly Wilkens, Plato Lions Club
Plato, Minnesota, USA

LEMON LUSH

1 stick margarine
1 c. flour
½ c. chopped walnuts
1 (8 oz.) container Cool Whip
1 c. powdered sugar

1 (8 oz.) pkg. cream cheese
2 (3.4 oz.) pkg. Jell-O instant
  lemon pudding
3 c. milk

Mix together 1 stick margarine, 1 cup flour, and ½ cup chopped walnuts. Pat into bottom of 8x8 inch baking dish. Bake at 350° for 15 minutes. Cool. Mix 1 cup Cool Whip, 1 cup powdered sugar, and one 8 ounce package cream cheese. Spread evenly on cooled crust. Mix 2 packages instant lemon pudding and 3 cups milk. Spread over ingredients in dish. Spread remainder of Cool Whip on top. Sprinkle with chopped nuts. Refrigerate overnight. Chocolate pudding may be used in place of lemon.

Frances Losey, Crandon Lions Club
Crandon, Wisconsin, USA

LEMON CAKE DESSERT

1 yellow or lemon cake mix
1 pkg. lemon jello or 1 pkg. lemon
    instant pudding

¾ c. salad oil
¾ c. water
4 eggs

Mix all ingredients together with electric mixer. Spray 9x13 inch cake pan. Pour batter in. Bake 40 minutes at 350°. Remove from oven. Prick entire top of cake with toothpick.

Have ready and mixed 2 cups powdered sugar, juice of 2 lemons, and 2 tablespoons water. Spoon on cake top and spread quickly as it tends to run off cake edges. Serve with Cool Whip if desired.

This has been a favorite dessert for our family for 30 years and has never been a failure!

C.M. "Tiny" Brandt, Wells Lions Club
Wells, Minnesota, USA

MILLIONAIRE'S PIE

1 pie crust shell, baked and cooled
1 c. powdered sugar
¼ c. butter or margarine, softened
1 egg
½ tsp. vanilla
¼ tsp. salt
2 c. frozen whipped topping,
    thawed

8 oz. can (1 c.) crushed pineapple,
    drained
½ c. pecans, chopped
1 Tbsp. milk
¼ c. maraschino cherries,
    chopped

Cream together sugar and softened butter or margarine. Add egg, vanilla, and salt. Beat until smooth and creamy. Spread mixture in baked pie crust shell. Chill. Combine whipped topping, pineapple, pecans, milk, and cherries until blended. Spread mixture over chilled filling. Chill pie until ready to serve. Delicious.

Georgette P. Amedeo, Airline Lioness Club
Metairie, Louisiana, USA

My mind works like lightning ... one brilliant flash and it's gone again!

ICE CREAM DESSERT

½ c. butter
2 sq. unsweetened baking
   chocolate
1 c. powdered sugar
3 egg yolks
3 egg whites

½ c. chopped nuts (optional)
1 tsp. vanilla
22 vanilla wafers
1 qt. vanilla ice cream
1 qt. orange sherbet

Melt together butter and chocolate. Add powdered sugar and stir. Add egg yolks and beat with electric mixer. Fold into above mixture 3 beaten egg whites. Add nuts and vanilla. Put wafer crumbs into 8x10 inch dish (save some for top). Pour chocolate mixture over crumbs. Add layer of vanilla ice cream and layer of orange sherbet. Sprinkle a few crumbs over top. Freeze. (Can use any flavor of ice cream that you want.)

Jean Lancaster, Moweaqua Lions Club
Moweaqua, Illinois, USA

STRAWBERRY ICE CREAM

1 large box strawberry Jell-O
⅔ c. hot water
6 eggs
2½ c. sugar

2 cans Milnot
1 qt. fresh unsweetened
   strawberries

Dissolve Jell-O into hot water. Add eggs, sugar, Milnot, and strawberries. (If using sweetened berries, cut back on sugar.) Pour into freezer and finish with milk to fill line.

Lynette Cutler, Moweaqua Lions Club
Moweaqua, Illinois, USA

FIG ICE CREAM

1 qt. fresh figs, peeled
8 egg yolks
¾ c. sugar
3 c. cream

2 Tbsp. lemon juice
4 Tbsp. Cointreau
¼ tsp. salt

Whip the eggs, salt, and sugar until well blended. Mix the figs, lemon juice, and Cointreau until it becomes a rough puree. Whip the cream until it peaks, then mix all together and place in the freezer. Stir about every ½ hour until frozen. It may also be placed in an ice cream churn and churned.

Alternate method for making Fig Ice Cream is to make your favorite vanilla ice cream recipe and add the fresh figs. Churn it as you would for any homemade ice cream.

William M. Davidson, IV, Statesboro Lions Club
Statesboro, Georgia, USA

HOMEMADE ICE CREAM

4 eggs
2½ c. sugar (if using unsweetened
fruit - 2 c. if plain)
1 can Eagle Brand milk

1 Tbsp. vanilla flavoring
1 to 2 c. fruit, chopped in food
processor (optional)

Beat together all ingredients. Pour into a 4 quart freezer can and add milk to reach fill line on container. Follow manufacturer's directions for making ice cream.

Mrs. Lion Robert (Margaret) Logan, Canton Lions Club
Canton, Georgia, USA

EGG BEATERS HOMEMADE ICE CREAM

3 qt. milk
6 eggs or the equivalent in Egg
Beaters
3½ pt. cream

3 c. sugar (scant)
1½ Tbsp. vanilla
Pinch of salt

Beat eggs and sugar together. Add vanilla and salt. Add the cream to the sugar and egg mixture. Add part of the milk. Pour into freezer container and fill the rest of the way with milk. Makes 1½ gallons. Our family could not tell the difference in real eggs or Egg Beaters.

Martha Walters, Emporia Noon Lions Club
Emporia, Kansas, USA

ICE CREAM CUSTARD
(Vanilla)

3 qt. milk
1¾ to 2 c. sugar
Pinch of salt

6 or 7 eggs
1 Tbsp. vanilla

Scald milk, then add some hot milk to sugar and egg mixture. Cook in double boiler until coats spoon. Add 1 can evaporated milk just before freezing. Crank ice cream freezer or electric freeze. Makes 1 gallon.

Variation: Reduce milk by 1 quart. Add fruit and 2 teaspoons lemon juice. Cook as above. Add fruit and lemon juice just before freezing in crank ice cream freezer or electric. Add the 1 can of evaporated milk too just before freezing.

From Father's mother's kitchen, Mrs. Loulie Watkins Bunch.
Glenn E. Bunch, Snow Hill Lions Club
Snow Hill, North Carolina, USA

The shadows are behind you if you walk toward the light.

MOM'S GREEN STUFF

16 large marshmallows
1 c. milk
3 oz. pkg. lime jello
2 (3 oz.) pkg. cream cheese
20 oz. can undrained crushed
    pineapple

1 c. cream, whipped
⅔ c. mayonnaise
Nuts (optional)

Melt marshmallows and milk in double boiler. Pour hot mixture over jello; stir till dissolved. Add cheese and stir till dissolved. Add pineapple and cool. Blend in cream and mayonnaise. Sprinkle nuts on top if desired.

Mom makes this for our family gatherings.

Julia Hughes, Craigsville Lions Club
Craigsville, West Virginia, USA

BAILEY'S IRISH CREME MOUSSE

½ lb. semi-sweet chocolate chips
3 oz. butter
½ c. powdered sugar
3 egg yolks

4 oz. Bailey's Irish Cream
2 c. whipping cream
3 egg whites

Melt chocolate and butter. Let stand in pan 5 minutes. Combine sugar, yolks, and Bailey's; blend in chocolate mixture. Whip cream and fold into chocolate mixture. Beat whites to soft peaks and fold them into the chocolate mixture. Divide into serving dishes and garnish with shaved chocolate. Serves 8 to 10.

If you haven't any charity in your heart,
you have the worst kind of heart trouble.

"MUD PIE"

A Colorado ski resort favorite. (I first learned to make it at a Colorado ski resort.)

1 premade chocolate crumb pie
   shell
½ gal. coffee ice cream

1 c. Hershey's chocolate syrup
1 can whipped cream

1. Scoop out sections of ½ gallon of coffee ice cream into a medium size cooking pan.
2. Place pan on stove at medium-low heat.
3. Constantly stir ice cream as it melts to avoid burning or cooking.
4. When ice cream is melted and *before* it starts to cook, pour ice cream into premade chocolate pie shell.
5. Place pie shell with ice cream in freezer for 3 to 5 hours, until ice cream re-freezes.
6. Take pie shell and ice cream out of freezer; pour over chocolate syrup for topping. Re-freeze for 3 hours.
7. Serve individual mud pie slices topped with whipped cream.

This is an out-of-this-world dessert treat that even non-coffee drinkers will love! Doesn't taste like coffee as much as it does chocolate.
O.J. Mooneyham, President, Cheyenne Mountain Lions Club
Colorado Springs, Colorado, USA

PEACH COBBLER

1 stick margarine
1 c. sugar
¾ c. plain flour
¾ c. sweet milk

Pinch of salt
1 tsp. baking powder
Sliced peaches (about 2 c.)

In a 9½ x 13 inch pan, melt margarine. Mix well the remaining ingredients and pour over butter. Place peaches on top of batter. Bake at 350° for 1 hour.
Bertha Smith, President, Parkway Lions Club
Panama City, Florida, USA

PINEAPPLE-ORANGE DESSERT

1 small pkg. instant coconut
   cream pudding
1 (20 oz.) can crushed pineapple
   (do not drain)

1 (11 oz.) mandarin oranges,
   drained
1 small (8 oz.) container Cool Whip
1 c. mini marshmallows

Combine pudding mix with pineapple; fold in oranges, Cool Whip, and marshmallows. Refrigerate to blend flavors.

Sliced bananas may be added just before serving.
Elaine B. Wymer, Rootstown Lions Club
Rootstown Township, Rootstown, Ohio, USA

GRAPES AND PINEAPPLE WITH SOUR CREAM

2 c. fresh seedless green grapes
13¼ oz. can pineapple chunks, drained
¼ c. brown sugar (set aside 1 Tbsp.)
⅓ c. sour cream

Combine grapes and pineapple. In small bowl, blend all but 1 tablespoon of the brown sugar and the sour cream. Toss with fruits and chill. Just before serving, sprinkle with remaining tablespoon of brown sugar. The sour cream-sugar mixture can be used on fresh mixed fruit, too, as a topping.

Rosemary Kish, Downriver Pride Lions Club
Lincoln Park, Michigan, USA

SCALLOPED PINEAPPLE

6 slices bread, cubed
3 eggs, beaten
1½ c. sugar
½ c. cream or milk
½ c. oleo, melted
1 can chunk pineapple, drained

Cube bread and place in 2 quart casserole. Pour over the sugar. Stir in the beaten eggs and milk. Pour the melted oleo over the top, then add the drained pineapple. Stir in lightly. Bake in 350° oven for 40 minutes. This is very good. Could be used as a dessert. Leave it cool and put a little Cool Whip on top.

Betty J. Wertz (member Evan Wertz), Bascom Lions Club
Tiffin, Ohio, USA

BONNIE'S PINEAPPLE SHEET CAKE

2 c. sugar
¼ c. Wesson oil
2 eggs
2 tsp. soda
2 c. all-purpose flour
1 large (16 oz.) can crushed pineapple (with juice)
Icing (recipe follows)

Mix all ingredients together well. Place in sheet cake pan and bake at 350° about 25 minutes or until it tests done. While cake is hot, frost with following icing.

Icing:

1 small can evaporated milk
1 stick margarine
1 c. sugar
1 c. nuts
1 c. coconut

Bring first 3 ingredients to boil slowly, stirring, and boil for 10 minutes. Add nuts and coconut. Pour over cake, spreading evenly, while cake is hot. Cut in squares.

Note: This recipe came from England.

Bertha Smith, President, Parkway Lions Club
Panama City, Florida, USA

POPPY SEED TORTE

1 c. flour	1 c. sugar
½ c. butter	¼ c. poppy seeds
½ c. grated nuts of choice	½ tsp. salt
1 pkg. gelatin	2 eggs, beaten
1½ c. milk	2 Tbsp. corn starch
½ tsp. vanilla	1 large container Cool Whip

Combine the flour and butter along with the nuts and press into a 9x12 inch baking dish. Bake for 15 minutes at 350° until brown. Dissolve the gelatin in 1½ cups water and set aside. Combine the remaining ingredients, except the Cool Whip, in a saucepan and cook on low to medium heat until thick. Remove from heat and add the gelatin mixture. Cool slightly and add ½ of the container Cool Whip. Pour mixture into the baking dish. When cool to cold, cover with the remaining Cool Whip and serve.

Credit for recipe goes to Todd Anderson and Kellie Musil.
William M. Davidson, IV, Statesboro Lions Club
Statesboro, Georgia, USA

PISTACHIO TORTE

First layer:

1½ c. flour	1 stick oleo
2 Tbsp. sugar	½ c. fine pecans

Mix together ingredients for first layer. Pat into bottom of 13x9 inch pan. Bake at 350° for 15 to 20 minutes. Cool!

Second layer:

8 oz. cream cheese	¾ c. powdered sugar
½ large Cool Whip	

Whip together ingredients for second layer. Pour over cool first layer and refrigerate.

Third layer:

2 pkg. instant pistachio pudding	2½ c. milk

Blend together ingredients for third layer. Pour over second layer. Cool.

Enjoy your own life without comparing it with that of another.

HOLIDAY STEAMED PUDDING

1 c. grated apples
1 c. grated carrots
1 c. grated potatoes
1 c. raisins
1 c. chopped walnuts

1 tsp. baking soda
1 tsp. salt
¼ tsp. cinnamon
¼ tsp. nutmeg

Mix together. Spoon into greased containers. Fill ⅔ full. Cover with foil and tie with string. Place on a trivet in a large pan with cover. Pour in water about ½ way up the sides of the containers. Cover. Bring water to a boil. Steam 1½ hours on moderate heat. Serve warm with your favorite sauce or ice cream. Can be frozen after steaming. Reheat to serve. Yield: 8 to 10 servings. No eggs, butter or other fat needed.

Jane Hansen, Ponderosa Lions Club
Auberry, California, USA

SCANDINAVIAN SOUR CHERRY PUDDING

1 c. flour
⅛ tsp. salt
1 tsp. baking powder
1 (16 oz.) can pitted sour red
  cherries

3 Tbsp. butter
1¼ c. white sugar
¾ c. milk
½ tsp. almond extract

Preheat oven to 350°. Sift together flour, salt, and baking powder. Drain cherries and save ½ cup juice. Cream butter, gradually adding 1 cup sugar until light and fluffy. Add flour mixture alternately with milk, mixing until smooth. Pour into buttered 8 inch square baking pan. Combine cherries, reserved juice, and remaining ¼ cup sugar. Bring to boil; stir until sugar dissolves. Add almond extract and pour over batter. Bake at 350° for 30 minutes. Good warm or cold with vanilla ice cream or whipped cream.

Walter E. Loomis, North Jackson Lions Club
Jackson, Michigan, USA

DATE PUDDING

1 c. flour
½ c. sugar
1 Tbsp. baking powder
½ c. milk
½ c. dates

½ c. nuts
1 c. brown sugar
2 c. boiling water
1 Tbsp. butter

Mix flour, sugar, baking powder, and milk together. Add dates and nuts to mixture; put in pan. Mix brown sugar, water, and butter together; pour over dough and bake at 350° for 35 minutes. Use a large, deep pan to allow for the rising of the dough. Serve with whip cream.

Mrs. Lion John (Helen) Jennings, Canton Lions Club
Canton, Georgia, USA

BAKED PEACH PUDDING

2 c. sliced peaches
¾ c. sugar
½ c. milk
4 tsp. butter

½ tsp. salt
1 tsp. baking powder
1 c. flour
1 tsp. vanilla

Topping:

1 c. sugar
1 Tbsp. cornstarch
¼ tsp. salt

¼ tsp. cinnamon
¼ tsp. nutmeg
1 c. boiling water

Slice peaches into 8x8 inch pan. Cream butter and sugar. Add dry ingredients with milk and vanilla. Spoon over peaches.

For topping: Mix sugar with cornstarch, salt, cinnamon, and nutmeg. Sprinkle over batter. Pour cup of boiling water over all. Bake 50 minutes at 325°. Serve with vanilla ice cream. Note: I use fresh peaches and cut back some on the sugar.

Nicki Florentine, Silver Run-Union Mills Lions Club
Westminster, Maryland, USA

RAISIN PUDDING

1 Tbsp. shortening
½ c. brown sugar
½ tsp. cinnamon
½ tsp. baking soda
¼ tsp. salt

½ tsp. vanilla
½ c. milk
1 c. flour
½ c. raisins
½ c. nuts

Mix as cake. Put in greased pan. Bake at 350° for 30 minutes. Bring to boil 1 cup brown sugar and 2 teaspoons butter. Pour over cake and bake at 400° for 10 minutes.

Evelyn Steele, Lyman Lions Club
Lyman, Wyoming, USA

BANANA PUDDING

3 to 5 bananas
1 large box vanilla pudding
   (instant)
1 box vanilla wafers

8 oz. sour cream
12 oz. Cool Whip
3 c. milk

Layer vanilla wafers and bananas. Mix vanilla pudding with milk (follow directions on box). Add sour cream and Cool Whip to pudding. Pour over bananas and wafers. Chill in refrigerator.

Lib Howard, Rock Hill Lions Club
Rock Hill, South Carolina, USA

ICEBOX BANANA PUDDING

2 small boxes vanilla instant
   pudding
3 c. milk
1 can Eagle Brand milk

1 small ctn. Cool Whip
5 bananas
Vanilla wafers

Beat pudding and milk together for 2 minutes. Add Eagle Brand milk and mix well. Fold in Cool Whip; layer wafers, bananas, and pudding in a 13x9 inch Pyrex. Top with wafers. Refrigerate.

Beverly Ryan, Decatur Lions Club
Decatur, Texas, USA

FUDGE PUDDING

1 c. flour
⅔ c. sugar
2 Tbsp. cocoa
½ c. milk
2 Tbsp. melted butter

½ c. nuts
1 c. brown sugar
¼ c. cocoa
1 tsp. vanilla

Mix together 1 cup flour, ⅔ cup sugar, and 2 tablespoons cocoa. Add to dry mixture. Beat till smooth the milk, vanilla, and butter. Stir in your nuts and spread in buttered casserole. Mix together and sprinkle over batter the brown sugar and cocoa. Pour 1½ cups boiling water over entire cake. Bake at 350° for 50 minutes.

My sister made this when she was a teen-ager and it was very good with ice cream or whipped cream. It was fairly easy to make. My sister is Edna Bunch Gibbs of Kilkenny, North Carolina, who gave me this recipe.

Glenn Bunch, Snow Hill Lions Club
Snow Hill, North Carolina, USA

MAGIC LEMON PUDDING

2 Tbsp. butter
1 c. sugar
6 Tbsp. flour
3 egg yolks, beaten
1½ c. milk

¼ tsp. salt
3 Tbsp. lemon juice
1 tsp. grated lemon rind
3 egg whites, beaten

Combine butter, sugar, flour, egg yolks, and salt; beat very smooth. Add lemon juice, grated rind, and milk; mix. Fold in stiffly beaten add whites. Place in custard cups and set in a pan of hot water. Bake in a 350° oven about 40 minutes. This mixture may also be baked in an unbaked pie shell.

This is a recipe of my mother's. She made it often on the farm where I grew up near Crown Point, Indiana.

Edwin J. Blume, Paris Lions Club
Paris, Illinois, USA

CHERRY PUDDING

½ c. sugar
½ c. milk
1 tsp. baking powder
2 Tbsp. butter
½ tsp. salt
¾ c. flour

1 (16 oz.) can sour cherries
¾ c. sugar
1½ c. water
2 Tbsp. butter
½ tsp. salt

Mix first 6 ingredients together. Pour in a greased 9 inch square pan and heat. Mix remaining ingredients together, then spoon over mixture in 9 inch pan. Bake 20 minutes at 450°. This recipe has been in our family for years.

Pat Lamb, Moweaqua Lions Club
Moweaqua, Illinois, USA

FRUITTY PUDDING DELIGHT

14 whole graham crackers
1 (6 serving) pkg. Jell-O Brand
   vanilla instant pudding and
   pie filling

1 c. Cool Whip (brand) non-dairy
   whipped topping
1 (21 oz.) can blueberry pie filling

Line 9 inch square pan with whole graham crackers, breaking crackers if necessary. Prepare a pudding mix as directed on package for pudding. Let stand 5 minutes, then blend in whipped topping. Spread half the pudding mixture over the crackers. Add another layer of crackers; top with remaining pudding mixture and remaining crackers. Spread pie filling over top layer of crackers. Chill 3 hours. Serves 9 people.

May substitute any fruit pie filling that you prefer, i.e., cherry, raspberry, etc.

Janine K. Cox, Bakersfield Pioneer Lions Club
Bakersfield, California, USA

RICE PUDDING

2 eggs
½ c. sugar
¼ tsp. salt
Dash of cinnamon
2 c. scalded milk

¾ c. cooked rice
1 tsp. vanilla
Nutmeg
Raisins

Beat eggs; add sugar, salt, milk, cinnamon, rice, vanilla, and raisins. Mix together; pour into baking dish. Place dish in 1 inch water. Bake for 1½ hours or until knife comes out clean in a 325° oven.

Recipe from my grandmother.

Carol A. Case, Manteno Lions Club
Manteno, Illinois, USA

BAKED INDIAN PUDDING

¼ c. yellow corn meal
4 c. hot water
½ c. maple syrup
¼ c. light molasses
2 eggs, slightly beaten
2 Tbsp. butter

⅓ c. brown sugar
1 tsp. salt
¼ tsp. cinnamon
¾ tsp. ginger
¼ c. cold milk
Vanilla ice cream

In top of double boiler, slowly stir corn meal into hot milk. Cook over boiling water, stirring occasionally for 20 minutes. Preheat oven to 300°. Lightly grease 2 quart (8½ inch) round pan. In small bowl, combine rest of ingredients, except cold milk. Stir into corn meal mixture; mix well. Turn into prepared dish; pour cold milk on top without stirring. Bake, uncovered, for 2 hours or just until set, but quivery on top. *Do not* overbake. Let stand for 30 minutes. Serve warm.

Dave Bernier, Westbrook Lions Club
Westbrook, Maine, USA

INDIAN PUDDING

6 Tbsp. unsalted butter
¾ tsp. ground allspice
¾ tsp. ground mace
½ c. + 3 Tbsp. brown sugar
2 (12 oz.) cans evaporated milk
½ tsp. salt

2 eggs
1 tsp. baking soda
1 tsp. vanilla
1 c. yellow corn meal
½ c. toasted pine nuts

In saucepan, melt butter; stir in allspice and mace. Cook for 2 minutes. Stir in sugar until dissolved. Add milk and salt. Cook until milk is ready to boil. Remove from heat. Whip the egg in bowl until fluffy; bring to a boil. Add baking soda and corn meal until well blended. Add milk in steady stream and whisk for 1 minute. Pour in casserole dish setting in pan of water; sprinkle nuts evenly and bake at 350° for 45 to 55 minutes.

Maggie Harnois, Westbrook Lions Club
Westbrook, Maine, USA

Avenge yourself... live long enough to become a problem to your children.

BREAD PUDDING

3 slices bread, toasted and
    buttered
½ c. granulated sugar
4 c. milk, scalded
½ tsp. nutmeg

4 eggs
1 tsp. vanilla extract
½ c. raisins (optional)
½ tsp. cinnamon

    Preheat oven to 350°. Butter 1½ quart casserole. Generously spread toasted bread with butter and tear into bite-size pieces. Place toast in buttered dish. Beat together eggs, sugar, and vanilla. *Slowly* add scalded milk to egg mixture and mix thoroughly. Stir in raisins. Pour mixture into dish over bread. Sprinkle with cinnamon and nutmeg. Set dish into pan of water that comes halfway up outside edge and bake for 45 to 60 minutes. Pudding is done when knife inserted in center comes out clean. Serve warm. Refrigerate any leftovers. Yields about 6 servings.

Donna S. Reitz, Sykesville Lions Club
Sykesville, Pennsylvania, USA

BREAD PUDDING

1 c. raisins (cover with hot water
    for a few minutes)
2 eggs, beaten slightly
¼ c. sugar
¼ tsp. salt

1 tsp. vanilla
2 c. milk
2 slices bread, broken in small
    pieces
Cinnamon and nutmeg to taste

    If you soak raisins in hot water, put bread in water. If not, soak bread in milk. Bake at 350° in pan of water at least 1 hour.

Florence Carter, Westbrook Lions Club
Westbrook, Maine, USA

APPLE-BREAD PUDDING

4 c. cubed bread
2 apples, sliced
½ c. raisins
½ c. sugar
1 Tbsp. cinnamon

4 eggs
1 c. milk
2 c. apple juice or as much needed
    to have it moist

    Mix all ingredients in a 2 quart casserole. Bake at 350° for 60 minutes.

Martha Cute, Blackstone Valley Lions Club
Forestdale, Rhode Island, USA

Become a chronic enthusiast!

PUMPKIN SQUARES

Crust:

1¾ c. graham cracker crumbs
⅓ c. sugar
½ c. melted butter

2 eggs
¾ c. sugar
1 (8 oz.) cream cheese

Pumpkin mix:

1 (16 oz.) canned pumpkin
3 egg yolks (save whites)
½ c. sugar
½ c. milk
½ tsp. salt

2 tsp. ground cinnamon
1 env. unflavored gelatin
¼ c. cold water
3 egg whites
¼ c. sugar

1. Mix cracker crumbs and ½ cup sugar; stir in melted butter. Pat in a 13x9 inch baking dish.

2. Beat 2 eggs, ¾ cup sugar, and cream cheese until light and fluffy. Pour over graham cracker crumbs and bake at 350° for 20 minutes.

3. Beat pumpkin, egg yolks, ½ cup sugar, milk, salt, and cinnamon in top of double boiler. Cook, stirring frequently, until thick (5 minutes).

5. In saucepan with ¼ cup cold water, sprinkle unflavored gelatin until dissolved.

5. Beat egg whites until foamy. Gradually beat ¼ cup sugar until stiff; gently fold in pumpkin. Pour over crust. *Refrigerate.* Garnish with whipped cream.

HOLIDAY FROZEN PUMPKIN SQUARES

3 c. graham cracker crumbs
½ c. sugar
½ c. melted butter
2 c. pumpkin (16 oz. can)
½ c. packed brown sugar
½ tsp. salt

1 tsp. cinnamon
¼ tsp. ginger
⅛ tsp. cloves
½ gal. softened vanilla ice cream
8 oz. container frozen whipped
  topping

Mix graham cracker crumbs with sugar and butter. Press into softened vanilla ice cream. Pour into crumb-lined pan. Cover with foil and freeze until firm. Thaw 10 to 15 minutes before cutting and serving. May top with a spoonful of whipped cream or frozen whipped topping if desired. Serves 12 to 15.

❦

Love is a friendship set to music.

RASPBERRY CRISP

1 qt. raspberries
½ c. sugar
¼ c. butter

⅓ c. flour
¾ c. oatmeal
½ c. brown sugar

Preheat oven to 350°. Wash raspberries and put in a 9x9 inch baking dish. Sprinkle the ¼ cup of white sugar over the berries. Stir butter into brown sugar, flour, and oats; sprinkle the mixture over the fruit. Bake at 350° for 30 minutes.

Dave Bernier, Westbrook Lions Club
Westbrook, Maine, USA

JELLY RITZ DESSERT

Crushed Ritz crackers
1 small pkg. red jello
1 small pkg. green jello

½ pt. whipped cream
Sugar
Lemon juice

Dissolve each package of jello in 2 different bowls as per package instructions. Let partially set. Whip cream with sugar and a few drops of lemon juice. Set in fridge until ready to use. Crush Ritz crackers and place in bottom of cake pan. Spread red jelly on top. Follow with crushed Ritz as third layer. Next, put on the whipped cream (not too thick) and repeat from the beginning, ending up with the Ritz layer. Let cool well in fridge.

Mrs. Laurie Kovach, Brandon Crocus Lions Club
Brandon, Manitoba, Canada

STRAWBERRY DELIGHT

1 large box instant vanilla pudding
    mix
1¾ c. milk
1 tsp. vanilla
1 large (12 oz.) Cool Whip

⅓ box graham crackers
2 (10 oz.) pkg. frozen strawberries
1 pkg. ready made strawberry
    glaze

Blend first 3 ingredients. Fold in Cool Whip. Place a layer of graham crackers (uncrushed) on bottom of 9x13 inch pan. Layer with pudding mixture. Drain part of liquid off strawberries, then top mixture in pan with strawberries, then spread on glaze. Refrigerate several hours before serving.

All sunshine makes the dessert.

Rexie Martin, Rock Hill Lions Club
Rock Hill, South Carolina, USA

Your smile is the most important thing you wear.

ANGEL BERRY DESSERT

1 angel food cake
1½ c. boiling water
2 (3 oz.) pkg. sugar-free
   strawberry jello

1 c. cold water
2 small or 1 large pkg. frozen
   strawberries
1 c. Cool Whip

Break the angel food cake into small pieces and put in a 9x13 inch pan. Put the boiling water in a bowl, then add the jello, stirring until dissolved. Add the cold water. Let jello slightly set, then add the strawberries and Cool Whip. Pour mixture on top of the angel food cake pieces. Put in the refrigerator until set.

Virginia L. Kelley, Sundowners Lions Club
Emporia, Kansas, USA

STRAWBERRY-ANGEL FOOD DESSERT

1 (6 oz.) strawberry jello (or sugar-
   free)
20 oz. frozen strawberries
2 Tbsp. sugar

Pinch of salt
1 angel food cake
1 pt. whipped cream (or 2 pkg.
   Dream Whip)

Break up angel food cake into 9x13 inch pan. Dissolve jello in 2½ cups boiling water. Stir in salt, berries, and sugar until cool. Fold in whipped cream. Pour over cake. Cool in refrigerator. Enjoy with sugar free jello and Dream Whip for a low cholesterol and low calorie dessert.

Peg Turner, Rootstown Lions Club
Rootstown Township, Rootstown, Ohio, USA

THREE-LAYER JELLO

3 oz. strawberry-flavored jello
10 oz. pkg. frozen strawberries
3 oz. orange-flavored jello
8 oz. pkg. Neufchatel or cream
   cheese, softened

11 oz. can mandarin oranges
   (undrained)
3 oz. lime-flavored jello
8¼ oz. can crushed pineapple
   (undrained)

Prepare strawberry jello with 1 cup boiling water; stir until dissolved. Stir in *frozen* strawberries. Pour into 8 cup mold or 9x9x2 inches. Chill until almost firm. Rinse out the bowl and begin second layer. Pour 1 cup boiling water on orange-flavored jello. Stir until dissolved. Gradually add the softened cheese (use a wire whisk to blend) until only small flecks of cheese remain. Add the oranges. Pour on strawberry layer. Chill until almost firm. Rinse out your mixing bowl for the last layer. Pour 1 cup boiling water on lime-flavored jello. Stir in the crushed pineapple with syrup. Chill until almost thickened, then pour on orange layer. Serves 9 to 12. The first layer sets very quickly because of the frozen fruit; use 1 bowl for making the jello and 1 measuring cup! The first layer can also be made with cherry or raspberry jello and matching frozen fruit.

Rosemary Kish, Downriver Pride Lions Club
Lincoln Park, Michigan, USA

TINY TARTS

1 (3 oz.) pkg. cream cheese   1 c. sifted flour
1 stick margarine

   Blend and then chill.

   Filling (1 teaspoon per tart):

¾ c. brown sugar   1 tsp. vanilla
1 Tbsp. melted butter   ¾ c. chopped nuts
1 egg

   Roll dough ½ inch and cut with 3 inch cutter. Fill tiny muffin tins. Mix filling and put 1 teaspoon in each muffin tin after you put dough in. Bake at 350° for 25 minutes.

Karen Brewer, Elburn Lions Club
Elburn, Illinois, USA

STAINED GLASS TORTE

2 c. graham wafer crumbs   ½ c. sugar
½ c. melted butter

   Press ⅔ of mixture into a 10 inch springform pan or a 9x13 inch pan. Chill.

1 pkg. orange Jell-O powder   ¼ c. cold water
1 pkg. lime Jell-O powder   1 c. hot pineapple juice
1 pkg. raspberry Jell-O powder   2 c. whipped cream or Cool Whip
3 c. boiling water   1 tsp. vanilla
1 pkg. plain gelatin (1 Tbsp.)   ½ c. sugar

   Dissolve each package of Jell-O separately in 1 cup boiling water. Pour into 3 greased 8x8 inch cake pans and chill until firm. Cut into ½ inch cubes. Soften gelatin in ¼ cup cold water, then add hot pineapple juice. Stir until gelatin is dissolved. Chill until partially set. Add vanilla. Fold gelatin-pineapple mixture into whipped cream. Gently fold in Jell-O cubes. Turn into prepared pans. Sprinkle with remaining wafer crumbs. Chill at least 6 hours to set. When firm, slice and serve with whipped cream. We served this at our Christmas tea this past year and everyone really enjoyed it.

Mabel Norquay, Jasper Mountain Lions Club
Jasper, Alberta, Canada

Sometimes the poorest man leaves his children the richest inheritance.

TIPSY LAIRD

2 Sara Lee pound cakes
2 large pkg. vanilla pudding mix
1 pkg. coconut macaroons
1 small jar raspberry jam

½ c. raspberry liquor
½ pt. whipping cream or small
pkg. Dream Whip

Slice the cake whole in ½ inch thick slices, then third each slice. Sprinkle the liquor over each slice and spread the jam over the slice of cake. Make the puddings as directed on the box. Crumble a few macaroons in the bottom of a large bowl and follow with a layer of cake slices and pudding. Continue layering the macaroons, cake, and pudding until gone or bowl is about ⅔ full, ending with a pudding layer. Cover and place in refrigerator. Just before serving, whip the cream with 3 teaspoons sugar and spread over the top. Keep cool until ready to serve.

LaGail H. Davidson (Mrs. W.M.D., IV), Statesboro Lions Club
Statesboro, Georgia, USA

WALNUT STRUEDEL

7 c. walnuts*
½ lb. margarine
1 egg
1 egg yolk

1 Tbsp. yeast
1 c. warm milk
4 c. flour
4 Tbsp. sugar

Put dry ingredients together and mix as pie dough with margarine. Make a well; add eggs and yeast mixture. Mix all together. Divide dough into 4 parts and set on floured cloth. Let rise for 1 hour at room temperature.

Roll each dough and spread with nut filling. Prick with toothpick, then roll as for jelly roll and let rise for about 45 minutes to 1 hour. Brush with beaten egg (note: Use whole egg) and bake at 350° for 40 minutes to 1 hour.

Filling: Mix nuts with 2½ cups sugar or a little more. Add a little cinnamon and 1 tablespoon cocoa, then add enough warm milk to make it spreading consistency. When you put dry yeast into milk, do not stir. Let set for 5 minutes.

* Note: Measure 7 cups whole nuts, not chopped.

Claude H. Ohlinger, Blandon Lions Club
Blandon, Pennsylvania, USA

Speak the truth, but leave immediately after.

Miscellaneous

FIRST AID IN HOUSEHOLD EMERGENCIES

POISONING: When a poison has been taken internally, start first aid at once. Call doctor immediately.
- Dilute poison with large amounts of liquid — milk or water.
- Wash out by inducing vomiting, when not a strong acid, strong alkali, or petroleum.
- For acid poisons do not induce vomiting, but neutralize with milk of magnesia. Then give milk, olive oil, or egg white. Keep victim warm and lying down.
- For alkali poisons such as lye or ammonia, do not induce vomiting.
- Give lemon juice or vinegar. Then give milk and keep victim warm and lying down.
- If poison is a sleeping drug, induce vomiting and then give strong black coffee frequently. Victim must be kept awake.
- If breathing stops, give artificial respiration.

SHOCK: Shock is brought on by a sudden or severe physical injury or emotional disturbance. In shock, the balance between the nervous system and the blood vessels is upset. The result is faintness, nausea, and a pale and clammy skin. Call ambulance immediately. If not treated the victim may become unconscious and eventually lapse into a coma.
- Keep victim lying down, preferably with head lower than body.
- Don't give fluids unless delayed in getting to doctor, then give only water. (Hot tea, coffee, milk, or broth may be tried if water is not tolerated.)
- Never give liquid to an unconscious person. Patient must be alert.
- Cover victim both under and around his body.
- Do not permit victim to become abnormally hot.
- Reassure victim and avoid letting him see other victims or his own injury.
- Fainting is most common and last form of shock. Patient will respond in 30-60 seconds by merely allowing patient to lie head down, if possible, on floor.

FRACTURES: Pain, deformity, or swelling of injured part usually means a fracture. If fracture is suspected, don't move person unless absolutely necessary, and then only if the suspected area is splinted. Give small amounts of lukewarm fluids and treat for shock.

BURNS: Apply or submerge the burned area in cold water. Apply a protective dry sterile cloth or gauze dry dressing if necessary. Do not apply grease or an antiseptic ointment or spray. Call doctor and keep patient warm (not hot) with severe burns.
- If burn case must be transported any distance, cover burns with clean cloth.
- Don't dress extensive facial burns. (It may hinder early plastic surgery.)

WOUNDS: Minor cuts — Apply pressure with sterile gauze until bleeding stops. Use antiseptic recommended by your doctor. Bandage with sterile gauze. See your doctor. **Puncture Wounds** — Cover with sterile gauze and consult a doctor immediately. Serious infection can arise unless properly treated.

ANIMAL BITES: Wash wounds freely with soap and water. Hold under running tap for several minutes if possible. Apply an antiseptic approved by your doctor and cover with sterile gauze compress. Always see your doctor immediately. So that animal may be held in quarantine, obtain name and address of owner.

HEAT EXHAUSTION: Caused by exposure to heat or sun. Symptoms: Pale face, moist and clammy skin, weak pulse, subnormal temperature, victim usually conscious.
Treatment: Keep victim lying down, legs elevated, victim wrapped in blanket. Give salt water to drink (1 tsp. salt to 1 glass water), ½ glass every 15 minutes. Call doctor.

GENERAL DIRECTIONS FOR FIRST AID

1. Effect a prompt rescue.
2. Maintain an open airway.
3. Control severe bleeding by direct pressure over bleeding site. No tourniquet.
4. Give First Aid for poisoning.
5. Do not move victim unless it is necessary for safety reasons.
6. Protect the victim from unnecessary manipulation.
7. Avoid or overcome chilling by using blankets or covers, if available.
8. Determine the injuries or cause for sudden illness.
9. Examine the victim methodically but be guided by the kind of accident or sudden illness and the need of the situation.
10. Carry out the indicated First Aid.

MISCELLANEOUS

HOW TO BOIL WATER

Some say most men can't even boil water. This recipe disproves that misconception.

Enough water   **Heat source**
1 pot (size of choice)

Put water in pot (somewhat similar to a cup in a shape, but larger, usually made of some sort of metal and often has a long handle as well). Pot should be long enough to hold all the water you want to boil. If it isn't, you can divide your water in half, but the first half gets cold while you boil the second half. Light burner under pot. Cook until bubbles appear. Keep your eyes closed during the latter part of this process as a watched pot never boils.

Lloyd E. Wright, Georgetown Lions Club
Georgetown, Ohio, USA

CORNCOB JELLY

12 corncobs from which sweet   **1 box fruit pectin**
** corn has been cut (raw)**   **4 c. sugar**
4 c. water

Boil the 12 corncobs in 4 cups water for 10 minutes, straining through a cloth for 3 cups. Add more water if needed. Put liquid into a pan. Add 1 box fruit pectin. Bring to boil. Add 4 cups sugar (all at once). Bring to rolling boil. Remove from heat and skim. Put into jars and seal.

This jelly is clear and tastes like honey. Food coloring may be added, if desired, but I like the pretty clear look.

Necessity is the mother of invention.
Lion Kathleen Schatz Dague, Aurora Eastgate Lions Club
Aurora, Colorado, USA

GREEN PEPPER JELLY

8 green peppers   **1½ c. cider vinegar**
7 c. sugar   **1 bottle Certo (or 2 pouches)**
1 tsp. turmeric   **Green food coloring**

Cut and core peppers. Grind in food processor. Put through sieve. Take 2 cups juice and pulp; boil with sugar, vinegar, and turmeric (rolling boil for 2 minutes). Add Certo and bring to boil (rolling boil for 3 minutes). Add green food coloring as desired. Pour into sterilized jars. Melt wax and seal tops.

The first U.S. postage stamp was issued in 1847.
Lion Kathleen Schatz Dague, Aurora Eastgate Lions Club
Aurora, Colorado, USA

RHUBARB REFRIGERATOR OR FREEZER JAM

5 c. diced fresh or frozen rhubarb
3 c. sugar

1 pkg. gelatin mix (your favorite flavor, such as grape)

Mix rhubarb and sugar in large bowl and let set overnight. Cook this mixture about 10 minutes in large saucepan. Remove from fire. Stir in gelatin mix. Put in jars and keep in refrigerator or freezer.

If I can make this, any man can do it!

Rollin Dillinger, Offerle Lions Club
Offerle, Kansas, USA

MARASCHINO CHERRIES
(Make your own)

10 c. light colored cherries
2 tsp. alum
4 Tbsp. salt
7 c. sugar

1 tsp. almond extract
8 c. cold water
2 oz. red or green food coloring

Wash and pit cherries. Drain cherries before measuring. Save juice. Dissolve alum and salt in 8 cups water. Add cherries and let stand 5 to 8 hours. (If cherries float, cover with plate weighted with a jar filled with water.) Drain and rinse cherries. Measure juice and water to it to make 2 cups. Add sugar and cook until sugar dissolves. Add cherries and boil 2 minutes. Remove from heat. Add food color and extract. Let stand 18 to 24 hours in a cool place. Boil 2 minutes; pour boiling hot into hot jars and seal at once.

Lion Kathleen Schatz Dague, Aurora Eastgate Lions Club
Aurora, Colorado, USA

MOTHER'S MAYONNAISE

3 eggs
1½ c. sugar
½ c. vinegar

1 tsp. dry mustard
Salt to taste
Dash of pepper

Mix sugar, mustard, and eggs. Add vinegar, salt, and pepper. Cook in double boiler until thick. May add lump butter.

Betty Groft (Mrs. Cyril), Silver Run-Union Mills Lions Club
Westminster, Maryland, USA

Thorough preparation makes its own luck.

SUBSTITUTE FOR SWEETENED CONDENSED MILK
(Not evaporated milk - similar to "Eagle Brand")

1 c. dry milk
⅔ c. sugar

3 Tbsp. butter or margarine
⅓ c. boiling water

Blend until smooth. Refrigerate until thick (or overnight). Equals 1 can of sweetened condensed milk. A good way to cut cooking costs.

Lion Kathleen S. Dague, Aurora Eastgate Lions Club
Aurora, Colorado, USA

HOMEMADE EAGLE BRAND MILK

1 c. instant dry milk
⅔ c. sugar
⅓ c. boiling water

3 Tbsp. melted butter or
margarine

Combine in blender and blend until very smooth. This is the same as 1 can of Eagle Brand milk.

Edna Eckel, Moweaqua Lions Club
Moweaqua, Illinois, USA

OLD-FASHIONED MUSTARD

1 gal. cider vinegar
1 c. dry mustard
1 c. sugar

½ c. salt
1 tsp. alum
Approx. 15 lb. tiny cucumbers

Mix cider vinegar with rest of ingredients, except cucumbers. Soak and wash cucumbers in cold water. Pat dry and pack them very tightly in any kind of jar. Can even be placed in a crock. Cover cucumbers with vinegar mixture. Place lids on and store in cool dark place.

Bev O'Clair, Westbrook Lions Club
Westbrook, Maine, USA

RECIPE FOR A HAPPY HOME

Combine happy hearts; melt in lots of love. Mix well with respect, gentleness, laughter, and joy. Faith, hope, and self-control. Pour in understanding. Forget not the patience. Blend in listening ears. Allow to grow and share. Sprinkle with smiles, hugs, and kisses; bake for a lifetime. Yields 1 happy home.

PDG Lloyd E. Wright, Georgetown Lions Club
Georgetown, Ohio, USA

❧

In every soul is deposited the seed of a great future.

CAJUN SPICE MIX

1 Tbsp. cayenne pepper
2 Tbsp. salt
3 Tbsp. paprika
1 Tbsp. onion powder
1 tsp. garlic powder

1 tsp. white pepper
2 tsp. black pepper
1½ tsp. thyme
1½ tsp. oregano

Mix all together and store in airtight container. Excellent spice for "blackened" fish or chicken or those delicious "blackened hamburgers." Just use as little or as much as you dare for that real "Cajun Country" taste.

Frances Cantrell, Bowie Evening Lions Club
Bowie, Texas, USA

PEAR MINCEMEAT

16 lb. pears, peeled
2½ lb. raisins
6 large apples, peeled
2 large oranges, peeled
2 large lemons, peeled
3 lb. sugar

3 lb. sorghum syrup
1 Tbsp. allspice
1 small can nutmeg
1 pt. vinegar
1 tsp. salt

Grind first 5 ingredients in food chopper or food processor. Add remaining ingredients and cook 1½ hours. Add 1 pint fruit juice or wine. Heat to boiling. Seal in jars. Makes a very good 2 crust pie. Add ¼ cup sugar and 2 tablespoons butter.

Roger Gage, Decatur Lions Club
Decatur, Texas, USA

PEAR PRESERVES

Peel pears and thinly slice. For each gallon of sliced pears, top with 1 quart of sugar. Cover and let set overnight. Thinly slice 2 lemons, peel and all. Stir mixture and cook slowly until pears become transparent and slightly red in color (approximately 1 to 1½ hours). No water ever needs to be added to this, the fruit and sugar makes the juice.

Pack in clear sterilized jars and seal. These are delicious with hot biscuits! I learned to make these by watching my mother when I was a little girl.

Frances Cantrell, Bowie Evening Lions Club
Bowie, Texas, USA

You only fail when you do less than your best.

HOW TO PRESERVE CHOICE CHILDREN

1 grassy field
½ doz. children
2 or 3 small dogs

Pinch of brooks
Some pebbles

Mix children and dogs together well and put them in the field, stirring constantly. Pour the brook over some pebbles. Sprinkle the field with flowers; spread over all a deep blue sky and bake in hot sun. When thoroughly brown, remove and set away to cool in a bathtub.

Life is what happens - just as you were making other plans.
Terry Pister, Prince Albert Downtown Lioness Club
Prince Albert, Saskatchewan, Canada
Hedgesville Lions Club
Hedgesville, West Virginia, USA

HOMEMADE MEAT COATING

Flour
Bread crumbs

Potato flakes (instant)

Use amount needed for size of meat serving. Mix all 3 ingredients together. Dip meat in and coat evenly on both sides, then fry. Excellent dip for fish or chicken.
Thelma Bankert (Mrs. Melvin), Silver Run-Union Mills Lions Club
Littlestown, Pennsylvania, USA

EASY CUCUMBER RELISH

20 large cucumbers, peeled and
seeded
2 large onions, peeled
4 Tbsp. salt (noniodized)
1 qt. white vinegar

1 c. sugar
2 tsp. mustard seed
2 tsp. celery seed
1 hot pepper, chopped

Grind cucumbers and onion. Add salt and let stand 1 hour. Drain thoroughly. Add remaining ingredients. Cook 20 minutes. Can and seal hot.
Lion Sharon Riggenbach, Graysville/Proctor Lions Club
Proctor, West Virginia, USA

A human being's first responsibility is to shake hands with himself.

INDIAN RELISH

12 green tomatoes
12 peeled cored tart apples
3 peeled onions
5 c. vinegar

1 tsp. red pepper
3 tsp. ginger
1 tsp. turmeric
1 tsp. salt

Put green tomatoes, apples, and onions through a food chopper or chop until very fine. Boil the next 6 ingredients. Add the chopped ingredients. Simmer for ½ hour. Pack the relish in sterile jars. Seal and process for 15 minutes in boiling water bath. Makes about 4 quarts.

Dr. Bill Buker, Westbrook Lions Club
Westbrook, Maine, USA

CHOW CHOW

2 gal. green tomatoes
1 gal. cabbage
1 doz. onions
1 doz. bell peppers
3 jalapeno peppers (more if you
    like it hot)

6 c. sugar
2 Tbsp. cinnamon
2 Tbsp. ginger
1 Tbsp. cloves
1½ Tbsp. celery seed
½ gal. vinegar (apple cider)

Grind first 5 ingredients. Mix together. Sprinkle ¾ cup salt. Let stand 2 hours. Drain. Add remaining ingredients. Bring to boil and cook 10 minutes. Put in jars and seal. Very good on cooked dry beans or peas.

Roger Gage, Decatur Lions Club
Decatur, Texas, USA

PICKLED BEETS

2 qt. red beets and juice

    Brine:

1 c. sugar
1 c. vinegar
1 c. beet juice

3 medium onions

½ Tbsp. salt
½ Tbsp. mixed pickling spices
1 Tbsp. lemon juice

Use canned or cooked beets; drain juice and use in brine. Add sliced onion. Heat and boil brine 2 to 4 minutes. Pour hot brine over beets and onions. Store in refrigerator. Beets are ready to eat in a day or two.

Alice E. Wood, Eden Lions Club
Eden, Wisconsin, USA

Have old memories but young hopes.

LIFE'S RECIPE

1 c. good thoughts
1 c. kind deeds
1 c. consideration for others

2 c. sacrifice for others
3 c. forgiveness
2 c. well-beaten faults

Mix thoroughly and add tears of joy, sorrow, and sympathy for others. Fold in 4 cups of prayer and add faith. After pouring all into your daily life, bake well and serve with a smile.

Taken from "Cooking With Pride" cookbook published by the Royalton Hills Lions Club in November, 1993.

Royalton Hills Lions Club
North Royalton, Ohio, USA

REFRIGERATOR PICKLES

25 medium cucumbers, sliced
3 onions, sliced
½ c. salt
4 c. vinegar
5 c. sugar

1 tsp. turmeric
1½ tsp. celery seed
1½ tsp. mustard seed
1 tsp. alum

Pour mixture over cucumbers. Seal and store in refrigerator.

Linda Theriault, Westbrook Lions Club
Westbrook, Maine, USA

BREAD AND BUTTER PICKLES

4 qt. medium, sliced cucumbers
   (unpeeled)
3 medium onions, sliced
2 green peppers, cleaned, cored,
   and sliced
2 cloves garlic

2 tsp. celery seed
2 Tbsp. mustard seed
⅓ c. pickling salt
5 c. sugar
3 c. white vinegar
2 tsp. turmeric

Gently mix cucumbers, onion, green peppers, and whole garlic cloves. Add salt and mix thoroughly. Cover with cracked ice. Let stand 3 hours. Drain well. Combine remaining ingredients. Pour over cucumber mix. Heat just to a boil. Seal in hot sterilized jars. Makes 8 pints.

A old Spanish proverb: When you are born, everyone is smiling, yet you are weeping, so live your life in such a way - when you die - everyone may weep and you may smile.

Sarah Wehling, Bothell Lions Club
Bothell, Washington, USA

Only those who see the invisible can do the impossible.

MUSTARD PICKLES

To 1 gallon of vegetables, add 1 cup salt to 1 gallon water. Soak vegetables in salt water 3 hours. Drain and wash. Boil vegetables in 2 cups vinegar and 1½ cups water. Mix 2½ cups sugar, 4 tablespoons flour, 4 tablespoons mustard, 1 tablespoon turmeric, 1 teaspoon celery seed, and 1 tablespoon mixed pickled spices tied in bag.

Vegetables include onions, cucumbers, cauliflower, peppers, etc.

Evelyn Steele, Lyman Lions Club
Lyman, Wyoming, USA

EASY CUCUMBER PICKLES

7 c. cucumbers (do not peel)　　　　**½ c. chopped green pepper**
1 c. onions, sliced

Put in large pan. Cover with water. Add 3 tablespoons salt. Let stand 1 hour. Drain. Mix 2 cups sugar, 1 cup vinegar, and 1 teaspoon celery seed. Pour over pickles. Let stand 3 days before eating. Will keep for weeks.

Jeanne Wait, Whitestown Lions Club
Whitestown, Indiana, USA

HORSERADISH DRESSING

4 to 6 oz. bottle horseradish　　　**2 Tbsp. white vinegar**
1 pkg. lemon jello　　　　　　　　**1 pt. whipping cream, whipped**
1 c. boiling water　　　　　　　　**1 Tbsp. sugar**
1 tsp. salt

Mix jello and boiling water. Stir till dissolved. Add salt, vinegar, and horseradish. Allow to gel in fridge. Meanwhile, whip cream, adding sugar until stiff. Add to jelled mixture. This is good on roasted meats and bar-b-ques.

Walter E. Loomis, North Jackson Lions Club
Jackson, Michigan, USA

BARBECUE SAUCE

½ c. tomato juice　　　　　　　**1 c. vinegar**
4 tsp. salt　　　　　　　　　　　**½ lb. butter or margarine**
1 Tbsp. ground red pepper

Combine the above ingredients and let come to boil. Makes enough sauce to barbecue 2½ chickens.

Edna K. Bunch, Snow Hill Lions Club
Snow Hill, North Carolina, USA

BARBECUE SAUCE

1 bottle catsup
¼ c. brown sugar
½ tsp. vinegar

1 onion, diced
Liquid smoke

Combine all ingredients and cook down or put on meat in oven.

Nancy Fausett, Lyman Lions Club
Lyman, Wyoming, USA

FROZEN SPAGHETTI SAUCE

16 c. peeled and chopped
   tomatoes
2 Tbsp. oregano
2 Tbsp. basil
¼ c. parsley (fresh, finely
   chopped, or dried)
¼ c. sugar

2 Tbsp. salt
4 onions (medium), chopped
4 cloves garlic, finely chopped
¾ tsp. black pepper
2 (12 oz.) cans tomato paste
½ c. oil

In a 6 to 8 quart pot, cook the onions and garlic in the oil until the onions are transparent. Add all remaining ingredients and simmer for 2 to 2½ hours. Divide the sauce into freezer containers in quantities suitable for your family requirements.

Note: While cooking, remember to stir the sauce frequently to prevent sticking and scorching. Longer cooking time will render a thicker sauce.

This is a handy freezer item to have when company (friends or relatives) show up unexpectedly near the supper hour. What a "hero or heroine" as the case may be!

A.J. and Wanda Groenendale, Fort Collins Lions Club
Fort Collins, Colorado, USA

Everything is changing.
People are taking the comedians seriously and the politicians as a joke.

FUNDRAISER SPAGHETTI SAUCE

4 (32 oz.) Prego spaghetti sauce
7 (12 oz.) tomato paste
7 (29 oz.) tomato sauce
8 tsp. oregano
8 tsp. basil
16 tsp. salt

4 tsp. pepper
4 tsp. garlic salt
8 lb. ground meat
2 bags frozen chopped onions
1½ c. white sugar

Brown meat and onions well. Drain in a large colander. Place in an electric roaster. Add Prego sauce and all spices including the sugar. Stir well. Have roaster set on high or 500°. Add paste and sauce. Stir well while cooking on high until sauce bubbles. Lower heat setting to 250° and simmer for 4 to 6 hours. One electric roaster serves 60 people. Cook 10 pounds spaghetti and drain. Put into a large container and refrigerate until needed. When ready to serve, place in boiling water 5 minutes. Drain well and put into another electric roaster. Add 2 quarts of the cooked sauce and mix well to coat. To serve, place portion of spaghetti on plate and top with sauce.

Jim and Pat Tulloch, Bedford Heights Lions Club
Bedford Heights, Ohio, USA

CHILI SAUCE

4 qt. ripe tomatoes
1½ c. ground onions
⅛ c. salt
1½ c. sweet peppers
2 or 3 small chili peppers

4 c. sugar
1½ tsp. celery seed
1½ tsp. cinnamon
1½ tsp. allspice
4 c. vinegar

Bring to boil and simmer to desired consistency. Can.

Evelyn Steele, Lyman Lions Club
Lyman, Wyoming, USA

CINNAMON APPLESAUCE

½ c. red hot cinnamon candies
1 c. water
2 pkg. jello (1 lemon, 1 raspberry)

1½ c. cold water
25 oz. or 1 lb. 9 oz. applesauce
  (unsweetened)

Simmer ½ cup red hot cinnamon candies in 1 cup water until dissolved. Add 2 packages jello to hot liquid, stirring until dissolved. Add 1½ cups cold water and applesauce. Blend well.

Alma Lemm, Huffman Lions Club
Huffman, Texas, USA

❦

Feed your faith and your doubt will starve to death.

BAKED PINEAPPLE HOT DISH
(Very good with ham)

1 (No. 2) can chunk pineapple
2 Tbsp. flour
2 Tbsp. shortening

⅓ c. sugar
1 c. grated Longhorn cheese
Bread or cracker crumbs

Drain pineapple (save the juice). In saucepan, stir flour, shortening, and juice; cook until it becomes thick. Add sugar to the hot sauce. Grease a casserole. Cut pineapple into tiny pieces and place in casserole. Add cheese and sauce; stir well. Cover mixture with crumbs. Bake at 300° for 15 to 20 minutes or until cheese is melted. Serve hot or cold.

Experience is a good school, but the fees are high.
Lion Kathleen Schatz Dague, Aurora Eastgate Lions Club
Aurora, Colorado, USA

CRANBERRY SAUCE

1½ c. sugar
⅔ c. orange juice
⅔ c. dry red wine

24 oz. fresh or frozen whole
cranberries

Combine sugar, juice, and wine in saucepan. Bring to a boil. Add cranberries that have been washed, drained, and picked over to remove spoiled ones. Reduce heat and boil gently until all skins have popped. Remove from heat and transfer to dish. Refrigerate. This may also be canned in sterile jars and sealed for storage.

Got this recipe from a Harrowsmith magazine while waiting for dentist. We love it. The color is beautifully different.
Lion Vivian Quinlan, Mathews Lions Club
Mathews, Virginia, USA

BROWN BUTTER AND SAGE SAUCE

Cheese ravioli is particularly good with this herb-scented sauce.

4 Tbsp. butter
1 Tbsp. fresh sage or 1½ tsp. dried
   sage

½ tsp. salt
¼ tsp. pepper

1. In a medium frying pan over medium-high heat, melt the butter. Cook butter until it becomes golden brown, 2 to 3 minutes. Do not let it scorch.
2. Add the sage, salt, and pepper. Makes ¼ cup (6 servings).
John J. Hess for Mrs. Joanne Brownell, Clarence Center Lions Club
Clarence Center, New York, USA

❧

Life is like a mirror - we get the best results when we smile at it.

RED EYE GRAVY

1 or more slices "country ham"
Hot liquid coffee

Light or dark brown sugar
(optional)

Use one or more slices of "country ham," depending on the quantity of red eye gravy desired. Fry ham slices until well done or all grease has been cooked out. To the hot grease in the pan, add 1 or more cups of hot liquid coffee (regular or decaffeinated). Lower the heat and keep warm till used. A teaspoon of light or dark brown sugar (for each cup of coffee used) may be desired to give the gravy a slightly sweet taste.

This "Deep South" item has just about disappeared, although the scarcity may be due in part to the necessity to use only "country-cured" ham, which may not always be available. Used to flavor meat, biscuits, scrambled eggs, grits.

Lion Seth Howard, Canton Lions Club
Canton, Georgia, USA

PARSLEY SAUCE

This is enough for one pound of pasta.

2 c. lightly packed parsley leaves
⅓ c. walnut pieces
2 cloves garlic, peeled
½ tsp. salt
¼ tsp. pepper

½ c. olive oil
1 oz. Parmesan (about ⅓ c.),
freshly grated
1 Tbsp. butter (at room
temperature)

1. In a food processor or blender, chop parsley, walnuts, garlic, salt, and pepper. While machine is running, gradually add olive oil.
2. Scrape into bowl and stir in Parmesan cheese and butter. Makes 1 cup (6 servings).

John J. Hess for Mrs. Joanne Brownell, Clarence Center Lions Club
Clarence Center, New York, USA

People need responsibility.
They resist assuming it, but they cannot get along without it.

YORKSHIRE PUDDING

To be eaten with roast beef. Recipe from England.

⅞ c. flour
½ c. milk
½ tsp. salt

2 eggs
½ c. water

Sift flour and salt into a bowl. Make a well in the center and pour in the milk. Beat 2 eggs until fluffy. Beat them into the batter. Add ½ cup water. Beat the batter well until large bubbles rise to the surface. You may permit this to stand for 1 hour and then beat it again. Have ready a hot ovenproof dish, about 10x10 inches, or hot muffin tins containing about ¼ inch hot beef drippings or melted butter. Pour in the batter. Bake the pudding in a 400° oven for about 20 minutes. Reduce the heat to 350° and bake it 10 to 15 minutes longer. (Some cooks recommend a 350° oven for ½ hour.) Serve it at once.

Sausage-Toad-In-The-Hole: Add 6 to 10 sausages to above batter, then cook as above.

For lump-free gravy, place all ingredients into jar with tight fitting lid and shake for a few seconds.

Mrs. Joyce Perkins, South Benton Lions Club
Monroe, Oregon, USA

OLIVE OIL-LEMON SAUCE

This sauce goes very well with meat tortellini.

¼ c. olive oil
2 Tbsp. lemon juice
⅛ tsp. crushed red pepper flakes
½ tsp. salt

¼ tsp. pepper
1 Tbsp. chopped parsley
½ tsp. lemon zest

1. In a frying pan, heat oil over medium-high heat. Add the lemon juice, red pepper flakes, salt, and pepper. Simmer 1 minute.
2. Stir in the parsley and the lemon zest. Makes ⅓ cup (6 servings).

John J. Hess from Mrs. Joanne Brownell, Clarence Center Lions Club
Clarence Center, New York, USA

❦

There are times when silence has the loudest voice.

BECKY'S SWEET AND SOUR SAUCE
(For steamed veggies)

1 c. honey
1 c. vinegar
1 c. tamari or soy sauce
5 c. soup stock
3 oz. ginger, chopped fine

2 cloves garlic, chopped fine
12 oz. can tomato sauce or 6 oz. paste
1 Tbsp. corn starch
1 c. orange juice or cider

Chop ginger and garlic. (If using ground ginger, add to desired taste.) Mix all but last 2 ingredients. Bring to a boil. Blend corn starch and orange juice. Add to mixture and boil to thicken.

Straight from the kitchens of Vancouver, British Columbia.
Rebecca Mergaert by Walter E. Loomis, North Jackson Lions Club
Jackson, Michigan, USA

COCKTAIL SAUCE FOR SHRIMP

2 c. catsup
½ c. lemon juice
1 tsp. salt

½ c. Worcestershire sauce
Dash of hot sauce
¼ c. horseradish

Combine all ingredients the day before using and store in the refrigerator. This yields enough sauce for about 5 pounds of raw shrimp in the shell. Yield: About 4 cups.

Mrs. Lion Robert (Margaret) Logan, Canton Lions Club
Canton, Georgia, USA

ROMESCO SAUCE

Serve with rotelle or other grooved shape.

¼ c. slivered almonds
¼ c. olive oil
1 small onion, chopped
1 clove garlic, minced
4 tsp. red wine vinegar
⅓ c. roasted red bell peppers

1 slice white bread, toasted
½ tsp. paprika
⅛ tsp. cayenne pepper
½ tsp. salt
¼ tsp. pepper

1. In a small frying pan over medium heat, toast nuts until golden, shaking pan occasionally so they don't burn, about 4 minutes. Remove nuts and set aside.

2. Stir 1 tablespoon of oil, the onion, and garlic into the pan; cook until onion is soft, 3 to 5 minutes.

3. In a food processor or blender, puree almonds and the onion mixture with vinegar, roasted peppers, bread, paprika, cayenne, salt, and pepper. Add remaining oil and puree until very smooth. Makes ¾ cup (6 servings).

John J. Hess for Mrs. Joanne Brownell, Clarence Center Lions Club
Clarence Center, New York, USA

VIVIAN'S PARSLEY PISTOU SAUCE

½ c. tomato shakes (minced sun-
    dried tomatoes)
1 c. fresh Italian parsley leaves
½ c. fresh grated Parmesan
    cheese

2 large cloves garlic
½ c. olive oil
½ to 1 c. pine nuts

Tomato shakes were purchased at Price Club.

Combine all ingredients in blender or in food processor until it is pureed. Store in refrigerator for at least 1 day while tomato shakes soften. Use a dollop of pistou in a bowl of hot soup or toss hot pasta with pistou for a taste different but as delightful as pesto sauce made with basil.

Hint: On recipe cards, I like to circle each ingredient. Each one stands out and is less likely to be missed. Ditto for shopping lists and using different colors for categories is even better for shopping - example green for veggies and red for meat.

Lion Vivian Quinlan, Mathews Lions Club
Mathews, Virginia, USA

MUSHROOM SAUCE
(Great on cheese ravioli)

1 Tbsp. butter
1 lb. mushrooms, halved and
    thinly sliced
2 cloves garlic, minced
¼ c. dry sherry

¾ tsp. salt
¼ tsp. pepper
1 c. heavy cream
1 Tbsp. chopped fresh parsley

1. In a large frying pan over high heat, melt the butter. Add mushrooms and cook until their liquid has evaporated and they just begin to brown, about 12 minutes.

2. Stir in the garlic and cook mixture until the mushrooms are completely brown, about 3 minutes longer. Stir in sherry, salt, and pepper; cook until sherry is almost evaporated, about 1 minute.

3. Add cream and cook until reduced and slightly thickened, 5 to 7 minutes. Stir in the parsley and serve. Makes 2 cups (6 servings).

John J. Hess for Mrs. Joanne Brownell, Clarence Center Lions Club
Clarence Center, New York, USA

If you had your life to live over again, you'd need more money.

MOTHER'S LIFETIME RECIPE

2 heaping c. of patience
1 heartful of love
2 handfuls of generosity

Dash of laughter
1 headful of understanding

Sprinkle generously with kindness. Add plenty of faith and mix well. Spread over a period of a lifetime, and serve to everybody you meet.

Taken from "Cooking With Pride" cookbook published by the Royalton Hills Lions Club in November, 1993.

Royalton Hills Lions Club
North Royalton, Ohio, USA

EDIBLE PLAY DOUGH

1 c. honey
1 c. peanut butter

1 c. instant dry milk

Mix. Keep adding more powdered milk until thick enough to mold into snakes, monsters, and other creations. Eat.

Fun to make; fun to eat.
Rev. Fred Gilbert, Dannemora, New York, Lions Club
Dannemora, New York, USA

PLAYDOUGH
(For children to play with)

The following recipe makes excellent playdough that can be stored unrefrigerated.

2 c. flour
¼ c. oil
Food coloring

2 c. water
4 tsp. cream of tartar
1 c. salt

Add wet ingredients to dry. Blend well. The dough should be the consistency of melted ice cream. Store in covered container.

The first state to enter the Union after the first 13: Vermont, 1791.
Lion Kathleen Schatz Dague, Aurora Eastgate Lions Club
Aurora, Colorado, USA

We don't know who we are until we see what we can do.

BIRD FEEDER

1 c. corn meal
1 c. peanut butter
1 c. sugar

½ c. flour
1 c. water
1 c. commercial bird seed

Mix all together, except the bird seed. Microwave on HIGH for 3 to 5 minutes or until mixture is very thick. Stir 1 cup commercial bird seed in. Cool. Press into a pie pan or mold around a pine cone. Refrigerate until cool and mixture has hardened. Unmold or tie string around pine cone and place outside for a holiday treat for our feathered friends.

Birds are our friends and need food in the winter when the ground is bare or covered with snow.

Lion Kathleen Schatz Dague, Aurora Eastgate Lions Club
Aurora, Colorado, USA

DOGGIE BONES

2½ c. whole wheat flour
6 Tbsp. margarine
1 Tbsp. salt
½ c. nonfat dry milk powder
1 egg
1 Tbsp. sugar

½ c. water
1 clove garlic, pressed, or ½ tsp.
    dried (optional)
1 beef cube
Parsley

Mix all together until dough can be rolled out. Roll to cracker thickness. Cut with dog bone shape cookie cutter or heart shape. Place on baking sheet. Bake 30 minutes at 350° or until golden brown. Pets need Christmas cheer too.

HOME BAKED DOG TREAT COOKIES

2 beef bouillon cubes
3 c. hot water
5 c. flour
1½ c. oatmeal

¼ c. vegetable oil
1 c. dry milk
1 egg (optional)

Set oven at 350°. Dissolve bouillon cubes in water. When dissolved, add the flour gradually, then add oatmeal and oil. If too thick to handle, add a bit more water. Dust hands with flour and roll pieces of dough into patties. Place on greased cookie sheet and bake until crisp and brown.

A dog is man's best friend.

Lion Kathleen Schatz Dague, Aurora Eastgate Lions Club
Aurora, Colorado, USA

If you believe, you can achieve.

RECIPE FOR HAPPINESS

Keep your heart free from hate,
Your mind free from worry;
Live simply; expect little,
Give much; fill your life with love;
Scatter kindness;
Forget self, think of others;
And do as you would be done by.

Paula Burns, Lyman Lions Club
Lyman, Wyoming, USA

A small town is a place where everyone knows
whose check is good and whose husband is not.

❦ ❦ ❦

The beauty of the old-fashioned blacksmith was
when you took your horse to be shod, he didn't find 40 other things that
needed to be done.

❦ ❦ ❦

Be curious always! For knowledge will not acquire you;
you must acquire it.

❦ ❦ ❦

If you are wondering about the difference
between attachment and enjoyment,
just ask yourself how you would react
if suddenly an object you valued was gone.

INDEX OF RECIPES

SNACKS, APPETIZERS, BEVERAGES

SNACKS AND APPETIZERS

ALL OCCASION CHEESE BALL 28
ARMADILLO EGGS (STUFFED
  JALAPENOS) 4
BACON CHEESE DIP 20
BAKED CREAM CHEESE APPETIZER....... 27
BARBECUE COCKTAIL WIENERS 9
BEAN DIP............................. 22
BOURBON HOT DOGS 9
BUENO SAUSAGE DIP 18
BURRITO BITES 4
CALIFORNIA CAVIAR 6
CANDIED WALNUTS 35
CARAMEL CORN........................ 34
CHEESE BALL......................... 29
CHEESE BALL......................... 29
CHEESE BALL......................... 28
CHEESE BALL OR SPREAD 30
CHEESE DUMPLINGS................... 32
CHEESE LOG 29
CHEESE PUFFS 32
CHEESE ROLL......................... 28
CHESTNUT WRAP AROUND 12
CHILI CON QUESO DE NEW MEXICO........ 3
CHILI CON QUESO DIP.................... 3
CHIPPED BEEF BALL 27
CHIPPED BEEF CHEESE SPREAD 26
COCKTAIL MEAT BALLS.................. 8
COCKTAIL MEATBALLS 7
COTTAGE CHEESE PINEAPPLE DIP........ 20
COWBOY JERKY........................ 7
CRABBIES 23
CRISP WON TON 5
CURRY DIP 18
DEVILED EGGS......................... 13
DILL DIP.............................. 17
FIVE LAYERED DIP 2
FRUIT PIZZA 11
GARBAGE MIX......................... 36
GREEN PEPPER APPETIZER............... 5
GUACAMOLE 2
HAM AND CHEESE BALL 30
"HANKY-PANKIES" 23
HEARTY PARTY RYES 25
HEAVENLY DIP (HOT)................... 26
HIDDEN VALLEY RANCH PINWHEELS 1
HOLIDAY PIE.......................... 25
HOMEMADE BEEF JERKY 7
HOT OLIVE CHEESE PUFFS 27
HOT SAUSAGE DIP...................... 19
ITALIAN PIE 10
JIM'S CHEESE BALL 29
KAHLUA CARAMEL CORN 33
LINDA'S DIP........................... 20
LIVERWURST SPREAD.................... 25
LOWER CALORIE GRANOLA.............. 36
MEXICAN LAYER DIP 2
MEXICAN MESS 1
MICROWAVE CURRIED FRUIT............. 12
MICROWAVE KARMEL CORN 33
MICROWAVE MEATBALL APPETIZERS....... 8
MINIATURE BACON-CHEESE QUICHE 33
NACHOS DELUXE....................... 4
ONION DIP............................ 17
PEOPLE CHOW......................... 36
PEPPERONI PIZZA DIP.................. 21

PINEAPPLE CHEESE BALL 31
PINEAPPLE CHEESE BALL 31
PINEAPPLE CHEESE BALL 31
PINEAPPLE CHUNKS 11
PIZZA DIP............................ 21
POLISH MISTAKES 24
POPCORN BALLS...................... 34
POPCORN CAKE....................... 34
POPCORN............................. 35
REUBEN DIP 18
ROAST BEEF ROLL-UPS 26
ROASTED GARLIC 13
SALMON MOLD 15
SAUSAGE BALLS 6
SAUSAGE DIP......................... 19
SAUSAGE DIP......................... 19
SHRIMP DIP........................... 16
SHRIMP DIP........................... 15
SHRIMP DIP........................... 16
SHRIMP MOUSSE 15
SMITHFIELD HAM SAUSAGE AND BACKFIN
  CRAB SPREAD...................... 24
SPECIAL CHEESE BALL................. 28
SPICED PEARS........................ 11
SPINACH BREAD....................... 16
SPINACH DIP.......................... 17
STUFFED CELERY 5
STUFFED EGGS 13
STUFFED MUSHROOMS 14
SUNGREN'S CHEESE BALL.............. 30
SUPER CHALUPA DIP................... 3
TACO DIP............................. 22
TEXAS CAVIAR 6
TORTILLA ROLL-UPS 1
TUNA FISH MOLD...................... 14
TUNA PATE 14
TUNA VEGETABLE SPREAD 23
VEGETABLE DIP 21
VEGETABLE PIZZA 9
VEGETABLE PIZZA 10
VEGGIE DIP 22
WATER CHESTNUT DIP 17
WATER CHESTNUTS 13
WRAPPED WATER CHESTNUTS.......... 12

BEVERAGES

BANANA SLUSH PUNCH 40
BLUE JAY PUNCH...................... 39
CAPPUCCINO MIX...................... 44
CRANBERRY-GRAPE SPRITZER 37
EGGNOG 41
FIRST NIGHT FREEZES 40
FLY ME TO CANCUN MARGARITA........ 42
FRESH HOMEMADE LEMONADE.......... 44
GRANDMA'S FERMENTED GRAPE WINE.... 42
HOT WASSAIL........................ 44
IRISH CREAM 42
KAHLUA 42
LIME PUNCH 37
LUSCIOUS PUNCH 39
MARGARITAS......................... 43
NEW YEAR'S NECTAR 43
PARTY FRUIT PUNCH................... 37
PERFECT PARTY PUNCH................ 38
PUNCH FOR 100 PEOPLE............... 38
RUM GOODIES 41
SLUSH 40
SPICED TEA MIX...................... 45

STRAWBERRY DAIQUIRI 43
WOODY'S REVENGE 41

BREAKFAST AND BRUNCH

ABBLESCIBERS. 47
ARMADILLO EGGS 60
BAKED CHEESE AND EGGS 61
BLIZZARD FRUIT. 66
BREAKFAST CASSEROLE 58
BREAKFAST CASSEROLE 57
BREAKFAST PIZZA 62
BREAKFAST PIZZA 61
BREAKFAST PIZZA 61
BRUNCH EGG CASSEROLE. 53
BRUNCHY EGG CASSEROLE 58
CHEESY EGG BAKE 50
CHEESY SAUSAGE QUICHE 48
CHEESY SPINACH BRUNCH 54
CHILI EGG PUFF. 53
CINNAMON FRENCH TOAST 64
COUNTRY BRUNCH CASSEROLE. 50
CRISP ZUCCHINI PANCAKES. 64
EASY BREAKFAST 55
EASY TURKEY QUICHE 48
EGG AND SAUSAGE SOUFFLE 56
EGG CASSEROLE. 59
EGG-SAUSAGE CASSEROLE. 59
EGGS O'BRIEN 60
EGG STRATA. 51
FARMER'S BREAKFAST 62
FAVORITE BREAKFAST CASSEROLE 51
FRENCH TOAST SUPREME 65
GREEN CHILI QUICHE 49
GRITS SOUFFLE. 56
HAM AND CHEESE OVEN BAKED
   OMELETTE. 55
HAM AND POTATO BREAKFAST 63
LEFSE 62
NANCY'S HOT FRUIT 47
ONE DISH BREAKFAST 52
OVEN OMELET 53
PANCAKES. 63
PIPERADE 66
POTATO PANCAKE 63
QUICHE LORRAINE. 47
QUICK BREAKFAST ROLLS 66
SAUSAGE AND EGG CASSEROLE 55
SAUSAGE AND EGG CASSEROLE 50
SAUSAGE BREAKFAST CASSEROLE 57
SAUSAGE-ONION SQUARES 56
SOUTHWESTERN QUICHE. 48
SPINACH QUICHE. 49
STUFFED FRENCH TOAST 65
TORTILLA EGG CASSEROLE. 54
WAFFLE RECIPE. 65
WALT'S FAVORITE HOT CAKES. 64
WALT'S VEGETABLE QUICHE 49
WINE AND CHEESE OMELET
   CASSEROLE 52

SOUPS AND SANDWICHES

SOUPS

BEAN, SAUSAGE, AND BRANDY SOUP 78
BEST EVER CROCK POT CHILI! 72
BRUNSWICK STEW. 69
BUTTER BEAN SOUP 77
CABBAGE PATCH SOUP 91
CHEDDAR CHOWDER 99

CHEESE SOUP 98
CHEESE SOUP 98
CHEEZY VEGETABLE CHILI. 76
CHICKEN CORN SOUP. 83
CHICKEN, MEAT, VEGE, NOODLE SOUP . . . 81
CHICKEN SUCCOTASH SOUP 83
CHICKEN TORTELLINI SOUP. 83
CHILI CHICKEN 77
CHILI WITH YELLOW BEANS 75
CHINESE EGG DROP SOUP - DUN FAR
   TONG 93
CHRISTMAS EVE SOUP 81
CLAM CHOWDER SOUP. 98
COCKA-LEEKIE SOUP 91
CREAM OF TOMATO SOUP 93
CREAMY CHICKEN-VEGETABLE
   CHOWDER. 82
CREAMY VEGETABLE SOUP 85
CREAMY WILD RICE SOUP 89
ELEPHANT SOUP 95
ELEPHANT STEW 70
FISH CHOWDER 97
FISH STEW 95
GARBANZO BEAN SOUP 79
GAZPACHO 101
GONE ALL DAY STEW 67
GONE ALL DAY STEW 67
GOULDSBORO STEAK SOUP 80
GRANMA JO'S CALICO BEAN SOUP AND
   MIX 78
HAMBURGER BARLEY SOUP 80
HEARTY MEATBALL AND VEGETABLE
   STEW 69
HOBO CHILE 73
ICED GAZPACHO - COLD SOUP 93
LEMON CHICKEN SOUP. 81
MAGIC BEAN SOUP 79
MEAT BALL CHOWDER 100
MEATLESS CHILI. 76
MEXICAN CHICKEN CORN CHOWDER. 100
MOM'S BEEF STEW 68
MOUNT SEYMOUR LENTIL SOUP 94
MUSHROOM SOUP. 91
NEW ENGLAND CLAM CHOWDER 97
OLD-FASHIONED POTATO SOUP 86
OLD-FASHIONED VEGETABLE SOUP 84
ONION SOUP. 90
OVEN STEW 68
PASTA FAGIOLI SOUP 94
PHEASANT STEW WITH BAKING POWDER
   DUMPLINGS. 70
PORTUGUESE BEAN SOUP. 79
POTATO SOUP 86
RED CABBAGE SOUP. 92
REGULATORS CHILI. 74
ROADKILL ELEPHANT SOUP 101
SEAFOOD BISQUE 96
SHRIMP BISQUE 96
SLOW COOKER TACO SOUP. 88
SOUP SUPREME 82
SPLIT PEA WITH HAM SOUP. 90
TACO SOUP. 87
TACO SOUP. 87
TEXAS JAILHOUSE CHILI. 72
TZVIVELLE RIVEZ SOUP - ONION RIVEL
   SOUP 90
VEGETABLE CHILI. 75
VEGETABLE CHOWDER. 99
VENUS DE MILO MINESTRONE SOUP 88
VOMACK - CZECH VEGETABLE AND CREAM
   SOUP 84
WEDNESDAY'S CHILI 71

666

WICKY WACKY STEW. 68
WILD RICE SOUP 89
WINTER VEGETABLE SOUP 85
WINTER WHITE CHILI. 71
ZUCCHINI SOUP 92

SANDWICHES
BURGER BUNS 106
CHICKEN BAR-B-Q SANDWICHES. 107
CHIPPED HAM SANDWICHES 102
CRABMEAT SPECIAL ON ENGLISH
  MUFFINS 106
CREAMED CHIPPED BEEF. 103
EGG SANDWICH FILLING. 102
HOT CRAB SANDWICH. 105
PIMENTO CHEESE SANDWICHES. 104
PIZZA SANDWICH 105
RUNZAS 103
SLOPPY JOES. 107
SLOPPY JOES. 107
SUPER BOWL SUPER SANDWICH 104
VEGETABLE SANDWICH 106

SALADS

AMBROSIA SALAD 135
APPLE-CRANBERRY SALAD 147
APRICOT SALAD. 134
BANANA SALAD 139
BEAN SALAD. 109
BLEU CHEESE DRESSING. 148
BLUEBERRY SALAD 142
BOILED BACON DRESSING. 151
BROCCOLI-CAULIFLOWER SALAD 110
BROCCOLI-CAULIFLOWER SALAD
  SUPREME 111
BROCCOLI SALAD 110
CABBAGE SALAD 111
CARROT MEDLEY SALAD 112
CARROT SALAD 112
CAULIFLOWER SALAD 112
CHEESE STUFFED LETTUCE 116
CHERRY COLA SALAD 141
CHERRY CONGEALED SALAD. 143
CHERRY NUT CONGEALED SALAD 143
CHERRY PORT JELLO 142
CHICKEN SALAD. 122
CHICKEN SALAD SUPREME 125
CHINESE CHICKEN SALAD 123
CHINESE CHICKEN SALAD 123
CHRISTMAS SALAD 142
"COMPANY'S COMIN'" MACARONI
  SALAD 128
CONGEALED BUTTERMILK SALAD. 137
CONGEALED CRANBERRY SALAD. 147
CONGEALED STRAWBERRY SALAD. 141
COOKED FRUIT SALAD 132
COOL CORN SALAD 115
CORN BREAD SALAD. 115
COUNTRY STUFFED TOMATOES 121
CRANBERRY SALAD. 148
CRANBERRY SALAD. 146
CUCUMBER SALAD 116
CURRIED FRUIT 131
CURRIED RICE SALAD. 119
DARK CHERRY SALAD. 136
DEWEY LIONS COLE SLAW. 113
DIET FRENCH SALAD DRESSING. 150
DILL POTATO SALAD 119
EASY FRUIT SALAD 134
EASY MANDARIN PINEAPPLE SALAD 143

EXOTIC CHICKEN SALAD. 125
FANTASTIC LUNCHEON SALAD. 126
FETA CHEESE SALAD DRESSING. 149
5-MINUTE FRUIT SALAD. 132
FREEZER COLE SLAW. 115
FREEZER SLAW 114
FROZEN CRANBERRY FRUIT SALAD 134
FROZEN FRUIT SALAD. 133
FRUIT SALAD. 131
FRUIT SALAD. 132
GEORGIA VEGETABLE SALAD 121
GERMAN POTATO SALAD 118
GOLDEN GLOW SALAD 141
GORGONZOLA AND APPLE SALAD 138
GRANDMA'S CRANBERRY SALAD 147
GREEK POTATO SALAD. 119
GRILLED TARRAGON CHICKEN SPINACH
  SALAD 124
HAM BROCCOLI SALAD. 111
HEAVENLY SALAD 140
HOT BACON DRESSING. 150
HOT BACON DRESSING. 150
HOT CHICKEN SALAD 125
ITALIAN SALAD 122
JAMES SALAD. 139
JELLIED SHRIMP SALAD 126
LENTIL SALAD 117
LETTUCE LAYERS 116
LOW CALORIE DUMP SALAD. 138
MACARONI SALAD 128
MARINATED COLE SLAW. 114
MARY SALAD. 135
MR. MAC'S SALAD DRESSING 149
MYSTERY SALAD 136
NOODLES WITH COTTAGE CHEESE 131
OLD WAREHOUSE SALAD DRESSING 149
OVERNIGHT COLESLAW 113
PASTA-APPLE SALAD. 130
PEA SALAD 117
PINEAPPLE FRUIT DRESSING. 151
PINK LEMONADE SALAD 137
PINK SALAD. 138
PINK SALAD. 139
POPPY SEED DRESSING. 149
POTATO SALAD. 118
POTATO SALAD. 118
PRETZEL SALAD. 145
PRETZEL SALAD. 146
PURPLE LADY SALAD 135
RASPBERRY DESSERT SALAD 139
RASPBERRY MOLD 140
RAW CRANBERRY SALAD. 148
REFRIGERATOR SLAW 114
ROSAMARINA SALAD 130
SALATA HORIATIKI - VILLAGE SALAD 121
SALMON SALAD 127
SEAFOOD SALAD 127
7-UP SALAD. 140
SHRIMP MOUSSE 127
SLEET SALAD 133
SPAGHETTI SALAD. 129
SPAGHETTI SALAD. 129
SPAGHETTI SALAD. 130
SPINACH SALAD. 120
SPINACH-STRAWBERRY SALAD. 120
STRAWBERRY PRETZEL SALAD. 144
STRAWBERRY PRETZEL SALAD. 145
SUNSHINE SALAD. 137
SUPER CHICKEN SALAD 124
SWEET AND SOUR BEAN SALAD 109
SWEET ONION SALAD 117
TACO SALAD. 122

TANGY CRANBERRY SALAD 146
THREE BEAN SALAD 109
TOMATO SALAD 120
TROPICAL ORANGE SALAD. 144
TUNA MACARONI SALAD. 128
24-HOUR SALAD 136
WEST INDIES CRAB SALAD. 126

VEGETABLES

ASPARAGUS HOT DISH 154
ASPARAGUS LUNCHEON BAKE 154
BAKED BEANS 155
BAKED BEANS 156
BAKED CARROTS. 170
BAKED EGGPLANT 175
BAKED LIMA BEANS. 176
BAKED RICE 185
BEET RUSSE. 162
BLACK BEANS AND RICE. 161
BORSCH. 162
BREADED ZUCCHINI 194
BROCCOLI AND CAULIFLOWER
   CASSEROLE 167
BROCCOLI AND CAULIFLOWER HOT
   DISH 167
BROCCOLI AND RICE CASSEROLE 166
BROCCOLI CASSEROLE 164
BROCCOLI CASSEROLE 164
BROCCOLI-CAULIFLOWER
   CASSEROLE 166
BROCCOLI DRESSING CASSEROLE. 164
BROCCOLI-EGG CASSEROLE 162
BROCCOLINI 163
BROCCOLI, RICE, AND CHEESE. 166
BROCCOLI RICE CASSEROLE 165
BROCCOLI-RICE CASSEROLE 165
BROCCOLI WITH TANGY SAUCE 163
BRUSSELS SPROUTS WITH ALMONDS 168
BUREK 197
CABBAGE AU GRATIN 169
CALICO BEANS. 159
CELERY CASSEROLE. 172
CHEESY BROCCOLI AND RICE
   CASSEROLE 164
CHEESY CORN CASSEROLE. 173
CHEESY POTATOES. 181
CHEESY SCALLOPED POTATOES. 184
CHIPPED POTATOES 178
COLD WATER BEANS. 158
COMPANY'S FAVORITE SIDE DISH 165
COPPER CARROTS 171
CORN CASSEROLE 172
CROCKERY COOKER BAKED BEANS. 155
CRUNCH-TOP POTATOES 179
CRUNCHY VEGETABLE CASSEROLE. 197
DRUNKEN BEANS. 156
ESCALLOPED ASPARAGUS. 153
FOUR BEAN CASSEROLE 157
FRED'S BAKED BEANS 155
FRIED CABBAGE. 168
FRIED GREEN TOMATOES 191
FROZEN CORN 174
GOURMET POTATOES 183
GRATER TATER CASSEROLE 182
GREEN BEAN SCANDIA 175
GREEN BEANS WITH LIME AND DILL. 176
GRIT PIE 199
HASH BROWN POTATO CASSEROLE. 182
HASH BROWN POTATO DISH 181
HAWAIIAN YAMS 193

HO BO BEANS. 159
HOBO BEANS. 159
HOLIDAY POTATO DISH. 184
HOLIDAY YAM CASSEROLE. 193
HOT FRUITED CABBAGE 170
HUSBAND PLEASING BEANS 157
ITALIAN POTATO CASSEROLE 182
KENTUCKY VEGETABLE CASSEROLE 198
LIMAS BAKED IN SOUR CREAM 176
MACARONI AND TOMATOES. 192
MAKE AHEAD POTATOES 177
MARINATED BROCCOLI. 163
MASHED POTATO CASSEROLE 179
MIXED VEGETABLES WITH WHITE
   SAUCE 198
MY FAVORITE CARROTS. 171
OLD-FASHIONED CORN PUDDING 174
ORANGE-GLAZED CARROTS 171
PINEAPPLE BOURBON SWEET
   POTATOES. 188
POTATO CASSEROLE. 183
POTATO CASSEROLE. 183
POTATOES AND GREEN CHILIES 178
POTATOES ELEGANTE. 185
POTATO LOAF. 180
POTATO STUFFING. 178
QUICK CHILI BEANS. 161
RALPH'S FAVORITE CABBAGE 168
RANCH BEANS 158
RATATOUILLA FROM MISSISSIPPI 196
RED BEANS AND RICE. 160
RED CABBAGE AND APPLES 170
REFRIED BEANS. 158
REFRIGERATED MASHED POTATOES 179
ROASTED ASPARAGUS 154
SANTA MARIA BBQ BEANS 160
SAUTEED PEPPERS 177
SCALLOPED CORN AND CARROT
   CASSEROLE 173
SCALLOPED TOMATO AND
   ARTICHOKES. 192
SETTLER'S BEANS 156
SEVEN-BEAN CASSEROLE 157
SPANISH RICE. 185
SPINACH BUREK FROM YUGOSLAVIA. 186
SPINACH SQUARES 186
SPINACH STRUDEL 187
SQUASH CASSEROLE 188
STUFFED ARTICHOKES WITH LEMON
   SAUCE 153
STUFFED BAKED POTATOES 180
STUFFED TOMATOES 192
SUGARY SAM YAMS. 194
SUMMER SQUASH CASSEROLE. 187
SWEET POTATO CASSEROLE 190
SWEET POTATO CASSEROLE 190
SWEET POTATO CASSEROLE. 189
SWEET POTATO CASSEROLE. 191
SWEET POTATO CASSEROLE. 190
SWEET POTATOES. 188
SWEET POTATOES WITH PECANS. 189
SWEET-SOUR CABBAGE 169
SWISS VEGETABLE MEDLEY 199
THOSE POTATOES. 181
THREE-BEAN BAKE 161
THREE CORN CASSEROLE. 173
TOM'S MARINATED CARROTS 172
TWICE BAKED POTATOES. 180
VEGETABLE CASSEROLE 199
VEGETABLE PAELLA. 196
VIDALIA ONION CASSEROLE 177
VIVIAN'S CORN BAKE. 174

YAM-YAM SWEET POTATOES 191
ZUCCHINI AND CAULIFLOWER
   SKILLET 195
ZUCCHINI FRITTERS 195

ENTREES

ENTREES - BEEF

BAKED CHUCK AND MUSHROOM
   SAUCE 209
BAKED SWISS 205
BARBEQUE BEEF 222
BARBEQUE BEEF LOAVES 225
BARBEQUE MEATBALLS 229
BBQ BEEF RIBS 218
BBQ CUPS 222
BBQ SPARERIBS, CHINESE STYLE 219
BEEF BRISKET BARBECUE 219
BEEF BURGUNDY 205
BEEF INTERNATIONAL 201
BEEF OR LAMB SHISH KABOBS 211
BUTTER BALL STEAK BARBEQUE 221
CARIBBEAN PICADILLO 203
CARUTHERS BBQ TRI-TIP 220
CHATEAUBRIAND 213
CHICKEN FRIED STEAK AND GRAVY 210
CHILI AND MEATBALL CASSEROLE
   MEATBALLS 228
EASY MEAT LOAF 224
EASY SLOPPY JOES 222
GOURMET MEAT BALLS 227
GOURMET SIRLOIN TIPS 211
GOVERNORS SAUERBRATEN 214
ITALIAN BEEF 204
KANSAS STYLE BAR-B-Q MEAT LOAF 225
KOREAN BARBEQUE BEEF BY CECILE
   PARK 221
LEAN BEEF AND VEGETABLE POT
   ROAST 206
LIONS BARBECUE RECIPE 223
LIONS PICNIC MEATBALLS AND
   SAUSAGE 228
LITTLE CHEDDAR LOAF 226
MAMIE'S MEAT PIE 208
MARINATED STEAK 217
MEAT BALLS 227
MEAT BALLS STROGANOFF 227
MEAT BARBECUE 222
MEAT LOAF ROLL 224
MEAT LOAF WELLINGTON 226
MEAT MARINADE 216
MEXICAN FLANK STEAK 201
MEXICAN ROAST 212
MIGAS MIGAS 208
MORCON - BEEF ROLL 207
ORIENTAL MEATBALLS 230
OVEN BEEF BURGUNDY 205
PEPPERED BEEF TENDERLOIN WITH
   MUSTARD AND HORSERADISH
   SAUCE 217
PEPPER STEAK 218
POLISH HAMBURGERS 224
POLYNESIAN ROAST 203
PORCUPINE MEATBALLS 229
PRETZEL MEATLOAF 226
"QUICK AND EASY" BARBECUED
   BURGERS 223
RICEBALLS 229
ROULADEN MIT SPAETZLE 202
SANTA MARIA BBQ TRI TIP 220
SAUERBRATEN 216

SAUERBRATEN - MARINATED BEEF 215
SIMPLE SALISBURY STEAK 206
SPICY ORIENTAL CARAMELIZED BEEF 202
STANDING RIB ROAST 212
STEAK 'N GRAVY 209
STEAK ROLLS 209
SWEET AND SOUR MEATBALLS 231
SWEET AND SOUR MEATBALLS 230
SWEET 'N' SOUR MEAT LOAF 225
SWEET SOUR SPARERIBS 210
TERIYAKI BURGERS 223
THAI BEEF WITH NOODLES 204

ENTREES - POULTRY

BAKED CHICKEN WITH WINE 257
BAKED PINEAPPLE CHICKEN 247
BOMBAY TURKEY 268
BRAZILIAN HOLIDAY CHICKEN 249
CAJUN CHICKEN WITH A TWIST 237
CAJUN GUMBO FILE 236
CASABLANCA CHICKEN 234
CHICKEN A-LA-BEE 248
CHICKEN ALMONDINE 251
CHICKEN AND RICE 262
CHICKEN AND RICE 262
CHICKEN AND SWISS CHEESE
   CASSEROLE 264
CHICKEN BOGG 261
CHICKEN BREAST IN HEAVY CREAM AND
   SPICY MUSTARD 242
CHICKEN BREAST IN WINE 242
CHICKEN BREASTS DIANE 240
CHICKEN CACCIATORE 248
CHICKEN CASSEROLE 262
CHICKEN CASSEROLE 263
CHICKEN COOKED IN WINE 257
CHICKEN DELITE 243
CHICKEN DIABLO 244
CHICKEN DISH 261
CHICKEN DISH 244
CHICKEN DISH 260
CHICKEN DIVAN 256
CHICKEN DRUMETTES 245
CHICKEN FETAAZINI 249
CHICKEN HAWAIIAN 233
CHICKEN KORMA 258
CHICKEN MARSALA 243
CHICKEN NAPOLEON 255
CHICKEN PENNY 260
CHICKEN PIE 260
CHICKEN TETRAZZINI 254
CHICKEN TETRAZZINI 249
CHICKEN WINGS 245
CHICKEN WINGS 244
CHICKEN WITH OLIVES 248
CHICKEN WITH PECANS 243
CHINESE STYLE OVEN ROASTED
   CHICKEN 238
CORNISH GAME HEN AND WILD RICE
   SUPREME 268
CORNISH HENS WITH WILD RICE 269
COUNTRY CLUB-STYLE HOT CHICKEN
   SALAD 264
CRISP BAKED DRUMSTICKS 246
CROCK POT DRESSING 265
CURRIED CHICKEN CASSEROLE 259
CURRIED CHICKEN 259
EVERYDAY BROCCOLI CHEESE
   CHICKEN 253
FOIL BAKED CHICKEN 252
GENO'S ITALIAN TURKEY SAUSAGE 267

GREEK CHICKEN AND TOMATO
   CASSEROLE 238
HAWAIIAN CHICKEN 233
HERBED CHICKEN CASSEROLE 263
HERB-SMOKED TURKEY 266
ISRAELI CHICKEN 232
ITALIAN CHICKEN 237
KOTOPOULO ME BAMYES - CHICKEN WITH
   OKRA 235
LEMON-GARLIC ROAST CHICKEN 258
LEMONY HERB DRUMSTICKS 245
LUAU CHICKEN 234
MANDARIN CHICKEN 254
MARINATED CHICKEN BREASTS 242
MEXICAN CHICKEN 232
MONTEREY CHICKEN 253
NUTTY CHICKEN BREAST 241
OLD-FASHIONED BREAD STUFFING 265
ORANGE-A-TANGY GOURMET
   CHICKEN 251
ORIENTAL CHICKEN 235
OVEN BUTTERED FRIED CHICKEN 252
PAPRIKA CHICKEN 256
PARMESAN CHICKEN AND WILD RICE 261
PENNE WITH CHICKEN, SUN-DRIED
   TOMATOES, AND ONIONS 241
POPPY SEED CHICKEN 255
POPPY SEED CHICKEN 255
PRETTY GOOD CHICKEN 247
RANCH CHICKEN 239
RO-TEL CHICKEN 238
SAUSAGE STUFFING 265
SAUTEEN BREAST OF CHICKEN IN CURRY
   SAUCE 259
SIMPLE SUNDAY CHICKEN 263
STUFFED CHICKEN BREAST 239
STUFFED CHICKEN BREAST WITH THREE
   CHEESES 240
SWEDISH MEATBALLS WITH SOUR CREAM
   SAUCE 266
SWEET AND SOUR CHICKEN 250
SWEET-AND-SOUR CHICKEN 250
SWEET AND SOUR DRUMSTICKS 246
THANKSGIVING STUFFING 264
TURKEY MEAT LOAF 267
TURKEY MEAT LOAF WITH HERBS 267

ENTREES - SEAFOOD
ANGEL HAIR SCALLOPS AND SHRIMP 273
ASIAN SHRIMP, VEGETABLES, AND
   NOODLES 273
BAKED FISH 283
BAKED FISH 284
BAKED GREEK FISH 283
BARBECUED SHRIMP 271
BERING SEA BAKED SALMON 280
CATFISH PARMESAN 282
CHEESY SALMON CHOWDER 280
CRAB AND SHRIMP BAKE 275
CRAB BURGERS 276
CRAB DELIGHT 276
CURRIED SHRIMP AND CHICKEN
   BREAST WITH ZUCCHINI AND
   CARROTS 272
DEEP-FRIED COUNTRY-STYLE
   PRAWNS 277
HADDOCK 283
HADDOCK-SHRIMP BAKE 270
HALIBUT CASSEROLE 285
HALIBUT SOUFFLE 285
LANDLUBBER'S CRABMEAT SPREAD 276
MAGGIE'S CLAM CAKES 277

MAINE JEMBALAYAK 271
MARYLAND LADY CRAB CAKES 275
MERMAID FISH FILLET 281
OUTDOOR GRILLED SALMON 279
POACHED SALMON ALA DISHWASHER 279
QUICK AND ELEGANT ORANGE
   ROUGHY 282
ROUGHY ROLL-UPS 281
SALMON LOAF 278
SALMON PIE 278
SALMON PIE 278
SCALLOPED OYSTERS 270
SCAMPI MARINARA 272
SEAFOOD STUFFED SHELLS 284
SHRIMP AND TORTELLINI 274
SHRIMP JAMBALAYA 275
SHRIMP RUMALDE 270
SHRIMP SCAMPI 274
SPICY CAJUN SHRIMP 274
WHITE CLAM SAUCE LINGUINE 277

ENTREES - PORK
B-B-Q PORK RIBS 286
DIFFERENT PORK CHOPS 292
HAM BALLS 289
HAM BALLS 289
HAM LOAF 289
HAM LOAF 288
HAWAIIAN GRILLED PORK CHOPS 292
HONEY-BAKED HAM 288
LION LARRY'S ROAST SUCKLING PIG 286
MANDARIN PORK AND VEGETABLES 287
MOM MICHAUD'S NEW YEAR RAGOUT 293
PORK CHOP AND POTATO
   CASSEROLE 291
PORK CHOP AND RICE CASSEROLE 291
PORK CHOPS AND POTATOES 291
PORK CHOPS WITH APPLES AND
   ONIONS 290
PORK TENDERLOIN WITH CINNAMON 287
SAUERKRAUT MEATBALLS 288
SICILIAN MEAT ROLL 290
SWEET AND SOUR PORK 287

ENTREES - MISCELLANEOUS
BARBECUE DEER 299
BARBECUED VENISON MEAT BALLS 295
BASIL VEAL AND PASTA 296
BRATWURST 299
BUFFALO STEAK BBQ 299
DEER MEAT IN SAUCE 300
FLAT ROAST LEG OF LAMB 295
FRANKS IN A LOAF 298
HOUDAH CURRY OF VEAL 297
HUNTER'S STEW - BOURGUIGNON 294
IRISH CORNED BEEF AND CABBAGE 298
LAMB STEW 296
LEG OF LAMB, BONED 301
SALAMI 300
SMALL GAME GOULASH 300
SUPER DOGS 297
VENISON STROGANOFF 294

CASSEROLES AND MAIN DISHES

AMERICAN CHOP SUEY 318
AMERICAN SPAGHETTI 341
AWESOME SPAGHETTI 337
BARBECUED SAUERKRAUT 358
BEEF AND BEAN BARBEQUE 368

BEEF STROGANOFF AND RICE
   CASSEROLE 374
BLUE RIBBON COMPANY CASSEROLE 328
BROCCOLI AND HAM CASSEROLE........ 329
BROCCOLI-LIMA CASSEROLE............ 356
BROWN RICE CHEESE.................. 331
BURGER CASSEROLE 376
BUSY DAY GOULASH.................. 354
CABBAGE AND BEEF CASSEROLE........ 360
CABBAGE LASAGNA.................. 345
CALICO BEANS AND-OR CORN........... 368
CHALUPAS.......................... 321
CHEESE AND SAUSAGE MANICOTTI...... 350
CHEESEBURGER PIE.................. 366
CHEESE 'N CHICKEN ENCHILADAS 324
CHICKEN AND BROCCOLI WITH MUSHROOM
   SAUCE 307
CHICKEN AND CRESCENT ROLL
   CREATION 313
CHICKEN AND DRESSING CASSEROLE.... 304
CHICKEN AND RICE SUPREME........... 308
CHICKEN CASSEROLE................. 305
CHICKEN CASSEROLE................. 305
CHICKEN CASSEROLE................. 306
CHICKEN CASSEROLE................. 310
CHICKEN CASSEROLE................. 310
CHICKEN CHALUPAS 321
CHICKEN CHEESE PIES................ 316
CHICKEN ENCHILADAS 324
CHICKEN NOODLE CASSEROLE......... 312
CHICKEN POT PIE 307
CHICKEN POT PIE 314
CHICKEN SPAGHETTI.................. 339
CHICKEN SPAGHETTI.................. 339
CHICKEN STRATA..................... 314
CHILI SQUARES 366
CHOP SUEY......................... 318
CLAM SPAGHETTI.................... 341
CLASSIC LASAGNA.................... 348
CORNISH PASTIES 370
COUNTRY COTTAGE CASSEROLE........ 364
COUNTRY HAM CASSEROLE 328
COW PLOPPES WITH SALAD 311
CRAB CASSEROLE.................... 330
CRAFTY CRESCENT LASAGNE.......... 347
DUTCH NOODLES..................... 317
DYNAMITE.......................... 364
EASY CASSEROLE 315
EASY FETTUCCINE ALFREDO............ 349
EASY FRIDAY CASSEROLE 331
FINNISH PASTY....................... 370
FRANKFURTER SCALLOP 362
FRENCH CANADIAN TOURTIERE 369
FRIED RICE.......................... 333
GOULASH 354
GREEK LASAGNA..................... 345
GREEN CHILI CASSEROLE.............. 357
GREEN ENCHILADAS 322
GROUND BEEF-VEGETABLE
   CASSEROLE 369
HAM AND CHEESE CASSEROLE.......... 328
HAM AND NOODLE CASSEROLE 329
HAMBURGER AND BEAN CASSEROLE 368
HAMBURGER AND MACARONI
   CASSEROLE 373
HAMBURGER AND MINUTE RICE
   CASSEROLE 375
HAMBURGER AND POTATO
   CASSEROLE 369
HAMBURGER CABBAGE CASSEROLE..... 360
HAMBURGER CASSEROLE 365
HAMBURGER DRESSING HOT DISH....... 367

HAMBURGER NOODLE CASSEROLE 373
HAMBURGER PIE 363
HARVEST SUPPER CHICKEN
   CASSEROLE 309
HOBO SPAGHETTI 338
HOMEMADE PIZZA 336
HOMEMADE RAVIOLI 353
HOT CHICKEN CASSEROLE 312
HOT CHICKEN SALAD CASSEROLE 312
HOT CHINESE CHICKEN 309
HUNGRY JACK CASSEROLE............ 371
IMPOSSIBLE BLT PIE 365
IMPOSSIBLE CHEESEBURGER PIE 362
IMPOSSIBLE ZUCCHINI-TOMATO PIE..... 356
JENNY'S SPAGHETTI 340
KASH VARNISHKAS 357
KING RANCH CHICKEN CASSEROLE...... 313
LASAGNA........................... 348
LASAGNA ROLLS 343
LASAGNE........................... 344
LASAGNE........................... 346
LAYERED CHICKEN ENCHILADA BAKE 323
LAZY DAY LASAGNA................... 342
LINGUINI WITH ESCAROLE AND
   CHICKPEAS....................... 349
LITTLE TOSTADA TARTS 320
LUMPIA............................ 320
MACARONI AND CHEESE 351
MARCETI 319
MARZETTI 374
MEATBALL CASSEROLE 372
MEATLESS MOUSSAKA 355
MEXICAN CABBAGE.................. 360
MEXICAN GOULASH.................. 325
MEXICAN HASH CASSEROLE 327
MEXICAN SKILLET SPAGHETTI 327
MISS MARIA'S MACARONI
   CASSEROLE 352
MONTEREY STYLE ENCHILADAS 322
MOUSSAKA 363
MOUTCHENTRA - LENTIL WITH RICE...... 356
NUTTY NOODLE CASSEROLE........... 372
ONE DISH CONNELLY RECIPE 367
ONE POT DINNER.................... 367
PASTITSIO - A GREEK MACARONI
   CASSEROLE 319
PIEROGI CASSEROLE 353
"PISSALADIERE A L'APPEL" - FRENCH
   PIZZA 334
POLISH STUFFED CABBAGE -
   GOLABKI 359
POPOVER PIZZA...................... 335
PORK CHOP AND POTATO BAKE......... 329
POWDERHOUSE CASSEROLE 315
QUICK CHICKEN CASSEROLE 306
QUICK PIZZA........................ 335
RATATOUILLE 354
RED BEANS AND RICE................ 332
RICE AND CHICKEN CASSEROLE........ 308
SAUSAGE AND MACARONI
   CASSEROLE 351
SAUSAGE AND RICE CASSEROLE....... 333
SAUSAGE SPAGHETTI 337
SHRIMP AND HAM JAMBALAYA 331
SICILIAN-STYLE SPAGHETTI WITH
   TUNA 341
SOUPER MEAT 'N POTATOES PIE 372
SOUR CREAM CHICKEN ENCHILADAS 323
SOUR CREAM NOODLE BAKE........... 350
SPAGHETTI BAKE..................... 338
SPAGHETTI WITH MEAT BALLS 340

SPAGHETTI WITH WALNUTS AND
  PARMESAN 336
SPANISH RICE 332
SPECIAL PIZZA 334
SPINACH LASAGNA 346
SUPER NACHOS 326
SWISS NOODLES 351
TALARINI 316
TALGARINI 317
TATER TOPPED CASSEROLE 361
TATER-TOPPED CHILI BEEF 362
TATER TOT CASSEROLE 361
TATER TOTS CASSEROLE 361
TEX-MEX MACARONI AND CHEESE 352
TICO-TACO 326
TOASTED RICE AND PASTA PILAF 332
TUNA BISCUIT BRAID 330
TUNA LASAGNA 343
TURKEY-CHEDDAR PIE 303
TURKEY DINNER PIE 303
TURKEY ENCHILADAS 325
TURKEY-WILD RICE CASSEROLE 304
UNSTUFFED CABBAGE ROLLS 358
VEGETABLE AND CHICKEN POT PIE 311
VEGETABLE CASSEROLE 355
VEGETABLES WITH BEEF OVER RICE 375
VERY HOT BANGERS AND MASH 371
WATSON GOULASH 373
ZUCCHINI CASSEROLE 357
ZUCCHINI LASAGNA 344

BREADS

ALASKA BREAD 385
AMERICAN INDIAN BREAD -
  "BANNOCK" 427
APPLE BREAD 413
BANANA BREAD 414
BANANA BREAD 413
BANANA BREAD SUPREME 414
BANANA MUFFINS 408
BARBADOS BREAD 386
BASIC ROLL DOUGH 378
BEER BREAD 386
BELFAST MUFFINS 409
BETTER ANGEL BISCUITS 383
BISCUITS 384
BLACK RASPBERRY DUMPLINGS 428
BLUEBERRY MUFFINS 409
BOHEMIAN KOLACHES 399
BROCCOLI BREAD 386
BROCCOLI CORN BREAD 388
BUNDT CARAMEL ROLLS 394
BUTTERMILK YEAST BISCUITS 429
CARAMEL-CREAM CHEESE CINNAMON
  ROLLS 395
CHEDDAR, BACON, AND OLIVE BREAD . . . 387
CHOCOLATE ZUCCHINI BREAD 422
CORN CUSTARD CAKE 429
CRANBERRY NUT BREAD 426
CREAM CHEESE BANANA BREAD 414
CRUMB-TOPPED COCOA BANANA
  BREAD 415
DANISH PUFF 397
DANISH ROLLS 393
DELICIOUS ROLL DOUGH 377
DILLY BREAD 388
DINNER ROLLS 378
DOLE RAISIN PINEAPPLE MUFFINS 411
EASY MONKEY BREAD 401
EDNA'S ROLLS 379

FINNISH CHRISTMAS RYE BREAD OR
  JOULULIMPPU 421
FRENCH BREAD STICKS 382
GINGERBREAD 417
GOOD CINNAMON ROLLS 397
GRAPE-NUTS BREAD 388
HALF-TIME SPOON ROLLS 379
HAWAIIAN COCONUT SPREAD 426
HOMEMADE WHITE BREAD 393
HONEY DEW BISCUITS 383
HOT MEXICAN CORN BREAD 387
HOT ROLLS (REFRIGERATED) 381
ICEBOX ROLLS 380
INSTANT MIRACLE ROLLS 381
ITALIAN BUTTER BREAD - CHRISTMAS FRUIT
  BREAD 416
LEMON NUT BREAD 425
LUCY'S BISCUITS 385
MAGIC BISCUITS 384
MAINE BLUEBERRY MUFFINS 409
MICROWAVE DUMPLINGS 428
MOTHER'S OATMEAL BREAD 420
NEVER-FAIL BUNS 377
NORTH TEXAS STATE UNIVERSITY COFFEE
  CAKE 408
OATMEAL ROLLS 380
OLD-FASHIONED CINNAMON ROLLS 396
OLD TIME DUMPLINGS 427
OLD WITCHES MAGIC NUT BREAD 425
ONION HARVEST BREAD -
  ZWIEBELKUCHEN 389
ORANGE BRAN MUFFINS 410
ORANGE BREAD 417
ORANGE, DATE, AND PECAN BREAD 417
PATE'S ELEPHANT EARS 400
PEACH CORIANDER BREAD 418
PEANUT BUTTER TEA RING 401
PERSIMMON BREAD 418
PINEAPPLE ZUCCHINI BREAD 424
PISTACHIO BREAD 418
PLUM BREAD 419
PLUM COFFEE CAKE 408
POPOVERS 428
POPPY SEED BREAD 389
POPPY SEED STOLLEN OR ALMOND TEA
  RING 403
PORK AND BEAN BREAD 390
PUMPKIN SWIRL BREAD 419
QUICK AND EASY ROLLS 382
QUICK STICKY BUNS 406
RAISIN CARROT MUFFINS 410
RAW APPLE BREAD 413
RHUBARB BREAD 420
SALT RISING BREAD 390
SANDBAKKLSE 398
SCANDINAVIAN COFFEE BREAD 407
SEMMEL - HARD ROLL 378
7-UP BISCUITS 385
SHEPHERD'S BREAD 391
SIX WEEK MUFFINS 412
SOURDOUGH WHITE BREAD 392
SOUTH PACIFIC MUFFINS 411
SPICE BREAD-IN-A-JAR 404
SPOON BREAD 392
STICKY BUNS 406
STOLLEN OR CHRISTMAS LOAF 402
STRAWBERRY BREAD 421
STUFFED SPINACH-CHEESE BREAD 391
SUGARLESS FRUIT AND NUT
  MUFFINS 412
SWEDISH COFFEE ROLL 407
SWEDISH OATMEAL BREAD 420

SWEET POTATO ROLLS.................. 379
TINY GEMS 412
TOASTED BUTTER PECAN LOAF 424
TORTILLAS 427
TRINITY EASTER BREAD 405
WHITE BREAD......................... 393
WHODONITS 404
YORKSHIRE PUDDING 426
ZUCCHINI BREAD 421
ZUCCHINI FRUIT BREAD 423
ZUCCHINI NUT BREAD.................. 422
ZUCCHINI NUT BREAD................. 423

CAKES AND FROSTINGS

ANGEL FLAKE CAKE.................... 484
ANGEL FOOD CAKE.................... 484
ANYTIME BRAN CAKE 435
APPLE CAKE.......................... 456
APPLE CAKE.......................... 459
APPLE CAKE.......................... 459
APPLE COFFEE CAKE 470
APPLE NUT CAKE...................... 459
AUNT MARGARET'S CHOCOLATE
    CAKE 497
AUNT MARTHA'S CHOCOLATE CAKE...... 497
BABY FOOD CAKE 485
BABY FOOD CAKE 485
BABY FOOD POUND CAKE 486
BACARDI RUM CAKE 482
BANANA NUT CAKE 434
BANANA SPLIT CAKE 444
BEST CAKE 466
BEST FRUITCAKE EVER 451
BLACKBERRY CAKE AND ICING 491
BLACK BOTTOM CUPCAKES.............. 490
BLENDER COCONUT CAKE.............. 449
BOHEMIAN COFFEE CAKE 469
BUTTERNUT POUND CAKE.............. 488
CALIFORNIA WINE CAKE................ 437
CARROT CAKE 479
CARROT CAKE 478
CARROT CAKE 477
CHEESE CAKE 483
CHEESE CAKE 483
CHEESE CAKE 482
CHERRY CAKE 463
CHERRY-GLAZED SPONGE CAKE......... 463
CHESS CAKE.......................... 447
CHOCOLATE BANANA CAKE............. 501
CHOCOLATE CAKE AND CHOCOLATE
    FROSTING......................... 495
CHOCOLATE CAKE..................... 499
CHOCOLATE CAKE..................... 495
CHOCOLATE CAKE..................... 498
CHOCOLATE FROSTING 503
CHOCOLATE FUDGE FROSTING.......... 503
CHOCOLATE KAHLUA CAKE 500
CHOCOLATE SAUERKRAUT CAKE 501
CHOCOLATE SHEET CAKE 496
CHOCOLATE SHEET CAKE 499
CHOCOLATE VINEGAR CAKE 501
CHOCOLATE ZUCCHINI CAKE........... 500
COCONUT-PINEAPPLE CAKE 465
COFFEE CAKE - RIVEL KUCHA 469
COKE CAKE........................... 433
COUNTRY POPPY SEED CAKE........... 474
CRANBERRY MINCEMEAT CAKE 468
CRAZY CAKE.......................... 432
CRAZY CAKE.......................... 432
CREAM CHEESE CAKE 483
CREAM CHEESE CAKE 484
CRUMB CAKE 444
DATE CAKE........................... 467
DATE CAKE........................... 466
"DELICIOUS" LEMON PUDDING CAKE..... 462
DEVILS FOOD CAKE.................... 494
DIABETIC FRUIT CAKE................. 450
DIRT CAKE........................... 431
"EARTHQUAKE CAKE".................. 435
EASY CARROT CAKE 478
EASY COFFEE CAKE 470
"EASY" COFFEE CAKE.................. 473
EASY GERMAN APPLE CAKE 458
EASY LEMON CAKE 461
EDENTON (NORTH CAROLINA) TEA PARTY
    CAKES 436
ENGLAND CAKE 455
FIVE FLAVOR CAKE 446
FLORIDA'S LIGHTEST ORANGE CAKE..... 452
FLOSSIE'S PISTACHIO LAYER CAKE 480
FRESH APPLE CAKE 458
FRESH APPLE CAKE 457
FRESH APPLE CAKE 456
FROSTING 502
FRUIT COCKTAIL CAKE 437
FUDGE CAKE 496
GAIL'S CHOCOLATE CAKE.............. 498
GERMAN APPLE CAKE.................. 458
HEATH COFFEE CAKE 471
HEREDITY POUND CAKE................ 487
HICKORY NUT CAKE 434
HOLIDAY PECAN CAKE 443
ICEBOX JELLO CHEESE CAKE 482
ICEBOX KRANTZ - CHRISTMAS CAKE 448
ICE CREAM FRUIT CAKE................ 451
INEXPENSIVE FRUIT CAKE 450
IRISH CREAM CAKE.................... 438
ITALIAN LOVE CAKE................... 446
JAM CAKE 445
JEWISH COFFEE CAKE 471
KING SIZE APPLESAUCE CAKE 460
LANE CAKE 441
LEMON MERINGUE CAKE 461
LEMON POPPY SEED CAKE 473
LEMON SHORTCAKE 462
LEMON SUPREME CAKE 462
MANDARIN CAKE 454
MAYONNAISE CAKE.................... 441
MEXICAN WEDDING CAKE 447
MISSISSIPPI MUD CAKE................ 502
MOTHER'S DATE CAKE 467
MYSTERY FRUIT CAKE BALLS 452
NO-CHOLESTEROL MILLION DOLLAR POUND
    CAKE 489
NOVA SCOTIA POUND CAKE............. 486
OATMEAL CAKE 448
OLD-FASHIONED JAM CAKE 445
OLD TIME POUND CAKE 489
ORANGE LIQUEUR CAKE 453
ORANGE MANDARIN CAKE 453
PEANUT BUTTER CAKE................. 449
PINEAPPLE CAKE...................... 463
PINEAPPLE SHEET CAKE 464
PLACEK 440
PLUM LEAKE CAKE 438
POPPY SEED BREAD (CAKE) 474
POPPY SEED CAKE 473
POUND CAKE 487
PRESSED FRUIT CAKE 450
PULL APART COFFEE CAKE 472
PUMPKIN CAKE....................... 476
PUMPKIN CAKE....................... 475

PUMPKIN CAKE. 475
PUMPKIN CAKE ROLL 477
PUMPKIN CHIFFON CAKE 476
QUICK APPLE DESSERT WITH SAUCE 457
QUICK BLACK FOREST CAKE 490
RASPBERRY-ALMOND COFFEE CAKE 468
RED VELVET CAKE 493
RED WALDORF CAKE AND FROSTING 492
RHUBARB CUSTARD CAKE 480
RHUBARB DUMP CAKE 480
RICH CRANBERRY COFFEE CAKE 469
ROSY APPLE CAKE 460
ROYAL BLACK CAKE 491
RUM CAKE. 481
SCRIPTURE CAKE 447
SIMPLE POUND CAKE 486
SOUR CREAM COFFEE CAKE 472
SOUTHERN BUTTERMILK POUND
   CAKE 488
STRAWBERRY CAKE 454
STRAWBERRY ICING 502
STRAWBERRY PECAN CAKE. 455
SUPER DELICIOUS CARROT CAKE 479
TEN EGG CAKE. 442
THE BEST WHITE CHOCOLATE CAKE 494
THREE-HOLE CAKE 442
TWINKIE CAKE 442
UGLY DUCKLING CAKE 443
VANILLA WAFER CAKE. 436
VANILLA WAFER CAKE. 503
WACKY CAKE 431
WEIGHT WATCHERS PISTACHIO CAKE 481
WHITE CHOCOLATE CAKE 493
WHOOPIE PIE CAKE. 439

PIES AND PASTRIES

APPLE DANISH 533
"APPLE PIE OH MY" 519
BEST EVER PIE. 510
BETTY'S PEANUT BUTTER PIE 515
BLUEBERRY CRUMB PIE 521
BLUEBERRY PINWHEEL COBBLER. 534
BROWN SUGAR PIE 505
BUTTER TARTS 534
CHEESE ROLL. 535
CHERRY BERRIES ON A CLOUD 535
CHESS CAKE PIE 505
COCONUT CUSTARD PIES 507
COCONUT PIE. 506
CRANBERRY PIE. 521
CRAZY CRUST APPLE PIE. 520
DONNA'S OIL PIE CRUST. 532
DONNA'S PECAN PIE 514
EGG PASTRY. 536
EXQUISITE PIE 507
15-MINUTE CUSTARD PIE 507
FREEZE-AHEAD PEACH PIE FILLING 525
FRENCH CHOCOLATE PIE. 505
FRESH STRAWBERRY PIE. 531
FRESH STRAWBERRY PIE. 532
FUDGE PIE 506
GIVE THANKS FOR PIE 528
"GRANDMA CROSBY'S MOLASSES
   DOUGHNUTS" 536
HERSHEY BAR PIE. 508
JAPANESE FRUIT PIE. 508
JAPANESE FRUIT PIE. 508
KENTUCKY PIE 508
LEMON BERRY PIE. 524
LEMON MERINGUE PIE 522

LEMON MILLIONAIRE 524
LEMON SOUR CREAM PIE. 523
LEMON SPONGE PIE 522
LEMON VELVET PIE 523
LIGHT 'N FRUITY PIE 509
MOIST SHOO-FLY PIE. 516
MOM'S APPLE PIE 520
MOM'S PIE CRUST 532
NANTUCKET CRANBERRY PIE 525
NEVER-FAIL-PIE-CRUST-OR-TURNOVERS. . 533
NOT-SO-DRY SHOO-FLY PIE 517
NUT MERINGUE PIE 509
NUTTY CHOCOLATE PIE 506
OUT OF THIS WORLD PIE 509
PARADISE PUMPKIN PIE 528
PEANUT BUTTER CUSTARD PIE. 515
PEANUT BUTTER-JELLY PIE 514
PEANUT BUTTER PIE 514
PEANUT STREUSEL PIE. 510
PECAN DELIGHT PIE 511
PECAN PIE. 512
PECAN PIE. 511
PECAN PIE. 513
PECAN PIE. 513
PECAN PIE DIXIE 513
PERFECT APPLE PIE 519
PIE CRUST. 533
PINEAPPLE CAKE PIE 526
PINEAPPLE CHIFFON PIE 526
PINEAPPLE PIE. 526
PRINCESS LEMON PIE. 525
PRUNE PIE 526
PUMPKIN CHESS PIE. 527
PUMPKIN FLUFF PIE 527
PUMPKIN PIE CRUNCH 528
RHUBARB CUSTARD PIE 529
RHUBARB PAN-PAN 529
RHUBARB PIE 529
SHOO-FLY PIE. 516
STRAWBERRY GLAZE PIE. 531
STRAWBERRY HEAVEN PIE 531
STRAWBERRY PIE 530
STRAWBERRY PIE 529
SUGAR FREE APPLE PIE. 520
SUGAR-FREE STRAWBERRY PIE 530
SWEET POTATO PECAN PIE 512
THE BEST PEANUT BUTTER PIE 515
UP 'N ADAM PIE 517
ZUCCHINI CHERRY PIE 518

COOKIES, BARS, CANDIES

COOKIES

ALMOND COOKIES 548
APPLESAUCE COOKIES. 549
APPLESAUCE OATMEAL COOKIES. 557
ART'S CHOCOLATE CHIP COOKIES 560
AUNT JANE'S SUGAR COOKIES 567
BAKE WHILE YOU SLEEP COOKIES. 553
BANANA OATMEAL COOKIES 557
BUCKEYES 542
BUFFALO CHIPS 563
BUTTER COOKIES 539
CHEESECAKE COOKIES 540
CHEWY CHOCOLATE COOKIES 537
CHEWY SKOR TOFFEE BITS COOKIES 546
CHOCOLATE CHIP COOKIES. 561
CHOCOLATE CHIP COOKIES. 561
CHOCOLATE CHIP COOKIES. 560
CHOCOLATE CHIP COOKIES. 562
CHOCOLATE CHIP COOKIES. 562

CHOCOLATE CHIP COOKIES. 560
CHOCOLATE MERINGUE COOKIES 554
CHOCOLATE OATSIES. 556
CHRISTMAS MOUNDS. 544
CHRISTMAS SUGAR COOKIE
  LOLLIPOPS. 564
CHRISTMAS SURPRISE BALLS 544
COCONUT COOKIES 548
COLORADO SNOW NEWTONS 544
CORN FLAKE COOKIES 543
CREAM FILLED CONFETTI COOKIES 540
CRISPIE COOKIES 541
"CROSBY'S COWBOY COOKIES" 545
DELUXE PECAN CHOCOLATE
  COOKIES 564
DINGBATS 552
DISHPAN COOKIES. 541
DROP SUGAR COOKIES 566
DROP SUGAR COOKIES 565
FORGOTTEN KISSES 553
GERMANTOWN OATMEAL COOKIES 556
GINGER SNAPS. 537
GINGERSNAPS 538
GRAND MA COOKIES. 556
GRANDMA'S SPICE COOKIES 549
ICEBOX DATE COOKIE. 552
KATHLEEN'S FAVORITE OATMEAL
  COOKIES 557
LAST MINUTE COOKIES. 558
LITTLE ROUND SWEDISH COOKIES. 541
M&M'S COOKIES. 562
MARY'S SUGAR COOKIE 566
MERINGUE COOKIES. 554
MOLASSES COOKIES. 550
MOLASSES CRINKLES 550
NO BAKE COCOA AND OATMEAL
  COOKIES 555
NO BAKE COOKIES 555
NO BAKE COOKIES 554
OATMEAL, PEANUT BUTTER,
  CHOCOLATE CHIP COOKIES WITH
  NUTS. 563
"OLD-FASHIONED" MOLASSES
  COOKIES 550
OLEO COOKIE. 538
PEANUT BUTTER COOKIES WITH A
  TWIST. 558
PEANUT BUTTER ICEBOX COOKIES 559
PEANUT BUTTER KISS COOKIES 559
PEANUT BUTTER SWIRLS. 558
"PIZZELLES" 538
PREACHER'S COOKIES 545
QUICK PEANUT BUTTER COOKIES 559
RAISIN COOKIES. 552
RAISIN FILLED COOKIES 551
RAISIN PUFF COOKIES 551
SNICKERDOODLES. 542
SOFT SUGAR COOKIES 565
SOUR CREAM COOKIES 547
SOUR CREAM COOKIES 546
SOUTHERN SOUR CREAM JUMBLES. 547
SUGAR COOKIES 565
SURPRISE MERINGUES. 553
TARTS 539
VINEGAR COOKIES 555
WELSH CAKES 543

BARS
"ALL-IN-A-PAN BROWNIES" 574
ANYTIME HOLIDAY BARS 581
APPLE BARS. 568
APRICOT BARS. 568

APRICOT M-M-MUMBLES. 569
BAKLAVA 569
BING CHERRY BARS 570
BLONDE BROWNIES. 570
BROWNIES 570
BROWNIES 575
CARAMEL-CHOCOLATE SQUARES. 575
CARROT BARS 576
CHOCOLATE AND OAT BARS 576
CHOCOLATE CHIP BROWNIES 571
CHOCOLATE DESSERT BARS. 576
CHOCO-NUT PIZZA. 577
CONGO BARS 577
CREME DE MENTHE BROWNIES 572
CREME DE MENTHE BROWNIES 573
DATE BARS 577
DIABETIC BROWNIES. 571
DISNEYLAND COOKIES 578
FAMILY-SIZED BROWNIES 574
FARMER'S SQUARES. 578
FROSTED CREAM BARS 579
FUDGE NUT BARS 579
GRANOLA BARS 579
HEATH BARS. 580
HEATH BARS. 580
HELLO DOLLIES 580
HOMEMADE TRIX CANDY BARS. 586
LEMON ANGEL BARS 581
LINZER TORTE BARS. 581
MOLASSES RAISIN BAR. 582
MOM'S BROWNIES 573
NUT BARS 582
ORANGE ZUCCHINI BARS. 582
PEANUT BUTTER CRISPS 583
PEANUT BUTTER FINGERS 584
PEANUT BUTTER LOGS. 584
QUICK FORTY-NINERS. 585
RASPBERRY SKOR BARS 585
SALTED PEANUT CHEWS 583
SPECIAL "K" BARS 586
TWICE BAKED PECAN SQUARES. 585

CANDIES
APPLETS CANDY 587
BERNICE'S PEANUT BUTTER FUDGE 598
BEST CARAMELS EVER. 588
BOURBON BALLS 592
CAN'T FAIL FUDGE 600
CHEEZY FUDGE 601
CHEWY PRALINES 592
CHOCOLATE BALLS. 589
CHOCOLATE FUDGE 601
CHOCOLATE FUDGE 601
CHOCOLATE MARSHMALLOWS 589
CHOCOLATE PEPPERMINT ROLL. 590
DATE AND NUT CHEWS. 587
DIVINITY FUDGE. 599
DIXIE PEANUT BRITTLE. 596
EASY CHOCOLATE FUDGE 601
ENGLISH TOFFEE. 591
ENGLISH TOFFEE. 591
KAHLUA PECAN FUDGE. 599
MAMIE EISENHOWER'S MILLION DOLLAR
  FUDGE 600
MARSHMALLOW ROLLS. 589
MY FUDGE SPECIAL. 600
O'HENRY'S. 590
OLD-FASHIONED PEANUT BRITTLE 595
PEANUT BRITTLE 595
PEANUT BUTTER BALLS 593
PEANUT BUTTER BONBONS. 594
PEANUT BUTTER BRITTLE 597

PEANUT BUTTER CANDY 594
PEANUT BUTTER CHEWS 593
PEANUT BUTTER EGGS. 593
PEANUT BUTTER FUDGE 598
PEANUT BUTTER FUDGE 597
PEANUT BUTTER FUDGE 597
PEANUT FUDGE 599
PECAN CANDY 591
RUM OR BOURBON BALLS 592
SEAFOAM CANDY. 588
STRAWBERRY CHEWS 588
STRAWBERRY DIVINITY. 587
SUE'S PEANUT BRITTLE 596
THREE MINUTE PEANUT BUTTER
    FUDGE 598

DESSERTS

ALMOND DELITE. 603
ALMOND FLOAT 603
ANGEL BERRY DESSERT. 644
APPLE-BREAD PUDDING 641
APPLE CRISP 604
APPLE CRISP 605
APPLE CRISP 603
APPLE CRISP 605
APPLE CRISP 604
APPLE LOAF 606
APPLE SQUARES 607
APPLE TORTE 607
BAILEY'S IRISH CREME MOUSSE. 632
BAKED INDIAN PUDDING. 640
BAKED PEACH PUDDING. 637
BANANA CHIFFON CAKE 609
BANANA CREAM DESSERT 610
BANANA PUDDING 637
BANANAS FOSTER 609
BANANAS IN WINE SAUCE 608
BANANA S'MORES 609
BERRY BAVARIAN CROWN 610
BLACK BOTTOM CUPCAKES 611
BONNIE'S PINEAPPLE SHEET CAKE 634
BREAD PUDDING 641
BREAD PUDDING 641
CARAMEL DESSERT. 612
CARAMEL DUMPLINGS 613
CHEDDAR CHEESE CAKE 615
CHEESECAKE 614
CHERRY PUDDING. 639
CHERRY TORTILLAS 616
CHOCOLATE AMARETTO
    CHEESECAKE 615
CHOCOLATE CHIP LOAF 616
CHOCOLATE CREAM CRUNCH. 617
CHOCOLATE ECLAIR DESSERT 622
CHOCOLATE ECLAIRS. 622
CHOCOLATE LAYER DESSERT. 617
CRANBERRY SOUR CREAM COFFEE
    CAKE 620
CRANBERRY SUPREME. 619
CREAM PUFF DESSERT. 619
CREAM PUFFS 618
CREAM PUFFS 618
CROWN CANTALOUPE WITH BANANA
    FLAMBE 612
DATE PUDDING. 636
DESSERT. 621
EASY EGG CUSTARD 620
ECLAIR CAKE 621
EGG BEATERS HOMEMADE ICE
    CREAM. 631

FIG ICE CREAM. 630
FOUR-LAYER DESSERT. 623
FRENCH APPLE DESSERT 606
FRESH BLUEBERRY DESSERT 611
FROZEN CHERRY DESSERT 616
FRUIT COBBLER 623
FRUIT COCKTAIL DESSERT. 626
FRUIT COCKTAIL DESSERT. 626
FRUIT CRUNCH. 625
FRUIT DELIGHT. 625
FRUIT JELLO 624
FRUIT PIZZA 624
FRUITTY PUDDING DELIGHT. 639
FUDGE PUDDING 638
GEORGIA FRUIT COBBLERS. 626
GERMAN CHOCOLATE DELIGHT 627
GINGERBREAD WITH HOT LEMON
    SAUCE. 627
GRAPES AND PINEAPPLE WITH SOUR
    CREAM. 634
GRASSHOPPER PIE 628
HOLIDAY FROZEN PUMPKIN SQUARES. . . . 642
HOLIDAY STEAMED PUDDING 636
HOMEMADE ICE CREAM 631
ICEBOX BANANA PUDDING. 638
ICEBOX FRUIT CAKE 625
ICE CREAM CUSTARD 631
ICE CREAM DESSERT 630
INDIAN PUDDING 640
JELLY RITZ DESSERT. 643
LEMON CAKE DESSERT 629
LEMON LUSH 628
LEMONY DESSERT. 628
MAGIC LEMON PUDDING. 638
MILLIONAIRE'S PIE 629
MOM'S GREEN STUFF 632
"MUD PIE" 633
PANNUKAKKUA - FINNISH CUSTARD 620
PEACH COBBLER 633
PEPPERMINT CHEESECAKE 614
PINEAPPLE-ORANGE DESSERT 633
PISTACHIO TORTE 635
POPPY SEED TORTE 635
PUMPKIN SQUARES 642
QUICK AND EASY CAKE DESSERT. 612
RAISIN PUDDING 637
RASPBERRY CRISP 643
RICE PUDDING 639
ROSE-BLUSH APPLE TORTE. 608
SCALLOPED PINEAPPLE 634
SCANDINAVIAN SOUR CHERRY
    PUDDING. 636
STAINED GLASS TORTE 645
STRAWBERRY-ANGEL FOOD DESSERT. . . . 644
STRAWBERRY DELIGHT 643
STRAWBERRY ICE CREAM 630
THREE-LAYER JELLO. 644
TINY TARTS 645
TIPSY LAIRD 646
WALNUT STRUEDEL. 646

MISCELLANEOUS

BAKED PINEAPPLE HOT DISH. 657
BARBECUE SAUCE. 655
BARBECUE SAUCE. 654
BECKY'S SWEET AND SOUR SAUCE 660
BIRD FEEDER 663
BREAD AND BUTTER PICKLES 653
BROWN BUTTER AND SAGE SAUCE 657
CAJUN SPICE MIX. 650

CHILI SAUCE 656
CHOW CHOW 652
CINNAMON APPLESAUCE 656
COCKTAIL SAUCE FOR SHRIMP 660
CORNCOB JELLY 647
CRANBERRY SAUCE 657
DOGGIE BONES 663
EASY CUCUMBER PICKLES 654
EASY CUCUMBER RELISH. 651
EDIBLE PLAY DOUGH. 662
FROZEN SPAGHETTI SAUCE. 655
FUNDRAISER SPAGHETTI SAUCE 656
GREEN PEPPER JELLY 647
HOME BAKED DOG TREAT COOKIES. 663
HOMEMADE EAGLE BRAND MILK. 649
HOMEMADE MEAT COATING 651
HORSERADISH DRESSING 654
HOW TO BOIL WATER 647
HOW TO PRESERVE CHOICE
    CHILDREN 651
INDIAN RELISH 652
LIFE'S RECIPE. 653
MARASCHINO CHERRIES 648

MOTHER'S LIFETIME RECIPE 662
MOTHER'S MAYONNAISE 648
MUSHROOM SAUCE. 661
MUSTARD PICKLES 654
OLD-FASHIONED MUSTARD 649
OLIVE OIL-LEMON SAUCE. 659
PARSLEY SAUCE 658
PEAR MINCEMEAT 650
PEAR PRESERVES 650
PICKLED BEETS 652
PLAYDOUGH 662
RECIPE FOR A HAPPY HOME. 649
RECIPE FOR HAPPINESS 664
RED EYE GRAVY 658
REFRIGERATOR PICKLES 653
RHUBARB REFRIGERATOR OR FREEZER
    JAM. 648
ROMESCO SAUCE 660
SUBSTITUTE FOR SWEETENED CONDENSED
    MILK. 649
VIVIAN'S PARSLEY PISTOU SAUCE 661
YORKSHIRE PUDDING 659

You may order as many single copies of **Kitchen Traditions, The Lions Clubs Cookbook,** as you wish. Simply contact your local Lions Club at the address or phone below:

If you are unable to obtain a book from the local Lions Club above, you may contact us at the address below for information on how to receive your new cookbooks:

Cookbooks Unlimited
P.O. Box 1865
Loveland, CO 80539
Phone: (303) 663-6767 ☎ Fax: (303) 663-6760

❖   ❖   ❖   ❖   ❖   ❖   ❖   ❖   ❖   ❖   ❖   ❖   ❖

Cook Up a Fundraising Success!

Lions Clubs are entitled to purchase these books at considerably reduced prices with easy payment terms, to enable you to use them as a great fundraising project for your local club. Using this cookbook to earn thousands of dollars is a great way to accomplish your club's goals quickly and easily with very little work on anyone's part. (Send a copy of this form to the address above, or just call for further information.)

☐ I am interested in using this book as a fundraising project for my club. Please send more information.

Name _____

Address _____

City, State, Zip _____